A PEACE
TO END ALL
PEACE

Also by David Fromkin

The Independence of Nations
The Question of Government

David Fromkin

A PEACE TO END ALL PEACE

CREATING THE
MODERN MIDDLE EAST
1914–1922

Henry Holt and Company
New York

Library of Congress Cataloging-in-Publication Data
Fromkin, David.
    A peace to end all peace.
    Bibliography: p.
    Includes index.
    1. Great Britain—Foreign relations—Middle East.
2. Middle East—Foreign relations—Great Britain.
3. Middle East—Politics and government—1914—1945.
I. Title.
DS63.2.G7F76   1989   327.41056   88—34727

ISBN 0-8050-0857-8

First American Edition

Printed in the United States of America
10 9 8 7 6 5 4 3 2 1

"After 'the war to end war' they seem
to have been pretty successful in Paris
at making a 'Peace to end Peace.'"

Archibald Wavell (later Field Marshal Earl
Wavell), an officer who served under Allenby
in the Palestine campaign, commenting on
the treaties bringing the First World War
to an end

CONTENTS

List of Illustrations and Maps   10
Photo Credits   11
Acknowledgments   12
A Note on Spelling   14
Introduction   15

PART I At the Crossroads of History

1   THE LAST DAYS OF OLD EUROPE   23
2   THE LEGACY OF THE GREAT GAME IN ASIA   26
3   THE MIDDLE EAST BEFORE THE WAR   33
4   THE YOUNG TURKS URGENTLY SEEK AN ALLY   45
5   WINSTON CHURCHILL ON THE EVE OF WAR   51
6   CHURCHILL SEIZES TURKEY'S WARSHIPS   54
7   AN INTRIGUE AT THE SUBLIME PORTE   62

PART II Kitchener of Khartoum Looks Ahead

8   KITCHENER TAKES COMMAND   79
9   KITCHENER'S LIEUTENANTS   88
10 KITCHENER SETS OUT TO CAPTURE ISLAM   96
11 INDIA PROTESTS   106
12 THE MAN IN THE MIDDLE   111

PART III Britain is Drawn into the Middle Eastern Quagmire

13 THE TURKISH COMMANDERS ALMOST LOSE THE WAR   119
14 KITCHENER ALLOWS BRITAIN TO ATTACK TURKEY   124
15 ON TO VICTORY AT THE DARDANELLES   130
16 RUSSIA'S GRAB FOR TURKEY   137
17 DEFINING BRITAIN'S GOALS IN THE MIDDLE EAST   146
18 AT THE NARROWS OF FORTUNE   150
19 THE WARRIORS   155
20 THE POLITICIANS   159
21 THE LIGHT THAT FAILED   163

22 CREATING THE ARAB BUREAU   168
23 MAKING PROMISES TO THE ARABS   173
24 MAKING PROMISES TO THE EUROPEAN ALLIES   188
25 TURKEY'S TRIUMPH AT THE TIGRIS   200

PART IV Subversion
26 BEHIND ENEMY LINES   207
27 KITCHENER'S LAST MISSION   216
28 HUSSEIN'S REVOLT   218

PART V The Allies at the Nadir of Their Fortunes
29 THE FALL OF THE ALLIED GOVERNMENTS: BRITAIN AND FRANCE   231
30 THE OVERTHROW OF THE CZAR   239

PART VI New Worlds and Promised Lands
31 THE NEW WORLD   253
32 LLOYD GEORGE'S ZIONISM   263
33 TOWARD THE BALFOUR DECLARATION   276
34 THE PROMISED LAND   284

PART VII Invading the Middle East
35 JERUSALEM FOR CHRISTMAS   305
36 THE ROAD TO DAMASCUS   315
37 THE BATTLE FOR SYRIA   332

PART VIII The Spoils of Victory
38 THE PARTING OF THE WAYS   351
39 BY THE SHORES OF TROY   363

PART IX The Tide Goes Out
40 THE TICKING CLOCK   383
41 BETRAYAL   389
42 THE UNREAL WORLD OF THE PEACE CONFERENCES   403

PART X Storm over Asia
43 THE TROUBLES BEGIN: 1919–1921   415
44 EGYPT: THE WINTER OF 1918–1919   417
45 AFGHANISTAN: THE SPRING OF 1919   421
46 ARABIA: THE SPRING OF 1919   424
47 TURKEY: JANUARY 1920   427

48 SYRIA AND LEBANON: THE SPRING AND SUMMER OF 1920   435
49 EASTERN PALESTINE (TRANSJORDAN): 1920   441
50 PALESTINE—ARABS AND JEWS: 1920   445
51 MESOPOTAMIA (IRAQ): 1920   449
52 PERSIA (IRAN): 1920   455

PART XI Russia Returns to the Middle East

53 UNMASKING BRITAIN'S ENEMIES   465
54 THE SOVIET CHALLENGE IN THE MIDDLE EAST   471
55 MOSCOW'S GOALS   475
56 A DEATH IN BUKHARA   480

PART XII The Middle Eastern Settlement of 1922

57 WINSTON CHURCHILL TAKES CHARGE   493
58 CHURCHILL AND THE QUESTION OF PALESTINE   515
59 THE ALLIANCES COME APART   530
60 A GREEK TRAGEDY   540
61 THE SETTLEMENT OF THE MIDDLE EASTERN QUESTION   558
Notes   569
Bibliography   607
Index   621

LIST OF ILLUSTRATIONS AND MAPS

1 Lord Kitchener
2 Sir Mark Sykes
3 Enver
4 Talaat
5 Djemal
6 Crowds gather outside the Sublime Porte, 1913
7 Turkish soldiers at Dardanelles fort, 1915
8 Allied fleet at entrance to Dardanelles
9 Pictorial map of the Dardanelles
10 H.M.S. *Cornwallis*
11 Anzac beach
12 Australian troops at Gallipoli
13 Winston Churchill
14 Russian troop column
15 Russian advance-guard in Turkey, 1916
16 Russian occupation of Erzerum
17 Russian troops in Trebizond
18 British camel column in the Jordan Valley
19 British survey party in Palestine
20 Transport camels
21 View of Beersheba
22 The Hejaz flag
23 Prince Feisal
24 King Hussein of the Hejaz
25 T.E. Lawrence with Lowell Thomas
26 David Ben-Gurion
27 Vladimir Jabotinsky
28 Chaim Weizmann with Lord Balfour
29 Union Jack hoisted above Basra
30 Street scene in Baghdad
31 Reading of General Allenby's proclamation of martial law, 1917
32 Australian Light Horse entering Damascus, 1918
33 General Allenby enters Aleppo, 1919
34 Ottoman soldiers surrender, November 1918
35 British sentry, Constantinople, 1920
36 Admiral Calthorpe's flagship, 1918

37 Woodrow Wilson
38 Lloyd George
39 Signing of the Treaty of Sèvres, 1920
40 British bluejackets in Constantinople, 1920
41 French quarter of Smyrna after the fall of the city, 1922
42 French troops enter Damascus, 1920
43 Bodies of Greek soldiers in a Turkish field, 1922
44 Mustapha Kemal
45 Reza Khan
46 Amanullah Khan
47 King Fuad of Egypt
48 Zaghlul Pasha
49 Sons of King Hussein of the Hejaz: Feisal, King of Iraq; Abdullah, Emir of Transjordan; and Ali, later briefly to be King of the Hejaz
50 Ibn Saud with Sir Percy Cox and Gertrude Bell

Photo Credits
1, 3, 4, 6, 7, 8, 9, 10, 11, 12, 13, 14, 15, 16, 17, 18, 19, 20, 21, 22, 23, 24, 29, 30, 31, 32, 33, 34, 35, 36, 37, 38, 39, 40, 41, 42, 43, 44, 46, 47, 80 are reproduced courtesy of *The Illustrated London News* Picture Library, London.
2, 5, 25, 45, 49 are reproduced courtesy of UPI/Bettmann Newsphotos, New York.
26 is reproduced courtesy of the Bettmann Archive, New York.
27 and 28 are reproduced courtesy of the Zionist Archives and Library.

Maps (Between pages 20 and 21)
The Middle East in 1914
The Campaign in Central Asia
The Greek-Turkish War
The Middle East in the 1920s
Cartography by Sue Lawes

ACKNOWLEDGMENTS

The idea of writing this book came to me in the course of a conversation with Timothy Dickinson in which he asked my views about the history of the Middle East. Later I put my ideas in written form. Jason Epstein suggested that the book be structured around a personality. I took his suggestion and chose Winston Churchill. Now I cannot think of how the book could have been structured any other way.

As books on my subject appeared in London, my friend and colleague Robert L. Sigmon would buy them for me and send them to me by airmail. And Professor Stanley Mallach of the University of Wisconsin-Milwaukee helped me find books I could not find elsewhere.

Alain Silvera, Professor of History at Bryn Mawr College and a lifelong friend, kept me abreast of the latest scholarship by supplying me with articles from learned journals as well as valuable ideas, information, and suggestions. He read and re-read the manuscript and offered detailed marginal corrections and comments. He showed the manuscript also to his Ph.D. student Kay Patterson, who offered extensive and careful comments. At my request, Professor Ernest Gellner of Cambridge University kindly arranged for me to meet Professor Elie Kedourie, whom I wanted to persuade to be the other academic reader of my manuscript. Professor Kedourie read the manuscript and gave me the benefit of his immense erudition and authoritative comments. I am grateful to him, and to Mrs Kedourie for her kindness and patience in putting up with my demands on her husband's time. Dr Nicholas Rizopoulos read the Greek-Turkish episodes and offered valuable suggestions. I hope I need not add that Professor Kedourie, Professor Silvera, Dr Rizopoulos, and Mrs Patterson are not responsible in any way for the opinions and conclusions I express in the book. Moreover, the manuscript has been extensively rewritten since they saw it, so there may well be factual or other statements in it they would have advised me to change.

Academic readers, in particular, will observe in reading the book that I owe an immense intellectual debt to the books and essays of many other scholars—more, indeed, than there is space to name here. Chief among those to whom I am thus indebted are Elie Kedourie, for his masterful studies of Middle Eastern and British history and politics, and Martin Gilbert, whose great life of Winston Churchill is essential to anyone writing about this period. I have leaned heavily on Gilbert's volumes—as everyone now must. And I was inspired by the example of Howard Sachar to believe that a history of the Middle East can be written—as I was attempting to do—on a very broad scale.

Samuel Clayton, the son of Sir Gilbert Clayton, was kind enough to spend the best part of an afternoon talking to me about his father. My thanks to him, and to his wife, the Lady Mary, for their hospitality in having me to tea at Kensington Palace.

In the course of my research in archives in Britain and elsewhere over the years, I have benefited from the kindness and patience of such unfailingly helpful librarians as Lesley Forbes of the University of Durham, Clive Hughes of the Imperial War Museum, Norman Higson of the University of Hull, Alan Bell of Rhodes House, Oxford, and Gillian Grant of the Middle East Centre, St Antony's College, Oxford. My heartfelt thanks to them all.

I owe an immense debt of gratitude to Rob Cowley, my editor at Henry Holt and an authority on the First World War, for his knowledgeable and helpful suggestions and for his constant encouragement and enthusiasm. Marian Wood at Henry Holt and Sara Menguç at André Deutsch saw me through the publication process with unfailing cheer and awesome efficiency.

For permission to reproduce quotations from documents I am indebted to the following:

—The Clerk of the Records, House of Lords Record Office, for permission to quote from the Lloyd George Papers in the Beaverbrook Collection in the custody of the House of Lords Record Office;

—the Sudan Archive of the University of Durham, on whose extensive collection I have drawn freely;

—Mrs Theresa Searight, and the Rhodes House Library, for permission to quote from the diaries of Richard Meinertzhagen;

—the Brynmor Jones Library of the University of Hull and Sir Tatton Sykes, Bart., for permission to quote from the papers of Sir Mark Sykes;

—the Middle East Centre, St Antony's College, Oxford, for permission to quote from their extensive collection, including the papers of Sir Hubert Young, T. E. Lawrence, Lord Allenby, William Yale, F. R. Somerset, C. D. Brunton, and the King Feisal and Balfour Declaration files;

—the Warden and Fellows of New College, Oxford, for permission to quote from Lord Milner's files;

—the Trustees of the Liddell Hart Centre for Military Archives at King's College, London, for permission to quote from Lord Allenby's papers.

Transcripts/Translations of Crown copyright records in the Public Record Office appear by permission of the Controller of H. M. Stationery Office.

For access to documentary material, I wish also to thank the British Library, London; Camellia Investments, Plc, London; the Weizmann Archives, Rehovot, Israel; the Bodleian Library, Oxford; the Imperial War Museum, London; the Houghton Library of Harvard University; and the New York Public Library.

A Note on Spelling

In spelling Turkish, Arabic, and Persian names and titles, I have used whatever form of spelling I am most familiar with from my reading over the years. So there is no system or consistency in it; but I would guess that the spellings most familiar to me will be the most familiar to the general reader as well.

INTRODUCTION

The Middle East, as we know it from today's headlines, emerged from decisions made by the Allies during and after the First World War. In the pages that follow I set out to tell in one volume the wide-ranging story of how and why—and out of what hopes and fears, loves and hatreds, mistakes and misunderstandings—these decisions were made.

Russian and French official accounts of what they were doing in the Middle East at that time were, not unnaturally, works of propaganda; British official accounts—and even the later memoirs of the officials concerned—were untruthful too. British officials who played a major role in the making of these decisions provided a version of events that was, at best, edited and, at worst, fictitious. They sought to hide their meddling in Moslem religious affairs (pages 96—105) and to pretend that they had entered the Middle East as patrons of Arab independence—a cause in which they did not in fact believe. Moreover, the Arab Revolt that formed the centerpiece of their narrative occurred not so much in reality as in the wonderful imagination of T. E. Lawrence, a teller of fantastic tales whom the American showman Lowell Thomas transformed into "Lawrence of Arabia."

The truth has come out over the course of decades in bits and pieces, and now, toward the end, in one great heap, with the opening of archives of hitherto secret official documents and private papers. It seemed to me—in 1979, when I started my research—that we had arrived at a point where at last it would be possible to tell the real story of what happened; hence this book.

During the past decade I have worked in the archives, studied the literature, and put together the findings of modern scholarship to show the picture that is formed when the pieces of the puzzle are assembled. The authors whose works I cite in the Notes at the end of the book made most of the new discoveries, though I have made some too: what the Young Turk leaders may have done in order to persuade the Germans to ally with them on 1 August 1914 (pages 60—6), for example, and why the Arab negotiator al-Faruqi may have drawn a line through inland Syria as the frontier of Arab national independence (page 178).

Then, too, I may be the first to disentangle, or at any rate to draw attention to, the many misunderstandings which in 1916 set off a hidden tug-of-war within the British bureaucracy between Sir Mark Sykes, London's desk man in charge of the Middle East, and his friend Gilbert Clayton, the head of intelligence in Cairo (page 193). I found that neither Sykes nor Clayton ever realized that Sykes, in the 1916 negotiations with France, misunderstood what Clayton had asked him to do. Sykes did the exact opposite, believing in all innocence that he was carrying out Clayton's wishes, while Clayton felt sure that Sykes had knowingly let him down. Since Clayton never mentioned the matter to him, Sykes remained unaware that differences had arisen between him and his colleague. So in the months and years that followed, Sykes mistakenly assumed that he and Clayton were still at one, when in fact within the bureaucracy Clayton had become an adversary of his policy—and perhaps the most dangerous one.

Getting the bureaucratic politics right—and I hope that is what I have done—has been one of my chief endeavors. But I have tried to do more than clarify specific processes and episodes. The book is meant to give a panoramic view of what was happening to the Middle East as a whole, and to show that its reshaping was a function of Great Power politics at a unique time: the exact moment when the waves of western European imperial expansionism flowed forward to hit their high-water mark, and then felt the first powerful tugs of the tide that was going to pull them back.

The Middle East, as I conceive it, means not only Egypt, Israel, Iran, Turkey, and the Arab states of Asia, but also Soviet Central Asia and Afghanistan: the entire arena in which Britain, from the Napoleonic Wars onward, fought to shield the road to India from the onslaughts first of France and then of Russia in what came to be known as "the Great Game."

Other studies of the First World War and its aftermath in the region have tended to deal with a single country or area. Even those dealing with European policy in the Arab or Turkish East as a whole have focused solely, for example, on the role of Britain, or of Britain and France. But I place the creation of the modern Middle East in a wider framework: I see what happened as the culmination of the nineteenth-century Great Game, and therefore show Russia, too, playing a leading role in the story. It was in whole or in part because of Russia that Kitchener initiated a British alliance with the Arab Moslem world (pages 97−8); that Britain and France, though they would have preferred to preserve the Turkish Empire in the region, decided instead to occupy and partition the Middle East (pages 137−42); that the Foreign Office publicly proclaimed British support for the establishment of a Jewish National Home in Palestine (pages 184–93); and that, after the war, a number of British officials felt that Britain was obliged to hold the line in the Middle East against crusading Bolshevism (pages 465–8). Yet, so far as I know, this is the first book to tell the story as that of the Middle East in the widest sense: the Great Game sense, in which Russia plays a central role.

As you will see when you read the book, Middle Eastern personalities, circumstances, and political cultures do not figure a great deal in the narrative that follows, except when I suggest the outlines and dimensions of what European politicians were ignoring when they made their decisions. This is a book about the decision-making process, and in the 1914–22 period, Europeans and Americans were the only ones seated around the table when the decisions were made.

It was an era in which Middle Eastern countries and frontiers were fabricated in Europe. Iraq and what we now call Jordan, for example, were British inventions, lines drawn on an empty map by British politicians after the First World War; while the boundaries of Saudi Arabia, Kuwait, and Iraq were established by a British civil servant in 1922, and the frontiers between Moslems and Christians were drawn by France in Syria-Lebanon and by Russia on the borders of Armenia and Soviet Azerbaijan.

The European powers at that time believed they could change Moslem Asia in the very fundamentals of its political existence, and in their attempt to do so introduced an artificial state system into the Middle East that has made it into a region of countries that have not become nations even today. The basis of political life in the Middle East—religion—was called into question by the Russians, who proposed communism, and by the British, who proposed nationalism or dynastic loyalty, in its place. Khomeini's Iran in the Shi'ite world and the Moslem Brotherhood in Egypt, Syria, and elsewhere in the Sunni world keep that issue alive. The French government, which in the Middle East *did* allow religion to be the basis of politics—even of its own—championed one sect against the others; and that, too, is an issue kept alive, notably in the communal strife that has ravaged Lebanon in the 1970s and 1980s.

The year 1922 seems to me to have been the point of no return in setting the various clans of the Middle East on their collision courses, so that the especial interest and excitement of the years with which this book is concerned, 1914 through 1922, is that they were the creative, formative years, in which everything seemed (and may indeed have been) possible. It was a time when Europeans, not implausibly, believed Arab and Jewish nationalism to be natural allies; when the French, not the Arabs, were the dangerous enemies of the Zionist movement; and when oil was not an important factor in the politics of the Middle East.

By 1922, however, the choices had narrowed and the courses had been set; the Middle East had started along a road that was to lead to the endless wars (between Israel and her neighbors, among others, and between rival militias in Lebanon) and to the always-escalating acts of terrorism (hijacking, assassination, and random massacre) that have been a characteristic feature of international life in the 1970s and 1980s. These are a part of the legacy of the history recounted in the pages that follow.

Two stories are told in the book and then merge into one. The first begins with Lord Kitchener's decision at the outset of the First World War to partition the Middle East after the war between Britain, France, and Russia, and with his appointment of Sir Mark Sykes to work out the details. The book then follows Sykes during the wartime years, as he worked out Britain's blueprint for the Middle East's future. It goes on to show that, in large part, the program Sykes had formulated was realized after the war, and was embodied in documents formally adopted (for the most part) in 1922.

This was the story that I originally set out to write. It was meant to show that if you put together a number of the documents and decisions of 1922—the Allenby Declaration establishing nominal independence for Egypt, the Palestine Mandate and the Churchill White Paper for Palestine (from which Israel and Jordan spring), the British treaty establishing the status of Iraq, the French Mandate for Syria and Lebanon, Britain's placing new monarchs on the thrones of Egypt and Iraq and sponsoring a new princely ruler for (what was to become) Jordan, the Russian proclamation of a Soviet Union in which Russia would re-establish her rule in Moslem Central Asia—you would see that when taken together they amounted to an overall settlement of the Middle Eastern Question. Moreover, this settlement of 1922 (as I call it, because most of its elements cluster in and around that year) flowed from the wartime negotiations which Sir Mark Sykes had conducted with France and Russia to agree upon a partition of the postwar Middle East between them. The French received a bit less than had been agreed, and the Russians were only allowed to keep what they had already taken before the war, but the principle of allowing them to share with Britain in the partition and rule of Moslem Asia was respected. Within the British sphere, all went according to the Sykes plan: Britain ruled for the most part indirectly, as protector of nominally independent Arab monarchies, and proclaimed herself the sponsor of both Arab and Jewish nationalism.

In addition to establishing that there had been a settlement of 1922 in the Middle East, I show that our quarrel with that settlement (to the extent that with hindsight we would have designed the new Middle East differently) is not what we sometimes believe it to be. It is not even that the British government at that time failed to devise a settlement that would satisfy the needs and desires of the peoples of the Middle East; it is that they were trying to do something altogether different. For Lord Kitchener and his delegated agent Mark Sykes the Middle Eastern Question was what it had been for more than a century: where would the French frontier in the Middle East be drawn and, more important, where would the Russian frontier in the Middle East be drawn?

That, as I say, is the story which I set out to tell. But in the telling of it, another emerged: the story of how, between 1914 and 1922, Britain changed, and British officials and politicians changed their minds, so that by 1922—when they formally committed themselves to their program for remaking the Middle East—they no longer believed in it. In the course of the narrative we see the British government of 1914, 1915, and 1916, which welcomed a Russian and a French presence in the postwar Middle East, turn into a postwar government that regarded Russia in the Middle East as a danger and France in the region as a disaster. We see the pro-Zionists of 1917 turn into the anti-Zionists of 1921 and 1922; and the enthusiasts for Feisal's Arab Movement turn against Feisal as untrustworthy and against his brother Abdullah as hopelessly ineffectual. Above all, we see Britain embarking on a vast new imperial enterprise in the Middle East—one that would take generations to achieve, if its object were to remake the Middle East as India had been remade—at the very time that the British public was turning to a policy of scaling down overseas commitments and was deciding it wanted no more imperial adventures.

It may well be that the crisis of political civilization that the Middle East endures today stems not merely from Britain's destruction of the old order in the region in 1918, and her decisions in 1922 about how it should be replaced, but also from the lack of conviction she brought in subsequent years to the program of imposing the settlement of 1922 to which she was pledged.

The book I intended to write was only about how Europe went about changing the Middle East; the book that emerged was also about how Europe changed at the same time, and about how the two movements interacted.

Lloyd George, Woodrow Wilson, Kitchener of Khartoum, Lawrence of Arabia, Lenin, Stalin, and Mussolini—men who helped shape the twentieth century—are among those who played leading roles in the drama that unfolds in *A Peace to End All Peace*, striving to remake the world in the light of their own vision. Winston Churchill, above all, presides over the pages of this book: a dominating figure whose genius animated events and whose larger-than-life personality colored and enlivened them.

For Churchill, as for Lloyd George, Wilson, Lenin, Stalin, and
the others—and for such men as Jan Christian Smuts, Leo Amery,
and Lord Milner—the Middle East was an essential component or a
testing area of their worldview. Their vision of the future of the
Middle East was central to their idea of the sort of twentieth century
they passionately believed would or should emerge as a phoenix from
the ashes of the First World War. In that sense, the history recounted
in the pages that follow is the story of how the twentieth century was
created, as well as the modern Middle East.

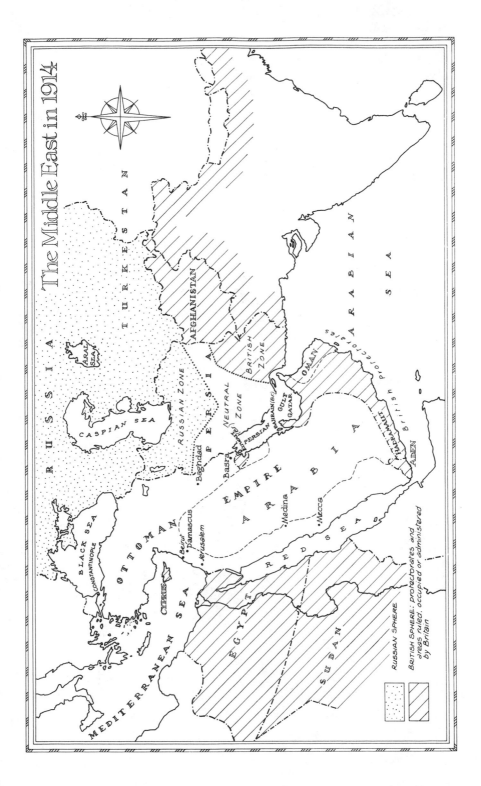

The Middle East in 1914

RUSSIA

TURKESTAN

BLACK SEA
CONSTANTINOPLE

CASPIAN SEA

ARAL SEA

AFGHANISTAN

RUSSIAN ZONE

PERSIA

NEUTRAL ZONE

BRITISH ZONE

OTTOMAN

EMPIRE

Baghdad

Basra

PERSIAN GULF

BAHRAIN (Br.)

GULF

QATAR

OMAN

British protectorates

ARABIA

CYPRUS

MEDITERRANEAN SEA

Beirut

Damascus

Jerusalem

Medina

Mecca

RED SEA

HADRAMAUT

ADEN

ARABIAN

SEA

EGYPT

SUDAN

RUSSIAN SPHERE

BRITISH SPHERE: protectorates and
areas ruled, occupied or administered
by Britain

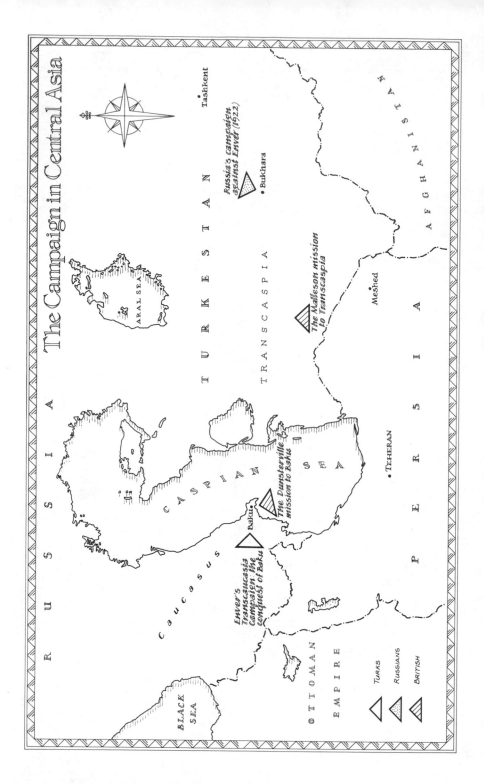

The Campaign in Central Asia

RUSSIA

TURKESTAN

ARAL SEA

Tashkent

Russia's campaign against Enver (1922)

Bukhara

TRANSCASPIA

The Malleson mission to Transcaspia

Meshed

AFGHANISTAN

CASPIAN SEA

Caucasus

The Dunsterville mission to Baku

Baku

Enver's Transcaucasia Campaign: the conquest of Baku

PERSIA

TEHERAN

BLACK SEA

OTTOMAN EMPIRE

TURKS

RUSSIANS

BRITISH

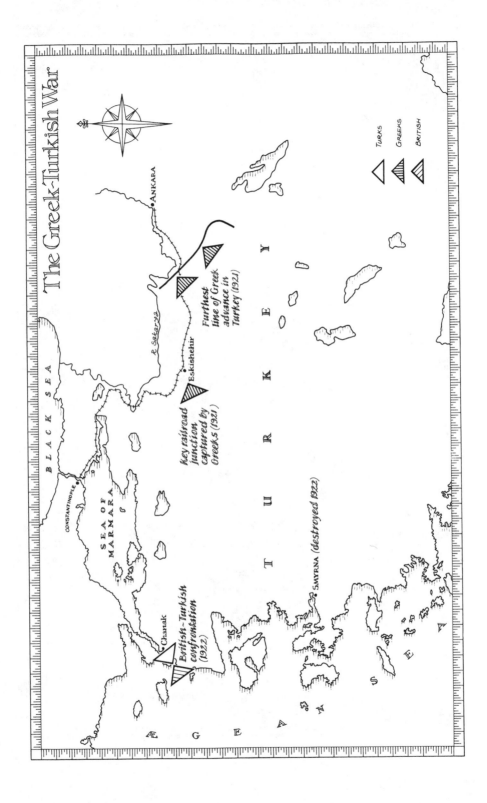

The Greek-Turkish War

TURKS

GREEKS

BRITISH

BLACK SEA

ANKARA

R. Sakarya

Furthest
line of Greek
advance in
Turkey (1921)

Eskishehir

Key railroad
junction
captured by
Greeks (1921)

T U R K E Y

SEA OF
MARMARA

CONSTANTINOPLE

SMYRNA (destroyed 1922)

Chanak

British-Turkish
confrontation
(1922)

A E G E A N   S E A

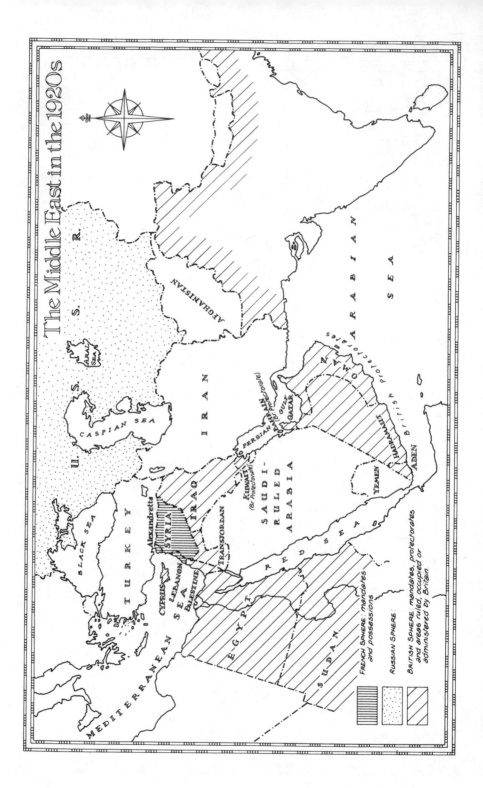

PART I

AT THE CROSSROADS OF HISTORY

1

THE LAST DAYS OF OLD EUROPE

I

In the late spring of 1912, the graceful yacht *Enchantress* put out to sea from rainy Genoa for a Mediterranean pleasure cruise—a carefree cruise without itinerary or time-schedule. The skies brightened as she steamed south. Soon she was bathed in sunshine.

Enchantress belonged to the British Admiralty. The accommodation aboard was as grand as that on the King's own yacht. The crew numbered nearly a hundred and served a dozen or so guests, who had come from Britain via Paris, where they had stayed at the Ritz. Among them were the British Prime Minister, Herbert Asquith; his brilliant 25-year-old daughter Violet; the civilian head of the Admiralty, Winston Churchill; and Churchill's small party of family members and close colleagues. In the final enchanted years before the First World War brought their world to an end, they were as privileged a group as any the world has known.

Violet Asquith kept a diary of her journey. In Pompeii she and her friends wandered "down the long lovely silent streets" that once had pulsated with the life of Imperial Rome; now, she noted, those once lively streets were overgrown with grass and vegetation.[1] In Sicily her party climbed to the ruins of an ancient Greek fortress and, amidst wild lavender and herbs, had a picnic lunch, sitting on blocks of stone from the fallen walls. Later they went higher still to watch the sunset over the sea from what remained of the old Greek theater on the heights. There they lay "among wild thyme and humming bees and watched the sea changing from blue to flame and then to cool jade green as the sun dropped into it and the stars came out."[2]

Rotations and revolutions—the heavenly movements that cause day to become night and spring/summer to become autumn/winter—were reflected in her observations of the landscape and its lighting; but a sense of the mortality of civilizations and of political powers and dominations did not overshadow Violet's cheerful vision of her youthful voyage to the lands of antiquity. Her father presided over an empire roughly twice as large as the Roman Empire at its zenith; she may well have thought that her father's empire would last twice as long too.

The Prime Minister, an enthusiastic sightseer, was inseparable from his Baedeker guidebook. An ardent classicist, he read and wrote with ease and pleasure in classical Greek and Latin. Winston Churchill, no scholar of ancient languages or literature, was as jealous as a child. "Those Greeks and Romans," he protested, "they are so overrated. They only said everything *first*. I've said just as good things myself. But they got in before me."[3]

Violet noted that, "It was in vain that my father pointed out that the world had been going on for quite a long time before the Greeks and Romans appeared upon the scene."[4] The Prime Minister was an intellectual, aware that the trend among historians of the ancient world was away from an exclusive concern with the European cultures of the Greeks and Romans. The American professor James Henry Breasted had won wide acceptance for the thesis that modern civilization—that is, European civilization—had its beginnings not in Greece and Rome, but in the Middle East: in Egypt and Judaea, Babylonia and Assyria, Sumer and Akkad. Civilization—whose roots stretched thousands of years into the past, into the soil of those Middle Eastern monarchies that long ago had crumbled into dust— was seen to have culminated in the global supremacy of the European peoples, their ideals, and their way of life.

In the early years of the twentieth century, when Churchill and his guests voyaged aboard the *Enchantress*, it was usual to assume that the European peoples would continue to play a dominating role in world affairs for as far ahead in time as the mind's eye could see. It was also not uncommon to suppose that, having already accomplished most of what many regarded as the West's historical mission—shaping the political destinies of the other peoples of the globe—they would eventually complete it. Conspicuous among the domains still to be dealt with were those of the Middle East, one of the few regions left on the planet that had not yet been socially, culturally, and politically reshaped in the image of Europe.

II

The Middle East, although it had been of great interest to western diplomats and politicians during the nineteenth century as an arena in which Great Game rivalries were played out, was of only marginal concern to them in the early years of the twentieth century when those rivalries were apparently resolved. The region had become a political backwater. It was assumed that the European powers would one day take the region in hand, but there was no longer a sense of urgency their doing so.

Few Europeans of Churchill's generation knew or cared what went on in the languid empires of the Ottoman Sultan or the Persian Shah. An occasional Turkish massacre of Armenians would lead to a public outcry in the West, but would evoke no more lasting concern than Russian massacres of Jews. Worldly statesmen who privately believed there was nothing to be done would go through the public motions of urging the Sultan to reform; there the matter would end. Petty intrigues at court, a corrupt officialdom, shifting tribal alliances, and a sluggish, apathetic population composed the picture that Europeans formed of the region's affairs. There was little in the picture to cause ordinary people living in London, or Paris, or New York to believe that it affected their lives or interests. In Berlin, it is true, planners looked to the opening up of railroads and new markets in the region; but these were commercial ventures.* The passions that now drive troops and terrorists to kill and be killed—and that compel global attention—had not yet been aroused.

At the time, the political landscape of the Middle East looked different from that of today. Israel, Jordan, Syria, Iraq, and Saudi Arabia did not exist then. Most of the Middle East still rested, as it had for centuries, under the drowsy and negligent sway of the Ottoman Empire, a relatively tranquil domain in which history, like everything else, moved slowly.

Today, toward the close of the twentieth century, the politics of the Middle East present a completely different aspect: they are explosive. No man played a more crucial role—at times unintentionally—in giving birth to the Middle East we live with today than did Winston Churchill, who before the First World War was a rising but widely distrusted young English politician with no particular interest in Moslem Asia. A curious destiny drove Churchill and the Middle East to interfere repeatedly in one another's political lives. This left its marks; there are frontier lines now running across the face of the Middle East that are scar-lines from those encounters with him.

---

* The Baghdad Railway project remains the best-known example of German economic penetration of the region. The story is a tangled one and often misunderstood, but the British originally encouraged and supported the project, little aware at the outset of the dangers it might pose. Eventually the project became a source of discord between Britain and Germany which, however, was resolved by an agreement reached between the two countries in 1914.

2

THE LEGACY OF THE GREAT
GAME IN ASIA

I

Churchill, Asquith, and such Cabinet colleagues as the Foreign Secretary, Sir Edward Grey, the Chancellor of the Exchequer, David Lloyd George, and, later, the War Minister, Lord Kitchener, were to play a decisive role in creating the modern Middle East; but in doing so they were unable to escape from a Victorian political legacy that Asquith's Liberal government thought it had rejected. Asquith and Grey, having turned their backs on the nineteenth-century rivalry with France and Russia in the Middle East, believed that they could walk away from it; but events were to prove them wrong.

II

The struggle for the Middle East, pitting England against European rivals, was a result of the imperial expansion ushered in by the voyages of Columbus, Vasco da Gama, Magellan, and Drake. Having discovered the sea routes in the fifteenth and sixteenth centuries, the European powers went on to vie with one another for control of the rest of the world. England was a relatively late starter in the race, but eventually surpassed the others.

During the eighteenth century the British Isles, despite their small size, finally established an empire that encircled the globe. Like the Spaniards and the Dutch before them, the British boasted that their monarch now reigned over dominions on which the sun never set. By 1912, when Winston Churchill and Herbert Asquith cruised aboard the *Enchantress*, their monarch, George V, ruled a quarter of the land surface of the planet.

Of none of their conquests were the British more proud than those in the storied East. Yet there was irony in these triumphs; for in besting France in Asia and the Pacific, and in crowning that achievement by winning India, Britain had stretched her line of transport and communications so far that it could be cut at many points.

Napoleon Bonaparte exposed this vulnerability in 1798, when he invaded Egypt and marched on Syria—intending, he later maintained, from there to follow the path of legend and glory, past Babylon, to India. Though checked in his own plans, Napoleon afterwards persuaded the mad Czar Paul to launch the Russian army on the same path.

Britain's response was to support the native regimes of the Middle East against European expansion. She did not desire to control the region, but to keep any other European power from doing so.

Throughout the nineteenth century, successive British governments therefore pursued a policy of propping up the tottering Islamic realms in Asia against European interference, subversion, and invasion. In doing so their principal opponent soon became the Russian Empire. Defeating Russian designs in Asia emerged as the obsessive goal of generations of British civilian and military officials. Their attempt to do so was, for them, "the Great Game,"[1] in which the stakes ran high. George Curzon, the future Viceroy of India, defined the stakes clearly: "Turkestan, Afghanistan, Transcaspia, Persia—to many these names breathe only a sense of utter remoteness ... To me, I confess, they are the pieces on a chessboard upon which is being played out a game for the dominion of the world."[2] Queen Victoria put it even more clearly: it was, she said, "a question of Russian or British supremacy in the world."[3]

III

It appears to have been a British officer named Arthur Conolly who first called it "the Great Game." He played it gallantly, along the Himalayan frontier and in the deserts and oases of Central Asia, and lost in a terrible way: an Uzbek emir cast him for two months into a well which was filled with vermin and reptiles, and then what remained of him was brought up and beheaded. The phrase "the Great Game" was found in his papers and quoted by a historian of the First Afghan War.[4] Rudyard Kipling made it famous in his novel *Kim*, the story of an Anglo-Indian boy and his Afghan mentor foiling Russian intrigues along the highways to India.[*]

The game had begun even before 1829, when the Duke of Wellington, then Prime Minister, entered into official correspondence on the subject of how best to protect India against a Russian

---

[*] These activities of the rival intelligence services are what some writers mean by the Great Game; others use the phrase in the broader sense in which it is used in this book.

attack through Afghanistan. The best way, it was agreed, was by keeping Russia out of Afghanistan. British strategy thereafter was to employ the decaying regimes of Islamic Asia as a gigantic buffer between British India and its route to Egypt, and the threatening Russians. This policy was associated especially with the name of Lord Palmerston, who developed it during his many years as Foreign Minister (1830–4, 1836–41, and 1846–51) and Prime Minister (1855–8 and 1859–65).

The battle to support friendly buffer regimes raged with particular intensity at the western and eastern ends of the Asian continent, where the control of dominating strategic positions was at stake. In western Asia the locus of strategic concern was Constantinople (Istanbul), the ancient Byzantium, which for centuries had dominated the crossroads of world politics. Situated above the narrow straits of the Dardanelles, it commanded both the east/west passage between Europe and Asia and the north/south passage between the Mediterranean and the Black Sea. So long as Constantinople was not in unfriendly hands, the powerful British navy could sail through the Dardanelles into the Black Sea to dominate the Russian coastline. But if the Russians were to conquer the straits they could not merely keep the British fleet from coming in; they could also send their own fleet out, into the Mediterranean, where its presence could threaten the British lifeline.

Toward the far side of the Asian continent, the locus of strategic concern was the stretch of high mountain ranges in and adjoining Afghanistan, from which invaders could pour down into the plains of British India. Britain's aim in eastern Asia was to keep Russia from establishing any sort of presence on those dominating heights.

Sometimes as a cold war, sometimes as a hot one, the struggle between Britain and Russia raged from the Dardanelles to the Himalayas for almost a hundred years. Its outcome was something of a draw.

IV

There were vital matters at stake in Britain's long struggle against Russia; and while some of these eventually fell by the wayside, others remained, alongside newer ones that emerged.

In 1791 Britain's Prime Minister, William Pitt, expressed fear that the Russian Empire might be able to overthrow the European balance of power. That fear revived after Russia played a crucial role in the final defeat of Napoleon in 1814–15, but diminished again after 1856, when Russia was defeated in the Crimean War.

From 1830 onward, Lord Palmerston and his successors feared

that if Russia destroyed the Ottoman Empire the scramble to pick up the pieces might lead to a major war between the European powers. That always remained a concern.

By the middle of the nineteenth century, British trade with the Ottoman Empire began to assume a major importance, and economic issues were added to the controversy, pitting free trade Britain against protectionist Russia. The deep financial involvement of France and Italy in Ottoman affairs, followed by German economic penetration, turned the area in which Russia and Britain conducted their struggle into a minefield of national economic interests.

Oil entered the picture only in the early twentieth century. But it did not play a major role in the Great Game even then, both because there were few politicians who foresaw the coming importance of oil, and because it was not then known that oil existed in the Middle East in such a great quantity. Most of Britain's oil (more than 80 percent, before and during the First World War) came from the United States. At the time, Persia was the only significant Middle Eastern producer other than Russia, and even Persia's output was insignificant in terms of world production. In 1913, for example, the United States produced 140 times more oil than did Persia.[5]

From the beginning of the Great Game until far into the twentieth century, the most deeply felt concern of British leaders was for the safety of the road to the East. When Queen Victoria assumed the title of Empress of India in 1877 formal recognition was given to the evolution of Britain into a species of dual monarchy—the British Empire and the Empire of India. The line between them was thus a lifeline, but over it, and casting a long shadow, hung the sword of the czars.

British leaders seemed not to take into account the possibility that, in expanding southwards and eastwards, the Russians were impelled by internal historical imperatives of their own which had nothing to do with India or Britain. The czars and their ministers believed that it was their country's destiny to conquer the south and the east, just as the Americans at the time believed it their manifest destiny to conquer the west. In each case, the dream was to fill out an entire continent from ocean to ocean. The Russian Imperial Chancellor, Prince Gorchakov, put it more or less in those terms in 1864 in a memorandum in which he set forth his goals for his country. He argued that the need for secure frontiers obliged the Russians to go on devouring the rotting regimes to their south. He pointed out that "the United States in America, France in Algiers, Holland in her colonies—all have been drawn into a course where ambition plays a smaller role than imperious necessity, and the greatest difficulty is knowing where to stop."[6]

The British feared that Russia did not know where to stop; and, as an increasingly democratic society engaged generation after generation in the conflict with despotic Russia, they eventually developed a hatred of Russia that went beyond the particular political and economic differences that divided the two countries. Britons grew to object to Russians not merely for what they did but for who they were.

At the same time, however, Liberals in and out of Parliament began to express their abhorrence of the corrupt and despotic Middle Eastern regimes that their own government supported against the Russian threat. In doing so, they struck a responsive chord in the country's electorate. Atrocities committed by the Ottoman Empire against Christian minorities were thunderingly denounced by the Liberal leader, William Ewart Gladstone, in the 1880 election campaign in which he overthrew and replaced the Conservative Prime Minister, Benjamin Disraeli, Earl of Beaconsfield.

Claiming that the Sultan's regime was "a bottomless pit of fraud and falsehood,"[7] Gladstone, in his 1880−5 administration, washed Britain's hands of the Ottoman involvement, and the British government withdrew its protection and influence from Constantinople. The Turks, unable to stand on their own, turned therefore for support to another power, Bismarck's Germany; and Germany took Britain's place at the Sublime Porte.

When the Conservatives returned to office, it was too late to go back. Robert Cecil, 3rd Marquess of Salisbury (Prime Minister: 1885−6, 1886−92, 1895−1900, 1900−2), aware that the Ottoman rulers were jeopardizing their own sovereignty through mismanagement, had thought of using such influence as Britain could exert to guide and, to some extent, reform the regime. Of Gladstone's having dissipated that influence, he lamented: "They have just thrown it away into the sea, without getting anything whatever in exchange."[8]

V

Germany's entry on the scene, at Constantinople and elsewhere, marked the beginning of a new age in world politics. The German Empire, formally created on 18 January 1871, within decades had replaced Russia as the principal threat to British interests.

In part this was because of Britain's relative industrial decline. In the middle of the nineteenth century, Britain produced about two-thirds of the world's coal, about half of its iron, and more than 70 percent of its steel; indeed over 40 percent of the entire world output of traded manufactured goods was produced within the British Isles at that time. Half the world's industrial production was then British-owned, but by 1870 the figure had sunk to 32 percent, and by 1910, to 15 percent.[9] In newer and increasingly more important industries, such as chemicals and machine-tools, Germany took the lead. Even Britain's pre-eminent position in world finance—in 1914 she held 41 percent of gross international investment[10]—was a facet of decline; British investors preferred to place their money in dynamic economies in the Americas and elsewhere abroad.

Military factors were also involved. The development of railroads radically altered the strategic balance between land power and sea power to the detriment of the latter. Sir Halford Mackinder, the prophet of geopolitics, underlined the realities of a new situation in which enemy railroad trains would speed troops and munitions directly to their destination by the straight line which constitutes the shortest distance between two points, while the British navy would sail slowly around the circumference of a continent and arrive too late. The railroad network of the German Empire made the Kaiser's realm the most advanced military power in the world, and Britain's precarious naval supremacy began to seem less relevant than it had been.

Walter Bagehot, editor of the influential London magazine, *The Economist*, drew the conclusion that, because of Germany, Russian expansion no longer needed to be feared: "... the old idea that Russia is already so great a power that Europe needs to be afraid of her ... belongs to the pre-Germanic age."[11] Russia's disastrous defeat by Japan (1904–5), followed by revolutionary uprisings in St Petersburg and throughout the country in 1905, suggested that, in any event, the Czar's armies were no longer strong enough to remain a cause for concern.

The Conservative government of Arthur James Balfour (1902–5) nonetheless continued to pursue the old rivalry as well as the new one, allying Britain not only with Japan against Russia, but also with France against Germany. But Sir Edward Grey, Foreign Secretary in the successor Liberal administration of Henry Campbell-Bannerman (1905–8), pictured the two policies as contradictory. "Russia was the ally of France," he wrote, "we could not pursue at one and the same time a policy of agreement with France and a policy of counteralliances against Russia."[12]

Grey therefore negotiated a treaty with Russia, executed in 1907, that reconciled the differences between the two countries in Asia. Tibet was neutralized; Russia gave up her interest in Afghanistan, and left control of that country's foreign policy in Britain's hands; and Persia was divided into a Russian zone, a neutral zone, and a British zone. The Great Game had seemingly been brought to an end.

It could have been anticipated that the settlement of 1907 would arouse fears in Constantinople that Britain would no longer protect

Turkey against Russia. A Palmerston or a Stratford Canning might have allayed such fears, but neither Sir Edward Grey nor his ambassador in Constantinople took the trouble to do so.

VI

There was an intellectual time lag between London and the outposts of empire. Grey, Asquith, and their Liberal colleagues saw Britain's traditional rivals, France and Russia, as British friends and allies in the post-Victorian age. But British officers, agents, and civil servants stationed along the great arc that swung from Egypt and the Sudan to India failed in many cases to adopt the new outlook. Having spent a lifetime countering Russian and French intrigues in the Middle East, they continued to regard Russia and France as their country's enemies. Events in 1914 and the succeeding years were to bring their Victorian political views back into unexpected prominence.

In one respect officers in the field and ministers in London were in agreement: both shared the assumption that what remained of the independent Middle East would eventually fall under European influence and guidance. Asquith and Grey had no desire for Britain to expand further into the Middle East, while junior British officers in Cairo and Khartoum harbored designs on the Arab-speaking provinces to their east. Both groups believed, however, that the Ottoman Empire in the Middle East would collapse one day and that one or more of the European powers would have to pick up the pieces. This assumption—that when the Ottoman Empire disappeared, Europe would have to take its place—proved to be one of those motors that drive history.

3

THE MIDDLE EAST BEFORE
THE WAR

I

For decades and indeed centuries before the outbreak of the First
World War in 1914, the native regimes of the Middle East had been,
in every sense, losing ground to Europe. The khanates of Central
Asia, including Khiva and Bukhara, had fallen to Russia, as had
portions of the Persian Empire. The Arab sheikhdoms along the
Gulf coast route from Suez to India had been brought under British
sway; and Cyprus and Egypt, though formally still attached to
Turkey, were in fact occupied and administered by Britain. The
Anglo-Russian Agreement of 1907 brought Afghanistan into the
British sphere, and divided most of Persia between Britain and
Russia. In the Moslem Middle East, only the Ottoman Empire
effectively retained its independence—though precariously, as its
frontiers came under pressure.

Indeed, the still-independent Turkish Sultanate looked out of
place in the modern world. Like a ruined temple of classical antiquity, with some of its shattered columns still erect and visible to
tourists such as those aboard the *Enchantress*, the Ottoman Empire
was a structure that had survived the bygone era to which it belonged. It was a relic of invasions from the east a millennium ago:
beginning around AD 1,000, waves of nomad horsemen streamed
forth from the steppes and deserts of central and northeast Asia,
conquering the peoples and lands in their path as they rode west.
Pagan or animist in religious belief, and speaking one or other of the
Mongolian or Turkish languages, they carved out a variety of principalities and kingdoms for themselves, among them the empires of
Genghis Khan and Tamerlane. The Ottoman (or Osmanli) Empire,
founded by Turkish-speaking horsemen who had converted to Islam,
was another such empire; it took its name from Osman, a borderland
ghazi (warrior for the Moslem faith) born in the thirteenth century,
who campaigned on the outskirts of the Eastern Roman (or
Byzantine) Empire in Anatolia.

In the fifteenth century Osman's successors conquered and replaced the Byzantine Empire. Riding on to new conquests, the
Ottoman Turks expanded in all directions: north to the Crimea, east
to Baghdad and Basra, south to the coasts of Arabia and the Gulf,
west to Egypt and North Africa—and into Europe. At its peak, in
the sixteenth century, the Ottoman Empire included most of the
Middle East, North Africa, and what are now the Balkan countries of
Europe—Greece, Yugoslavia, Albania, Rumania, and Bulgaria—as
well as much of Hungary. It stretched from the Persian Gulf to the
river Danube; its armies stopped only at the gates of Vienna. Its
population was estimated at between thirty and fifty million at a time
when England's population was perhaps four million; and it ruled
more than twenty nationalities.[1]

The Ottomans never entirely outgrew their origins as a marauding
war band. They enriched themselves by capturing wealth and slaves;
the slaves, conscripted into the Ottoman ranks, rose to replace the
commanders who retired, and went on to capture wealth and slaves
in their turn. Invading new territories was the only path they knew
to economic growth. In the sixteenth and seventeenth centuries,
when the conquests turned into defeats and retreats, the dynamic of
Ottoman existence was lost; the Turks had mastered the arts of war
but not those of government.

Ottoman leaders in the nineteenth century attempted programs of
sweeping reform. Their goals were the centralization of government;
the establishment of an executive branch under the Sultan's chief
minister, the Grand Vizier; the rationalization of taxation and conscription; the establishment of constitutional guarantees; the found-
ing of secular public schools offering technical, vocational, and other
training; and the like. A start—but not much more—was made along
these lines. Most of the reforms took place only on paper; and as an
anachronism in the modern world, the ramshackle Ottoman regime
seemed doomed to disappear.

The empire was incoherent. Its Ottoman rulers were not an ethnic
group; though they spoke Turkish, many were descendants of once-
Christian slaves from Balkan Europe and elsewhere. The empire's
subjects (a wide variety of peoples, speaking Turkish, Semitic,
Kurdish, Slavic, Armenian, Greek, and other languages) had little in
common with, and in many cases little love for, one another.
Though European observers later were to generalize about, for
example, "Arabs," in fact Egyptians and Arabians, Syrians and
Iraqis were peoples of different history, ethnic background, and
outlook. The multinational, multilingual empire was a mosaic of
peoples who did not mix; in the towns, Armenians, Greeks, Jews,
and others each lived in their own separate quarters.

Religion had some sort of unifying effect, for the empire was a theocracy—a Moslem rather than a Turkish state—and most of its subjects were Moslems. The Ottoman Sultan was regarded as caliph (temporal and spiritual successor to the Prophet, Mohammed) by the majority group within Islam, the Sunnis. But among others of the seventy-one sects of Islam, especially the numerous Shi'ites, there was doctrinal opposition to the Sultan's Sunni faith and to his claims to the caliphate. And for those who were not Moslem (perhaps 25 percent of the population at the beginning of the twentieth century), but Greek Orthodox, Roman Catholic, Armenian Catholic, Armenian Gregorian, Jewish, Protestant, Maronite, Samaritan, Nestorian Christian, Syrian United Orthodox, Monophysite, or any one of a number of others, religion was a divisive rather than a unifying political factor.

The extent to which religion governed everyday life in the Middle East was something that European visitors in the nineteenth and early twentieth centuries found remarkable; for religion had played no such role in Europe for centuries. Indeed, Europeans visited the Middle East largely to see the past. They came to see Biblical sites, or excavated wonders of the ancient world, or nomads who lived as they had in the time of Abraham.

The Porte, too, appeared to live in the past. Ottoman officials continued to pretend, for example, that Bulgaria formed part of the empire long after losing control of that territory in 1878, and counted Egyptians as among its subjects even after Britain occupied Egypt in 1882. For this and other reasons, Ottoman statistics were unreliable, and it is only in the roughest sense that we can say that the empire's population in the early twentieth century may have been about twenty to twenty-five million, in a territory—depending on how it is defined—about six times the size of Texas. It comprised, broadly speaking, most of the Arabian peninsula and what is now Turkey, Israel, Lebanon, Jordan, Syria, and Iraq.

Until the early twentieth century, the Ottoman Empire was for most of the time under the absolute personal rule of the Sultan. In at least one respect he was quite unlike a European monarch: as the son of a woman of the harem, he was always half-slave by birth. Under his rule civil, military, and Holy Law administrations could be discerned in an empire carefully divided into provinces and cantons. But the appearance of orderly administration—indeed of effective administration of any sort—was chimerical. As Gertrude Bell, an experienced English traveler in Middle Eastern lands, was later to write, "No country which turned to the eye of the world an appearance of established rule and centralized Government was, to a greater extent than the Ottoman Empire, a land of make-believe."[2] There were army garrisons, it is true, scattered about the empire, but otherwise power was diffuse and the centralized authority was more myth than reality. Gertrude Bell, in the course of her travels, found that outside the towns, Ottoman administration vanished and the local sheikh or headman ruled instead. There were districts, too, where brigands roamed at will. The rickety Turkish government was even incapable of collecting its own taxes, the most basic act of imperial administration. On the eve of the First World War, only about 5 percent of taxes was collected by the government; the other 95 percent was collected by independent tax farmers.[3]

Foreign countries exercised varying degrees of influence and control within the empire. It was not only that Egypt and Cyprus were in fact governed by Britain, which had occupied them in the late nineteenth century; and that the sheikhdoms along the Gulf coast were under British control. Lebanon, a separate canton under arrangements established in 1864, was governed by a Christian military governor directly serving under the Porte which, however, was obliged to act only in consultation with six European powers. Russia and France reserved to themselves the right to protect, respectively, the Orthodox and Catholic populations of the empire; and other powers also asserted a right to intervene in Turkish affairs on behalf of the groups they sponsored.

What was more than a little unreal, then, was the claim that the Sultan and his government ruled their domains in the sense in which Europeans understood government and administration. What was real in the Ottoman Empire tended to be local: a tribe, a clan, a sect, or a town was the true political unit to which loyalties adhered. This confused European observers, whose modern notions of citizenship and nationality were inapplicable to the crazy quilt of Ottoman politics. Europeans assumed that eventually they themselves would take control of the Ottoman domains and organize them on a more rational basis. In the early years of the twentieth century it was reasonable to believe that the days of Turkish dominion were numbered.

By 1914 the much-diminished Ottoman Empire no longer ruled North Africa or Hungary or most of southeastern Europe. It had been in a retreat since the eighteenth century that finally looked like a rout. For decades, in the Ottoman army and in the schools, discontented men had told one another in the course of clandestine meetings that the empire had to be rapidly changed to meet the intellectual, industrial, and military challenges of modern Europe. Stimulated but confused by the nationalism that had become Europe's creed, intellectuals amongst the diverse Turkish-speaking and Arabic-speaking peoples of the empire sought to discover or to forge some sense of their own political identity.

In the final years before the outbreak of the First World War, obscure but ambitious new men took power in the Ottoman Empire, relegating the Sultan to a figurehead position. The new men, leaders of the Young Turkey Party, were at once the result and the cause of ferment in Constantinople, the Ottoman capital, as they tried to meet the challenge of bringing Turkey's empire into the twentieth century before the modern world had time to destroy it.

II

Constantinople—the city originally called Byzantium and today known as Istanbul—was for more than eleven centuries the capital of the Roman Empire in the East, and then for more than four centuries the capital of its successor, the Ottoman Empire. Like Rome, Constantinople was built on seven hills and, like Rome, it was an eternal city: its strategic location gave it an abiding importance in the world's affairs.

Constantinople is a collection of towns located principally on the European side of the great waterway that links the Mediterranean to the Black Sea, at a point where the channel separating Europe from Asia narrows to widths of as little as a half-mile. The site is a natural fortress, difficult to conquer or even to attack. A bay some four miles long, known as the Golden Horn, forms a magnificent natural harbor that provides shelter and protection for a defending fleet.

In 1914 the population of Constantinople stood at about a million. It was a cosmopolitan and polyglot population: most residents of the city were Moslem, Greek, or Armenian, but there was also a considerable colony of European and other foreigners. A European influence was evident in the architectural style of the newer buildings, in the style of dress, and in such innovations as street lights.

Rudimentary modernization had only just begun. In 1912 electric lighting had been introduced into Constantinople for the first time.[4] A start had been made toward constructing a drainage system for the city's narrow, filthy streets; and the packs of wild dogs that for centuries had patrolled the city were, by decision of the municipal council, shipped to a waterless island to die.[5] Some work had been done on the paving of roads, but not much; most streets still turned to mud in the frequent rainstorms, or coughed dry dust into the air as winds blew through the city.

Violent alternating north and south winds dominated the city's climate, bringing sudden changes of extreme heat or cold. The political climate, too, was subject to sudden and extreme changes at the beginning of the twentieth century; and for many years prior to 1914 British observers had shown that they had no idea where the winds were coming from or which way they were blowing. Political maneuverings at the Sublime Porte, the gate to the Grand Vizier's offices from which the Ottoman government took its name, were conducted behind a veil of mystery that the British embassy time and again had failed to penetrate.

III

The British embassy, like those of the other Great Powers, was located in Pera, the European quarter of the city, which lay to the north of the Golden Horn. Foreign communities had grown up in proximity to their embassies, and lived their own lives, separately from that of the city. In Pera, French was the language of legation parties and entertainments; Greek, not Turkish, was the language of the streets. Three theaters offered revues and plays imported from Paris. The Pera Palace Hotel offered physical facilities comparable with those available in the palatial hotels of the major cities of Europe.

Most Europeans succumbed to the temptation to live in the isolation of their own enclave. Few were at home in the narrow, dirty lanes of Stamboul, the old section of the city south of the Golden Horn, with its walls and fortifications crumbling into ruin. One of the few who felt at ease on either side of the Golden Horn was an Englishman named Wyndham Deedes, who had come to play an important role in the new Young Turkey administration.

Deedes was from a county family of Kent: four centuries of English country gentlemen had preceded him. After Eton, he took a commission in the King's Own Rifles, and for twenty-two years thereafter he remained a British officer. (When asked once about the horrors of the Boer War, he replied, "Well, anything was better than Eton.")[6] Early in his military career, Deedes volunteered to serve in the Ottoman Gendarmerie, a newly created Turkish police force commanded by European officers. Its creation was a reform forced upon the Sultan by the European powers, for the old police force had become indistinguishable from the robber bands it was supposed to suppress. Deedes and his European colleagues were commissioned as officers of the new force while, at the same time, retaining their commissions in their respective national armies.

As viewed in old photographs, Deedes looked an oddity in the oriental surroundings in which service in the Gendarmerie placed him. Small, painfully thin, and light-complexioned, he did not blend into the Ottoman landscape. Ascetic and deeply Christian, he had little use for sleep, rest, or food. He worked fifteen hours a day, indifferent to comfort and careless of danger; nobody could have been more unlike the Turkish officers who, if European accounts were to be believed, were in many cases corrupt and cowardly. He made a success of his challenging assignment, and won popularity with the Turks.

Deedes was an unknown figure when he entered the Gendarmerie in 1910. Four years later he had achieved such high standing that he was co-opted by the leading figure in the new Ottoman government to help run the Ministry of the Interior. By the time of his thirty-first birthday in 1914, Deedes, who had learned to speak Turkish fluently, was one of the few Englishmen who understood Turkish affairs. Yet his government did not make real use of his experience and knowledge. One of the continuous themes of the years to come was that Deedes was a Cassandra: his government chose to disregard his warnings and to ignore his accurate analyses of Turkish political motives.

The minister under whom Deedes served in the Ottoman government in 1914 was Mehmed Talaat. Most of what the British government thought it knew at the time about Talaat and about the political party that Talaat led was erroneous; and at least some of it could have been corrected by Deedes. But the British embassy in Constantinople believed that it knew the truth about Ottoman politics already, and therefore that it did not have to inquire further.

IV

Mehmed Talaat, the Minister of the Interior and the leader of the largest faction within the governing political party, was a figure whom British diplomats did not regard as a gentleman. They believed that he lacked race and breeding; they scornfully reported that he was of gypsy origin. He had thick black hair, heavy black eyebrows, a hawk-like nose, and what one of the few sympathetic British observers described as "a light in his eyes, rarely seen in men but sometimes in animals at dusk."[7]

Talaat was the single most important figure in Turkish politics. He was very much a self-made man. Little is known of his origins and background except that they were humble. He began life as a minor employee of the Post and Telegraph Office and is believed to have been a *Bektashi*, that is, a member of the largest of the Turkish Dervish orders. (The Dervishes were Moslem religious brotherhoods.) He is believed to have joined a Freemason lodge, is known to have organized a secret political society, and to have been imprisoned for a time for his underground activities.

Joining a secret organization was a common activity in the Ottoman Empire of Talaat's youth. Under the autocratic Sultan Abdul Hamid, who reigned from 1876 to 1909, open political activity was dangerous.

The Sultan, who suspended the constitution and disbanded Parliament, was intolerant of dissent and employed a secret police force to deal with it. The political life of the empire was driven underground, where secret societies proliferated. The earliest ones took their inspiration from nineteenth-century European revolutionary groups, especially the Italian *carbonari*, and organized themselves into cells of a handful of members, only one of whom, typically, would know a member of another cell. Many of them, including the forerunner of the Young Turkey Party, were founded by university and military academy students. The army, too, was an especially fertile breeding ground for such societies; its younger members were shamed by their empire's disastrous showing on one battlefield after another.

Abdul Hamid's police forces succeeded in smashing the secret societies in Constantinople and elsewhere. Beyond their grasp, however, was Salonika, the bustling and un-Turkish Macedonian port in what is now Greece. Salonika is where a number of the secret societies established their headquarters, developing close relationships with members of the Ottoman Third Army, which had its headquarters there. The disorder and disintegration with which the Third Army had to deal in Macedonia—a frontier region of the empire—in itself was a formative experience that helped the secret societies to enlist recruits within the ranks of the army.

Talaat, who lived and worked in Salonika, was one of the founders of one such secret society which eventually became the principal faction within a merged group that called itself the Committee of Union and Progress—the C.U.P. as it will be called hereafter. It was known, too, as the Young Turkey Party, and later its members were called the Young Turks. Upon joining it, initiates swore an oath on the Koran and a gun. Djemal Bey, a staff officer who later played a major role in Middle Eastern politics, was Talaat's initial recruit among the leadership of the Third Army.

One day in 1908 a junior army officer named Enver, who was stationed in Salonika and who had also joined Talaat's group, was ordered to return to Constantinople. Afraid that his membership had been discovered by the secret police, he slipped out of Salonika and took to the hills, to which another Young Turkey army colleague had already escaped. Then another army officer followed his example, taking troops and ammunition with him. The Sultan sent troops against them, but the troops joined the rebels. There was a spontaneous combustion of a bloodless revolution in Salonika: the C.U.P. took control. The Young Turks seized control of the Telegraph Office—it may have been no coincidence that Talaat was one of its officials—and established contact with C.U.P. cells that honeycombed the army and the empire. When the smoke had cleared the constitution had been restored, parliamentary and party politics had resumed, and the following year the Sultan abdicated in favor of his brother.

The old politicians took office, while the Young Turks remained in the background. But the C.U.P. had become a force with which to reckon, and not merely because of its strong representation in the officer corps of the army. In a disorganized society, the strength of the C.U.P. was that it had branches everywhere, criss-crossing the empire.

The leaders of the successful uprising at first enjoyed a good-enough press in the western world so that in common parlance "Young Turks" came to mean any brash group of young people with dynamic ideas who rebel against an outmoded leadership. They were viewed with sympathy by the Foreign Office in London, but were disliked and disdained in the British embassy in Constantinople. The ambassador, Sir Gerard Lowther, seems to have fallen completely under the influence of Gerald FitzMaurice, his First Dragoman, or official interpreter and adviser on oriental affairs; and FitzMaurice detested the C.U.P. almost from the very outset.

FitzMaurice's interpretation of the events of 1908 was colored by the fact that they had occurred in Salonika, about half of whose 130,000 inhabitants were either Jews or Dunmehs (members of a Jewish sect that had converted to Islam in the seventeenth century). Salonika was also a city in which there were Freemason lodges. Emmanuel Carasso (or Karasu), a Jewish lawyer, had founded an Italian Freemason lodge in which he apparently allowed Talaat's secret society to meet when it was in hiding from the Sultan's secret police. FitzMaurice concluded that the C.U.P. was a Latin-influenced international Jewish Freemason conspiracy; and Lowther duly reported this to the Foreign Office in London. Lowther referred to the C.U.P. as "the Jew Committee of Union and Progress."[8]

FitzMaurice later conducted an investigation of the C.U.P., the results of which were reflected in a confidential report sent by Lowther under his own name on 29 May 1910, to the official head of the Foreign Office, Sir Charles Hardinge. In his report, Lowther pointed out that *liberté, égalité, fraternité* (liberty, equality, fraternity), words drawn from the French Revolution, were both the slogan of the Italian Freemasons (hence Karasu's lodge) and of the Young Turkey movement. The Young Turks, he claimed, were "imitating the French Revolution and its godless and levelling methods. The developments of the French Revolution led to antagonism between England and France, and should the Turkish revolution develop on the same lines, it may find itself similarly in antagonism with British ideals and interests."[9]

In his detailed report of more than 5,000 words, Lowther alleged that Jews had taken over a Freemason network ("The Oriental Jew is an adept at manipulating occult forces . . .") and through it had taken control of the Ottoman Empire. Amongst the ringleaders of the Jewish Freemason conspiracy, according to Lowther, was the U.S. ambassador to Turkey, Oscar Straus, whose brothers owned the New York department stores Macy's and Abraham & Straus.

The danger to England, wrote Lowther, is that "The Jew hates Russia and its Government, and the fact that England is now friendly to Russia has the effect of making the Jew to a certain extent anti-British . . . a consideration to which the Germans are, I think, alive."[10] Indeed, Lowther concluded, "I have reason to believe that my German colleague is aware of the extent to which Jewish and Latin Masonry inspires the Committee, and that he has confidentially kept his Government informed as to this feature of Young Turkey politics."[11]

However, when the 288-man Ottoman Parliament was elected in 1908, only four Jews were elected to it, and when the C.U.P. created a Central Committee in 1909, Karasu was not elected to membership on it, nor did he ever rise to a leadership position either in the party or in the government; he was never the influential figure that foreigners supposed him to be. As deputies in Parliament, Karasu and the three other Jews bent over backwards to prove that they were Turks first and Jews only second; indeed, they supported the C.U.P.'s measures against Zionist settlement in Palestine.* Lowther explained this away by claiming that the new goal of Zionism was to create a Jewish homeland not in Palestine but instead in a section of what is now Iraq.

The FitzMaurice and Lowther report won wide acceptance among British officials and led the British government into at least three profound misconceptions that had important consequences.

The first of these concerned the inner workings of the C.U.P. FitzMaurice and Lowther misled their government into believing that the Young Turks were controlled by two men. Talaat and Djavid ("who is a Crypto-Jew") were, according to FitzMaurice and Lowther, "the official manifestations of the occult power of the Committee. They are the only members of the Cabinet who really count, and are also the apex of Freemasonry in Turkey."[12] In fact the C.U.P. was split into factions—factions with which the British government could have intrigued, had it known that they existed.[13] It was an ironic coincidence that Djavid, whom FitzMaurice and Lowther feared as a Crypto-Jew, was the leader of the pro-British faction; but FitzMaurice and Lowther did not know that.

A second misconception was that a group of Jews wielded political

---

* Karasu, however, did attempt at various times to reconcile the aims of Zionism with those of C.U.P. nationalism.

power in the Ottoman Empire—or indeed anywhere else in the world at that time. A few years later FitzMaurice drew an obvious conclusion from his misconception: that the world war (in which Britain was by then engaged) could be won by buying the support of this powerful group. Its support could be bought, he decided, by promising to support the establishment of a Jewish homeland in Palestine (he had by then determined that the Zionist movement desired to return to Zion, not to Iraq). This reasoning helped to persuade the Foreign Office that it ought to pledge British support to the Zionist program—which it eventually did in 1917.

FitzMaurice's misinformation led to yet another conclusion with important consequences: that the Young Turk leaders were foreigners, not Turks, and that they served foreign interests. This was the opposite of the truth, and led British observers to miscalculate what the Young Turk government would do. In fact, as even FitzMaurice and Lowther saw, a principal failing of the C.U.P. was its Turkish chauvinism. It discriminated against Jews, Armenians, Greeks, Arabs, and others. Its strength was that it was opposed to all foreign interests; its anti-European bias attracted wide popular support.

The British government never learned that Lowther and FitzMaurice had supplied it with a warped view of Ottoman politics. John Buchan, who became wartime Director of Information for the British government, described the C.U.P. leaders as "a collection of Jews and gipsies," pictured the Ottoman government as the tool of world Jewry, and called Enver Pasha "a Polish adventurer"—confusing him with another Turkish officer whose name was similar and whose father was Polish though not Jewish.[14]

V

The years after 1908 proved to be a disaster for the Ottoman Empire, in a war against Italy and in another against a Balkan coalition; and, in 1913, it was in the process of losing a second Balkan War when the C.U.P. suddenly seized control of the government. Young Enver— the same officer who had precipitated the events of 1908 in Salonika— impetuously led a raid on the Sublime Porte; his raiding party killed the Minister of War. Enver and his friends took office; he was promoted to a field command in which he covered himself with glory, and on 4 January 1914, he took over the War Ministry for himself. Thirty-one years old, Enver married the niece of the Sultan, moved into a palace, and became the center of attention in Turkish politics.

Djemal Pasha became Military Governor of Constantinople, and in that position consolidated the C.U.P.'s hold on the seat of government. Halil Bey, President of the Chamber of Deputies, also assumed an important role, as did Mehmed Djavid, an economics teacher who was appointed Minister of Finance. Talaat, the principal C.U.P. leader, became Minister of the Interior and the real leader of the government. The courtly Prince Said Halim provided respectability as Grand Vizier and Foreign Minister.

The British government sent out a new ambassador, Sir Louis Mallet, who was sympathetic to the Young Turks. He too, however, was uninformed about what was happening in Constantinople. Where his predecessor had detected Jewish and German control, Mallet sent dispatches to London that radiated a misleading optimism about the Porte's intentions. Like the previous ambassador, Mallet failed to understand what the C.U.P. leaders believed Turkey's interests to be.

In London the Cabinet persisted in accepting Lowther and FitzMaurice's mistaken notion that the C.U.P. was a monolithic body. Lowther and FitzMaurice had reported that it was controlled by Talaat and Djavid, while according to later reports—followed by most historians—it was ruled by a dictatorial triumvirate of Enver, Talaat, and Djemal. In fact, as the German archives now show, power was wielded by the C.U.P.'s Central Committee of about forty members, and especially by its general directorate of about twelve members who functioned as a sort of politburo, in which personal rivalries abounded. Decisions of the Central Committee were reflected in the positions taken by party members in the Cabinet and in the Chamber of Deputies.

The C.U.P. encompassed a variety of opinions, and was rife with faction and intrigue. There was, however, a consensus about the nature of the threat that the Ottoman Empire faced and about the nature of the policy that ought to be adopted to counter it.

4

THE YOUNG TURKS URGENTLY SEEK AN ALLY

I

The Young Turk outlook on current affairs was colored by the trauma of continuing territorial disintegration. The provinces of Bosnia and Hercegovina (in what is now Yugoslavia), nominally still Turkish, were formally annexed by Austro-Hungary in 1908—a troubling move that provided the background in 1914 to the assassination of the Archduke Francis Ferdinand and the outbreak of the First World War. Italy, a latecomer to imperial expansion, made no secret of her designs on Ottoman territory and, on a flimsy pretext, attacked Turkey and in 1911—12 captured the coast of what is now Libya, as well as Rhodes and other islands off the Turkish coast. At about the same time, Albania revolted against Ottoman rule, raising a serious question as to whether the empire could hold the loyalties of its non-Turkish subjects.

Meanwhile, in the First Balkan War (1912—13) the Balkan League (Bulgaria, Greece, Montenegro, and Serbia) defeated Turkey and annexed almost all of the territory the Ottoman Empire still held in Europe. In the Second Balkan War (1913), the Ottoman Empire managed to regain some territory in Thrace, immediately across the water from Asiatic Turkey; but that looked to offer merely a brief respite in the empire's continuing disintegration. In Constantinople, the band of Young Turk adventurers who had seized power and who ruled the empire as the Sultan's ministers, feared that their domains were in mortal danger and that the European predators were closing in for the kill.

Only a short time before, the nations of Europe had divided up the African continent among themselves. Some of them were now hungry for new conquests. There were not many directions in which they could look. Much of the surface of the globe was already taken: a quarter by the British Empire and a sixth by the Russian Empire. The western hemisphere fell within the ambit of the Monroe Doctrine and thus was shielded by the United States. The Middle East was the only vulnerable region left. There were rumors of French ambitions in Syria; of Italian and Russian designs further north; and of rival Greek, Bulgarian, and Austrian claims to the west. Beyond the campfires, the C.U.P. leaders could sense the animals in the dark moving in for the attack.

II

The C.U.P. leadership was convinced that its program of freeing the empire from European control—a program that British statesmen, among others, either did not know about or did not understand—would precipitate the attack. Ambivalent in its attitude toward Europe—scorning it as non-Moslem, while admiring its modern ways and achievements—the C.U.P. intended to throw off the shackles of Europe in order to imitate Europe more closely. The Young Turks seem to have had no coherent plan for bringing European economic domination to an end, but they wanted, somehow, to do it.

A vital item on the C.U.P.'s internal agenda was the modernization of transport and communications. European interests were willing to supply the networks and systems which the Ottoman Empire lacked, but of course wanted to own them, preferably on the basis of exclusive concessions. The C.U.P. leaders, like other Ottoman leaders before them, wanted the European technologies to be introduced but were determined to avoid European ownership or control. During the nineteenth century, Turkey had created her own postal service, even though it coexisted within the empire alongside postal services maintained for themselves by various European powers.[1] Rejecting an offer from a British company, the Ottoman Empire also created its own telegraph network.[2] A few telephones were in use in Constantinople and Smyrna in 1914; a foreign group had been given a concession to install a telephone system in Constantinople in 1911, but had not made much progress.[3]

The coming of the steamship had put Ottoman maritime traffic largely in the hands of foreign interests.[4] Such as they were, the empire's few railway lines were also in foreign hands.* There were few roads and still fewer automobiles to make use of them: 110 in Constantinople and 77 elsewhere by 1914. The traditional form of transportation was the caravan of camels, horses, mules, and animal-drawn carts—and it could not compete against the foreign-owned

---

* "It is a measure of the low degree of development of the Ottoman Empire that in 1914, its 1,900,000 square kilometers had only 5,991 kilometers of railways," all of it single-track.[5]

railroads. The usual speed of a mixed caravan was between two and three miles an hour, and its daily stage was only between fifteen and twenty miles.[6] Railroad speeds were at least ten times greater, and the railroad cost of transporting goods was perhaps only 10 percent of the caravan cost.[7]

The C.U.P. dilemma lay in wanting to switch from caravan to railroad without allowing the empire to pass into the control of the Europeans who owned the railroads. Europeans already exercised an economic preponderance which the C.U.P. resented but could do nothing about. Turkey was in the unequal position of being able to supply only natural resources and having to import her manufactured needs. Industrialization was necessary in order to redress the balance; but the Porte had no program to achieve it. The empire could supply only unskilled labor; as the Europeans constructed railroads and other types of machinery, they brought along Europeans to maintain them. Technical training for the local population was what was needed; again the Porte had no program to provide it.

Europeans also shared in the control of what is at the heart of a political entity: its finances. Because the Porte had defaulted on a public debt of more than a thousand million dollars in 1875, the Sultan was obliged to issue a decree in 1881 that placed administration of the Ottoman public debt in European hands. A council was created for the purpose and was given control of almost one-quarter of the Ottoman Empire's revenues. It wielded exclusive authority over the customs duties on such basic items as alcoholic spirits, stamps, salt, and fish.[8] The Sublime Porte was no longer master even of its own Treasury or Customs House. The C.U.P. wanted to take back control in these areas, though it had no refinancing program to propose.

Bitterly resented by all Ottoman leaders were the Capitulations, the concessions that provided Europeans with a privileged economic position within the empire and which placed them for many purposes under the jurisdiction of their own consuls rather than of the Ottoman courts. No Turkish policeman could enter the premises of a European or American without the permission of the latter's consul. The C.U.P. wanted to cancel these Capitulation privileges.

Another ground for C.U.P. resentment was that the European powers had, on occasion, violated Ottoman sovereignty in intervening in defense of Christian minorities and Christian rights. The European disposition to do so posed a threat to the C.U.P.'s secret agenda, for the Young Turks proposed to assert their power not only against foreigners but also against other groups inhabiting the empire. This ran contrary to what they had pledged in 1908. The public program of the C.U.P. had called for equal rights for all the many religious, ethnic, and linguistic groups that resided within the empire. Once in power the C.U.P. showed the dark side of its nationalism by asserting instead the hegemony of Turkish-speaking Moslems over all others. The Turkish-speaking and Arabic-speaking populations of the empire were roughly equal—each about 10 million people, or about 40 percent of the total population apiece—yet in the Ottoman Chamber of Deputies there were perhaps 150 Turks as against only about 60 Arabs. (The figures are not exact because it is not clear in every case who was Arab and who was Turk.) The remaining 20 percent of the population, including the important Greek, Armenian, Kurdish, and Jewish communities, was discriminated against even more severely than were the Arabs. According to the eleventh edition of the *Encyclopaedia Britannica* (1910−11), the Ottoman Empire at the time was inhabited by twenty-two different "races", yet "no such thing as an Ottoman *nation* has ever been created." If ever there were a chance of creating one, the C.U.P. leaders threw it away by excluding 60 percent of the population from its purview.

Talaat, Enver, and their colleagues were nationalists without a nation. Within the empire (as distinct from the steppes to its east), even those who spoke Turkish were often of non-Turkish origin. Sir Mark Sykes, a British Member of Parliament who had traveled extensively in Asia, began one of his books by asking: "How many people realize, when they speak of Turkey and the Turks, that there is no such place and no such people . . . ?"[9] The ancient homeland of the Turkish peoples, Turkestan, was in the possession of Russia and China. More than half the Turkish peoples of Asia lived either there or elsewhere outside the Ottoman Empire, so that the Czar could lay greater claim to speak for the ethnic Turks than could the Sultan. Enver Pasha was later associated with the dream of reuniting all the Turkish-speaking peoples and domains of Asia, and certainly the idea was familiar to him in 1914—intellectually it was in the air—but, as of then, it did not enter into his plans. A small man, much addicted to theatrical gestures and to large programs that began with the prefix "pan-," Enver was also supposed to harbor pan-Islamic ambitions. His treatment of Arab fellow-Moslems shows that this, too, was a slogan that he did not translate into policy.

In the view of the C.U.P. leadership, Europe would not let the empire survive in any event—and certainly would not allow the C.U.P. to carry through its program—unless one of the Great Powers could be induced to become Turkey's protector. Thus the search for a European ally was the urgent and overriding item on the C.U.P. agenda. Djemal Pasha was pro-French, but when eventually he heard that Enver had proposed an alliance with Germany, he approvingly commented that "I should not hesitate to accept any alliance which rescued Turkey from her present position of isolation."[10]

III

All shades of opinion within the C.U.P. were in agreement that the most urgent item on Turkey's agenda was to secure a powerful European ally. The Young Turks believed that one of the European blocs or indeed any one of the leading Great Powers—Britain, France, or Germany—could protect the Ottoman Empire against further encroachments on its territory. Other than Russia, the countries that were most likely to invade the Ottoman Empire were powers of lesser strength: Italy, Austria-Hungary, Greece, or Bulgaria.

Djavid, the pro-British C.U.P. Minister of Finance, had already appealed to Britain. His appeal had been made in 1911, at the time of the initial Italian attack on Turkey. Churchill was the only senior Cabinet minister who had wanted to respond positively. Arguing that Turkey's friendship was more important than Italy's, Churchill wrote to the Foreign Secretary that Turkey "is the greatest land weapon wh the Germans cd use against *us*."[11] At the end of 1911, when Djavid wrote to propose a permanent alliance with Britain, Churchill wanted to send an encouraging reply, but the Foreign Office would not agree to his doing so.[12]

Between May and July 1914, with increasing urgency the C.U.P. leaders secretly approached three other European Great Powers in search of an ally.[13] Djemal, the Minister of Marine, who was pro-French, made overtures to France but was rebuffed. Talaat, in desperation, approached Russia—which was like asking the chief burglar to become chief of police—and his proposal, too, was rebuffed. Finally, the C.U.P. leaders conferred together at the villa of the Grand Vizier and authorized Enver, who had served in Berlin, to approach Germany with a request for an alliance. Enver made his approach on 22 July 1914. His proposal was turned down by Hans von Wangenheim, Germany's ambassador in Constantinople. The Ottoman Empire's diplomatic isolation was complete; no Great Power would agree to protect it.

The Ottoman War Minister was quite open in explaining to the German ambassador why the Young Turks were seeking an ally. Enver explained to von Wangenheim that the domestic reforms planned by the C.U.P. could be carried out only if the Ottoman Empire were "secured against attacks from abroad."[14] He expressed his belief that the empire could be secured against such attacks only by "the support of one of the groups of Great Powers."[15] Apparently he was unable to persuade the German ambassador that the Ottoman Empire had anything of sufficient value to give in return.

The government of Britain, meanwhile, was unaware of the flurry of Turkish diplomatic activity and did not realize that the Porte was urgently seeking a Great Power alliance. A few days after the German ambassador in Constantinople rejected the Ottoman proposal, British ministers received their first intimation that a war crisis might arise in Europe that could involve Britain. Between 23 July 1914, when Austria-Hungary sent an ultimatum to Serbia, and 4 August, when Britain unexpectedly found herself at war alongside the Entente Powers (France and Russia) and against the Central Powers (Germany and Austria-Hungary), few thoughts were spared for the Ottoman Empire; but to the extent that they were, the common assumption was that Germany might attempt to entice the Ottoman Empire into an alliance.

British leaders at the time never suspected that it was the other way around: that Turkey was seeking an alliance with Germany, and that Germany was reluctant to grant it. Even after the war was over, when it was discovered that Talaat and Enver had sought the alliance, details of how the Ottoman Empire and Germany forged their alliance remained obscure. Contemporaries and a number of historians blamed Winston Churchill, who was said to have driven the Turks into Germany's arms; but the still-emerging evidence from diplomatic archives tells a different and more complex story—which began in 1914, on the eve of a sudden war crisis that neither Churchill nor his Cabinet colleagues had foreseen.

5

WINSTON CHURCHILL ON THE EVE OF WAR

I

In 1914, at the age of thirty-nine, Winston Churchill was about to begin his fourth year as First Lord of the Admiralty in the Liberal government of Prime Minister Herbert Asquith. Though he administered his important departmental office ably and vigorously, he was not then the imposing figure the world later came to know. His energy and talent—and his gift for publicizing his own exploits—had brought him forward at an early age; but it was largely the amused indulgence of the Prime Minister and the powerful sponsorship of David Lloyd George, the Chancellor of the Exchequer, that sustained him in his governmental position. He was a decade or more younger than the other members of the Cabinet, and the opinion was widespread that he was not sufficiently steady or mature to have been entrusted with high office.

He still spoke with the trace of a schoolboy lisp. His face had just begun to lose its last hints of adolescence. Only recently had the belligerent tilt of the head, the brooding scowl, and the thrusting cigar started to take command; and his sandy hair had begun to thin a bit. He had put on some weight in recent years, but was not yet portly. Of ruddy complexion, medium height, and with a hint of rounded lines, he was physically unprepossessing; only with hindsight could it have been seen that he would one day appear formidable.

It was not his person but his driving personality that fascinated those who encountered him. He was a mercurial figure, haunted by the specter of his brilliant, diseased father who had died a political failure at the age of forty-five. Fearing that he, too, would die young, Churchill had shamelessly elbowed friend and foe aside in his dash to the top in the short time that he believed still remained to him. Some suspected that, like his father, he was emotionally unbalanced, while others regarded him as merely too young. He combined aspects of greatness with those of childishness; but his colleagues recognized the childishness more readily than they did the greatness. He was moody; he took things personally; and he often embarked on lengthy tirades when instead he should have been listening or observing. Though generous and warm-hearted, he was not sensitive to the thoughts and feelings of others, and often was unaware of the effect produced by his own words and behavior. He was noisy; he brought passion into everything he undertook. Colleagues who aimed at detachment and understatement found him tiresome.

He often changed his views; and since he always held his views passionately, his changes of mind were as violent and extreme as they were frequent. He had been a Tory and now was a Liberal. He had been the most pro-German of ministers and had become the most anti-German. He had been the leading pro-Turk in the Cabinet and was to become the most anti-Turk. To his enemies he appeared dangerously foolish, and even his friends remarked that he allowed himself to be too easily carried away.

Unlike the others, he disdained to play it safe. He had soldiered in India, seen war in Cuba and the Sudan, and become a hero by escaping from a prisoner-of-war camp in South Africa. Taking risks had brought him fame and had catapulted him to the top in politics. He was happy in his marriage and in his high government office, but his temperament was restless: he sought worlds to conquer.

Three years before—in the summer of 1911—an unexpected opportunity had opened up for him to fulfill some of his ambitions. At that time, during the course of a brief international crisis, the Asquith government had been shocked to learn that the Admiralty was not prepared to carry out wartime missions in support of the army. To their amazement, Cabinet ministers at the time were told that the Royal Navy was unable to transport a British Expeditionary Force across the English Channel. They also learned that the Admiralty was unwilling to create a Naval War Staff. It became clear to Asquith and his colleagues that a new First Lord of the Admiralty had to be appointed to institute basic reforms.

Churchill, then Home Secretary, angled for the job, and his mentor, Lloyd George, proposed him for it. Predictably, his candidacy was hampered by his youth. At thirty-six he was already, with a solitary exception, the youngest person ever to serve as Home Secretary; and his many enemies, who claimed that he had pushed himself forward with unseemly haste, argued that he had run ahead of himself. To them he appeared to possess in excess the characteristic faults of youth: obstinacy, inexperience, poor judgment, and impulsiveness. The other leading contender for the position of First Lord expressed warm admiration for Churchill's energy and courage, but echoed the usual accusation that the young Home Secretary was too apt to act first and think afterward.[1]

For whatever reason, the Prime Minister decided to take a chance on Churchill; and the record of the Admiralty from the summer of 1911 to the summer of 1914 showed that he had won his wager. Inspired by Lord Fisher, the retired but still controversial Admiral of the Fleet, Churchill had transformed the coal-burning nineteenth-century fleet into an oil-burning twentieth-century navy.

II

Elected to Parliament for the first time in 1900, Churchill took his seat (in 1901) as a member of the Conservative Party: a Unionist (the term usually used at this period), or a Conservative, or (using the older word) a Tory. But on the bitterly disputed issue of free trade, in 1904, he crossed the floor of the House and joined the Liberals.

As a political renegade, Churchill was distrusted by both parties—not entirely without reason, for his political instincts were never wholly at one with either of them. He tended toward Liberalism on social and economic issues, but on questions of foreign and defense policy his instincts were Tory. Churchill was belligerent by nature and out of sympathy with the streak of idealistic pacifism that ran through the Liberal Party. He inherited a genius for warfare from Britain's greatest general, his ancestor the Duke of Marlborough; he had been schooled at a military academy rather than at a university; he had served on active duty as an army officer; and he was enthralled by the profession of arms. When Violet Asquith, aboard the *Enchantress* in 1912, looked out at the lovely Mediterranean coastline and exclaimed, "How perfect!", he replied, "Yes—range perfect—visibility perfect—If we had got some six-inch guns on board how easily we could bombard ..."[2]

As war clouds suddenly gathered over the summertime skies of 1914, Liberal pacifists seemed to be out of touch with events while Churchill at the Admiralty seemed to be the right man at the right place at the right time.

6

CHURCHILL SEIZES TURKEY'S
WARSHIPS

I

On the outbreak of war, Winston Churchill briefly became a national hero in Britain. Although the Cabinet had refused him permission to do so, he had mobilized the fleet on his own responsibility in the last days of peacetime and had sent it north to Scapa Flow, where it would not be vulnerable to a German surprise attack. What he had done was probably illegal, but events had justified his actions, which in Britain were applauded on all sides.

Margot Asquith, the Prime Minister's wife, once wondered in her diary what it was that made Winston Churchill pre-eminent. "It certainly is not his mind," she wrote. "Certainly not his judgment—he is constantly very wrong indeed ..." She concluded that: "It is of course his courage and colour—his amazing mixture of industry and enterprise. He can and does always—all ways puts himself in the pool. He never shirks, hedges, or *protects* himself—though he thinks of himself perpetually. *He takes huge risks* [original emphasis]."[1]

Mobilizing the fleet despite the Cabinet's decision not to do so was a huge risk that ended in triumph. In the days following Britain's entry into the war even his bitterest political enemies wrote to Churchill to express their admiration of him. For much of the rest of his life, his proudest boast was that when war came, the fleet was ready.

At the time, his commandeering of Turkish battleships for the Royal Navy was applauded almost as much. An illustrated page in the *Tatler* of 12 August 1914 reproduced a photograph of a determined-looking Churchill, with an inset of his wife, under the heading "BRAVO WINSTON! The Rapid Mobilisation and Purchase of the Two Foreign Dreadnoughts Spoke Volumes for your Work and Wisdom."[2]

The battleships were the *Reshadieh* and the larger *Sultan Osman I*. Both had been built in British shipyards and were immensely powerful; the *Osman* mounted more guns than any battleship ever built before.[3] Each originally had been ordered by Brazil, but then had been built instead for the Ottoman Empire. The *Reshadieh*, though launched in 1913, had not been delivered because the Turks had lacked adequate modern docking facilities to accommodate her. With Churchill's support, Rear-Admiral Sir Arthur H. Limpus, head of the British naval mission, had lobbied successfully with the Ottoman authorities to secure the contract to build docking facilities for two British firms—Vickers, and Armstrong Whitworth. The docking facilities having been completed, the *Reshadieh* was scheduled to leave Britain soon after the *Sultan Osman I*, which was to be completed in August 1914.

Churchill was aware that these vessels meant a great deal to the Ottoman Empire. They were intended to be the making of the modern Ottoman navy, and it was assumed that they would enable the empire to face Greece in the Aegean and Russia in the Black Sea. Their purchase had been made possible by patriotic public subscription throughout the empire. The tales may have been improved in the telling, but it was said that women had sold their jewelry and schoolchildren had given up their pocket-money to contribute to the popular subscription.[4] Admiral Limpus had put out to sea from Constantinople on 27 July 1914, with ships of the Turkish navy, waiting to greet the *Sultan Osman I* and escort her back through the straits of the Dardanelles to the Ottoman capital, where a "navy week" had been scheduled with lavish ceremonies for the Minister of Marine, Ahmed Djemal, and for the cause of British-Ottoman friendship.

Churchill, who was reckoned the most pro-Turk member of the Asquith Cabinet, had followed with care, and had supported with enthusiasm, the mission of Admiral Limpus in Turkey ever since its inception years before. The British advisory mission to the Ottoman navy was almost as large as the similar German mission to the Ottoman army, led by the Prussian General of Cavalry, Otto Liman von Sanders. The two missions to some extent counter-balanced each other. British influence was thought to be strong in the Marine Ministry. German influence was strongest in the War Ministry. In London little was known of Middle Eastern politics, but Churchill enjoyed the rare advantage of having personally met three of the five leading figures in the Ottoman government: Talaat, Enver, and the Minister of Finance, Djavid. He therefore had been given an opportunity to learn that Britain's conduct as naval supplier and adviser could have political repercussions in Constantinople.

The European war crisis, however, propelled the newly built Turkish vessels into significance in both London and Berlin. The *Reshadieh* and *Sultan Osman I* were battleships of the new Dreadnought class. As such, they overshadowed other surface vessels and, in a sense, rendered them obsolete. By the summer of 1914 the

Royal Navy had taken delivery of only seven Dreadnoughts. Since the European war was expected to be a short one, there seemed to be no time to build more of them before battle was joined and decided. The addition of the two Dreadnoughts built for Turkey would increase the power of the Royal Navy significantly. Conversely, their acquisition by the German Empire or its allies could decisively shift the balance of forces against Britain. It was not fanciful to suppose that the *Reshadieh* and *Sultan Osman I* could play a material role in determining the outcome of what was to become the First World War.

Early in the week of 27 July 1914, as the First Lord of the Admiralty took precautionary measures in the war crisis, he raised the issue of whether the two Turkish battleships could be taken by the Royal Navy. The chain of events which apparently flowed from Churchill's initiative in this matter eventually led to him being blamed for the tragic outbreak of war in the Middle East. In turn he later attempted to defend himself by pretending that he had done no more than to carry into effect standing orders. The history of these matters has been confused ever since because *both* Churchill's story and the story told by his detractors were false.

According to Churchill's history of the First World War, British contingency plans adopted in 1912 provided for the taking of all foreign warships being built in British yards in the event that war should ever occur. When the war broke out in 1914, warships were being built in British yards for Turkey, Chile, Greece, Brazil, and Holland. According to Churchill, he did nothing more than follow the regulations adopted in 1912. His version of the matter implied that he did not single out the Ottoman vessels, but instead issued orders applicable to all foreign warships then under construction; he wrote that the arrangements for the taking of such vessels "comprised an elaborate scheme" that had been devised years before and had been brought up to date in 1912.[5]

This account was not true. Seizing the Turkish warships was an original idea of Churchill's and it came to him in the summer of 1914.

During the week before the war, the question of taking foreign vessels was raised for the first time on Tuesday, 28 July 1914, in an inquiry that Churchill directed to the First Sea Lord, Prince Louis of Battenberg, and to the Third Sea Lord, Sir Archibald Moore. "In case it may become necessary to acquire the 2 Turkish battleships that are nearing completion in British yards," he wrote, "please formulate plans in detail showing exactly the administrative action involved in their acquisition and the prospective financial transactions."[6]

Admiral Moore looked into the matter, and found no administrative or legal procedure that would justify seizing the Turkish ships. He consulted one of the legal officers of the Foreign Office, who told him that there was no precedent for taking any such action. The Foreign Office lawyer said that if Britain were at war it could be argued that national interests take precedence over legal rights, but that since Britain was not at war* it would be illegal for Churchill to take the foreign-owned vessels. The lawyer advised the Admiralty that, if it really needed the ships, it should try to persuade the Ottoman government to sell them.[7]

The Turks suspected what Churchill had in mind, for on 29 July the Foreign Office warned the Admiralty that the *Sultan Osman I* was taking on fuel and was under orders to depart for Constantinople immediately, even though unfinished.[8] Churchill immediately ordered the builders of both battleships to detain them. He also ordered British security forces to guard the vessels and to prevent Turkish crews from boarding them or from raising the Ottoman flag over them (which would have converted them, under prevailing international law, into Ottoman territory).

The following day the Attorney-General advised Churchill that what he was doing was not justified by statute, but that the welfare of the Commonwealth took precedence over other considerations and might excuse his temporarily detaining the vessels.[9] A high-ranking permanent official in the Foreign Office took the same point of view that day but placed it in a broader and more practical political perspective. "I think we must let the Admiralty deal with this question as they consider necessary," he minuted, "and afterwards make such defence of our action to Turkey as we can."[10]

On 31 July the Cabinet accepted Churchill's view that he ought to take both Turkish vessels for the Royal Navy for possible use against Germany in the event of war; whereupon British sailors boarded the *Sultan Osman I*. The Ottoman ambassador called at the Foreign Office to ask for an explanation, but was told only that the battleship was being detained for the time being.[11]

Toward midnight on 1 August Churchill wrote instructions to Admiral Moore, in connection with the mobilization of the fleet, to notify both Vickers and Armstrong that the Ottoman warships were to be detained and that the Admiralty proposed to enter into negotiations for their purchase.[12]

For the first time Churchill noted that warships were also being built in British shipyards for countries other than Turkey. Admiral Moore had brought this to the First Lord's attention several days before, but Churchill had not responded; now—although the other

---

* This opinion was rendered a week before the outbreak of war between Britain and Germany.

foreign vessels were not of equal importance—he ordered them to be detained, too, for completion and eventual purchase.

On 3 August the Admiralty entered into arrangements with Armstrong for taking the *Sultan Osman I* into the Royal Navy immediately.[13] That evening the Foreign Office cabled the British embassy in Constantinople with instructions to inform the Ottoman government that Britain desired to have the contract for the purchase of the *Osman* transferred to His Majesty's Government.[14] The following day Sir Edward Grey sent a further cable to Constantinople, saying that he was sure the Turkish government would understand Britain's position, and that "financial & other loss to Turkey will receive all due consideration."[15]

A key, but overlooked, point is that the Ottoman government did not learn for the first time of Churchill's seizure of the battleship when officially informed of it in the 3 August cable. The Turks knew that the battleships were being taken on 31 July, and on or before 29 July strongly suspected that they were going to be taken. The significance of these dates will become clear presently.

II

In Berlin the onset of the war crisis on 23 July led to some second thoughts about the value of Turkey as an ally. On 24 July 1914, Kaiser Wilhelm II personally overruled the negative decision of his ambassador to Constantinople, and ordered that Enver's offer of an alliance should be explored. An Austrian ultimatum to Serbia—the ultimatum that initiated the war crisis in Europe—had been delivered the previous evening, and the Kaiser decided that "at the present moment" Ottoman interest in contracting an alliance should be taken advantage of "for reasons of expediency."[16]

Secret talks began at once in Constantinople. On the Ottoman side, the negotiators were Prince Said Halim, the Grand Vizier and Foreign Minister; Talaat Bey, Minister of the Interior; and Enver Pasha, Minister of War. Although Enver had told the German ambassador that a majority of the members of the C.U.P. Central Committee were in favor of an alliance with Germany, the three Ottoman leaders kept their negotiations secret from the Central Committee and even from their powerful colleague Djemal Pasha, Minister of the Marine.[17]

On 28 July the Ottoman leaders forwarded their draft of a proposed treaty of alliance to Berlin. Despite the Kaiser's views, the German Prime Minister, Chancellor Theobald von Bethmann Hollweg, remained unenthusiastic about the potential entanglement. On 31 July, the day the General Staff told him to issue the order to go to war,

Bethmann Hollweg sent a wire to his ambassador in Constantinople, instructing him not to sign a treaty of alliance with the Ottoman Empire unless he was certain that "Turkey either can or will undertake some action against Russia worthy of the name."[18]

August 1 was the crucial day in the negotiations. Details of what was said in the course of the bargaining are still not known. On the German side, von Wangenheim was operating under direct instructions from the head of his government: the Chancellor in Berlin had made it quite clear that the Ottoman proposal should be rejected unless the Turks had something unexpectedly significant to contribute to the German cause in the war. In fact, the Turks did not want to join in the fighting at all. As later events were to show, the Grand Vizier and his associates hoped that they would not be dragged into the war. Thus on the face of it they had little to offer. Yet by the end of the day the three Young Turks had wrung an alliance agreement from the Germans, which both sides signed the following afternoon.

Not merely had the negotiations been conducted in secret, but Article 8 of the treaty provided that the agreement should continue to be kept secret. Article 4 was what the C.U.P. leaders had chiefly sought: "Germany obligates itself, by force of arms if need be, to defend Ottoman territory in case it should be threatened."[19] Germany's obligation was a continuing one for the length of the treaty, which was scheduled to expire on 31 December 1918.

The Ottoman Empire in turn undertook to observe strict neutrality in the then current conflict between Serbia and Austria-Hungary and to go to war only if Germany were required to enter the fighting by the terms of her treaty with Austria.* In such circumstances, and in such circumstances only, the Ottoman Empire pledged that it too would intervene, and would allow the German military mission in Constantinople to exercise "effective influence" over the conduct of its armies.

The day after the treaty was signed, the Porte ordered general mobilization to begin, but also proclaimed neutrality in the European conflict. The treaty remained a secret; and Enver and his co-conspirators claimed that the program of mobilization was not directed against the Allied Powers. The Ottoman leaders went out of their way in conversations with Allied representatives to stress the possibility of friendly relationships, and Enver went so far as to suggest that Turkey might join the Allies.

* The treaty was signed the day *after* Germany had declared war on Russia. Germany had *not* been required to declare war by the terms of her treaty with Austria; as it happened, Germany declared war several days before Austria-Hungary did. The oddly drawn treaty with the Ottoman Empire therefore did not—if read literally—obligate the Turks to enter the war.

Berlin, hitherto skeptical of what the Ottoman Empire could contribute, now became anxious to obtain Turkish assistance. On
5 August the Chief of the German General Staff, who only weeks
before had said that the Ottoman Empire at Germany's side would
not be an "asset," began to press for Turkish aid against Britain as
well as Russia;[20] but the Turks refused to be hurried into taking
action. Indeed the lack of transportation facilities made it impossible
for the empire to mobilize swiftly.

The army had been guided for several years by a German military
mission, so the German ambassador presumably had been informed
that it would be physically impossible for the Ottoman Empire to
enter the war until the late autumn or the winter. Since almost
everybody's assumption on 1 August was that the war would be
over within a few months, von Wangenheim had granted the
Young Turks an alliance even though he must have believed that the
Ottoman Empire would not be ready to fight until the war was
almost over. Yet his instructions from Berlin were that he should not
conclude an alliance unless the Young Turks could prove to him that
they had something meaningful to contribute to the German war
effort. What was that "something meaningful"?

The common assumption of historians seems to be that the Turks
offered nothing new that day—that, in effect, von Wangenheim
ignored his instructions from Berlin. If so, he may have been seeking
to please the Kaiser; or it may be that the threatened outbreak of a
general European war led him to view the Ottoman Empire as more
significant militarily than he had believed ten days before. If, however, von Wangenheim *did* attempt to follow the instructions he had
received from Berlin, then the question which historians have not
asked becomes intriguing: what did Enver offer Germany on 1 August
that was so important that the German ambassador changed his
mind and agreed that, in return, Germany would protect the Ottoman
Empire?

III

A couple of decades ago, a curious fact came to light. A student of
the German diplomatic archives disclosed that they showed that on
1 August 1914 Enver and Talaat, in a meeting with Ambassador
von Wangenheim, suddenly offered to turn over to Germany the
most powerful warship in the world: the *Sultan Osman*.[21] Von
Wangenheim accepted the offer; and British Intelligence reports
from behind German lines two weeks later showed that officers of
the German fleet had eagerly expected to receive the vitally important

new warship—and apparently were bitterly disappointed when Churchill seized the vessel instead.[22]

Historians have not examined this episode in any great detail, possibly because on the surface it seems so difficult to explain. Enver and Talaat could not possibly have intended to give away Turkey's prize battleship, in which the populace had invested so much emotion as well as money, and in which the empire took such pride; it would have been political suicide for any Ottoman leader to even propose to do so. Yet the evidence cannot be disputed; in secret, they made von Wangenheim the offer.

In another connection, some twenty years ago a student of the Ottoman archives mentioned, in passing, a conversation that might provide an explanation. On the same day that Enver and Talaat made their offer to Germany—1 August 1914—Enver revealed to fellow Young Turk leaders that Britain had seized the *Osman*.[23] Thus on 1 August he already knew! Indeed—since it is now known that, in London, the Turks suspected on 29 July that Churchill was about to seize the *Osman*, and on 31 July protested that he had already done so—it is entirely possible that even *before* 1 August Enver knew that the battleship had been taken by Britain.

Might this not provide the answer to an earlier question? Von Wangenheim was not supposed to grant the Ottoman Empire an alliance unless the Turks could show that they would make a material contribution to the defeat of the Allies. But nonetheless he agreed to an alliance on 1 August, when the week before he had not believed that the Ottoman armed forces could make such a contribution. Was not the offer of the *Osman* on 1 August, therefore, the material contribution that bought Enver and Talaat their German alliance?

If Enver and Talaat knew before making their secret offer that they had already lost the *Osman* to Britain—that it was therefore no longer theirs to dispose of—they *could* have made the offer; they could have made it with impunity. In fact the Germans never discovered that they had been duped. They seem to have assumed that Enver and Talaat meant to keep their side of the bargain, and only learned they could not do so when they received official notification of Churchill's action several days later—*after* Germany had already signed a pledge to protect the Ottoman Empire against its enemies, largely in return (it is speculated here) for Enver's and Talaat's worthless promise.

7

AN INTRIGUE AT THE SUBLIME PORTE

I

In the course of the secret negotiations between Germany and the Young Turks in Constantinople on 1 August, Enver, the Minister of War, held a private meeting in the German embassy in Constantinople with the German ambassador, Hans von Wangenheim, and with the head of the German military mission, Otto Liman von Sanders.[1] The three men discussed the form that military collaboration between their countries might take if Turkey and Bulgaria should contract with each other to join in a war against Russia on Germany's side. It seemed to them that naval mastery was essential if a successful campaign were to be mounted. They concluded that the German Mediterranean fleet, consisting of the powerful *Goeben* and its sister ship, the *Breslau*, should come to Constantinople to strengthen the Ottoman fleet in the Black Sea so as to give the Turkish-Bulgarian armies a free hand in invading Russia. Significantly, none of the three men appears to have believed that the *Osman* might be available to fulfill that function. Presumably Enver already knew that he had lost the battleship to Britain; while the Germans believed that the vessel—under orders from Enver—was going to join the German fleet at a North Sea port, so that the *Goeben* and the *Breslau*, which already were in the Mediterranean, could more conveniently come to Constantinople.

After the conference, Liman and von Wangenheim requested their government to send the German ships to Turkey. On 3 August the German Admiralty dispatched orders to that effect to Rear-Admiral Wilhelm Souchon, commander of the Mediterranean Squadron. The wireless message reached Souchon in the early morning of 4 August, when he was close to the coast of Algeria where he intended to disrupt the flow of troops from French North Africa to the mainland of France. Deciding not to turn back immediately, Souchon first shelled two port cities of Algeria, and only then turned back to refuel in the neutral Italian port of Messina in Sicily, where German coaling-stations awaited him. Slowed down by defective boilers on the *Goeben*, the squadron did not reach Messina until the morning of 5 August.

At his refueling stop, Souchon received a telegram from Berlin apparently changing his orders again. Enver had not consulted his colleagues before inviting the German warships to Constantinople; they were by no means anxious to be drawn into the fighting, and when the Ottoman government learned that the ships were *en route*, it warned Berlin not to let them come. Berlin cabled Souchon that his call on the Ottoman capital was "not possible"; but Souchon chose to interpret this merely as a warning rather than as an order, and determined to proceed to Turkey to force the issue. This personal decision of the German admiral was a turning point in events.

Meanwhile, the British, whom Churchill had ordered to shadow the *Goeben*, had lost sight of her under cover of night on 4 August; but on the 5th she was sighted again, and the commanding English admiral positioned his naval squadron to intercept her when she should come out of the straits of Messina after refueling. He placed his squadron west of Sicily, to meet her as she returned to attack North Africa again, which is what he supposed she would do. A much smaller force was already stationed in the Adriatic Sea, far to the northeast, to block her should she attempt to return to her home port of Pola (in what was then Austria, but is now Yugoslavia).

On the British side there was as massive a failure of political imagination in London, as there was of military competence at sea. It seems never to have occurred to the Foreign Office, the War Office, or the Admiralty that the Ottoman Empire ought to figure in strategic calculations. Neither in London nor in the field did anybody in command consider the possibility that Admiral Souchon might be headed toward Constantinople. They assumed that when he headed east it was in order to elude them and double back toward the west.

When the *Goeben* and her sister ship, the *Breslau*, emerged from the straits of Messina on 6 August, Admiral Souchon expected to find his way blocked by a superior British force. Instead he found the way clear, and set his course toward the Aegean.

"It was all the Admirals' fault," the Prime Minister's daughter later told Churchill. "Who but an Admiral would *not* have put a battle-cruiser at both ends of the Messina Straits, instead of putting two at one end and none at the other?"[2] She advised him to retire all his admirals and promote captains in their place.

Souchon did encounter a British naval contingent as he steamed eastward, but it withdrew rather than risk battle with the formidable *Goeben*. After prodigies of exertion on the part of the Germans, and of blundering on the part of the English pursuers, Souchon's force arrived at the entrance to the straits of the Dardanelles.

II

At 1:00 in the morning on 6 August, the Grand Vizier discussed the fate of the *Goeben* and *Breslau* with the German ambassador. The British Mediterranean Squadron was following close behind the two German ships, so that if Turkey refused them admittance to the straits, they would be trapped between the Turkish forts in front of them and the British squadron behind them. The Grand Vizier, Said Halim, announced that his government had decided to allow the German ships to enter the straits so that they could make good their escape. But, he said, conditions were attached to this permission; and when he announced what they were, it became clear that his terms were steep. They showed that—contrary to what British observers believed—the Young Turk government intended to escape domination by the Germans, as well as other Europeans. The Porte demanded that Germany accept six far-reaching proposals, the first of which was high on the list of C.U.P. priorities—abolition of the Capitulations, and thus of privileges hitherto accorded to the Germans and other Europeans. Other proposals guaranteed Turkey a share of the spoils of victory if Germany won the war. From a German point of view these proposals were outrageous, but unless von Wangenheim wanted to abandon the *Goeben* and *Breslau* to the long-range guns of the British navy, he had no choice but to agree. The Turks had him at gun point.

At the Admiralty in London, Turkey's decision to admit the German warships looked like collusion between Constantinople and Berlin. Churchill and his colleagues had no idea that what really was going on was extortion; and Churchill angrily dashed off a telegram to his forces ordering them to institute a blockade of the Dardanelles.[3] He had no authority to issue such an order on his own and, had the order been carried out, it could have been construed in Constantinople as an act of war. In reply to a request for clarification, the Admiralty cabled back that there had been a "mistake in wording" and "no blockade intended."[4] Instead the British ships were to wait in international waters for the German ships to come out.

Britain protested to the Sultan's government that under accepted conventions of international law Turkey, as a neutral, was obliged either to send the German ships back out or to intern them. The Ottoman government did neither. Instead, the legal situation prompted the Porte to extract further concessions from the Germans.

Von Wangenheim had barely recovered from the extortionate demands of 6 August when, on 9 August, the Grand Vizier had more news for the German ambassador. Said Halim announced that the Ottoman Empire might join with Greece and Rumania in a public pact of neutrality in the European conflict. If so, something would have to be done about the continuing presence of the *Goeben* and the *Breslau* in Turkish waters so as not to compromise Turkish neutrality. The Porte proposed a fictitious purchase of the two warships: the Turks would take over ownership of the vessels, and would pretend to have paid for them. In that way there could be no objection to the ships remaining in Turkey; there would be no breaching of the laws of neutrality.

On 10 August the German Chancellor cabled von Wangenheim from Berlin rejecting this Turkish proposal and urging immediate Turkish entry into the war. The Young Turk leaders, however, were reluctant to involve the empire in the European conflict. Von Wangenheim was summoned that day to the Sublime Porte, where the Grand Vizier angrily reproached him for the premature arrival of the *Goeben* and the *Breslau*. Ignoring his own government's complicity in the affair of the German warships, Said Halim repeated his proposal that the ships should be transferred to Turkish ownership. Von Wangenheim refused the proposal.

The Ottoman government thereupon unilaterally issued a public declaration falsely claiming that it had bought the two German cruisers and had paid eighty million marks for them. Public opinion throughout the empire was elated, and on 14 August a frustrated von Wangenheim advised Berlin that there was no choice but to go along with the "sale"; to disavow it risked turning local sentiment violently around against the German cause. His advice was heeded, and at a ceremony on 16 August the Minister of the Marine, Djemal Pasha, formally received the vessels into the Ottoman navy.

The Turks did not have the trained officers and crews that were needed to operate and maintain such sophisticated vessels, and decided that, for the time being, the Germans should do it for them. Admiral Souchon was appointed commander of the Ottoman Black Sea Fleet, while his sailors were given fezzes and Ottoman uniforms, and went through the forms of enlisting in the Sultan's navy.[5] In London the entire episode was viewed as a calculated German maneuver designed to show that Germany was generously restoring to the Ottoman Empire the type of modern warships that Churchill had wrongfully taken away; and, even today, historians continue to repeat that account of the affair.

It was little more than a week since angry schoolchildren had poured into the streets of Constantinople to protest at Churchill's seizure of the battleships that had been purchased with their money.[6] British government leaders were certain that there was a connection between the two events. The Prime Minister's comment about Turkey's "purchase" of the German ships was that "The Turks are very angry—not unnaturally—at Winston's seizure of their battleships here."[7]

In turn, Churchill became angry at the Turks. On 17 August the

Prime Minister noted that "Winston, in his most bellicose mood all for sending a torpedo flotilla thro' the Dardanelles—to threaten & if necessary to sink the *Goeben* & her consort."[8] Cabinet opinion, however, was swayed by the views of the Secretary of State for War and the Secretary of State for India, who argued that it would be damaging for Britain to appear to be the aggressor against the Ottoman Empire.

It appeared, however, that the Ottoman Empire was moving toward the enemy camp, and the plausible explanation commonly accepted in London was that it was Churchill's seizure of the Turkish battleships which had caused that to happen. Wyndham Deedes, who had returned from Turkey to England in a daring journey via Berlin, went to see his friend, the Ottoman ambassador, in London and discovered that, in fact, that explanation was untrue: the battleships were not at the heart of the problem. Of course the Porte was upset about the seizure of the ships, but would not change its pro-German policy even if the ships were returned.

Fear of Russian expansionism was at the heart of the Porte's policy. The Turkish ambassador told Deedes that if the Allies won the war, they would cause or allow the Ottoman Empire to be partitioned, while if Germany won the war, no such partition would be allowed to occur.[9] That was why the Porte had become pro-German. Deedes denied that the Allies would allow the Ottoman Empire to be partitioned, but the ambassador had been told by Enver that the Allied Powers had given similar assurances years before but had not kept their word. (Enver did not mention that, in addition, Germany had given a written guarantee to protect Ottoman territory. He and his colleagues continued to keep their treaty of alliance with Germany a secret, and its existence was not revealed until many years later.)

Deedes was alarmed by his conversation with the Turkish ambassador, and warned the new British War Minister, Lord Kitchener, that Turkey was drifting into the enemy camp because of her fears of Allied intentions. Since Britain had allied herself with Russia—Russia, which had been attempting to dismember the Ottoman Empire for a century and a half—it would be no easy task to reassure the Porte, but Deedes urged that the effort should be made.

Churchill, meanwhile, was increasingly belligerent toward the Ottoman Empire, which he regarded as becoming enemy territory. Information reaching him in the last half of August indicated that German officers and men were moving overland, through neutral Bulgaria, to assume positions in the Ottoman armed forces. As early as 26 August Admiral Limpus had reported to Churchill that "Constantinople is almost completely in German hands at this moment."[10]

Churchill continued to press for action. On 1 September he initiated staff talks between the Admiralty and the War Office to plan an attack on Turkey in the event of war. The following day he received authority from the Cabinet to sink Turkish vessels if they issued from the Dardanelles in company with the *Goeben* and *Breslau*. Later he authorized his Dardanelles squadron commander to use his own discretion as to whether to turn back Turkish vessels attempting to come out from the Dardanelles by themselves. This was a blunder: it drove the Turks to strike back with stunning effectiveness.

Pursuant to Churchill's authorization, the squadron stopped a Turkish torpedo boat on 27 September and turned it back; for, in violation of Ottoman neutrality, it had German sailors aboard. In retaliation, Enver Pasha authorized the German officer commanding the Turkish defenses of the Dardanelles to order the straits to be sealed off and to complete the laying of minefields across them. This cut off the flow of Allied merchant shipping and thus struck a crippling blow. The Dardanelles had been Russia's one ice-free maritime passageway to the west. Through them she sent 50 percent of her export trade, notably her wheat crop which, in turn, enabled her to buy arms and ammunition for the war.[11] Had the Allied leaders realized that the First World War was going to develop into a long war of attrition, they could have seen that Turkey's mining of the straits threatened to bring down Czarist Russia and, with her, the Allied cause.

Free passage through the Dardanelles had been assured by treaty; once again the Ottoman authorities were violating their obligations under international law, and once again they appeared to have been provoked to do so by the actions of Winston Churchill.

Yet the Ottoman Empire made no move to declare war. Its position of passive hostility left Churchill baffled and frustrated.[12]

III

Though Churchill did not know it, from the point of view of the German government, too, the situation was baffling and frustrating; German military officers attempting to bring Turkey into the war found themselves driven to anger and despair.

Berlin was bitterly disappointed that the continuing presence of the *Goeben* and *Breslau* did not provoke Britain into declaring war; and the German and Austrian ambassadors received repeated demands from their home governments to push the Turks into taking action. Both ambassadors recognized, however, that whatever the Young Turks' ultimate intentions might be, the Grand Vizier and his colleagues had valid reasons for not moving toward intervention in the European conflict immediately. Mobilization of the armed forces was not yet completed; and it was not clear, once mobilization had been completed, how the fragile Ottoman exchequer could continue to support it. Moreover, Turkish negotiations with neighboring Balkan countries, and particularly with Bulgaria, had not yet come to fruition.

From the beginning, the Porte had made clear its view that Turkey could intervene in the war only in partnership with Bulgaria. Indeed, the campaign plan that had been worked out on 1 August by Enver, Wangenheim, and Liman von Sanders presupposed that Bulgaria and the Ottoman Empire would combine forces. Bulgaria sat astride Turkey's principal land route to the rest of Europe and—of more immediate importance—was a neighbor who coveted additional territory. Were Bulgaria to invade Turkey while the Ottoman armies were away fighting the Russians, the empire would be helpless. "Surely," the Grand Vizier remarked to the German ambassador, "Germany would not want Turkey to commit suicide."[13]

The Bulgarians, however, were reluctant to commit themselves, and while Talaat succeeded in negotiating a defensive treaty with Bulgaria, signed on 19 August, which provided for mutual assistance in certain circumstances in case either country was attacked by a third party, the terms of the treaty were inapplicable to the situation that would arise if Turkey should join Germany in the war against Russia. Bulgaria was not prepared to intervene in the Russo-German conflict; and, as the Germans in Constantinople had been made to understand, this meant that the Ottoman Empire, too, would continue to maintain its neutrality.

Berlin and London both viewed Constantinople with despondency. Churchill, it will be recalled, no longer believed in Turkish neutrality and had proposed to the Cabinet that a flotilla be sent up to the Dardanelles to sink the *Goeben* and *Breslau*. But in Constantinople only two days later, General Liman von Sanders—from the opposite point of view—despaired of bringing Turkey into the war and sent a request to the Kaiser that he and his military mission be allowed to return home. Like Churchill, he raged against the Young Turks; he spoke of challenging Enver and Djemal to duels.[14] In his request to the Kaiser, Liman pointed out that Enver's recent statements and military dispositions indicated that the C.U.P. intended to keep Turkey on the sidelines until the war was over, or at least until it became clear beyond a doubt that Germany was going to win it. He also pointed out that the Ottoman armies might collapse even before entering the war, for lack of money and food, if the Porte continued to keep them in a state of mobilization.[15] At roughly the same time that Admiral Limpus was reporting to

Winston Churchill that Constantinople was almost completely in German hands, General Liman von Sanders was reporting to the Kaiser that the whole atmosphere of Constantinople made it almost unbearable for German officers to continue their service there.[16]

The Kaiser, however, refused Liman's request that he should be allowed to return to Germany. Germany's plan to win the war quickly by a rapid victory in western Europe had collapsed at the first Battle of the Marne in early September; and thereafter Berlin stepped up the pressure to bring Turkey into the war. The German ambassador, von Wangenheim, was unable to explain to his home government how unrealistic, at least for the time being, that project appeared to be in Constantinople. Even Enver, whom the ambassador had once described as standing "like a rock for Germany,"[17] believed that the time for action had not yet come: Turkey was not ready militarily and, in any event, Enver's colleagues were still opposed to intervention.

The difference between the ultimate objectives of the two governments became vividly evident on 8 September 1914, when the Porte suddenly announced its unilateral abrogation of the Capitulations privileges of all foreign powers—including Germany. The German ambassador flew into a rage upon receiving the news, and threatened that he and the military mission would pack up and leave for home immediately. In the event, however, neither he nor the mission left. That they stayed illustrated the improvement in the Turkish bargaining position since late July.

In an extraordinary maneuver, the German and Austrian ambassadors joined with their enemies in the war, the British, French, and Russian ambassadors, in presenting a joint European protest to the Porte, whereupon it became evident how skillful the Turkish leaders had been in flirting without committing themselves. For the German and Austrian ambassadors privately intimated to the Porte that they would not press the issue for the time being, while the Allied ambassadors, in turn, intimated that they would accept the Turkish decision if Turkey continued to remain neutral.

The Porte went ahead to put its decision into effect. In early October all foreign post offices in the empire were closed; foreigners were made subject to Turkish laws and courts; and customs duties on foreign imports not only were taken over, but were also raised.

IV

Considering the tangible benefits that had begun to flow from the policy of non-intervention, it seems astonishing that at about this time Enver Pasha began to plot against that policy and against its leading proponent, the Grand Vizier. The substantial German military presence in Constantinople, supported by the *Goeben* and *Breslau*, may have played a role in his calculations; but what Enver had in mind is more likely to have been the course of the Russo-German war. In July and August his policy had been motivated by fear of Russian seizures of Turkish territory; but in September, in the wake of the Russian collapse, he seems to have turned to thoughts of Turkey seizing Russian territory. He switched from a defensive to an aggressive policy. His switch was a turning point in Ottoman and Middle Eastern affairs.

It may be surmised that the spectacular German military triumphs over the Russians at the battle of Tannenberg at the end of August, and in the ongoing battle of the Masurian Lakes that began in September, persuaded Enver that, if Turkey wanted to win a share of Russian territory, she would have to intervene soon, before Germany had won an unaided victory. Hundreds of thousands of Russian troops had been killed or captured by the Germans, and even a less impetuous observer than Enver might have concluded that Russia was about to lose the war. The German victory train was leaving the station, and the opportunistic Enver seems to have been jolted into believing that it was his last chance to jump aboard. On 26 September Enver personally ordered the closing of the Dardanelles to all foreign ships (in effect, to Allied shipping) without consulting his colleagues. A week later he told von Wangenheim that the Grand Vizier was no longer in control of the situation.

A bid for power was taking place in Constantinople behind closed doors. The British Foreign Office, which knew next to nothing about the internal politics of the C.U.P., took a simplistic view of the affair. Sir Edward Grey, the Foreign Secretary, later remembered remarking that "nothing but the assassination of Enver would keep Turkey from joining Germany," and adding "that, in times of crisis and violence in Turkey, there were apt to be two classes of person— assassins and assassinated, and that the Grand Vizier was more likely than his opponent to belong to the latter class."[18]

Would it have been possible for a well-informed British ambassador to have exerted some influence on the evolution of events in Constantinople? Historians continue to debate the question, and of course there is now no way to put the matter to the test.[19]

Obscure though the details remain, what was going on in the autumn of 1914 was a process in which rival factions and personalities maneuvered for support within the C.U.P. Central Committee. Enver's growing influence came from winning over Talaat Bey to his point of view, for Talaat headed the principal faction in the party.

Other C.U.P. leaders, while sharing Enver's belief that Germany would probably win the war, until now had seen no reason to hazard their empire's future on the accuracy of that prediction. They were politicians, while Enver was a warrior, younger and more impetuous than Churchill but filled with much the same passion for glory. As War Minister and Germany's best friend, he stood to benefit personally from the many opportunities to increase his fame and position that war at Germany's side would offer. A dashing figure who had enjoyed almost unlimited luck but had demonstrated only limited ability, he failed to see that bets can be lost as well as won. In putting his chips on Germany, he thought he was making an investment—when he was doing no more than placing a wager.

On 9 October, Enver informed von Wangenheim that he had won the support of Talaat and of Halil Bey, President of the Chamber of Deputies. The next move, he said, would be to try to gain the support of Djemal Pasha, Minister of the Marine. Failing that, he said, he planned to provoke a Cabinet crisis; he claimed, on the basis of his following in the Central Committee—which, in reality, was Talaat's following—that he could install a new pro-interventionist government. Overstating his political strength, Enver assured the Germans that he could bring Turkey into the war by mid-October. All he needed, he told them, was German gold to support the army.[20] The Germans, of course, were already aware that the Ottoman forces would need money; Liman had reported to the Kaiser that they would be in imminent danger of collapse without it.

On 10 October, Djemal joined the conspiracy. On 11 October, Enver, Talaat, Halil, and Djemal conferred, and informed the Germans that their faction was now committed to war and would authorize Admiral Souchon to attack Russia as soon as Germany deposited two million Turkish pounds in gold in Constantinople to support the armed forces. The Germans responded by sending a million pounds on 12 October and a further million on 17 October, shipping the gold by rail through neutral Rumania. The second shipment arrived in Constantinople on 21 October.

Talaat and Halil then changed their minds: they proposed to keep the gold but, nonetheless, to remain neutral in the war. Enver reported this to the Germans on 23 October, but claimed that it did not matter as long as he could still count on the other military service minister, Djemal. Though he later announced that Talaat had swung back again to the pro-interventionist cause, Enver gave up attempting to persuade his party and his government to intervene in the war. He could not get Turkey to declare war on the Allies so he pinned his hopes on a plan to provoke the Allied governments to declare war on Turkey.

Enver and Djemal issued secret orders allowing Admiral Souchon to lead the *Goeben* and *Breslau* into the Black Sea to attack Russian vessels. Enver's plan was to claim that the warships had been attacked by the Russians and had been forced to defend themselves. Admiral Souchon, however, disobeyed Enver's orders and openly started the fighting by bombarding the Russian coast. Once again the German admiral gave history a push. His purpose, he stated later, was "to force the Turks, even against their will, to spread the war."[21] As a result of his actions, it was all too clear that the *Goeben* and *Breslau* had struck a premeditated blow; there was now no lie behind which Enver could conceal what he had allowed to happen.

The incident led to an open showdown in Constantinople. The Grand Vizier and the Cabinet forced Enver to cable an order to Admiral Souchon to cease fire. A political crisis ensued that lasted for nearly two days, the details of which were veiled even from the normally well-informed Germans and Austrians. There were meetings of the Ottoman Cabinet and of the C.U.P. Central Committee. Debate was joined, threats were issued, coalitions were formed, resignations were tendered, and resignations were withdrawn. Apparently the consensus approximated the thinking of Asquith in Britain just before the outbreak of war: that the first priority was to maintain party unity. Even though a majority in the Central Committee supported the newly formed triumvirate of Talaat, Enver, and Djemal in the view that the Ottoman Empire now ought to enter the war, it deferred to the views of the minority, led by the Grand Vizier and the Minister of Finance, rather than allow a party split to occur.

On 31 October Enver reported to the Germans that his colleagues in the Cabinet insisted on dispatching a note of apology to the Russians. From the German point of view this was a dangerous proposal, but Enver said that, having "duped" his colleagues about the attack on Russia, he now found himself isolated in the Cabinet; his hands, he said, were tied.[22]

Though Enver and his German co-conspirators did not yet know it, there was no need for alarm: in London the British Cabinet had already risen to the bait. The British were unaware of the deep split in Young Turk ranks and believed the Porte to have been in collusion with Germany all along. Responding to Souchon's attack even before the Porte drafted its apology, the Cabinet authorized the sending of an ultimatum requiring the Turks immediately to expel the German military mission and to remove the German officers and men from the *Goeben* and *Breslau*. When the Turks did not comply, Churchill did not bother to refer the matter back to the Cabinet; on his own initiative he dispatched an order to his forces in the Mediterranean on the afternoon of 31 October to "Commence hostilities at once against Turkey."[23]

The British admiral who received Churchill's order did not carry it out immediately and, in consequence, Turkey was unaware that

Britain had gone to war against her. In Constantinople, Enver still feared that the Turkish apology to Russia might be accepted. To prevent that from happening, he again foiled the intentions of his Cabinet colleagues by inserting into the Turkish note an outrageous allegation that Russia had provoked the attack.[24] Predictably the Czar's government rejected the allegation, issued an ultimatum to the Porte, and on 2 November declared war.

British naval forces commenced hostile operations against the Ottoman Empire on 1 November. At a dramatic meeting of the Ottoman Cabinet on the night of November 1–2, even the Grand Vizier's peace faction was obliged to recognize that the empire was now at war, like it or not. Yet no declaration of war was issued from London.

On 3 November, on instructions from Churchill, British warships bombarded the outer forts of the Dardanelles. Critics later charged that this was a piece of childish petulance on Churchill's part which alerted Turkey to the vulnerability of the forts. There is no evidence, however, that Turkey responded to the warning. At the time, the chief significance of the bombardment seemed to be its demonstration that hostilities had commenced.

On 4 November, Asquith confided that "we are now frankly at war with Turkey."[25] The formalities, however, were neglected. It was not until the morning of 5 November that, at a meeting with the Privy Council, the proclamations of war against the Hohenzollern and Habsburg empires were amended to include the Ottoman Empire.

The relative casualness with which the British drifted into the Ottoman war reflected the attitudes of British Cabinet ministers at the time: it was not a war to which they attached much importance, and they made no great effort to prevent it. They did not regard Turkey as an especially dangerous enemy.

V

In London it was still not known—indeed it would not be known until years later—that Enver had taken the initiative in proposing, negotiating, and executing a secret treaty of alliance with Germany *before* the Admiralty had seized the Turkish battleships. It also was not known that it was the Porte that had seized the *Goeben* and *Breslau*, and that it had done so over German protest. In Downing Street the official account was believed, according to which the Kaiser had initiated the transfer to Turkey of the German vessels to replace the *Osman* and *Reshadieh* in order to win over to Germany the Turks whom Churchill had alienated.

It was the common view, therefore, that it was Churchill who had brought about the war with Turkey. Indeed, Lloyd George continued to level the charge against him as late as 1921.[26] Souchon and Enver had in fact started the war between Turkey and the Allies, but in the public imagination of the British it was Churchill who had done so.

Churchill, for his part, began to point out in August 1914—and continued to point out thereafter—that having the Ottoman Empire for an enemy had its advantages. Free at last to cut up the Ottoman Empire and to offer portions of its territory to other countries at the eventual peace settlement, Britain could now hold out the lure of territorial gains in order to bring Italy and the Balkan countries into the war on her side.

Italy, a latecomer to the pursuit of colonial empire, had come to see the vulnerable Ottoman domains as the principal territories still available for acquisition. She remained anxious to acquire even more Ottoman territory. Eventually, the lure of acquisition helped to bring her into the war on the Allied side.

The Balkan countries, too, coveted additional territorial gains. For Britain to forge an alliance with all the Balkan countries by the promise of Ottoman territory required the reconciliation of some of their rival ambitions; but if this could be achieved, such a combination would bring powerful forces to bear against the Ottoman and Habsburg empires, and offered the prospect of helping bring the war against Germany to a swift and successful conclusion.

Already on 14 August, Asquith noted that "Venizelos, the Greek Prime Minister, has a great scheme on foot for a federation of Balkan States against Germany and Austria . . ."[27] On 21 August, Asquith characterized a number of his ministers as looking to Italy, Rumania, or Bulgaria as potential allies of importance; Lloyd George as being "keen for Balkan confederation"; and "Winston violently anti-Turk." He himself, however, was "very much against any aggressive action *vis-à-vis* Turkey wh. wd. excite our Mussulmans in India & Egypt."[28] Churchill was not so impetuous as that made him sound. In fact he had taken the time and trouble to communicate personally with Enver and other Ottoman leaders who were hoping to keep their country neutral. He had given up on them two months too soon; but it was only when he had become convinced that there was no chance of keeping Turkey out of the war that he had swung around to pointing out the advantages of having her in it.

By the end of August, Churchill and Lloyd George were enthusiastic advocates of the Balkan approach. On 31 August Churchill wrote a private letter to Balkan leaders urging the creation of a confederation of Bulgaria, Serbia, Rumania, Montenegro, and Greece to join the Allies. On 2 September he initiated private talks with the Greek government to discuss the form that military cooperation between their two countries might take in an offensive operation against the Ottoman Empire.

At the end of September, Churchill wrote to Sir Edward Grey that "in our attempt to placate Turkey we are crippling our policy in the Balkans. I am not suggesting that we should take aggressive action against Turkey or declare war on her ourselves, but we ought from now to make arrangements with the Balkan States, particularly Bulgaria, without regard to the interests or integrity of Turkey." He concluded his additional remarks by adding that "All I am asking is that the interests and integrity of Turkey shall no longer be considered by you in any efforts which are made to secure common action among the Christian Balkan States."[29]

Grey and Asquith were more cautious in their approach, and less enthusiastic about the proposed Balkan Confederation than were Churchill and Lloyd George, but in at least one respect their thinking evolved in a parallel way. In order to persuade Turkey to remain neutral, the representatives of the British government eventually had been instructed to give assurances that, if she did so, Ottoman territorial integrity would be respected. From this there followed a converse proposition, that Grey had made explicit as early as 15 August, "that, on the other hand, if Turkey sided with Germany and Austria, and they were defeated, of course we could not answer for what might be taken from Turkey in Asia Minor."[30]

When the Ottoman Empire entered the war—pulled into it by Churchill as it seemed then, pushed into it by Enver and Souchon as it seems now—the conclusion that British policy-makers drew therefore seemed to be inescapable. In a speech delivered in London on 9 November 1914, the Prime Minister predicted that the war had "rung the death-knell of Ottoman dominion, not only in Europe, but in Asia."[31]

Earlier in 1914, Sir Mark Sykes, the Tory M.P. who was his party's leading expert on Turkish affairs, had warned the House of Commons that "the disappearance of the Ottoman Empire must be the first step towards the disappearance of our own."[32] Wellington, Canning, Palmerston, and Disraeli had all felt that preserving the integrity of the Ottoman Empire was of importance to Britain and to Europe. Yet in a little less than a hundred days the British government had completely reversed the policy of more than a hundred years, and now sought to destroy the great buffer empire that in times past British governments had risked and waged wars to safeguard.

The Cabinet's new policy was predicated on the theory that Turkey had forfeited any claim to enjoy the protection of Britain. In the turmoil of war the Asquith government had lost sight of one of the most important truths about traditional British foreign policy: that the integrity of the Ottoman Empire was to be protected not in order to serve the best interests of Turkey but in order to serve the best interests of Britain.

In turn, the British decision to dismantle the Ottoman Empire finally brought into play the assumption that Europeans had shared about the Middle East for centuries: that its post-Ottoman political destinies would be taken in hand by one or more of the European powers.

Thus the one thing which British leaders foresaw in 1914 with perfect clarity was that Ottoman entry into the war marked the first step on the road to a remaking of the Middle East: to the creation, indeed, of the modern Middle East.

PART II

KITCHENER OF KHARTOUM LOOKS AHEAD

8

KITCHENER TAKES COMMAND

I

During the summer and autumn of 1914, as the Ottoman Empire was drifting into the war, an important new governmental appointment in London was beginning to affect British policy in the Middle East. It began, as so many things did, with Winston Churchill.

On 28 July 1914, the same day that he initiated the seizure of the Turkish vessels, Churchill held a luncheon meeting with Field Marshal Horatio Herbert Kitchener to discuss the deepening international crisis. As proconsul in Egypt, the veteran commander of Britain's imperial armies was responsible for the security of the Suez Canal and of the troops from India who were to be transported through it in the event of war. Churchill, the First Lord of the Admiralty, was responsible for the naval escort of the troopships on their long voyage to Europe; and over lunch the young politician and the old soldier exchanged views.

Churchill told Kitchener that "If war comes, you will not go back to Europe."[1] It was not what the field marshal wanted to hear. Kitchener had come to Britain intending to stay only long enough to attend the 17 July ceremonies elevating him to the rank and title of Earl Kitchener of Khartoum; he was anxious to return to his post as British Agent and Consul-General in Egypt as soon as possible. His eyes had always been turned toward the East; he told King George that he wanted to be appointed Viceroy of India when that post became available as scheduled in 1915, though he feared that "the politicians" would block his appointment.[2] The crusty, bad-tempered Kitchener loathed politicians.

Even the disintegrating international situation could not keep him in London. Early in August he traveled to Dover to catch a Channel steamer; the plan was that he would take the train from Calais to Marseilles, and there would board a cruiser for Egypt. Shortly before noon on 3 August, he boarded the steamer at Dover, and complained impatiently when it failed to set off for Calais at the scheduled departure time.

As it happened, his departure was about to be cancelled rather than delayed. The previous evening, in the smoking room of Brooks's, a London club, someone who fell into conversation with a Conservative Member of Parliament remarked that the War Office was in an absolutely chaotic state and that it was a pity that Kitchener had not been asked to take it over. Later that evening, the M.P. reported his conversation to two of his party's leaders who were in a semi-private room of the club discussing the international situation. Andrew Bonar Law and Sir Edward Carson—the leaders to whom the conversation was reported—took the matter up with Arthur Balfour, the former Conservative Prime Minister, who passed the suggestion on to Churchill, with whom he was on good terms.

On the morning of 3 August—the day Germany declared war on France—an article appeared in *The Times*, written by its military correspondent, urging the appointment of Kitchener to head the War Office. That same morning, Churchill saw the Prime Minister and proposed Kitchener's appointment, though apparently without indicating that the proposal came from the Conservatives as well as from himself. Churchill's notes indicate that he thought that Asquith had accepted the proposal at the time; but in fact the Prime Minister was reluctant to make the appointment, and decided instead to keep Kitchener in Britain merely in an advisory position.

On board the Channel steamer, which had not yet left Dover, Kitchener received a message from the Prime Minister asking him to return immediately to London. The field marshal at first refused; and it was with difficulty that he was persuaded to disembark. His fears were justified; back in London he found that Asquith did not seem to be thinking of a regular position for him, let alone one with clearly defined powers and responsibilities. Urged on by his colleagues, Kitchener decided to force the issue; he went to see the Prime Minister for a one-hour meeting on the evening of 4 August—the night Britain decided to go to war, by which time German armies were already overrunning Belgium—and stated that, if obliged to remain in London, he would accept no position less than Secretary of State for War.

Pushed by politicians and the press, the Prime Minister gave way the next day, and Kitchener was appointed War Minister. As he wrote: "K. was (to do him justice) not at all anxious to come in, but when it was presented to him as a duty he agreed. It is clearly understood that he has no politics, & that his place at Cairo is kept open—so that he can return to it when peace comes. It is a hazardous experiment, but the best in the circumstances, I think."[3] Assuming, as did nearly everybody else, that the war would last no more than a few months, Asquith did not replace Kitchener as Agent and Consul-General in Egypt; he thought that the field marshal would be returning to his post there shortly. On 6 August Kitchener took up his new duties in the War Office in Whitehall.

Lord Kitchener lived in a borrowed house in London, making it plain that he did not intend to stay.* It was located just off the intersection of Carlton House Terrace and Carlton Gardens, less than a five-minute walk from the War Office, which meant that he could spend almost every waking moment on the job. He arose at 6:00 a.m., arrived at his office at 9:00 a.m., generally took a cold lunch there, returned to his temporary home at 6:00 p.m. to read the evening papers and nap, and then after dinner would read official cables until late at night.[4] The glass or two of wine with dinner and the nightly scotch and soda that had been his comforts in Egypt were forsworn; at the request of George V he had pledged to set a national example by drinking no alcoholic beverages during the war.

Asquith's reluctance to bring the famous soldier into the Cabinet seems to have been prompted by the fear that, as Secretary for War, Kitchener, rather than the Prime Minister, would emerge as Britain's wartime leader. No great soldier had served in a major office of state since the Duke of Wellington's ministry nearly a century before; and no serving army officer had been included in a Cabinet since General George Monk, who in 1660 restored the monarchy and then was rewarded with high office. The principle of civilian authority had been upheld jealously since then; but Asquith felt obliged to subordinate it to his urgent need for Field Marshal Kitchener's services.

Kitchener was a figure of legend—a national myth whose photo hung on walls throughout the kingdom. After he took up his Cabinet appointment, large crowds would gather to watch him enter and leave the War Office each day. As the Prime Minister's daughter later wrote:

> He was an almost symbolic figure and what he symbolized, I think, was strength, decision, and above all success ... [E]verything that he touched 'came off'. There was a feeling that Kitchener could not fail. The psychological effect of his appointment, the tonic to public confidence, were instantaneous and overwhelming. And he at once gave, in his own right, a national status to the government.[5]

The public, it was said, did not reason about Kitchener, but simply trusted him completely, saying "Kitchener is there; it is all right."[6]

In the past he had always brought things to a successful conclusion.

---

* In March 1915 he moved into York House, St James's Palace, a residence provided for him by King George.

He had avenged the murder of General Charles George Gordon in the fall of Khartoum by destroying the empire of the Dervishes and reconquering the Sudan. The French had then attempted to intrude upon Britain's imperial domains, but in 1898 Kitchener firmly confronted them at the fort of Fashoda in the Sudan, and the French contingent backed down and withdrew from the fort. In South Africa the Boer War had begun badly; then Kitchener came to take charge and brought it to a victorious conclusion. As commander of the armies of India in the early twentieth century, he had imposed his will as decisively as he had done in Egypt.

The far-off outposts of empire in which he won his brilliant victories lent him their glamor. Distance made him seem at once magical and larger-than-life, like a sphinx presiding over the desert. A lone, insecure, and secretive figure who used a small group of aides as a wall against the world, he appeared instead to be the strong and silent hero of popular mythology. His painful shyness was not seen as such; his fear of his political colleagues appeared to be disdain. A young Foreign Office clerk who watched the field marshal at a gathering with the Prime Minister, Sir Edward Grey, and David Lloyd George, recorded in his diary that "Kitchener looked like an officer who has got mixed up with a lot of strolling players and is trying to pretend he doesn't know them."[7]

Tall, broad-shouldered, square-jawed, with bushy eyebrows, bristling moustache, cold blue eyes set widely apart, and an intimidating glower, he towered physically over his fellows and looked the part for which destiny and the popular press had cast him. From his earliest campaigns, he was fortunate in the journalists who followed his career and who created his public image. He was fortunate, too, in the timing of his career, which coincided with the rise of imperial sentiment, literature, and ideology in Britain. Disraeli, Kipling, A. E. W. Mason (author of *Four Feathers*), Lionel Curtis (a founder of the *Round Table*, the imperialist quarterly), John Buchan, and others created the tidal wave of feeling on the crest of which he rode.

George Steevens of the *Daily Mail*, who was perhaps the leading war correspondent of his time, told his readers in 1900 that Kitchener's "precision is so unhumanly unerring he is more like a machine than a man."[8] Steevens wrote a book about the Sudan campaign, telling how Kitchener (then sirdar, or commander, of the Egyptian army) led his armies south over nearly a thousand miles of rock and sand, from the waters of the Nile Valley to lands where rain never falls, to conquer a country of a million square miles. Ignoring the episodes in which Kitchener's generalship was open to criticism, the book dwelt at length on the characteristic organizational ability that derived from the sirdar's background as an engineering officer. According to Steevens, Kitchener prepared his movements with such care that "he has never given battle without making certain of an annihilating victory . . ."[9] Steevens wrote that "the man has disappeared . . . there is no man Herbert Kitchener, but only the Sirdar, neither asking affection nor giving it. His officers and men are wheels in the machine: he feeds them enough to make them efficient, and works them as mercilessly as he works himself."[10]

When he joined the Cabinet, and indeed for many months afterward, its other members—to most of whom he was a stranger—were in awe of him. Although they were jolted by his military pronouncements, which ran counter to everything which they had been led to believe, they accepted his judgments without demur. They had believed the professional British army to be of adequate size, but during his first day at the War Office, Kitchener remarked, "There is no army."[11] The accepted view was that the war would be a short one, but Kitchener with unerring foresight told an astonished (and, according to Churchill, a skeptical) Cabinet that Britain would have to maintain an army of millions of men in the field; that the war would last at least three years; and that it would only be decided by bloody battles on the continent of Europe and not at sea.[12] Defying the conventional view that a large army could be created only by conscription, Kitchener instead raised his mass army by a volunteer recruitment campaign, which surprised his contemporaries as much as it has amazed posterity.

Kitchener proposed to win the war by organizing his forces as thoroughly as he had done in advance of the Khartoum campaign. He would spend the first years methodically creating, training, and equipping an army of overwhelming strength, and would concentrate his forces, not dissipate them in sideshows. The impending Ottoman war, he felt, would be a sideshow; it would be a waste of resources to send additional troops to fight the Turks. He feared a Turkish attack on the Suez Canal—his only military concern in the Middle East— but he believed that the British forces in Egypt could deal with it. The Middle East played no role in his plans for winning the war. But that did not mean that Kitchener had no Middle Eastern policy; as will be seen presently, he held strong views about what role Britain should play in the region once the European war was won.

II

It was pure accident that the military hero brought into the government to preside over the war effort should have been one who regarded himself, and was regarded by others, as having the East for his special province. From that accident came the distinctive outlines of the policy that emerged.

Most recently, Kitchener had governed Egypt, a country officially still part of the Ottoman Empire, but which had in effect been an independent country until the British had occupied it in 1882, with the stated aim of restoring order and then leaving. Instead of leaving, the British stayed on. As of 1914, Egypt was a relatively recent addition to the British sphere of influence, and British officers who served there with Kitchener had begun to develop a distinctive outlook on events. Stationed as they were in an Arabic-speaking country, they had come to regard themselves, mistakenly, as experts on Arab affairs, and were all the more frustrated to be excluded from foreign policy making by the Foreign Office and by the Government of India—the two bodies that traditionally dealt with the Arabic-speaking portions of the Ottoman Empire. Neither Kitchener nor his aides demonstrated any real awareness of the great differences between the many communities in the Middle East. Arabians and Egyptians, for example, though both Arabic-speaking, were otherwise different—in population mix, history, culture, outlook, and circumstances. Even had they been the experts on Egypt which they believed themselves to be, that would not necessarily have made Kitchener's aides the experts on Arabia they claimed to be.

In the Sudan campaign, undertaken in the face of misgivings within both the Foreign Office and Lord Cromer's Egyptian administration, Kitchener had greatly expanded the area of Britain's control of the Arabic-speaking world. It may have been during the Sudan campaign that Kitchener first began to dream of carving out a great new imperial domain for Britain in the Middle East, in which he would serve as her viceroy.

As early as the end of the nineteenth century, British officials were aware that the Khedive—the native prince from behind whose throne Britain ruled Egypt—was ambitious to expand his authority. Although in theory he was the Ottoman Sultan's viceroy in Egypt, there were persistent rumors that he considered the possibility of taking the Sultan's place as temporal and spiritual lord—Sultan and Caliph—of the Arabic-speaking provinces of the empire, thereby splitting the empire in half. A variant was the rumor that he planned to annex the Moslem Holy Places in Arabia and establish a caliph there under his protection.[13] The British and Egyptian officers attached to him would understand that the achievement of any such plan would bring greatly enlarged authority to themselves.

At the time—the end of the nineteenth century—the Great Power principally opposed to the expansion of British Egypt was France, which had aligned herself with Russia. As viewed from Britain's outposts bordering the Mediterranean, the alliance seemed to be directed against Britain. But Russia was far away; and in Egypt and the Sudan, France was the enemy whose threatening presence was felt close at hand. Rivalry with France for position and influence in the Arabic-speaking world: that was the policy in the service of which Kitchener's officers had been reared.

Larger combinations and considerations in world politics were beyond the range of the typical officer in British Cairo, an enclave that possessed (wrote one of Kitchener's aides) "all the narrowness and provincialism of an England garrison town ..."[14] The local community of British officials and their families was tight and homogeneous. Its life centered around the Sporting Club, the Turf Club, and the balls given at a leading hotel six nights out of seven.

It was from this provincial garrison community—its views on Arab policy hitherto ignored by the makers of British world policy—that Lord Kitchener emerged.

III

The outbreak of the war against the Ottoman Empire made it necessary to clarify the nature of Britain's presence in Egypt and Cyprus, for both were nominally still part of the Sultan's empire. The Cabinet was in favor of annexing both countries and, indeed, according to what officials in Cairo were told, had already made the decision. Ronald Storrs, the Oriental Secretary (which is to say, the staff specialist in Eastern affairs) to Lord Kitchener in Cairo, protested that, in the case of Egypt, such a decision violated forty years of promises by British governments that the British occupation was merely temporary. The Agency (that is, the office of the British Agent in Egypt, Lord Kitchener) advocated a protectorate status for Egypt, with at least token reference to eventual independence—a case argued effectively by Milne Cheetham (acting chief of the Agency in Kitchener's absence). The Cabinet abandoned its own views in deference to those of the Agency, and thus showed the direction of things to come.

The Cabinet, in this instance, allowed Kitchener's Agency to establish the prototype of the form of rule that the field marshal and his staff eventually wanted Britain to exercise throughout the Arabic-speaking world. It was not to be direct rule, such as was practiced in parts of India. In Kitchener's Egypt a hereditary prince and native Cabinet ministers and governors went through the motions of governing. They promulgated under their own name decisions recommended to them by the British advisers attached to their respective offices; that was the form of protectorate government favored by the Kitchener group. In the artful words of Ronald Storrs: "We deprecated the Imperative, preferring the Subjunctive, even the wistful, Optative mood."[15]

The Egyptian decision was the forerunner of others in which Storrs and other members of Kitchener's entourage made policy decisions for the Middle East under cover of the reclusive field marshal's authority. When the views of the government about the East came into conflict with those of Lord Kitchener, it was the latter that were likely to prevail. Decisions that normally would have been made by the Prime Minister, the Foreign Secretary, the Viceroy of India, or the Cabinet were instead made by relatively junior officials who represented Kitchener and purported to represent his views. Only the field marshal's unique prestige made this possible.

On one telegram from Cairo, Sir Edward Grey, the Foreign Secretary, minuted "Does Lord Kitchener agree? If so, I will approve."[16] He could have written the same inscription on them all. Kitchener was scrupulous in clearing foreign-policy decisions with Grey, but Grey deferred to him, and approved even those proposals of the War Minister with which he disagreed.

One reason that Members of Parliament and the Cabinet left eastern questions so much to Kitchener and his entourage was that they themselves knew little about them. To a government official in the 1980s, accustomed to bulging reference libraries, to worldwide press coverage, and to the overwhelming supply of detailed information about foreign countries gathered by the major governments, British ignorance of the Middle East during the 1914 war would be unimaginable. Shortly after Britain found herself at war with the Porte, Sir Mark Sykes, one of the few M.P.s who had traveled in the East, complained that in the English language there was not so much as one authentic history of the Ottoman Empire.[17] Of the histories then current, none was based on original research, and all were based on a German work that left off in the year 1744, and were therefore long out of date.[18] As late as 1917, when British armies were poised to invade northward toward Syria, British Intelligence, asked by the army to provide a guide to conditions there, reported that there was no book in any European language that provided a survey of the social and political conditions of the area.[19]

The British government lacked even the most elementary type of information—including maps—of the empire with which it was at war. In 1913–14, one of Kitchener's intelligence officers had secretly surveyed and mapped a wilderness area close to British Egypt's Sinai frontier; it was one of a mere handful of surveys gathered by British Intelligence.[20] For the most part, British officers conducting operations in Ottoman territory in the first years of the war were operating in the dark. One of the many reasons for the failure of Britain's invasion of Turkey in 1915 was that the British invasion force was supplied with only one map of the peninsula it was to attack—and that map, it turned out, was inaccurate. When it came to the Middle East, the politicians, like the soldiers, were aware that they were moving in areas that were literally uncharted.

But the Cabinet ministers who deferred to Kitchener in Middle Eastern matters were unaware of how little was really understood about the Middle East either by the War Minister or by the aides in Cairo and Khartoum on whom he relied for advice and information.

9

KITCHENER'S LIEUTENANTS

I

Avoiding not merely women (as he had always done) but the outside world as a whole, the War Minister lived in a masculine preserve with his personal Military Secretary, Lieutenant-Colonel Oswald FitzGerald, as his almost sole and constant companion. FitzGerald corresponded and conversed on Kitchener's behalf; when people said they had written to or heard from Kitchener, they meant that they had written to or heard from FitzGerald.

Kitchener had always relied heavily on his staff. Now that he had moved into the center of power in London, not only FitzGerald, but also the staff remaining in Egypt and the Sudan moved toward the center of power with him. Thus Lord Kitchener imposed his design on policy not merely by shaping a new approach toward the Middle East, but also by delegating power to chosen officers in the field who would guide and execute that policy. Instead of being ignored or neglected, as they felt they had been in the past, British officials in Egypt and the Sudan were given a chance to make their weight felt.

Kitchener's old lieutenants in the Arabic-speaking world rose with him to pre-eminence in Eastern policy-making. What was conspicuous at the end of 1914 was that Kitchener had stamped his personal brand on the government's policies, but what turned out to be of more lasting importance was that he had chosen the people who were to inform and to advise the British government about the Middle East throughout the war—and afterward. By tranferring authority to them, Kitchener moved much of the evaluation of information and the making of policy from the capital city of a world empire, where officials—even though not specifically knowledgeable about Middle Eastern affairs—tended toward a broad and cosmopolitan view of matters, to the colonial capitals of Egypt and the Sudan, where the prejudices of old hands went unchallenged and unchecked. The British enclaves in Cairo and Khartoum were the environment to which the War Minister longed to return and from which spiritually he had never departed.

The War Minister's weakness, according to one observer, was that "He is more or less a foreigner" in England.[1] To him, London was more alien than Cairo or Calcutta. The field marshal was profoundly ill at ease with unfamiliar faces. Instead of relying on the War Office and the Foreign Office in London for information and advice about the Middle East, he continued to fall back on his staff in Egypt. When he was appointed War Minister, he asked Ronald Storrs, his Oriental Secretary, to stay on in London with him. Storrs pointed out that governmental regulations would not allow it but, when Storrs returned to Egypt, Kitchener continued to be inspired by his suggestions. Storrs, the son of an Anglican clergyman, was an intellectually elegant graduate of Pembroke College, Cambridge, then in his mid-thirties. Although he had no more than an undergraduate education in Eastern languages and literature, service as Oriental Secretary of the Agency in Cairo for more than a decade had established him as a specialist in Middle Eastern affairs. His lowly rank—after the outbreak of war, he finally obtained diplomatic standing, though only as a second secretary—gave no indication of his high position in the field marshal's esteem.

II

By the end of 1914, it was clear that the war was not coming to a quick conclusion, that the field marshal would not be able to return to Cairo for some time, and that therefore a new British proconsul had to be selected for Egypt. Kitchener, in order to keep the position in Cairo vacant for his return, personally selected Sir Henry McMahon to serve as his replacement (under the new title of High Commissioner, rather than Agent); McMahon was a colorless official from India, on the verge of retirement.

Despite McMahon's appointment, Ronald Storrs and his colleagues in Egypt and the Sudan continued to look upon the War Minister as their real chief. Sir John Maxwell, commanding general of the British forces in Egypt, reported directly to Kitchener at the War Office rather than to, or through, the new High Commissioner.

The senior figure in the War Minister's following in the Middle East was Lieutenant-General Sir Francis Reginald Wingate, who had succeeded Kitchener as sirdar of the Egyptian army and Governor-General of the Sudan. Wingate's entire career had been one of military service in the East, principally in Military Intelligence. He passed for a master of Arabic. Of his role in Kitchener's Khartoum campaign, the journalist George Steevens wrote that "Whatever there was to know, Colonel Wingate surely knew it, for he makes it his business to know everything ... As for that mysterious child of lies, the Arab, Colonel Wingate can converse with him for hours, and at the end know not only how much truth he has told, but exactly what truth he has suppressed ... Nothing is hid from Colonel Wingate."[2]

Wingate governed the Sudan from Khartoum, a sun-scorched capital city of some 70,000 inhabitants that had been completely rebuilt to the specifications of Lord Kitchener. By steamer and railroad, it was 1,345 miles away from Cairo, and Wingate felt cut off and neglected. On 18 February 1915, he sent a letter marked *Very Private* to his Agent in the Egyptian capital that cried out with his sense of hurt:

> The more that I think over the Arabian Policy question & the peculiar situation into which it has drifted owing to the number of "cooks" concerned in its concoction—the less I consider it desirable we should show our hands unless we are officially called upon for a statement of our views.
>
> Speaking for myself—you must remember that in spite of my position in Egypt & the Sudan & the number of years I have been in the country, little use has been made of my experience in this, or in other matters connected with the situation.
>
> . . .
>
> As I have often said before, I think that our geopolitical position & our connection with the Arabian Provinces nearest to us, has given us opportunities for understanding the situation there—and the views of the Moslems of the Holy Places—better than many others; but clearly that view is not shared by either the Home or Indian authorities & therefore, I prefer to keep silent for the time being.[3]

In fact Wingate could not bear to keep silent, and only twelve days later he wrote that he had changed his mind and had decided "that we ought not to keep entirely to ourselves information & views which may be helpful" to those responsible for making policy.[4]

Wingate's Agent in Cairo—the official representative in Egypt of the Sudan government—was Gilbert Clayton, who had also served under Lord Kitchener in the Sudan campaign. After receiving his commission in the Royal Artillery in 1895, Clayton went out to Egypt and had been stationed there or in the Sudan ever since. From 1908 to 1913 he served as Private Secretary to Wingate. From 1913 onward he served as Sudan Agent in Cairo and, at the same time, as Director of Intelligence of the Egyptian army. Clayton moved into a central position in making Britain's Arab policy on 31

October 1914, when, by decision of the Commanding General in Egypt, Sir John Maxwell, who reported directly to Kitchener, he became head of all intelligence services in Cairo—of the British civil authority and the British army, as well as the Egyptian army. Thus London heard only one version of intelligence data from Egypt—Clayton's—instead of three. A former army captain, Clayton rapidly moved up the ranks during the war and by the end of it was a general.

In this fatherly way, Clayton served as mentor to the adventurous young archaeologists and orientalists who flocked to Cairo to serve in the intelligence services during the war. He must have had outstanding human qualities, for his young men, though diverse in other regards, all liked and respected him. They saw him as shrewd, sober, sensible, and steady. He was about ten years older than most of them and, whether or not they took it, they listened to his advice. For them he was the incarnation of the old hand.

III

Although the Foreign Office and the India Office often disputed the views or proposals that Wingate and Clayton espoused, nobody during the war questioned their professional ability or their expert knowledge based on long experience in the Middle East. It was not until years after the war had ended that David Lloyd George, using information that became available from the German side, made a case for the proposition that they were dangerously incompetent.

According to Lloyd George, the British authorities in Cairo were blind to what was happening behind enemy lines. In particular, he wrote, there was a point in 1916 when the Ottoman Empire was too exhausted to continue fighting. If the British forces in Egypt had launched an attack on Sinai and Palestine then—or even in 1915— little effort would have been needed, according to Lloyd George, to "have crumpled . . . up" the Turks, which in turn would have allowed Britain to move through the Balkans to defeat Germany.[5] The opportunity was missed, according to him, because the intelligence services either did not know, or failed to report, what was going on inside the Ottoman Empire. As a result, he claimed, the British government failed to win the war during the years when the war still could have been won on British terms.

A more easily proved failing of Cairo Intelligence was that it was unaware of the extent to which the Egyptian government had been infiltrated by enemy agents. It was not until that expert on Ottoman affairs, Wyndham Deedes, went to work in Cairo in 1916, and discovered that the Egyptian police forces were honeycombed with spies, that the Turkish network was smashed.

An early sign of the inadequacy of Cairo's intelligence apparatus that ought to have sent up a warning signal, but did not, appeared in the autumn of 1914, about a month before the Ottoman war began, when the local British army commander, General Maxwell, wrote from Egypt to Lord Kitchener that "It is very difficult to put a true value on all the reports from Constantinople, Asia Minor and Syria ... I can get no information direct as the Turks guard the frontier very closely—our agents cannot get through—those we had on the other side have been bagged." He added a disquieting note about the intelligence imbalance: "The East is full of German spies and they get fairly good information."[6]

At least Maxwell was aware that he did not know what was going on in Constantinople. Wingate and Clayton fell into the trap of believing that they did. They accepted Gerald FitzMaurice's mistaken theory that the Ottoman government was in the hands of a group of pro-German Jews. At the end of 1914 General Wingate blamed the war on "a syndicate of Jews, financiers, and low-born intriguers" in Constantinople.[7]

He and his colleagues compounded the error by linking it to misleading information about the state of Moslem opinion. Just after the war began, Storrs sent Maxwell a report of remarks made by a Syrian informant about public opinion behind enemy lines. According to the informant, the inhabitants of Syria were filled with hatred of the Ottoman government because they believed it would support Zionism. "These Zionists are closely connected with Berlin and Constantinople and are the most important factor in the policy of Palestine," the informant stated.[8] The false rumor that Berlin and Constantinople were about to back Zionism echoed back and forth through the years, and later in the war misled the British Cabinet into believing that it had to issue a pro-Zionist Declaration immediately.

Storrs wrote to Kitchener (which is to say, to his personal military secretary, Lieutenant-Colonel Oswald FitzGerald) at the end of the year. He commented on plans for the postwar Middle East, and claimed that Moslems would oppose a Jewish Palestine because they blamed Jews for the war. "Again would not Islam be extremely indignant at the idea of handing over our conquests to a people which has taken no part as a nation in the war, and a section of which has undoubtedly helped to thrust the Turks over the precipice."[9] In fact, as Foreign Office and Arab Bureau reports later were to show, Moslem opinion, even in non-Turkish areas, generally supported the Ottoman Empire and its alliance with Germany. Storrs was wrong, too, in supposing that Moslems were opposed to a Jewish Palestine because of the war; Moslem opposition to a Jewish Palestine had arisen long before the war, in the wake of Zionist colonization at the end of the nineteenth century.

A characteristic flaw in the information-gathering conducted by Clayton and Storrs was that they frequently accepted information supplied by a single informant without testing and checking it. Instead they seemingly relied on the sort of intuitive ability that Steevens had ascribed to Wingate: the gift of being able to divine the extent to which any native is telling the truth. John Buchan, who later became wartime Director of Information in London, wrote in the second chapter of his adventure novel *Greenmantle* that "the truth is that we are the only race on earth that can produce men capable of getting inside the skin of remote peoples. Perhaps the Scots are better than the English, but we're all a thousand percent better than anybody else." Wingate, Clayton, and Storrs acted as though they understood the natives of the Ottoman Empire as well as did the Scots hero of Buchan's novel. As it transpired, their ability to understand the natives was quite limited.

In evaluating reports that there was dissatisfaction with Ottoman rule in some sections of the empire, British Cairo particularly misunderstood one of the salient characteristics of the Moslem Middle East: to the extent that it was politically conscious, it was not willing to be ruled by non-Moslems. Behind enemy lines there were Moslems who were dissatisfied with the Young Turk government, but they proposed to replace it with a different Turkish government, or at any rate a different Islamic government. They regarded rule by a Christian European power, such as Britain, as intolerable.

Storrs apparently believed that he could get around that by pretending that it was Egyptian rule that would be substituted for Turkish rule. He proposed to create what would appear to be a new Egyptian empire to replace the Ottoman Empire in the Arabic-speaking Middle East; it was behind that façade that Lord Kitchener would rule as Britain's viceroy. Storrs derived particular satisfaction from reports that Ottoman rule had become unpopular in Syria; he believed that he could offer the Syrians a popular alternative. Accurate reports, received with some frequency, indicated that—other than the Maronites, a Christian sect with ties to the French—most Syrians who held political views objected to the prospect of being ruled in the postwar world by France, and since Storrs and his colleagues took it for granted that the Arabic-speaking peoples could not govern themselves, the only possibility left was the one advocated by Storrs: the incorporation of Syria into British Egypt.

Seen in that light, reports that Syrians considered the Germans and Turks to be Zionists and the French to be detestable meant that the Syrians must be pro-British. Summarizing a memorandum submitted by a Syrian leader who called for Arab independence, Clayton stated that "it is to England, and to England alone, that both Syrian Christians and Pan-Arabs are turning."[10] On 2 February 1915, Storrs wrote to FitzGerald/Kitchener that "There is no doubt that local Syrian feeling, both Christian and Muslim, is strongly in favor of our adding that country to the Egyptian Sultanate ..."[11] The question was whether actively to promote that feeling. The newly arrived High Commissioner in Cairo, McMahon, writing the same day to FitzGerald/Kitchener to seek guidance, outlined the alternatives as they had undoubtedly been described to him by Storrs and Clayton: "The Syrians want our intervention and say that unless we can give them some assurance of support they will have to turn to the French altho they would prefer us to the French."[12]

Wrong-headed and professionally ambitious, Britain's men on the spot supposed that Arabs wanted to be ruled by Europeans, and buoyed by this mistaken belief, Kitchener's lieutenants aimed at taking control of Syria. France's men on the spot were wrong-headed and ambitious too; and they also aimed to take Syria.

IV

During the Crusades, French knights won kingdoms and built castles in Syria; and in 1914—a millennium later—there were still French-men who regarded Syria as properly part of France. France maintained close ties with one of the Christian communities along the Mount Lebanon coast of Syria, and French shipping, silk, and other interests eyed commercial possibilities in the area. Thus for religious, economic, and historical reasons, France saw herself as having a role to play in Syria's affairs.

The moment that the Ottoman Empire entered the war, French officials in the Middle East (like their British counterparts, Wingate, Clayton, and Storrs) therefore formulated plans to annex Turkey's Syrian provinces. France's minister in Cairo and Consul-General in Beirut immediately joined in urging their government to invade the Lebanese coast. Their quixotic plan called for a landing of only about 2,000 French troops, who would be joined—they believed—by 30,000 local volunteers. Speed was of the essence, in their view; France would have to strike before Turkey could raise an army and before Britain could strike first.[13]

Their proposal could hardly have been more inopportune. It reached the French government in November 1914, when it was still in exile in Bordeaux, having fled from Paris in the face of the German advance to the Marne. While there were powerful colonialist figures in Parliament, the Foreign Ministry, and the Cabinet, November was a month in which everyone's attention was still focused on the mortal struggle in northern France and Belgium. The proposal to dispatch troops to Syria was rejected.

The following month, however—the contending armies in Europe having settled down in their trenches, and the government having returned to Paris—the proposal to invade Syria did receive attention. A delegation of colonialist politicians secured the agreement, in principle, of Alexandre Millerand, the Minister of War, to support a Syrian expedition. Foreign Minister Theophile Delcassé, however, remained vehemently opposed: "Nothing appears less desirable than intervention in Syria," he said.[14] Delcassé was one of the many French officials who believed that annexing Syria would be of much less value to his country than preserving the Ottoman Empire would be. As of 1914 France supplied 45 percent of the foreign capital in the private sector of the Ottoman economy and 60 percent of the Ottoman public debt, and thus had an enormous stake in the empire's continued existence and vitality.[15]

On 30–31 December 1914, Sir Henry McMahon, who was about to take up his duties as Kitchener's replacement in Cairo, visited Paris. He met with officials of the Foreign Ministry and War Ministry but failed to reply coherently to their questions about Britain's Middle Eastern policy. McMahon was notoriously dull-witted and ineffectual, but the French, who did not know him, assumed he must be clever and astute: his incompetent replies were interpreted by Millerand, the War Minister, as deliberate and subtle evasions, masking a secret British plan to invade and occupy Syria by themselves.[16]

Millerand immediately reported these conversations to the French Cabinet, which authorized him to create an expeditionary force to invade Syria whenever Britain did, whether invited by her to participate or not. In February 1915, Delcassé went over to London and took up the matter of Syria with Sir Edward Grey. The French Foreign Minister was reassured that Britain would not invade Syria without giving prior notice. The two foreign ministers appear to have agreed that if the Ottoman Empire were to be partitioned, Britain would not oppose France's designs on Syria, but that it would be far preferable for the empire not to be broken up.

Thus the foreign ministers settled the differences between their two countries—temporarily. But their men on the spot in the Middle East continued to stir up trouble between Britain and France; and, misunderstanding the region, Kitchener and his lieutenants also went on to pursue other dangerous designs there.

KITCHENER SETS OUT TO CAPTURE ISLAM

I

The West and the Middle East have misunderstood each other throughout most of the twentieth century; and much of that misunderstanding can be traced back to Lord Kitchener's initiatives in the early years of the First World War. The peculiarities of his character, the deficiencies of his understanding of the Moslem world, the misinformation regularly supplied to him by his lieutenants in Cairo and Khartoum, and his choice of Arab politicians with whom to deal have colored the course of political events ever since.

To appreciate the novelty of Kitchener's approach to the Middle East, it must be remembered that when the Ottoman Empire entered the First World War, Asquith, Grey, and Churchill did not intend to retaliate by seizing any of its domains for Britain. They did propose to allow Britain's allies to make territorial gains in Europe and Asia Minor at Turkey's expense; but Asquith's Britain had no territorial designs of her own on Ottoman lands, either in the Middle East or elsewhere. Kitchener, however, maintained that when the war was over, it was in Britain's vital interest to seize much of the Ottoman Empire for herself: the Arabic-speaking part. This would mean a total reversal of Britain's traditional policy.

Kitchener, like most Britons who had lived in the East, believed that in the Moslem world religion counts for everything. But the field marshal and his colleagues in Cairo and Khartoum mistakenly seemed to believe that Mohammedanism was a centralized, authoritarian structure. They regarded Islam as a single entity: as an "it," as an organization. They believed that it obeyed its leaders. Centuries before, Cortez had won control of Mexico by seizing the Aztec emperor; and medieval French kings had tried to control Christendom by keeping the pope captive in Avignon. In much the same spirit, Kitchener and his colleagues believed that Islam could be bought, manipulated, or captured by buying, manipulating, or capturing its religious leadership. They were intrigued by the notion that whoever controlled the person of the Caliph—Mohammed's successor—controlled Islam.

Central to Kitchener's analysis was the contention that the Caliph might hurl Islam against Britain. Since Sunni Moslems (who predominated in Mohammedan India) regarded the Turkish Sultan as a Caliph, Kitchener perceived this as a continuing threat. In Cairo and Khartoum it was believed that, as of 1914, the Caliph had fallen into the hands of Jews and Germans; the War Minister worried that once the world war was won, the Caliph might become a tool in the hands of Britain's Middle East rivals, particularly Russia.

In enemy hands, the caliphate could be used (Kitchener believed) to undermine Britain's position in India, Egypt, and the Sudan. Britain ruled over half of the world's Moslems.[1] In India alone there were almost seventy million of them, and Mohammedans constituted a disproportionately large part of the Indian Army. In Egypt and the Sudan, Britain ruled millions more, who lived alongside the Suez Canal sea road to India. Tiny British garrisons policed these tens of millions of natives, but Kitchener knew that they could not even begin to deal with a revolt.

The British imagination was haunted by the Indian Mutiny (1857–9), the mysterious uprising, incited by religion, that had brought down the rule of the East India Company. More recently the uprising in the Sudan, which Kitchener had so brilliantly avenged, was inspired by a new religious leader who called himself the Mahdi, a title Europeans translated as "Messiah." Pan-Islamic unrest in Egypt in 1905–6 had caused Britain deep concern. For Kitchener and his entourage, the possibility of a Moslem Holy War against Britain was a recurring nightmare.

The Director of Information, John Buchan, dramatized these fears in his 1916 novel *Greenmantle*, in which Germany makes use of a Moslem prophet in a plot to destroy Britain's empire. The prophet appears in Turkey; there are portents of his coming; there is an ancient prophecy; there is a modern revelation; and the region in which he intends to ignite a rebellion is made explicit. "There is a dry wind blowing through the East, and the parched grasses wait the spark. And the wind is blowing towards the Indian border."[2]

Kitchener believed that a call to arms by the Caliph against Britain during the 1914 war could perhaps be offset by the words or actions of other Moslem religious leaders. After Britain had won the war, however, more decisive action would be necessary. The reason was that when the war had been won, Russia was sure to take possession of Constantinople and—unless something were done about it—of the Caliph. Kitchener saw a German-controlled Caliph as merely

Fear(?) Russian in Asia intervention (handwritten marginalia)

dangerous—he would attempt to foment unrest in India to throw Britain off balance in the European war. But he saw a Russian-controlled Caliph as a mortal danger to the British Empire; for (unlike Asquith and Grey) Kitchener believed that Russia still harbored ambitions of taking India away from Britain. In Kitchener's view, Germany was an enemy in Europe and Russia was an enemy in Asia: the paradox of the 1914 war in which Britain and Russia were allied was that by winning in Europe, Britain risked losing in Asia. The only completely satisfactory outcome of the war, from Kitchener's point of view, was for Germany to lose it without Russia winning it—and in 1914 it was not clear how that could be accomplished. So the War Minister planned to strike first in the coming postwar struggle with Russia for control of the road to and into India.

Kitchener's proposal was that, after the war, Britain should arrange for her own nominee to become Caliph. Mohammed had been an Arabian; Kitchener proposed to encourage the view that Mohammed's successors as Caliph should be Arabian, too. The advantage of this was that the coastline of the Arabian peninsula could easily be controlled by the British navy; Britain would be able to insulate the Caliph from the influence of Britain's European rivals. Once Britain could install the Caliph within her sphere of influence in Arabia, Kitchener believed she could gain control of Islam. And even before the Ottoman Empire entered the war, Kitchener's lieutenants in Cairo reminded the War Minister that an obvious candidate to be the Arabian caliph—the ruler of Mecca—had already been in touch with him.

II

Toward the end of the summer of 1914, as the Ottoman war approached, Gilbert Clayton recalled that Abdullah, the favorite son of Hussein, the ruler of Mecca, had visited Cairo some months earlier and had suggested that Arabia might be ripe for revolt. At the time, Abdullah had been afraid that the Young Turks were about to move against his father; and Abdullah, whose indolent disposition hid a bold intelligence, looked about for possible support from abroad. But shortly afterward his father and the Porte composed their differences, so that British assistance was no longer needed.

Even now, it is not certain what Abdullah said in Cairo and what was said to him. Abdullah apparently first met Lord Kitchener there in 1912 or 1913. He met Kitchener in Cairo again in February and April 1914, and also met with Ronald Storrs. Abdullah seems to have sought assurances of British help if the Porte were to seek to depose his father. At the time, Kitchener, who inquired in detail about the difficulties in Arabia, seems to have disclaimed any interest in interfering in internal Ottoman affairs. Abdullah may have been less impressed by the disclaimer of interest than by the expression of concern.[3]

To Storrs, Abdullah apparently claimed—falsely—that the rival chiefs of the Arabian peninsula were prepared to follow his father in opposing the Porte's designs. He suggested a future relationship between Arabia and Britain similar to that between Afghanistan and Britain, in which the former exercised internal self-rule and the latter administered all foreign relations. Though the idea was attractive to him, Storrs, like his chief, was unable to offer Abdullah the encouragement that he sought.[4]

Several Arabian emirs had indeed been in conflict for years with the Young Turk leadership in Constantinople. But Gilbert Clayton failed to appreciate the extent to which religious, dynastic, and other differences divided them. Arabic-speaking émigrés in Cairo, with whom he met, may have misled him in this connection. In fact none of the Arabian emirs was willing to accept one of the others as a leader.

Prominent among the Arabic-speaking exiles living in Cairo with whom Clayton spoke was a colorful former Ottoman army officer and C.U.P. politician named Aziz Ali al-Masri. Al-Masri, of Circassian ancestry,* was born and brought up in Egypt; he had attended military school in the Ottoman Empire. After military service in the field, he had emerged as a leader of the Young Turkey Party. Yet he was a mere major attached to the General Staff at a time when Enver, a classmate of whom he held a low opinion, had become Minister of War. Discontented, al-Masri responded by organizing al-'Ahd, a small secret society of army officers who objected to the C.U.P.'s centralizing policies and its failure to give those who spoke Arabic their fair share of high office. The officers of al-'Ahd were united in their opposition to the Turkifying policies adopted by the C.U.P. They advocated either admitting the Arabic-speaking populations to a greater share of power in the central government, or else decentralizing and allowing them greater autonomy at the local level, or perhaps both.[5]

Enver Pasha was responsible for having had Major al-Masri arrested and convicted on trumped-up charges in early 1914. Thus al-Masri unwillingly found himself cast in the role of an Arab revolutionary— unwillingly, because he aspired to leadership of the Ottoman Empire as a whole, not a mere section of it. Responding to opinion in Cairo,

---

* The Circassians were a people from the Caucasus, once ruled by Turkey and later by Russia.

Lord Kitchener intervened on his behalf; and Djemal Pasha arranged to have him pardoned and exiled to his native Egypt. An opponent, since his childhood, of British rule in Egypt, anti-British, pro-German, a supporter of the Ottoman Empire who was opposed only to its government, a military politician who numbered a mere handful of colleagues among his supporters, al-Masri was misunderstood by the British intelligence officers who wrongly regarded him both as powerful and as a potential ally.

In early September 1914, it appears that al-Masri visited the British Agency in Cairo, and met with Clayton.[6] Al-Masri knew that Abdul Aziz Ibn Saud and other Arabian leaders had in the past considered rising against the Porte. Perhaps he told Clayton so. Perhaps Clayton was reminded of Abdullah's visit and of what he had said to Storrs and Kitchener.

After seeing al-Masri, Clayton met with Ronald Storrs and made arrangements for him to forward a secret memorandum to Lord Kitchener. The Clayton memorandum was enclosed in a letter that Storrs was to send to his old chief on the relatively innocuous subject of camels.

III

It was a common British concern in 1914 that the Ottoman Empire, if it entered the war, might launch an attack against the Suez Canal; and, like officials in the war ministries of Europe who analyzed the military potential of neighboring enemy countries in terms of railroad facilities, Ronald Storrs focused attention on the supply of camels available to the Ottoman forces. The Ottoman army, he wrote in his letter to Kitchener, would count on obtaining its animals from the camel-breeders of the western district of Arabia, the Hejaz, and what Storrs proposed was to encourage the local ruler—the Emir of Mecca—not to deliver them.

The message about camels served as his cover: with it Storrs forwarded Clayton's secret memorandum of 6 September 1914 to Kitchener which urged him to enter into conversations with the ruler of Mecca for other purposes. One of the issues raised in Clayton's memorandum was whether the Ottoman Sultan could be replaced as Caliph of Islam by an Arabian leader friendly to Britain. If so, the Emir of Mecca, the guardian of the Moslem Holy Places, was an obvious candidate, the more so as he was in a position to provide Britain with important assistance in the matter of pilgrimages.

In the rhythm of life in the Islamic East, no activity was more important than the mass pilgrimage each year to the Holy Places of Arabia—a pilgrimage that every Moslem able to do so is commanded to make at least once in his lifetime. The world war interfered, particularly in 1915. Even if Indian Moslems were to forgive Britain for going to war against the only significant independent Islamic power, there was a question as to whether they would forgive the disruption of the pilgrimage that played so large a role in their lives.

The Holy Places of Arabia, Mecca, and Medina are located in the Hejaz, whose ruler therefore was in a position to safeguard the right of British Moslems to continue visiting their shrines despite the war. Claiming descent from the Prophet's family, the Emir of Mecca—in addition to being ruler of the Hejaz—was in a position to assume the mantle of the Caliph.

In his secret memorandum, Clayton made the erroneous assertion that the rival regional leaders of the Arabian peninsula—the rulers of Asir and the Yemen, as well as Ibn Saud and perhaps Ibn Rashid of Nejd—were coming together with the ruler of Mecca to work for "an Arabia for the Arabs."[7] According to Clayton's memorandum, the movement was encouraged by the Khedive, the nominal ruler of Egypt under the Sultan, who also regarded himself as a candidate to succeed the Sultan as Caliph of Islam. It is not clear how Clayton intended to reconcile the conflicting ambitions of this diverse group.

The claim that the other rival leaders would unite behind the Emir of Mecca was one that Abdullah had advanced on his father's behalf some five months before in conversations with Ronald Storrs. In presenting it as fresh information, Clayton may have been indicating that the information had been recently confirmed to him by al-Masri or by some other exiled Ottoman figure. The novelty of the memorandum lay in the suggestion that the Arabians could be of service to Britain during the war, and not merely afterward.

Kitchener responded immediately. He sent a cable to Cairo on 24 September 1914, in which he ordered that Storrs be told to send a trusted messenger to Abdullah to ask a question in confidence: in the event of war, would the Hejaz be for or against Britain? Before sending his cable, Kitchener cleared it with Sir Edward Grey, who was impressed by Clayton's memorandum, which he termed "very important."[8]

A few weeks later the messenger returned from his undercover journey to Ottoman Arabia with a vague but encouraging reply. It invited the War Minister to spell out what he had in mind. Cairo cabled Kitchener that "Communication is guarded, but friendly and favourable."[9]

Meanwhile the Agency had again been in communication with Major al-Masri and also other Arabic émigrés in Cairo. These exiles from the Ottoman Empire continued to carry on the decades-old discussion of who the various and diverse Arabic-speaking peoples of the empire were, or ought to be. This question of national identity was one which had been raised in the coffee houses of Damascus and Beirut, and in the student quarters of Paris from the nineteenth century onward, and had given rise to a variety of literary clubs and secret societies within the Ottoman Empire.

In the context of Ottoman politics, the Arabic-speaking exiles in Cairo were responding to those policies of the Young Turk government which subjected the majority of the inhabitants of the Ottoman Empire to the hegemony of the roughly 40 percent of the population who spoke Turkish. In one way or another, what the exiles advocated was a greater say in governmental matters, and more and higher official positions for those who spoke Arabic—about the same percentage as spoke Turkish.

Though often referred to as nationalists, these men are more accurately described as separatists.[10] They did not ask for independence; they asked for a greater measure of participation and local rule. They were willing to be ruled largely by Turks because the Turks were fellow-Moslems. Unlike European nationalists, they were people whose beliefs existed in a religious rather than secular framework. They lived within the walls of the city of Islam in a sense in which Europe had not lived within Christendom since the early Middle Ages; for, like the cities built in the Arab world in medieval times, the lives of Moslems circle around a central mosque. They did not represent an ethnic group, for historically, the only ethnic or "true" Arabs were the inhabitants of Arabia, while the Arabic-speaking populations of such provinces as Baghdad or Damascus, or of such cities as Algiers or Cairo, were of mixed ethnic stock and background, spanning the vast range of ancient peoples and cultures that extended from the Atlantic Ocean to the Persian Gulf.

There were only a few dozen people who were active partisans of Arabic nationalism (separatism) in October 1914, as members of one or more of the secret societies, such as al-Fatat and al-'Ahd, of which the British Agency in Cairo was becoming increasingly aware.[11] A great deal more is now known about these men and what they represented than was known to the British at the time. In large part they were members of the Arabic-speaking élites who had been well connected with the regime which had been overthrown by the Young Turks and who felt threatened by the pro-Turkish and centralizing trends in C.U.P. policy.[12] Milne Cheetham, the acting Agent and Consul-General in Cairo, cabled an intelligence memorandum about the secret societies to Kitchener on 26 October 1914, as the field marshal pondered the terms of his next message to Arabia.

IV

Kitchener's telegram, which was cleared and sent by Grey at the Foreign Office, told the Agency that Storrs should reply to Abdullah that "If the Arab nation assist England in this war that has been forced upon us by Turkey, England will guarantee that no internal intervention take place in Arabia, and will give Arabs every assistance against foreign aggression." (By "Arabs," Kitchener here meant those who lived in Arabia.) In other words, if the Arabian leaders freed their peninsula from the Sultan and declared their independence, Britain would help to protect them against any invasion from abroad.

At the Agency, Cheetham and Storrs were responsible for supervising the translation of this message into Arabic. Apparently with the encouragement of Clayton, they broadened its language to pledge British support for "the emancipation of the Arabs."[13] This went far in the direction pointed out by Reginald Wingate. Wingate believed in stirring up the tribes of Arabia on Britain's behalf. Unlike Kitchener, who proposed to deal with Arabia at the end of the war, the impatient Wingate urged immediate action at the beginning of the war. His goal was to lure the Arabs away from the Ottoman Empire and as early as 14 January 1915 he wrote to Clayton that "I fear British action has been so long delayed that it is doubtful if we shall now succeed in detaching the Arabs ..."[14] His familiar complaint was that his superiors had not heeded his advice in time.

As the Kitchener message was being sent out in Arabic translation, the émigré groups with which Clayton kept in contact in Cairo seem to have told him that Arabs in the Hejaz would be suspicious of British intentions, and that some sort of clarification of what was being promised would be in order. Kitchener, with Grey's approval, immediately authorized the Agency to issue a further statement. Again the Agency went beyond its instructions, and issued proclamations directed not merely to Arabia, but to practically all of Arabic-speaking Asia ("Palestine, Syria and Mesopotamia"), promising that if their inhabitants threw off the Turks, Britain would recognize and guarantee their independence.[15]

Although the Agency exceeded its instructions in making this public offer, the pledge itself was a reasonable one. Britain had not yet made any conflicting commitment to the Allied Powers regarding the future of Arabic-speaking Asia. If the Arabic-speaking provinces, in defiance of all the probabilities, had struck a major blow for the Allied cause by seceding from the Ottoman Empire and by successfully winning their freedom by their own exertions, there was no reason why Britain should not have guaranteed help in protecting their future independence. It would have been in Britain's national interest, with respect both to wartime and to postwar rivalries, to do so.

It was rather the message that Kitchener *had* authorized that was troubling, for—reflecting his belief that Arabia was important not for the role it could play in the war but for the role it could play after the war—he had closed his message to Mecca with his bombshell: "It may be that an Arab of true race will assume the Khalifate at Mecca or Medina, and so good may come by the help of God out of all the evil that is now occurring."[16] Restoring the caliphate to Arabia, where it and Mohammed were born thirteen centuries before, was Kitchener's strategy for preparing for the rivalry with Russia which was bound to follow the conclusion of the war against Germany. But Arabians, living within the political confines of their own peninsula, were not likely to understand what he had in mind. They would not know that at the outset of one great conflict between European powers he was already thinking ahead to the next. They would be even less likely to recognize that Kitchener, Wingate, Clayton, and Storrs did not understand the nature of the caliphate.

Scholars have been kept busy ever since explaining to western students of the Middle East that the split between temporal and spiritual authority, that in medieval Europe pitted pope against emperor, did not occur in the world of Islam. Kitchener, Wingate, Clayton, and Storrs were mistaken in believing that the Caliph could be a spiritual leader only. In Islam, all of life, including government and politics, falls within the governance of the Holy Law; so that in the eyes of Sunni Moslems, such as the Ottoman Sultan and the Emir of Mecca, the dominion of the Caliph as upholder of the Holy Law is pervasive. What British Cairo did not see is that the Caliph is also a prince: a governor and a leader in battle as well as a leader in prayer.

Kitchener's followers, for all their supposed knowledge of the Islamic world, missed the importance of another point: they ignored the extent of Islamic disunity and fragmentation. Thus the Kitchener plan called for Ibn Saud, leader of the fierce puritanical Wahhabi sect, to recognize the spiritual authority of the Sunni ruler of Mecca; but that was not a realistic possibility, for like so many of the dozens of contending sects into which Islam is divided, theirs were at daggers drawn.

The proposal which Kitchener and his followers sent off to Mecca misled its recipient, who read it as an offer to make him ruler of a vast kingdom; for that, of course, is what the new Caliph of Islam would have been. As will be seen, when the ruler of Mecca opened the discussion of what the boundaries of his new kingdom were to be, Storrs was appalled; for he and Kitchener had not intended that the area ruled by the Emir should be expanded. In the summer of 1915, Storrs wrote to FitzGerald/Kitchener that if the ruler of Mecca could conciliate the other ruling emirs and chieftains of the Arabian peninsula, and impress upon them that "he has no idea of pretending to any temporal rights within their territories, his chances of a general—though hardly yet of a universal—recognition as Caliph will be good."[17]

The British intended to support the candidacy of Hussein for the position of "Pope" of Islam—a position that (unbeknown to them) did not exist; while (unbeknown to them too) the language they used encouraged him to attempt to become ruler of the entire Arab world—though in fact Storrs believed that it was a mistake for Hussein to aim at extending his rule at all. Kitchener and his lieutenants would have been astonished to learn what their communication signified to Moslems in Arabia.

11

INDIA PROTESTS

I

Arthur Hirtzel, Secretary to the Political Department of the India Office, was not shown the Kitchener messages to Hussein until 12 December 1914—*after* they had reached Mecca. He was aghast. Hirtzel quickly criticized "a very dangerous correspondence" which, in hinting at an Arab caliphate, "does the very thing which this Office has always understood that H.M.G. would *not* do."[1] The Secretary of State for India, Lord Crewe, privately told the Viceroy that Kitchener refused to see that the spiritual prestige of the existing Caliph—the Turkish Sultan—remained intact, and that Moslems in India, who held him in high regard, even if they accepted his being replaced would never accept his being replaced as a result of foreign meddling.[2]

When he saw Kitchener's pledge to protect Arabian independence, Hirtzel protested that it was "a starting document," "a guarantee given . . . in writing without the authority of H.M.G."[3] Hirtzel's protest was buttressed by an earlier memorandum from the Foreign Department of the Government of India, forwarded to the India Office with support from the governors of Aden, Bombay, and elsewhere, which explained that, "What we want is not a United Arabia: but a weak and disunited Arabia, split up into little principalities so far as possible under our suzerainty—but incapable of coordinated action against us, forming a buffer against the Powers in the West."[4] This misunderstood British Cairo's intentions: as Clayton later wrote to Wingate, "India seems obsessed with the fear of a powerful and united Arab state, which can never exist unless we are fool enough to create it."[5]

Attempting to soothe feelings in the India Office and in the Government of India, Lord Crewe explained that there had been no prior consultation about the Kitchener pledge because "this was a private communication of Lord Kitchener's" rather than an official communication from His Majesty's Government.[6] But the jurisdictional dispute that had flared up was not extinguished by such assurances; it flamed on heatedly throughout the war and afterward.

II

India's institutional outlook was that of a beleaguered garrison spread too thin along an overextended line. Her instinct was to avoid new involvements. Her strategy for the Middle East was to hold the bare minimum—the coastline of the Gulf, to keep open the sea road to and from Britain—and to refuse to be drawn inland.

Nonetheless the unwanted war against the Ottoman Empire opened up the possibility of annexing nearby Basra and Baghdad. Colonization and economic development of these provinces would bring great riches, it was believed; and the Government of India was tempted, even though in the past its officials had often warned against assuming further territorial responsibilities. Whatever she did, British India was determined to identify her interests with those of her subjects, many of whom were Moslem; and Lord Kitchener's Islamic policy posed a threat to this vital interest.

Kitchener's initiatives also intruded into a foreign policy sphere in which the Government of India jealously guarded its rights against competitors within the British government. The Foreign Department of the Government of India exercised responsibility for relations with such neighboring areas as Tibet, Afghanistan, Persia, and eastern Arabia; and the Government of India also administered Britain's protectorate over Aden and the Gulf sheikhdoms through a network of governors and resident agents. Thus when Kitchener entered into discussions with the ruler of Mecca, he intervened in an area of Indian concern and activity.

Though the Government of India had long followed a policy of holding the coastal ports along the Persian Gulf sea route to Suez, it had avoided involvement in the politics of the interior. Even so, Captain William Henry Shakespear, an officer in the Indian Political Service, had, as Political Agent in Kuwait, entered into relations of political and personal friendship with Abdul Aziz Ibn Saud, an emir and a rising power in central Arabia, in the years immediately preceding the outbreak of war.[7] Like Abdullah in Cairo, Ibn Saud had expressed a willingness for his domain to become a British client state; and like Kitchener and Storrs, Shakespear was obliged to indicate that his government was unwilling to interfere in matters of purely domestic Ottoman concern. This was even more true at the time because the Foreign Office backed the pro-Turkish House of

Rashid, the paramount rulers of central Arabia and the House of Saud's hereditary enemy. But with the outbreak of war, India was free to back her protégé Ibn Saud, only to find Cairo backing a rival in Mecca.

Cairo, in turn, found its own projects thwarted by India. In November 1914, the month that the Ottoman Empire entered the war, Cairo proposed (with the approval of Sir Edward Grey) to send Major al-Masri on an expedition to organize agitation and perhaps revolution in Mesopotamia. Ever fearful of igniting a conflagration that could blaze out of control, India blocked the proposal.

India believed that if the Arabs ever were to turn against the Turkish government, Ibn Saud should lead this revolt; but as of December 1914, the Viceroy argued that action along these lines would be premature.[8] Taking a contrary view, Kitchener and his followers in Cairo and Khartoum looked to Sherif Hussein as Britain's important Arabian ally, and issued proclamations urging Arabs to revolt. Apart from this difference in overall strategy, Simla,* on the basis of prewar dealings, was aware of others in the Arabic-speaking world who might be alienated by British support for the Emir of Mecca's pretensions. There was Sheikh Mubarak of Kuwait, long a friend of Britain; there was the friendly ruler of the Persian port of Muhammara; there was even Sayyid Talib, the magnate of Basra, "dangerous scoundrel" though Hirtzel believed him to be.[9] A Foreign Office official, in warning of repercussions in Arabia, noted that the Emir of Mecca's two enemies there—Ibn Saud and Seyyid Mohammed al-Idrisi, the ruler of Asir—were, in his view, Britain's friends.[10]

Indian officials made the point that Cairo's policies were reckless; worse, they would not work. Britain's sponsorship of an Arab caliphate would not only adversely affect Moslem opinion in India (and Moslem opinion in India was, from the British point of view, what the caliphate issue was principally about); it would also do no good in the Arab world. Percy Cox, of the Indian Political Service, reported in December 1915 that he had held meetings with the Sheikh of Kuwait and Ibn Saud, and that he had found the caliphate question to be of no interest to them. Ibn Saud said that among the Arabian chiefs "no one cared in the least who called himself Caliph," and claimed that his Wahhabi sect did not recognize any caliphs after the first four (the last of whom had died more than a thousand years before).[11]

---

* "Simla" is often used to mean the Government of India, whose summer capital it was.

III

Oddly, nobody in London or in Simla seems to have drawn the appropriate conclusion from an episode at the end of 1914 that showed the power of the Caliph had been put to the test and had been shown to be illusory.

In November 1914, upon entering the First World War, the Sultan/ Caliph proclaimed a *jihad*, or Holy War, against Britain, amidst well-planned demonstrations in Constantinople. There were crowds, bands, and speeches. The Wilhemstrasse ordered copies of the proclamation to be forwarded immediately to Berlin for translation into "Arabic and Indian" (*sic*) for leaflet propaganda among Moslem troops in enemy armies.[12] The staff of the German Foreign Ministry predicted that the Sultan's actions would "awaken the fanaticism of Islam" and might lead to a large-scale revolution in India.[13]

The German military attaché in Constantinople believed that the proclamation would influence Moslem soldiers in the British and French armies not to fire on German troops. However, the skeptical German ambassador proved a better prophet: he wrote in a private letter that the proclamation would "coax only a few Moslems"[14] to come over to the side of the Central Powers. He was right. The *jihad* proved to be, in a coinage of the First World War, a "dud": a shell that was fired, but failed to explode.*

Enthusiasm for a Holy War was low, even in Constantinople. The *jihad* was proclaimed, but nothing happened. The British, however, continued to be wary and feared that any jolt might cause the unexploded shell suddenly to go off. In October 1915 Gilbert Clayton wrote a memorandum arguing that although the *jihad* until then had been a failure, it still might come alive.[15] According to Lord Crewe, Secretary of State for India, the only reason it had not worked was because the Porte did not control the Holy Places of the Hejaz: "If the Committee of Union and Progress get control of Mecca, they might be able to declare a regular Jehad [*sic*], probably affecting Afghanistan, and giving serious trouble in India."[16]

Meanwhile Wingate, Clayton, and Storrs were actively pursuing the Kitchener plan that called for an association in the postwar world with Arabia and with an Arabian religious primate. The cautious Clayton warned that the Arab caliphate was a delicate matter and should be proposed by Arabs themselves;[17] but Wingate, as always impatient to move forward, assured FitzGerald/Kitchener that "We shall do what we can to push the Arab movement & I have got various irons in the fire in this connection."[18]

---

* Troubles caused by groups such as the nomadic Senussi on Egypt's Libyan frontier were minor, and might well have occurred in any event.

But the India Office continued to fear that, as a result of these activities, Mecca would be drawn into the vortex of world politics—an eventuality that might disturb opinion in India at a time when any disturbance could prove fatal. During the course of the war, Simla was going to send many of its European soldiers to Europe, and large numbers of Indian troops as well. For the duration of the war it was in a weak position to quell whatever uprisings might occur. Cairo and Constantinople both seemed to Simla to be pursuing policies that threatened to inflame Moslem passions in India and thus to imperil the Indian Empire.

As the war progressed, British officials who ruled India increasingly came to believe that their most dangerous adversaries were neither the Turks nor the Germans, but the British officials governing Egypt; for despite India's protests, British Cairo went ahead with its intrigues in Mecca.

12

THE MAN IN THE MIDDLE

I

Mecca, where Mohammed was born, and Medina, to which he emigrated, are the holy cities that for Moslems everywhere give unique importance to the mountainous Hejaz, the long and narrow western section of the Arabian peninsula bordering the Red Sea. Hejaz means "separating"—a reference to the highlands that divide it from the plateau to the east. In the early twentieth century Arabia was an empty and desolate land, and the Hejaz, in the words of the 1910 *Encyclopaedia Britannica*, was "physically the most desolate and uninviting province in Arabia." Whole sections of it were unwatered and uninhabited wilderness. About 750 miles long and, at its widest, about 200 miles across, the Hejaz precariously supported a population estimated at 300,000, half-Bedouin and half-townsmen. Although it formed part of the Ottoman Empire, its distance from Constantinople, magnified by the primitive state of transportation and communications, had always lent it considerable autonomy.

Dates, of which a hundred varieties were said to grow, were the staple crop; but the real industry of the province was the annual pilgrimage. About 70,000 pilgrims made the journey to Mecca each year. Protecting the pilgrims from marauding Bedouin tribes was a principal function of the local representative of the Ottoman government; and the authorities made a practice of offering subsidies to the tribes in the hope of persuading them that there was better pay in safeguarding than in molesting the visitors.

Mecca was a two-day camel journey, or about forty-five miles, from the nearest coastal port. It lay in a hot and barren valley, and controlled the passages through the surrounding hills. Its population was estimated at 60,000. Entrance into its precincts was prohibited to non-Moslems, and exercised the powerful lure of the forbidden. Only a few European travelers had succeeded in penetrating the city in disguise and bringing back detailed descriptions of it.

111

These Europeans reported that even in the holy city certain dark practices lingered from a primitive past. According to the *Encyclopaedia Britannica*, "The unspeakable vices of Mecca are a scandal to all Islam, and a constant source of wonder to pious pilgrims. The slave trade has connexions with the pilgrimage which are not thoroughly clear; but under cover of the pilgrimage a great deal of importation and exportation of slaves goes on."

Yet European travelers also reported that the people of the Hejaz, and indeed of all Arabia, were among nature's aristocrats. According to the *Britannica*:

> Physically the Arabs are one of the strongest and noblest races of the world ... Thus, physically, they yield to few races, if any, of mankind; mentally, they surpass most, and are only kept back in the march of progress by the remarkable defect of organizing power and incapacity for combined action. Lax and imperfect as are their forms of government, it is with impatience that even these are borne ...

The job of the Emir of Mecca, if the *Britannica* was to be believed, was not an easy one.

For Moslems, Mecca had always been the center of the world. Now, the ambitions of Kitchener's Cairo and of the C.U.P.'s Constantinople brought the arid Hejaz into the center of twentieth-century politics. The new attentions that Mecca received in the 1914 war brought it into the center in other ways, less welcome to its Emir; he found himself caught in the middle.

Hussein ibn Ali, who ruled the Hejaz on behalf of the Ottoman Sultan, was styled the Sherif of Mecca and its Emir. To be a sherif, or notable, was to be a descendant of Mohammed; and Hussein, like Mohammed himself, was a member of the House of Hashem.* For some time it had been the practice of the Ottoman regime to appoint the Emir of Mecca from among rival sherifs. In 1908 Hussein, of the Dhawu-'Awn clan, was personally selected by the Sultan, over the opposition of the C.U.P., which backed the candidate of a rival clan.

Hussein, like his courtly friend the Grand Vizier and like the Sultan himself, was a man of old-fashioned breeding and learning whose style of expression was ornate. Of medium height, with a white beard, and about sixty years of age in 1914, he had spent much of his life in glorified captivity at the court in Constantinople. There, even the prying eyes of enemies were unable to detect him in any improper conduct; he spent his time in meditation.

Hussein continually expressed strong personal loyalty to the Sultan. The Sultan, however, was a figurehead. Real power at the Porte was

---

* Hussein referred to himself and his family as "Hashemites."

wielded by the Young Turks, new men without family background, with whom he was out of sympathy. Though loyal to the Sultan, he found himself increasingly at odds with the Sultan's government, and in particular with its policy of centralization.

Hussein's ambition was to make his position as Emir secure for himself and, in perpetuity, for his family. He strove to increase his independence, while the centralizing C.U.P. government conspired to decrease it. The government pushed forward with construction of the Hejaz railroad, aimed, among other things, at curtailing the Emir's autonomy. The railroad already ran from Damascus, capital of what is now Syria, to Medina in the Hejaz. What the government proposed was to extend the line to Mecca and to the port of Jeddah. This was a threat to the camel-owning Bedouin tribes of the Hejaz and to their lucrative control of the pilgrim routes to the Holy Places. Using the railroad and also the telegraph, the C.U.P. threatened to exercise direct rule over Medina, Mecca, and the rest of the Hejaz. If carried into effect, the Turkish government's plan would make Hussein into a mere subordinate functionary. Hussein responded by inspiring civil disturbances.

For Hussein, who had begun his administration of affairs by using Turkish troops against the Arabian tribes, this represented a change in policy, but not a change in allegiance. He remained in the ambiguous position of supporting the Ottoman Empire while opposing its government.

In the years just before the beginning of the European war, the secret societies in Damascus and the various rival lords of Arabia were in frequent touch with one another; they explored the possibility of uniting against the Young Turks in support of greater rights for the Arabic-speaking half of the empire. At one time or another most of the principal Arabian chiefs were involved in such conversations. In 1911, the Arab deputies in the Ottoman Parliament asked Hussein to lead the Arabic-speaking peoples in throwing off the Turkish yoke; he refused. A year later the secret societies seem to have approached his rivals, but not Hussein. By 1913 Arab nationalists apparently regarded him as "a tool in the hands of the Turks for striking the Arabs."[1] Yet the Turkish government also strongly distrusted him, and explored the possibility of deposing him.

Two of Hussein's sons were active politically. Abdullah, his favorite, was a deputy from Mecca in the Ottoman Parliament, while Feisal was a deputy from Jeddah. Abdullah counselled his father to resist the government; he believed that with the support of the secret societies and of Britain it could be done. Feisal advised against opposing the government. Abdullah, a short, heavy-set, astute man with a politician's conciliating manner, was for boldness. Feisal, tall, quick, and nervous, was for caution.

Hussein, who had played off his enemies against one another for years, was inclined to temporize and delay. With each year in office as Emir he had increased his prestige and his mastery over the complex web of personal, family, and tribal relationships that made for authority in the Hejaz. He had reduced the political influence of the local C.U.P. lodges in Mecca and Medina. His primacy within his own emirate was established firmly.

In 1913 and 1914, however, he found himself surrounded by external enemies. There were his neighbors and traditional rivals, the Arabian lords to his south and east, whom he had threatened and who threatened him. There were the Arab nationalists, some of whom regarded him as an essentially Turkish official. There were the British, whose navy could easily dominate the long coastline of the Hejaz once they went to war against the Ottoman Empire—and he knew that they would become his enemies if he threw in his lot with the empire. Finally, there was the Ottoman government which threatened a showdown on the issue of the Emir's autonomy.

Now, for the duration of the war, the C.U.P. postponed completion of the railroad and the adoption of its new governmental regulations, as well as its secret plan to appoint a new emir in Hussein's place. But it ordered Hussein to supply manpower for the army. Hussein and Abdullah may well have suspected a C.U.P. plot: the men of the Hejaz would be sent as soldiers to distant battlefields, while regular Turkish troops would be sent to take their place in garrisoning the Hejaz, and would then seize control of it.

Hussein assured all his dangerous neighbors that he would act in accordance with their wishes—but put off doing so until some time in the future. He asked the advice of Abdul Aziz Ibn Saud, his rival and a powerful warlord to the east, as to whether or not he should associate Mecca with the Sultan's call for a Holy War against Britain and her allies; and he discussed with Arabic nationalist leaders from Damascus the possibility of joint action against the Porte. In reply to requests and demands from the Porte, he asked for money to raise troops and supplies for the Ottoman Empire, but continued to postpone sending any contingents to the Turkish army.

He gave Kitchener's messages and promises a warm response. At the same time—at the end of 1914—when Djemal Pasha prepared to attack the British at the Suez Canal, Hussein wrote to him, promising to send troops to join in the attack; while Abdullah replied to Storrs in British Cairo that the Hejaz had decided to side with Britain in the war. Abdullah explained, however, that this would have to be kept a secret. For the moment, it was not possible for the Emir to reveal his intention of allying with Britain, nor could he take action. According to Abdullah and Hussein, the time was not yet ripe.

II

Storrs was pleased that his correspondence had placed the Residency, the office of the British High Commissioner, on terms of close cordiality with Mecca. On 27 January 1915, he wrote FitzGerald/ Kitchener that "I am still in very friendly and intimate contact with the Sherif of Mecca, and am firmly convinced that he is a more paying proposition for our care and attention than any purely local Chieftain (however powerful in himself) who cannot enjoy the prestige of receiving the annual homage of the representatives of Islam throughout the world."[2]

For the moment all that Kitchener and the Residency really asked of Hussein was neutrality. Since Hussein's desire was to avoid being drawn into the perilous war, the two parties to the correspondence were in accord. Hussein did nothing to associate himself or Mecca with the proclamation of a Holy War. For the Residency, the correspondence therefore had accomplished everything that could reasonably have been desired. The High Commissioner, Sir Henry McMahon, reported to Kitchener on 2 February 1915, that "there is no need for immediate action . . . as all that is necessary for the moment, with the Sherif of Mecca—had been done."[3]

The War Minister was satisfied. He did not share Wingate's belief that a tribal revolt in Arabia could affect Britain's fortunes in the war; he gave no sign of disappointment when Hussein did not propose to lead such a revolt. Kitchener believed that Germany was the enemy that mattered and that Europe was the only battlefield that counted. His long-term plan to capture the caliphate was designed for the postwar world. In his view, he and it—and the Middle East—could wait until the war was over.

PART III

BRITAIN IS DRAWN INTO THE MIDDLE EASTERN QUAGMIRE

13

THE TURKISH COMMANDERS
ALMOST LOSE THE WAR

I

At the time of his appointment as War Minister, Kitchener did not intend Britain to be drawn into any involvement in the Middle East during the war. When he started along the road that led to such an involvement, he was not aware that this was what he was doing. Later, in 1915–16, when he found his country fully engaged in the Middle East, he must have wondered how he had allowed such a situation to come about. From the outset of the war, it had been his unwavering doctrine to disregard the East while focusing on the western front.

Kitchener's opinion that Turkey and the Middle East could safely be ignored for the duration of the European conflict derived in part from the assumption that the Ottoman Empire did not pose a significant military threat. This was an assumption that was widely shared.

British officials viewed Ottoman military capability with contempt; and the record of the first six months of warfare in the East confirmed them in their view. From October 1914, when the *Goeben* and *Breslau* opened fire on the Russian coast, until February 1915, when an avenging British fleet began its bombardment of the straits of the Dardanelles and then steamed toward Constantinople, the Ottoman armies blundered from one defeat to another.

The Supreme Commander of the Turkish armed forces was Enver Pasha, who a week before the war began had proclaimed himself "vice-generalissimo." In theory this placed him second only to the figurehead Sultan. In practice it placed him second to none.

Enver had the qualities of a lone adventurer, not those of a general. Though audacious and cunning, he was an incompetent commander. Liman von Sanders, the Prussian army adviser with whom he frequently found himself at odds, regarded Enver as a buffoon in military matters.

Enver, however, pictured himself as a leader of a wholly different character. He portrayed himself as an heir to the founders of the Ottoman Empire: the band of *ghazis*—crusading warriors for the Islamic faith—who in the fourteenth century had galloped from the obscurity of the Byzantine frontier onto the center stage of history.

At the outset of the war, he hastened to attack the Russian Empire.[1] There was an obstacle in his path: the forbidding Caucasus mountain range, which formed the land frontier between the two empires. Against the advice of Liman von Sanders, he determined to launch a frontal attack across that daunting natural frontier, which the Russians, in secure possession of the high ground, had heavily fortified—and to do so in the depths of winter. He proposed initially to group his forces along an enormous territory within Turkey, 600 miles long and 300 miles wide, through which there was no railroad to transport troops or supplies. The few roads were steep and narrow. The rivers could be crossed only by fording, the bridges having collapsed long before and having never been repaired. Because the nearest railhead was over 600 miles away, every bullet, every shell, had to be transported by camel—a journey of six weeks. Much of the territory was without track or habitation, unexplored and uncharted. Long winters and mountain snowstorms made whole sections of it unpassable much of the year.

Enver's plan, as he explained it to Liman von Sanders, was to then move out of this staging area, cross the frontier into Czarist territory, and attack the fortified Russian position on the Caucasus plateau by the sort of orchestrated movement pictured in military textbooks, with some columns attacking directly, and others moving out at an angle and then wheeling about to flank or encircle. He was unmoved by the reminder that, without railroads or other transport, the strategic mobility required for the military movements that he envisaged would be unavailable. He entertained no doubts of his success. Having crushed the Russians, said Enver, he would then march via Afghanistan to the conquest of India.

On 6 December 1914, Enver left Constantinople and on 21 December took command of the Ottoman Third Army. He led the attack on the Caucasus plateau in person. The Russians were terrified and appealed to Britain to help somehow; they had no idea they faced a foe who was utterly inept.

Enver left his artillery behind because of the deep snow. His troops were forced to bivouac in the bitter cold (as low as minus thirty degrees Fahrenheit without tents). They ran short of food. An epidemic of typhus broke out. With routes blocked by the winter snows, they lost their way in the tangled mountain passes. Enver's plan was for his forces to launch a coordinated surprise attack on the Russian base called Sarikamish, which blocked the invasion highway;

but, having lost touch with one another, the various Turkish corps arrived at different times at Sarikamish to attack and to be destroyed piecemeal.

The remnants of what had once been an army straggled back into eastern Turkey in January 1915. Of the perhaps 100,000 men who took part in the attack,[2] 86 percent were lost. A German officer attached to the Ottoman General Staff described what happened to the Third Army by saying that it had "suffered a disaster which for rapidity and completeness is without parallel in military history."[3]

Yet even as he rode back from the catastrophe in the northeast, Enver ordered another ill-conceived offensive. In command was Djemal Pasha, the Minister of the Marine. Jealous of Enver, whose prestige and power had begun to overshadow those of the other Young Turks, Djemal took the field as commander of the Ottoman Fourth Army, based in Syria and Palestine. On 15 January 1915, he began his march toward Egypt to launch a surprise attack across the Suez Canal.

Again, the logistical problems were ignored. The roads of Syria and Palestine were so bad that not even horse-drawn carts could move along many of them;[4] and the wastes of the 130-mile wide Sinai desert were trackless. The Ottoman soldiery nonetheless performed prodigies of endurance and valor. Somehow they transported themselves and their equipment from Syria to Suez. Kress von Kressenstein, a German engineering officer, dug wells along the route, which enabled them to survive the march through the desert. The time of year, for once, was well chosen: January is the best month in Egypt for avoiding the terrible heat.

But when the Fourth Army reached the banks of the Suez Canal, Djemal discovered that most of his troops could not use the bridging pontoons that were meant to transport them to the other side. The German engineers had brought the pontoons from Germany, but the troops had not been trained in their use. Djemal ordered the attack to commence nonetheless. Early in the morning of 3 February, while the sky was still half-dark, it began. The British, from behind their fortifications, awoke to discover an Ottoman army on the opposite bank of the enormous ditch; and with their superior weaponry they opened fire upon it. In the battle and the subsequent rout, 2,000 Ottoman troops—about 10 percent of Djemal's forces—were killed. Djemal ordered a retreat; and kept on going all the way back to Syria.[5]

Turkish generalship became a joke. Aubrey Herbert wrote from Shepheard's Hotel in Cairo to his friend Mark Sykes that the latest Ottoman plan was "that the Turks are to bring thousands of camels down to the Canal and then set a light to their hair. The camel, using its well known reasoning powers, will dash to the Canal to put the fire out. When they have done this in sufficient quantities the Turks will march over them."[6]

In London the Prime Minister lightly dismissed the Ottoman invasion by saying that "The Turks have been trying to throw a bridge across the Suez Canal & in that ingenious fashion to find a way into Egypt. The poor things & their would-be bridge were blown into smithereens, and they have retired into the desert."[7]

II

Enver had assumed that the war would be short, and that it would be decided in a few lightning campaigns. He had neither a plan for a war of attrition nor an understanding of what such a war might entail. He had no gift for organization, no head for logistics, and no patience for administration. As War Minister he thoughtlessly led his country into chaos.[8]

He began by ordering all eligible men throughout the imperial domains to report for induction into the army immediately, bringing with them enough food for three days. When they reported as ordered—which is to say, all at the same time—their numbers dwarfed the conscription offices, which could not deal with so many at once. Having flooded in from the countryside, the draftees ate up their three days' supply of food and then had nothing to eat. Soon they began to drift away, labeled as deserters, afraid to return either to the conscription offices or to their homes.

Bringing in the manpower from the countryside ruined what would have been the bountiful harvest of 1914. It set a terrible pattern: throughout the war, the draft of men and pack animals brought famine in good years as well as bad. During the war years, the supply of draft animals fell, horses to 40 percent and oxen and buffaloes to 15 percent of what they had been. The shrinkage in agricultural activity was equally dramatic: cereal acreage was cut in half, and cotton fell to 8 percent of its prewar production level. Control of the scarce supplies of food and other goods became the key to wealth and power. In the sprawling metropolis of Constantinople, a Chicago-style political boss with gangland connections fought against Enver's General Director of the Commissariat for effective control of the economy.

The transportation system of the empire was also shattered by the war. In the absence of railroads and usable roads, in the past goods had been mostly shipped by sea. Now the empire's 5,000 miles of coastline were under the guns of the Allied navies. In the north the Germans and Turks pulled back the *Goeben* and *Breslau* for the defense of the Dardanelles, abandoning the Black Sea to the newly built battleships of the Russians. The Mediterranean was dominated by the French and British navies. Allied ships cut off the Ottoman coal supply; thereafter the empire depended for its fuel on the meagre supplies that could be brought overland from Germany.

On the eve of war, there were only about 17,000 industrial workers in an empire of 25 million people; for practical purposes, the country had no industry.[9] All that it had was agriculture, which was now ruined. By the end of the war, the export trade was down to a quarter and the import trade down to a tenth of what they had been.

The Porte ran up huge budget deficits during the wartime years, and helplessly ran paper money off the printing presses to pay for them. During the war prices rose 1,675 percent.

Before long, the war had brought the Ottoman economy almost to its knees; and the Young Turk government had no idea what to do about it.

KITCHENER ALLOWS BRITAIN TO ATTACK TURKEY

I

The British government, too, encountered unexpected problems with which it had no idea how to deal. At the outset of war nobody in Britain had foreseen that the warring armies would dig trenches across western Europe. Now that they had done so, nobody in Britain had any idea of how to break through enemy lines.

As 1914 turned into 1915, the British Cabinet became increasingly unhappy about the direction of the war. Lord Kitchener's strategy of concentrating all forces in western Europe seemed to offer no hope of victory in the foreseeable future. The wiliest politician in the Cabinet—David Lloyd George—was conspicuous among those who looked for a way out.

Lloyd George, after Asquith the most powerful politician in the Liberal Party and in the Cabinet, was not one who willingly goes down with a sinking ship. He was, above all, a survivor: years later it could be seen that he was the only British minister who succeeded in staying in the Cabinet from the outbreak of the First World War until its end.

The glowing, dynamic political wizard from Wales was the supreme strategist—or, some would say, opportunist—of his time. "To Lloyd George no policy was permanent, no pledge final," wrote one of his contemporaries; the zig-zags in his policy forced him to seek support first from one group then from another, so that "He became like a trick rider at the circus, as he was compelled to leap from one back to another ..."[1] His deviousness was a byword, so that even an admirer said that his truth was not a straight line but "more of a curve."[2] The way he himself put it was that, "I never believed in costly frontal attacks either in war or politics, if there were a way round."[3]

No minister felt more greatly frustrated than he did by the way Allied commanders were fighting the war in France and Flanders: hopeless direct assaults on entrenched enemy positions. Every time that he sought a way out or a way around, he found the route blocked either by the War Office on behalf of Britain's generals, or by the Foreign Office on behalf of Britain's allies.

From the beginning, Lloyd George looked for a solution in the East. He was among those who favored entering into Balkan alliances, notably with Greece, in order to defeat the Ottoman Empire and to turn the German flank. Other Cabinet ministers agreed. So did Maurice Hankey, Secretary of the War Cabinet and most influential of the civil servants. Hankey's memorandum of 28 December 1914, proposing an assault on the Dardanelles in collaboration with Balkan allies, cogently outlined the arguments underlining the Cabinet's belief that "Germany can perhaps be struck most effectively, and with the most lasting results on the peace of the world through her allies, and particularly through Turkey."[4]

The Foreign Secretary, Sir Edward Grey, blocked this approach. It was Grey, according to Lloyd George's associates in the left wing of the Liberal Party, who had closed off Britain's alternative of remaining neutral in the war; he had done this, they claimed, by his secret prewar arrangements with France.* (The philosopher Bertrand Russell later wrote: "I had noticed during previous years how carefully Sir Edward Grey lied in order to prevent the public from knowing the methods by which he was committing us to the support of France in the event of war.")[6] Now again it was Grey, who had entered into secret prewar arrangements with Russia regarding the Dardanelles, who argued that Allied claims to postwar territorial gains precluded bringing the Balkan states into the war. It was the Foreign Office's view not only that Bulgaria's rivalry with Rumania and Greece rendered an alliance that included all three states unfeasible, but that Greek help in capturing Constantinople was unacceptable because it would offend the Russians.

Yet it was agreed by the Admiralty, the War Office, and the Cabinet alike that Constantinople could not be captured by the Royal Navy alone. An army, they argued, was needed as well. If the Greek army or another Balkan army were not to be allowed to help, then the British army would be needed; but Lord Kitchener supported those Allied field commanders who decreed that no troops should be diverted from the trenches of the western front until the war in Europe was won.

Yet, notwithstanding the hopeful views of Allied commanders in the field, nothing in the first months and years of the war suggested to the leading members of the Cabinet that on the western front the war was being won or even could be won. As early as 7 October

---

* The historical evidence now shows that this was not true.[5] But the left wing of the Liberal Party continued to believe that it was.

1914, Asquith noted that Kitchener "thinks it is not improbable that
... the big opposing armies may in some months' time come to
something like stalemate."[7] By the end of December, Winston
Churchill (as he informed the Prime Minister) thought it "quite
possible that neither side will have the strength to penetrate the
other's lines in the Western theatre"; while, at the same time, Lloyd
George, in a memorandum to Cabinet colleagues, dismissed the
prospects of a breakthrough on the western front as an "impossibility."[8]

History had seen nothing like the trench warfare that spontaneously
emerged in the autumn of 1914; and Kitchener, though he quickly
divined the problem, admitted that he saw no solution. The Entente
Powers and the Central Powers manned parallel lines of fortifications
that soon stretched all the way from the Atlantic Ocean to the Alps.
Each side thus decisively barred the way to the other.

Trench warfare began as an endurance contest and ended as a
survival contest. Beneath the ground, in the perhaps 35,000 miles of
trenches that they eventually dug, the opposing armies lived in
bloody squalor and subjected one another to punishing and almost
ceaseless artillery barrages, punctuated by suicidally futile charges
against the other side's barbed wire and machine guns. Alternately
executioners and executed, one side played the role of the firing
squad whenever the other side launched one of its frequent attacks.
No ground was gained. It was a deadlock.

The civilian ministers turned for guidance to the military oracle in
their midst, but the oracle sometimes was awkwardly silent and at
other times spoke a gibberish that undermined belief in his powers of
divination. In the Cabinet, unfortunately, FitzGerald was not available to speak and listen for him. Field Marshal Kitchener always had
found it immensely difficult to *explain* his military views, even to
close colleagues; in the company of those whom he feared—strangers,
civilians, politicians—he was struck dumb. To break the silence, he
sometimes launched into long discourses on nonmilitary subjects of
which he knew little or nothing. He spoke of Ireland to the Irish
leader, Carson, and of Wales to Lloyd George; both men were
surprised to find him ignorant and foolish.

There was genius within him, but it manifested itself only on
occasion. Years after the war, having remarked that Kitchener "talked
twaddle," Lloyd George took it back by adding:

> No! He was like a great revolving lighthouse. Sometimes the
> beam of his mind used to shoot out, showing one Europe and
> the assembled armies in a vast and illimitable perspective, till
> one felt that one was looking along it into the heart of reality—
> and then the shutter would turn and for weeks there would be
> nothing but a blank darkness.[9]

Kitchener's failure to show them a way out of the deadlock on the western front led the country's civilian leaders to devise plans of their own. The plans resembled one another in proposing to swing around the fortified western front in order to attack from the north, the south, or the east. The doctrine of the generals was to attack the enemy at his strongest point; that of the politicians was to attack at his weakest.

Lloyd George's mind inclined toward collaboration with Greece in the vulnerable southeast of Europe. Churchill, inspired by Admiral Lord Fisher (whom he had brought back from retirement to serve as First Sea Lord), proposed a landing in the northwest of Europe, on an island off Germany's Baltic Sea coast. Maurice Hankey, however, carried all before him with his persuasive memorandum of 28 December 1914.

Hankey proposed that Britain should move three army corps to participate with Greece, Bulgaria, and Rumania in an attack on Turkey at the Dardanelles that would lead to the occupation of Constantinople and the subsequent defeat of Germany's two allies, the Ottoman and Habsburg empires. The political problem of reconciling Bulgaria with Greece and Rumania, he pointed out, would have to be overcome; but he believed that this could be done as a result of Allied military participation in the campaign and Allied guarantees that all three states would receive a fair share of the spoils of victory.

When shown the memorandum, Churchill commented that he himself had advocated an attack at the Dardanelles two months earlier, but that Kitchener had refused to supply the needed manpower; and that such an action would be much more difficult to mount in January than it would have been in November. Churchill continued to believe that the Baltic Sea project was a more promising move, but recognized that he and Hankey thought alike in espousing some sort of flanking attack.

Hankey's plan, however, was never put to the test. It foundered on the usual shoals: Kitchener's unwillingness to divert troops from the west, and Sir Edward Grey's worry that a Greek march on Constantinople might be troubling to Russia. Grey was not hopeful of reconciling Bulgarian claims with those of the other Balkan states but, above all, what led him to oppose a Greek attack at the Dardanelles was the fear that it might succeed; for if the Greeks were to conquer their old imperial capital, Constantinople, the Byzantium of their great days, they would be unlikely to give it up; while Russia, rather than let any other country seize it, might well (in Grey's view) change sides in the war.

The situation in Athens was that the Prime Minister, Venizelos, who at the outset of the world war had offered to enter into a war with Turkey, was still inclined to join the Allies, while his political adversary, the Kaiser's brother-in-law, pro-German King Constantine, acted to prevent him from doing so. Instead of throwing its weight behind Venizelos, the British Foreign Office, like King Constantine, opposed Greek entry into the war.

In retrospect it seems clear that if the Greek army had marched on Constantinople in early 1915, alongside the British navy, the Ottoman capital would have been defenseless. The anguish of Winston Churchill when this was not allowed to happen is evident in the phrases of a letter that he wrote to Grey in the winter of 1915 but never sent:

> I beseech you ... Half-hearted measures will ruin all—& a million men will die through the prolongation of the war ... [N]o impediment must be placed in the way of Greek cooperation—I am *so* afraid of your losing Greece, & yet paying all the future into Russian hands. If Russia prevents Greece helping, I will do my utmost to oppose her having Cple ... PS If you don't back up this Greece—the Greece of Venizelos—you will have another who will cleave to Germany.[10]

II

When 1915 began, Lord Kitchener suddenly changed his mind and proposed that Britain should attack the Dardanelles. The Russian high command had urgently asked him to stage a diversionary attack there, and he was fearful that if he did not comply Russia might be driven out of the war—which at that point would have been fatal for Britain and France, for it would have allowed the Germans to concentrate all their forces in the west. Kitchener insisted, however, that the attack had to be mounted by the Royal Navy on its own: he would make no troops available. No matter; civilian members of the Cabinet leaped at the chance to escape from the western front strategy which they (unlike the Allied generals) regarded as hopeless.

Enver's attack on the Caucasus was responsible for the Russian plea and hence for Kitchener's change of mind. Russia's cry for help came before her quick, easy, and decisive victory over Enver's Turks in January 1915. Logically, after crushing the Ottoman invaders that month, the Russians should have told Lord Kitchener that it was no longer necessary for him to launch a diversionary attack on Constantinople—or Kitchener should have drawn that conclusion for himself. Instead, throughout January and February, Britain's leaders considered how best to attack Constantinople in order to relieve Russia from a Turkish threat that no longer existed.

Thus began the Dardanelles campaign, which was to so alter the fortunes of Churchill and Kitchener, Asquith and Lloyd George, Britain and the Middle East.

15

ON TO VICTORY AT THE DARDANELLES

I

When Lord Kitchener proposed that an expedition to the Dardanelles should be mounted by the Royal Navy alone, Churchill's reply from the Admiralty echoed what every informed person in the military and in government said: that the Dardanelles could be forced only by a combined operation in which the navy was joined by the army. A glance at the map would show why. The 38-mile-long straits are at no point more than 4 miles wide. Warships attempting to force their passage against the strong current would face lines of mines in front of them and a crossfire of cannon barrages from the European and Asian shores. Thirteen miles after entering the waterway, ships reach the Narrows, a mere 1,600 yards across, which can be dominated by the guns of the forts on shore. Only if an attacking army took possession of the coastline could it silence the artillery on shore and give its fleet a chance to sweep the mines ahead of it; the forts, in other words, had to be stormed or destroyed to allow the navy to get through.

Kitchener met with his advisers at the War Office to ask them to reconsider their position about the opening of the new front, but they were adamant in reiterating that no troops could be made available. In turn, Churchill, on the morning of 3 January 1915, met with his War Group at the Admiralty to reconsider whether, given the importance of keeping Russia in the war, it really would be out of the question to mount a wholly naval operation. The idea of employing only warships that were old and expendable was raised; and the War Group decided to ask the commander on the spot for his views.

Soon after the meeting adjourned, Churchill sent an inquiry to the commander of the British naval squadron off the Dardanelles, Admiral Sackville Carden. In his cable Churchill asked: "Do you consider the forcing of the Dardanelles by ships alone a practicable operation?"— adding that older ships would be used, and that the importance of the operation would justify severe losses.[1]

To everybody's surprise, Admiral Carden replied to Churchill that, while the Dardanelles could not be "rushed"—in other words, could not be seized in a single attack—"They might be forced by extended operations with a large number of ships."[2] Carden had been in command at the Dardanelles for months, and his views carried the day.

The Cabinet overruled Churchill—who argued in favor of a naval strike in the Baltic instead—and authorized him to put Carden's Dardanelles plan into operation. Churchill was not opposed to the Dardanelles plan; it was simply that he preferred his Baltic plan. Once the Dardanelles decision had been taken, he moved to carry it out with all of his energy and enthusiasm.

II

Though gifted in many other ways, Churchill was insensitive to the moods and reactions of his colleagues, and oblivious to the effect he produced upon others. When he gave orders that naval officers felt ought properly to have been issued by one of themselves, he inspired a collegial and institutional hostility of which he was unaware; he did not know that they viewed him as an interfering amateur, and that his imprecision in the use of their technical language fueled their resentment.

He also did not know (for they did not tell him) how much his colleagues in the Cabinet were alienated by his other traits. He bubbled over with ideas for their departments, which they regarded as meddling. He talked at such length that they could not endure it. Neither subordinates nor colleagues dared to tell him to his face that he was often impossible to work with. Even Fisher, his naval idol and mentor, whom he had chosen as First Sea Lord, found it difficult to communicate with him; though, it should be said, the problem was mutual.

Lord Fisher, whose intuitive genius and extreme eccentricity were rather like Kitchener's, had a sudden hunch, on or before 19 January, that sending a naval expedition to the Dardanelles was a mistake. But he was never able to articulate the basis for his foreboding, so he could not persuade Churchill to change course.

Support for the Dardanelles expedition initially had been unanimous, but from that rising high tide of enthusiasm there had been a turn, an ebbing, so that within days the tide had reversed direction and was flowing swiftly the other way.

Maurice Hankey, to whom Fisher had complained of Churchill in January, began establishing a record that he, too, was opposed to the expedition unless the army participated in it. As the most skillful bureaucrat of his time, Hankey was more sensitive to the currents of opinion that prevailed in Churchill's Admiralty than was Churchill himself. He was aware that by the middle of February, Admiralty opinion had turned against the idea of a purely naval venture, although the attack was scheduled to begin in a matter of days.* On 15 February, Sir Henry Jackson, who a month earlier had urged Churchill to implement Carden's plans immediately, circulated a memorandum in which he said that the purely naval plan "is not recommended as a sound military operation."[6] Captain Herbert William Richmond, Assistant Director of Operations, was also associated with this criticism, having written a memorandum of his own along similar lines the day before, a copy of which he had forwarded to Hankey.

Early in the morning of 16 February Fisher sent a similar warning to Churchill, who was thunderstruck: he was driven to seek an immediate emergency session with whatever members of the War Council of the Cabinet were available. The dire situation was this: the British naval armada off the Turkish coast was due to commence its attack within forty-eight to seventy-two hours; the armada could not postpone its attack while remaining in the area, for enemy submarines might soon be sent to sink it;[7] but if the armada proceeded to attack, it would fail, according to this suddenly revised opinion of the naval leadership of the Admiralty, unless a substantial body of troops was sent to support it—troops that Kitchener had repeatedly refused to send and which, in any event, could hardly be expected to arrive in time even if dispatched immediately.

Before attending the War Council, Kitchener spoke with Wyndham Deedes, the officer who had served in the Ottoman Gendarmerie before the war, now a captain in intelligence serving in London, and asked his opinion of a naval attack on the Dardanelles. Deedes replied that in his view such a plan would be fundamentally unsound. As he began to explain why that would be so, an enraged Kitchener cut him short, told him he did not know what he was talking about, and abruptly dismissed him.

---

* He told the Cabinet so; he told the Prime Minister so; and he recorded his opinion in letters and memoranda. In a diary entry for 19 March he recorded that "On the first day proposal was made I warned P. M., Lord K, Chief of Staff, L. George and Balfour that Fleet could not effect passage and that all naval officers thought so."[3] Hankey indeed had issued such warnings, but a month later than he claimed. It was not on 13 January (when the Cabinet committee decided on the Dardanelles expedition) but on 10 February that he wrote to Balfour along those lines.[4] Later still he spoke to Asquith. On 13 February, the Prime Minister noted that "I have just been having a talk with Hankey, whose views are always worth hearing. He thinks very strongly that the naval operations . . . should be supported by landing a fairly strong military force. I have been for some time coming to the same opinion . . ."[5]

Yet the interview with Deedes changed Kitchener's mind. A few hours later, Kitchener told members of the War Council that he would agree to send the 29th Division—the only regular army division that remained in Britain—to the Aegean to support the navy's attack. In addition, the new Australian and New Zealand troops who had arrived in Egypt could be dispatched if necessary. The plan, which now met the requirements of Fisher, Jackson, Richmond, and the others, was that once the navy's ships had won the battle for the straits, the troops would come in behind them to occupy the adjacent shore and, thereafter, Constantinople. According to a diary entry, "Lord K's words to Winston were: 'You get through! I will find the men.' "[8]

The plan was flawed. If the Turkish defenders had competent leadership and adequate ammunition, a combined assault was called for. Instead of waiting for the navy to win the battle, the army ought to have helped by attacking the Dardanelles forts. The civilian Maurice Hankey saw this clearly; the admirals and generals did not.

On 22 February, the Admiralty issued a public communiqué announcing that the Dardanelles attack had begun and describing it in detail. The newspapers took up the story, focusing attention on the attack and arousing public expectations. *The Times* noted that "bombardment from the sea will not carry such a project very far unless it is combined with troops"; and warned that "The one thing the Allies dare not risk in a persistent attack on the Dardanelles is failure."[9]

Kitchener issued a similar warning of his own to Cabinet colleagues. Although he had originally proposed to "leave off the bombardment if it were ineffective,"[10] when Lloyd George argued in favor of adhering to that plan ("If we failed at the Dardanelles we ought to be immediately ready to try something else"), Kitchener changed his mind. At a meeting of the War Council on 24 February, the War Minister cited the Admiralty's public communiqué as his reason for the change. "The effect of a defeat in the Orient would be very serious. There could be no going back. The publicity of the announcement had committed us." If the fleet failed, he said, "the army ought to see the business through."[11]

First he had suggested sending in the navy. Now he had decided to send in the army. Step by step, without meaning to, Kitchener was allowing Britain to be drawn into a major engagement in the Middle East.

III

The Turks expected Churchill's attack on the Dardanelles; but for the moment they had no means to defend against it. Not even

Wyndham Deedes—usually so well informed on Ottoman affairs—knew this secret, although the Germans were well aware of it. At the outset of the war, the Ottoman forces and their German advisers had begun to strengthen the forts on both sides of the straits of the Dardanelles, but saw their efforts nullified by the lack of ammunition. At the end of 1914 and at the beginning of 1915, Berlin learned that the supply of ammunition at the straits was enough to fight only about one engagement, and that some of the Ottoman gunboats had enough shells to fire for about one minute each.

During the next six weeks, the Ottoman high command received a number of intelligence reports indicating that an Allied naval attack on the straits was imminent. On 15 February 1915, detailed information was received on a concentration of British and French war vessels in the eastern Mediterranean.

On the morning of 19 February, Admiral Carden's British warships fired the opening shots in the Dardanelles campaign. The U.S. ambassador to Turkey noted that the success of the Allied forces seemed inevitable, and the inhabitants of Constantinople thought that their city would fall within days.[12]

It was a measure of the Porte's despair that it even considered seeking help from Russia, its age-old enemy. The day after the British attack began, the Turkish ambassador to Germany suggested the creation of a Russian-Turkish-German alliance: Russia, he proposed, should be offered free passage through the Dardanelles in return for switching sides in the war.[13] As the Grand Vizier explained to the German ambassador in Constantinople, "One ought to make peace with Russia so that one could then hit England all the harder."[14] The Germans relayed the proposal to Russia, but nothing came of it. For the Turks there seemed to be no way out of a losing battle for the straits.

The roar of the British naval guns at the mouth of the Dardanelles echoed politically through the capital cities of the strategically crucial Balkan countries. In Athens, in Bucharest, and in Sofia politicians started moving toward the Allied camp. It was evident that all of them, even Bulgaria, would enter the war alongside the Entente Powers if the Dardanelles campaign were won.[15] As Lloyd George had repeatedly argued, with the Balkan countries as allies, Britain could bring the war to an end by moving through the disaffected Austro-Hungarian Empire to invade Germany from the relatively undefended south.

When the armada of British warships, supported by a French squadron, opened fire at long range on the morning of 19 February, the Turkish shore batteries at the mouth of the Dardanelles lacked the range even to reply. In order to inflict greater damage on the Turkish shore fortifications, Carden moved his warships closer to shore. That night the weather turned, and the navy was obliged to discontinue operations for five days because of poor visibility and icy gales. On 25 February the attack resumed. British marines who were put on shore at the tip of the peninsula found the forts at the entrance of the straits deserted; the Turks and Germans had withdrawn to the Narrows, where the artillery defenses of the Dardanelles were concentrated.

The British mission in Sofia reported that the Bulgarian army might join in the attack on Turkey. The Prime Minister of Rumania indicated to the British representative in Bucharest that not only was his own country a friend to the Allies but that "Italy would move soon."[16] In early March a joyful and excited Churchill received a secret cable from Venizelos—still serving as Prime Minister—promising Greek support, including three army divisions for Gallipoli; and, according to Venizelos, even the pro-German King Constantine was prepared to join the Allies.[17]

Victory was in the air. Though suffering from influenza, Churchill was elated. He confessed to Violet Asquith, the Prime Minister's daughter, that "I think a curse should rest on me because I am so happy. I know this war is smashing and shattering the lives of thousands every moment—and yet—I cannot help it—I enjoy every second I live."[18]

According to a cable from Admiral Carden to Churchill dated 4 March, the fleet could expect to arrive at Constantinople, weather permitting, in about fourteen days.[19] The postwar fate of the Ottoman Empire leaped to the top of the international agenda; even the Italians, who had not yet entered the war, began to claim their "share in the eventual partition of Turkey."[20] Churchill seems to have sensed that such claims were premature: in a confidential letter to the Foreign Secretary, he proposed that European Turkey should be captured but that the Allies should dictate an armistice that would leave Ottoman Asia in Ottoman hands at least temporarily.[21]

Only Fisher remained skeptical for a few days more. *"The more I consider the Dardanelles, the less I like it!"* (original emphasis), he wrote.[22] But on 10 March, even he was converted when intercepted German wireless messages revealed that the remaining Dardanelles forts, including the key ones dominating the Narrows, were about to run out of ammunition. Shifting suddenly to great enthusiasm, Fisher proposed to go out to the Aegean and personally assume command of the armada. The rush to take credit for the impending victory was on.

One evening after dinner—a rare social occasion for the War Minister—Violet Asquith spoke with Lord Kitchener, and told him that it was Churchill who would deserve the accolades of triumph. She said that "If the Dardanelles comes off W. will deserve full and almost sole credit. He has shown such courage and consistency in taking the responsibility throughout all the vacillations of Fisher and others." In her diary she recorded that "Lord K. replied indignantly: 'Not at all—I was always strongly in favour of it.' "[23]

16

RUSSIA'S GRAB FOR TURKEY

I

It was at Russia's urging that Kitchener and Churchill had launched the expedition to the Dardanelles, but when it looked as though that expedition might succeed, the Czar's government panicked. An Allied victory at the Dardanelles might seem an occasion for rejoicing; but it would mean that Constantinople would fall into British hands—and suddenly a century of Great Game fears and jealousies revived in Russian minds. The Russian government worried that once the British captured Constantinople they might decide to keep it.

On 4 March 1915 the Russian Foreign Minister, Sergei Sazanov, sent a secret circular telegram to London and Paris conveying a message from Czar Nicholas II, demanding that the Allies turn over Constantinople and the straits—and also adjacent territories—to Russia. In return, the Czar and Sazanov promised to listen with sympathetic understanding to British and French plans to achieve their own national ambitions in other regions of the Ottoman Empire and elsewhere.

In Paris the Russian demand was received with dismay. Afraid that possession of Constantinople would enable Russia to become France's rival in the Mediterranean, the French government attempted to put off the Russians with vague expressions of "goodwill."[1] Delcassé suggested that a detailed territorial settlement should await the eventual peace conference.

Sir Edward Grey undercut the French position. In his sympathy for the susceptibilities of his country's Allies, Grey, who had allayed French suspicions of British intentions in Syria, now moved to allay Russian suspicions of British intentions at the Dardanelles. In doing so he opened Pandora's box. If Russian claims were granted in advance of the peace conference, then France would be moved to submit her claims, and Lord Kitchener would be moved to submit his. However alive he may have been to such dangers, Grey gave priority to the need to reassure Russia.

II

According to the British Foreign Office, the position of the pro-Allied ministry in Petrograd might be undermined by pro-German opponents if Russia were not given satisfaction in the Constantinople matter.

Grey later explained how pro-German elements at the Russian court—whom he seems to have genuinely feared—would misrepresent British military operations at the Dardanelles if such an assurance were not given:

> It had always been British policy to keep Russia out of Constantinople and the Straits ... of course it was our policy still. Britain was now going to occupy Constantinople in order that when Britain and France had been enabled, by Russia's help, to win the war, Russia should not have Constantinople at the peace. If this were not so, why were British forces being sent to the Dardanelles at a time when the French and British armies were being so hard pressed in France that the Russian Armies were making unheard of sacrifices to save them?[2]

Grey and Asquith, the leaders of the Liberal administration, were, in any event, disposed to make the concession that Britain's wartime ally requested. Heirs to the political tradition of Gladstone, they were anti-Turk and sympathetic to Russian aspirations; and they could point to the conclusion of the Committee of Imperial Defence, arrived at in 1903 during a Conservative administration, that to exclude Russia from Constantinople was no longer a vital British interest. At the outset of the Ottoman war, the Prime Minister wrote that "Few things wd. give me greater pleasure than to see the Turkish Empire finally disappear from Europe, & Constantinople either become Russian (which I think is its proper destiny) or if that is impossible neutralised ... "[3] In March 1915, when the issue arose, he wrote of Constantinople and the straits that "It has become quite clear that Russia means to incorporate them in her own Empire," and added that "Personally I have always been & am in favour of Russia's claim ... "[4]

Unbeknownst to the rest of the Cabinet, Sir Edward Grey had already committed the country to *eventual* Russian control of Constantinople, having made promises along these lines to the Russian government in 1908.[5] His view was that if Russia's legitimate aspirations were satisfied at the straits, she would not press claims in Persia, eastern Europe, or elsewhere.

The month before, Grey had refused to encourage an anti-German *coup d'état* in Constantinople, aimed at taking Turkey out of the war, because it would have prevented him from giving Constantinople to Russia.[6] What he had done was in line with British decisions regarding Greece and the Balkan states, not bringing them into the war on the Allied side because doing so might have meant, in Grey's words, "the unsettlement of Russia's wholeheartedness in the war."[7]

Churchill dissented. He was opposed to issuing anything more than a general statement of sympathy for Russian aspirations, and wrote to Grey that he had instructed the Admiralty to undertake a study of how Russian control of Constantinople and the straits would affect British interests. He urged looking beyond immediate wartime concerns: "English history will not end with this war," he cautioned.[8]

Despite Churchill's counsel, the government, moved by an overriding fear that Russia might seek a separate peace, agreed to the terms proposed by Sazanov and the Czar. The British (12 March 1915), belatedly followed by the French (10 April 1915), formally accepted the secret proposal, reiterating that their acceptance was conditional on their own desires with respect to the Ottoman Empire being realized, and on the war being prosecuted by all of them to a final successful conclusion.

In an additional British memorandum, also dated 10 March 1915, Grey provided Sazanov with a number of other British comments and qualifications. Observing that Russia had originally asked only for Constantinople and the straits but was now asking for adjacent territories as well, Grey also pointed out that before Britain had been given a chance to decide upon her own war goals, "Russia is asking for a definite promise that her wishes shall be satisfied with regard to what is in fact the richest prize of the entire war." Grey repeatedly emphasized that in agreeing to the Czar's proposals, the British government was giving the greatest possible proof of its friendship and loyalty to Russia. It would be impossible, wrote Grey, for any British government to do any more than Asquith was doing in meeting Russia's desires, for the commitment into which he had just entered "involves a complete reversal of the traditional policy of His Majesty's Government, and is in direct opposition to the opinions and sentiments at one time universally held in England and which have still by no means died out."

Grey went on to outline what Russia might be expected to concede in return. He made it clear that his government had not yet formulated most of its own objectives in the East, but that one of them would be revision of the 1907 Anglo-Russian Agreement so as to give Britain the hitherto neutral third of Persia in addition to the third she already occupied. He emphasized, too, that the Constantinople agreement they had just reached was to be kept secret.

The agreement was to be kept secret because Grey was worried about the effect on Moslem opinion in India if its terms were revealed. He feared that Britain would be seen as a party to the destruction of the last remaining independent Mohammedan power of any consequence. Accordingly, Grey told the Russians that if the terms of their agreement were to become known, he would want to state publicly "that throughout the negotiations, His Majesty's Government have stipulated that the Mussulman Holy Places and Arabia shall under all circumstances remain under independent Mussulman dominion."[9]

As Grey viewed it, Britain would have to compensate Islam for destroying the Ottoman Empire by establishing a Moslem state elsewhere, and Mecca and Medina made it unthinkable from a religious point of view that it should be established anywhere but in Arabia. Besides, the promise was an easy one to make; it was a territory that none of the Great Powers coveted. David Lloyd George later wrote that "no one contemplated that foreign troops should occupy any part of Arabia. It was too arid a country to make it worth the while of any ravenous Power to occupy as a permanent pasture."[10] It was not then known that there were immense deposits of oil in the region.

III

Arabia did, however, play a role in the postwar plans of the powerful British Secretary of State for War. Russia's demands of 4 March 1915, and their acceptance by Britain on 12 March, led Lord Kitchener to warn the Cabinet in a memorandum dated 16 March that after the war "old enmities and jealousies which have been stilled by the existing crisis in Europe may revive" and that Britain might be "at enmity with Russia, or with France, or with both in combination."[11] What he anticipated was no less than a revival of the Great Game. He, too, urged the creation of an independent Arabian kingdom to include Mecca and Medina, but he added that it should exist under British auspices. It was essential that it should do so in order to give Britain a hold on the spiritual leadership of the Moslem world.

In Kitchener's comprehensive design for the postwar Middle East, Britain, from its recently annexed Mediterranean island of Cyprus, would control a convenient land route to India safe from disruption by France or Russia. The War Minister's plan was for Britain to take possession of Alexandretta,[*] the great natural port on the Asian mainland opposite Cyprus, and to construct a railroad from it to the Mesopotamian provinces (now in Iraq), of which Britain would also

---

[*] Now called Iskenderun, and located in the extreme south of what is now Turkey, near the frontier of what is now Syria.

take possession. It was generally believed (though not yet proven) that the Mesopotamian provinces contained large oil reserves which were deemed important by Churchill and the Admiralty. It was believed, too, by Kitchener and others, that the ancient Mesopotamian lands watered by the Tigris and Euphrates rivers could be developed so as to produce agricultural riches; but in Kitchener's view the principal advantages of his proposal were strategic. The British railroad from the Mediterranean to the head of the Persian Gulf would enable troops to move to and from India rapidly. The broad swath of British-owned territory it would traverse would provide a shield for the Persian Gulf, as well as a road to India. If Britain failed to take possession of it, he feared that Russia would.

Sir Arthur Hirtzel of the India Office wrote a similar memorandum at about the same time, with one significant difference in emphasis: he urged that the Mesopotamian provinces should be incorporated into the Indian Empire.[12] He viewed it as an area that could be irrigated and made rich by colonists from India. In his scheme, the administration of the area would be entrusted to the Government of India and would fall within the jurisdiction of the India Office. It was becoming increasingly clear that in London two of the contending rival powers fighting one another for a share of the Ottoman Empire were the British High Commissioner in Cairo and the British Viceroy in Simla.

Underlying both Hirtzel's and Kitchener's memoranda was the assumption, shared by most members of the government, that it was now in Britain's interest to carve up the Ottoman Empire and to take a large piece of it. The Prime Minister was practically alone in seeing a need to examine that assumption in a critical light. He admitted, however, that politicians such as Churchill, who felt that Britain ought to do as well out of the war as her allies, spoke for practically everybody else on this issue.

Asquith wrote:

> I believe that, at the moment, Grey and I are the *only* two men who doubt & distrust any such settlement. We both think that in the real interest of our own future, the best thing would be if, at the end of the War, we could say that ... we have taken & gained nothing. And that not from a merely moral & sentimental point of view ... but from purely material considerations. Taking on Mesopotamia, for instance—with or without Alexandretta ... means spending millions in irrigation & development with no immediate or early return; keeping up quite a large army white & coloured in an unfamiliar country; tackling every kind of tangled administrative question, worse than we have ever had in India with a hornet's nest of Arab tribes.[13]

The Prime Minister told members of his Cabinet that when they discussed the future of the Ottoman territories, their "discussion had resembled that of a gang of buccaneers."[14] But it was typical of him that he did not take a stand against them. What he told the Cabinet was that, while he was in sympathy with Grey's view "that we have already as much territory as we are able to hold," he did not regard himself and his colleagues as "free agents" who were entitled to hold back from taking more. If "we were to leave the other nations to scramble for Turkey without taking anything ourselves, we should not be doing our duty." [15]

In the correspondence that comprised the Constantinople agreement, Russia in effect had challenged the western powers to formulate their own territorial demands. Asquith took up the challenge: he appointed an interdepartmental group under the chairmanship of a career diplomat, Sir Maurice de Bunsen, to study the matter and to recommend what Britain ought to ask from an Ottoman peace settlement.

Largely unnoticed and undiscussed, another major step had been taken. In the 100 days between the outbreak of the German war and the outbreak of the Ottoman war, Britain had overturned the foreign policy of more than a century by abandoning any commitment to the preservation of the territorial integrity of the Ottoman Empire. Now, in the 150 days since the outbreak of the Ottoman war, the Asquith government had come around to the view that dividing up the Ottoman Empire was positively desirable, and that Britain would benefit from taking part in it.

IV

The Asquith government's move to plan the breakup of the Ottoman Empire was prompted by the Russian demand for Constantinople. Lord Kitchener had anticipated that demand at the outset of the war. Months before Asquith appointed the interdepartmental committee chaired by the diplomat Sir Maurice de Bunsen to outline Britain's aims in the postwar Middle East, Kitchener had initiated informal inquiries of his own along these lines, which his lieutenants pursued before, during, and after the de Bunsen proceedings.

Kitchener turned to his former staff in Cairo to elaborate the details of his plans for the postwar Middle East, with special reference to the possibility that Russia and France might resume their traditional hostility to Britain in that part of the world.

Apparently Oswald FitzGerald, Kitchener's aide, wrote to Storrs asking for comments on the role of Palestine after the war with respect to a probable French and/or Russian position further north. It was one of the first times that Zionism—the movement to create a Jewish homeland in Palestine—entered into British wartime speculations. Storrs replied at the end of 1914:

> With regard to Palestine, I suppose that while we naturally do not want to burden ourselves with fresh responsibilities as would be imposed upon us by annexation, we are, I take it, averse to the prospect of a Russian advance Southwards into Syria, or of a too great extension of the inevitable French Protectorate over the Lebanon, etc. France would be a better neighbour than Russia, but we cannot count on the permanence of any Entente, however Cordiale, when the generation that is full of war memories passes away. A buffer State is most desirable, but can we get one up? There is no visible indigenous elements out of which a Moslem Kingdom of Palestine can be constructed. The Jewish State is in theory an attractive idea; but the Jews, though they constitute a majority in Jerusalem itself are very much in a minority in Palestine generally, and form indeed a bare sixth of the whole population.

After considering the alternatives, Storrs concluded that the most attractive approach would be to annex and incorporate Palestine into Egypt. He ended by saying, "Please remember me to the Chief. Egyptians are hoping that he will continue to direct their fate from afar."[16]

Storrs wrote again at the beginning of March 1915, proposing that after the war Kitchener should return to a new "North African or Near Eastern Vice-Royalty including Egypt and the Sudan and across the way from Aden to Alexandretta."[17] This, he suggested, would offer Kitchener an attractive alternative to becoming Viceroy of India. In effect he was proposing that most of the Arabic-speaking world should be organized into a confederation that would be a British protectorate ruled by Kitchener from Cairo.[18]

As he developed a Middle Eastern policy for Britain, the War Minister based it on the Storrs proposal. On 11 November 1914, Kitchener wrote to Sir Edward Grey that the French should be persuaded to forego their traditional interest in Syria, and should in exchange be given more of North Africa after the war; while Syria should be nominally independent under a British protectorate and should be joined to Arabia under the spiritual leadership of an Arab caliph. (This was the matter about which Kitchener had corresponded with Hussein of Mecca months before.)

Kitchener later suggested to Grey that negotiations might be opened with Arabic-speaking leaders without telling the French government; but Lord Crewe, the Secretary of State for India, told

Grey that such a course of proceedings would not be "feasible."[19] In any event, Kitchener, Storrs, and Sir Mark Sykes, the Tory M.P. who joined the Kitchener entourage in 1915, all wrongly believed that the French could be persuaded to abandon their interest in Syria (except for the Christian areas of Mount Lebanon, where their presence might prove to be, according to Storrs, "inevitable").[20]

As to the Arabic-speaking peoples, it long had been an article of faith among the British officials who dealt with oriental affairs that they were incapable of genuine independence. Gertrude Bell, the most famous of prewar British travelers in Arabian lands, repeated what was regarded as obvious when she wrote that "the Arabs can't govern themselves."[21] As used by British officials among themselves during the war, "independence" for Arabic-speaking areas merely meant independence from the Ottoman Empire, and indicated that such areas would move instead into the orbit of some European power.[22]

Throughout the next two years, Kitchener and his colleagues continued to press their scheme. On 26 August 1915, the field marshal's colleague, Reginald Wingate, Governor-General of the Sudan, wrote the Governor-General of India that "I conceive it to be not impossible that in the dim future a federation of semi-independent Arab States might exist under European guidance and support, linked together by racial and linguistic grounds, owing spiritual allegiance to a single Arab Primate, and looking to Great Britain as its patron and protector."[23]

Taking the lead in pushing for an Arab caliphate, Wingate corresponded with Kitchener's candidate for the position—Hussein, the ruler of Mecca and Medina—through an Arab religious leader in the Sudan, Sir Sayyid Ali al-Mirghani. Captain G. S. Symes, Wingate's private secretary, produced a detailed memorandum outlining the pan-Arab scheme of which the caliphate would be part; and Storrs submitted another memorandum supporting the Arab caliphate on 2 May 1915. Gilbert Clayton, the Cairo Intelligence chief, supporting the plan for Britain to take Syria and for the caliphate to be brought to Arabia, made it seem that many voices were urging the scheme, when in fact it was only a single faction speaking, though with several voices.[24]

In London, Lord Kitchener explained to his colleagues—including the representative of India, which had been alarmed by his correspondence with Hussein months before—why the moving of the caliphate was central to his strategy for the postwar world. At a meeting of the War Committee of the Cabinet on 19 March 1915, Lord Crewe said that two different views were taken in the India Office about the future of the Ottoman Empire. The Political Department wanted to sacrifice Turkey to Arabia, while the Military

Department wanted to make Turkey as strong as possible as a barrier against a potential Russian threat. Minutes of the meeting record that

> LORD KITCHENER objected to the Military Department's plan. The Turks, he said, would always be under pressure from their strong Russian neighbour, with the result that the Khalifate might be to a great extent under Russian domination, and the Russian influence might indirectly assert itself over the Mohammedan part of the population of India. If, on the other hand, the Khalifate were transferred to Arabia, it would remain to a great extent under our influence.[25]

The Foreign Office deemed it unwise to interfere in Moslem religious affairs; the India Office went further and called it dangerous. But the Foreign Office would not, and the India Office could not, overrule the judgment of Herbert Kitchener. He was more than the head of the War Office, more than a Cabinet minister, more than an old hand at African and Asian affairs, more than the empire's greatest soldier. He was a living legend west and east of Suez. He was Kitchener of Khartoum; and in the sunset of his career, the tall old soldier cast a long shadow over the future of the Middle East.*

---

* The image is one used by Lord Beaverbrook.

17

DEFINING BRITAIN'S GOALS IN THE MIDDLE EAST

The de Bunsen committee—the interdepartmental group that Asquith created to advise the Cabinet as to what Britain ought to want in the Middle East—was appointed on 8 April 1915, and produced its report on 30 June 1915. The committee was composed of one representative each from the Foreign Office, the Admiralty, the India Office, and other relevant departments. Kitchener's War Office was represented on the committee by General Sir Charles Calwell, Director-General of Military Operations. In addition, Kitchener placed Sir Mark Sykes on the committee as his personal (as distinct from his departmental) representative; and through Sykes, the War Minister dominated the committee's proceedings. Thereafter Sykes remained the London bureaucrat charged with responsibility for Middle Eastern affairs throughout the war.

Sykes, a wealthy, 36-year-old Roman Catholic Tory baronet, had been elected to the House of Commons in 1911. During and after his undergraduate years at Cambridge, he had traveled widely in Asiatic Turkey and had published accounts of his journeys. This had made him one of the Conservative Party's experts on Ottoman affairs, but as Ottoman affairs had not played any significant role in British politics between 1911 and 1914, and as his party was out of office, Sykes was not well known either to the public or to his fellow politicians.

Sykes was the product of a curious background. He was the only child of an unhappy marriage: his warm-hearted but wanton mother and his harsh elderly father lived apart. At the age of three, when his mother converted to Roman Catholicism, he became a Catholic, too. When he was seven his father took him on a trip to the East. His religion and his travels in the East remained lifelong passions.

His education was fitful. He was moved from school to school and there were times when he was not at school at all. He spent two years at Jesus College, Cambridge, but did not stay to take his degree. He was restless. The vast estates that he inherited and his horse-breeding stables did not keep him at home. He roamed the East, and spent

four years attached to the embassy in Constantinople. He was welcomed everywhere for his talents. He was a caricaturist and a mime,
in both cases of almost professional quality. He was amusing and
made friends easily. He held opinions strongly, but changed them
rapidly.

When the war came, Sykes made an effort to find a job that would
make use of his Middle Eastern expertise. In the summer of 1914 he
wrote a letter to Winston Churchill asking for a job "on the spot"
working against Turkey, offering to "raise native scallywag corps,
win over notables, or any other oddment." He wrote that "I know
you won't think me self-seeking if I say all the knowledge I have of
local tendencies and possibilities, are at your disposal . . .";[1] but
Churchill either did not have a position for him or did not offer it.

Sykes fell into Kitchener's orbit as a result of meeting Lieutenant-
Colonel Oswald FitzGerald, the field marshal's close friend and
personal military secretary. FitzGerald arranged for Sykes to
be brought into the War Office early in 1915, where he served under
Calwell preparing information booklets for troops in the Mediterranean
area. While there, he made an especial friend of G. M. W. Macdonogh,
a fellow Roman Catholic who had attended the same public school;
as Director of Military Intelligence, Macdonogh proved a valuable
ally in advancing Sykes's career.

Shortly after his arrival at the War Office, Sykes was given his de
Bunsen assignment. Kitchener required a young politician who knew
the Middle East, and young Sir Mark Sykes was one of the handful
of Members of Parliament who knew the area. As a Tory, he shared
many of Kitchener's sentiments and prejudices. In every sense they
were members of the same club.*

Yet, at the time of his appointment, he barely knew Kitchener;
and was never to know him much better. Sykes was directed to call
FitzGerald every evening to give a full report of the de Bunsen
committee's discussions. FitzGerald would later tell him what
Kitchener wanted him to say or do at the meetings that followed. His
few attempts at actually seeing the reclusive national legend evidently
proved unsatisfactory; Sykes later commented that "The less I saw
of him, the easier it was to do what he required . . ."[2]

From the outset, though, the other members assumed that he
spoke with the full weight of Lord Kitchener's authority. The relatively inexperienced M.P. controlled the interdepartmental committee. He was outspoken and opinionated. He was the only member
of the committee who had been to most parts of the Ottoman
Empire; he alone could speak from first-hand knowledge. Then, too,

* Both belonged to the Other Club, founded by Winston Churchill and F. E.
Smith.

he was a politician. He made the other key member of the committee, Maurice Hankey, into a friend and personal supporter. Hankey, also in his thirties, was Secretary to the Committee of Imperial Defence and Secretary to the War Council of the Cabinet, and was to become the first holder of the office of Secretary of the British Cabinet. Controlling the agenda, and writing the minutes of what was said and decided at meetings, Hankey was on the road to becoming the most valuable and important man in the bureaucracy, and his support proved invaluable to Sykes.

In the de Bunsen proceedings, it was Sykes who outlined the alternatives that were available to Britain. He explored the relative advantages of several different kinds of territorial settlement: annexation of the Ottoman territories by the Allied Powers; dividing the territories into spheres of influence instead of annexing them outright; leaving the Ottoman Empire in place, but rendering its government submissive; or decentralizing the administration of the empire into semi-autonomous units. (Eventually the committee recommended trying the last choice first, as being the easiest.)

In order to discuss these matters, the committee had to decide what names to give to the various areas into which they might want to divide the Ottoman Empire. It is indicative of the spirit in which they approached their task that they saw no need to follow the lines of existing political subdivisions of the empire, the *vilayets* (or provinces), and felt free to remake the face of the Middle East as they saw fit. In any event, the tendency of the committee members, like that of the British governing class in general, was to be guided in such matters by the Greek and Latin classics they had studied at public school: they employed the vague Greek terms used by Hellenistic geographers two thousand years earlier. The Arabic-speaking areas of Asia to the north of Arabia thus collectively were referred to as "Mesopotamia" in the east and "Syria" in the west, though the areas to be included in each were unclear. The southern part of Syria was called "Palestine," a corruption of "Philistia," the coastal strip occupied by the Philistines more than a thousand years before Christ; and while no country had ever called itself Palestine, it was a geographic term current in the Christian western world to describe the Holy Land.

The committee, led by Mark Sykes, proposed the creation of five largely autonomous provinces in the decentralized Ottoman Empire which they envisaged. They were to be Syria, Palestine, Armenia, Anatolia, and Jazirah-Iraq (the northern and southern parts of Mesopotamia). As the committee saw it, British influence or control would be desirable in a wide swath across the Middle East from the Mediterranean to the Persian Gulf. A British railroad was to be constructed from a Mediterranean port to Mesopotamia, to provide the overland road to the East. Kitchener continued to insist on Alexandretta as the port, but Sykes demanded that it be Haifa, and FitzGerald, mediating between the two, let Sykes have his way.

In all other respects Sykes hewed close to the Kitchener line, though with slight modifications of his own. Like Kitchener, he advocated moving the caliphate to the south to put it out of the reach of Russia's influence; but he added that it also would put it out of reach of financial control by France, for he assumed that Ottoman finances would be largely controlled by the French in view of the large French investment in the Ottoman public debt.[3]

The overall approach, however, was Kitchener's. Sykes, who had been a conspicuous member of the pro-Turkish bloc in Parliament, abandoned his conviction that the integrity of the Ottoman Empire ought to be maintained. To his intimate friend and fellow pro-Turkish M.P., Aubrey Herbert, he wrote on April Fool's Day:

> I perceive by your letter that you are pro-Turk still. I got a summons from Field to attend a meeting of the Ottoman Society to which I never belonged ... I immediately wired to McKenna [Home Secretary] and I have every hope that the whole crowd have been clapped into barbed wire—ha! ha! How furious this must make you ha! ha! again. Your Policy is wrong. Turkey must cease to be. Smyrna shall be Greek. Adalia Italian, Southern Taurus and North Syria French, Filistin [Palestine] British, Mesopotamia British and everything else Russian—including Constantinople, ... and I shall sing a *Te Deum* in St. Sophia and a *Nunc Dimittis* in the Mosque of Omar. We will sing it in Welsh, Polish, Keltic, and Armenian in honour of all the gallant little nations.

After more of the same, Sykes closed with a note:

> To the Censor
> This is a brilliant letter from one genius to another. Men of base clay cannot be expected to understand. Pray pass on without fear.
>
> Mark Sykes Lt. Col. FRGS, MP, CC, JP.[4]

18

AT THE NARROWS OF FORTUNE

I

London was dealing quickly with the political consequences of the impending victory at the Dardanelles but, at the scene of battle, the fleet moved slowly. The weather kept the warships from bringing their full fire power to bear. As the days went by, the Turkish troops along the shore began to regain their confidence, and learned to harass the British minesweepers by firing on them with howitzers and small mobile guns. On 13 March Churchill received a cable from Carden saying that minesweeping was not proceeding satisfactorily due to what Carden claimed was heavy Turkish fire, although no British casualties had been suffered. This, noted Churchill, "makes me squirm"; "I do not understand why minesweeping should be interfered with by fire which causes no casualties. Two or three hundred casualties would be a small price to pay for sweeping up as far as the Narrows."[1]

Part of the problem—and it was one of the defects in Admiral Carden's original plan—was that the minesweepers were manned by civilian employees, who were not willing to operate under fire; but the major problem was that Admiral Carden was losing his nerve. Churchill had cabled him on 13 March reporting that "we have information that the Turkish Forts are short of ammunition and that the German officers have made desponding reports,"[2] to which Carden replied that he would launch the main attack into the straits and wage the battle for the crucial Narrows on or about 17 March, depending on the weather; but the admiral worried, and could neither eat nor sleep. He had lost no ships and reported that he had suffered no casualties, but the strain of anxiety proved too much for him and suddenly his nerves broke.

On the eve of the main battle for the straits, Admiral Carden told his seconds-in-command that he could no longer go on. He summoned a fleet physician, who examined him and certified that he was suffering from indigestion and that he should be placed on the sick list for three or four weeks. On 16 March Carden cabled Churchill "Much regret obliged to go on the sick list. Decision of Medical Officer follows."[3]

Churchill promptly appointed John de Robeck, the second-in-command, to take his place. De Robeck, according to his cabled report to the Admiralty, then commenced the main attack at 10:45 on the morning of 18 March.

The day began to go badly when a French battleship mysteriously exploded and disappeared just before 2:00 in the afternoon. Two hours later two British battleships struck mines. A vessel sent to rescue one of them, the *Irresistible*, also struck a mine; and it and the *Irresistible* both sank. Then a French warship damaged by gunfire was beached. De Robeck reported to the Admiralty, however, that the rest of his ships would be ready to recommence action in three or four days. At the Admiralty in London, there was elation, for Naval Intelligence had discovered that when the action recommenced, the enemy would collapse. On the afternoon of 19 March, Captain William Reginald Hall, the Director of Naval Intelligence, brought Churchill and Fisher an intercepted, decoded message from the German Kaiser; they grasped its significance immediately. Churchill cried out in excitement that "they've come to the end of their ammunition," as indeed they had. Fisher waved the message over his head and shouted, "By God, I'll go through tomorrow" and then repeated "Tomorrow! We shall probably lose six ships, but I'm going through."[4] Churchill and Fisher did not tell the Cabinet, for fear of compromising their intelligence sources, nor did they tell de Robeck; they merely cabled him that it was important not to give the impression that operations were suspended.

Unknown to Churchill and Fisher, at Maurice Hankey's suggestion, the Director of Naval Intelligence, Captain Hall, had initiated negotiations with Talaat Bey, the young Turk leader, aimed at inducing the Ottoman Empire to leave the war in return for a large payment of money. The British and Turkish negotiators met at a seaport in European Turkey on 15 March.[5] The negotiations failed because the British government felt unable to give assurances that the Ottoman Empire could retain Constantinople—so deeply were the British now committed to satisfying Russia's ambitions. Captain Hall had not yet learned of the collapse of the negotiations when, on the night of 19 March, he told Churchill of the plan to offer four million pounds to Turkey if she would leave the war. Churchill was aghast and Fisher was furious. At their insistence, Hall cabled his emissaries to withdraw the offer. Hall later recalled that Fisher started up from his chair and shouted "Four million? No, no. I tell you I'm going through tomorrow."[6]

II

All that stood between the British-led Allied fleet and Constantinople were a few submerged mines, and Ottoman supplies of these were so depleted that the Turks were driven to catch and re-use the mines that the Russians were using against them.

Morale in Constantinople disintegrated. Amidst rumors and panic, the evacuation of the city commenced. The state archives and the gold reserves of the banks were sent to safety. Special trains were prepared for the Sultan and for the foreign diplomatic colony. The well-to-do sent wives and families ahead to the interior of the country. Talaat, the Minister of the Interior, requisitioned a powerful Mercedes for his personal use, and equipped it with extra petrol tanks for the long drive to a distant place of refuge. Placards denouncing the government began to appear in the streets of the city. The Greek and Armenian communities were expected by the authorities to welcome the Allies, but now the police began to arrest suspects within the Turkish-speaking community as well.

Meanwhile those members of the Enver-Talaat faction who had supported it to the bitter end gathered up petrol and prepared to burn down the city when the Allies arrived, and wired St Sophia and the other great monuments with dynamite. The *Goeben* made ready to escape into the Black Sea.

Enver bravely planned to remain and defend the city, but his military dispositions were so incompetent that—as Liman von Sanders later recalled—any Turkish attempt at opposing an Allied landing in Constantinople had been rendered impossible.

III

London rejoiced and Constantinople despaired, but in the straits of the Dardanelles, the mood of the British command was bleak. The casualties and losses from mines on 18 March had left Admiral de Robeck despondent. He feared for his career. According to one report, when evening came on the 18th and de Robeck surveyed the results of the day's battle, he said "I suppose I am done for."[7]

De Robeck was unnerved because he did not know what had caused his losses. In fact his ships had run into a single line of mines running parallel to the shore rather than across the straits. They had been placed there the night before and had escaped notice by British aerial observers. It was a one-time fluke.

Fate now appeared in the charming person of General Sir Ian Hamilton, whom Kitchener had sent out in advance of the forthcoming troops. Hamilton was to be their commander, with orders to let the navy win the campaign and then to disembark and take possession of the shore. If the navy failed to win through on its own, Hamilton's alternative orders were to invade the European shore of the straits, capture the Narrows, and let the navy through.

Once Admiral de Robeck realized that he had an alternative to going back into battle—that in London it was regarded as acceptable for him to turn over the responsibility to Hamilton and the army if he chose to do so—he saw no reason to run further risks. Whoever said it first, de Robeck and Hamilton agreed that the navy should wait until the army could come into action. Hamilton had already cabled his views to Kitchener, who on 18 March showed the cable to the Prime Minister; the cable persuaded Asquith that "The Admiralty have been over-sanguine as to what they cd. do by ships alone."[8] De Robeck cabled Churchill, after meeting with Ian Hamilton on 22 March, that "having met General Hamilton . . . and heard his proposals I now consider" that the army has to enter the campaign.[9]

On the morning of 23 March the War Group met at the Admiralty to discuss de Robeck's decision. Winston Churchill was appalled and shocked, but the First Sea Lord, Admiral Fisher, took the view that the decision of the man on the spot had to be accepted, like it or not, and in this view he was supported by Admiral of the Fleet Sir Arthur Wilson and Admiral Sir Henry Jackson. Churchill violently disagreed, and took the matter to the Cabinet when the War Group meeting ended. He had drafted a strong cable to de Robeck which he brought along for the Cabinet's approval, and which in no uncertain terms ordered the admiral to renew the attack. At the Cabinet meeting Churchill received support from both the Prime Minister and from Kitchener, who drafted appropriately strong cables to Sir Ian Hamilton.

Returning to the Admiralty that afternoon, Churchill found that Fisher, Wilson, and Jackson remained adamantly opposed to his sending the cabled order to de Robeck. As a civilian minister attempting to overrule the First Sea Lord and his fellow admirals on a naval matter, Churchill felt obliged to return to Asquith and ask for the Prime Minister's consent. Asquith, however, refused to give it. His personal view was that the attack should be resumed, but he would not order it over the opposition of the Sea Lords at the Admiralty.

Knowing as he did that the ammunition crisis in Turkey meant that the road to Constantinople was open, Churchill fought back against the decision to let the navy abandon the campaign. Since he could not give de Robeck orders to resume the attack, he attempted to get him to do it through persuasion. He sent cables in which he attempted to reason with the admiral and to show him why a resumption of the naval attack was important. He spoke again with the

Prime Minister who expressed his "hope" that the attack would resume soon.[10] It was to no avail. Only a few hundred casualties had been suffered, but the Admiralty's Dardanelles campaign was over.

IV

After the battle of 18 March—the battle that so alarmed de Robeck that he decided to turn his ships around and steam away—the Ottoman commanders concluded that their cause was lost. While Admiral de Robeck, aboard ship, was giving his orders to give up the fight, on shore the Turkish defending forces, unaware of de Robeck's decision, received orders to fire their remaining rounds of ammunition and then to abandon their coastal positions. If Admiral de Robeck, who had led his fleet in battle for only one day, had plunged back into battle for a second day he would have seen the enemy forces withdraw and melt away. In a few hours his minesweepers, working without interruption or opposition, could have cleared a path through the Narrows; and once the lines of mines surrounding the Narrows had gone, there were no more laid. The fleet would have steamed into Constantinople without opposition.

For Winston Churchill, who was only hours away from victory, the nearness of it—the knowledge that he was almost there, that it was within his grasp—was to become the torment of a lifetime. It was more than a personal triumph that had slipped through his fingers. It was also his last chance to save the world in which he had grown up: to win the war while the familiar, traditional Europe of established monarchies and empires still survived.*

It was also the lost last chance for Britain, France, and Russia to impose their designs on the Middle East with ease. Though they would continue to pursue their nineteenth-century goals in the region, thereafter they would do so in the uncongenial environment of the twentieth century.

The Ottoman Empire, which had been sentenced to death, had received an unexpected last-minute reprieve. Its leaders rushed to make use of the time that Britain had allowed them before the new trial of arms began.

---

* Historians still debate the question of whether victory in the Ottoman war in 1915 would have led to a rapid Allied victory in the German war. The "Easterners," led by Lloyd George, never doubted that it would have done so.

19

THE WARRIORS

I

Shaken by the Allied bombardment of 18 March, Enver Pasha announced an uncharacteristic and important decision: he relinquished command of the Ottoman forces at the Dardanelles to the German general, Liman von Sanders. It ran counter to all of Enver's instincts to turn over his Moslem warriors to a foreign—and Christian— commander. Until that moment he had resisted pressures to turn over authority, even to the German experts who served as departmental and staff advisers. Although he had allowed German officers in his War Ministry to move into key posts in the Departments of Operations, Intelligence, Railroads, Supply, Munitions, Coal, and Fortresses, he had jealously questioned the judgments and circumscribed the authority of his German colleagues; and in many areas he continued to do so. Yet under the guns of the Allied armada he finally stepped aside on the battlefield that most mattered.

Liman had little time, and wasted none. He assembled such forces and supplies as were to be found amidst the wreckage of the empire's resources. He made his own command appointments, notably giving a responsible position to Mustapha Kemal, a Turkish officer who admired European ways and whose scorn of Ottoman backwardness and bitter consciousness that he was superior to those advanced over his head had, until then, kept him in obscure and unrewarding assignments. Kemal was to prove the battlefield genius of the coming combat: the commander with the eye for the key tactical position, who would seize the high ground and dominate the field.

Liman was kept well informed of British progress in organizing an invasion force. News of the British expedition's assembly and embarkation in Egypt was published by newspapers in Cairo and reported to the Turks by merchants in Alexandria. Later, Ottoman agents in neutral Greece could hardly have missed noticing the vast fleet as it moved through the islands of the Aegean, its lights and signal lamps shining brightly through the night, its military bands blaring above the sound of winds and waves by day.

Well-officered for once, the Ottoman defending forces under Liman's workmanlike direction were waiting for the British invasion when it came. It was the type of engagement in which the steadfastness of the Ottoman soldiery could be employed to best advantage. Sir Mark Sykes had pointed this out in late February in a letter to Churchill. He wrote that though they could be routed by a surprise attack, "Turks always grow formidable if given time to think."[1]

II

For Sir Ian Hamilton, the British Commander, the campaign began the morning of 12 March when Lord Kitchener unexpectedly—and without explanation—summoned him to the War Office to offer him the command. He told the War Minister that he knew nothing about Turkey, and therefore that he needed at least some word of explanation and guidance.

As Hamilton later recalled, at their meeting the War Minister, while giving him command of the division that initially was being sent out to the Dardanelles in support of the navy, warned that the troops were "only to be a loan and are to be returned the moment they can be spared." He explained that "all things earmarked for the East are looked on by powerful interests both at home and in France as having been stolen from the West."[2]

The Director of Military Operations at the War Office then briefed Hamilton by showing him a map and a plan of attack borrowed from the Greek General Staff. The War Office had not taken the time or trouble to work out one of their own.

General Hamilton was sent out with an inaccurate and out-of-date map, and little else to guide him. On seeing the Gallipoli peninsula for the first time, he remarked immediately that "the Peninsula looks a tougher nut to crack than it did on Lord K.'s small and featureless map."[3] It was a rugged landscape of ravines, and hills that divided the shoreline into tiny beaches cut off from one another.

Having traveled on a fast naval cruiser from Marseilles, Hamilton reached the coast of Gallipoli on 18 March, in time to influence de Robeck to call off the naval campaign. By late April he was steaming back toward the straits to command the army's attack. He carefully followed the instructions that the War Minister had given him for the campaign. He was to attack only the European side of the straits: the Gallipoli peninsula. He was not to attack until he had his whole force, which is why (despite his own misgivings) he had ordered the navy to take him back from Turkey to Egypt to assemble his forces. It took him about three weeks to organize his expeditionary force;

then the navy took him back to Turkey to launch his invasion of Gallipoli, the western (or European) shore of the Dardanelles.

It was a risky venture: indeed prewar British military studies that were revealed to the Cabinet by Asquith at the end of February had concluded that an attack on Gallipoli by the British army was too risky to be undertaken.[4] Kitchener had ordered that it should be done nonetheless, saying that he believed the Ottoman generals had left the European side of the straits more or less undefended.

At a War Council meeting, its only Tory member—the former Prime Minister Arthur Balfour—asked "whether the Turks were likely, if cut off, to surrender or to fight with their back to the wall." Lloyd George said he "thought it more probable that they would make a stand"; but Kitchener replied that they would probably surrender.[5]

A year later, a verdict on the matter was returned by Allied armies serving in the field. Compton Mackenzie, the young novelist-turned-war correspondent, reported from the Dardanelles that "French officers who have fought in the West say that as a fighting unit one Turk is worth two Germans; in fact, with his back to the wall the Turk is magnificent."[6]

III

At dawn on 25 April 1915, the British, Dominion, and Allied armies waded ashore onto six narrow, unconnected beaches on the Gallipoli peninsula. The Turks, who had known when but not where the Allies would attack, were taken by surprise and probably could have been overwhelmed that day.

The northernmost invasion site, Ari Burnu, also proved a surprise to the Australian and New Zealand troops who landed there—the navy had taken them to the wrong beach. Ascending the steep slopes to the ridge above, they encountered Turkish soldiers who fled until rallied by their commander, Mustapha Kemal. The battle raged all day. There were moments when it could have gone either way; but in the end the Turks drove the invaders back down the slope.

At the tip of Gallipoli, the five other Allied landings were at beachheads code-named S, V, W, X, and Y. At Y there were no Turks, and the invaders climbed unopposed to the top of the cliff that dominated the beach; but instead of marching on, they stopped because of confusion as to who was in command. At X, meeting little opposition, the attackers also mounted the cliff—and also stopped there. At S, the landing party met little opposition, but made camp on the beach without attempting to ascend to the top of the slope that overlooked it.

The Allies held an overwhelming numerical superiority that day—

most of Liman's forces were held in reserve at a distance from the battlefield—and at beaches Y, X, and S the invasion forces could have exploited their surprise attack by advancing and destroying the small Turkish garrison in the vicinity.

By 26 April the situation had changed. Turkish reinforcements started to pour in, and in a sense it was all over: a cheap victory at Gallipoli was no longer in sight for the Allies. General Birdwood, commander of the ANZAC forces, on the advice of his officers, recommended re-embarking and abandoning the positions his forces occupied. But Sir Ian Hamilton, Birdwood's commanding officer, decided instead to dig in.

Unknowingly, Hamilton thereby conceded that the expedition he led—and which was intended to break the military stalemate in the war—was doomed to fail. As had been shown in France and Flanders, digging in was more likely to produce a stalemate than break one; and indeed, in futile, bloody assaults on fixed positions, Gallipoli was to become a drawn-out replay of the trench warfare on the western front.

Hamilton had positioned his troops at best to fight the Turks to a draw, but at worst to suffer disaster. While the Turks dug in on the dominating heights, the British commanders ordered their troops to entrench on the beaches; and there at the water's edge the Allied fight eventually became one for survival. Soon most members of the British government in London came to view evacuation as the only solution, but Churchill and Kitchener fought against it: Churchill because he was never willing to accept defeat, and Kitchener because he believed it would be a disaster for a British army to be seen to be defeated by a Middle Eastern one.

20

THE POLITICIANS

I

Winston Churchill's dogged determination to fight on at Gallipoli until victory was won kept him in the spotlight even after the army had taken over the Dardanelles campaign from the navy. He appeared to be both the man who had brought the Ottoman war about, and the man who had caused Britain to suffer one defeat after another in that war.

Although from April onward the battle for the straits was no longer the Admiralty's operation, Churchill was made the scapegoat for the continuing casualties and setbacks as the Allied armies fought on hopelessly at Gallipoli. Kitchener's prestige was so great that the press, the public, and Parliament found it inconceivable that he had been responsible for the blunders that had been committed; but Churchill was an interfering civilian and it was easy to believe the admirals who claimed that his amateurish meddling in naval matters had been the cause of British setbacks. *The Times* gave voice to a gathering consensus in 1915 when its 18 May editorial proclaimed that

> What long ago passed beyond the stage of mere rumour is the charge, which has been repeatedly and categorically made in public, that the First Lord of the Admiralty has been assuming responsibilities and overriding his expert advisers to a degree which might at any time endanger the national safety ... When a civilian Minister in charge of a fighting service persistently seeks to grasp power which should not pass into his unguided hands, and attempts to use that power in perilous ways, it is time for his colleagues in the Cabinet to take some definite action.[1]

Outside of the War Cabinet, it was not generally known that Lord Kitchener was the author of the plan to send the navy on its own to attack the Dardanelles. Churchill was blamed for the decision, and therefore for the several weeks of advance warning that had been given to Enver and Liman von Sanders, which enabled them to entrench their armies to repel the Allied assault on Gallipoli. The officers on the Gallipoli beaches saw the earlier naval attack as a show-off stunt by the First Lord of the Admiralty, a *coup* that had failed and threatened to lose them their lives. Aubrey Herbert, who served in the armed forces there, wrote in his diary that "Winston's name fills everyone with rage. Roman emperors killed slaves to make themselves popular, he is killing free men to make himself famous. If he hadn't tried that *coup* but had cooperated with the Army, we might have got to Constantinople with very little loss."[2] Later he wrote that "As for Winston, I would like him to die in some of the torments I have seen so many die in here."[3]

Abuse was heaped on Churchill from all quarters, and his political position deteriorated rapidly. A final split between Churchill and Britain's greatest sailor, Admiral of the Fleet Lord Fisher, the First Sea Lord, brought matters to a head. Churchill and Fisher had conferred and had reached agreement on a program of reinforcements of the fleet supporting the Gallipoli campaign on Friday, 14 May. Early the following morning Fisher received several memoranda from Churchill summarizing the points on which they had agreed, but also adding new suggestions of his own. Infuriated, Fisher, who had announced that he was resigning on eight previous occasions, walked over from the Admiralty to nearby 11 Downing Street and told the Chancellor of the Exchequer, David Lloyd George, that he was resigning his office. Lloyd George sent for the Prime Minister, who was next door at 10 Downing Street, and the two of them attempted to persuade Fisher that he had to remain at his post at least temporarily. Fisher refused, and then went back to his room at the Admiralty, locked the door, and drew the blinds. Later, he disappeared from view for a time.

Churchill learned of the situation from his colleagues, for Fisher refused to see him. The immediate problem was that the navy—in the middle of a war—was without its chief commanding officer, and that the intentions of the other members of the Admiralty Board were unknown. Churchill was assured on Sunday, 16 May, that the Second, Third, and Fourth Sea Lords were all willing to continue in their positions. He also secured the agreement of Admiral of the Fleet Sir Arthur Wilson to return to his prewar position of First Sea Lord in Fisher's place. Since the press and the political world did not yet know of Fisher's resignation, Churchill planned to announce both Fisher's resignation and the new dispositions at the Admiralty to the House of Commons on Monday morning—before the Opposition had time to disrupt his plans.

Fisher, however, sent a hint of what he had done to Andrew Bonar

Law, leader of the Opposition. Bonar Law guessed what it meant, and called on Lloyd George first thing Monday morning. He asked the Chancellor whether Fisher had resigned. When Lloyd George confirmed that he had, Bonar Law explained his own view of the grave political consequences that could be expected to ensue. The Opposition theretofore had refrained from challenging the government in wartime, but Bonar Law said that he could no longer restrain his followers: Fisher was their hero, and they would not let Churchill stay at the Admiralty if Fisher went. Nor would they stop their attacks there, for the Tory Members of Parliament, in the face of one military failure after another, no longer felt that they could give the Liberal government their unqualified support.

Bonar Law's solution was to broaden the government. He proposed that the Liberal government should be replaced by a coalition government, representing the two major parties in Parliament, and Labour.

Lloyd George instantly saw the force of the argument. He asked Bonar Law to wait at 11 Downing Street while he went next door to consult the Prime Minister. Lloyd George then put the case for a coalition forcefully to Asquith, who abruptly agreed.

Churchill knew none of this. Early that afternoon he went to the House of Commons to announce that the Sea Lords had agreed to stay on with Admiral of the Fleet Wilson as their new head. He arrived to find that Lloyd George and Asquith would not let him make his speech. Asquith said that he did not want the scheduled debate between the parties to take place. He told Churchill that he would form a new government in which the Liberals would share office with the Conservatives and with Labour.

On 19 May 1915, the new government was announced. Churchill was removed from the Admiralty and given the minor position of Chancellor of the Duchy of Lancaster—in effect, Minister Without Portfolio—although he remained in the War Cabinet.

The political world did not know at the time that, if Churchill had been listened to, the Dardanelles campaign could have been won at a time when only a few hundred casualties had been incurred; and that it was because the admirals and generals had overruled him that Britain had embarked on a campaign that was in the process of costing her more than 200,000 casualties. Thus it failed to grasp the essential fact that Britain's generals and admirals were losing the war for her and that the country urgently needed not less but more civilian control of the military.

The political world in Britain also failed to grasp another essential fact: the war in the East was not merely being lost by the Allies, it was being won by the other side. The results of the campaign were a reflection of the fact that the courage and tenacity of the Australian,

New Zealand, British, and French soldiery was being matched by the courage and tenacity of their Ottoman opponents.

II

Lloyd George had brought about the creation of this first coalition government, which excluded Churchill from a major Cabinet position. He claimed that "he had fought to get Winston high office . . . His colleagues would not, however, agree to Winston's having anything but a minor position."[4] Lloyd George was aware, however, that a hurt and angry Churchill placed the blame on him.[5] Churchill's wife, even years later, spoke bitterly of the Chancellor as a Judas whose "Welsh trickiness" had shattered the First Lord's career; and the Duke of Marlborough, Churchill's cousin, sent a note on 24 May saying "Pro tem LG has done you in."[6] Churchill himself exclaimed: "I am the victim of a political intrigue. I am finished!"[7]

Lloyd George had always regarded the Ottoman war as Churchill's fault. In the spring of 1915 the Chancellor took an even wider view of his former protégé's failings. When it became clear that Churchill would have to leave the Admiralty, Lloyd George commented: "It is the Nemesis of the man who has fought for this war for years. When the war came he saw in it the chance for glory for himself, & has accordingly entered on a risky campaign without caring a straw for the misery and hardship it would bring to thousands, in the hope that he would prove to be the outstanding man in this war."[8]

21

THE LIGHT THAT FAILED

I

The Unionist-Conservative members of the new British government took office in the belief that their task would be to protect the country's military leadership from civilian interference. Having succeeded in removing Churchill from the Admiralty, they took it that the next item on the agenda should be the defense of Lord Kitchener against his principal adversary, the Liberal politician Lloyd George.

David Lloyd George, the Chancellor of the Exchequer, held the distinction of having been the first member of the Cabinet to question a decision of Field Marshal Kitchener's after the latter became Secretary of State for War. Once started on questioning Kitchener's judgments, Lloyd George never stopped. Avoiding the pitfall that was Churchill's undoing at the Admiralty, the Liberal politician did not at first dare to challenge the field marshal on issues that were strictly military. Instead the Chancellor of the Exchequer waged his campaign on grounds of his own choosing. The issue that he raised was the shortage of munitions and other supplies. Involving questions of labor, production, and finance, it was an issue regarding which his qualifications to speak were greater than Kitchener's.

On 19 May 1915, the day on which formation of the new government was announced, Lloyd George inaugurated the final phases of a campaign that succeeded in detaching the munitions and supply functions from Kitchener's War Office and placing them under himself as Minister of Munitions. In his new ministry he succeeded in starting to do what Kitchener had not been able to do: expanding civilian production of war material and finding new sources of supply.

The Unionist-Conservative M.P.s who entered the new coalition government began to take another look at Lloyd George and Lord Kitchener, whose quarrel they had prejudged. As Minister of Munitions, Lloyd George became a tornado twisting with elemental force to destroy the enemy. The Tories came to admire and applaud his efforts. Bonar Law and his colleagues had come into the Cabinet to protect Kitchener and the military from interference by amateurish Liberal civilians, but to their surprise found themselves ranged alongside Lloyd George in questioning Kitchener's competence.

The immediate military decision facing the new government was what to do about the Gallipoli expedition. The War Council of the Cabinet reconstituted itself as the Dardanelles Committee, and held its first meeting in Asquith's rooms at the House of Commons on 7 June 1915, to deliberate the matter. Thereafter it met often. The Tories discovered that the Secretary of State for War did not supply them with the information they required in order to form a judgment. Kitchener was secretive and reluctant to disclose military information to civilians. At times he avoided answering questions because he was not fully and accurately informed. At times he espoused positions that were contradictory.

Bonar Law and his principal Tory colleague, the new Attorney-General, Sir Edward Carson, were inclined either to abandon the venture or else to send enough reinforcements to Gallipoli to ensure success. The question was what level of reinforcements would ensure success, but Kitchener would not say how many troops the Turks had at Gallipoli or how many British troops were needed in order to win. Instead he continued to talk in terms of how many troops could be spared from the western front. In exasperation, by early September Carson was writing that "What I feel so acutely about is that all our calculations (if we can dignify them by that name) are absolutely haphazard—we are always told what we can send & not how many are necessary ..."[1]

By questioning the War Office on one occasion, ministers found that an important piece of cabled information had been received there although the War Minister denied all knowledge of it. Either Kitchener had forgotten the cable or had misunderstood it. On 10 Downing Street stationery, Carson penned a note and passed it along the Cabinet table to Lloyd George: "K doesn't read the telegrams—& we don't see them—it is intolerable."[2]

Carson began cross-examining Kitchener in Cabinet meetings as though he were an accused criminal in the dock. The field marshal's evasiveness, combined with hopeful predictions from Sir Ian Hamilton that never seemed to be fulfilled, brought the Tory leaders to frustration and despair. Typical comments during sessions of the Dardanelles Committee were "SIR E. CARSON said that the slaughter which had gone on was no success, and inquired if it were to be continued" and "MR. BONAR LAW asked if Sir Ian Hamilton was to continue attacking when such action was obviously hopeless."[3]

The question of what to do dragged on into the late autumn. Cabinet opinion began to harden in favor of withdrawal from Gallipoli; for Kitchener failed to offer an alternative that promised success. Kitchener dissented, arguing that Britain should soldier on. He claimed that "abandonment would be the most disastrous event in the history of the Empire," though he admitted that he "would like to liquidate the situation."[4]

The Cabinet was unwilling to order a withdrawal from Gallipoli without Lord Kitchener's sanction, the more so as the commander on the spot, Sir Ian Hamilton, remained hopeful. On the Gallipoli beaches the situation was desperate, and Wyndham Deedes, the officer who had warned Kitchener against the Dardanelles adventure but who was serving there, joined together with two other officers, George Lloyd and Guy Dawnay, to do something about it. They schemed to get one of their number sent back to London to tell the Cabinet the truth about their situation. Dawnay had the chance, and seized it.

Back in London, Dawnay saw Kitchener and other British leaders, even including the recently demoted Churchill. He tried to get his message through to them, but they were reluctant to accept the unpalatable truth. Deedes had also guessed what Dawnay would discover, and told him so: "And I bet the best you found was Winston after all!"[5]

In the end, Ian Hamilton was replaced; and the new British commander saw at once that the situation was hopeless and called for an immediate evacuation. But the Cabinet continued to hesitate; the problem, as always, was Lord Kitchener.

II

In Lloyd George's vivid image, Kitchener's mind was pictured as the moving, turning turret of a lighthouse; but somewhere in the raging storm of the Gallipoli campaign the light had suddenly gone out. The field marshal's colleagues waited with growing anger and impatience in the darkness for the powerful beam of light that never again swung around to dispel the night.

Even the Tory Bonar Law had come around so far as to propose that Lloyd George should replace Kitchener at the War Office, but the Prime Minister resisted the proposal. Only the inner group in the government was aware of the field marshal's failings; he retained his following in the country, and Asquith felt that to replace him would be politically impossible. The Prime Minister's typical solution was to send Kitchener out to the Dardanelles on a fact-finding expedition in the hope that he would be detained there indefinitely.

In the event, once he went out and saw the battlefield himself, Kitchener felt compelled to agree that Gallipoli should be abandoned. Armed with Kitchener's approval, the Cabinet finally issued the necessary authorization; and, at the beginning of 1916, the evacuation—which was far and away the most brilliant operation of the campaign—was completed. Deedes called the evacuation "one of the most remarkable things in history."[6]

III

On 25 April 1915, the Allies could have won an easy, bloodless victory by their surprise attack; but 259 days later, when they withdrew in defeat from their last positions on the blood-soaked beaches of the Dardanelles, it emerged that they had lost one of the costliest military engagements in history. Half a million soldiers had been engaged in battle on each side, and each had suffered a quarter of a million casualties.

It was a decisive battle, in that the Allies could have won it, and, with it, the Middle Eastern war—but did not. It foreshadowed, too, things to come; a supposedly backward Asian army had defeated a modern European one.

It had the effect of drawing Europe into Middle Eastern affairs on a long-term basis. The military involvement which Kitchener had feared but failed to prevent was suspended temporarily by the Allied evacuation, but would resume a year later. More important, the setback to Allied fortunes drove Britain both in a specific and a general sense to involve herself more deeply in Middle Eastern affairs. In a specific sense, as will be seen presently, it drove Kitchener's lieutenants to ally themselves with a Middle Eastern ruler they believed could help to save Sir Ian Hamilton's armies at Gallipoli from perishing. And in a general sense, the sheer magnitude of Britain's commitment and loss at Gallipoli made it seem vital years later that she should play a major role in the postwar Middle East to give some sort of meaning to so great a sacrifice.

IV

On 18 November 1915, having resigned as Chancellor of the Duchy of Lancaster, Winston Churchill crossed over to France to serve, at his own request, as an army officer on the western front. The political world continued to place the blame for Gallipoli on him. In the Cabinet, however, Kitchener was blamed too; and Kitchener knew it.

Lord Kitchener was aware that his Cabinet colleagues hoped he would not return from his trip to the Dardanelles, but deliberately disappointed them. On returning to London at the end of 1915, he spoke frankly with the Prime Minister about his loss of support within the Cabinet, and offered to resign. When an acceptable replacement could not be found for him, he adopted a different approach. With the Prime Minister's approval, he arranged for a basic change in the nature of the position he held as War Minister, reducing the powers and responsibilities of the job. A fighting soldier from the western front, Field Marshal Sir William Robertson, was then brought into office as Chief of the Imperial General Staff with widely expanded powers that until then had fallen within Kitchener's domain as War Minister.

Yet Kitchener retained authority in formulating political policy for the Middle East. When he returned to London at the end of 1915, his aide Sir Mark Sykes also returned to London from a long fact-finding trip, bringing with him exciting news of a Middle Eastern ruler who might ally himself with Britain, and a revolutionary program on the basis of that alliance for turning the tide in the Ottoman war—a program that Kitchener was to push through the Cabinet.

22

CREATING THE ARAB BUREAU

I

In the winter of 1915—16, as the Allies planned and executed their evacuation of Gallipoli and as Lord Kitchener took a lesser role in the conduct of the war, British policy in the Middle East took a new turn: Kitchener and his colleagues began to focus in an organized way on the uses Britain might make of discontented Arab leaders and soldiers within the Ottoman Empire. They acted on the basis of recommendations brought back from the East by Sir Mark Sykes, Kitchener's personally appointed Middle East expert. Sykes was returning home from a long mission of inquiry into how the Allies should deal with the defeated Middle East—a mission without much urgency after Turkey's victory at Gallipoli.

Projects often develop a momentum of their own: in the winter of 1915 the British naval attack on the Dardanelles had gone forward even after the Russian problem it was meant to alleviate had been solved, and when the winter was over the planning of how to carve up the Middle East went forward even though Churchill's expected conquest of Constantinople—which was the reason for doing the planning—had not materialized.

After the de Bunsen committee—which Sir Mark Sykes had guided—submitted its report on the postwar Middle East on 30 June 1915, the British government sent Sykes out to the East to discuss the committee's recommendations with officers and officials on the spot. He traveled to the Balkans, to Egypt twice (on the way out and on the way back), to the Persian Gulf, to Mesopotamia, and to India. It was a major undertaking; Sykes's journey lasted half a year. It gave him a unique exposure to a range of different points of view, but it was almost 1916 before he was able to meet with Cabinet members in London to tell them in person what he had learned.

In his first stop in Cairo—on the way out, in the summer of 1915—Sykes met with Kitchener's Middle East advisers in Egypt. Ronald Storrs, whom he had known before the war, introduced him to Gilbert Clayton. Religion formed an instant bond: Clayton was a devout Christian whose seriousness impressed Sykes deeply. They became friends as well as colleagues, although Sykes was more open in his dealings with Clayton than Clayton was in return.

Sykes was introduced by his friends to Arabic-speaking personalities of engagingly pro-British views, and became an advocate of Clayton's view that Syria should become British. He was led by Clayton and Storrs to believe that the populations of the region would welcome such a development. France could be given compensation elsewhere, he said; and, in any event, the only groups in France that wanted Syria were clerics or promoters of commercial concessions.[1] Attracted by the plan espoused at that time by his friends and by Wingate for the Sherif Hussein to be elevated to the caliphate, a plan that accorded perfectly with his own view that the caliphate should be moved south, Sykes was won over to the Storrs "Egyptian Empire" scheme. This proposed a single Arabic-speaking entity, under the spiritual rule of the Sherif and the nominal temporal rule of the figurehead monarch of Egypt, to be governed from Cairo by the British High Commissioner—who was to be Lord Kitchener.

There was, however, a current of opinion in Cairo that Sykes found disturbing: the talk of rivalry between Britain and France in the Middle East. Sykes did not believe that there were any serious grounds for disagreement between the two wartime allies; he thought that France did not really care about Syria, and could be induced to look elsewhere for her share of the winnings. His assumption was that the talk of rivalry was inspired by enemy propagandists. Only many months later did he learn that the anti-French talk (and more than talk) came from some of his own friends in Cairo; and he never learned that one of the ringleaders of the group was his friend Gilbert Clayton.

II

In India, at the opposite political pole, Sykes found a reception that was less than cordial. He was a young man, halfway through his first year in his first governmental job, and he had come out from London to tell India about the East. The man he had come to see was two decades his senior, had spent a lifetime in government service, and was one of Britain's most distinguished foreign policy professionals. Charles Hardinge, a former ambassador to Russia, had been the career official in charge of the Foreign Office before coming out to India as Viceroy. As Governor-General, he served in a family tradition that harked back to the previous century; his grandfather had been Governor-General of India in the 1840s, the decade before the

Mutiny. Hardinge's policy was for India to occupy and annex Mesopotamia, and his view of Cairo's proposals was that they were "absolutely fantastic" and "perfectly fatal." He rejected the notion of Arab independence, however nominal; he wrote that "Sykes does not seem to be able to grasp the fact that there are parts of Turkey unfit for representative institutions."[2]

More inclined than ever to support Cairo against Simla, Sykes also came to believe that the conflict in views and in jurisdictions was harmful in itself. He argued that "our traditional way of letting various offices run their own shows, which was allright in the past when such sectors dealt with varying problems which were not related, but it is bad now that each sector is dealing in reality with a common enemy."[3] There was no central policy: Simla, Cairo, the Foreign Office, the War Office, and the Admiralty each ran its own operation, as did officials in the field, each working in ignorance of what the others were doing, and often at cross-purposes. The obstacles in the way of arriving at a policy were formidable: Sykes once counted eighteen agencies that would have to be consulted before an agreed decision could be reached.[4]

During the course of his trip, Sykes explored the idea of establishing an overall bureau to assume charge of Arab affairs. Cairo was enthusiastic; on 13 December 1915, Clayton reported that he had started to assemble the nucleus of a Near East Office and hoped that Sykes would press forward with the project.[5] Returning to London at the end of 1915, Sykes did press forward by proposing the creation of a central agency to coordinate policy: an Arab Bureau, to be established in Cairo under his own direction. The new Secretary for India, Austen Chamberlain, at the same time urged the creation of an Islamic Bureau, to combat seditious enemy propaganda in India, Persia, and Afghanistan. The Viceroy of India, in response, made it clear that he opposed the creation of any bureau that planned to intrude into areas within his jurisdiction, especially if Sykes and his friends were to be in charge. Early in January 1916 Asquith ordered an interdepartmental conference to consider the creation of an Islamic Bureau.

At the conference, agreement was reached to accept the Sykes proposal, but with a major modification that cut the substance out of it. The Arab Bureau (as it was to be called) was not to be a separate body, but merely a section of the Cairo Intelligence Department. This was insisted on by Kitchener (represented by FitzGerald) and by the Foreign Office; they did not intend to surrender the control they exercised over British policy. Cairo was authorized to establish and staff a new entity; but a central agency to take charge of overall policy was not created—and that had been the point of the Sykes proposal. The various departments of government continued to make and carry out their independent and often conflicting policies. The leading role continued to be played by Kitchener, to whom the Foreign Secretary deferred. Sykes continued to make policy only as a representative of Kitchener, and not in his own right as chief of an independent agency; Kitchener, who did not wish to relinquish control, insisted that the situation should remain that way.

The head of Naval Intelligence questioned the desirability of creating the new bureau in Cairo along the lines that Sykes and Clayton proposed; to placate him, his candidate, David G. Hogarth, an Oxford archaeologist serving as a Naval Intelligence officer, was named to be its head. Hogarth was a shadowy figure who had worked with British intelligence agencies before the war.

Hogarth replaced the acting head of the Arab Bureau, Alfred Parker, a career army officer who was Kitchener's nephew. From the outset Hogarth worked directly under Clayton, whose principal views he seems to have shared. Under Hogarth, the bureau fought to assert the views of Wingate and Clayton—who wanted to expand British Egypt's control of the Arab world—as against those of the Foreign Office and the Government of India.

An even-tempered, low-keyed officer of the Sudan government named Kinahan Cornwallis became Hogarth's deputy, and Wingate's secretary, an officer named G. S. Symes, came over to the Arab Bureau from the Sudan. Philip Graves, a former *Times* correspondent, also joined the bureau; and Hogarth brought in Thomas Edward ("T. E.") Lawrence, a young man who had worked for him at the Ashmolean Museum in Oxford and over whose career he had presided ever since.* Lawrence was later to win renown as "Lawrence of Arabia."

At the beginning Clayton did not have an expert in Turkish affairs—and in waging an intelligence war against Turkey that was an evident disadvantage. Then he had a stroke of luck. On 10 December 1915, Wyndham Deedes—who had served in the Ottoman Gendarmerie before the war—arrived in Cairo from Gallipoli; in early January Clayton succeeded in co-opting him as deputy head of Egyptian Intelligence, where his knowledge of Turkish affairs proved an invaluable asset.

Soon Cairo was bustling with young Members of Parliament and others ambitious to have a say in Middle Eastern policy, revolving around the Arab Bureau. Among them were Aubrey Herbert, M.P., and George Lloyd, M.P., both Mark Sykes's friends from before the

---

* Lawrence worked closely with the Arab Bureau, but was not officially posted to it until the end of 1916.

war. At last Cairo had become a center of British policy-making for the Middle East; and Clayton had the satisfaction of knowing that in London the real makers of Britain's Middle East policy were Cairo's leader, Lord Kitchener, and his representative, Mark Sykes.

23

MAKING PROMISES TO THE ARABS

I

When Sykes returned from the East at the end of 1915, he brought back to London something more immediately startling and of more lasting importance than his idea of creating an Arab Bureau. What he brought was news of a mysterious young Arab who claimed that he and his friends could help Britain win the war. The young man's name was Muhammed Sharif al-Faruqi.

Nothing was known of al-Faruqi then; and little is known of him now. He emerged from obscurity in the autumn of 1915, and held the attention of the British government well into 1916, before slipping back into obscurity and dying young, killed on a road in Iraq in 1920 during a tribal raid. During his months in the spotlight in 1915–16, he directly or indirectly led Britain to promise concessions to France, Russia, Arabs, and others in the postwar Middle East. As middleman between British officials and Arab leaders, he was either misunderstood or else misrepresented each to the other. One can only guess at his motives. To the twentieth-century Middle East, he left a legacy of misunderstanding that time has not yet entirely dissipated.

II

The background to the astonishing al-Faruqi episode was the quasi-agreement Lord Kitchener had reached with the Emir Hussein of Mecca at the outset of the war. As noted earlier, Lord Kitchener, regarding the Emir Hussein as a spiritual rather than a material force,* had initiated a correspondence with him in the autumn of

---

* Reginald Wingate, who governed the Sudan, was alone among Kitchener's followers in believing from the very outset of the Ottoman war that Hussein could be of *military* assistance to Britain.

173

1914 that had been concluded on terms satisfactory to both men. Hussein* was to do nothing for the moment; he would not use his spiritual prestige against Britain in the Ottoman war (as Kitchener had feared he might do) and, at some future point, he would use it in favor of Britain (as Kitchener hoped he would do when the war was over and British rivalry with Russia resumed).

Matters having been settled early in 1915, the British Residency in Cairo was surprised to receive another letter from Hussein half a year later, in the summer of 1915, suddenly demanding—without explanation—that almost all of Arab Asia should become an independent kingdom under his rule. (As indicated earlier, British officials were unaware that Hussein would understand that they were offering him a kingdom when they suggested that he should become the Arab caliph; and it was the kingdom, not the caliphate, that tempted him at the time.)

Hussein's unexpected demand, coming without explanation after months of silence, aroused wonder and mirth in British Cairo. An amused Ronald Storrs commented that Hussein ought to be satisfied to be allowed to keep the province of the Hejaz. Storrs commented that Hussein "knows he is demanding, possibly as a basis of negotiations, far more than he has the right, the hope, or the power to expect."[1] Sir Henry McMahon, the British High Commissioner in Egypt, not wishing to discourage Hussein, gently replied to him that discussion of Middle Eastern frontiers ought to be postponed until the end of the war.

But Hussein's sudden demand for an independent Arab kingdom was by no means the unreasonable act that it appeared to be at the time in Cairo. Unbeknownst to McMahon and Storrs, what had happened in Mecca was that in January 1915 Hussein had discovered written evidence that the Ottoman government was planning to depose him at the end of the war—and indeed had postponed deposing him only because of the coming of the war.[2] He promptly sent his son Feisal to see the Grand Vizier in Constantinople, but learned that there was little chance of persuading the Porte to reverse this decision.

The Young Turk plan to depose him forced Hussein, against his inclinations, to consider opposing Turkey in the war. Fearing that to do so might isolate him in the Arab world, Hussein sent Feisal to Damascus to sound out the possibility of obtaining support from the Arab secret societies headquartered there. In carrying out this mission, Feisal stopped in Damascus twice: *en route* to

---

* Hussein ibn Ali, the Sherif of Mecca and its Emir, is referred to variously as Hussein, the Sherif, the Sherif Hussein, the Emir Hussein and, later, King Hussein. He is also referred to as the ruler of the Hejaz and, later, as King of the Hejaz.

Constantinople to see the Grand Vizier, and again on his way back from Constantinople afterwards.

On his first stop in Damascus, in late March 1915, Feisal was told that there were three Ottoman army divisions with mainly Arab soldiers concentrated in the Damascus area, and that the secret society conspirators believed that these divisions would follow their lead. Though they talked of leading a revolt against Turkey, the members of the secret societies also expressed reservations about doing so. For one thing, most of them believed Germany would soon win the war; they were bound to ask themselves why they should join the losing side. For another, as between the Ottoman Empire and the European Allies, they preferred to be ruled by Moslem Turks than by European Christians.

Although evidence of what they were planning is scanty, the secret societies apparently were inclined to set up a bidding competition between Britain and Turkey for Arab loyalties. They advised Hussein (through Feisal) not to join the Allies unless Britain pledged to support independence for most of Arab western Asia. With such a British pledge in hand, the secret societies could then have asked the Ottoman Empire to match it.

After his meetings in Damascus, Feisal proceeded to Constantinople to meet with the Grand Vizier. When he returned to Damascus on 23 May 1915, on his way home, he found the situation considerably changed. Djemal Pasha, the Turkish governor of Syria, had scented an Arab plot and taken steps to smash it. He had crushed the secret societies, arresting many of the ringleaders and dispersing others. He had broken up the three Arab army divisions, and had sent many of their officers away to Gallipoli and elsewhere.[3]

A handful of the remaining conspirators—six men according to one account, nine according to another[4]—now told Feisal that they could no longer initiate a revolt against the Ottoman Empire; Hussein should do it, and they would follow him—*if* Hussein could first induce the British to pledge support for Arab independence.

The men of the secret societies had drafted a document defining the territories that were to be Arab and independent. The document was called the Damascus Protocol. Feisal brought it back from Damascus to Mecca. It set forth the demands that the Emir Hussein was to submit to Britain. Hussein had nothing to lose in making the demands. Doing so would help him obtain support from the secret societies—for whatever that might be worth—when he launched his revolt; it would also stake his claim to leadership in Arabian and Arab politics, and would help to justify his support of Christians against Moslem Turkey. So in the summer of 1915 he sent his letter incorporating the Damascus Protocol demands to the British Residency in Cairo, where the demands—as has been seen—were not taken seriously.

III

Lieutenant Muhammed Sharif al-Faruqi, a 24-year-old Arab Ottoman staff officer from Mosul (in what is now Iraq), was a secret society member stationed in Damascus at the time of Feisal's first stop there in early 1915. He may have been among those who met with Feisal there at that time; if not, he learned what had been said from colleagues who had attended the meeting.

Al-Faruqi was one of the secret society officers ordered out of Damascus and sent by Djemal Pasha to the Gallipoli front, where casualties were high. Sending suspected Arab plotters to the front lines to be killed looked to be a deliberate policy of Djemal's in crushing sedition. On the other hand, there were valid military reasons for sending troops to reinforce the Gallipoli front where the Ottoman regime was fighting for survival. Al-Faruqi may have suspected, but could not have been sure, that his posting to Gallipoli showed that Djemal suspected him of treason.

Al-Faruqi kept in touch with secret society officers who remained in Damascus. From them he learned further details of what Feisal and Hussein were doing. He learned that the remnant of the secret societies in Damascus had encouraged Hussein to lead an Arab revolt against the Ottoman Empire if Britain would first agree to support the Damascus Protocol: the secret society program for Arab independence. He learned, too, that Hussein had in fact written to the British in Cairo in the summer of 1915 incorporating the Damascus Protocol in his letter and presenting it as his own set of demands for his establishment as monarch of an Arab kingdom comprising almost all of Arab western Asia.

In the autumn of 1915, Lieutenant al-Faruqi deserted the Ottoman forces at Gallipoli and crossed over to Allied lines. He claimed to have important information for British Intelligence in Cairo, and was promptly sent to Egypt for interrogation. Perhaps he feared that Djemal was about to obtain proof of his membership in the anti-Turkish conspiracy, and decided to escape while there was time. Perhaps he hoped to win glory by playing a lone hand in world politics. Whatever his motives, he acted on an impulse of his own: nobody had entrusted him with a mission.

Al-Faruqi spoke little English, and it is difficult to tell from the fragmentary historical record the extent to which he was correctly understood or the extent to which words were put in his mouth by those who wanted to hear what they claimed he said. Under interrogation by British Intelligence officials, the young officer claimed to be a member of the secret Arab military society al-'Ahd. He invoked the name of its leading figure stationed in Damascus, General Yasin al-Hashimi, Chief of Staff of the Ottoman 12th Division, and although al-Faruqi admitted that "I am not authorized to discuss with you officially" the proposals of al-'Ahd, the young deserter pretended—for whatever reason—to be a spokesman for the organization and was accepted as such by Gilbert Clayton, the head of British Intelligence in Cairo.[5] Though his story was unverified, British Intelligence believed it and did not investigate further. He was not in fact a representative of al-'Ahd or indeed of any other group: Clayton had been duped.

What gave plausibility to al-Faruqi's claim to represent al-'Ahd was that—from his colleagues in Damascus—he knew the details of the British correspondence with Sherif Hussein and knew about the demands that Hussein had sent to Cairo in the summer of 1915.

Al-Faruqi, purportedly speaking for the Arab army officers in Damascus, demanded that Britain give a pledge to support an independent Arab state within the frontiers that Hussein had outlined. When he did so the pieces suddenly seemed to fall into place for British Intelligence. Clayton grasped the essential fact it was no coincidence that the two sets of demands were identical and that both were the same as those that al-Masri—the founder of al-'Ahd—and other Arab exiles in Cairo had been making since the outset of the war. If the secret societies were backing Hussein, the Emir of Mecca was no longer to be thought of as representing merely his section of the Arabian peninsula. For if the Arab secret societies were as powerful as al-Faruqi represented them to be and as Clayton erroneously imagined them to be, Hussein would be speaking for hundreds of thousands of Ottoman troops and millions of Ottoman subjects.

Al-Faruqi warned Clayton and his colleagues that they must reply to Hussein immediately. According to al-Faruqi, the British had to guarantee the independence of the Arabic-speaking Middle East if they wanted al-'Ahd to lead an Arab rising within the Ottoman Empire. Presenting an ultimatum, the young man gave Britain only a few weeks to accept the offer; otherwise, he said, the Arab movement would throw all of its support behind Germany and the Ottoman Empire.

Cairo was seized with excitement. Ronald Storrs wrote to FitzGerald/Kitchener on 10 October 1915, that "The Arab question is reaching an acute state."[6] At about the same time Clayton composed a memorandum outlining his conversations with al-Faruqi for General Maxwell, the British army commander in Egypt, who urgently cabled Kitchener on 12 October that a "powerful organisation" existed behind enemy lines, that Hussein's proposals had actually come from that organization, and that unless agreement were reached with it, the Arabs would go over to the enemy.[7*]

Kitchener's followers in Cairo apparently believed that an Arab

---

* A curious assertion, since the Arabs were already in the enemy camp.

rebellion would enable them to save the Allied armies who were fighting for their lives at the edges of the Gallipoli peninsula in the Dardanelles. The British army commander at Gallipoli was Ian Hamilton, a Kitchener protégé, and Kitchener's Cairo followers may well have been in touch with him to help them persuade the reluctant High Commissioner in Egypt, Sir Henry McMahon, to meet the Arab demands. That they did so is suggested by a statement made by McMahon a year later, disavowing responsibility for the (by then unsuccessful) Arab Revolt. According to McMahon,

> It was the most unfortunate date in my life when I was left in charge of the Arab movement and I think a few words are necessary to explain that it is nothing to do with me: it is purely military business. It began at the urgent request of Sir Ian Hamilton at Gallipoli. I was begged by the Foreign Office to take immediate action and draw the Arabs out of the war. At that moment a large portion of the forces at Gallipoli and nearly the whole of the force in Mesopotamia were Arabs ...[8]

While urgently pleading with London for authorization to meet al-Faruqi's demands, the Residency reported that those demands were open to negotiation: the young Arab would make concessions where necessary. In the weeks and months that followed, al-Faruqi succeeded in remaining at the center of the dialogue. In what was becoming a great hoax, the young man drew and redrew the frontiers of countries and empires, in the course of exchanges among the British Residency, the Emir of Mecca, and Arab nationalist leaders, each of whom took al-Faruqi to be the emissary of one of the other parties. Al-Faruqi introduced himself in a letter to Hussein as an al-'Ahd member who had the ear of the British, while in Cairo he purported to negotiate for Hussein. Feisal tried to discover the identity of the mysterious Arab who had become so important in Cairo, but learned only his name, which told him nothing: "I did not know him," Feisal wrote in a report to Hussein.[9]

IV

Clayton, who was strongly disposed to oppose French claims to the interior of Syria (on a line that runs from Aleppo to Damascus through Homs and Hama), reported that al-Faruqi said Hussein would never allow France to have Aleppo, Homs, Hama, and Damascus. Whether Clayton was quoting, misquoting, or paraphrasing what al-Faruqi actually told him may never be known. Clayton recognized that France could not be excluded from the coast of Syria-Lebanon, where Christians under French patronage resided; and again he reported that al-Faruqi fell in with his views, and seemed willing, in Hussein's name, to surrender Arab claims in that area. Al-Faruqi informed Hussein that he had been asked to make such a concession—and had refused.

Based on Clayton's reports, the High Commissioner, Sir Henry McMahon, in a cable to the Foreign Office quoted al-Faruqi as saying that the Emir of Mecca would not insist on maintaining his original demand that his western frontier should extend to the sea, but that he would oppose "by force of arms" any French attempt to occupy the districts of Aleppo, Homs, Hama, and Damascus.[10] McMahon and Clayton wanted authorization to accept these terms.

But the geographical references made by McMahon were hazy. Was reference made, for example, to the city of Damascus, the environs of Damascus, or the province of Damascus? Did "districts" mean *wilayahs* (environs) or *vilayets* (provinces)? Was it al-Faruqi who spoke of districts, or was it McMahon or Clayton? By districts, did the British mean towns?

The significance of the Aleppo-Homs-Hama-Damascus demand has been bitterly debated ever since. For decades afterward partisans of an Arab Palestine argued that if these four geographical terms were properly understood, British Cairo had promised that Palestine would be Arab; while partisans of a Jewish Palestine argued the reverse. In a sense the debate was pointless; as will be seen, when the time came to make pledges, McMahon deliberately used phrases so devious as to commit himself to nothing at all.

If Clayton was the author of the Aleppo-Homs-Hama-Damascus geographical definition, he was probably thinking of Syria and Lebanon and of how to split off the interior of the country from the French-influenced coast. The seacoast represented one of the two north-south lines of civilization in Syria; the four towns represented the other. Situated between mountain and unrelieved desert, they defined the long narrow corridor which was the agriculturally cultivated region of inland Syria. On the map of Syria in the then-current (1910) edition of the *Encyclopaedia Britannica*, Damascus, Aleppo, Homs, and Hama are shown as the only towns of inland Syria; so they were the towns an Englishman might specify if he sought to define the territory of inland Syria. Granted, the towns are dissimilar, so that leading historians[*] have thought it illogical to group them together; but to a reader of the *Encyclopaedia* the logic of grouping them together would be evident.

The towns had another important feature in common: they constituted the railroad line. The French-built line of the Société Ottomane

---

[*] Professor Elie Kedourie among them.

du Chemin de Fer Damas-Hama et Prolongements, which was opened in 1895, connected Aleppo in the north of Syria to Damascus in the south.[11] Damascus, Aleppo, Homs, and Hama were its four stops. At Damascus one made the connection with the Hejaz railroad, which ran south to Medina, connecting Syria with Hussein's domain. Surely this would have appeared to be of immense significance at the time; and if al-Faruqi, not Clayton, was the one who first mentioned the four towns by name, surely it was this that he had in mind.

In an era in which railroads were considered to be of prime military and political importance, any soldier or politician representing Hussein in a territorial negotiation would presumably have insisted on gaining control of the railroad stations: not merely of Damascus, as the metropolis of the south, and of Aleppo, as the metropolis of the north, but also of the two railroad towns that connected them: Homs and Hama.

Recent experience dictated the demand. The Young Turks (before the war intervened) had planned to dominate the Hejaz by control of the railroad line running from Damascus down to the main cities of the Hejaz. It was only to be expected that if Hussein were on the winning side of the war he would pursue the mirror opposite of their strategy: he would dominate inland Syria by control of its railroad line.

Whether or not they formulated al-Faruqi's Aleppo-to-Damascus demands, Clayton and his friends were afraid that other British officials might not understand the importance of meeting them. Referring to Sir Milne Cheetham, his superior at the Residency who had been acting head until McMahon arrived, Ronald Storrs wrote to FitzGerald/Kitchener at Christmas imploring them to give priority to the Arab negotiation and adding "Excuse my worrying you with these difficulties, but if you knew the difficulty Clayton and I had all last autumn in getting Sir Milne to make any proposal about, or take any interest in, the Arab question, you would understand our anxiety."[12]

Clayton's luck was that Sir Mark Sykes—as mentioned earlier—had stopped in Cairo again on his way back from India to London in November 1915. Having told Sykes the al-Faruqi story, Clayton and his colleagues infected Sykes with their belief in the electrifying possibility that the Arab half of the Ottoman Empire might come over to the Allied side of the war. This was the amazing news that greeted Sykes on his arrival, and that necessarily altered all calculations.

That the Arabic-speaking world could be a major factor in the war came as especial news to Sykes. His view of politics in the area had been that arrangements were made between the rival foreign Great Powers; the interests and aspirations of native populations had not entered in any significant way into his calculations. He had always admired the Turkish-speaking ruling class but had not thought much of the subject populations of the Ottoman Empire in Asia. His undergraduate descriptions of them had been an exercise in pejorative vocabulary.

Of town Arabs, he had written that they were "cowardly," "insolent yet dispicable [sic]," "vicious as far as their feeble bodies will admit." Bedouin Arabs were "rapacious, greedy . . . animals."[13] Yet these were to be Britain's key allies in the Middle Eastern fighting, according to the new information supplied by Clayton. Sykes, who had a reputation for picking up opinions and arguments without taking the time to think them through, now showed that he could discard them with equal ease. He became a sudden convert to the cause of the native peoples of the Middle East.

From school days onward, Sykes had harbored an abiding and almost obsessive fear of Jews, whose web of dangerous international intrigue he discerned in many an obscure corner. Yet there was another group about which his feelings had been even more violent. "Even Jews have their good points," he had written, "but Armenians have none."[14] Now Sykes met with Armenian leaders in Cairo, and enthusiastically proposed the creation of an Armenian army, to be recruited from prisoners-of-war and Armenians in the United States, to invade Turkey. He gave it as his opinion that he could have the army in being in about eight weeks.[15]

Newly enthusiastic about Middle Easterners, Sykes was entirely won over to Clayton's view that Arab armies could supply the key to victory. Clayton primed him to return to London prepared to argue Cairo's new thesis that Hussein could be more important than the French in bringing the war in the East to a swift conclusion.

Clayton also coached Aubrey Herbert, an M.P. serving in Cairo Intelligence, who was returning to London, and who undertook to see Lord Kitchener and the Foreign Secretary, Sir Edward Grey, to explain matters to them. Herbert, with Clayton's help, drafted a strong memorandum urging the French to give up their claim to Damascus, Aleppo, Homs, and Hama, so that the towns could be ceded to Hussein.

V

With much that was new to report and to advocate, Sykes returned to a warm welcome in London in December 1915. It was then that he proposed creating an Arab Bureau and took the first steps leading to its establishment (see Chapter 22).

No other man had met with every important British officer from the Balkans and Egypt to India. Maurice Hankey arranged an audience for him with King George. Hankey also arranged for Sykes to go before the inner War Committee of the Cabinet, of which he was Secretary.

The principal message that Sykes brought back to the Cabinet was that the Arabs—whom he had previously disregarded as a factor in the war—were now of prime importance to the Allies; and that it was vitally and urgently important to reach agreement with Hussein.

Although Cairo and Sykes seemed unaware of the fact, in London it was recognized that Britain would have to pay a price—and a high one—to obtain France's consent to the making of promises to Hussein; she would have to make major concessions to the French in return for the privilege of being allowed to make concessions to the Arabs. Kitchener and Grey were willing to pay the price. Others were not.

It was the view of Lord Curzon, former Viceroy of India, that no promises should be made to the Arabs because they were "a people who are at this moment fighting against us as hard as they can."[16] The new Secretary of State for India, Austen Chamberlain, was also opposed to doing so; but Kitchener, backing Sykes, Clayton, and Storrs, vehemently insisted on authorizing Cairo to respond immediately and to reach agreement with Hussein; and Kitchener's views carried the day. Authorized and directed to do so by London, Sir Henry McMahon then resumed the correspondence with Mecca—the famous McMahon letters, the meaning of which has been debated so much and so long by partisans of Arab and Jewish causes in Palestine.*

In the interim, Hussein had written McMahon a second letter. In it he accused McMahon of "lukewarmth and hesitancy" because of his reluctance to discuss frontiers and boundaries. Had they been merely his own claims (the Emir continued) such a discussion indeed could have been postponed until the end of the war. But they were not his own claims. They did not even represent his own suggestions. They were demands that had been formulated by others: by "our people."[17] Cairo Residency officials now knew that this meant the mysterious secret society conspirators whom they imagined had a mass following in the Arab world.

On 24 October 1915 McMahon replied in a quite different spirit to Hussein. Instructed by Lord Kitchener to make the necessary pledges, he reluctantly agreed to enter into a discussion of specific territories and frontiers; but as he evidently was unwilling to assume

---

* As noted earlier, advocates of an Arab Palestine have argued for decades that the geographical terms employed by McMahon, if properly interpreted, indicate that McMahon was pledging that Palestine would be Arab; and advocates of a Jewish Palestine have argued the reverse.

personal responsibility for making definite commitments, he used language evasively. On the one hand, he agreed that after the war the Arabs should have their independence; but, on the other, he indicated that European advisers and officials would be needed to establish the administration of Arab countries, and insisted that these advisers and officials should be exclusively British. In other words, any "independent" Arab kingdom in the postwar Middle East would have to be a British protectorate.

What territories should be included in the British-protected independent Arab kingdom? McMahon replied by dividing the lands claimed by Hussein into four areas and explaining that Britain could not bind herself to support Hussein's claims in any one of them.

McMahon began by remarking that Hussein must give up claim to territory west of the districts of Damascus, Aleppo, Homs, and Hama. Al-Faruqi already had agreed (or at least McMahon thought he had) that Hussein would concede this point. McMahon later wrote that he intended to say that the territories Hussein and the Arabs were not to have were coastal Syria, Lebanon, and Palestine, with an eastern frontier that might be drawn somewhere in what is now Jordan. His language can be read that way, but on a more natural reading he was referring only to Syria-Lebanon here, not Palestine.

In the eastern portion of the Arabic-speaking Middle East, the Mesopotamian provinces of Basra and Baghdad, McMahon observed that the established position and interests of Britain were such that she would have to establish "special administrative arrangements" with respect to them; whether such arrangements would leave any room for an assertion of Arab sovereignty—and if so when and to what extent—was left unsaid.

In the western portion—Syria and Palestine—Britain could extend assurances to Hussein only in those territories "in which she can act without detriment to the interests of her ally France." Since France at the time claimed those territories in their entirety (indeed Sykes discussed France's claim to Palestine with al-Faruqi in November 1915) it followed that Britain could not pledge support for Arab claims with respect to them either—not even to Damascus, Aleppo, Homs, and Hama.

That left only Arabia, which at the time was divided among a number of leaders, of whom Hussein was one. Britain at the time enjoyed treaty relationships with other Arabian chiefs, including Hussein's rival, Ibn Saud. In his letter, McMahon pointed out that he could not promise anything to Hussein that would prejudice Britain's relationships with other Arab chiefs. By process of elimination, therefore, Britain did not bind herself to support Hussein's claims anywhere at all.

According to a summary later published in the secret *Arab Bulletin* (no. 5, 18 June 1916), for Britain's military, political, and intelligence leaders, the upshot of the correspondence was that His Majesty's Government had indicated a willingness to promote independence in Arabic-speaking Asia but had refused to commit itself with respect to the forms of government that would be installed in the area or with respect to precise boundaries.

McMahon, an experienced bureaucrat, had seen the need to be completely noncommittal. The negotiations between Sykes and the French about the future of the Middle East—to be described presently—had not yet taken place, and nobody in the British government knew with any certainty what would have to be conceded to France or, afterwards, to Russia. McMahon was under orders from Kitchener not to lose the alliance with Hussein; but the High Commissioner must have feared that he would be made the scapegoat if he did go ahead to meet Hussein's demands, and later it was discovered that those demands clashed with other conflicting commitments Britain might be called upon to make.

Such fears were by no means unreasonable. As Wyndham Deedes—the Cairo Intelligence expert on the Ottoman Empire—analyzed the situation early in 1916, there were three groups of Arabs; and in all honesty Britain could not agree to satisfy the demands of any one of the three. There were the Syrians, whose main aim was that the hated French should not be allowed in ("It is difficult rather to account for this extraordinary dislike ...," he wrote, but nonetheless it was there); and of course that ran counter to the demands of France. There was Hussein, whose aim was to head an Arab kingdom; but Deedes said that most Arabs and all Turks would be opposed to this. He wrote that "I think it is the view of most of us, and is the view of many of the Arabs and all of the Turks themselves" that "this idea is not a practical one." Other Arabs, wrote Deedes, were unwilling to accept Hussein as their leader. Finally, there were the Arabs of Iraq, who (he believed) wanted independence for themselves, but were up against the intention of the Government of India to annex and rule them. Deedes feared that the difficulties in the way of arriving at an understanding with the Arabs accordingly might prove "insuperable."[18]

It therefore would have been dangerous for McMahon as High Commissioner to have made any firm commitments to Hussein. He believed that the impatient Wingate had tried to push him into doing so. But Reginald Wingate wrote to Clayton that McMahon had misinterpreted his views, as had Lord Hardinge, the Viceroy of India:

I am afraid both the High Commissioner and Lord Hardinge are under the impression that I am a believer in the creation of a consolidated Arab Kingdom under the Sherif—Of course any such notion is altogether remote from my real views, but it has suited me, as I believe it has suited all of us, to give the leaders of the Arab movement this impression and we are quite sufficiently covered by the correspondence which has taken place to show that we are acting in good faith with the Arabs as far as we have gone.[19]

Gilbert Clayton, who strongly opposed defining Britain's relations with the Arabs until the war was over, believed that the McMahon letters had succeeded in putting the matter off and in avoiding the giving of any meaningful commitment. Months later Clayton summarized what McMahon had done by writing that "Luckily we have been very careful indeed to commit ourselves to nothing whatsoever."[20]

Hussein replied to McMahon that he could not accept the Aleppo-Homs-Hama-Damascus formula. He insisted on having the provinces of Aleppo and Beirut. Noting France's claim to Lebanon, he wrote that "any concession designed to give France or any other Power possession of a single square foot of territory in those parts is quite out of the question." So he failed to reach agreement with McMahon, but felt compelled to support the Allies nonetheless: the Young Turks were going to depose him, so he had to rebel against them whether Britain met his terms or not. In a conversation some years later with David Hogarth, of the Arab Bureau of British Intelligence in Cairo, Hussein indicated that with regard to Palestine and also with regard to Lebanon and the other lands in the Middle East, he did not regard matters as having been settled. He indicated that he regarded all matters as being subject to negotiation at the Peace Conference. According to Hogarth, "He compared ourselves and himself . . . to two persons about to inhabit one house, but not agreed which should take which floors or rooms."[21]

In London the Foreign Office took the view that the promises would never become due for payment: that Britain had pledged herself to support Arab independence only if the Arab half of the Ottoman Empire rose against the Sultan—which (the Foreign Office believed) it would never do. Since the Arabs would not keep their side of the bargain (so ran the argument), the British would be under no obligation to keep theirs. The Foreign Office, which did not rely on Clayton, but had its own sources of information, did not believe that the Arabic-speaking world was about to change sides in the war, but the Foreign Secretary, Sir Edward Grey, saw no harm in letting Kitchener and his lieutenants promise anything they wanted as an inducement to the Arabs to defect. Grey told Austen Chamberlain not to worry about the offers being made by Cairo as "the whole thing was a castle in the air which would never materialize."[22]

McMahon, on the other hand, worried that the whole thing might *not* be a castle in the air. He came, after all, from the Government of India, whose constant anxiety was the prospect of nationalist agitation. McMahon confided to Wyndham Deedes that his fear was not that the plan for an Arab revolt would break down, but rather that it would succeed—and then would pose a danger to Britain.[23]

To the Viceroy of India, who claimed that India's interests were neglected in the correspondence with Hussein, McMahon explained that "I had necessarily to be vague as on the one hand HMG disliked being committed to definite future action, and on the other hand any detailed definition of our demands would have frightened off the Arab." He claimed that the negotiations with Hussein would neither "establish our rights . . . or bind our hands."[24]

This explanation disturbed the Viceroy, who wrote to the Secretary of State for India about McMahon's claim "that the negotiations are merely a matter of words and will neither establish our rights, nor bind our hands in that country. That may prove eventually to be the case, especially if the Arabs continue to help the enemy, but I did not like pledges given when there is no intention of keeping them."[25]

In early 1916 Aziz al-Masri, the Arab secret society leader, wrote to Lord Kitchener approaching the argument from the other side. He wrote (in French, the language of diplomacy) that Britain could not achieve her objectives in the Arabic-speaking Middle East unless she were willing to leave its peoples free to exercise full and genuine independence. Those for whom he spoke wanted from Britain "*non pas une domination ou un protectorat*," that is, they did not want British domination or a British protectorate.[26] They would not accept what McMahon and Clayton called Arab independence: they demanded the real thing. They would not support Britain, he wrote, if she intended to govern them—which of course was exactly what McMahon and Clayton intended Britain to do.

Al-Masri had spotted the falseness in the British position. Kitchener and his followers badly wanted to win Arab support but were unwilling to pay the price the Emir Hussein demanded for it; so instead they were attempting to cheat, by pretending to meet Hussein's demands when in fact they were giving him the counterfeit coin of meaningless language.

Though Clayton and his colleagues did not know it, al-Masri, al-Faruqi, and the Emir Hussein were offering Britain coin that was equally counterfeit. Hussein had no army, and the secret societies had no visible following. Their talk of rallying tens or hundreds of thousands of Arab troops to their cause, whether or not they believed it themselves, was sheer fantasy.

Al-Faruqi, who had promised an Arab revolt when he first arrived, changed his story by 15 November, when he met Sir Mark Sykes: he now said that there could be no Arab uprising until and unless Allied armies first landed in force on the Syrian coast. Hussein, too, hoping Britain would take the military lead, refused to go into action by claiming it would be premature to launch an uprising. The Arabs, in other words, would do nothing until British armies arrived on the scene. Sykes, accepting these statements at face value, concluded that it was urgent for Britain to invade Syria and Palestine.

24

MAKING PROMISES TO THE EUROPEAN ALLIES

I

In December 1915 Sykes reported to his government that in Cairo he had been told by al-Faruqi that if British Egypt were to launch an invasion of Palestine and Syria, it would trigger a revolt in which the Arabic-speaking troops and provinces of the Ottoman Empire would come over to the Allied side. The problem was that Britain needed France's permission to divert the resources from the western front to launch such an offensive; and what Sykes told the Cabinet ministers was that they ought to seek such permission from the French immediately. (France was reluctant to allow any diversion of resources from Europe, and not without reason; early in 1916 Germany attacked Verdun in what by 1918 was to become the biggest battle in world history. Seven hundred thousand men on both sides were to be killed, wounded, gassed, or captured at Verdun in 1916, and 1,200,000 at the Somme; it was not a year in which the Allies could easily afford to send manpower elsewhere.)

At the same time, Sykes raised a related matter: the Sherif Hussein hesitated to come over to the Allied side (Sykes reported) for fear of French ambitions in the Arabic-speaking world. Negotiations with France aimed at allaying such fears were the answer, he said. If these problems with France were not resolved soon, Sykes warned, the Sherif might be deposed and killed by the Turks, and events in the Holy Places might ignite a *real* Holy War.[1]

The radical new view that Sykes had brought back with him from the Middle East was that in terms of winning the war, the Arabs were more important than the French.[2] France was a modern industrial power that had mobilized eight million men to fight the war, while Hussein, without industrial, financial, military, or manpower resources, brought with him only an uncertain prospect of subverting loyalty in the Ottoman camp; in retrospect, Sykes's new view was unbalanced, but his government nonetheless attempted to persuade France to make the concessions Sykes believed to be necessary.

In fact, the British government already had initiated talks with France. Britain could not make promises about Syria to the Emir Hussein without France's permission, for the Foreign Secretary, Sir Edward Grey, had recognized France's special interest in that area. Moreover, al-Faruqi had persuaded Lord Kitchener and his followers that Hussein's claims to Syria also had to be accommodated, at least to some extent. The Foreign Office, having authorized McMahon to make pledges to Hussein on 20 October 1915, therefore immediately requested the French government to send a delegate over to London to negotiate the future frontiers of Syria so as to define the extent to which Britain was free to deal with Hussein. Thus not only the McMahon letters, but also—and more importantly— the negotiations with France, Russia, and later Italy that ultimately resulted in the Sykes-Picot-Sazanov Agreement and subsequent Allied secret treaty understandings were among the results of Lieutenant al-Faruqi's hoax.

II

The French representative, François Georges Picot, came over to London and commenced negotiations on 23 November 1915. The British negotiating team was at first headed by Sir Arthur Nicolson, Permanent Under-Secretary at the Foreign Office, and included senior representatives from the Foreign, India, and War Offices. The talks had deadlocked by the time Sykes returned to London in December; late that month the British government delegated Sykes—Kitchener's man—to take the place of the Nicolson team in order to break the deadlock. In effect the Foreign Office turned the responsibility over to Lord Kitchener.

Sykes possessed some of the qualifications necessary to carry out his assignment. He passionately wanted to succeed in reaching an agreement with the other side. He was pro-French. As a result of early schooling abroad, he spoke French—though it is not clear how well. As a Roman Catholic himself, he was not prejudiced against France's goal of promoting Catholic interests in Lebanon. He had lived and traveled in the East, and had met with and knew the views of Britain's soldiers and civil servants there.

On the other hand, he had held government office for less than a year, and it was his first diplomatic assignment. He had no experience in negotiating with a foreign government, and was in a weak bargaining position because he wanted too much from the other side, too obviously.

Until 3 January 1916 Sykes went to the French embassy on a daily basis to negotiate. He reported in detail at night to FitzGerald and through him continued to receive the ghostly guidance of Kitchener.[3] It is impossible to know what Sykes said or was told: Kitchener and FitzGerald kept no proper files, and none of the three men left a record of what occurred. There may have been a misunderstanding between them as to what Sykes was instructed to demand and what he was told to concede. Later, in describing his dealings with Lord Kitchener, Mark Sykes remarked that "I could never make myself understood; I could never understand what he thought, and he could never understand what I thought."[4]

There is more evidence from the French side of the negotiations than from the British side as to the secret hopes and plans that were involved. Documents exist that establish what Picot and his political associates hoped to gain from the negotiations and how they hoped to achieve their goals.

Picot, the scion of a colonialist dynasty in France—his father was a founder of the Comité de l'Afrique Française, and his brother was treasurer of the Comité de l'Asie Française, of which his father was also a member—acted effectively as the advocate of the colonialist party within the Quai d'Orsay and was as dedicated a proponent of a French Syria as his government could have chosen to represent it.[5] Earlier in 1915 Picot had inspired a parliamentary campaign in Paris against the ministers who were prepared to give way to Britain in the Middle East. The mixture of domestic French commercial, clerical, and political interests in support of Picot's position proved potent. The Lyons and Marseilles Chambers of Commerce sent resolutions to the Quai d'Orsay in support of a French Syria. Proponents of a French Syria took control of the Committee on Foreign Affairs of the Chamber of Deputies.[6]

Pierre-Etienne Flandin, leader of the French Syria movement in the Senate, issued a report on Syria and Palestine in 1915 that became the manifesto of the "Syrian Party" in French politics—the party that Picot championed. Syria and Palestine form one country, he argued, that for centuries had been shaped by France, to such an extent that it formed the France of the Near East. (His argument harked back nearly a thousand years, to the Crusades and the establishment of Latin Crusader kingdoms in Syria and Palestine.) It was incumbent upon France to continue its *mission historique* there, he wrote. The potential wealth of the country was immense, he claimed, so that for commercial reasons, as well as historic and geographic ones, it was vital for the French Empire to possess it. Then, too, according to Flandin, it was vital for strategic reasons. Paralleling Kitchener's views about Mecca and the caliphate, Flandin claimed that Damascus was the third holiest city in Islam and was the potential center of an Arabic Islam; France dared not let another power direct it and perhaps use it against France.[7] Flandin claimed that at heart Syria-Palestine was French already. Its inhabitants, according to him and his colleagues, were unanimous in desiring to be ruled by France.

The French deluded themselves. Opposition to French rule was intense among the educated classes in Syria (other than the Maronites, the Eastern-rite Roman Catholic community sponsored by France). Sykes and his friends in Cairo believed that the French were blinding themselves when they ignored this opposition. (Clayton and his colleagues did not see, however, that they were deluding themselves in the same way by thinking that the peoples of those areas ardently desired to be governed by Britain.)

Picot drafted his own negotiating instructions outlining a strategy to win the concessions that he wanted from the British. They show that he would have preferred to preserve the Ottoman Empire intact, for its "feeble condition" offered France "limitless scope" to expand her economic influence.[8] Partition had become inevitable, however; it therefore was advisable to take control of Syria and Palestine, even though France would dismember the Ottoman Empire by doing so.

The French Foreign Office recognized that policing inland Syria would strain French resources; what Picot and his government most desired was to assert direct French rule only over the Mediterranean coastline and an enlarged Lebanon, and to control the rest of Syria indirectly through Arab puppet rulers. Picot's plan was to pretend to Sykes that France insisted on obtaining direct rule over all of Syria, so that when he moderated the claim he could obtain some concession in return. What he hoped to get was an extension of the French sphere of influence eastward from Syria to Mosul (in what is now Iraq).

In secretly planning to take Mosul, Picot was unaware that Kitchener and Sykes were secretly planning to give it to him. They wanted the French sphere of influence to be extended from the Mediterranean coast on the west all the way to the east so that it paralleled and adjoined Russian-held zones; the French zone was to provide Britain with a shield against Russia. France and Russia would be balanced one against the other, so that the French Middle East, like the Great Wall of China, would protect the British Middle East from attack by the Russian barbarians to the north. This concept had appeared in the de Bunsen proceedings. It had been suggested to Kitchener, perhaps by Storrs, and it became central to his strategic plan for the postwar East. Even Britain's claim to Mosul, with the oil riches strongly suspected to exist there, was to be sacrificed in order to place the French in the front line, at a point where the Russians might be expected one day to attack. The War Office point of view was that "From a military point of view, the principle of inserting a wedge of French territory between any British zone and the Russian Caucasus would seem in every way desirable."[9]

On the British side of the negotiations Sykes also wanted France's agreement to an Egyptian offensive; Kitchener wanted Alexandretta, and an agreement that Britain could invade the Ottoman Empire at Alexandretta; Sykes held a brief from Cairo to reserve the towns in Syria that were being promised to the Sherif Hussein; and nobody in the British government wanted to see any other Great Power established in the postwar world astride the road to India. It was a challenging agenda, especially for Sykes, a neophyte in diplomacy.

The British feared that Picot would not compromise on France's claim to exercise direct rule over all of Syria, while the French feared that they would not be allowed to rule any of it, not even coastal Lebanon. Picot argued that Christian Lebanon would not tolerate even the nominal rule of the Emir of Mecca, while Paul Cambon, the French ambassador in London, warned that French rule would be necessary to avert the outbreak of a religious war: "It is enough to know the intensity of rivalries between the various rites and religions in the Orient to foresee the violence of the internal strife in Lebanon as soon as no external authority is there to curb it."[10]

In the end both Sykes and Picot obtained what they wanted from one another: France was to rule a Greater Lebanon and to exert an exclusive influence over the rest of Syria. Sykes succeeded in giving, and Picot succeeded in taking, a sphere of French influence that extended to Mosul. Basra and Baghdad, the two Mesopotamian provinces, were to go to Britain.

Palestine proved to be a stumbling block. Sykes wanted it for Britain, even though Lord Kitchener did not, while Picot was determined to get it for France. In the end a compromise was reached: Britain was to have the ports of Acre and Haifa (rather than Alexandretta, north of Syria, the harbor that Kitchener preferred) and a territorial belt on which to construct a railroad from there to Mesopotamia, while the rest of the country was to fall under some sort of international administration.

Except for Palestine and for the areas in which France or Britain exercised direct rule, the Middle East was to form an Arab state or confederation of states, nominally independent but in reality divided into French and British spheres of influence.

The agreement reached by Sykes and Picot was to come into effect only after the Arab Revolt was proclaimed. Picot and the French ambassador, Cambon, were not persuaded that Hussein would contribute anything of value to the Allied cause; they told their Foreign Minister to ratify the preliminary Sykes-Picot Agreement (concluded on 3 January 1916) as soon as possible, before the British had a chance to become disillusioned about the Arabs, and therefore to regret the extensive concessions they had made to France in order to be free to deal with Hussein.[11]

III

Sir Mark Sykes believed that he had won for the Arabs what Hussein and al-Faruqi had demanded. Sykes characterized Arabs as wanting recognition of their essential unity, but only as an ideal; in practice, he said, such unity would not be in harmony with their national genius, nor would it prove feasible from the point of view of finance and administration. He had told the War Cabinet that Arabs "have no national spirit in our sense of the word, but they have got a sense of racial pride, which is as good."[12] They should be content, he said, with a "confederation of Arabic speaking states, under the aegis of an Arabian prince."[13] Sykes failed to recognize that Hussein and the secret societies were asking for a unified Arab state, just as they were asking for a state that was fully independent rather than a European protectorate.

Sykes also had misunderstood his British friends and colleagues in Cairo. Under his veneer of worldliness, Sykes was an innocent: he believed that people meant what they said. Clayton, directly, and also through Aubrey Herbert, had told him that it was important to the Allied cause to promise Damascus, Aleppo, Homs, and Hama to Hussein's independent Arab confederation. Sykes therefore asked Picot to agree to this (and imagined that he had won Picot's consent, not knowing that Picot wanted to give it). The Sykes-Picot Agreement provided that the four towns should be excluded from the area of direct French rule and instead should fall within the scope of an independent Arab state or states—though subject, of course, to exclusive French influence. To Sykes it appeared that he had tailored the commitments to France and to the Arabs to fit together, and also that he had secured precisely the concession from France that his friends in Cairo had asked for.

Sykes had concentrated on satisfying what Cairo had told him were Hussein's claims, and did not see that behind them Cairo was advancing claims of its own. What Sykes did not understand was that when Clayton and Storrs said they wanted inland Syria for the Arabs, they really meant that they wanted it for Britain, and for themselves as Britain's representatives in the region, advancing behind an Arab façade; and when they said they wanted it to be independent, they meant that they wanted it to be administered by Britain rather than France.

Sykes did not see that Hussein's Syrian domains would be any the less independent for being advised by French rather than by British officials. In Cairo, however, a world of difference was seen between British and French administration. Not entirely without reason, Clayton and his colleagues believed French colonial administrators to be incapable of allowing a country to retain its own character. What the French termed their "civilizing mission" was seen as annex-ationism by the British; often it seemed to involve imposing the French language and culture on a native society. The British, on the other hand, in Egypt and elsewhere, kept to themselves, dwelt in their own clubs and compounds, and, apart from supervising the administration of the government, left the country and its people alone. In the eyes of Clayton and his colleagues, this was the greatest degree of independence to which Arabic-speaking peoples could as-pire. As one of Clayton's colleagues told students at a British Military Staff College a few years later, educated Arabs regarded British rule as "the only decent alternative" to Ottoman rule.[14]

Equating, as they did, a French presence with annexation and a British presence with independence, Clayton and his colleagues (though they did not tell Sykes so) regarded the Sykes-Picot Agree-ment as a betrayal of the pledge to grant independence to the pro-posed Arab confederation. Kitchener's followers aspired to rule Syria themselves, and believed that Sykes had let them down. But that is not the way they put it. What they said was: Sykes has let down *the Arabs* (as though it were the Arabs rather than themselves who desired Britain to rule Syria).

For whatever it meant to them politically, and perhaps even per-sonally, Clayton and Storrs saw that Sykes had foreclosed the possi-bility of their creating a new Egyptian empire. Simla had already staked out a claim to the nearby Mesopotamian provinces, so Baghdad and Basra—the principal British zone in the Sykes-Picot Agree-ment—would be ruled by their adversary, the Government of India; while Syria, which could have been in Cairo's sphere, was instead surrendered to France. The agreement allowed Cairo and Khartoum to expand their influence only in arid, inhospitable Arabia. Kitchener, after the war, could go out to India as Viceroy; but Clayton and Storrs were Arabists, tied emotionally and professionally to the fortunes of the Cairo Residency. They could hardly help but be dismayed by what Sykes had done.

Sykes never understood that his friends in Cairo held these views; he thought that he had done what they had asked. He thought he had won inland Syria for the Arabs; he did not realize that they thought he had lost it. He never suspected that Cairo was going to try to undermine the Sykes-Picot Agreement. He was proud of the agreement, and it was ironic that the Arab Bureau which he had created became the center of the plot to destroy it.

His old friend Aubrey Herbert worked with the Arab Bureau in Cairo and so Herbert knew (while Sykes did not) that Clayton bitterly believed that the Sykes-Picot Agreement had reduced Cairo's Arab policy to tatters. Herbert cast the blame on Picot. He wrote:

> I am afraid that swine Monsieur P[icot] has let M.S. [Mark Sykes] badly down. I told him I thought it would happen. It is an awful pity both for the thing itself, and for M. and also because it is one up to the old early Victorians who are in a position to say "We told you so. This is what comes of disregarding the ABC of Diplomacy, and letting Amateurs have a shy at delicate and important negotiations."[15]

IV

The Sykes-Picot Agreement was approved by the British and French Cabinets at the beginning of February 1916. But its terms and even its existence were kept secret; the very fact that the Allies had reached an agreement about the postwar Middle East was not revealed until almost two years later. Some of the few officials in London who knew of the agreement expressed reservations about it. The common British complaint was that it gave away too much to the French.

For Sykes, some of the justification for giving way to the French was soon destroyed. Sykes had wanted to win France's approval of Cairo's proposal to invade Syria and thereby spark al-Faruqi's promised Arab Revolt. But the Prime Minister, deferring to the generals who insisted on concentrating all forces on the western front in Europe, ruled out a new Middle Eastern campaign because of the diversion of resources that it would entail.

A furious Sykes delivered a speech in the House of Commons denouncing Asquith's leadership as muddled, and demanding the establishment of a four-member Cabinet committee to run the war. Delivered at a time when the Prime Minister was faltering as a leader, the speech attracted wide and favorable publicity. It also led Sykes to two meetings that proved important in his climb up the political ladder: one with Lloyd George, and one with the former proconsul in South Africa, Lord Milner, and his influential coterie, including Geoffrey Robinson, editor of *The Times*.

Despite his failure to win approval for an invasion of Syria, Sykes believed that it was important to conclude the arrangements with France on the basis that had been agreed. The Sykes-Picot Agreement achieved what Kitchener, at least, wanted to achieve: the containment of Russia in the postwar Middle East. Moreover, Sykes seemed to believe that for the Allies to resolve their differences and arrive at a definite agreement was in itself a good thing. Russian ratification was required, so the immediate assignment for Sykes was to join Picot—who was already in Petrograd—to help secure Russian approval of their agreement.

V

There was a curious omission in the agreement Sykes and Picot were bringing to Petrograd. As regards Palestine, the document took account of the interests of France, Britain, the other Allies, and the Moslem Arab leader Hussein of Mecca; but no reference was made to the interests of the people of the Biblical Holy Land—the Jews. Yet political Zionism—the organized Jewish movement aiming at a national return of the Jewish people to Palestine—had been an active force in the world for two or three decades. Jewish resettlement of Palestine had gone on in the nineteenth and early twentieth centuries, and by 1916 there was a substantial Jewish population living and working there.

Before Sykes embarked for Russia, his attention was caught by an observation made about this by Captain William Reginald Hall, the head of intelligence at the Admiralty. Hall objected to the inducements being offered to Hussein's Arabs, saying that the British should land troops in Palestine, for only then would the Arabs come over to the Allies. "Force is the best Arab propaganda," claimed Hall, and besides promises to the Arabs might be opposed by Jews, who had "a strong *material*, and a very strong *political*, interest in the future of the country [original emphasis]."[16] Sykes was struck by the mention of Jews. Until then they had not figured in his calculations. Before leaving for Russia, Sykes therefore contacted Herbert Samuel, the Home Secretary, who was Jewish, hoping to learn about Zionism.

It will be remembered that in their negotiations, Sykes and Picot had compromised their differences about Palestine by agreeing that most of it would be placed under an international regime, the precise form of which would be determined after consultation with the other interested Allies—Russia and Italy—and with Hussein of Mecca. Captain Hall's comments led Sykes to worry, however, that the compromise at which he and Picot had arrived had left a principal factor out of account: they had not taken into consideration the possibility that Jews might be concerned in the political future of Palestine.

Evidently Sykes was afraid that when he brought this omission to the attention of Picot, the Frenchman would think that he was doing so in order to back out of their agreement. Accordingly, on his arrival in Petrograd he was at pains to establish his good faith. In his innocence he did not know—or even suspect—that the French government had already gone behind his back to renege on the Palestine compromise they had agreed upon. In secret negotiations with the Russians initiated by the French Premier, Aristide Briand, on 25 March 1916, the French secured Russian agreement that an international regime for Palestine—the arrangement Sykes had agreed upon with Picot—would be impractical and that instead a French regime ought to be installed. A secret Franco-Russian exchange of notes on 26 April 1916 outlined an agreement between the governments as to their respective spheres of influence in the Ottoman territories, and embodied a Russian pledge to France "to support in negotiations with the British government the designs of the government of the Republic [France] on Palestine."[17]

The Russians had no sympathy for Jews or for Jewish claims, and when Sykes arrived in Petrograd, his Czarist hosts persuaded him that Zionist Jews were a great and potentially hostile power within Russia. Thereafter Sykes was seized with the conviction that Jews were a power in a great many places and might sabotage the Allied cause. But unlike the Russians, Sykes believed in attempting to win them over. He reported to the Foreign Office that he had told Picot that, while Britain had no interest in taking possession of Palestine, it was what the Zionists wanted, and that they ought to be propitiated if the Allies were to have a chance of winning the war.[18] His own notion was to offer the Zionists an incorporated land company in Palestine; his question to the Foreign Office was "Is a land company enough?"—to which the brusque response from the Foreign Office was that he should keep his thoughts to himself.[19] (Evidently the Foreign Office did not want Sykes to meddle in a matter about which—it was clear—he knew nothing.)

Returning to London in April 1916, Sykes took further steps to learn about Zionism. He again saw Samuel, who introduced him to Dr Moses Gaster, chief Rabbi of the Sephardic Jewish community.* According to Sykes, Gaster "opened my eyes to what Zionism meant."[20] Sykes then introduced Gaster to the French negotiator, Georges Picot, and suggested to Picot that France and Britain, instead of operating independently of one another in the Middle East, should work together as patrons of Arabs and Jews. Picot was impressed neither by Gaster nor by Sykes's proposal, and held fast to his territorial designs.

Sykes began to worry, at a time when a decisive Allied victory seemed at best a remote possibility, that Jewish forces would tilt the scales in favor of the Germans and Turks. He attempted to persuade

---

* Jews whose ancestors in the Middle Ages lived in Spain and Portugal.

Picot that if the Allies failed to offer Jews a position in Palestine, France might lose the war and, with it, cities and provinces in France herself, of much more consequence to Frenchmen than Palestine. He urged Picot to tell his government that saving Paris and Verdun and regaining Alsace were worth concessions in the Middle East.

While Sykes was in the process of discovering the Zionist issue—before, during, and after his Petrograd trip—so was the Foreign Office in London, prompted by Sykes's old friend Gerald FitzMaurice. FitzMaurice, who had attended the same public school (Beaumont) and had acquired many of the same views and prejudices as had Sykes, was—it will be remembered—the principal source within the British government of the fallacy that the Sublime Porte had fallen into the hands of Jews. At the Admiralty early in 1916, FitzMaurice hit upon the converse of that proposition: he inspired a Foreign Office colleague—another Old Boy of Beaumont, named Hugh O'Beirne—to suggest that "if we could offer the Jews an arrangement as to Palestine which would strongly appeal to them we might conceivably be able to strike a bargain with them as to withdrawing their support from the Young Turk Government which would then automatically collapse."[21] Just as Cairo believed in powerful, mysterious Arab societies that could overthrow the Young Turks, London believed in powerful, mysterious Jewish societies that could do so, too.

O'Beirne evidently intended to pursue the matter within the Foreign Office himself, but did not get the chance to do so: he died in the spring of 1916. So it was, after all, left to Sykes to raise the issue of Zionism within the British bureaucracy, little though he knew of Jews or their affairs.

Like FitzMaurice, Sykes retained his childhood belief in the existence of a cohesive world Jewish community that moved in hidden ways to control the world. Britain's foremost academic authority on the Middle East, Edward Granville Browne, Adams Professor of Arabic at Cambridge University, who had known Sykes as a pupil, though he had praise for him in other respects, commented that Sykes "sees Jews in everything."[22]

VI

Zionism, however, was far from being the chief issue with which Sykes dealt in wintry Petrograd in 1916. The broad outlines of the Middle Eastern settlement were at issue, and when he arrived he found that the Russian leaders—like British officials in London—claimed that France was being promised too much. In response, the

French ambassador, Maurice Paléologue, explained to the Russian Foreign Minister that the reason Britain had pushed France to extend her claims so far to the east was to provide Britain with a buffer against Russia.[23] This was perfectly true, but the Foreign Office in London was furious at being given away, and bombarded Petrograd with official denials. Privately, Foreign Office officials described Paléologue as "really incorrigible."[24]

It was because Cairo, taken in by al-Faruqi's hoax and believing fully in the potency of Arab secret societies, had persuaded London that Hussein of Mecca could tear down the Ottoman Empire that all of these commitments, mortgaging the future of the postwar Middle East, had been made by the Asquith coalition government. Was it worth the price? Within a few weeks of the Sykes-Picot-Sazanov Agreement, Britain was to find out.

TURKEY'S TRIUMPH AT THE TIGRIS

I

As the Arab Bureau in Cairo waited and hoped for an Arab rebellion that would bring down the Ottoman Empire, it was called upon to help British India liquidate yet another disastrous and muddle-headed enterprise in the war against Turkey: a smaller-scale but more shameful Gallipoli by the shores of the Tigris river in Mesopotamia.[1]

A month before the outbreak of the Ottoman war in the autumn of 1914, London had ordered a standby force to be sent from India to the Persian Gulf to protect Britain's oil supplies from Persia in case they should be threatened. Its initial objective in case of war was to protect the oil refinery at Abadan, a Persian island in the Shatt al-'Arab, the waterway at the head of the Persian Gulf where the Euphrates and Tigris rivers meet. On 6 November 1914, the day after Britain declared war on Turkey, this force, by now augmented, moved forward. The Turkish fort at Fao at the mouth of the Shatt al-'Arab fell after a brief bombardment by a British gunboat, the river sloop *Odin*; and a fortnight later, several thousand British troops occupied the Mesopotamian city of Basra seventy-five miles upriver. Although the British Indian force had landed in Mesopotamia, it did so to shield neighboring Persia from attack.

Turkish resistance was feeble, for the Basra front was hundreds of miles from the main concentrations of Ottoman troops and supplies near Baghdad. As the British Indian expeditionary force went about rounding out its position in Basra province, it parried Turkish counterattacks with ease.

Drawn into the interior of marshy lower Mesopotamia by the Turkish retreat, an ambitious newly appointed British commanding officer, Sir John Nixon, who had arrived in April 1915, sent his officer in the field, Major-General Charles Vere Ferrers Townshend, further and further upstream in quest of new victories but with no great sense of direction or strategic purpose. Finally, Nixon ordered the troops—despite Townshend's misgivings—to keep on marching all the way to Baghdad.

A successful advance from Basra to Baghdad would have required a mastery of logistics and an abundance of troops, river transport, hospital equipment, artillery, and supplies that British India did not make available to the expeditionary force. The troops were advancing into a country of swamps and deserts, without roads or railroads, and were therefore obliged to follow the meandering course of the shallow, treacherous Tigris river. For this they needed flotillas of riverboats suited to the Tigris. The country was pestilential—there were maddening, sickening swarms of flies and mosquitos—so mobile hospitals and medical supplies would be required. Whereas in Basra the weakened Turks were at the end of their long supply line, in front of Baghdad Townshend's forces would be at the end of theirs—and would need to have brought with them adequate supplies of food and ammunition.

Though his forces lacked these apparent necessities, Townshend, whose talent for generalship was close to genius, almost fought his way through to victory. But his final triumph, if it can be so termed—at Ctesiphon, about twenty-five miles southeast of Baghdad, and hundreds of river miles from the base of his supply line at Basra—was Pyrrhic: he lost half of his small force. On the night of 25 November he began his retreat.

Townshend had learned that Field Marshal Colman von der Goltz, whom he regarded as one of the great strategists of his time, had assumed overall command of Ottoman forces in Mesopotamia. He had learned, too, that 30,000 Turkish troops were about to reinforce the 13,000 that had opposed him at Ctesiphon. Townshend's own fighting forces now numbered 4,500; and they were short of ammunition and food.

Townshend believed—with good reason—that the closest safe place for him to make a stand was some 250 miles downstream, but decided—unwisely—that his exhausted troops could not go that distance. After a punishing week-long retreat of nearly a hundred miles, punctuated by battles with the pursuing Turks, Townshend, who had suffered a thousand more casualties, chose to stop and make his stand at Kut el-Amara.

Kut was a mud village caught in a loop in the Tigris river, and surrounded by water on three sides. Sheltering within it and entrenching the fourth side, Townshend imprisoned himself in a fortress-like position. It made it difficult for the Turks to get in or for him to get out. In the event, von der Goltz's Ottoman armies left a sufficient force at Kut to guard against a British breakout, and then marched on to entrench themselves downriver so as to block any force Britain might send to the rescue.

Townshend planned to be rescued, but ruined his own chances. Although he had supplies sufficient to last until April 1916, he cabled that he could only hold out until January. The full forces available to rescue him could not be assembled by then—a few weeks more were required—but driven on by Townshend's inconsistent and increasingly unbalanced cables, the partial forces available launched one premature attack after another and were beaten back. Had they waited until they could attack in force, they might have fought their way through.

II

On 26 April 1916, the garrison at Kut having exhausted its last rations of food, the War Office in London offered Townshend the services of Captains Aubrey Herbert and T. E. Lawrence in negotiating a surrender. Both were associated with the Arab Bureau in Cairo, and Herbert, a Member of Parliament, had been a well-known friend of the Ottoman Empire before the war. Both had just arrived in Mesopotamia, and Lawrence had already been stricken with the prevalent local fever.

The siege of Kut had by then lasted 146 days, exceeding the records previously set by the famous sieges of Ladysmith (in the Boer War) and Plevna (in the Russo-Turkish war of 1877). It was an epic of heroism—as the defenders faced disease, starvation, and floods—and of heartbreak, as supplies parachuted to them were blown offcourse into the river, and riverboats sent to their aid went aground or were stopped by chains the Turks stretched across the river.

Townshend, who had never quite recovered from a fever contracted in 125-degree heat the summer before, had become emotionally unbalanced. At some point during the siege he had decided that the Turks might let him and his men go free on parole in return for a payment of a million pounds. Herbert and Lawrence, who went with him on 27–8 April to negotiate terms, were authorized by London to offer even more: ashamed though they were of doing so, they offered the Turks two million pounds. On orders from Enver, who apparently enjoyed Britain's humiliation in begging to buy the freedom of her troops, the Turkish commander rejected the offer.

The British defenders of Kut thereupon destroyed their guns and unconditionally surrendered. Townshend was treated with courtesy, and sent by the Turks to live in comfort—and indeed luxury—in Constantinople. His diseased, starving troops, however, were sent on a death march—100 miles to Baghdad, then 500 more to Anatolia—and then were put to work on railroad chain gangs. Few of them survived.

Townshend's forces suffered more than 10,000 casualties between the start of their advance on Baghdad and their surrender. Twenty-three thousand casualties were suffered by the British forces seeking to rescue them from Kut; yet the garrison was carried off into captivity and found death along the way.

It was another national humiliation inflicted upon Britain by an Ottoman foe British officials had always regarded as ineffectual—and whom the Arab Bureau proposed to bring crashing down by internal subversion later in 1916.

PART IV

SUBVERSION

BEHIND ENEMY LINES

I

In 1916 the question seemed to be: which of the warring coalitions, Germany and her allies or Britain and her allies, would collapse first under the enormous strains imposed by the war? Cairo, with its own special point of view, was betting that Turkey would be the first to crack. Would Hussein's revolt, scheduled to occur in mid-1916, be able to subvert the loyalty of hundreds of thousands of Ottoman soldiers and millions of Ottoman subjects? British Intelligence thought it not improbable, always having regarded the Sultan's regime as feeble.

In the western world it had been assumed for decades that one day or another the ramshackle Ottoman Empire would collapse or disintegrate. By such reckoning, the strain of waging war against Britain, France, and Russia would bring it crashing down; and subversion from within would add to the strain.

Yet the record as of mid-1916 suggested otherwise. As nationalists who campaigned against foreign influence and to eradicate the vestiges of colonialism, the Young Turk leaders were sensitive to any alien presence in their midst—even that of their allies. Both Enver and Talaat expressed concern about the reach of German influence in the administration of Turkey's wartime effort.* Yet no serious wedge was driven between Turks and Germans.

Although many Germans serving with the Ottoman forces expressed frustration and disgust at the obstacles placed in the way of getting their orders executed, they did not allow their relationship

---

* After Gallipoli, Enver resumed his earlier campaign to curb German influence. In early 1916 he indicated that even the 5,500 German troops then in the Ottoman Empire were too many, and should be withdrawn. To demonstrate that Turkey had no need of them, he insisted on sending seven Ottoman divisions to southern Europe to fight alongside the armies of other of the Central Powers. His efforts were not entirely successful; indeed, by the end of the war, there were 25,000 German officers and men serving in the Ottoman Empire.

with the Turks to break down. Germany exerted influence only with a view toward winning the war and made no move to subvert the independence of the Ottoman government or the position of the C.U.P. leaders. More than any other Great Power on either side, Germany demonstrated an ability to keep postwar ambitions in Asia from intruding into wartime decisions; and as a result she was best able to take advantage of opportunities to stir up trouble behind enemy lines. The Habsburg and Ottoman governments were suspicious of each other, as well as of the Germans, and there was the inevitable bickering in the field between jealous officers; but, on the whole, the Germans imposed upon their allies, in the first years of the war in Asia, a sense that winning the war took priority over other objectives.*

Afghanistan was an exception: where it was concerned, officers in the field let their mutual mistrust get the better of them. Their mission was to subvert British control of that fierce Islamic country—a control exercised under the terms of the agreement of 1907 that ended the Great Game between Russia and Britain. As a result of bickering between Germans and Turks and between Germans and other Germans, only one of the four overland expeditions to Afghanistan sent out at the beginning of the war went on to reach Kabul, where the Germans spent six months vainly attempting to persuade the Emir to come into the war against Britain. The Emir declined to act unless the Central Powers could place armies in the field to ensure the success of his rebellion. They could not do so, so the Emir quietly remained within the British fold.

In Persia, however, the Central Powers enjoyed a considerable success. The Germans, long before the war, had solidified their relations with leading Persian politicians, and in 1915 they succeeded in inducing the Prime Minister to sign a secret treaty of alliance. The German ambassador also secured the support of the 7,000-strong Swedish-officered gendarmerie, while his secret agents built up support among the various tribes that constituted about 20 percent of the total population. By the end of 1915 the Allies found the situation so menacing that the Russians, supported by the 8,000-strong

---

* It was not easy. As the archives of Austria-Hungary show, Habsburg officials expressed deep distrust of the ambitions for expansion that they ascribed to the German and Turkish empires.[1] For centuries, Austria-Hungary had been encroaching on Ottoman territories in Europe. Her annexation of Ottoman Bosnia had brought on the Balkan Wars and set the stage for Sarajevo. She continued to dispute the Ottoman title to Albania, which she occupied in the earlier part of the world war. Harboring territorial designs of their own, Habsburg officials suspected that Hohenzollern officials were thinking along similar lines, so that Djemal's Suez campaign brought expressions of concern from them that Germany might attempt to annex Egypt; while Ottoman officials, as always, distrusted their European partners.

Russian-officered Persian Cossacks, occupied the north of the country, taking over the capital city of Teheran and, with it, the weak, recently crowned young Shah. The most pro-German of the politicians fled, initially to the holy city of Qum, and later to Kermanshah, near the Ottoman frontier, where a German puppet government was established, backed by Ottoman troops.

In the south, the most successful of the German agents, Wilhelm Wassmuss, stirred up a fierce tribal uprising that was quelled only with the utmost difficulty by Brigadier General Sir Percy Sykes, of the Government of India, who in 1916 created an 11,000-man British-officered native force, the South Persia Rifles, and took command of the south with a base of authority in Shiraz. The South Persia Rifles, the Persian Cossacks, the tattered remnants of the gendarmerie, and the German-sponsored tribal confederations were the only organized armed forces that remained in what had been at one time a sovereign, and indeed considerable, country. The Shah had no effective forces at his disposal to uphold Persia's neutrality, enforce her laws, or defend her territorial integrity. In the north the province of Azerbaijan had been a battlefield between Turkey and Russia ever since Enver's attack on the Caucasus at the outset of the war; and as the war went on, Russian and Ottoman troops surged back and forth, moving through and occupying Persian territory at will.

The German-Ottoman allies converted Persia, which had been an Allied preserve, into a contested battlefield. By 1915–16 the country had, for all practical purposes, disappeared as a sovereign entity, let alone one fully controlled by the Allied Powers.

II

Britain's efforts to subvert the Arabic-speaking population behind Ottoman lines had met with no comparable success. But Djemal Pasha, the C.U.P. triumvir operating out of Damascus, took the subversion threat seriously enough to crack down on those he suspected of treason. In the wake of his raids in 1915 on the Arab secret societies in Syria, he published in Stamboul in 1916, under the imprint of the Ottoman Fourth Army, a book entitled *La Verité sur la question syrienne*, setting forth the evidence that he claimed would justify his treatment of the alleged plotters. In the book he discussed the secret societies and their aims in some detail, and argued that the convicted men were traitors, not nationalists.

Whether because or in spite of Djemal's crackdown, the Arabic-speaking population did not waver in its loyalty. More important to the Porte, Arab soldiers demonstrated loyalty not only to Islam but also to the Ottoman government. A British Intelligence memorandum based on interviews with captured Arabic-speaking officers in prisoner-of-war camps reported that most of the officers actually supported the Young Turks, and that even the minority who did not were "unable to square their consciences with a military revolt in the face of the enemy."[2]

III

In the eyes of the Young Turks, the loyalty of non-Moslem inhabitants of the empire was open to question. The Porte was suspicious, not only of Christians, but also of Jews—especially the 60,000 or more of them in Palestine.

It disturbed Talaat and his colleagues that at least half of the Jews in Palestine were not Ottoman subjects. Almost all of those who were not Ottoman subjects had come from the Russian Empire, mostly during the half century before 1914 and remained—in theory—subjects of the Czar.

The Young Turkey movement had no reason to mistrust them; they had left Europe to escape from politics and conspiracies, not to engage in them. Fleeing the pogroms of Russia, the Ukraine, and Poland, they could have found a new home—as many Jews did—in lands of opportunity such as the United States, which welcomed immigrants. Those who chose instead the hardships of pioneer life in barren Palestine were dreamers who asked only to be allowed to practice their religion or their ideals in peace.

Some were drawn to the Holy Land by religion; others were inspired to re-create the Judaean nationality that the Romans had detroyed 2,000 years before; but most were socialist idealists who aimed at establishing an egalitarian, cooperative society in self-sufficient agricultural settlements in a country distant from European anti-Semitism. Once arrived, they revived the ancient Hebrew language, restored the depleted soil, and cultivated self-reliance. By the early part of the twentieth century their settlements had begun to flourish; more than forty of them dotted the landscape of the Holy Land. They constructed towns as well; in 1909, on barren sand dunes by the sea, they began to build what is now Tel Aviv. They were encouraged and supported from abroad by the relatively small group of Jews whose program called for a return to Zion: the Zionist movement.

At the end of 1914, just after the Ottoman Empire entered the First World War, Djemal Pasha, who became Turkey's ruler of Syria and Palestine, took violent action against the Jewish settlers. Influenced by a bitterly anti-Zionist Ottoman official named Beha-ed-din,

Djemal moved to destroy the Zionist settlements and ordered the expulsion of all foreign Jews—which is to say, most of Jewish Palestine. The expulsions had already begun before the German government—fearful of alienating Jewish opinion in neutral countries—induced Talaat and Enver to intervene. The American ambassador, Henry Morgenthau, acted together with von Wangenheim in the matter.

Though the American and German governments were able to influence the Porte, the Porte was not always able to control the actions of Djemal, who frequently played a lone hand and looked upon the Palestinian Jewish community as potentially seditious. To some extent this proved to be a self-fulfilling prophecy. While most Palestinian Jews chose to avoid involvement in the world war, David Ben-Gurion and Itzhak Ben Zvi, former law students at the University of Constantinople who were leaders of the Labor Zionist movement, offered to organize a Palestinian Jewish army in 1914 to defend Ottoman Palestine. But, instead of accepting their offer, Djemal deported them and other Zionist leaders in 1915. Ben-Gurion and Ben Zvi went to the United States, where they continued to campaign for the creation of a pro-Ottoman Jewish army. But early in 1918 they rallied to a Jewish army formation that was to fight in Palestine on the British side against the Ottoman Empire. Nothing the wartime Ottoman government had done had given them cause to remain pro-Turk.

Yet despite Djemal's capricious and often cruel measures, most Jewish settlers in Palestine did nothing to subvert the Ottoman Empire; and only a tiny minority—albeit a highly effective one—worked against it. Of that tiny minority, led by an agricultural scientist named Aaron Aaronsohn, more will be said later.

IV

According to the Turks, in 1914—15 Russian efforts at subversion behind Ottoman lines were directed across the frontier at the Armenians of northeastern Anatolia, adjacent to Russian Armenia. The episode has been a subject of violent controversy ever since.

Turkish Armenia was the staging area for Enver's initial attack on the Caucasus plateau, and it was the initial objective of the Russian armies when, in turn, beginning in 1915, they streamed down from the Caucasus to invade Turkey. As Christians, the Armenians were inclined to prefer the Russian to the Turkish cause. Nothing in the history of Ottoman rule predisposed them to remain loyal to Constantinople. The Turkish massacres of Armenians in 1894, 1895, 1896, and 1909 were still fresh in their minds. Then, too, Enver had sent their blood enemies, the Kurds, into Armenia in

Ottoman military units, rekindling ancient feuds and giving rise to
new ones.

In early 1915, Enver, as Minister of War, and Talaat, as Minister
of the Interior, claimed that the Armenians were openly supporting
Russia, and had taken to mob violence. In reprisal they ordered the
deportation of the entire Armenian population from the northeastern
provinces to locations outside of Anatolia. Turkish government representatives even today insist that "At the instigation and with the
support of Czarist Russia, Armenian insurgents sought to establish
an Armenian state in an area that was predominantly Turkish" and
that, prior to the deportations, "Armenian forces had already massacred the Moslem population of the city of Van and engaged in hit-
and-run actions against the flanks of the Turkish army."[3]

The deportations, organized by Talaat as Minister of the Interior,
are still remembered as the Armenian Massacres of 1915. Rape and
beating were commonplace. Those who were not killed at once were
driven through mountains and deserts without food, drink, or shelter.
Hundreds of thousands of Armenians eventually succumbed or were
killed; Armenian sources have put the figure as high as 1,500,000,
and though the figures are still the subject of bitter dispute, there can
be no disputing the result: Turkish Armenia was destroyed, and
about half its people perished.

There are historians today who continue to support the claim of
Enver and Talaat that the Ottoman rulers acted only after Armenia
had risen against them.[4] But observers at the time who were by no
means anti-Turk reported that such was not the case. German officers
stationed there agreed that the area was quiet until the deportations
began.[5]

At the German and Austrian embassies, the first reports of the
deportations were ignored: officials clearly believed that massacres of
Christians were about to take place, but did not want to know about
them. They accepted Talaat's reassurances eagerly.

By May 1915 massacre reports were too persuasive to be ignored
any longer. The Austrian ambassador told his government that he
thought he ought to "alert the Turkish statesmen in a friendly
manner" to the possible adverse repercussions of their proceedings.[6]
He later reported that he had in fact spoken with Talaat, had urged
that the matter be handled carefully, and had suggested avoiding
"persecution of women and children" because it would play into the
hands of Allied propagandists.[7] On 24 May the Allied governments
denounced the Porte's policy of "mass murder"; to which the Porte
replied that responsibility rested on the Allies for having organized
the insurrection in Armenia.[8] (Whether there had been such an
insurrection, and, if so, whether Russia organized or merely encouraged it, remain, as noted earlier, controversial issues.)

Reports poured in from German officials in the field with gruesome details of atrocities; von Wangenheim, the German ambassador, found it increasingly difficult to overlook what was going on. By the middle of June, he cabled Berlin that Talaat had admitted that the mass deportations were not being carried out because of "military considerations alone."[9] Though they received no guidance from their home governments, von Wangenheim and his Austrian counterpart, Pallavicini, communicated to the Porte their feelings that the indiscriminate mass deportations, especially when accompanied by pillagings and massacres, created a very bad impression abroad, especially in the United States, and that this adversely affected the interests that Germany and Turkey had in common.[10]

In July, von Wangenheim reported to the German Chancellor that there no longer was any doubt that the Porte was trying to "exterminate the Armenian race in the Turkish empire."[11] He and Pallavicini both concluded that attempting to interfere did no good. His recommendation to his government was to build a record showing that Germany was not responsible for what was happening.[12] Other German officials disagreed, and tried to interfere, as did the German Pastor Johannus Lepsius, but the Wilhelmstrasse accepted von Wangenheim's advice. In October it asked the Porte to issue a public statement clearing Germany of complicity and stating that German representatives in the Ottoman Empire had tried to save the Armenians.[13] When the Porte refused, the Wilhelmstrasse threatened to issue such a statement on its own, but then backed down for fear of damaging the Turkish alliance.

The Armenian Massacres provided useful and effective propaganda for the Allied Powers, as the German and Austrian ambassadors had feared.* Perhaps the massacres also affected Allied thinking about the terms of a future postwar settlement, for they reinforced the argument that the Ottoman Empire could not be left in control of non-Moslem populations, and possibly not even of non-Turkish-speaking populations.

It was evident to neutral opinion that Talaat and Enver were happy to have rid themselves of the Armenians. Their public position was that they had foiled an attempt at subversion. Certainly they had succeeded in eliminating unrest; Armenia became as quiet as death itself.

---

* The Liberal statesman, historian, and jurist, James Bryce, a pro-Armenian who headed a commission to investigate the 1915–16 Armenian Massacres during the war, issued a report that was damning to the C.U.P. government. Turkish spokesmen still claim that the Bryce report was a one-sided and distorted work of wartime propaganda, and cite the admission of Arnold Toynbee, one of Bryce's assistants, that the report was intended to further Britain's propaganda and policy objectives.[14] In this it succeeded.

V

The Allies did have one clear opportunity to subvert the Ottoman Empire, but they deliberately passed it up. It was offered to them by Djemal Pasha.

Alone among the Young Turk triumvirs, Djemal took steps to distance himself from the Armenian Massacres. His apparent aim was to keep open his avenues to the Allied Powers. Since his defeat at the Suez Canal in early 1915, Djemal had settled in Damascus and had come to rule Greater Syria—the southwestern provinces that today comprise Syria, Lebanon, Jordan, and Israel—almost as his private fiefdom. At the end of 1915, while the Armenian Massacres were taking place, he proposed, with Allied help, to seize the Ottoman throne for himself.

Making use of the representative of the dominant Armenian political society, the Dashnaktsutium (Armenian Revolutionary Federation), to convey his proposals, Djemal appears to have acted on the mistaken assumption that saving the Armenians—as distinct from merely exploiting their plight for propaganda purposes—was an important Allied objective. In December 1915 Dr Zavriev, a Dashnak emissary to the Allies, informed the Russian government that Djemal was prepared to overthrow the Ottoman government. This was the month that the Allied evacuation from Gallipoli began; in the wake of that disastrous expedition it could have been expected that the Allies would be willing to pay a price to bring hostilities with Turkey to an end.

Djemal's terms, as outlined by Sazanov, the Russian Foreign Minister, envisaged a free and independent Asiatic Turkey (consisting of Syria, Mesopotamia, a Christian Armenia, Cilicia, and Kurdistan as autonomous provinces) whose supreme ruler would be Djemal as Sultan. Djemal agreed in advance to the inevitable Russian demand to be given Constantinople and the Dardanelles. He also offered to take immediate steps to save the surviving Armenians. He proposed, with Allied help, to march on Constantinople to depose the Sultan and his government; and in return he asked financial aid to help reconstruct his country after the war.

The Russians proposed to accept Djemal's proposal, and Sazanov seemed confident that his allies would agree to do so.[15] But, in March 1916, France rejected the proposal and insisted on having Cilicia (in the south of what is now Turkey) and Greater Syria for herself.

Sir Edward Grey, the British Foreign Secretary, also showed himself to be unwilling to encourage revolt behind enemy lines if doing so meant foregoing the territorial gains in Asiatic Turkey that Britain had promised to her allies. In their passion for booty, the Allied governments lost sight of the condition upon which future gains were predicated: winning the war. Blinded by the prize, they did not see that there was a contest.

Djemal's offer afforded the Allies their one great opportunity to subvert the Ottoman Empire from within; and they let it go. Enver and Talaat never discovered Djemal's secret correspondence with the enemy, and Djemal continued the fight against the Allies at their side.

VI

The Ottoman Empire benefited from the fact that it was not the principal theater of war for any of its opponents, all of whose forces and energies were concentrated elsewhere. Even so, its wartime performance was surprisingly successful. Engaged in a three-front war, the Ottoman Empire defeated Britain and France in the west in 1915—16, crushed the advancing armies of British India in the east at the same time, and in the north held off the Russian invasion forces.

Behind enemy lines, the Ottoman performance was equally outstanding. Turkish and German subversion had made a shambles of the Allied-controlled Persian Empire. In striking contrast, as of mid-1916 Britain had failed in her efforts to win over the Arabic-speaking peoples of the Ottoman Empire, and Russia's appeal to the Armenians had been followed only by their dreadful massacre.

Would Hussein's imminent revolt in June 1916 turn the situation around? Would it prove any more successful than previous Allied efforts to stir up trouble behind Ottoman lines? On the basis of the record to mid-1916 the chances would have had to be rated as low, but Clayton and his colleagues were hopeful, and if they were right they stood to win a great prize. For Hussein's imminent revolt was Cairo's chance to win the war in the East, and to salvage the wartime reputation of its leader, Lord Kitchener.

KITCHENER'S LAST MISSION

In London direction of the war was now entrusted not to the War Minister, but to the Chief of the Imperial General Staff. The Cabinet had reason to believe that Kitchener had lost his touch even in the area he was supposed to know best—the East. The only British military operation he had opposed there until the end—the evacuation from Gallipoli—was the only one to have proved a brilliant success.

Asquith, who believed it politically impossible to let Kitchener resign and yet found it awkward to retain him in office, hit on the expedient of sending the War Minister away on another long mission— a mission to Russia. A trip there—he of course was obliged to travel by ship—would take most of the last half of 1916. A long, dangerous voyage in arctic seas was much to ask of the aging soldier from the tropics, but he accepted his new assignment and made his preparations to depart.

His long run of luck had finally run out. If he had died in 1914 he would have been remembered as the greatest British general since Wellington. Had he died in 1915 he would have been remembered as the prophet who foretold the nature and duration of the First World War and as the organizer of Britain's mass army. But in 1916 he had become the aging veteran of a bygone era who could not cope with the demands placed upon him in changing times. "They expect too much of me, these fellows," he is supposed to have confided to a Cabinet colleague; "I don't know Europe, I don't know England, and I don't know the British Army."[1] His heart and mind remained with the colonial armies of Egypt and India that he had reorganized and that were trained to do his bidding. In modern Europe he was lost.

Shortly before noon on Friday, 2 June 1916, Lord Kitchener went to the King's Cross railroad station almost unattended and unnoticed. The train was a minute and a half late in starting, and he was seized with impatience; he hated delay. Once started, the train sped him to his port of embarkation.

At Scapa Flow, the headquarters of the Grand Fleet off the

northern tip of Scotland, Kitchener and the faithful FitzGerald boarded the armored cruiser *Hampshire* the afternoon of 5 June 1916, bound for the Russian port of Archangel. The departure route of the *Hampshire* had already been plotted, but should have been changed. Naval Intelligence, which earlier had broken the German radio code, intercepted a message to the German minelaying submarine U75 in late May. It indicated that the submarine was to mine the passage that the *Hampshire* intended to follow. Two further intercepts confirmed the information, as did sightings of the submarine. In the confusion at British headquarters at Scapa Flow, Admiral Sir John Jellicoe, the British naval commander, and his staff somehow failed to read or to understand the warnings that Naval Intelligence sent to their flagship. (At a court of inquiry that convened later in 1916 to look into the matter, Admiral Jellicoe succeeded in hiding the existence of these intelligence warnings, which were revealed only in 1985.)[2]

The seas were stormy, but Kitchener refused to delay his departure. Admiral Jellicoe's officers had misread the weather charts, which should have shown them that the storm would intensify, and they believed that it would abate. At 4:45 p.m. the *Hampshire* put out to sea into a raging gale. The weather proved too much for the destroyers assigned to escort duty; after two hours, they turned back. The *Hampshire* steamed ahead alone. Sometime between 7:30 and 7:45 it struck one of the U75's mines and went down with almost all hands.

As soon as the mine exploded, Kitchener and FitzGerald came out on the starboard quarterdeck, followed by officers of their staff. One survivor later recalled that the "Captain was calling to Lord K to go to a boat but Lord K apparently did not hear him or else took no notice."[3] Escape from the doomed vessel seemed out of the question, and the field marshal made no move to attempt it. He stood on deck, calm and expressionless, for about a quarter of an hour. The only survivor of the *Hampshire* who is still alive has never forgotten a last glimpse of him, dressed in a greatcoat, standing on deck and waiting impassively for the ship to sink.[4] Then Lord Kitchener and his ship went down beneath the turbulent waves.

FitzGerald's body was washed ashore, but Kitchener disappeared into the depths of the sea. A popular legend sprang up in Britain soon afterward, according to which Lord Kitchener had escaped from death and would one day return.

HUSSEIN'S REVOLT

I

By a coincidence that often has been remarked upon, Lord Kitchener was lost at sea just as the Emir Hussein of Mecca proclaimed his rebellion against the Ottoman Empire. Hussein ordered it when he discovered that the Young Turks intended to depose him. But British officialdom in Cairo and Khartoum, unaware of this, regarded the rebellion as an accomplishment of the school of Kitchener—of Wingate, Clayton, and Storrs—and of their tactic of dangling vague but grandiose prospects of future glory in front of the Emir's eyes. The Residency had been working to generate the uprising for almost nine months. When the news of the desert uprising reached Cairo, Wyndham Deedes called it "a great triumph for Clayton."[1]

For Hussein, it was something closer to an admission of defeat; his policy had been to remain neutral and collect bribes from both sides. He moved to the Allied side reluctantly, forced to do so by the imminent danger that the Young Turks would overthrow him. Having already discovered that they intended to depose him eventually, he found himself exposed to new risks, starting in the summer of 1915, when Djemal Pasha began to crush dissent in the Arab circles with which Hussein (through his son Feisal) had been in contact in Damascus. Djemal acted on the basis of documents obtained from the French consulates in Beirut and Damascus that betrayed the names of Arab conspirators and of at least one key British agent. Arrests were made. Interrogations, torture, and trials by military court took place. On 21 August 1915 eleven persons convicted of treason were executed. In the following months there were more arrests and more trials. A number of those arrested were prominent figures in Arab life. Among those undergoing torture and interrogation in jail were people who could have revealed details of Feisal's conversations with the secret societies al-'Ahd and al-Fatat, and of Hussein's promises to Kitchener and McMahon. The Emir could not be sure that they would remain silent. He sent pleas to

Djemal and to the Porte asking that they show mercy to the prisoners. The pleas only compromised him further.

Then, in April 1916, Hussein learned from Djemal that a picked and specially trained Ottoman force of 3,500 men was about to march through the Hejaz to the tip of the Arabian peninsula, where an accompanying party of German officers planned to establish a telegraph station. The Ottoman force was sufficiently strong to crush Hussein as it marched through his domain. The news threw the Emir into hasty and improvised activity; it obliged him to strike first, and to seek the protection of the Royal Navy along his coast. On 6 May there were twenty-one new executions in Beirut and Damascus; the news was unexpected, and speeded up Hussein's schedule.

Prudently, Hussein had already obtained more than 50,000 gold pounds from the Porte with which to raise and equip forces to combat the British. To this he added the first installment of a substantial payment from Britain with which to raise and equip forces to combat the Turks.[2] The revolt in the Hejaz was proclaimed sometime between 5 and 10 June 1916. The Royal Navy immediately moved along the Hejaz coastline, which deterred the German-Turkish force from advancing further.

The Arab Bureau believed that the uprising would draw support throughout the Moslem and Arabic-speaking worlds. Most important of all, it believed that the revolt would draw support from what the British believed to be a largely Arabic-speaking Ottoman army. Feisal and Hussein reported that they expected to be joined by about 100,000 Arab troops.[3] That would have been about a third of the Ottoman army's fighting strength. According to other reports, Hussein expected to be joined by about 250,000 troops, or almost the whole of the Turkish army's functional combat troops.[4]

In the event, the Arab revolt for which Hussein hoped never took place. No Arabic units of the Ottoman army came over to Hussein. No political or military figures of the Ottoman Empire defected to him and the Allies. The powerful secret military organization that al-Faruqi had promised would rally to Hussein failed to make itself known. A few thousand tribesmen, subsidized by British money, constituted Hussein's troops. He had no regular army. Outside the Hejaz and its tribal neighbors, there was no visible support for the revolt in any part of the Arabic-speaking world. The handful of non-Hejazi officers who joined the Emir's armed forces were prisoners-of-war or exiles who already resided in British-controlled territories.

An initial military problem was that the Emir's small band of tribal followers were helpless against Ottoman artillery. Their attacks on the Turkish garrisons in Mecca and nearby Taif were repulsed, as were their attacks on Medina and on the port of Jeddah. British ships and airplanes came to the rescue by attacking Jeddah. Once the port was secured the British landed Moslem troops from the Egyptian army, who moved inland to help Hussein take Mecca and Taif. The port of Rabegh, defended by fewer than thirty Turks, was captured with ease, as was the port of Yanbo. Thus the British Royal Navy won control of the Red Sea coast of Arabia, and established a British presence ashore in the ports.

Hussein would not allow Christian British military units to move inland. His expressed view, which the British found parochial, was that it would compromise his position in the Moslem world and would be deeply resented if non-Moslems were to enter the land that embraced the Holy Places.

The problem was that Hussein on his own was no match for the Turks. The activist Reginald Wingate, Governor-General of the Sudan, wrote to Clayton that Britain ought to send in troops whether Hussein wanted them or not. He noted that he had been in favor of sending a British expeditionary force to the Hejaz all along.[5] But Wingate's superiors disagreed with him, and it became British policy, insofar as it was possible, to supply professional military assistance to the Hejaz from among Moslem officers and troops. In a land of intrigue, this policy was also beset with difficulties.

Major al-Masri, strongly recommended by the British authorities, was appointed Chief of Staff of the forces nominally commanded by the Emir's son Ali. He took up his position in late 1916, and within a month was removed from command as a result of a murky intrigue. He was replaced by the able Jaafar al-Askari, an Arab general in the Ottoman army whom the British had taken prisoner.

According to one account, al-Masri was plotting to take over control from Hussein in order to negotiate to change sides. He spoke of coming to an arrangement whereby the Hejaz forces would return to the Ottoman fold in return for an agreement by the Porte to grant local autonomy to Arabic-speaking areas.[6]

It was not merely that al-Masri and his colleagues believed that Germany would win the war. Two years later, when it had become clear that it was the Allies who were going to win, the one-time Arab secret society commander in Damascus (whom al-Faruqi had purported to represent when he duped Clayton and the others in Cairo), General Yasin al-Hashimi, still refused to change sides. Gilbert Clayton had misread the politics of the Arab secret societies: they were profoundly opposed to British designs in the Middle East. At the beginning of the war they had resolved to support the Ottoman Empire against the threat of European conquest.[7] They remained faithful to their resolve. They preferred autonomy or independence if they could get it; but if they could not, they preferred to be ruled by Turkish Moslems rather than by Christians.

Hussein himself, from the opening days of his revolt, continued to

1 Lord Kitchener

2 Sir Mark Sykes at his desk in 1916

3 Enver, who led the *coup d'état*

4 Talaat, civilian strongman of the Young Turk regime

5 Djemal, a leading military figure in the
Young Turk Party

6 Crowds gather outside the Sublime Porte after the Young Turk
coup d'état in 1913

7 Turkish soldiers at Dardanelles fort with stone cannon balls, 1915

ADRIANOPLE

DÉDÉ-AGATCH   Enos   Tchatal Tepé

Gulf o

Isle of Samothrace

PENINSU

Isle of Imbros

Fort Ertogrul
Cape Helles   Eski Hissarlik

SEDDUL-BAHR

STRAITS OF THE DARDANEL

KUM KALE

Cape Yeni

Æ G E A N   S E A

8 Allied fleet off the entrance to the Dardanelles

9 Pictorial map of the Dardanelles

10 H.M.S. *Cornwallis* firing at the Turks at Gallipoli

11 A view of Anzac beach

12 Australians charging uphill

13 Winston Churchill, as First Lord of the Admiralty

14 Russian column pressing forward

15 Russian advance-guard on snow-clad slopes in Turkey, 1916

16 Russian occupation of Erzerum

17 Russian troops in Trebizond

18 A British camel column in the Jordan Valley

19 A British survey party in southern Palestine

20 A chain of transport camels

21 View of Beersheba with inset of General Allenby

22 The Hejaz flag

23 Prince Feisal (second from right)

24 King Hussein of the Hejaz

25 T.E. Lawrence (left) with Lowell Thomas near Aqaba in
Palestine in the autumn of 1917

26 David Ben-Gurion

27 Vladimir Jabotinsky

28 Chaim Weizmann (left) with Lord Balfour

communicate with the Young Turks with a view to changing back to the Ottoman side of the war. The *Arab Bulletin* (no. 25, 7 October 1916) quoted the Arabian warlord Abdul Aziz Ibn Saud as charging that "Sherif's original intention was to play off the British against the Turks, and thus get the Turks to grant him independence guaranteed by Germany."

Hussein's basic program remained constant: he wanted more power and autonomy as Emir within the Ottoman Empire, and he wanted his position to be made hereditary. Although the British were not yet aware of his correspondence with the enemy, they rapidly became disenchanted with the Emir for other reasons. As they came to see it, Hussein, far from being the leader of a newly created Arab nationalism, was a ruler who took little interest in nationalism and whose only concern was for the acquisition of new powers and territories for himself. David Hogarth, the intelligence officer who headed the Arab Bureau, drily commented that, "It is obvious that the King regards Arab Unity as synonymous with his own Kingship ..."[8]

The Emir insisted on proclaiming himself king of the Arabs, although Ronald Storrs on behalf of Cairo had warned him not to do so. Storrs later wrote that "he knew better than we that he could lay no kind of genuine claim" to be the king of all the Arabs.[9] In this respect, Storrs found that "his pretensions bordered on the tragicomic," yet felt that Britain was now obliged to support him as far as possible.[10] The Arab Bureau was deeply disappointed by the failure of Hussein's leadership to take hold.

II

It is due to T. E. Lawrence, a junior member of the Arab Bureau, that its real views were recorded in convenient form, providing an account of the contemporary observations and private thoughts of the small band of Kitchener's followers who had organized Hussein's revolt and who had placed so much hope in it. It was Lawrence who suggested that the Arab Bureau publish an information bulletin. Originally issued under the title *Arab Bureau Summaries*, it then became the *Arab Bulletin*. It appeared at irregular intervals, commencing 6 June 1916, and continuing until the end of 1918. The first issue was edited by Lawrence. For most of the next three months, issues were edited by Lieutenant-Commander David Hogarth, the Oxford archaeologist who served as Director of the Arab Bureau. At the end of the summer, Captain Kinahan Cornwallis, Hogarth's deputy, took over as the regular editor.

Issued from the Arab Bureau offices in the Savoy Hotel, Cairo, the *Arab Bulletin* was labeled "Secret." Only twenty-six copies were printed of each issue. The restricted distribution list included the Viceroy of India and the British commanders-in-chief in Egypt and the Sudan. A copy each also went to the War Office and to the Admiralty in London. The issues provided a wide range of confidential current and background information about the Arab and Moslem worlds.

Lawrence, in the first issue (6 June 1916), which appeared just as the revolt in the Hejaz began, indicated that there were problems in holding Arabs together even for the purposes of revolt. He wrote that whenever there were large tribal gatherings, dissensions soon arose; and, knowing this, the Turks held back and did nothing. They delayed "in the sure expectation that tribal dissension would soon dismember their opponents."

The *Arab Bulletin*, no. 5 (18 June 1916), reported the beginning of Hussein's proclaimed revolt a week or two earlier. This issue and issue no. 6 (23 June 1916) indicate that Hussein's military operations had achieved only modest success, and that even this had been due to British forces. According to issue no. 6, the Turks on the coast were caught between British ships and seaplanes, and the Arabs. Seeking cover behind walls, the Turks were driven to surrender for lack of food and water, for their wells were outside the walls. Turkish prisoners taken at Jeddah were quoted in the *Arab Bulletin*, no. 7 (30 June 1916), as saying that English "shells and bombs it was that really took the town."

Hussein's troops were belittled as soldiers. According to issue no. 6, "They are presumably tribesmen only"; and "They are all untrained, and have no artillery or machine guns. Their preference is for the showy side of warfare, and it will be difficult to hold them together for any length of time, unless the pay and rations are attractive." A detailed analysis and description written by T. E. Lawrence, which appeared in issue no. 32 (26 November 1916), was in the same vein: "I think one company of Turks, properly entrenched in open country, would defeat the Sherif's armies. The value of the tribes is defensive only, and their real sphere is guerilla warfare." He wrote that they were "too individualistic to endure commands, or fight in line, or help each other. It would, I think, be impossible to make an organized force out of them."

Hussein's call to revolt fell on deaf ears throughout the Arab and Moslem worlds, according to the *Arab Bulletin*. Soundings of opinion around the globe, as reported in issues throughout 1916, elicited responses ranging from indifference to hostility. Issue no. 29 (8 November 1916), which reported Hussein's proclamation that he was assuming the title of King of the Arabs, commented icily that "the prince, claiming such recognition, is very far from being in a position to substantiate his pretension," and that His Majesty's

Government was not going to sign a blank check on the future political organization of the Arab peoples. In issue no. 41 (6 February 1917), Hogarth wrote that "the prospect of Arabia united under either the King of the Hejaz or anyone else seems very remote. The 'Arab Cause' is evidently a very weak cement in the peninsula; dislike of the Turk is stronger; and a desire to stand well with us is perhaps stronger still."

Nearly a year after Hussein proclaimed the Arab Revolt, Hogarth was prepared to write it off as a failure. In reviewing what he called "A Year of Revolt" in the Hejaz for the *Arab Bulletin*, no. 52 (31 May 1917), he concluded that it had not fulfilled the hopes placed in it nor did it justify further expectations: "That the Hejaz Bedouins were simply *guerillas*, and not of good quality at that, had been amply demonstrated, even in the early sieges; and it was never in doubt that they would not attack nor withstand Turkish regulars." The best that could be hoped for in the future from Hussein's Arab Movement, he wrote, was that it would "just hold its own in place."

It was not much of a return on the British investment. According to a later account by Ronald Storrs, Britain spent, in all, 11 million pounds sterling to subsidize Hussein's revolt.[11] At the time this was about 44 million dollars; in today's currency it would be closer to 400 million dollars. Britain's military and political investment in Hussein's revolt was also considerable. On 21 September 1918 Reginald Wingate, who by then had succeeded Kitchener and McMahon as British proconsul in Egypt, wrote that "Moslems in general have hitherto regarded the Hejaz revolt, and our share in it, with suspicion or dislike"; and that it was important to make Hussein look as though he had not been a failure in order to keep Britain from looking bad.[12]

III

Three weeks after Hussein announced his rebellion, the British War Office told the Cabinet in London that the Arab world was not following his lead. In a secret memorandum prepared for the War Committee of the Cabinet on 1 July 1916, the General Staff of the War Office reported that Hussein "has always represented himself, in his correspondence with the High Commissioner, as being the spokesman of the Arab nation, but so far as is known, he is not supported by any organization of Arabs nearly general enough to secure ... automatic acceptance of the terms agreed to by him."[13] As a result, according to the memorandum, the British government ought not to assume that agreements reached with him would be honored by other Arab leaders.

In a secret memorandum entitled "The Problem of the Near East," prepared at about the same time, Sir Mark Sykes predicted that if British aid were not forthcoming, the Sherif Hussein's movement would be crushed by early 1917. Gloomily, Sykes foresaw that by the close of the war, Turkey would be the most exhausted of the belligerent countries and, as a result, would be taken over by her partner, Germany. The Ottoman Empire, wrote Sykes, would become little more than a German colony.[14] His analysis in this respect foreshadowed the new views about the Middle East that were to become current in British official circles the following year under the influence of Leo Amery and his colleagues.

Sykes had become an assistant to his friend Maurice Hankey, Secretary of Asquith's War Cabinet. In his new position Sykes continued to concern himself with the East. He had published an *Arabian Report*, a London forerunner of Cairo's *Arab Bulletin*. When his friend Gilbert Clayton arrived from Egypt in the latter half of 1916, the two men went before the War Committee to urge support for Hussein's revolt in the Hejaz. They also urged that Sir Henry McMahon should be replaced as High Commissioner in Egypt; for McMahon had been appointed only to keep the position available for Kitchener, and when the field marshal died, Kitchener's followers wanted the job for Reginald Wingate, one of their own.*

During the summer of 1916, Sykes spent a good deal of time making public speeches. In his speeches he gave currency to the new descriptive phrase, "the Middle East," which the American naval officer and historian Alfred Thayer Mahan had invented in 1902 to designate the area between Arabia and India;[15] and he added to his public reputation as an expert on that area of the world.

In September, as intelligence reports from Cairo indicated that the revolt in the Hejaz was collapsing even more rapidly than he had anticipated, Sykes advocated sending out military support to Hussein immediately—a plan vigorously advanced by McMahon and Wingate. His urgings were in vain: Robertson, the all-powerful new Chief of the Imperial General Staff, refused to divert troops or efforts from the western front.

The late summer and autumn of 1916 appeared to be desperate times for Hussein's cause, though in retrospect Britain's naval control of the Red Sea coastline probably ensured the survival of the Emir's supporters. The British hit on the idea of sending a few hundred Arab prisoners-of-war from India's Mesopotamian front to join Hussein. When Sir Archibald Murray, commanding general (since January 1916) of the British army in Egypt, reiterated that he could

---

* In the end, they succeeded. Wingate was appointed High Commissioner, but not until January 1917.

spare no troops to send to Hussein's defense, the High Commissioner, Sir Henry McMahon, suggested asking for help from France. He also sent Ronald Storrs, his aide at the Residency, on a mission to Arabia to inquire as to what else could be done.

IV

At the end of the summer of 1916, the French government sent a mission to the Hejaz to attempt to stop the Sherif Hussein's revolt from collapsing. Lieutenant-Colonel Edouard Brémond, heading the French mission, arrived in Alexandria 1 September 1916, and from there took ship for Arabia, arriving at the Hejazi port of Jeddah on 20 September.[16]

Brémond's opposite number in Jeddah was Colonel C. E. Wilson, the senior British officer in the Hejaz and representative of the Government of the Sudan—which is to say of Wingate, who was soon to assume operational control of the British side of the Hejaz revolt. His assistant, Captain Hubert Young, was at the British consulate in Jeddah (which called itself the Pilgrimage Office, as it dealt with the affairs of Moslem pilgrims from British India and elsewhere) to greet Brémond when he arrived. Brémond also met Vice-Admiral Sir Rosslyn Wemyss, whose British fleet controlled the Red Sea passage between Egypt and the Sudan and Arabia, and who ferried officers and men across it.

Brémond's assignment was to shore up the Hejaz revolt by supplying a cadre of professional military advisers from among the Mohammedan population of the French Empire who, as Moslems, would be acceptable to the Sherif. The French mission led by Brémond comprised 42 officers and 983 men. The size of the French mission prompted the rival British to send out a further complement of officers of their own to serve under Wilson. Brémond, in turn, contemplated increasing the size of his forces in order to strengthen the forces of the Sherif, which were dangerously weak. Indeed, Abdullah, the son closest to the Sherif's thinking, was fearful that the Ottoman forces based in Medina might attack and overrun the rebel positions on the road to Mecca.

In the middle of October, Ronald Storrs, of the British Residency in Cairo, took ship from Egypt to the Hejaz with an alternative approach. He came in support of Major Aziz al-Masri, the nationalist secret society leader, whom Cairo had nominated to take in hand the training and reorganization of the Hejaz forces, and whose brief tenure in command was described earlier (see page 220). Al-Masri was of the opinion that it would be a political disaster to allow Allied troops, even though Moslem, to become too visibly involved in the

Sherif's campaign. His view was that the forces of Mecca could fight effectively on their own if trained in the techniques of guerrilla warfare.

Storrs arranged for his young friend, the junior intelligence officer T. E. Lawrence, to come along on the ship to Jeddah. Lawrence had accumulated a few weeks of leave time, and wanted to spend them in Arabia, which he had never visited. Storrs obtained permission for Lawrence to come along with him; so they arrived in Jeddah together.

Thomas Edward Lawrence was twenty-eight years old, though he looked closer to nineteen or twenty. He had been turned down for army service as too small; he stood only a few inches above five feet in height. Hubert Young called him "a quiet little man."[17] Ronald Storrs, like most others, called him "little Lawrence," though Storrs also called him "super-cerebral."[18]

His personal circumstances seemed undistinguished. He was apparently of a poor family and of modest background, in an Arab Bureau group that included Members of Parliament, millionaires, and aristocrats. He had attended the City School at home in Oxford rather than a public school (in the British sense): Eton, Harrow, Winchester, or the like. In Arab Bureau circles he ranked low, and had no military accomplishments to his credit.

Lawrence had worked for the archaeologist David Hogarth at the Ashmolean Museum, and Hogarth—who later became head of the Arab Bureau—had gotten him into the geographical section of the War Office in the autumn of 1914 as a temporary second lieutenant-translator.[19] From there he went out to the Middle East to do survey maps. He stayed on in Cairo to do other jobs.

When Storrs and Lawrence arrived in Jeddah, the Emir Hussein's son Abdullah met them. Abdullah proved an immediate disappointment to Lawrence, but Lawrence so impressed Abdullah that he won coveted permission to go into the field to meet the Emir of Mecca's other sons. For Lawrence this was a major *coup*. Colonel Alfred Parker, who had been the first head of the Arab Bureau and who served as head of Military Intelligence in the Hejaz revolt, wrote to Clayton on 24 October 1916, that "Before Lawrence arrived I had been pushing the idea of going up country and had hoped to go up. Don't think I grudge him, especially as he will do it as well or better than anyone. Since he has been gone" the Hejaz government "is not inclined to agree to other trips."[20]

In the field, Lawrence visited Feisal and the other leaders and found Feisal enchanting: "an absolute ripper," he later wrote to a colleague.[21] Lawrence decided that Feisal should become the field commander of the Hejaz revolt. Among his other qualities, Feisal looked the part.

On his own initiative, Lawrence sent a written report to Reginald Wingate, Governor-General of the Sudan, who was soon to be sent to Egypt to replace McMahon as High Commissioner. When Lawrence left the Hejaz in November, instead of returning directly to Cairo, he embarked for the Sudan to introduce himself to Wingate.

Lawrence—through his friendship with Gilbert Clayton, the Sudan's representative in Cairo—must have been familiar with Wingate's outlook on the future of Middle Eastern politics. He would have known that Wingate aimed at securing British domination of the postwar Arab Middle East and (like himself) at preventing France from establishing a position in the region. Although Wingate wanted Hussein's forces to be saved from defeat and possible destruction, he could not have wanted the rescue to be undertaken by Frenchmen— for that would risk bringing Hussein's Arab Movement under long-term French influence.

Lawrence proposed to Wingate an alternative to Brémond's project of employing French and other Allied regular army units to do the bulk of Hussein's fighting for him: Hussein's tribesmen should be used as irregulars in a British-led guerrilla warfare campaign. Aziz al-Masri had originally suggested the guerrilla warfare idea to Lawrence, intending to exclude France and Britain from Arabia; Lawrence modified the plan so as to exclude only France. Lawrence added that Feisal should be appointed to command the Sherifian striking forces, and claimed that he himself was the only liaison officer with whom Feisal would work.

Wingate tended to agree. Back in 1914 he had been the first to urge that the Arabian tribes should be stirred up to make trouble for Turkey. In a sense it was Wingate's own plan that Lawrence was advocating. Indeed, writing to a fellow general some two decades later, Wingate claimed that it was he—and not "poor little Lawrence"—who had launched, supported, and made possible the Arab Movement.[22]

Lawrence's proposals were also congenial to the British military authorities in Cairo. They did not expect his guerrilla warfare campaign to be a great success—quite the contrary—but they had no troops to spare for the Hejaz and therefore were delighted to hear that none were needed. Lawrence rose high in their estimation by not asking for any.

Lawrence left Cairo again on 25 November 1916, and by early December had taken up his position with Feisal. Wingate became High Commissioner in January 1917, and supplied Lawrence with increasingly large sums of gold with which to buy support from the Arab tribes. Yet the winter and spring of 1917 went by with no news of any significant military success that Lawrence's tribesmen had won.

V

The most conspicuous failure of the Mecca revolt was its failure to carry with it Medina, the other large holy city of the Hejaz. Medina lay some 300 miles to the northeast of Mecca, blocking the route that continued northward toward Syria. Followers of the Sherif Hussein attacked it in the first days of the revolt, but were beaten off with ease; and the Sherif's forces were unable to capture it during the war. Nor could they by-pass it and allow its large Turkish garrison to attack them on the flank or from the rear.

Medina was surrounded by a solid stone wall, said to date from the twelfth century, dominated by towers and, at the northwest, by a castle manned by the Ottoman garrison. The terminal of the Hejaz railroad from Damascus was situated within its walls, and provided access to supplies and reinforcements. Although the railroad track was repeatedly dynamited during the war by Allied-led Bedouin raiding parties, the Ottoman garrison continued to repair it and keep it in use.

The Ottoman presence at Medina, blocking the line of advance that the Sherifian tribesmen would have to follow in order to participate in the main theater of operations of the Middle Eastern war, seemed to demonstrate that Hussein was not going anywhere. The rebellion that streamed forth from Mecca was visibly brought to a halt by the centuries-old walls of Medina. The structure of Ottoman authority held firm. It had not been in the state of advanced decay that European observers had reported it to be.

PART V

THE ALLIES AT THE NADIR OF THEIR FORTUNES

THE FALL OF THE ALLIED GOVERNMENTS: BRITAIN AND FRANCE

I

Between autumn 1916 and autumn 1917, the Ottoman Empire held firm while the governments of its adversaries, the Allied Powers, collapsed. This was very much contrary to what European political and military leaders had expected.

The Ottoman army's success in holding the Dardanelles played a direct role in the overthrow of Prime Minister Asquith's government in Britain and that of Czar Nicholas in Russia. The overthrow of the British and Russian governments, and of the French government in 1917, brought to power in the three Allied capitals new leaders who held strong views about the Middle East which were totally at variance with those of their predecessors.

The Prime Minister who had brought Britain into the war was the first Allied leader to fall victim to it. Bonar Law once observed, in a letter to Asquith, that "In war it is necessary not only to be active but to seem active."[1] Asquith, with his indolent patrician ways, seemed the reverse. He had achieved a towering position in British politics, but it was an aspect of his special genius to make his triumphs appear effortless. In the transaction of political and governmental business he was unhurried: he always seemed to have time for another dinner party, another visit to the countryside, or—all too often—another cognac.

As military catastrophes multiplied in Mesopotamia, Gallipoli, and on the western front, the Prime Minister's method of Cabinet government by consensus seemed indecisive, while his unwillingness to call upon the nation for such strong measures as compulsory military service suggested that he was less than completely dedicated to winning the war.

Lloyd George, in dramatic contrast, made the conscription issue his own. In taking the lead on this issue he showed how much his political position had changed. While Asquith, who had brought the country into the war, continued to uphold peacetime civil liberties and Liberal values, Lloyd George, the one-time Radical who until the last moment had opposed entry into the war, emerged as a leader prepared to sacrifice individual rights for the sake of victory. Traditional Liberals, who had always opposed compulsion, felt that Lloyd George was going over to the other camp.

As he lost his old political friends, Lloyd George acquired new ones, two of whom proved to be especially important. One was Sir Edward Carson, the rebel Irish Tory who led the fight for conscription in the House of Commons. The other was the champion of imperialism, Alfred Milner, who led the fight for conscription in the House of Lords and, as chairman of the National Service League, in the country. Milner, an outstanding colonial administrator, had been largely responsible for launching the Boer War, the venture in South Africa at the turn of the century that Lloyd George as a young idealist had vigorously opposed.[2] At the time Lloyd George had attacked Milner bitterly. As a Radical, the young Welshman had opposed imperial expansion, foreign involvement, and military ventures; while Lord Milner, as a Liberal Unionist who became the inspiration of right-wing Tories, made himself the center of imperialist thought. His ideal was imperial union.* Together with the young men assembled in South Africa under his leadership—"Milner's Kindergarten"—he had stimulated the movement for integration of the far-flung empire into one organic unit.** Milner was a superb administrator whose skills were later to prove invaluable to Lloyd George in winning the war.

II

In 1916, Lloyd George became Secretary of State for War when Kitchener died, but found himself powerless to put an end to the sickening military disasters of that year. It has been estimated that the total of military and civilian casualties in all of Europe's domestic and international conflicts in the 100 years between 1815 and 1915 was no greater than a single day's combat losses in any of the great battles of 1916.[3] Coming after Gallipoli and Mesopotamia, and such

---

* Milner's ideal was a union of the white peoples of the British Empire. Other members of the Milner circle, however, advocated a multiracial imperial union.
** Lionel George Curtis, his former secretary, in 1910 helped to found the quarterly review the *Round Table* which advocated British imperial federalism. Another former secretary, John Buchan, was a fervent imperialist who won over a vast public by his popular adventure novels. Another graduate of the Kindergarten, Geoffrey Robinson, edited *The Times*.

gory episodes as the 142,000 British casualties suffered in just four days of fighting at Arras in France, the terrible Somme offensive of July 1916 aroused a climax of despair. On 1 July the British lost 60,000 men, the heaviest casualties ever suffered in a single day by a British army.[4] By the time the offensive was over, British casualties at the Somme had mounted to 420,000. Among them was Raymond Asquith, the Prime Minister's son.

Lloyd George despaired of victory as he observed the lengthy and inefficient meetings of Asquith's large War Cabinet, debating end-lessly and deciding nothing. On 9 November he told Maurice Hankey that "We are going to lose this war."[5]

At about the same time, the Gallipoli controversy was revived, reminding the political world how ineptly the Asquith government had waged war. Unwisely, the government had sanctioned an official inquiry in June into the Dardanelles campaign. Churchill, now out of office, devoted himself to documenting the case that his colleagues were to blame for the Gallipoli disaster. The alarmed Prime Minister managed to have the report restricted to the Commission of Inquiry's conclusions, omitting the testimony and other evidence on which they were based. Nonetheless, the political damage was done and the Gallipoli inquiry contributed to the collapse of the first coalition government.

The story of Asquith's overthrow has been told too often for it to need retelling here at any length. A principal role in his downfall was played by the British press, dominated then, as it never has been before or since, by one man. Alfred Harmsworth, Viscount Northcliffe, controlled half the London press, at a time, before radio or television, when publications were the only media of mass com-munication. His ownership of *The Times*, with its prestige, and of the *Daily Mail*, with its popular appeal, gave him both "the classes and the masses."[6] Northcliffe used his immense power to dramatize the case that Asquith and his civilian colleagues were preventing the generals and admirals from winning the war.

Northcliffe's newspapers ranged themselves behind Sir Edward Carson, Britain's leading trial lawyer, who led the revolt against the government in Parliament and in the country. Carson on the attack was the most dangerous animal in the political jungle. As he lashed out against the government, the lean, dark, and bitter Irishman seemed to be everything the Prime Minister was not. As a historian has written of him, "The notion became current that he possessed a drive, a remorseless determination, and unrelenting hostility to the Germans, which contrasted strongly with the dismal procrastination attributed to Asquith and his colleagues."[7]

Although he denied it, in the autumn of 1916 Lloyd George began working closely with Carson; and Sir Max Aitken (later Lord

Beaverbrook) brought Bonar Law into a political combination with them. After intricate maneuverings, Asquith resigned and went into Opposition, taking half of his Liberal Party—and all of its leaders except Lloyd George—with him. Pushed by Aitken ("It was he who made B.L. decide to break up the Asquith government," said Lloyd George),[8] Bonar Law threw the weight of the Unionist-Conservative Party behind Lloyd George. (A major condition imposed by the Conservatives was that Churchill should be excluded from the new government.) A substantial number of backbench Liberals joined with them, as did the tiny Labour Party. On 7 December 1916, David Lloyd George became Prime Minister of Britain as head of the second coalition government.

Lloyd George moved quickly to impose a war dictatorship. Direction of the war was entrusted to a War Cabinet, composed initially of five members. The new Prime Minister headed it himself. Bonar Law, who also became Leader of the House and Chancellor of the Exchequer, became a member, as did Labour's Arthur Henderson. The work of the War Cabinet was done principally by its other two members, Lord Milner, on whom Lloyd George especially relied, and to a lesser extent, Lord Curzon. Maurice Hankey became Secretary to the War Cabinet, and took charge of seeing that its decisions were carried out.

It was a sweeping, revolutionary change in the way the country was governed. Arthur Balfour, the former Prime Minister who became Foreign Minister in the new government, remarked of Lloyd George at the time: "If he wants to be a dictator, let him be. If he thinks that he can win the war, I'm all for his having a try."[9]

A chance effect of the change in government was that it changed Britain's objectives in the Middle East. Asquith and Grey, the only two men in the government who doubted the desirability of acquiring new territories in the East, had been driven from office. Lord Kitchener, who had imposed his own Middle Eastern views on the Cabinet, was dead; and the new Prime Minister had been an opponent of Kitchener's views all along.

Unlike Kitchener, Lloyd George had believed, and continued to believe, that the East could be of great importance in winning the war. Typically, only a few days after Lloyd George took office as Prime Minister, Hankey recorded in his diary that "I lunched along with Ll. G., who discoursed mainly on his plans for a big military coup in Syria."[10]

As for the future of the area, he was moved in large part by his hatred of the Turkish regime. From his first political leader, the nineteenth-century Liberal, William Ewart Gladstone, he had inherited an abhorrence of the Ottoman Empire for its cruelty toward its

Christian subjects. He was sympathetic to Greece, which had territorial ambitions in Asia Minor, and espoused Zionist aspirations in the Holy Land. In the latter case he had made clear, however, that he expected the Jewish National Home to develop within the context of British rule. What became clear only after Lloyd George had been in office for a year or two was that he envisioned the Middle East, not just as the road to India, but as a prize worth seeking in itself. Unlike British ministers of the nineteenth century, whose aim was limited to excluding other European powers from the region, Lloyd George therefore sought British hegemony in the Middle East.

As Prime Minister, Lloyd George moved ever closer to Milner and imperialism. Hankey later wrote that Milner "was Lloyd George's most trusted colleague; except, perhaps Bonar Law—but he was more for political advice."[11] Lloyd George was a pragmatic, intuitive opportunist who improvised; Milner, with his German background, was methodical in action and systematic in thought, supplying what the Prime Minister lacked.

Milner further strengthened his hold on the Lloyd George government by placing his own followers within Hankey's secretariat. Hankey was able to retain Sir Mark Sykes, his personal choice, as one of his three assistants,* but the other two were Leo Amery, one of Milner's leading adherents, and William Ormsby-Gore, Milner's Parliamentary Secretary.

When Lloyd George, after the fashion of an American president in the White House, set up his own informal staff, Milner had a hand in including some of his own followers, such as Lionel Curtis, a founder of the magazine *Round Table*, which espoused imperial union, and Philip Kerr, the magazine's editor. The staff was set up in temporary buildings in the garden of 10 Downing Street and was dubbed the "Garden suburb."

A sort of dictatorship of two emerged from the early days of the new Prime Minister's period of office: at 11:00 each morning Lloyd George would meet with Milner, along with Hankey and the Chief of the Imperial General Staff, and only at noon would they meet with the other members of the War Cabinet. In 1918 Milner became War Minister in name as well as reality. He had the experience needed for the job: he had run the civilian side of the Boer War and now, under Lloyd George, ran the civilian side of the First World War.

Lloyd George's association with the Milner circle was intellectual as well as practical and bureaucratic. The Prime Minister came to

---

* Hankey wrote to Lloyd George that Sykes was "mainly an expert on Arab affairs" but that he was "by no means a one-sided man" and that his breadth of vision could be "invaluable in fixing up the terms of peace."[12]

social gatherings where the Round Tablers met to exchange views. In the middle of 1917 Hankey observed that "Among the most influential at the present moment I would place the Round Table group. They dine every Monday ... Milner is the real leader in this group ... Lloyd George sometimes attends their gatherings."[13]

The influence was mutual. Shortly afterward Hankey noted that Milner had "come completely round to Ll. G.'s view ... that it is necessary to devote our main efforts against Turkey."[14]

III

In France, several governments had fallen during the course of the war, but the differences between one government and another were not dramatic. In 1917 that changed.

The mutiny of the French army in May 1917 brought about the fall of the last of France's wartime governments with which her politicians felt comfortable. The traditional leadership was discredited. The Viviani, Briand, and Ribot governments had been allowed to resign, but the Paul Painlevé government had not been: in November of 1917 the French Parliament overthrew it. There was only one potential premier yet untried who might fight on to victory, but he was the most feared and detested man in public life. As Lloyd George remarked of him, "There was only one man left, and it is not too much to say that no one wanted him."[15] He was the man who had exposed the corrupt practices of his political colleagues—and they had never forgiven him.

Georges Clemenceau was, like Lloyd George, a political "loner." He, too, was a Radical, though in France the label had rather a different meaning. Like Lloyd George, he was believed to have abandoned the leftist tenets of his youth.[16] Like Lloyd George, the man of "the knock-out blow," he had denounced proponents of a compromise peace, and indeed had brought an end to discussions along those lines initiated by the Germans through Aristide Briand in 1917. He was growing deaf and fat and was seventy-six years old, but he remained the fighter he had been all his life; and the President, who felt obliged to offer him the premiership, noted that this "devil of a man has all patriots on his side, and if I did not call on him his legendary strength would make any alternative cabinet weak."[17]

Clemenceau was above all a hater, and in all the world what he most hated was Germany. He was the last survivor of the National Assembly that in 1871 had protested against the harsh peace terms Germany had imposed upon a vanquished France. He had never given up. It had always been his view that France should concentrate on building up her strength against Germany, and therefore that diverting strength into colonial adventures was a mistake. Thus the senators and deputies who aimed at annexing Syria and Palestine to France saw in him their chief enemy.

Between 1881 and 1885, over Clemenceau's protests, France had led the way in new colonial expansion. On a pretext, the French first invaded and conquered Tunisia in North Africa, and then the states that became Indochina in Asia. Prince Otto von Bismarck, the German leader, supported and indeed encouraged such French ventures. On 27 November 1884, Clemenceau told the French Chamber of Deputies that "Bismarck is a dangerous enemy, but even more dangerous perhaps as a friend; he showed us Tunis, placing us in conflict with England."[18]

In Parliament and in his journal, *La Justice*, Clemenceau denounced the acquisition of colonies as a financial and military burden, a distraction from the problem of the German frontier, and a clever German-inspired move that Berlin hoped would drive France into quarrels with Britain. In opposing the policy, he exposed the financial corruption that accompanied French colonial politics. *La Justice's* suggestion of sinister manipulations in the Tunisia affair were not far off the mark: there were speculations in real estate, railway concessions, and submarine cable telegraph concessions, whatever their relation might have been to the formulation of government policy. The financial corruption surrounding the adventure in Indochina was even more lurid. Clemenceau's accusations and exposures destroyed reputations and brought down governments. He became known as "the wrecker" even before he became known as "the tiger."

Of French parliamentary life at the time, Winston Churchill later wrote, "The life of the French Chamber, hectic, fierce, poisonous, flowed through a succession of scandals and swindles, of exposures, of perjuries, and murders, of plottings and intriguings, of personal ambitions and revenges, of crooking and double-crossing, which find their modern parallel only in the underworld of Chicago."[19] Clemenceau strode through it all in a murderous rage. In an age when it was still the custom to settle quarrels on the field of honor, he was a feared duellist. A speaker in the Chamber taunted the other members by saying of Clemenceau that "he has three things you fear: his sword, his pistol, and his tongue."[20]

For fear of him the French government in 1882 hesitated to join in the occupation of Egypt, with the result that Britain took Egypt entirely for herself. His opposition to colonial expansion could easily be portrayed—and was portrayed—as benefiting the British Empire. That was the line his opponents took when he became vulnerable to political attack. They produced a forgery to prove that he had sold out to Britain. Hecklers were hired to follow him around shouting

"Aoh yes," and free copies of a newspaper were circulated containing a cartoon showing him juggling with sacks of pounds sterling.[21] In 1892 one leading British politician wrote to another that "A Frenchman was here yesterday who told me an extraordinary cock and bull which is apparently believed in Paris where they will believe anything ... It is to the effect that Clemenceau's paper *La Justice* which is said to be losing money is financed from England on behalf of Germany and England."[22] In 1893 he was defeated for re-election and was driven out of parliamentary life for a decade.

This was the man whom a despairing France turned to in the darkest moment of 1917, and who soon imposed his will upon the government of his nation. Like Lloyd George, he became a sort of war dictator, incarnating a driving determination to fight on until Germany was totally crushed. Like Lloyd George, too, he happened to bring to office a special view about policy in the Middle East.

As premier, he continued to have no territorial goals for France outside of Europe. Of the traditional French claim to Syria, reflected in the Sykes-Picot Agreement, Clemenceau said that if Lloyd George could get France the right to install a protectorate regime there he would not refuse it, "as it would please some reactionaries," but that he himself attached no importance to it.[23]

The fortunes of war and politics had brought into power in their respective countries the first British Prime Minister who wanted to acquire territory in the Middle East and the only French politician who did not want to do so.

30

THE OVERTHROW OF THE CZAR

I

It was an improbable chain of circumstances that led France to rally behind a leader who was opposed to French imperialism in the Middle East, and an even odder chain of circumstances that led Russia in the same month to fall under the sway of a leader who also claimed to oppose Russian imperialism in the region.

If one thing seemed clear by the beginning of 1917, it was that Russia held the edge in the Middle Eastern war against Turkey. Enver's catastrophic defeat in early 1915 on the Caucasus front was followed by a successful Russian invasion of eastern Anatolia in 1916. The Russians had strengthened their strategic position by winning mastery of the Black Sea and by constructing railroad lines from the Caucasus toward their new front line in eastern Turkey. The Grand Duke Nicholas, the Russian commander, planned to mount a new offensive as soon as the railroad lines were completed. According to a German staff officer attached to the Ottoman armed forces, the grand duke's offensive would "have led to a complete victory and perhaps driven Turkey out of the war in the summer of 1917."[1]

Yet years later, Lloyd George told the House of Commons that "the collapse of Russia was almost entirely due" to the Ottoman Empire.[2] The basis of Lloyd George's opinion was that by closing off most of Russia's imports and exports, the Young Turk masters of Constantinople had deprived her of armaments and revenues. Those who disagree with Lloyd George's assessment are able to argue that even if the Constantinople trade route had remained open, wartime Russia, with her peasant farmers away in the army, produced less than the normal amount of food and so had less to export, and her Allies had little ammunition to send her. But either observation points to the paradoxical truth that Russia's military successes on the Caucasus front were in a sense irrelevant: the real war had become an economic and social survival contest.

The industrialist Walter Rathenau in Germany was the pioneer in understanding this. In 1914 he organized a Division of Raw Materials for a skeptical Ministry of War in Berlin. He was given a secretary and one small room at the back of the ministry. By the end of 1918 it was the largest unit in the ministry; it had spread over several blocks of buildings and almost overshadowed the rest.[3] In Rathenau's prescient vision, warfare was undergoing its industrial revolution, becoming a matter of financing, moving, and supplying on a gigantic scale, and therefore required central allocation, planning, and control over the whole economy.

Lloyd George in his pragmatic way learned to see things much the same way. He brought war socialism to the hitherto individualistic British economy. When he started the Ministry of Munitions in a requisitioned hotel, he had no staff at all. By the end of the war, the ministry had 65,000 employees and it exercised control over three million workers.[4] In industry after industry, supplies were requisitioned and allocated. New workers, including large numbers of women, were brought into the labor force.

In Russia, as in Germany and Britain, the violent and rapid social changes that accompanied this wartime industrial revolution tugged at the structure of society, straining pillars and supports never designed to carry a great weight. There were displacements in morals, politics, employment patterns, investment patterns, family structure, personal habits, and language. Some idea of the magnitude of the changes may be suggested by the length of the Carnegie Endowment's postwar survey of the economic and social changes that had occurred in twenty-one countries: it ran to 150 volumes. The British series alone ran to 24 volumes.

Of the principal European belligerents in the First World War, Czarist Russia proved the least able to cope with these challenges for it was weak in the elements of infrastructure—transportation systems, communication systems, engineering industries, and capital markets—that make a modern economy resilient and adaptable. More than anything else, however, Russia's failure was a failure of leadership.

The consequences of the Turkish stranglehold on the Dardanelles underscored the lack of patriotism in some elements of the governing classes and the lack of competence in others. There was no excuse for the terrible shortages that developed in 1916 and 1917. Russia was a country naturally rich in agriculture: the peasantry made up 80 percent of the population, and cereals alone constituted half of her exports.[5] With the export trade cut off at Constantinople, all the food formerly sent out of the country was available to be consumed at home; and though there was a fall in the production of agricultural estates caused by the loss of labor to the army, more than enough food was produced to feed the country.[6] The shortages resulted instead from disruption of transportation and distribution, due in part to bottlenecks and breakdowns, but due also to deliberate maneuvers: speculation, profiteering, and hoarding.

The Czar's government recklessly ignored the need to crack down on the profiteers who accentuated the consequences of Turkey's stranglehold on Russia's trade route to the West. Widespread industrial strikes and the onset of financial chaos failed to move the government to act. By 1917 current interest and sinking fund payments due on its public debt were greater than the total revenues of the state in 1916, a national insolvency with which the government dealt by printing paper money, so that prices during wartime years rose by 1,000 percent.[7]

An obvious way out of the crisis was to bring the war to an end. In 1915 the Ottoman Empire and Germany had offered Russia right of passage through the Dardanelles if she would abandon the Allies. Throughout 1916 Germany continued to sound out the possibility of concluding a separate peace with Russia. Many of the soundings took place in neutral Sweden. The stumbling block, some have said, was the Czar's unwillingness to relinquish his grip on Poland.[8] However, the Russian Minister to Sweden explained to the Germans that in his "personal opinion" Russia would have to continue in the war on the Allied side until she received the "key to the Black Sea": which is to say, Constantinople and the Dardanelles.[9] On the field of battle the Czar's hungry and tattered soldiery were struggling for survival, but his response to the German overtures shows that Nicholas II continued to give priority to his imperial ambitions—above all, perhaps, to the conquest of the long-sought-for Dardanelles.

II

The history of the Russian revolutions of 1917, which is still being written and which remains timelessly relevant to the world's condition, falls outside the scope of the present study. One aspect of that history, however, is of concern here and will be pursued in the following pages: the plot to promote the fortunes of the then-unknown Lenin that was hatched in the Ottoman Empire.

In the disastrous course of Russia's participation in the European war, those in control of Russia's government, finance, and industry demonstrated that their interests diverged from those of the population at large. At the leftward fringe of the outlawed revolutionary underground, an obscure and isolated figure had said as much—though for theoretical reasons of his own—from the moment the war began. During the war he lived, studied, and wrote in penniless exile in Zurich, Switzerland. He was in his mid-forties and was not yet famous beyond police and revolutionary circles.

Vladimir Ilyich Ulyanov, who in 1901 had adopted the pseudonym of Lenin, was a former attorney who had devoted his life to Marxist theory and factional disputes. Stocky, muscular, with the hunched shoulders of a fighter, he was a brilliant but abrasive and intolerant man who fearlessly followed the juggernaut of his logic wherever it might lead. At the outset of the war he was shocked to see his socialist colleagues flock to the support of their respective countries. Lenin's theory led him to stand alone in opposition to the war and therefore in opposition to his country. It set him apart from the others. Even his own political faction, the Bolsheviks, did not fully understand his views on the war.

At the beginning of September 1914, he drafted his *Seven Theses on the War*, in which he wrote that: "From the point of view of the laboring class and the toiling masses of all the peoples of Russia, the lesser evil would be the defeat of the tsarist monarchy and its army, which oppresses Poland, the Ukraine, and a number of other peoples of Russia." In his *Theses* he repeatedly denounced the empire exercised by the Russians over the other peoples ruled by the Czar.[10] He was a Russian; but it was his duty, as he saw it, to aim at Russia's defeat and at the dismemberment of the Russian Empire.

In Constantinople at the time there lived a former colleague of Lenin's, a fellow leader of the Socialist Second International, who had arrived at similar conclusions. Alexander Israel Helphand, who had adopted the underground pseudonym of "Parvus," was a Russian Jew whose professed political objective was the destruction of the Czarist Empire.[11] Where Lenin was merely indifferent to the prospect of a German victory, Helphand was positively enthusiastic about it. As it happened, Helphand possessed the money and political contacts that enabled him to pursue his pro-German inclinations.

Of the same generation as Lenin (Helphand was born in 1869, Lenin in 1870), Parvus had been one of the other intellectually commanding figures on the left wing of the revolutionary socialist movement. Leaving Russia for Germany in the early 1890s, he had made his name as a theorist and journalist fighting alongside the Polish-born German Jewess Rosa Luxemburg for a pure revolutionary position. In the early years of the twentieth century, he had become the mentor of Leon Trotsky, and in 1905 he had originated what was to become Trotsky's theory of the "permanent revolution." Returning to Russia, Parvus was banished to Siberia, but soon escaped to western Europe.

But there was another side to Helphand/Parvus, which showed itself only gradually: he was a shady promoter who, from the point of view of his fellow-idealists, did suspiciously well for himself. He had set up publishing ventures that were meant to serve the revolutionary cause but seemed to serve his personal interests even better. Lenin and his Bolshevik faction had good reason for believing that in 1904 Parvus had embezzled perhaps 130,000 marks* (roughly 30,000 dollars) in literary royalties that the writer Maxim Gorky had contributed to the Social Democratic Party. They confronted him with it and the explanations that he offered were unconvincing.

Abandoning publishing and revolutionary activities, he had turned full-time to a variety of businesses, moving on via Vienna to the Balkans and the Ottoman Empire, where he became interested in the Young Turkey movement and began dealing in corn and other commodities. By 1912 he had established close contact with Young Turk government officials, with whose aid he obtained contracts to provide supplies for the Ottoman armies in the Balkan Wars.

When the First World War broke out in Europe, Helphand published an article in the Turkish press advising the Ottoman government that its interests would be served by a German victory. He also helped foment pro-German feeling in the Balkan countries. When the Ottoman Empire entered the war, he helped the Porte obtain vital supplies of grain and railroad parts, though of course at a profit to himself; he also advised the government on various aspects of mobilizing its economy for the war effort. Destroying the government of Russia was his goal, and his home in Constantinople became a meeting place for plotters against the Czar.

Through his contacts, Helphand managed to arrange an interview with the German ambassador to the Ottoman Empire. He met von Wangenheim on 7 January 1915, and told him that "The interests of the German government are identical with those of the Russian revolutionaries."[12] Von Wangenheim cabled a report of the meeting to the German Foreign Office two days later, in which he reported that Helphand had told him "that the Russian Democrats could achieve their aim only by the total destruction of Czarism and the division of Russia into smaller states."[13] Helphand proposed that Germany should help him unite the revolutionaries behind a program of subverting the Russian Empire.

At a high level, the German government evinced interest in his proposal. At the end of February 1915 Helphand went to Berlin to meet with officials at the Foreign Ministry. They asked him to recapitulate his proposal in writing; in response, on 9 March, he submitted a memorandum to them embodying a vast plan for the subversion of Czarist Russia by encouraging socialist revolutionaries and nationalists. He told the Germans about Lenin and his Bolshevik faction, reported that Lenin and some of his followers were in

---

* There is some dispute about the exact figure.

Switzerland, and singled them out as especially worth German support. Thus Helphand discovered and identified Lenin for the Germans.

The German leaders agreed to adopt Helphand's proposals and at the end of March gave him an initial payment of a million marks (equal at that time to roughly 240,000 dollars in U.S. currency) to begin the work of attempting to unify the various revolutionary groups.

His initial overtures to his former comrades were rebuffed. In Berlin, Rosa Luxemburg did not even give him an opportunity to speak: she showed him to the door. Lev Davidovich Bronstein, who called himself Trotsky, admitted that Parvus had once been an important figure, a friend and teacher, but concluded that in 1914 he had changed, and that he was now "politically deceased."[14] The attitude of Parvus's former socialist-revolutionary colleagues was described by one of them who said they regarded him as "a Russian informer, a scoundrel, a confidence trickster, ... and now a Turkish agent and speculator."[15]

In the spring he made his most important approach. He went to Zurich and set up court at the luxurious Baur au Lac Hôtel. There he lived ostentatiously, drinking a bottle of champagne each morning at breakfast, smoking cigars of enormous size, and surrounding himself with showy women.[16] He also began spreading money around among the poorer exiles, persuading them that he had become the paymaster of the revolution.

At the end of May he sought out Lenin at the restaurant where the Bolshevik theorist usually was to be found, went over to the table where Lenin and his associates were lunching, spoke to them, and accompanied them back to Lenin's apartment. Helphand explained his mission. Lenin, having listened to his presentation, accused him of having turned into a German "chauvinist," and ordered him to leave and never come back.[17]

Yet a friend of Lenin's left with Helphand to start putting the plan of subversion into effect. Their base of operation was to be Stockholm. Through his friend, Lenin was able to learn of developments as they occurred. Moreover, Lenin and the Bolshevik Party accepted money from Helphand via a Polish and a Russian Social Democrat; Lenin later denied this, but his correspondence shows that his denials were untrue.[18]

The business in which Helphand ostensibly engaged was a trading firm, whose activities in fact enriched him enormously. Secretly he organized subversion and published a revolutionary newspaper, which the German government financed. The publication was not a great success. He attempted to organize a general strike in Russia, even without the aid of Lenin and the others. It was a much greater success; he did not achieve a general strike, but brought as many as 45,000 protesters into the streets of Petrograd (as St Petersburg, the Russian capital, had been called since 1914).

But Helphand had focused the German government's attention on the particular importance of Lenin as a disruptive force and, through other agents, the Germans arranged to watch over the Bolshevik theorist and to lend him additional money when he needed it without his necessarily having to acknowledge the source of the funds.

Thus Helphand, the Constantinople-based intimate of the Young Turks, had brought into play a strange new weapon with which Turkey's ally Germany could attempt to bring their common Russian foe crashing down.

III

Petrograd was a long distance away from the granary of the south, and its population suffered from food shortages and soaring food prices throughout 1916 and 1917. During that time strikes and protests became a way of life: including those inspired by Helphand, between mid-1915 and February 1917, there were 1,163 strikes.[19] Over half of these were politically rather than economically motivated, which showed that the revolt against the regime had begun to transcend the issue of shortages.

On 8 March 1917 a demonstration took place in celebration of International Women's Day. Housewives, protesting against food shortages, joined the demonstration; so did many of the roughly 90,000 workers then on strike in about fifty factories. The next day there were about 200,000 on strike, and the day afterward the strike became general. Two days later four regiments of soldiers joined the populace, strengthening the demonstrators against the increasingly helpless police. The army mutiny proved decisive, only because effective government had long since vanished. The governor of the city ordered proclamations of martial law to be put up, but there was no glue to hold the posters on the walls.[20]

On 15 March Czar Nicholas II abdicated, effective from the following day, in favor of his brother, the Grand Duke Michael. The following day the Grand Duke Michael declined to accept the throne, and Russia became a republic governed by a Provisional Government originally led by Prince G. E. Lvov and later by Alexander Kerensky.

Politicians of all shades of opinion were surprised to find that what the population of Petrograd had pushed against was an open door. As a leading historian of these events has written, "The revolutionary parties played no direct part in the making of the revolution. They did not expect it . . ."[21] Were the events in Petrograd instead the fruition of the conspiracy conceived by Parvus, the associate of the Young Turks? Helphand and the German General Staff, through their agents and their gold, did play a role in inciting Russians to strike and to rebel, though surely not to the extent suspected by British Intelligence. At first it was not even clear whether the overthrow of the Czar could help them to achieve their goal—which was to defeat Russia. At the time all political parties, including the Bolsheviks, were in favor of prosecuting the war; now that they no longer had a government they detested, as Russian patriots they wanted to defeat their enemies, the Germans and Turks.

But, as Helphand alone understood, Lenin was of a different persuasion—and was beside himself with frustration. He was in Zurich, cut off from participation in the great events in Russia; and his followers in Petrograd misunderstood what he wanted them to do. Helphand had anticipated the Bolshevik theorist's reaction. Without asking Lenin, Helphand went ahead to make arrangements with the German General Staff to have a railroad train placed at Lenin's disposal to take him and his closest political associate, Gregori Zinoviev, back to Petrograd. When he then issued the invitation to Lenin, the latter warily refused and attempted instead to make arrangements that did not involve Helphand. He also posed conditions: between twenty and sixty Russian exiles should be allowed on the train, without regard to their views about the war, and the train should enjoy extraterritorial rights. The German Minister in Berne cabled the German Foreign Office that Lenin and Zinoviev "believed that they had, in this way, insured themselves against being compromised in Russia."[22] The German government understood and agreed. In April of 1917 Lenin was sent in his sealed train on his way to Russia.

From the moment that he arrived at the Finland station in Petrograd, with typically acerbic greetings to those who met him, Lenin set about positioning his Bolshevik faction—as Helphand had expected—as the only political group in Russia that advocated ending the war immediately. His followers had believed that they should support their country now that it had a republican government of the political left. They had fallen, according to Lenin, into error. In his view, the war demonstrated that capitalism had entered into its imperialist stage, which he regarded as its final stage; it therefore was the right time for socialist parties throughout Europe to launch revolutions. It was not the time to wage international war, especially in alliance with governments such as those of France and Britain that ought to be overthrown.

In the autumn of 1917, when Lenin—with the aid of additional financial subsidies from Germany—seized power in Petrograd and made himself dictator of what remained of the shattered Russian state, he moved immediately to take his country out of the war. In March 1918 he accepted defeat by agreeing to a peace treaty that met Germany's terms. It appeared that Helphand had served his friends in Constantinople and Berlin well; as he had foretold, backing Lenin had helped to drive Russia out of the war.

IV

British observers of the Russian revolutions in 1917 were struck by the apparent conjunction of Bolsheviks, Germans, and Jews. Many of the Bolshevik leaders were of Jewish origin. So was Helphand, who had brought them German money and support—and who had come from Constantinople and was an intimate of the Young Turks. The Young Turks—according to the doctrine long held by British officials—were controlled by Jewish Freemasons who had brought the Ottoman Empire into alliance with Germany. It was a long-standing British belief that Jews and Germans were intimately related. It all seemed to fit.

John Buchan, the popular novelist of imperialism, who had been Milner's Private Secretary in South Africa and who, on Milner's recommendation, later became director of information services for Lloyd George's government, expressed this view in the first chapter of his classic novel of suspense, *The Thirty-Nine Steps* (1915):

> Away behind all the governments and the armies there was a big subterranean movement going on, engineered by very dangerous people ... [T]hat explained a lot ... things that happened in the Balkan War, how one state suddenly came out on top, why alliances were made and broken, why certain men disappeared, and where the sinews of war came from. The aim of the whole conspiracy was to get Russia and Germany at loggerheads ... [T]he Jew was behind it, and the Jew hated Russia worse than hell ... [T]his is the return match for the pogroms. The Jew is everywhere ... with an eye like a rattle-snake ... [H]e is the man who is ruling the world just now, and he has his knife in the empire of the Tsar.

Thus the Bolsheviks came to be viewed, not as Russians or even as ideological extremists, but as enemy secret agents called into existence by Germans doing the work of Jews who were devoted to the vengeful destruction of Russia. In 1917 and for many years afterward British officials continued to believe that the Bolsheviks were not principals in their own right, with their own agenda and their own objectives, but were mere employees of the German General Staff who took their orders from Jews and Prussians in Berlin.

The possibility that Russia might collapse had been Britain's nightmare ever since September 1914, just as it had been the dream of Enver Pasha—a dream which inspired him to bring the Ottoman Empire into the war on the side of the Central Powers. The Bolshevik Revolution had turned the one's nightmare and the other's dream into reality. Scholars still differ in their accounts of how it came about, but without question Russia's leaving the war in 1917 was a severe blow to Britain and her allies, and an enormous victory not only for Germany but also for Ottoman Turkey.

V

During the Gallipoli adventure, Winston Churchill had said, "This is one of the great campaigns in history. Think what Constantinople is to the East. It is more than London, Paris, and Berlin all rolled into one are to the West. Think how it has dominated the East. Think what its fall will mean."[23]

Yet its capture—which had seemed imminent to Churchill in March 1915—continued to prove elusive. After the Allies' failure to win through to Constantinople in 1915, it was the turn of the Russians, who scored successes in Turkish Armenia in 1916 and were poised to march toward Constantinople in 1917. Then came the revolutions in Petrograd, and the Russian armies on Turkish soil, believing the war was coming to an end, gave up all thought of launching an attack.

By then the Turks were too exhausted to exploit the situation by launching an attack of their own on the Russians. But their opponents were exhausted too; sufficiently so to consider giving up such ambitious goals as winning Constantinople. In 1917 Milner, and perhaps Lloyd George, flirted with the idea of coming to an understanding with Germany, in which the Russian Empire rather than the Ottoman Empire could be partitioned as the spoils of victory.[24]

Against all odds, the Ottoman Empire had held its own. The governments that had brought the Allied Great Powers into the war against Turkey—the Asquith government in Britain, the René Viviani government in France, and the Czar and his minister Sazanov in Russia—had all been overthrown. In some measure it was Turkey's successful defense of the Dardanelles that was responsible for bringing them down. Though at first it had seemed a madly reckless act of Enver and Talaat to bring the tottering Ottoman Empire into the war, they had brought it off; they had lost some territory but they also seemed poised to gain some, and at the end of 1917 they were more powerful than ever within the Sublime Porte. They no longer felt the need to cloak themselves in the respectability of Prince Said

Halim and finally allowed him to resign as Grand Vizier. The self-made party boss Talaat Bey boldly took the title into his own un-aristocratic hands.

Yet for Talaat and Enver the road ahead was perilous. Though the threat from Russia was removed, the threat from Britain was renewed. Their enemy, the new Prime Minister of Britain, was a dynamo and a war leader of genius. Though Lloyd George was willing to explore the possibility of a compromise peace with the Young Turks, he was a fighter—and his heart was in the fight to destroy Turkey's empire.

PART VI

NEW WORLDS AND PROMISED LANDS

31

THE NEW WORLD

I

In 1916—17, the shadow of the United States first fell over Lloyd George's imperial ambitions in the Middle East.

By the last quarter of 1916, the Allies had become dependent upon the United States not merely for supplies but for financing. They were running out of money, and the economist John Maynard Keynes, speaking for the British Treasury, warned the Cabinet that by the end of the year "the American executive and the American public will be in a position to dictate to this country."[1] President Woodrow Wilson underlined the point by interfering with a J. P. Morgan financing for Britain in December 1916—demonstrating that he could destroy the market for Allied loans in the United States and thereby drive Britain and France into insolvency.[2]

The Allies were unsure of Wilson's intentions. In fact he was opposed to their imperialist ambitions and intended to thwart them. "England and France have not the same views with regard to peace that we have," he noted, and he proposed to "force them to our way of thinking."[3] The conflict between his goals and theirs—in the Middle East as elsewhere—was to shape the politics of the years that followed. The entry of Wilson's America onto the world stage therefore opened up dangers as well as opportunities for Lloyd George.

As a public figure, Wilson was not easy for them to understand. The grandson of a pastor and the son of a Presbyterian minister, Wilson had studied law and government, became a professor, then President of Princeton University, Governor of New Jersey, and finally President of the United States. Yet in character, thought, and temperament, he was not so much a lawyer, a scholar, or a politician as he was, like his father and grandfather, a theologian.[4] He aimed at converting or—failing that—defeating rather than appeasing. A politician takes professional pride in achieving compromises, but Wilson—who did not wish to appear a politician—prided himself on avoiding them.

A man of high mind, character, and principles, he often saw moral issues in a controversy when others did not; he frequently inspired others to share his vision. He was, and still remains, a controversial figure: prim and bespectacled, the aloof and scholarly President, whose features appeared finely ascetic to his admirers, appeared priggish and self-righteous to others. He was a complex and forbidding figure.

The Allies at times misinterpreted the President's words and actions as a show put on for purposes of domestic politics, and failed to appreciate the sincerity of his desire to keep the United States out of the world war—and to keep *them* out of the new colonies they planned to establish for themselves in such areas as the Middle East. Thus they misunderstood Wilson's attempt to mediate an end to the war—a mission that he undertook at the request of the German Chancellor at the end of 1916.

Bethmann Hollweg, the civilian Chancellor of Germany, who for months had desired a negotiated settlement, forwarded a note to the United States on 12 December 1916, expressing a willingness to talk peace. Bethmann, for reasons of domestic politics, was unable to make the note more specific; but Wilson went ahead to issue a peace note of his own on 18 December, asking the Allies to define their war goals in the hope of narrowing the differences between the two sides.

Lloyd George had just become Prime Minister, and he and the French believed that Wilson was really asking for a program on the basis of which he could bring the United States into the war—which is what Secretary of State Robert Lansing allowed them to understand. Lansing, who was pro-intervention, in fact was undercutting the President's peace policy by suggesting to the Allies the terms of their reply. The Allies obliged; they defined their goals in sweeping terms, among them—"The liberation of the peoples who now live beneath the murderous tyranny of the Turks, and the expulsion from Europe of the Ottoman Empire, which has proved itself radically alien to Western civilization."[5] This was not a peace proposal but a war cry; clearly the Ottoman Empire would not negotiate a compromise peace on the basis of it. It was contrary to what the President had sought, and it is not clear how he would have proceeded if Germany had not suddenly pushed him into the arms of the Allies.

II

Bethmann lost all control of his government in early 1917. The new Chief of the General Staff, Paul von Hindenburg, and his animating military genius, Erich Ludendorff, believed that the war could be won speedily and that compromise was unnecessary. German policy was dictated by the military leaders, who assured the Kaiser in January 1917 that unrestricted submarine warfare could force the British into submission within six months, and that American intervention in the war, if it came, would come too late.

The German submarine campaign, exacerbated by the notorious Zimmerman telegram,* pushed the United States toward a declaration of war, though substantial numbers of Americans resisted the logic of events and remained adamantly opposed to involvement in the war. Swept against his will into the Allied camp, the President faced the challenge of uniting his country behind him.

The President's political problem—which was about to play a role in shaping his goals in the Middle East and elsewhere—was that he was the leader of a minority party. In 1912 he had won the presidency only because the majority party—the Republicans—had split in two, with some voting for William Howard Taft's Regulars and others for Theodore Roosevelt's Progressives; and in 1916 he had been re-elected only with the support of the Progressives in the normally Republican Middle and Far West. To carry the country behind his candidates and his program in future elections he would need to hold the same swing voting groups that had thrown the 1916 race to him: the big-city Irish Catholics who were anti-British and the mainly Republican, Middle Western German-Americans (many of them born in Germany) who were pro-German. How was he to bring the United States into the Allied camp without alienating these groups?

Yet the U-boats left him no choice: on 17 March 1917, German submarines sank three American merchant vessels. On 20 March the President met with his Cabinet to solicit advice. He listened to the views of his Cabinet and said little, although he remarked on the "apparent apathy of the Middle West"[6] as a problem to be overcome. He did not tell the Cabinet whether he had made up his mind what to do.

On 24 March Joseph Patrick Tumulty, the President's long-time private secretary, wrote to him that the opinion of the American public, as revealed by editorials in newspapers all over the country, was that if the United States went to war against Germany, "it should be on an issue directly between us and them."[7] America should not be tied to Allied war goals, whatever their merits; Americans should not be asked to die for other people's causes.

---

* The German Foreign Secretary, Arthur Zimmerman, sent a secret cable instructing his Minister in Mexico to seek an alliance with Mexico against the United States. Mexico was to be given Texas, New Mexico, and Arizona. The British government turned over an intercepted copy of Zimmerman's cable to President Wilson, who published it.

When Wilson went before Congress the evening of 2 April to ask for a declaration of war against the German Empire, it became evident that he was thinking along the same lines, for he devoted much of his speech to the United States' special goals. In explaining why he felt compelled to ask for a declaration of war, he narrowed the focus of the quarrel with Germany to grounds on which it was difficult to fault him: the Germans had sunk three American merchant vessels and proposed to sink more. Acts of war were being committed against the United States, to which she had no honorable choice but to respond in kind.

To emphasize that the quarrel was about the sinking of American ships, the President postponed consideration of relations with Germany's ally, the Habsburg Empire. He said that since Austria-Hungary had not made war on the United States, the United States, at least for the moment, would not make war on her. (In the event, the United States did not declare war against the Habsburg Empire until the end of 1917.) Emphasizing even further that he proposed to enter the war on political grounds of his own choosing, the President did not mention the Ottoman Empire at all, nor Bulgaria, which had recently joined the Central Powers. In fact the United States never declared or made war against them, although the Porte—as a result of German pressure—broke off diplomatic relations with the United States.

But he departed from the specific quarrel about the merchant vessels to challenge the German government—and the Allied governments too—on more general grounds. The actions of the Kaiser's government, he told Congress, constituted "a war against all nations"; and so "The challenge is to all mankind."[8] The United States, he said, would fight "for the ultimate peace of the world, and for the liberation of its peoples, the German peoples included"; and, in a phrase that became famous, he asserted that "The world must be made safe for democracy."[9] Implicitly distinguishing American policy from that of the Allied Powers, Wilson proclaimed that "We have no selfish ends to serve. We seek no indemnities for ourselves, no material compensation for the sacrifices we shall freely make."[10]

The point was later made explicit when the United States—keeping her distance from the Europeans and their suspect political ambitions—declined to become one of the Allies, and chose to be designated as an associate rather than as an ally. This was an extraordinary decision: to fight alongside Britain, France, Italy, and Russia, but to refuse to be their ally; and to fight against Germany, but to refuse to fight against Germany's allies. It was an indication of a fundamental conflict between the European belligerents and Wilson's America as to the purpose of the war and the shape of the peace. The intervention of the United States was to cast a long shadow over the gains with which the Entente Powers had promised to reward one another at the end of the war, especially in the Middle East.

III

The President was concerned about the attacks on his war policy by Progressive and Socialist leaders in the Middle West, for they represented voting blocs he could not ignore. They denounced his policy as aiding imperialism, and claimed the war was being fought in the service of major financial interests. They pictured the war as a greedy struggle for spoils.

They attacked where the President felt vulnerable, for he believed, correctly, that the Allied governments had entered into secret agreements with one another to aggrandize their empires, and feared that if these agreements were made known they might confirm the charge leveled against him that he had associated the United States with a war that served essentially imperialistic interests. The secret Sykes-Picot Agreement, for example, provided for Britain and France to divide up the Arabic-speaking Middle East. Other agreements provided for Russia and Italy to annex portions of what is now Turkey. Wilson inquired into the details of the secret treaties—even though his political confidant, Edward Mandell House, felt these were matters best not gone into until the war was won. In response to the President's inquiry, the British Foreign Secretary, Arthur Balfour, sent copies of the secret agreements to Washington on 18 May 1917. House (who used his honorary Texas title of colonel) was dismayed by their contents. Of the plan to partition the Middle East, Colonel House presciently remarked that "It is all bad and I told Balfour so. They are making it a breeding place for future war."[11]

The Allies would not renounce the claims that they had staked out for themselves in their secret agreements. The President could not use coercion to make them do so: while fighting alongside them he could not hurt them without hurting the United States. Yet he knew that if news of the agreements leaked out it would hurt them all. As an opponent, on principle, of secret treaties, he was pushed into the paradoxical position of trying to keep the Middle Eastern agreements a secret; but he was not able to do so. When the Bolsheviks seized power in Petrograd, they published the copies of the secret agreements that they discovered in the Russian archives. Fearful of the effect on American public opinion, Wilson tried—but failed—to prevent the publication of the treaties in the United States.

Falling back on a suggestion by his brilliant young journalist supporter Walter Lippmann, then an editor of the *New Republic*, Wilson took the offensive by redefining the goals for which the war was being fought, in a way that he judged would purify the Allied cause, in the hopes of boosting public morale on his own side and of again appealing to the German people over the heads of their leaders.[12]

Wilson defined the new war goals in several ways and on a number of occasions. Most famous were the Fourteen Points, which he outlined to a joint session of Congress on 8 January 1918. Of these, some were of a general nature: no more secret agreements between countries; diplomacy and negotiation always to take place in the public view; freedom of the seas; freedom of trade, and an end of tariff and other economic barriers; general disarmament; and the establishment of an association of nations to guarantee the independence and territorial integrity of all nations. Others dealt with specific issues; and, of these, Point Twelve, although the United States was not at war with the Ottoman Empire, outlined American objectives with respect to it: "12. The Turkish portions of the present Ottoman empire should be assured a secure sovereignty, but the other nationalities which are now under Turkish rule should be assured an undoubted security of life and an absolutely unmolested opportunity of autonomous development." In an earlier draft, Wilson had proposed that Turkey be wiped off the map;[13] his main interest in the Middle East was missionary and, like Lloyd George, he seems to have kept in mind the Turkish massacres of Christians. The final version, however, drafted by his advisers, was in line with the President's claim that the United States was fighting the governments rather than the peoples of her adversaries.

Point Twelve expressed the view, shared by Wilson and House, that the Middle East should not be divided among the belligerent powers; that peoples hitherto ruled by the Turks should become autonomous.[14] Only a year before, however, Wilson and House had agreed that it would be unwise for the President to discuss in public his plans for displacing the Ottoman regime because his words might endanger the American missionary colleges in Beirut and outside Constantinople.[15]

A month later, on 11 February 1918, Wilson spoke to Congress and defined in a general way the Four Principles upon which the peace settlement should be made. The second and third principles were:

2. That peoples and provinces are not to be bartered about from sovereignty to sovereignty as if they were chattels or pawns in a game, even the great game, now for ever discredited, of the balance of power; but that

3. Every territorial settlement involved in this war must be made in the interest and for the benefit of the populations concerned, and not as a part of any mere adjustment or compromise of claims amongst rival states . . .

In a speech on 4 July 1918, Wilson defined the Four Ends for which the United States and its associates were fighting as including

The settlement of every question, whether of territory or sovereignty, of economic arrangement, or of political relationship, upon the basis of the free acceptance of that settlement by the people immediately concerned, and not upon the basis of the material interest or advantage of any other nation or people which may desire a different settlement for the sake of its own exterior influence or mastery.

Wilson's peace proposals were received with ardent enthusiasm, but, revealingly, not by the Allied governments. As Walter Lippmann's biographer has written,

At first this puzzled Lippmann, for he had assumed that Wilson had coordinated his plan with the Allies before making it public. He had not, and for a good reason: he knew they would turn it down. Defeated in his efforts to persuade the Allies to repudiate the secret treaties, he had tried to induce the peoples of Europe to put pressure on their own governments. The tactic failed, and as a result the Fourteen Points were simply a unilateral American pronouncement rather than a declaration of Allied policy.[16]

Indeed they represented a challenge to the Allied as well as to the enemy governments.

IV

Point Twelve was not only unilateral but also anomalous: the President was proposing to dismember the Ottoman Empire, with which the United States was not at war. It also seemed an anomaly that the United States should have declared war against Germany and later against Austria-Hungary without also declaring war against their allies.

The Senate Foreign Relations Committee appeared to be in favor of issuing the additional declarations of war. Its chairman asked Secretary of State Lansing for a fuller explanation of the Administration's reasons for not doing so. In a lengthy memorandum submitted by Lansing in reply, the Secretary of State cited a number of reasons.[17] At the time, the United States held no significant trade, economic, or political stakes in the Middle East other than two Protestant missionary-supported colleges—Robert College and the Syrian Protestant College—with which Wilson's friend and chief financial supporter, Cleveland Dodge, was intimately concerned. But Lansing argued that safeguarding these institutions in itself was of sufficient importance to justify the Administration's policy. He indicated that these institutions were worth millions of dollars and might be confiscated in the event of war. He also warned that, in the event of war, Christians and Jews in the Ottoman Empire might become the victims of new massacres. Lansing saw no particular advantage to be gained by declaring war, and pointed out that Turkey had not attacked the United States.

Despite the many reasons cited by Lansing for the Administration's decision, Congress remained unconvinced, and a resolution was introduced in the Senate in 1918 calling for the additional declarations of war. Testifying before the Senate Foreign Relations Committee, Lansing said that the decision was essentially one for Congress to make. At the request of the committee, he agreed to sound out the Allies as to whether they believed the additional declarations of war would help or hinder the war effort.

In May, Lansing reported to the President that the Allies were of the opinion that it would be helpful if the United States were to issue the additional declarations of war. Lansing pointed out to the President, however, that more than a million dollars a month was being sent to American missionaries in the Ottoman Empire to feed and care for Syrians and Armenians, and that this aid would be cut off in the event of war.[18]

The President reaffirmed his decision not to declare war. The Senate Foreign Relations Committee was so informed and reluctantly accepted his decision. Thus the United States remained at peace with the Ottoman Empire while the President continued to formulate his plans for breaking it up.

V

At the President's request, Colonel House, by-passing the State Department, began in early September 1917 to assemble a group of assistants to help him formulate America's plans for the postwar world. It was to be an independent group to which no publicity was to be given: it was code-named "the Inquiry." It met at first in the New York Public Library. At Wilson's suggestion, House drew participants principally from the academic world, beginning with names recommended by the president of Harvard University and by the editor of the *New Republic*. President Wilson personally chose

Walter Lippmann. At its peak, the group assembled by House numbered 126. The vast majority of its members had received their final academic degrees from one of four élite universities—Chicago, Columbia, Harvard, and Yale—and many were recruited directly from the faculties of those or similar institutions.[19]

Yet the Inquiry—apart from its professionally drawn maps—[20] was conducted amateurishly. The Middle Eastern group, composed of ten scholars operating out of Princeton University, did not include any specialists in the contemporary Middle East; its chairman was a student of the Crusades. The chairman's son, also a member, was a specialist in Latin American studies. Among other members were an expert on the American Indian, an engineer, and two professors who specialized in ancient Persian languages and literature.[21]

The choice of the New York Public Library as its first headquarters symbolized the approach adopted by the Inquiry: having raised all the political questions that divide the human race, the Inquiry proceeded to look them up. Many of the researchers did no more than summarize the information that they found in an encyclopaedia. Many delved into questions of literature and architecture that could have no conceivable bearing on the terms of an eventual peace treaty. Few of the reports had any bearing on the question of American national interests.[22]

It was typical that even in the economic section of the Middle Eastern group's report, there was no mention of the possibility that significant deposits of petroleum might be found in that part of the world. Yet in 1918, in waging a twentieth-century war in which tanks and airplanes made their appearance, the United States discovered (as did France that same year, and as Winston Churchill had done in Britain before the war) that the vast quantities of petroleum required in modern warfare had rendered the potential oil resources which were suspected to exist in the Middle East of considerable importance. That the Inquiry's reports on the Middle East ignored the oil issue was an indication of the unworldliness of the President's men that boded ill for the future Peace Conference.[23]

VI

While the President's peace program was in some respects quixotic, the extraordinary response that it evoked throughout the world showed that it expressed a widespread yearning to understand why the war was being fought. Britain's Foreign Secretary, Balfour, said that the war "was perhaps the biggest event in history" but that, beyond that, his mind would not go: "Coming generations might find it possible to see the thing as it really existed," but he and his generation could not.[24] The war, by 1917, had grown so much larger than the events that caused it that its causes seemed almost absurdly insignificant by comparison.

The day after Woodrow Wilson delivered his speech to Congress asking for a declaration of war, Walter Lippmann wrote to him (in words that were to appear in the *New Republic* later in the week): "Only a statesman who will be called great could have made America's intervention mean so much to the generous forces of the world, could have lifted the inevitable horror of war into a deed so full of meaning."[25] Lippmann, as he so often did, had found the word for it: the President, by adopting the goals that he did, had given the war a *meaning*.

Years later, in off-the-record comments aboard ship *en route* to the peace conferences in 1919, Wilson told his associates that "I am convinced that if this peace is not made on the highest principles of justice, it will be swept away by the peoples of the world in less than a generation. If it is any other sort of peace then I shall want to run away and hide ... for there will follow not mere conflict but cataclysm."[26]

However, neither Wilson nor those who took part in his Inquiry had formulated concrete programs that would translate promises into realities: the President's program was vague and bound to arouse millennial expectations—which made it practically certain that any agreement achieved by politicians would disappoint.

32

LLOYD GEORGE'S ZIONISM

I

As human beings, no two men could have been less alike than the austere American President and the charming but morally lax British Prime Minister. As politicians, though, they were similar: loners who had won power through the fluke of a party split. Each carried on a personal foreign policy, by-passing the Department of State and the Foreign Office. Both Wilson and Lloyd George had been reluctant to let their countries enter the war and, after opting for war, had found it difficult to keep their pacifist and anti-war supporters in line. Both men were of the political left; but there the similarities came to an end, for while Wilson was moving in an ever more progressive and idealistic direction, Lloyd George was doing just the opposite.

Had his political past been a guide to his future performance, Lloyd George could have been expected to share the United States' aversion to imperialist designs on the Middle East. In his Radical youth he had opposed British imperialism and it would have been in character for him, on becoming Prime Minister, to have overturned the Asquith Cabinet's agreement with the Allies to expand their empires—but he did not do so.

Lloyd George felt much the same need to reformulate war goals that Wilson did, but arrived at different conclusions. Wilson proclaimed that the enormity of the war required peace without annexations. Lloyd George took the other view: the enormity of the war required indemnities and annexations on an enormous scale.

Both Wilson and Lloyd George promised the peoples of the Ottoman Empire a better life, but where Wilson held out the hope of self-government, Lloyd George, while employing the rhetoric of national liberation, proposed to give the Middle East better government than it could give itself. In this the Prime Minister's goals coincided with those of Kitchener's lieutenants who exercised day-to-day control of British Cairo's Middle Eastern policy; thus the chances that his policy would actually be carried out were improved.

Taking office as 1916 turned into 1917, the new Prime Minister brought old-fashioned Radical fervor to such emerging war goals as the destruction of the reactionary Ottoman Empire—goals that harked back to the glorious days of nineteenth-century Liberalism. One of Lloyd George's first actions on becoming Prime Minister was to order his armies in Egypt onto the offensive. One of the others was to order John Buchan, whom he installed at Milner's suggestion as Director of Information, to launch a propaganda campaign portraying the destruction of the Ottoman Empire as a major purpose of the war. The campaign captured the imagination of the public: "The Turk Must Go!" proved to be an effective slogan.[1] Like Wilson's proclaimed points and principles, it also proved, at least in the short run, good politics.

Lloyd George's program of sending troops to fight in the East brought him into immediate conflict with his generals; they continued to demand supreme control over military decisions, and in this were supported by King George. Their strategy, as always, was to concentrate all resources on the western front, and they complained that their professional judgment was being defied by the new Prime Minister. Their newspaper friends on Fleet Street took up the cause. In early January the press lord, Lord Northcliffe, in a heated conversation threatened "to break" Lloyd George unless he called off his eastern strategy.[2] Northcliffe gave himself the credit for having overthrown Asquith in December, and appeared confident that he could bring down Lloyd George in January if he chose.

At about the same time, the War Office asked someone close to Lloyd George to warn him that the generals were going to fight him and that he *"might not* get the best of it [original emphasis]."[3] In Germany the General Staff was in the process of sweeping aside the civilian Chancellor. With the King, the leaders of his own Liberal Party, the press, and the generals against him, the Prime Minister could not be certain that the British Imperial General Staff would not attempt something similar. It was one of those times in world politics when anything, even the previously unimaginable, seemed possible.

Yet he stood as firm as he could on his eastern strategy, scornful of his military advisers. Long afterward, he wrote that "nothing and nobody could have saved the Turk from complete collapse in 1915 and 1916 except our General Staff."[4] According to Lloyd George, a victory over the Ottoman Empire before the end of 1916, when Bulgaria entered the war, would "have produced a decisive effect on the fortunes of the War."[5] It would have been easy to beat Turkey at any time, he said: "the resolute façade the Turks presented to the Allies ... had nothing behind it. It was part of the War Office game to pretend that the Turks had formidable forces with ample reserves.

They may have believed it, but if so, either their information was defective, or they were easily taken in."[6]

From the beginning of the war, Lloyd George had argued that Germany could be beaten by an attack through the Balkans. Defeating Turkey would open up the Balkans to such an attack. Writing long afterward, he was able to support his position by quoting von Hindenburg, the chief of the German General Staff: "If ever there was a prospect of a brilliant strategic feat, it was here ... Why did England never make use of her opportunity? ... Some day history will perhaps clear up this question ..."[7]

Lloyd George wanted to do it, but his problem was that he lacked the political strength to face down the generals and to commandeer troops and equipment in sufficient quantity to do the job. Throughout 1917 and well into 1918, he and Britain's military leaders fought a war of maneuver and intrigue against each other. Lloyd George's position was precarious; he had no depth of support in Parliament, where he was sustained for the time being by former enemies and distrusted by former friends. The most dangerous politician to attack the government was his one-time protégé Winston Churchill. "His tone was rather bitter in speaking of Lloyd George whom he had evidently come to consider as his detested antagonist," noted a friend of the two men.[8] Churchill had cause to be bitter; Lloyd George had excluded him from the Cabinet. "He brought Turkey into the War," the Prime Minister said. "Such men are too dangerous for high office."[9]

In speeches and newspaper articles, Churchill brought to bear his vast knowledge of military affairs and his grasp of detail in criticizing the conduct of the war. As Lloyd George knew well, there was much to criticize; he was powerless to impose his own views on the Allied commanders, yet as Prime Minister he was responsible to Parliament for their continuing costly failures. Keeping his lines of communication open, Churchill sent a private warning to the Prime Minister that, dissatisfied with the conduct of the war, the disparate opposition groups in the Commons might unite to bring him down.

On 10 May 1917 Churchill and Lloyd George happened to meet after a session of the House of Commons, and the Prime Minister spoke of his desire to have Churchill in the Cabinet. Though he still thought Churchill had "spoilt himself by reading about Napoleon," Lloyd George confided to Frances Stevenson, his secretary and mistress, that he needed Churchill to cheer him up and encourage him at a time when he was surrounded by colleagues with gloomy faces.[10]

As always, it was a question of whether it was a greater risk to leave Churchill out or to bring him in. In mid-July he appointed Churchill Minister of Munitions; and, even though the post did not carry with it membership in the War Cabinet, the appointment immediately aroused such opposition that for a time it endangered the government's existence.*

Churchill's aunt, writing to congratulate him on becoming Minister of Munitions, added "My advice is stick to munitions & don't try & run the government!"[12] The new appointment prompted *The Times* to warn that the country "is in no mood to tolerate even a forlorn attempt to resuscitate amateur strategy."[13] Churchill's family and friends, who were worried for him, and his legions of enemies and detractors, who were worried for the country, would have been dismayed but not surprised to learn that, within a week of his appointment, he had approached the Secretary of the War Cabinet with a revived plan to invade the Middle East. He proposed to land British armies at the port of Alexandretta to invade northern Syria and cut across the lines of transportation and communication of the Ottoman Empire.[14] The War Cabinet ignored his proposal, and it came to nothing.

II

Within months of taking office, Lloyd George was engaged in secret negotiations with the Young Turk leader, Enver Pasha. The Prime Minister's agent in the negotiations was Vincent Caillard, financial director of the giant armaments firm Vickers, who had spent many years in Constantinople as president of the council of administration of the Ottoman Public Debt. Caillard, in turn, acted through his close business associate, Basil Zaharoff, who had risen from the underworld of Smyrna to become the world's most notorious arms salesman, known in the popular press as the "merchant of death." Zaharoff journeyed to Geneva in 1917 and 1918 and reported that he was able to conduct negotiations there with Enver Pasha, at first through a go-between and then face-to-face.[15]

Through his emissary, the Prime Minister offered bribes—large bank accounts—to Enver and his associates to leave the war on Britain's terms, which were: Arabia to be independent; Armenia and Syria to enjoy local autonomy within the Ottoman Empire; Mesopotamia and Palestine to become *de facto* British protectorates,

---

* Lloyd George was saved by Bonar Law, who held his angry Conservatives in line. Bonar Law disliked Churchill, and was bitter about not having been consulted in the matter. Nonetheless, he remained loyal to the Prime Minister. Lloyd George cleverly told him that Asquith had pledged, if he came back as Prime Minister, to bring Churchill back to power as First Lord of the Admiralty.[11] The implied message was that a Lloyd George government, with Churchill confined to a relatively less important position, was preferable.

like Egypt before the war, though under formal Ottoman suzerainty; and freedom of navigation through the Dardanelles to be secured. In return, Lloyd George offered to pledge that the Capitulations (the treaties giving preferential treatment to Europeans) would remain abolished, and that generous financial treatment would be given to Turkey to aid her economic recovery. The terms offered by Lloyd George differed in two important ways from those envisaged by the prior Asquith government: France, Italy, and Russia were to get nothing; and Britain was to take Palestine as well as Mesopotamia.

Zaharoff's reports—the veracity of which it is difficult to judge—indicate that Enver, after mercurial changes of mind and mood, did not accept Lloyd George's offer. It does not sound as though he ever seriously intended to do so. But the instructions that Zaharoff received reveal Lloyd George's intentions with regard to the Middle East.

III

In a secret session of the House of Commons on 10 May 1917, the Prime Minister surprised even a close collaborator by saying unequivocally that Britain was not going to give back the German colonies in Africa captured during the war, and that Turkey would not be allowed to keep Palestine or Mesopotamia.[16] Though Lloyd George had definite ideas about the future of the liberated Ottoman lands, few of his colleagues were aware of them. He avoided official channels and made his ideas known in detail only in the course of the secret negotiations with Enver Pasha; hence the importance of what they revealed.

The Prime Minister intended to deny France the position that Sir Mark Sykes had promised her in the postwar Middle East, and took the view that the Sykes-Picot Agreement was unimportant; that physical possession was all that mattered. Regarding Palestine, he told the British ambassador to France in April 1917 that the French would be obliged to accept a *fait accompli*: "We shall be there by conquest and shall remain."[17]

Lloyd George was the only man in his government who had always wanted to acquire Palestine for Britain. He also wanted to encourage the development of a Jewish homeland in Palestine. His colleagues failed to understand how strongly he held these views.

There was a background to Lloyd George's beliefs of which his colleagues were largely ignorant. He was not, like Asquith and the other members of the Cabinet, educated in an exclusive public school that stressed the Greek and Latin classics; he was brought up on the Bible. Repeatedly he remarked that the Biblical place names were better known to him than were those of the battles and the disputed frontiers that figured in the European war. He expressed himself about these places with fervor. In his later memoirs he wrote that he had objected to the division of Palestine in the Sykes-Picot Agreement (most of it going to France or into an international zone) on the grounds that it mutilated the country. He said it was not worth winning the Holy Land only to "hew it in pieces before the Lord."[18] He asserted that "Palestine, if recaptured, must be one and indivisible to renew its greatness as a living entity."[19]

IV

Unlike his colleagues he was keenly aware that there were centuries-old tendencies in British Nonconformist and Evangelical thought toward taking the lead in restoring the Jews to Zion. Indeed they formed the background of his own Nonconformist faith. He was only the latest in a long line of Christian Zionists in Britain that stretched back to the Puritans and the era in which the *Mayflower* set sail for the New World. Promised lands were still much thought about in those days, whether in the United States or in Palestine.

In the mid-seventeenth century, two English Puritans residing in Holland—Joanna and Ebenezer Cartwright—petitioned their government "That this Nation of England, with the inhabitants of the Netherlands, shall be the first and the readiest to transport Izraell's sons and daughters in their ships to the Land promised by their forefathers, Abraham, Isaac, and Jacob for an everlasting Inheritance."[20] Guided by the Scriptures, the Puritans believed that the advent of the Messiah would occur once the people of Judaea were restored to their native land.

The idea recurred: in the mid-nineteenth century, the social reformer Anthony Cooper, who became Earl of Shaftesbury, inspired a powerful evangelical movement within the Church of England that aimed at bringing the Jews back to Palestine, converting them to Christianity, and hastening the Second Coming. Shaftesbury also inspired Palmerston, the Foreign Secretary and his relation by marriage, to extend British consular protection to Jews in Palestine: "Palmerston had already been chosen by God to be an instrument of good to His ancient people," Shaftesbury noted in his diary.[21]

Palmerston acted from a mixture of idealistic and practical reasons not unlike those of Lloyd George in the next century. He pressed a Jewish Palestine on the Ottoman Empire in the context of the Great Game rivalry with France, at a time in the 1830s and 1840s when the rebelling Viceroy of Egypt, Mehemet Ali, backed by France, marched from Egypt on Syria to threaten the territorial integrity of the empire and the throne of its Sultan. As usual, Palmerston upheld the Ottoman cause. One of his purposes in advocating a Jewish Palestine was to strengthen the Ottoman regime, by providing it with Jewish support. Another was to foil the French and their protégé Mehemet Ali by placing along their line of march a British-backed Jewish homeland which would block their advance. Another was to provide Britain with a client in the Middle East, and therefore an excuse for intervention in Ottoman affairs. The Russians, as defenders of the Orthodox faith, and the French, as champions of the important and strategically located Maronite (Roman Catholic) community in Lebanon, claimed to represent significant Middle Eastern interests and communities. For the want of Protestants in the area, Britain had to adopt some other protégé in order to be able to make a similar claim.

Palmerston's notion of restoring the Promised Land to the Jewish people also proved to be shrewd domestic politics. It struck a responsive chord in British public opinion that harked back to Puritan enthusiasm.* According to the leading authority on Palmerston's diplomacy, his policy "became connected with a mystical idea, never altogether lost in the nineteenth century, that Britain was to be the chosen instrument of God to bring back the Jews to the Holy Land."[22] This somehow coexisted, at least in Britain's upper classes, with pervasive anti-Semitism.

In 1914 the entry of the Ottoman Empire into the war appeared to have brought about the political circumstances in which the Zionist dream at last could be realized. "What is to prevent the Jews having Palestine and restoring a real Judaea?" asked H. G. Wells in an open newspaper letter penned the moment that Turkey came into the war.

A similar thought occurred soon afterward to Sir Herbert Samuel, Postmaster General in Asquith's Cabinet, one of the leaders of the Liberal Party, and the first person of the Jewish faith to sit in a British Cabinet. In January 1915 he sent a memorandum to Prime Minister Asquith proposing that Palestine should become a British protectorate—because it was of strategic importance to the British Empire—and urging the advantages of encouraging large-scale Jewish settlement there. The Prime Minister had just been reading *Tancred*— a novel by Benjamin Disraeli, the nineteenth-century British leader (baptized a Christian, but born of a Jewish family), who advocated a Jewish return to Palestine—and Asquith confided that Samuel's memorandum "reads almost like a new edition of *Tancred* brought up to date. I confess I am not attracted by this proposed addition

---

* It was a vision that inspired secular idealists as well. George Eliot, in her novel *Daniel Deronda* (1876), proposed a Zionist program.

to our responsibilities. But it is a curious illustration of Dizzy's [Disraeli's] favourite maxim that 'race is everything' to find this almost lyrical outburst proceeding from the well-ordered and methodical brain of H.S. . . ."[23]

In March 1915 a revised version of Samuel's memorandum was circulated to the Cabinet. It did not attract support, and Asquith's private comment was that "Curiously enough the only other partisan of this proposal is Lloyd George, who, I need not say, does not care a damn for the Jews or their past or their future . . ."[24] The Prime Minister was unaware of the complex of motives behind the position taken by Lloyd George, who told the Cabinet that it would be an outrage to let the Christian Holy Places in Palestine fall into the hands of "Agnostic Atheistic France."[25] Asquith found it odd that Samuel and Lloyd George should advocate a British protectorate for Palestine for such different reasons: "Isn't it singular that the same conclusion shd. be capable of being come to by such different roads?"[26] It was a prescient remark for, in the years to come, British officials traveling along many different roads happened to arrive at the same conclusion: a distinctive characteristic of Britain's evolving Palestine policy was that there was no single reason for it.

Kitchener threw the great weight of his authority against Samuel's proposal. He told the Cabinet that Palestine was of little value, strategic or otherwise, and that it did not have even one decent harbor.[27] Samuel's proposal, therefore, was not adopted; but Lloyd George continued to disagree with Kitchener about the strategic importance of Palestine.

V

Lloyd George, though of a Welsh family, was born in Manchester, Britain's second-largest city, and the home of the Radical Liberal tradition which he was to uphold throughout much of his political life. Manchester was also, next to London, the home of Britain's largest Jewish community; and Members of Parliament from the area, such as Balfour and Churchill, were aware of the special concerns of their Jewish constituents.

C. P. Scott, editor of the great Liberal newspaper the *Manchester Guardian*, was converted to Zionism in 1914 by Chaim Weizmann, a Russian Jewish chemist who had settled in Manchester. Scott, who was considered to be Lloyd George's closest political confidant, took up the cause with all the force of his idealistic nature. The military correspondent of the *Guardian*, Herbert Sidebotham, saw a complementary aspect of the matter: a military advantage to Britain. In the issue of 26 November 1915, he wrote that "the whole future of the British Empire as a Sea Empire" depended upon Palestine becoming a buffer state inhabited "by an intensely patriotic race."[28]

The *Manchester Guardian*'s conversion was brought about in the context of the First World War, but Lloyd George had come to Zionism—or rather it had come to him—more than a decade before. In 1903 he had been retained as the British attorney for the Zionist movement and for its founder, Dr Theodore Herzl, in connection with an issue that caused an agonizing split in Zionist ranks: whether a Jewish state necessarily had to be located in Palestine. As one who represented Herzl at the moment of decision, he was in a position to understand the movement's dilemmas.

The Zionist movement was new, but its roots were as old as Judaea, whose independence was undermined and later crushed by ancient Rome, and most of whose inhabitants were driven into foreign lands in the second century AD. Even in exile the Judaeans—or Jews, as they came to be known—clung to their own religion, with its distinctive laws and customs, setting them apart from the peoples amongst whom they lived and moved. Inferior status, persecutions, frequent massacres, and repeated expulsions from one country after another further reinforced their sense of separate identity and special destiny. In the end—according to their religious teachings—God would bring them back to Zion, and in the course of their Passover ceremony each year they would repeat the ritual prayer, "Next year in Jerusalem!"

The future return to Zion remained a Messianic vision until the ideology of nineteenth-century Europe converted it into a contemporary political program. A representative idea of that time—which had been planted everywhere by the armies of the French Revolution and had flourished—was that every nation ought to have an independent country of its own (though, of course, what constituted a nation was an open question). The Italian revolutionary Giuseppe Mazzini was the outstanding proponent of this doctrine, according to which each nation should be freed to realize its unique genius and to pursue its particular mission in the service of mankind. Thus the nationalism of each nation serves not merely its own interests but also those of its neighbors; and in the service of this creed Mazzini's colleague Giuseppe Garibaldi—Italy's greatest hero—fought for Uruguay and France as well as Italy.

A converse of this proposition was that a fundamental cause of the world's ills was that some nations were being kept from achieving unity or independence—a situation that Mazzini and his followers proposed to change by war or revolution. Their program was taken over from the left by the right—Italy and Germany were formed into countries by Cavour and Bismarck respectively—and became a common theme of European political discourse. Nationalism was taken a step further in the Swiss (1847) and American (1861–5) civil wars, when seven confederated Swiss cantons and eleven Confederated States of America attempted to secede—and were crushed by the armies of their respective federal governments. Thus peoples were to be unified into one nation, like it or not.

This suggested there might be a dark side to the new nationalism: intolerance of groups different from the majority. Jews encountered this at once. In the nationalist environment of western Europe, the Jewish question assumed new guises: were the Jews of Germany Germans? were the Jews of France French?—and, if so, what of their special identity? By the end of the nineteenth century, the Jews of western Europe had achieved legal emancipation from many of the restrictions that had confined them for centuries: they could move out of their ghettos, practice the trade or profession of their choice, buy land, and enjoy the rights of citizenship—but they still encountered a wave of hostility from their neighbors who considered them alien.

In eastern Europe—the Russian Empire, including Poland, the Baltic lands, and the Ukraine—the Jewish situation was perilous. Most of the world's Jews then lived within the section of the Russian Empire to which they were confined so long as they lived within the Czar's domains: the Pale, or enclosure (from the word for a wooden stake used in building fences). Only a few of them—some illegally, some by special permission—lived in St Petersburg, Moscow, or elsewhere outside the Pale. The six million within the Pale were Russian Jews who were not allowed to be Jewish Russians. They were not only shackled by legal restrictions, but were victimized by the organized massacres called pogroms. In the last half of the nineteenth century and the first years of the twentieth century, these grew so terrible that Jews in large number fled the Russian Empire in search of refuge.

Since nationalism was then considered the cure-all for political ills, it was inevitable that somebody would propose it as the answer to the Jewish problem. National unity and self-determination within an independent Jewish commonwealth were, in fact, proposed in a number of eloquent books whose authors had arrived at their conclusions independently.* So Theodore Herzl was not the first to formulate such a program, but he was the first to give it tangible political expression, at a time when Jewish pioneers from Russia were beginning to colonize Palestine without waiting for the politics to be thrashed out.

* Among them were Moses Hess's *Rome and Jerusalem* (1862) and Leo Pinsker's *Auto-Emancipation* (1882).

When Herzl, an assimilated Jew, conceived the idea of political Zionism, his notion had been that Jews needed to have a national state of their own—but that its location was not of primary importance. Of Jews and Judaism Herzl knew next to nothing. He was a fashionable journalist, the Paris correspondent of a Viennese newspaper who had forgotten his Jewish origins until the shock of French anti-Semitism in the Dreyfus case convinced him of the need to rescue the world's Jews from their historical plight.

As a man of the world, he knew how political business was transacted in the Europe of his time and began by establishing a Zionist organization. He then commenced negotiations on its behalf with officials of various governments. Only after he had come into working contact with other Jews, and with Jewish organizations that for years had been fostering settlements in the Holy Land, did he come to recognize the unique appeal of the country that the world called Palestine—the Land of the Philistines—but that Jews called the Land of Israel.

By the beginning of the twentieth century, Herzl's negotiations with the Ottoman Empire had convinced him that the Sultan would not agree to the Zionist proposals—at least for the time being. So he looked elsewhere. In 1902 Herzl held an important meeting with Joseph Chamberlain, the powerful Colonial Secretary in the Salisbury and Balfour Cabinets and the father of modern British imperialism. Chamberlain, too, believed in a national solution to the Jewish problem, and listened sympathetically to Herzl's fall-back proposal that a Jewish political community should initially be established across the frontier from Palestine, in the hope that Palestine would eventually become available, somehow or other. Herzl was talking in terms of either Cyprus or the El Arish strip at the edge of the Sinai peninsula, next to Palestine, both areas nominally parts of the Ottoman Empire but in fact occupied by Britain. Chamberlain ruled out Cyprus but offered to help Herzl obtain the consent of the British officials in charge of Sinai.

To apply for this consent, Herzl, through his British representative, Leopold Greenberg, decided to retain the services of a politically knowledgeable lawyer, and chose David Lloyd George, who personally handled the matter on behalf of his London firm, Lloyd George, Roberts & Co. The proposal foundered as a result of opposition from the British administration in Egypt and the Foreign Office sent letters to Dr Herzl on 19 June and 16 July 1903 informing him that his proposal was not practical.

Chamberlain then suggested that he could offer an area for Jewish settlement within the jurisdiction of his own department and offered the prospect of settlement in Uganda in British East Africa. The

Prime Minister, Arthur James Balfour, who had also thought deeply about the Jewish question and had concluded that it required a national solution, supported Chamberlain's proposal. Herzl agreed, and Lloyd George accordingly drafted a Charter for the Jewish Settlement, and submitted it formally to the British government for approval. In the summer of 1903 the Foreign Office replied in a guarded but affirmative way that if studies and talks over the course of the next year were successful, His Majesty's Government would consider favorably proposals for the creation of a Jewish colony. It was the first official declaration by a government to the Zionist movement and the first official statement implying national status for the Jewish people.[29] It was the first Balfour Declaration.

A meeting of the World Zionist Congress convened shortly thereafter, where Herzl presented the Uganda proposal, urging the settlement of East Africa as a way-station and refuge along the road to the Promised Land, where the Jews of the Czarist Empire could escape the terrors of the pogroms. Herzl's arguments swayed heads but not hearts. Though they let their leader win the vote on the issue, most delegates were not interested in any land other than that of their ancestors. The Zionist movement was at a dead-end: Herzl did not know how to lead it to Palestine but it would not follow him anywhere else. In the summer of 1904 Herzl died, leaving behind a fragmented and deeply divided leadership.

In 1906, with a new Liberal government in Britain, Lloyd George again submitted the Sinai proposal for consideration, at the instigation of Leopold Greenberg. Again the British government rejected it, and Sir Edward Grey wrote on 20 March 1906 to say that the Foreign Office position had not changed.[30]

During its formative years, then, David Lloyd George had represented the Zionist movement as it sought to define itself. It was no more than one of his many clients—and not a major one at that—yet, as a result of his professional representation of it, no other British political leader was in a better position than he to understand its character and its goals. As he contemplated the conquest of Palestine in 1917 and 1918, nobody had a clearer idea than he of what to do with it once it was his.

Like Woodrow Wilson, whose concern in the Middle East was for American Protestant schools and missions, Lloyd George wanted his country to carry out what he regarded as the Lord's work in the region. But, unlike the President, the Prime Minister planned to aggrandize his country's empire by doing so.

Lloyd George had followed his own intellectual path to the conclusion that Britain should sponsor Jewish nationalism in the postwar Middle East. A number of his colleagues within the British government arrived at the same conclusion in 1917, though by different paths—many roads led to Zion. The odd thing was that, just as they had supported the Emir Hussein because of mistaken notions about Arabs and Moslems, they were now about to support Zionism because of mistaken notions about Jews.

TOWARD THE BALFOUR DECLARATION

I

Lloyd George—an "Easterner" both in his war strategy and in his war goals—succeeded in winning support for his views from important civilian members of the government, who came to view the Middle East in general, and Palestine in particular, as vital imperial interests, and who arrived independently and by various paths at the conclusion that an alliance with Zionism would serve Britain's needs in war and peace.

Lloyd George persuaded Lord Milner and his associates of the strategic importance of the war in the East in the winter of 1917, when it was by no means clear that the Allies would be able to win a decisive victory there or anywhere else. Even after the United States entered the war in the spring, it seemed entirely possible that the Americans might not arrive in time to stave off a negotiated peace agreement that would leave the belligerent countries more or less in their existing positions. There were also those who were worried about allowing the Germans and Turks to retain control of an area whose vital importance had been underscored by the Prime Minister.

The assistant secretaries of the War Cabinet, Leo Amery and Mark Sykes, worried that in the postwar world the Ottoman Empire might fall completely into the clutches of Germany. Were that to happen, the road to India would be in enemy hands—a threat that the British Empire could avert only by ejecting the Turks and Germans, and taking into British hands the southern perimeter of the Ottoman domains. The Cabinet, from the beginning, had thought of annexing Mesopotamia. As for Arabia, arrangements had been made with the local rulers who had asserted their independence: they were subsidized and could be relied upon to remain pro-British. That left Palestine as the only point of vulnerability. As the bridge between Africa and Asia, it blocked the land road from Egypt to India and, by its proximity, it threatened the Suez Canal and hence the sea road as well.

Amery, the leading figure among Milner's associates in the government, discussed the matter in a memorandum to the Cabinet dated 11 April 1917. Warning against allowing Germany to strike again at Britain through domination of Europe or the Middle East after the war, he argued that "German control of Palestine" was one of "the greatest of all dangers which can confront the British Empire in the future."[1]

Amery, along with Mark Sykes and, later, William Ormsby-Gore, had been appointed assistant to Maurice Hankey in heading the secretariat of the War Cabinet. A Member of Parliament and an army officer who had been serving in the War Office, Amery had become one of the inner band directing the war effort. In the division of responsibilities within the secretariat, the Middle East fell outside Amery's sphere and within that of Sykes. Yet Amery had already involved himself in a matter affecting Middle Eastern policy by lending a hand to an old friend.

An army officer whom Amery had known in South Africa, Lieutenant-Colonel John Henry Patterson, had commanded a Jewish corps in the Gallipoli campaign, and asked Amery to help get permission from the War Office to create a regiment of non-British Jews to fight under British command. This regiment would then be sent to fight in Palestine if and when Britain invaded the Ottoman Empire from Egypt and the Sinai. Patterson was an Irish Protestant, a student of the Bible, a professional army officer and amateur lion hunter, known for his best-selling book *The Man-eaters of Tsavo* and for his buccaneering spirit. The idea of a Jewish regiment had come from Vladimir Jabotinsky, a fiery Russian Jewish journalist who believed that Englishmen resented the presence in Britain of a large immigrant population of able-bodied Russian Jews who were not yet British subjects and who did not undertake military service. While he did not at first say so, Jabotinsky was inspired by the thought that a Jewish military unit helping to liberate Palestine would go far toward making the Zionist dream a reality.[2] Patterson was enthusiastic; the Jewish corps he had commanded at Gallipoli had been created in large part through the efforts of Jabotinsky's associate, Captain Joseph Trumpeldor, and Patterson had enjoyed commanding it.[3]

Amery agreed to help Patterson, but it was not an easy undertaking. Official Jewish community leaders opposed the project bitterly; in their view it endangered Jews who lived in the German, Austro-Hungarian, and Ottoman empires by suggesting that Jews, as such, were on the Allied side. The Zionist leadership, though at odds with the British Jewish community in most other matters, joined in deploring the identification of the Zionist cause with one or the other of the warring European coalitions. When Jabotinsky raised the issue for the first time in 1915, the British authorities also saw little merit in his proposal that the Jewish unit should help to liberate Palestine. "But nobody knows yet when we shall go to Palestine," said one high official, "and Lord Kitchener says never."[4]

Amery persisted throughout 1916 and 1917 and succeeded in laying Jabotinsky's petition before the War Cabinet. The British government then went forward to negotiate a convention with the other Allied governments, allowing each country to take into military service the resident nationals of the others; in other words, Russian Jews living in Britain could join the British army. Parliament authorized the convention, and in the summer of 1917 the Jewish unit (later called the Jewish Legion) was formed within the British army under the command of Lieutenant-Colonel Patterson. Lloyd George was enthusiastic: "The Jews might be able to render us more assistance than the Arabs" in the Palestine campaign, he said.[5]

Until his colleague Mark Sykes spoke to him about Zionism, Amery had not put his strategic concerns about Palestine and his support of the Jewish Legion into a unified focus, even though his general leanings were toward Zionism. A Jewish national entity had behind it the authority of his political mentor, the late Joseph Chamberlain, and was viewed favorably by his leader, Lord Milner, who had acquired a sympathy for Zionism early in life. Amery himself felt a similar sympathy; he later wrote that, apart from the United States, "Bible reading and Bible thinking England was the only country where the desire of the Jews to return to their ancient homeland has always been regarded as a natural aspiration which ought not to be denied."[6]

When William Ormsby-Gore joined Amery and Sykes as one of the three assistant secretaries of the War Cabinet, he brought with him a more concrete interest in the immediate prospects of the Zionist idea. Ormsby-Gore, a Member of Parliament and secretary to Lord Milner, had gone out to the Middle East to work with the Arab Bureau. Under his personal command was Aaron Aaronsohn, leader of a highly effective, intelligence-gathering group operation working behind Ottoman lines in Jewish Palestine to provide information about Turkish troop movements. Like Jabotinsky, Aaronsohn was attacked by fellow Jews for identifying Zionist interests with those of the Allies—and thus endangering the Palestinian Jewish community, which Djemal Pasha was tempted to treat as his colleagues had treated the Armenians. Aaronsohn's information about Turkish defenses and military dispositions proved to be of great value to the British military command in Egypt, however, and was appreciated by Ormsby-Gore.

Another aspect of Aaronsohn's life that fascinated Ormsby-Gore was his agricultural exploration and experimentation—the career in which he had become famous. A decade earlier, Aaronsohn had joined in the search for the original strain of wild wheat that had flourished thousands of years ago. Since that time the plant had deteriorated as a result of intensive inbreeding, becoming increasingly vulnerable to disease. To save the planet's basic grain food by finding nature's original plant was a romantic quest for the blue-eyed, fair-haired Aaron Aaronsohn. In the spring of 1906 he made the find of a lifetime: wild wheat blowing in the breezes at the foot of Mount Hermon, near the Jewish settlement of Rosh Pina.

Ormsby-Gore was struck by the work Aaronsohn had done at his station for agricultural research in Palestine, for it went to the heart of the argument about Zionism. The case against Zionism, which was made in the Cabinet by Lord Curzon, was that Palestine was too barren a land to support the millions of Jews who hoped to settle there. The argument made later by Arab groups, who claimed there was no room in the country for additional settlers, was that "no room can be made in Palestine for a second nation," as George Antonius, an eloquent Arab spokesman, wrote long afterward, "except by dislodging or exterminating the nation in possession."[7] Aaronsohn's experiments rebutted that argument.[*] His work tended to show that, without displacing any of the 600,000 or so inhabitants of western Palestine, millions more could be settled on land made rich and fertile by scientific agriculture. His work had wider applications: Ormsby-Gore brought back with him to London the idea that Zionist Jews could help the Arabic-speaking and other peoples of the Middle East to regenerate their region of the globe so that the desert could once more bloom.

II

As soon as Lloyd George became Prime Minister, Leo Amery initiated a move that placed Palestine within the context of the future of the British Empire. At the end of 1916 Amery proposed creating an Imperial War Cabinet, and sent a note on the subject to Lord Milner, who arranged for Lloyd George to put the idea in motion.[8]

The war had created a need for such a body: the empire had contributed so much manpower to the war effort that troops from outside Britain constituted a substantial part of the British armed forces. The Dominions alone contributed more than a million men to the armed forces, while the Indian Empire contributed at least a half million fighting men and hundreds of thousands of support troops.

---

[*] At the end of 1984 the population of Israel was 4,235,000 and that of the West Bank was 1,300,000—a total of 5,535,000 people now living in about 25 percent of the territory of Palestine as defined by the British Mandate.

Yet Canada, Australia, New Zealand, India, and Britain's other partners in the fighting had never been consulted about whether to go to war. George V had declared war, and his governor-generals in his Dominions overseas had promulgated declarations on their behalf. Neither the parliaments nor the governments of the Dominions had been involved in those decisions. Amery's proposal was to recognize, however belatedly, the importance of these partners by giving them representation in a central body in London dealing with the overall direction of the war.

Amery was convinced, as were Lord Milner's other friends, that the structure of the British Empire had to be changed fundamentally; and by the end of 1916, as the political situation in London became fluid, and party and other divisions were breaking down, much seemed possible that would not have seemed so before.

Until the time of Disraeli, the creation of the empire had been a haphazard and, it was said, an absent-minded affair. Disraeli gave it glamor and focused attention on it. Coming afterward, Amery and his friends in the Milner circle, who had worked in concert with Cecil Rhodes and Joseph Chamberlain, were among the first conscious and systematic proponents of empire, while their associates Rudyard Kipling and John Buchan were among its deliberate glorifiers. Many among them advocated the creation of an empire-wide economic system, closed to outsiders by tariffs. Others, who recognized that various parts of the empire often appeared to occupy economic positions in conflict with one another, advocated closer political association. Lionel Curtis, a founder of their publication, the *Round Table*, claimed that the British Empire had no choice but federation or disintegration. He spoke for those in the Milner circle whose program was organic, political union of the empire, with an imperial parliament elected from the Dominions as well as from Britain, giving rise to an imperial Cabinet which would rule the empire as a whole. The program had been rejected at an imperial conference in 1911, but the breakdown of world political structures during the First World War seemed to offer a second chance.

On 19 December 1916, acting on Amery's suggestion, Lloyd George told the House of Commons that "We feel that the time has come when the Dominions ought to be more formally consulted" on the issues of war and peace.[9] Accordingly, he convoked an Imperial War Conference, confusingly also called the Imperial War Cabinet, to meet in London three months later.

Nobody was more suspicious of the government's intentions than the delegate from South Africa, Jan Christian Smuts, a lawyer-turned-general who had fought against the British in the Boer War; he had no desire to be ruled from London. He arrived in London for the conference on 12 March 1917, and his suspicions were deepened when, the same day, he received an invitation to dine at Brooks's with Lord Milner, his former adversary.

When the conference opened, issue was joined at once and Smuts won a lasting victory. On 16 March 1917 he pushed through a resolution that postponed consideration of the details of how the British Empire should be reorganized until the end of the war, but committed the participants in advance to the proposition that the basis of the reorganization would be the independence of South Africa, Canada, Australia, and New Zealand.

Lloyd George may have been less disappointed at this outcome than were his colleagues in Milner's circle. The Prime Minister had purposes of his own, and saw ways in which Smuts, in particular, could serve them. Smuts was a superb administrator of the calibre of Milner, Amery, and Hankey, and could help them to run the war effort. As a successful general in his Boer War days and more recently in East Africa, and a representative of the Dominions, he could also help Lloyd George by throwing his weight against the British generals. Lloyd George prevailed upon Smuts to stay on in London and serve in the War Cabinet "on loan" from his own country's Cabinet. Thus he served not only as a member of the British Cabinet, but also as the South African representative in the Imperial War Cabinet (or Imperial War Conference). He was the only Cabinet minister in modern British history to have no connection with either House of Parliament; and spent the rest of the war away from home, living in a hotel room at the Savoy.[10]

"General Smuts had expressed very decided views as to the strategical importance of Palestine to the British Empire," Lloyd George later wrote,[11] and became immediately involved with the issue. Perhaps because it had been decided that the political links of the empire were not to be tightened, Smuts and Amery moved at the same time to cement the geographical links of the entities comprising the British system; and both men concentrated on the importance of Palestine. If broadly defined, and in conjunction with Mesopotamia, Palestine gave Britain the land road from Egypt to India and brought together the empires of Africa and Asia. The capture of German East Africa by Botha and Smuts had already created a continuous stretch of British-controlled territories between, on the one hand, Cape Town, the Atlantic Ocean port at the southern tip of Africa, and, on the other, Suez, which bridged the Mediterranean and the Red Sea at the continent's northeastern tip. With the addition of Palestine and Mesopotamia, the Cape Town to Suez stretch could be linked up with the stretch of territory that ran through British-controlled Persia and the Indian Empire to Burma, Malaya, and the two great Dominions in the Pacific—Australia and New Zealand. As of 1917, Palestine was the key missing link that could join together the parts of the British Empire so that they would form a continuous chain from the Atlantic to the middle of the Pacific.

The Prime Minister, of course, saw it the same way. As he wrote later, "For the British Empire, the fight with Turkey had a special importance of its own ... The Turkish Empire lay right across the track by land or water to our great possessions in the East—India, Burma, Malaya, Borneo, Hong Kong, and the Dominions of Australia and New Zealand."[12]

Amery, who was about to advise the Cabinet that continued Ottoman (and thus German) control of Palestine was a future danger to the British Empire, believed, with the Prime Minister, that Palestine ought to be invaded immediately—and that Smuts was the general to do it. For Smuts was not only a brilliantly successful general, but also shared their immediate strategic and broader geopolitical goals.

On 15 March 1917, the day that Smuts won his victory at the Imperial Conference, Amery wrote to him that

> The one thing, however, that is essential if we are going to do a big thing quickly in the Palestine direction, is a more dashing general ... If I were dictator, I should ask you to do it as the only leading soldier who had had experience of mobile warfare ... and has not yet got trenches dug deep in his mind.[13]

Lloyd George offered the command to Smuts, who hesitated and asked the advice of the South African Prime Minister, General Louis Botha. Smuts, who was in favor of accepting, reasoned that "Position on the other fronts most difficult and Palestine is only one where perhaps with great push it is possible to achieve considerable success."[14] After consultation, Botha and Smuts decided that the offer should be accepted if the campaign were to be mounted "on a large scale," "a first class campaign in men and guns."[15]

Smuts then conferred with Sir William Robertson, Chief of the Imperial General Staff, who made clear that he was not going to release the necessary troops and supplies from the western front, and dismissed the Middle East as a private obsession of the Prime Minister's, and at best "only a sideshow."[16] Lloyd George had been in office only a few months and his position was tenuous; his authority over the military was limited; and his promise of full support, Smuts concluded, was not one that he would be able to keep. Thus Smuts turned down the offer of the Palestine command, feeling that the campaign in the East would be sabotaged by Robertson and his colleagues.

Smuts continued, though, to take a keen interest in Palestine. He and Amery later went out together to the Middle East to study the situation and report; and both of them came back urging a strong Palestine offensive.

As a Boer, steeped in the Bible, Smuts strongly supported the Zionist idea when it was raised in the Cabinet. As he later pointed out, the "people of South Africa and especially the older Dutch population has been brought up almost entirely on Jewish tradition. The Old Testament ... has been the very marrow of Dutch culture here in South Africa."[17] Like Lloyd George, he had grown up believing that "the day will come when the words of the prophets will become true, and Israel will return to its own land,"[18] and he fully agreed with Lloyd George that the Jewish homeland should be established in Palestine under British auspices. Whether or not he originated the idea, Smuts was responsible for finding the formula— acceptable to Woodrow Wilson—under which countries like Britain would assume responsibility for the administration of territories such as Palestine and Mesopotamia: they would govern pursuant to a "mandate" from the future League of Nations. The territories would be held in trust for their peoples—a formula designed to be compatible with American anti-imperialist notions.

Amery put together the pieces of this new imperial vision at the end of 1918, when he wrote to Smuts that Britain's hold on the Middle East should be permanent, and not terminate when the mandates did. Without spelling out the details, he wrote that even when Palestine, Mesopotamia, and an Arabian state became independent of British trusteeship, they should remain within the British imperial system. The British Empire of the future, as he saw it, would be like a smaller League of Nations; and other such mini-leagues would emerge elsewhere in the world. Woodrow Wilson's overall League of Nations would therefore have relatively few members: there would be one representative from the British system, and one from each of the several other sub-systems.[19]

Thus Amery saw no incompatibility between a British Palestine and a Jewish Palestine. He also saw no reason why either British or Jewish aspirations should not be in harmony with Arab aspirations. Decades later, he wrote of the proponents of the Zionist dream in 1917—18 that "Most of us younger men who shared this hope were, like Mark Sykes, pro-Arab as well as pro-Zionist, and saw no essential incompatibility between the two ideals."[20]

34

THE PROMISED LAND

I

As the eventful year 1917 ran its course, Britain's Palestine policy continued to be shaped by many hands: Cabinet ministers at one level; bureaucrats, little known beyond official circles and little known today, at another.

Within the powerful secretariat of the War Cabinet, the Middle East fell within the domain of Kitchener's protégé Sir Mark Sykes, as it had done since shortly after the outset of the war. Maurice Hankey, his superior, held no strong views about the Middle East, and since the deaths of Kitchener and FitzGerald, Sykes had been acting without any real direction from above. He did not know that the new Prime Minister held decided views about a Middle Eastern settlement which were considerably different from his own; nor was he involved in the secret negotiations through Zaharoff in which the Prime Minister's terms for peace in the Middle East were revealed.

On his own, then, and unguided, Sykes continued to circle uncertainly around the question of Palestine. His instructions from Kitchener and FitzGerald had been to regard it as of no strategic importance to Britain, and those instructions had never been cancelled. Yet he had been made aware in the course of his negotiations with France and Russia in 1916 that the Holy Land held a passionate interest for many Jews whose support, Sykes felt, might be vital to the Allies. Yet Jewish opinion might be alienated by some of the arrangements for the postwar Middle East that he was negotiating with Britain's allies and potential supporters. As he held discussions with Frenchmen and Russians, Armenians and Arabs, he was haunted by a fear—groundless, but real to him nonetheless—that each of his transactions risked running afoul of Jewish opposition.

At the beginning of 1917 Sykes was engaged in a dialogue with James Malcolm, an Armenian businessman, about establishing an independent Armenian national state. They considered inviting Russia into the postwar Middle East as the protecting power for a united Armenia; but, as Sykes believed Jewish opinion to be violently anti-Russian, he suggested that something ought to be done in advance to disarm potential Jewish opposition to a scheme that allowed imperial Russia to expand. Sykes asked Malcolm to find out for him who the leaders of Zionism were so that he could approach them about this.

Malcolm had met Leopold Greenberg, editor and co-owner of the *Jewish Chronicle* who, as it happened, had also served as Theodore Herzl's British representative. Malcolm wrote to ask him who were the leaders of the Zionist organization, and passed on the information he received in reply to Sykes. Two names appeared to be of especial importance: Nahum Sokolow, an official of the international Zionist movement; and Dr Chaim Weizmann, an official of the British Zionist Federation, who was opposed to the decision of the Zionist movement to remain neutral in the world war.* Malcolm introduced himself to Weizmann and shortly afterward, on 28 January 1917, introduced Weizmann to Sykes.

Weizmann—although he did not know that the Allies were already making plans for the postwar Middle East—wanted to secure a commitment from Britain about Palestine while the war was still in progress. As a chemist, he made a significant contribution to the war effort by donating to the government his discovery of a process to extract acetone from maize—acetone being a vital ingredient in the manufacture of explosives.** But, despite his war work and his increasing acquaintance with the circle of high-ranking officials who were directing the war effort, he did not know that Britain had an official whose brief was to negotiate the design of the postwar Middle East. Another British Zionist leader, Rabbi Gaster, knew Sykes—and knew that Sykes held that job—but, seeing Weizmann as a rival, jealously kept the information to himself. Thus Weizmann learned of Sykes only by accident—in early 1917 when Sykes mentioned his job to James de Rothschild in the course of a chance conversation about their respective horse-breeding stables. Rothschild passed on the information to Weizmann, and Weizmann was about to arrange to meet Sykes when James Malcolm arranged for Sykes to meet Weizmann.

---

* Born in Russia and naturalized a British subject, he was passionately pro-Allied and believed that only the western democracies were compatible with Jewish ideals. Since he held no official position in the international Zionist movement, he was free to depart from its neutrality; but as an official of the British Zionist Federation, he could nonetheless speak in a representative capacity.
** Years after the war, Lloyd George—in writing his memoirs—invented the story that he had given the Balfour Declaration in gratitude for Weizmann's invention. Weizmann's important invention was real, but Lloyd George's story was a work of fiction.

Each wanted to do what the other wanted done. Sykes wanted to find someone with whom he could negotiate an alliance between British and Zionist interests; and Weizmann wanted to be that person.

Their first meetings were on an unofficial basis. From the start, Sykes, as he always did, tried to fit all Middle Eastern projects within the existing—but still secret—Sykes-Picot-Sazanov Agreement, of which Weizmann knew nothing. In the agreement, the Holy Places were to be placed under an international administration; so Sykes began by proposing that a Jewish entity in Palestine should be under joint Anglo-French rule ("condominium")—though he could not reveal to Weizmann why he was making the proposal. Though Sykes did not realize it, he was out of step not only with the Zionist leaders but also with the Prime Minister. Lloyd George—like Weizmann and his colleagues—wanted Palestine to be British. C. P. Scott, editor of the *Manchester Guardian* and Lloyd George's confidant, advised Weizmann to take the matter up with the Prime Minister; but Weizmann decided to concentrate on changing Sykes's mind rather than going over his head.[1]

In London, on 7 February 1917, Sykes met with Weizmann and other British Zionists who told him that they were opposed to the condominium idea and wanted Palestine to be ruled by Britain. Sykes replied that all the other difficulties could be resolved ("the Arabs could be managed," he said) but that rejection of the condominium approach brought them up against a problem for which he had no sure solution: France, he said, was "the serious difficulty."[2] France, he explained, refused to recognize that concessions to Zionism might help win the war; and he confessed to the Zionist leaders that he could not understand French policy in this respect. "What was their motive?" he asked.[3]

The next day, at his London residence at 9 Buckingham Gate, Sykes introduced the worldly Zionist leader Nahum Sokolow to François Georges Picot, who told Sokolow that, having seen the results of Jewish colonization in Palestine, he believed the program of Jewish settlement was feasible. Sokolow told Picot that Jews greatly admired France but "had long in mind the suzerainty of the British government."[4] Picot replied that the question of suzerainty was one for the Allies to decide among themselves. He said that he would do his best to make the Zionists' aims known to his government, but that in his view there was no possibility of his government deciding to renounce its claim to Palestine. Indeed, he said, 95 percent of the French people wanted France to annex Palestine.[5]

All concerned agreed to wait upon events, which were not slow in coming. Within two months the Czar was overthrown and the United States had entered the war. Sykes quickly saw the implications of both events for his arrangements with Picot. Millions of Jews lived within the Czarist Empire; their support, Sykes argued after the Russian Revolution in March, could help induce the new Russian government to remain in the war.[6] At the same time, the American entry into the war strengthened his conviction that the European Allies would have to validate their claims to a position in the postwar Middle East by sponsorship of oppressed peoples, such as Jews, Arabs, and Armenians. On both counts he felt he had new arguments with which to persuade the French government to adopt a more sympathetic attitude toward Zionism.

Meanwhile his conversations with Picot were about to reopen: Lloyd George succeeded in ordering the British army in Egypt to attempt an invasion of Palestine in 1917, leading the French government to insist on sending Picot to Egypt to accompany the British invasion forces—to which the British government responded by ordering Sykes to go there, too, to interpose between Picot and the British commanding general. Picot viewed the proposed British invasion as an attack on French interests. He reported that "London now considers our agreements a dead letter. English troops will enter Syria from the south"—from Egypt and Palestine—"and disperse our supporters."[7]

Lloyd George, impatient with France's pretensions in the Middle East, told Weizmann that the future of Palestine was a question that would be resolved between Britons and Jews.[8] He professed to be unable to understand why Sykes was so concerned about French objections and told Weizmann that Palestine "was to him the one really interesting part of the war."[9]

On the afternoon of 3 April 1917 Sykes, newly appointed as head of the political mission to the General Officer Commanding-in-Chief the Egyptian Expeditionary Force, went to 10 Downing Street to receive his parting instructions. There he met with the Prime Minister, Lord Curzon, and Maurice Hankey. Sykes proposed to try to raise an Arab tribal rebellion behind enemy lines, but Lloyd George and Curzon impressed upon him the importance of not committing Britain to an agreement with the tribes that would be prejudicial to British interests. Specifically they told him not to do anything that would worsen the problem with France, and to bear in mind the "importance of not prejudicing the Zionist movement and the possibility of its development under British auspices."[10] According to notes of the conference, "The Prime Minister laid stress on the importance, if possible, of securing the addition of Palestine to the British area in the postwar Middle East."[11] The Prime Minister warned Sykes not to make pledges to the Arabs "and particularly none in regard to Palestine."[12]

Sykes stopped first in Paris, where he stayed at the Hôtel Lotti on the Rue Castiglione, only a few steps away from the Place Vendôme, with its monumental reminder of Napoleon Bonaparte and his conquests. While there, Sykes told Picot that France would have to change her way of thinking and come around to a nonannexationist approach, and that this might involve American or British sponsorship of a reborn Judaea, and French sponsorship of a reborn Armenia. He was surprised that Picot appeared disconcerted by what he said.[13]

From the Hôtel Lotti, Sykes wrote on 8 April 1917 to the Foreign Secretary, Arthur Balfour, that the French were hostile to the notion of bringing the United States into Palestine as a patron of Zionism; they feared that, if introduced into the Middle East, the United States might become France's commercial rival there. "As regards Zionism itself," he continued, "the French are beginning to realize they are up against a big thing, and that they cannot close their eyes to it."[14]

The French Foreign Ministry, like Sykes, now believed that Russia's Jews might help to keep Russia in the war at a time when military disasters on the western front made the eastern front especially crucial. Nahum Sokolow, whom Sykes introduced to the Quai d'Orsay, seemed willing to help in this respect. His discussions with the French officials went well. On 9 April Sykes wrote to Balfour that "The situation now is therefore that Zionist aspirations are recognized as legitimate by the French."[15]

France remained adamant, however, in maintaining her own claims in the Middle East. Sykes met with the leader of the French colonialist bloc, Senator Pierre-Etienne Flandin; and on 15 April wrote to the Foreign Office that Flandin continued to insist that France must have the whole sea-coast of Syria, Lebanon, and Palestine down to El Arish in the Egyptian Sinai. Flandin claimed that "Picot was a fool who had betrayed France" by compromising with Britain in the Sykes-Picot Agreement.[16]

From Paris, Sykes went on to Rome, where he arranged for Nahum Sokolow to plead the Zionist case with the Pope and other Vatican officials. Whatever inspiration he may have derived from these meetings was counterbalanced by the emergence of a new problem: Italy's Foreign Minister, Baron Sidney Sonnino, strongly asserted Italian claims to a share in the postwar Middle East.

Once in Cairo, Sykes brought together his diverse allies to persuade them to work together. He introduced Picot to Arab leaders in Cairo, and later arranged for Picot to come with him on a journey to Arabia to meet with Sherif Hussein to outline for him, at least in a general way, the terms of the secret Sykes-Picot-Sazanov Agreement. Sykes optimistically believed that he had got Hussein to admit that the French could prove helpful to the Arabs in Syria; that he had persuaded Arab leaders to see that the Arabs were too weak to assume responsibility for an area of such complex interests as Palestine; and that he had reached an understanding that Palestinian Arabs would agree to a national status* for the Jewish community in Palestine if the Arab community received the same designation.[17]

In Cairo, Sykes was warned by Clayton and his friends at the Arab Bureau that a French presence in the Middle East would cause trouble.[18] But Sykes, faithful and good-hearted as ever, continued to maintain that his friends had fallen victim to "Fashodism"—a desire to best the French, as Kitchener had done at Fashoda—and that they ought to show more loyalty to their ally. He continued to attempt to convert Picot into a genuine partner, and suggested that the French representative work out a common policy with Hussein's sons so that Britain and France could pursue parallel, constructive, cooperative relationships with the new Arab rulers of the postwar Middle East. On 12 May he cabled London that "Picot has come to terms with the Arab representatives."[19] A few weeks later he wrote to a colleague: "I think French will be ready to co-operate with us in a common policy towards the Arab speaking people . . ."[20]

II

In the first half of 1917, General Sir Archibald Murray, commander of the British army in Egypt—the Egyptian Expeditionary Force— sent his troops lurching in fits and starts toward Palestine. Whether because London kept issuing and then countermanding instructions, or because he himself was inept, or a combination of both, Murray allowed the German commanders and their Turkish troops time to regroup. But then he hastily attacked—at Gaza, which dominated the coastal road to Palestine—in the early morning fog on 26 March, and was beaten. Kress von Kressenstein, the brilliant German commander, who had fortified Gaza effectively, suffered only half as many casualties as the British.

Calling up reinforcements from Egypt, Murray launched a second attack on fortified Gaza on 29 April, and Kressenstein defeated him even more decisively: the ratio of British to Turkish casualties was three to one. Weary and discouraged, the British armies withdrew; and within weeks Sir Archibald Murray was relieved of his command. Lloyd George was determined to renew the battle for Palestine in the autumn but, for the moment, London was unwilling to commit fresh troops to the campaign.

* The reference was to "*millet,*" a term used in the Ottoman Empire to designate a community entitled to a certain amount of autonomy in administering the affairs of its members.

Murray's two defeats led Sir Mark Sykes to worry that the Turks—in the breathing space before Britain resumed the attack in the autumn—might retaliate against the Jewish, Arab, and Armenian populations whose support he had been enlisting on behalf of the Allies. He cabled the Foreign Office suggesting that Britain should not go forward with Zionist, Arab, and Armenian projects so long as they exposed these peoples to jeopardy.[21] His suggestion met with no response.

Discouraged by the war news—the failure of the French offensive in Champagne, the mutiny of French army units there, the disintegration of Russia, and Murray's failure to invade Palestine—Sykes attached even greater importance to winning the support of the peoples of the Middle East. To him it seemed, as it did to Leo Amery and his colleagues, that even if the Allies were to win the war, their victory might be an inconclusive one; and that such positions as they might win for themselves in the Middle East could be subject to continual pressure by a German-controlled Turkey that would make full use of the Sultan's leadership of Islam. In his view, that made the annexationist claims of pre-Clemenceau France and of Baron Sonnino's Italy all the more short-sighted. In a "Memorandum on the Asia-Minor Agreement" he wrote that

> The idea of annexation definitely must be dismissed, it is contrary to the spirit of the time, and if at any moment the Russian extremists got hold of a copy they could make much capital against the whole Entente, this is especially so with the Italian claim which runs counter to nationality, geography, and common sense, and is merely Baron Sonnino's concession to a chauvinist group who only think in bald terms of grab.

He went on to say that France, if she were wise, would deal with her areas of influence in the Middle East as Britain planned to deal with hers: in Syria and the Lebanon France should sponsor Arab independence. If she did *not* do so, wrote Sykes, Britain should do nothing to help France deal with the troubles she would have brought on her own head.

Outlining his own vision of the future, Sykes wrote that "I want to see a permanent Anglo-French entente allied to the Jews, Arabs, and Armenians which will render pan-Islamism innocuous and protect India and Africa from the Turco-German combine, which I believe may well survive Hohenzollerns."[22]

Sykes had won over Amery to this point of view, and Amery later wrote that "the Jews alone can build up a strong civilisation in Palestine which could help that country to hold its own against German-Turkish oppression ... It would be a fatal thing if, after the war, the interests of the Jews throughout the world were enlisted on the side of the Germans."[23]

III

Chaim Weizmann was elected President of the British Zionist Federation in February 1917, enabling him to propose officially that the British government should make a public commitment to support a Jewish homeland in Palestine. After his meetings with Sykes he continued to meet with public officials who expressed sympathy with his ideas.

Lord Robert Cecil, Parliamentary Under-Secretary of State for Foreign Affairs, and the third son of Lord Salisbury, Victoria's last Prime Minister, became a devoted convert. Five young Cecils were killed in the First World War, and Lord Robert was moved to draft a memorandum outlining a plan for perpetual peace: the first draft of what later became the Covenant of the League of Nations. His ideas of self-determination disconcerted his political colleagues, who pointed out that logically his plan would lead to the dissolution of the British Empire.[24] A contemporary essayist wrote in wonder that "He took the cross in an odd international crusade for peace; and he found his allies in places where Cecils normally look for their enemies."[25] In a similar crusading spirit he took up the cause of a Jewish Palestine.

Another sympathizer was Sir Ronald Graham, an Arabist who had come back to the Foreign Office after more than a decade of service in Egypt, where he had been the first British official to discuss with Vladimir Jabotinsky the creation of a Jewish unit within the British army. Now, having returned to London, he urged the Foreign Office to make its support of Zionism public. While the notion of committing Britain to Zionism was inspired by Gerald FitzMaurice and Mark Sykes, Graham was probably more responsible than anyone else in the government for actually embodying the commitment in an official document, though his role tends to be passed over by historians—possibly because he failed to leave a significant archive of private papers behind him.

Graham and other officials of the Foreign Office were keenly aware that France was the obstacle in the way of giving Chaim Weizmann the public commitment he requested. Graham concluded, as had Sykes, that Zionism was weakened by its exclusive attachment to Britain. He worried that the Zionists were gambling everything on the prospect that Britain would govern Palestine—in ignorance of the secret Sykes-Picot Agreement in which Britain had pledged not to do so. On 19 April 1917 Graham wrote to Sykes that it was disquieting that the Zionist movement relied so completely on the prospect of Britain having Palestine.[26]

However it was difficult to see how the Zionist movement could turn to France for support. Within the French Foreign Ministry Zionism was spoken of with scorn, and important segments of French opinion had expressed hostility all along to the movement, which was regarded as pro-German. Zionism had attracted little support among France's Jews and, as a result, the French government held a low opinion of its strength—until the revolution in Russia made Jews seem much more politically important than they were. Even after events in Russia made it seem desirable to win Zionist support, the Quai d'Orsay hesitated to bid for it, fearing that an Allied commitment to Zionism might amount to an abandonment of France's claim to Palestine.

The problem was solved by Nahum Sokolow who, in his negotiations with the French Foreign Ministry, pointedly did not raise the question of which country should be the protecting power for Palestine. Officials at the Quai d'Orsay therefore were led to assume that Zionists would remain neutral on that issue. French officials were not prepared to support Zionism in a postwar Palestine—and did not envisage allowing Jews to achieve a separate national status—but they saw no harm in offering the Zionists words of encouragement so long as they were meaningless. They believed that those who held Zionist "daydreams" might be won over by granting them some form of verbal encouragement that did not constitute a real commitment.[27] In return for Sokolow's agreement to go to Russia to use his influence with the Jews there, on 4 June 1917 Jules Cambon, Director-General of the French Foreign Ministry, gave him a written formal assurance from the French government of its sympathy in the following terms:

> You were good enough to present the project to which you are devoting your efforts which has for its object the development of Jewish colonization in Palestine. You consider that, circumstances permitting, and the independence of the Holy Places being safeguarded on the other hand, it would be a deed of justice and of reparation to assist, by the protection of the Allied Powers, in the renaissance of the Jewish nationality in that land from which the people of Israel were exiled so many centuries ago.
>
> The French Government, which entered this present war to defend a people wrongfully attacked, and which continues the struggle to assure the victory of right over might, cannot but

feel sympathy for your cause, the triumph of which is bound up
with that of the Allies.

I am happy to give you herewith such assurance.[28]

It was subtly phrased. Omitted from the pledge was the crux of
the Zionist idea: that the renaissance of the Jewish nation should
occur within the context of a political entity of its own. Moreover,
the Holy Places, which were to remain independent of the pledge of
sympathy, had already been defined by the French in the Sykes-
Picot Agreement as a large enclave that took in most of inhabited
Palestine west of the Jordan river. If that definition were to apply,
French sympathy for the Jewish nation in Palestine would be restricted to Haifa, Hebron, northern Galilee, and the Negev Desert.
The Cambon letter was, as it was intended to be, noncommittal.*

Nonetheless, the French had outmaneuvered themselves. Their
formal assurance was too cautiously phrased to be meaningful, but
its existence licensed the British to issue an assurance of their own.
Once it became common ground that the Allies supported Jewish
aspirations in Palestine, however defined, the Zionist movement
would have an important role in selecting its protector, and would
choose Britain. This was a matter of less concern to Graham and
Sykes, whose principal objective at that time was to secure a homeland
in Palestine for the Jews, than to Leo Amery and his friends, to
whom Zionism was attractive mainly because it ensured that Palestine
would be British.

Armed with the written French statement that Sokolow had
brought back with him from Paris, Graham and Cecil advised a
willing Balfour in mid-June 1917 that the time had come to issue a
written public British commitment to Zionism. Balfour invited
Weizmann to participate in the process of drafting an appropriate
document. It was what Weizmann and Sykes had sought all along.

The process of drafting the appropriate language, and deciding to
whom it should be addressed, went on through the summer until
September, when Milner and Leo Amery took charge of it. Almost
all the governmental figures who mattered were disposed favorably
toward the proposed declaration. Sykes, fortified by Ormsby-Gore,
had converted the War Cabinet secretariat to Zionism. Balfour, the
Foreign Secretary, had long sympathized with Zionism and now
believed that Britain should go on record in its favor; and within his
own department he was pushed forward in this by Cecil and Graham.

---

* It is sometimes pointed out that the Balfour Declaration was equally vague.
But, unlike the Cambon letter, the Balfour Declaration (a) was published, (b) referred to the whole of Palestine, and (c) referred to the creation of an entity that was to
have a distinctly Jewish national identity—a National Home.

Smuts was deeply pro-Zionist. Milner and his set, including Philip Kerr of the Prime Minister's secretariat, had come to view the establishment of a Jewish Palestine as a vital British imperial interest. The Prime Minister had always planned to carry through a Zionist program; and while he did not express an interest in declaring Britain's intentions in advance, neither did he place any obstacle in the way of his government's doing so once his colleagues thought it useful.

Yet the proposal that Balfour should issue his pro-Zionist declaration suddenly encountered opposition that brought it to a halt. The opposition came from leading figures in the British Jewish community. Edwin Montagu, Secretary of State for India, led the opposition group within the Cabinet. He, along with his cousin, Herbert Samuel, and Rufus Isaacs (Lord Reading) had broken new ground for their co-religionists: they had been the first Jews to sit in a British Cabinet.* The second son of a successful financier who had been ennobled, Montagu saw Zionism as a threat to the position in British society that he and his family had so recently, and with so much exertion, attained. Judaism, he argued, was a religion, not a nationality, and to say otherwise was to say that he was less than 100 percent British.

Montagu was regarded as by far the most capable of the younger men in the Liberal ranks, and it was deemed a political masterstroke for the Prime Minister to have taken him and Churchill away from Asquith. Yet a typical political comment at the time (from Lord Derby, the War Minister) was, "The appointment of Montagu, a Jew, to the India Office has made, as far as I can judge, an uneasy feeling both in India and here"; though Derby added that "I, personally, have a very high opinion of his capability and I expect he will do well."[29] It bothered Montagu that, despite his lack of religious faith, he could not avoid being categorized as a Jew. He was the millionaire son of an English lord, but was driven to lament that "I have been striving all my life to escape from the Ghetto."[30]

The evidence suggested that in his non-Zionism, Montagu was speaking for a majority of Jews. As of 1913, the last date for which there were figures, only about one percent of the world's Jews had signified their adherence to Zionism.[31] British Intelligence reports indicated a surge of Zionist feeling during the war in the Pale of Russia, but there were no figures either to substantiate or to quantify it.[32] In Britain, the Conjoint Committee, which represented British Jewry in all matters affecting Jews abroad, had been against Zionism from the start and remained so.[33]

Montagu's opposition brought all matters to a halt. In disgust,

* Disraeli, of course, though of Jewish ancestry, was baptized a Christian.

Graham reported that the proposed declaration was "hung up" by Montagu, "who represents a certain section of the rich Jews and who seems to fear that he and his like will be expelled from England and asked to cultivate farms in Palestine."[34]

The sub-Cabinet officials who were pushing for a pro-Zionist commitment attempted to allay such fears. Amery, who was helping Milner redraft the proposed Declaration, explained the concept behind it to a Cabinet member as not really being addressed to British subjects of the Jewish faith, but to Jews who resided in countries that denied them real citizenship. "Apart from those Jews who have become citizens of this or any other country in the fullest sense, there is also a large body, more particularly of the Jews in Poland and Russia ... who are still in a very real sense a separate nation ..."[35] Denied the right to become Russians, they would be offered a chance to rebuild their own homeland in Palestine.

Montagu, however, took little interest in the position of Jews in other countries. It was the position of Jews in British society that concerned him; feeling threatened, he fought back with a ferocity that brought the Cabinet's deliberations on the matter to a standstill.

Montagu was aided by Lord Curzon, who argued that Palestine was too meagre in resources to accommodate the Zionist dream. More important, he was aided by Andrew Bonar Law—leader of the dominant party in the Coalition government and the Prime Minister's powerful political partner—who urged delay. Bonar Law argued that the time was not yet ripe for a consideration of the Zionist issue.

Montagu was also aided by the United States, which, until mid-October 1917, cautiously counselled delay. President Wilson was sympathetic to Zionism, but suspicious of British motives; he favored a Jewish Palestine but was less enthusiastic about a British Palestine. As the British Cabinet considered issuing the Balfour Declaration, it solicited the advice, and by implication the support, of President Wilson. The proposed Declaration was described by the Cabinet to the American government as an expression of sympathy for Zionist aspirations, as though it were motivated solely by concern for the plight of persecuted Jews. Wilson's foreign policy adviser, Colonel House, translated this as follows: "The English naturally want the road to Egypt and India blocked, and Lloyd George is not above using us to further this plan."[36]

This was a fair interpretation of the views of the Prime Minister and of the Milner circle which advised him. According to Chaim Weizmann, Philip Kerr (the former Milner aide who served as Lloyd George's secretary) "saw in a Jewish Palestine a bridge between Africa, Asia and Europe on the road to India."[37] It was not, however, a fair interpretation of the views of the Foreign Office, which had been won over by the argument that a pro-Zionist declaration would prove a crucial weapon against Germany in the war and afterward. The Foreign Office believed that the Jewish communities in America and, above all, Russia, wielded great power. The British ambassador in Petrograd, well aware that Jews were a weak and persecuted minority in imperial Russia and of no political consequence, reported that Zionists could not affect the outcome of the struggle for power in Russia. His home government persisted in believing, however, that the Jewish community in Russia could keep the government that ruled them in the Allied camp. As the crisis in Russia deepened, the Foreign Office was seized by a sense of urgency in seeking Jewish support.

IV

Fear begets fear. In Germany the press was aroused by rumors of what the British Foreign Office intended to do. In June 1917 Sir Ronald Graham received from Chaim Weizmann an issue of a Berlin newspaper known for its close relationship to the government, reporting that the British were flirting with the idea of endorsing Zionism in order to acquire the Palestinian land bridge on the road from Egypt to India, and proposing that Germany forestall the maneuver by endorsing Zionism first. (Though the British did not know it, the German government took little interest in adopting a pro-Zionist stance; it was the German press that took an interest in it.)

That summer Graham communicated his fears to Balfour. In his minute, Graham wrote that he had heard there was to be another postponement which he believed would "jeopardise the whole Jewish situation." This endangered the position in Russia where, he asserted, the Jews were all anti-Ally and, to a lesser extent, it would antagonize public opinion in the United States. Warning that Britain must not "throw the Zionists into the arms of the Germans," he argued that "We might at any moment be confronted by a German move on the Zionist question and it must be remembered that Zionism was originally if not a German Jewish at any rate an Austrian Jewish idea."[38]

Graham attached to his minute a list of dates showing how extensive the government's delays had been in dealing with the Zionist matter. In October, Balfour forwarded the minute to the Prime Minister, along with the list of dates which he said showed that the Zionists had reasonable cause to complain, to which he added his own recommendation that the question be taken up by the Cabinet as soon as possible.[39]

On 26 October 1917, *The Times* published a leading article attacking the continuing delay. Stating that it was no secret that British and Allied governments had been considering a statement about Palestine, *The Times* argued that the time had come to make one.

Do our statesmen fail to see how valuable to the Allied cause would be the hearty sympathy of the Jews throughout the world which an unequivocal declaration of British policy might win? Germany has been quick to perceive the danger to her schemes and to her propaganda that would be involved in the association of the Allies with Jewish national hopes, and she has not been idle in attempting to forestall us.

On 31 October 1917 the Cabinet overrode the opposition of Montagu and Curzon and authorized the Foreign Secretary to issue a much-diluted version of the assurance of support that Weizmann had requested. An ebullient Sykes rushed over with the news, "Dr. Weizmann, it's a boy"; but the Zionist leader was unhappy that the original language had been so watered down.[40]

Addressed to the most illustrious name in British Jewry, the Foreign Secretary's letter of 2 November 1917 stated:

Dear Lord Rothschild,
I have much pleasure in conveying to you, on behalf of His Majesty's Government, the following declaration of sympathy with Jewish Zionist aspirations which has been submitted to, and approved by, the Cabinet: "His Majesty's Government view with favour the establishment in Palestine of a national home for the Jewish people, and will use their best endeavours to facilitate the achievement of this object, it being clearly understood that nothing shall be done which may prejudice the civil and religious rights of existing non-Jewish communities in Palestine, or the rights and political status enjoyed by Jews in any other country." I should be grateful if you would bring this declaration to the knowledge of the Zionist Federation.

Britain's leaders anticipated no adverse reaction from their Arab allies; they had seen France as their only problem in this connection, and that had been resolved. The Prime Minister later wrote of the Arab leaders that "Palestine did not seem to give them much anxiety."[41] He pointed out that his government had informed King Hussein and Prince Feisal of its plans to re-create a Jewish homeland in the Holy Land. He caustically added that "We could not get in touch with the Palestinian Arabs as they were fighting against us."[42]

The public announcement of the Balfour Declaration was delayed until the following Friday, the publication date of the weekly *Jewish*

Chronicle. By then the news was overshadowed by reports from Petrograd that Lenin and Trotsky had seized power. The Foreign Office had hoped the Balfour Declaration would help to swing Russian Jewish support to the Allied side and against Bolshevism. This hope remained alive until the Bolsheviks decisively won the Russian Civil War in the early 1920s. In November of 1917 the battle against Bolshevism in Russia had just begun, and those Britons who supported the Balfour Declaration, because they mistakenly believed Russian Jews were powerful and could be valuable allies, were driven to support it all the more by the dramatic news from Petrograd.

It was not until 9 November that *The Times* was able to report the announcement of the Balfour Declaration, and not until 3 December that it published comments approving it. The comments followed upon a celebration at the London Opera House on 2 December organized by the British Zionist Federation. In addition to the Zionist leaders, speakers included Lord Robert Cecil, Sir Mark Sykes, and William Ormsby-Gore, as well as a Syrian Christian, an Arab nationalist, and spokesmen for Armenia. The theme of the meeting, eloquently pursued by many of the speakers, was the need for Jews, Arabs, and Armenians to help one another and to move forward in harmony. The opinion of *The Times* was that "The presence and the words of influential representatives of the Arab and Armenian peoples, and their assurances of agreement and cooperation with the Jews, would alone have sufficed to make the meeting memorable."[43]

Of the meeting, *The Times* wrote that "its outstanding features were the Old Testament spirit which pervaded it and the feeling that, in the somewhat incongruous setting of a London theatre, the approaching fulfillment of ancient prophecy was being celebrated with faith and fervour."[44] It was appropriate that it should be so: Biblical prophecy was the first and most enduring of the many motives that led Britons to want to restore the Jews to Zion.

The Prime Minister planned to foster a Jewish home in Palestine, in any event, and later wrote that the peace treaty would have provided that Palestine should be a homeland for the Jews "even had there been no previous pledge or promise."[45] The importance of the Balfour Declaration, he wrote, was its contribution to the war effort. He claimed that Russian Jews had given invaluable support to the war against Germany because of it. The grateful Zionist leaders had promised to work toward an Allied victory—and had done so. Writing two decades later, as the British government was about to abandon the Balfour Declaration, he said that the Zionists "kept their word in the letter and the spirit, and the only question that remains now is whether we mean to honour ours."[46]

The Prime Minister underestimated the effect of the Balfour Declaration on the eventual peace settlement. Its character as a public document—issued with the approval of the United States and France and after consultation with Italy and the Vatican, and greeted with approval by the public and the press throughout the western world—made it a commitment that was difficult to ignore when the peace settlement was being negotiated. It took on a life and momentum of its own.

V

The Declaration also played a role in the development of the Zionist movement in the American Jewish community. American Zionism had been a tiny movement when the war began. Of the roughly three million Jews who then lived in the United States, only 12,000 belonged to the often ephemeral groups loosely bound together in the amateurishly led Zionist Federation.[47] The movement's treasury contained 15,000 dollars;[48] its annual budget never exceeded 5,200 dollars.[49] The largest single donation the Federation ever received prior to 1914 was 200 dollars.[50] In New York the movement had only 500 members.[51]

Louis D. Brandeis, an outstanding Boston lawyer not previously identified with specifically Jewish causes, had become a Zionist in 1912 and took over leadership of the movement in 1914. As the intellectual giant of the Progressive movement in American politics, he was believed to exert great influence over President Wilson. Brandeis was perhaps the first Jew to play an important part in American politics since the Civil War. Only one Jew had ever been a member of a president's cabinet,[*] and Brandeis himself was to become the first Jewish member of the U.S. Supreme Court.

The great waves of Jewish immigration into the United States were recent, and most immigrants were anxious to learn English, to shed their foreign accents and ways, and to become American. American-born Jews, too, wanted to distance themselves from any foreign taint and feared that attachment to Zionism on their part might make them seem less than wholehearted in their loyalty to the United States.

It was this issue, above all, that Brandeis set out to address. As he saw it, American Jews lacked something important that other Americans possessed: a national past. Others could point to an ancestral homeland and take pride in it and in themselves. Brandeis especially admired Irish-Americans in this respect and for manifesting their opposition to continued British rule in Ireland.

Arguing that this kind of political concern and involvement is

[*] Oscar Straus, Secretary of Commerce and Labor from 1906 to 1909.

entirely consistent with American patriotism, and indeed enhances it, he proclaimed that "Every Irish-American who contributed towards advancing home rule was a better man and a better American for the sacrifice he made. Every American Jew who aids in advancing the Jewish settlement in Palestine ... will likewise be a better man and a better American for doing so."[52]

The ethical idealism of Brandeis made a powerful impression on Arthur Balfour when the British Foreign Secretary visited the United States in 1917 and discussed the future of Palestine. In turn, the Balfour Declaration vindicated the arguments that Brandeis had used in his appeals to the American Jewish community. It showed that Zionism was in harmony with patriotism in wartime because a Jewish Palestine was an Allied war goal. Soon afterward it also became an officially supported American goal. On the occasion of the Jewish New Year in September 1918, President Wilson endorsed the principles of the Balfour Declaration in a letter of holiday greetings to the American Jewish community.[53]

Whether because of the Balfour Declaration or because of Brandeis's effective and professional leadership, support for Zionism within the Jewish community grew dramatically. In 1919 membership of the Zionist Federation grew to more than 175,000, though Zionist supporters remained a minority group within American Jewry and still encountered fierce opposition from the richer and more established Jews—opposition that was not really overcome until the 1940s. But Brandeis had made American Zionism into a substantial organization along the lines pioneered by Irish-Americans who supported independence for Ireland; and the Balfour Declaration had helped him to do so—even though the Foreign Office had issued the declaration in part because they supposed such a force was already in existence and needed to be appeased.

VI

A measure of how far British war goals had moved in the year since Lloyd George replaced Asquith is provided by Leo Amery's reflections in his diary at the end of 1917. Looking back and evaluating what he had been able to accomplish during the year, he wrote that one of his main achievements in dealing with British government colleagues had been "all the work on Peace terms which gradually drove into their heads the importance of East Africa, Palestine, and Mesopotamia and the Imperial outlook generally."[54]

As Amery indicated, Britain's main objectives by now were not in Europe. The destruction wrought in the first three years of the war made a meaningful victory in Europe impossible. The rival warring

European coalitions were ruined. It was not feasible to look for an annexation or acquisition in Europe to make up for what had been lost. Even the destruction of Germany would not meet Britain's needs. In a wartime speech Smuts pointed out that Germany had to remain a substantial power in order to uphold the European balance of power, which it was in Britain's vital interest to maintain.[55]

It was an open question as to whether the Britain that sailed onto the world ocean and around the globe under Sir Francis Drake had perished forever with the generation of 1914 on the western front. If that Britain could be revived, it would have to be through imperial expansion, partly in Africa but principally in the Middle East—that was the direction in which the Prime Minister and the Milner circle were looking.

This shift in outlook brought the Ottoman war, which had begun as an accidental irrelevance, from the periphery to the very center of the Prime Minister's world policy. From the beginning he had said that the Great War could be won there. Now he was saying that his postwar objectives could be won there too. With his political instinct, he felt that it was an area in which he could win tangible rewards for his countrymen, and with his strategic vision he saw—as did Milner, Amery, Smuts, Kerr, and Ormsby-Gore—that, by supplying the missing section of the line that led from Cape Town to India and on to Australia and New Zealand, it offered a new lease on Britain's empire in Africa, Asia, and the Pacific. Where the Asquith Cabinet eventually came to see hegemony over portions of the Middle East as something that Britain merely wanted, the Lloyd George government came to see it as territory that Britain *needed*.

PART VII

INVADING THE MIDDLE EAST

35

JERUSALEM FOR CHRISTMAS

I

At the end of 1916, when David Lloyd George took office as Prime Minister, British fortunes in the East took a turn for the better. The blundering incompetence of the Government of India in conducting the Mesopotamian campaign—the advance on Baghdad late in 1915 that ended in the spring of 1916 in the defeat and surrender of the British Indian Army at Kut el-Amara—had shocked London into making a clean sweep at the top. Thus a new chief of the expeditionary army, who understood its logistical requirements, re-opened the campaign under a new Secretary of State for India, a new Viceroy, and a new commander-in-chief of the Indian Army. Major-General Stanley Maude led his Anglo-Indian Army of the Tigris forward into the Mesopotamian provinces in December 1916, and in a methodical campaign captured Baghdad on 11 March 1917.

Although it had never been clear as to what purpose the Baghdad campaign was meant to serve in the overall strategy of the world war, the capture of the ancient capital, glamorous from its association with the *Arabian Nights*, caught the imagination of the new Prime Minister. It brought him cheer at a time when it was badly needed, and inspired him to aim at Jerusalem for Britain's next great triumph.

The successes of the Army of the Tigris raised the question of what was to be done with the Ottoman provinces that it had occupied. The Government of India, although wary of committing itself, had envisaged all along that the Mesopotamian provinces of Basra and Baghdad would fall within its sphere if they were detached from the Ottoman Empire. To Sir Mark Sykes and his Arab Bureau friends, the notion that such areas should be administered in what they regarded as India's paternalistic way was abhorrent. In a memorandum written in 1916, Sykes warned the Cabinet that "if you work from India you have all the old traditions of black and white, and you can not run the Arabs on black and white lines."[1]

To mark the capture of Baghdad, Sir Percy Cox, chief political ificer of General Maude's expeditionary force, drafted a proclamation to the populace that essentially limited itself to calling for cooperation with the provisional British-Indian administration; but London ordered him not to issue it. Several drafts were written in London, and after discussion the War Cabinet chose one written by Sir Mark Sykes as a basis for the text that was finally approved. The proclamation invited the Arabs' leaders—though it was unclear who they were to be—to participate in the government in collaboration with the British authorities. It spoke—as was Sykes's wont—in high-flown phrases of liberation and freedom, of past glory and future greatness, and expressed the hope that the Arabic peoples might find unity north, south, east, and west. It pointed, however vaguely, toward an Arab Middle Eastern confederation under the leadership of King Hussein—a Sunni Moslem, although most of the inhabitants of the provinces of Basra and Baghdad were Shi'ite, and the differences between Sunnis and Shi'ites were profound and more than a thousand years old.

General Maude objected to the Sykes draft. As a military man, he deemed it essential to install a British administration to maintain security while the war continued. Moreover, he observed that in offering a measure of self-government to the Arabs of Baghdad, the proclamation took no note of the fact that—according to him—a majority of the inhabitants of the city were not Arabs but Jews.[*]

The Sykes draft nonetheless was imposed on General Maude and Sir Percy Cox by London, and caused widespread confusion. Apparently intended to assert that the occupying forces of British India were not going to rule the provinces of Mesopotamia, the proclamation did not make clear who was going to rule in their place.

On 16 March 1917 the War Cabinet created a Mesopotamian Administration Committee under the chairmanship of Lord Curzon to determine what form of government should be installed in the captured provinces. The committee decided that the province of Basra should become British—not British-Indian—while the province of Baghdad should join or should become an Arab political entity subject to a British protectorate. Meanwhile Indian personnel should be withdrawn from the occupied provinces.

General Maude had cabled to his superiors that "local conditions

---

[*] Whether or not they constituted a majority in the city—and the then-current *Encyclopaedia Britannica* indicated that they did not—the Jews were economically preponderant. Baghdad, along with Jerusalem, was one of the two great Jewish cities of Asia, and a thousand years before had become the seat of the exilarch—the head of the Jewish religion in the eastern diaspora— and thus the capital of oriental Judaism. Jews in large numbers had lived in the Mesopotamian provinces since the time of the Babylonian captivity—about 600 BC—and thus were settled in the country a thousand years before the coming of the Arabs in AD 634.

do not permit of employing in responsible positions any but British officers competent to deal with Military authorities and with people of the country. Before any truly Arab facade can be applied to edifice it seems essential that foundation of law and order should be well and truly laid."[2] Sir Percy Cox raised the same issues in a different way when he asked who the Arab leader of Baghdad was going to be.

It was evident that London either was not aware of, or had given no thought to, the population mix of the Mesopotamian provinces. The antipathy between the minority of Moslems who were Sunnis and the majority who were Shi'ites, the rivalries of tribes and clans, the historic and geographic divisions of the provinces, and the commercial predominance of the Jewish community in the city of Baghdad made it difficult to achieve a single unified government that was at the same time representative, effective, and widely supported.

Cox raised other immediate and practical issues that obviously had not been thought through in London. The laborers and other noncombatant support groups of the Army of the Tigris were Indian; if the Cabinet were serious in ordering the Indians out of the Mesopotamian provinces, who would take their place? Moreover, under Turkey, the system of law courts in the provinces had operated under, and with a right of appeal to, the high court in Constantinople, while under General Maude the court system of India offered similar rights; but if the connection with India were to be broken, what would happen to the administration of justice?

The Mesopotamian Administration Committee had no ready replies, for the Ottoman administration of Mesopotamia had been driven out, and no body of experienced officials other than those of British India existed in the provinces to replace it. The war continued, and orders had to be given and administrative decisions taken daily. Public facilities and utilities had to be managed. Who was to do it?

London was driven to reconsider, and to accept the administration of the Government of India so long as it was agreed that it should not be permanent. General Maude, in whose name the Sykes proclamation had been issued, was put in the position of preaching self-rule while discouraging its practice. The compromise formula at which the British had arrived might have been expressly designed to arouse dissatisfaction and unrest: having volunteered what sounded like a pledge of independence to an area that had not asked for it, the military and civil authorities of the occupying power then proceeded to withhold it.

The Mesopotamian provinces were the first to be captured from the Ottoman Empire by Britain during the war. Whitehall's failure to think through in practical detail how to fulfill the promises gratuitously made to a section of the local inhabitants was revealing, and boded ill for the provinces that were the next to be invaded: Palestine, Syria, and Lebanon. It showed that Sir Mark Sykes and his colleagues had adopted policies for the Middle East without first considering whether in existing conditions they could feasibly be implemented, and, if so, whether British officers on the spot would actually allow them to be implemented.

It was an inauspicious beginning and suggested the extent to which the British government did not know what it was getting into when it decided to supersede the Ottoman Empire in Asia. If there was this much muddle when British India occupied nearby Mesopotamia, it was reasonable to suppose there would be even more muddle when British Egypt marched on an area of such complex international interests as Palestine.

II

The new commanding officer sent out to Egypt was General Sir Edmund Allenby, a cavalry officer who had served and commanded with distinction in France. He was chosen in June 1917, after Smuts had definitely decided that he would not accept the appointment. Allenby's commission from the Prime Minister was to invade and occupy Palestine and to take Jerusalem before Christmas.

Allenby brought drive and discipline to the Egyptian Expeditionary Force, and a new professionalism. As head of Military Intelligence he chose Colonel Richard Meinertzhagen, who had distinguished himself in a similar capacity with Smuts in East Africa. Meinertzhagen chose Wyndham Deedes, the expert on Ottoman affairs, to serve under him in charge of the political section of the division.

Meinertzhagen took charge of espionage operations behind enemy lines—operations meant to pave the way for Allenby to invade Palestine. Though he had been strongly anti-Jewish, Meinertzhagen was moved to change his mind by Aaron Aaronsohn, whose spy network in Jewish Palestine he regarded as invaluable. But Aaronsohn paid a high price for winning the respect and friendship of British Military Intelligence: his spy ring exposed the Jewish settlers in Palestine to possible Turkish reprisals—at the worst of times, for the local Ottoman administration was inclined to strike out against the Jewish community in any event. In the spring of 1917, on the feast of Passover, Djemal expelled the Jews and Arabs of Jaffa; it was not clear where he meant them to go, although he spoke vaguely of the Syrian hinterland. The plight of the refugees, without means or supplies, evoked memories of the Armenians. Soon afterward Djemal indicated that he meant to deport the civil population of Jerusalem, of which the majority was Jewish. Only the firm intervention of the German Foreign Ministry kept the tragedy from occurring.

In these circumstances, the Palestinian Jewish community faced catastrophe if the extent and effectiveness of Aaronsohn's activities were uncovered—as eventually they were. Aaron's sister Sarah and a number of her associates were arrested by the Turks in October 1917, tortured and interrogated. Some were hanged. Sarah Aaronsohn, after four days of torture, succeeded in committing suicide. Reprisals against the Jewish population might have followed had not the Germans and Talaat intervened. As it was, only about a third of the Jewish population remained in Jerusalem by the end of 1917; most of the rest had died of starvation or disease.

III

Meinertzhagen was impressed by the effectiveness of Aaronsohn's Jews in contributing to the preparations for a British invasion of Palestine, but was less impressed by the effectiveness of Feisal's Arabs.

The British civil authorities in Cairo had little contact with T. E. Lawrence, their liaison with Feisal's Arabian guerrillas: and in the spring of 1917 he disappeared into the desert. The British military authorities in Cairo showed little concern for whatever Lawrence and Feisal might be doing, having given up interest in the Arab Revolt the previous year.

Lawrence had gone off with Auda abu Tayi, the fighting chief of the Bedouin tribal confederation of northern Arabia, whose adherence Lawrence had secured by the payment of 10,000 pounds sterling. Their objective was Aqaba, a sleepy, tiny port at the southern tip of Palestine, situated at the head of a channel of the Red Sea so narrow that the Royal Navy dared not enter it while its shore batteries were in enemy hands. Its several hundred Ottoman defenders and their gun positions faced out to sea, so Auda's band planned to steal up from behind to take Aqaba by a surprise attack.*

It was Auda who led the expedition, though Lawrence rode with him. With Bedouin cunning, Auda led his followers from the Arabian coastline northward into the desert, where their movements were lost from view. When they reappeared in southern Palestine two months later, their coming was a total surprise. On 6 July they overwhelmed

---

* It was probably Lawrence's idea, though Auda and/or Feisal may have thought of it independently.

Aqaba's small and unprepared Turkish garrison. Despite his two punishing months in the desert, Lawrence immediately set off on an arduous and dangerous trip across a wilderness of enemy-held territories to Suez to report Auda's capture of Aqaba. He astonished everyone by unexpectedly emerging from the Sinai desert, in Arab dress, creating a sensation at headquarters just after General Allenby came to take up his new command.

Lawrence possessed many virtues but honesty was not among them; he passed off his fantasies as the truth. A few months before, he had sent a letter to General Clayton that contained an almost certainly fictitious account of an expedition he claimed to have undertaken on his own.[3] Now he had real personal exploits to announce and to exaggerate, as he allowed his listeners to understand that he had played the chief role in the Aqaba campaign. Lawrence's arrival with the news from Aqaba completed his nine months' transformation into a military hero. Auda abu Tayi, sheikh of the eastern Howeitat, who had in fact won the victory, did not have a name that tripped easily off the tongues of British officers. Instead they said, as historians did later, that "Lawrence took Aqaba."

Whoever deserved credit, the capture of Aqaba transformed the Hejaz rebellion which had hitherto been bottled up in the Arabian peninsula by the Turkish garrison at Medina. Now the Royal Navy could transport Arabian tribesmen to Palestine; and thus, for the first time, Hussein's forces could reach a battlefield on which the British-Turkish war was actually to be fought, for Lawrence persuaded Allenby that Arab irregulars could assist British forces in the coming Palestine and Syria campaigns.

Feisal still remained at headquarters in the Hejaz when Allenby approved Lawrence's plan to transport him and a small striking force of his tribesmen by sea from the British-held coast of Arabia to Aqaba—a sea voyage of 250 miles. There they could act as a diversionary force on the right flank of the British army in the coming Palestine campaign which Allenby planned to launch in the autumn. Feisal accepted the plan, although it meant cutting himself off from the Hejaz, his father, and his brothers; he was deputized as a British general and came under Allenby's command.

A few months earlier, the Arab Bureau had considered the problems that would arise from any attempt to employ Feisal's forces in the Palestine and Syria campaigns. The bureau had reported to Clayton on 16 May 1917 that Feisal's Bedouins could not stand up to regular troops, and that an additional disadvantage of employing them was that their going into settled districts would be unwelcome to town dwellers. According to the Arab Bureau, the problem could be solved by recruiting Syrian deserters from the Ottoman army to serve under Feisal. This would "change the character of Sherif

Feisal's campaign from a series of desultory raids against the railway to an organized attempt to free the country."[4]*

IV

In the autumn of 1917 Allenby invaded Palestine. The Turks and their German commanders expected him to launch his attack on coastal Gaza, the obvious gateway to Palestine; but its defenses and defenders were well prepared and Allenby merely feinted at it while, with stealth and speed, his main forces swung around through the desert to attack inland at Beersheba instead. The Ottoman forces were taken by surprise, and fell back in disarray.

One reason for the Turks' surprise was a ruse devised and executed by Meinertzhagen. On 10 October he rode into no man's land; when an Ottoman cavalry patrol fired at him he pretended to be hit, and dropped a blood-stained sack that contained apparently confidential British documents indicating that the main attack would be at Gaza. "Meinertzhagen's device won the battle," David Lloyd George later wrote; he was "One of the ablest and most successful brains I had met in any army." Lloyd George added that "Needless to say he never rose in the war above the rank of Colonel."[6]

While Allenby's forces were rolling up the Gaza-to-Beersheba line, Feisal's forces harassed the Turks on the British right flank. As liaison officer between the British and Arab officers, first as a major and then as a colonel, T. E. Lawrence enjoyed a colorful campaign that later won him great publicity—but also much envy.

Brémond, the French representative in the Hejaz, later jealously observed that Lawrence "represented" 200,000 pounds sterling,[7] but it was more than that: by the end of the war, the Arab Revolt had cost Britain more than fifty times that amount. Whatever the sum, it was immense in those days—and more so by desert Bedouin standards. The tribes had never known such wealth as Lawrence brought them. Eventually the wealth transformed not merely the face of

---

* British officers put this program into effect when Feisal came to Aqaba, and served with him to provide professional advice and guidance. Lieutenant-Colonel Pierce Charles Joyce, stationed at Aqaba, was the senior British officer serving with Feisal's corps, as O.C. (Officer Commanding) Hejaz operations, reporting to Colonel Alan Dawnay of Allenby's General Staff. Dawnay at the planning level and Joyce at the operations level were the principal British officers placed in charge of the Arab army corps. General Harry Chauvel, commander of the Australian army in the Palestine and Syria campaigns, later wrote that "Joyce was the organiser of the only fighting force of any real value in the whole of the Arab Army and I always thought that he had more to do with the success of the Hejaz operations than any other British officer."[5]

tribal allegiances but also the appearance of the young Englishman who served as paymaster; his Arab wardrobe grew to be even more splendid than Feisal's. Nearly half a century later, when asked if he remembered Lawrence, a Bedouin sheikh replied "He was the man with the gold."[8]

The sheer logistics of getting the gold safely to Lawrence posed a problem, for not many people could be trusted with the possession of it. In Cairo, Wyndham Deedes used to spend his Saturday afternoons personally packing gold sovereigns into cartridge cases and watching them being loaded onto camels for the journey to Lawrence in the desert.

Apart from the tribes, whose role was sporadic, Feisal's army consisted of about 1,000 Bedouins supplemented by about 2,500 Ottoman ex-prisoners of war. British expectations that the ex-prisoners of war would transform Feisal's forces into something akin to a regular army were, at first, a disappointment. A representative of the U.S. Department of State in Cairo reported at the end of 1917 that Feisal's army remained "incapable of coping with disciplined troops"; and his report undoubtedly echoed official British opinion in Cairo at the time.[9]

Another disappointment was the performance of Lawrence's raiding party when assigned a specific operational task by Allenby: they were to dynamite a high-arched viaduct to cut the railroad communications of the Ottoman forces headquartered in Jerusalem. Lawrence and his men failed in the task, but Allenby, having pushed the Turkish right flank north of Jaffa, then thrust through the Judaean hills, and captured Jerusalem anyway—even earlier than Christmas. Though Lawrence bitterly blamed himself for his failure, Allenby did not—and showed it by inviting Lawrence to attend, as staff officer of the day to General Clayton, the ceremony of entrance into Jerusalem.

V

On 11 December 1917 General Sir Edmund Allenby and his officers entered the Holy City of Jerusalem at the Jaffa Gate, on foot. At the Citadel, Allenby read out a proclamation placing the city under martial law. To the French representative, Picot, Allenby explained that the city fell within the military zone, so that authority in the area was vested solely in the commanding general. As commanding general, Allenby would decide how long the area would remain under an exclusively military administration. Only when he deemed that the military situation permitted him to do so, said Allenby, would he allow civil administration to be instituted. Until then, the question of the Sykes-Picot Agreement and the ultimate disposition of Palestine would be deferred.

The liberation of what he called "the most famous city in the world" was what the Prime Minister had wanted for Christmas; with it, he later wrote, Christendom had been able "to regain possession of its sacred shrines."[10] The capture of Baghdad and Jerusalem had produced a tremendous psychological effect, he claimed, but also a material one. "The calling of the Turkish bluff was not only the beginning of the cracking-up of that military impostership which the incompetence of our war direction had permitted to intimidate us for years; it was itself a real contribution to ultimate victory."[11]

After the capture of Jerusalem, Feisal's Arab forces, under various Arab and British officers, showed their worth. Campaigning in Transjordan, the raiding parties continued their hit-and-run attacks, while the regulars, trained by Joyce and transported by his colleague Hubert Young, disproved the contention—frequently advanced by British intelligence officers in the past—that they could not stand up to the Turkish army. A significant role was planned for them in the next phase of the campaign by Allenby, who intended them to spread disorder among the Turks on his right flank.

Allenby was now in a position to march on Damascus, and then on Constantinople to deliver the knock-out blow to the Ottoman Empire, but just at that moment his hand was stayed. The Germans were preparing an offensive against western Europe, made possible by Russia's surrender, which allowed Ludendorff to bring back Germany's armies from the eastern front. Suddenly Allenby was obliged to send back to Europe almost all of his British troops. On the first day of spring 1918, German troops launched a surprise attack that smashed through Allied lines in northern France and threatened to win the war before American reinforcements could arrive. It was not until the summer that the fury of Ludendorff's offensive was spent. Meanwhile Allenby remained in Palestine, rebuilding his forces for the future.

From Christmas until summer's end, as Allenby awaited a chance to resume his offensive, political battle lines were forming within the British government and the Allied camp as to the ultimate disposition of the lands composing the Ottoman Empire. Meanwhile Enver Pasha was starting on a sort of Ludendorff offensive of his own in the north, designed to capture the Turkish-speaking lands of the Czarist Empire—Azerbaijan and Turkestan—and perhaps then to descend on Persia, Afghanistan, and India to destroy Britain's eastern empire while all of her British troops were away in Europe.

In retrospect, Enver's offensive, like Ludendorff's, looks like having been a last desperate throw of the dice. But at the time the Ottoman

Empire's capabilities and intentions were less easy to assess; and the Ottoman offensive brought vast areas of the northern Middle East, hitherto uncontested in the war, into the spotlight of world war and politics.

While Enver was attacking north and east, Allenby was at last able to resume his attack on Enver's forces in the west.

THE ROAD TO DAMASCUS

I

Between Christmas of 1917 and the summer of 1918, Allenby laid the foundation for resuming his campaign against the Turks. In January and February he restored and extended Jerusalem's railway connections to the coast, so as to relieve his army's dependence upon pack animals and ruined roads. He raided enemy forces to keep them off balance. Meanwhile he trained his raw Indian troops for the coming campaign.

Damascus was the next objective on his line of march. Even more than Baghdad and Jerusalem, it was an important city for all historical ages. Believed to be the oldest continuously inhabited urban center in the world, its origins were lost in the mists of time. Damascus was a flourishing oasis town before there were Jews or Arabs, Moslems or Christians, Englishmen or Germans. The capture of Damascus would symbolically complete not merely the British occupation of the Arabic-speaking Ottoman Empire, but also assure Britain's place in the line of legitimate succession from the ancient world conquerors who had sealed their triumphs by achieving mastery of the oases of Syria.

Britain claimed to be something other than a traditional conqueror, for she was acting on behalf of an array of associated powers and causes. Allenby was an Allied commander, and his armies were prepared to advance under many flags. Among their banners was one designed by Sir Mark Sykes for Hussein and the Arab cause. Its colors—black, white, green, and red—were meant to symbolize the past glory of Moslem Arab empires and to suggest that Hussein was their contemporary champion. Hussein's only modification of the design was to change the hue of the red.[1] Sykes had ordered flags to be made up by the British military supply offices in Egypt, and then had them delivered to the Hejaz forces.

The British-designed, British-produced flag of Arab nationalism signaled a critical issue as Allenby's armies prepared to march on

Damascus: the extent to which the particular British officials who mattered most in shaping Middle Eastern policy were sincere or cynical in their espousal of the various causes to which they had supposedly been converted along the way. Sir Mark Sykes, who before 1914 had admired the Turks as a ruling people, had become converted during the war to the cause of liberating the subject peoples from Ottoman tyranny. An outspoken anti-Semite, he had come to express his concern for the Jews, as did Meinertzhagen, also an avowed anti-Semite. Colonial officials such as Storrs and Clayton, who had always maintained that Arabic-speaking natives were incapable of self-government, appeared to support Sykes as he hailed the renaissance of Arab independence. Not all of these conversions were genuine.

At one end of the spectrum was Sykes, who believed in honoring the pledges of which, in large part, he was the author. At the other end were operational officers who deplored the pledges, and at times deprecated the causes in whose names they had been made. At the beginning of 1918 Sykes, in London, moved into a Foreign Office position in charge of the politics of the Ottoman theater of war. Those in charge of the politics of the Ottoman theater of war in the field—Clayton in Palestine, Wingate in Egypt, and the Government of India in Baghdad—were skeptical of the politics of idealism that Sykes had come to espouse, though they did not tell him so openly. Beneath the surface civility of British government interchanges in 1918 there ran a hidden line on which the Foreign Office and officers in the field pulled in opposite directions. Baghdad, Jerusalem, and, beyond Allied lines, Damascus, awaited word of their eventual fate, unaware that a tug of war within the British bureaucracy might decide it.

II

Brigadier General Gilbert Clayton served as chief political officer to General Allenby, but remained the political *alter ego* of Sir Reginald Wingate, the British High Commissioner in Cairo. He thus occupied a commanding position in determining the politics of both Egypt and the Sudan, as well as those of the army of occupation in Palestine. Clayton was a career army officer whose professional caution often kept him from expressing his views freely when they contradicted those of his superiors. He therefore expressed his views candidly to Wingate, with whom he agreed, but guardedly to Sykes, with whom he did not.

Clayton and Storrs envisaged an Arab kingdom or confederation guided by the British in a Middle East in which there was no room for France (except perhaps in Lebanon). Clayton denied that he was anti-French; it was not, he explained, as though he *wanted* to exclude the French from Syria. It was the fault of the French themselves: they were detested by the Syrians and, if given a chance to rule Syria, would bungle it. Clayton said he would not connive at bringing about that result; it was simply that he was predicting it. "You need not be afraid of any Fashoda-ism on my part," he wrote to Sykes on 20 August 1917.[2] It was rather that he feared Britain would be blamed for France's failure, and told Sykes that the important thing was to establish a record showing that it was not Britain's fault.

Though denying anti-French bias, he did admit having reservations about Britain's other Middle Eastern allies. Even by the standards of the time, Clayton and his colleague, Wingate, were strongly disposed to be anti-Jewish. Wingate had blamed Jews for inciting the outbreak of the Ottoman war. In 1916 Clayton reported to Wingate that Jews were behind the movement to make peace with the Ottoman Empire as well.[*]

But when the issue of a compromise peace with Turkey again came to the fore in 1917, Clayton argued that Britain had no moral right to negotiate because "We are committed to the support of Arabs, Syrians, Jews, and Armenians" and therefore had to press forward to complete victory.[4] At the same time, he opposed entering into just such commitments, including the commitment to Zionism. As the Balfour Declaration was being drafted, he wrote to Sykes that it would be best to keep Aaron Aaronsohn and the Jews "in play" without making any statement of British intentions.[5] Politics, he wrote, tended to distract Jews and Arabs from the war effort. By nature cautious, he saw no need in any event to make pledges in advance.

A month after the issuance of the Balfour Declaration, Clayton wrote to Sykes suggesting that it might have been a mistake.

I am not fully aware of the weight which Zionists carry, especially in America and Russia, and of the consequent necessity of giving them everything for which they may ask, but I must

---

[*] In the summer of 1916, when the Tory leader Lord Lansdowne privately argued in favor of a compromise peace, Clayton was in London; and on returning to Cairo wrote Wingate that "One impression I gained which confirmed what I have always thought, and which I know you take an interest in, was the widespread influence of the Jews. It is everywhere and always on the 'moderation' tack. The Jews do not want to see anyone 'downed'. There are English Jews, French Jews, German Jews, Austrian Jews & *Salonika* Jews—but all are JEWS ... You hear peace talk and generally somewhere behind is the Jew. You hear pro-Turk talk and desires for a separate peace with Turkey—again the Jew (the mainspring of the C.U.P.) [original emphasis]."[3]

point out that, by pushing them as hard as we appear to be doing, we are risking the possibility of Arab unity becoming something like an accomplished fact and being ranged against us.[6]

Nonetheless, Clayton was not pro-Arab, in the sense of favoring Arab independence. On the contrary, early in 1917 he and Wingate proposed to abolish even the nominal independence of Egypt and to move toward outright annexation—a judgment which the Foreign Office successfully opposed. Writing to Sykes at the time, in support of his own proposal and against the officials in London who had blocked it, Clayton claimed that

It is strong and I know dead against their policy, but, mark my words, I *know* I am right. All this claptrap about Sultans & self government for Egypt is rot. They are not nearly ready for it and if you have a Palace, every ounce of power and self government which you think you are giving to the People will go straight into the hands of the Sultan & his minister to be used against you. Beautiful theories are all very nice, but hard facts remain.[7]

Although Clayton had been the first to make much of the Arab secret societies, even before the outbreak of the Ottoman war, he consistently ignored what they told him: they did not want to be ruled by Christians or Europeans—not even the British. A reminder of this came in early 1918 in the diplomatic pouch from Madrid, where the British ambassador had seen Aziz al-Masri, the secret society leader, and reported receiving a proposal from him to organize the overthrow of the Enver-Talaat government in Constantinople. The Ottoman Empire would then be reorganized along federal lines, offering local autonomy to Arabs and others, and reconciling the reorganized empire with the Allied Powers.[8] Al-Masri had often said much the same thing to Clayton in Cairo at the beginning of the war, but it did not seem to register on Clayton that it meant that those for whom al-Masri spoke, though willing to be ruled by the Turkish Porte, refused to be ruled by the British Residency. What Clayton was proposing—a British protectorate for the Arab Middle East—was what al-Masri indicated he would never accept.

Thus Clayton, the officer who advised Allenby about the policies to be pursued in occupied Palestine, Transjordan, Lebanon, and Syria, though he claimed he was not an enemy of the French, and insisted he was a friend of both the Zionists and the Arabs, in practice opposed the ambitions of all three.

* * *

III

Sir Mark Sykes was a novice in government—in 1917 he had held executive office for only two years—and was a mercurial personality who remained subject to sudden enthusiasms. As remarked earlier, he was quick to take up a cause or to put it down. But though inconsistent, he was not dishonest: he did not dissemble. Having converted from anti-Arab, anti-Jew, anti-Armenian to pro-Arab, pro-Jew, pro-Armenian, he knew no way but one to keep faith with his new friends—with a whole heart.

Sykes, who believed in keeping the promises he had made to Arabs, Jews, Armenians, and Frenchmen, continued to labor in 1917–18 to keep his disparate coalition together. Chaim Weizmann described his outstanding qualities by writing that "He was not very consistent or logical in his thinking, but he was generous and warm-hearted."[9] Because of his role in helping to fulfill Jewish national aspirations, it was appropriate that the door to Sykes's office was known to the Zionist leader Nahum Sokolow as "the Door of Hope."[10] But within his own government there were those who objected to this generosity to foreigners. Indeed Sykes's principal problem was to secure the support of his own colleagues, who were puzzled by his views—puzzled, because it seems not to have occurred to them that he was, by their standards, naive.

Part of Sykes's problem was that he did not know which of his colleagues were in favor of what; he did not understand that some of them kept their motives and plans hidden. In confidential conferences and correspondence with trusted British government colleagues, he felt that he could express his views openly and fully, and wrongly assumed that they felt the same way. Civil servants and career army officers like Clayton were cautious by profession and, unlike Sykes, were disposed not to show their hands. Sykes was a House of Commons man; it was his trade to make speeches. By profession he spoke up; while, by profession, men like Clayton kept their own counsel.

Returning to London in the summer of 1917, Sykes discovered that pro-Ottoman members of the Foreign Office, in combination with the former American ambassador in Constantinople, Henry Morgenthau, had attempted in his absence to negotiate a separate peace with Turkey—an attempt aborted by the prompt opposition of Chaim Weizmann, among others. Sykes wrote to Clayton that "On my arrival I found that the Foreign Office had been carefully destroying everything I had done in the past 2 years. Stimulating anti-Entente feelings [i.e., anti-French feelings] and pushing separate negotiations with Turkey ideas. Indeed I just arrived in the nick of time. Luckily Zionism held good ..." He was right about Zionism, but wrong about the Foreign Office, which was not anti-French; the anti-French organization was Clayton's Arab Bureau, which Sykes himself had created.

David Hogarth, director of the Arab Bureau, had been in London in 1917 just before Sykes returned; and had lobbied against the Sykes-Picot Agreement, against a French role in the Middle East, and in favor of a British protectorate over a Hussein-led Arab confederation. In private Gilbert Clayton's views were almost identical to those expressed by the more candid Hogarth, but Sykes was unaware of that. Sykes wrote to Clayton that "Hogarth arrived and played hell by writing an anti-French and anti Agreement memorandum. Pouring cold water on the Arab movement and going in for ... a British Mecca." Sykes gleefully reported: "He got trounced ..."

Repeating that "The main thing is never to yield to Fashoda-ism French or British," Sykes announced that he and Picot (referred to as P) were going to force both the French and British governments to be honest with one another and honest with the Arabs: "... there is only one possible policy, the Entente first and last, and the Arab nation the child of the Entente." The Arabs, too, had to be taken in hand and made to see that they should not try to split the Anglo-French Entente. "Get your Englishmen to stand up to the Arabs on this and never let them accept flattery of the 'you very good man him very bad man' kind. I am going to slam into Paris to make the French play up to the Arab cause as their only hope. Colonialism is madness and I believe P and I can prove it to them."[11] Sykes did not seem to suspect that Picot himself remained a colonialist, who saw Britain as his country's rival in the Middle East, nor did he suspect that Clayton hoped to keep France out of the region altogether.

Clayton proved to be quite unwilling even to work with Picot and protested against carrying out an agreement—reached with the French during the Asquith government—whereby a joint Anglo-French administration would be introduced into the territories in the Middle East occupied during the war. Picot, acting as the French representative at Allenby's headquarters, asserted that Sir Edward Grey had promised it to him; but Clayton wrote to Sykes that "If this is so, I have heard nothing of it, and I cannot protest too strongly against any such unworkable and mischievous arrangement."[12] In any event, General Allenby exercised his authority to postpone consideration of such matters until the military situation was deemed suitable by him, which, in effect, cancelled that particular agreement for the time being.

With respect to Arabs, Jews, and Armenians, Clayton expressed his views to Sykes more guardedly. In the week following the publication of the Balfour Declaration, an exuberant Sykes sent a cypher cable to an unenthusiastic Clayton informing him that the Zionist movement was prepared to work on behalf of Arabs and Armenians and that he, Sykes, was in process of forming a joint committee to unify the three groups.[13] Chaim Weizmann would represent the Zionists; James Malcolm, the Armenians; and a Syrian Christian and an Arab Moslem would jointly represent the Arabs. It was important that more Arabs should join, added Sykes, for it would help Arabs everywhere.

A few weeks later Sykes cabled Clayton again, reporting that he had prevailed on the Zionist leadership to adopt a strong pro-Arab line.[14] He asked Clayton to tell the Syrian Arab groups in Cairo that if the Turks and Germans captured Zionist support, it would be bad for them as well as everyone else whose hopes rode with the Allies. He thus implied that the Balfour Declaration was issued in the Arab as well as in the British interest. Shortly after cabling Clayton, Sykes sent a message to Picot, telling him that Arab interests were being amply safeguarded and that Jews in Palestine would pay scrupulous attention to Arab rights.[15] Sykes also sent a letter to Clayton telling him that the Zionist and Armenian leaders were in complete accord and that it was important that Arab leaders should also join "the combine."[16]

Pouring cold water, Clayton in reply cabled that "in spite of all arguments Mecca dislikes Jews and Armenians and wishes to have nothing to do with them, while Arabs of Syria and Palestine fear repetition of the story of Jacob and Esau. In any case an Arab-Jewish-Armenian combination is so foreign to any previous experience and to existing sentiment that we must proceed with great caution."[17] He added that it would not be feasible to send an Arab delegation to London to join the committee, as Sykes had asked, because the Arabs were too divided.

A few days later he wrote to Sykes in a more conciliatory vein that "I quite see your arguments regarding an Arab-Jew-Armenian combine and the advantages that would accrue if it could be brought off. We will try it, but it must be done very cautiously and, honestly, I see no great chance of any real success. It is an attempt to change in a few weeks the traditional sentiment of centuries." Cautioning especially against the Jewish aspect of the combine, he added that "We have . . . to consider whether the situation demands out and out support of Zionism at the risk of alienating the Arabs at a critical moment."[18]

The next day Clayton's closest associate, the High Commissioner in Egypt, Sir Reginald Wingate, wrote to Allenby that "Mark Sykes is a bit carried away with 'the exuberance of his own verbosity' in regard to Zionism and unless he goes a bit slower he may quite unintentionally upset the applecart. However Clayton has written him an excellent letter which, I hope, may have an anodyne effect."[19]

Nonetheless Clayton held a meeting with Syrian representatives in Cairo, as Sykes had asked, and appears to have told them, as he had been instructed, that only if Jewish support for the Allied side were forthcoming would the Arab cause, which was bound up with that of the Allies, stand a chance of winning. He told them that Jews desired a home in Palestine but had no intention of creating a Jewish state there.[20]

The Syrian Arabs responded favorably, and an Arab Bureau report to Clayton quoted a spokesman for the Syrian committee as saying that its members "fully realized that their best and only policy was to co-operate with the Jews on the lines you suggested. He assured me that the Syrians quite understand the power and position of the Jews and that they now wish to disseminate propaganda to emphasize Syrian-Jewish fraternity and unity as regards Palestine."[21]

Clayton reported to Sykes that he believed Jews and Arabs were in fact coming together. He also reported that he had instructed T. E. Lawrence, the British liaison officer with Feisal, to impress upon Feisal his need to form an entente with the Jews.[22]

In administering the liberated areas of Palestine, however, British officials made no attempt to take advantage of this favorable disposition. Although the Balfour Declaration was published in London a month before Allenby entered Jerusalem, the British military authorities refused to publish it in Jerusalem. Thus it did not enter into the policy of the provisional military administration established by Allenby under Ronald Storrs, who declined to raise potentially disturbing issues while the war was being fought. Cairo Intelligence told the Foreign Office that applications by Jews to proceed to settle in Palestine should be denied until the military situation was resolved and until an organization had been created to deal with the various problems that might be expected to arise.[23]

There was an evident tendency on the part of military administration officials to believe that officials at home in London did not appreciate the very real difficulty of reconciling Moslems in Palestine to the prospect of an increase in Jewish settlement in the country. They therefore gave the impression of being unwilling to carry the Balfour Declaration into effect. Some observers noted, too, a tendency to prefer Moslems, who were treated as "natives," to Christians and Jews, whom it was more difficult to treat as such. William Ormsby-Gore, one of the three assistant secretaries of the War Cabinet, wrote to his colleague Mark Sykes from Tel Aviv in the summer of 1918 that the military occupation officers, drawn from service in Egypt and the Sudan, were persons "whose experience . . . does not make for a ready realisation of the very wide questions of world policy which affect Palestine. One can't help noticing the ineradicable tendency of the Englishman who has lived in India or the Sudan to favour quite unconsciously the Moslem both against Christian and Jew." He added that "The Arabs in Palestine are, I gather, showing their old tendency to corrupt methods and backsheesh and are endeavouring to 'steal a march' on the Jews."[24]

Clayton forwarded the Orsmby-Gore letter to Sykes with a covering letter of his own, saying that he felt it was somewhat misleading. Clayton protested that he personally was in favor of Zionism.[25] Apparently he had come around to the view that an agreement between Arabs and Jews could be worked out. He held no high opinion of the local Arabs and he wrote to Gertrude Bell, the author and traveler in the East who was serving in the British administration in Baghdad, that the "so-called Arabs of Palestine are not to be compared with the real Arab of the Desert or even of other civilised districts in Syria and Mesopotamia."[26]

Ronald Storrs, who was appointed military governor of Jerusalem, wrote to Sykes in the summer of 1918 that non-Jewish elements in the population, having eventually to take "a lower place in the land which the others are in the end absolutely certain to possess, the transaction should be effected so far as possible with decency, gentleness, and tact, and that the outgoing garrison should be allowed something of the honours of War." Urging a policy of going slowly, he wrote that "It will take months, possibly years, of patient work to show the Jews that we are not run by the Arabs, and the Arabs that we are not bought by the Jews."[27]

In the same letter, Storrs wrote that "it is one thing to see clearly enough the probable future of this country, and another thing to fail to make allowances for the position of the weaker and probably disappearing element. The results of the changes will be more satisfactory and more lasting if they are brought about gradually with patience, and without violent expressions of illwill, leaving behind them an abiding rancour."[28]

The question this raised for Sykes and his colleagues in London was whether this policy advocated by the man on the spot was better calculated to achieve, or to defeat, their objectives.

IV

In early 1918 Sykes and his colleagues at the Foreign Office took steps to carry their Palestine policy into effect. On 13 February the Foreign Office dispatched a cable to Sir Reginald Wingate at the Residency in Cairo to inform him that a Zionist Commission had been created and was being sent out to the Middle East. Composed of representatives from British and other Zionist movements, it was headed by Dr Chaim Weizmann and was to be placed in the charge of William Ormsby-Gore. Its object was to prepare the way to carry out the Balfour Declaration.[29]

Inaugurating the work of the Zionist Commission, Alan Dawnay, of Allenby's staff, arranged for Weizmann to meet Prince Feisal, and wrote to Lieutenant-Colonel P. C. Joyce, the senior British officer with Feisal, that "From what I gathered of the Zionist aims, in rather a short conversation, I think there should be no difficulty in establishing a friendly relationship between them."[30]

Weizmann was introduced to Prince Feisal and was enthusiastic about him. Of Feisal, Weizmann wrote to his wife that "He is the first real Arab nationalist I have met. He is a leader! He's quite intelligent and a very honest man, handsome as a picture! He is not interested in Palestine, but on the other hand he wants Damascus and the whole of northern Syria ... He is contemptuous of the Palestinian Arabs whom he doesn't even regard as Arabs!"[31]

This was in line with what Ormsby-Gore told a Zionist meeting in London some months later. According to a summary of his speech, he told the Zionist Political Committee that

> the true Arab movement really existed outside Palestine. The movement led by Prince Feisal was not unlike the Zionist movement. It contained real Arabs who were real men. The Arabs in trans-Jordania were fine people. The west of the Jordan the people were not Arabs, but only Arabic-speaking.[*] Zionists should recognise in the Arab movement, originally centered in the Hejaz, but now moving north, a fellow movement with high ideals.[32]

Feisal's senior British military adviser, Lieutenant-Colonel Joyce, attended the Weizmann-Feisal meeting and reported his personal opinion that Feisal welcomed the prospect of Jewish cooperation and in fact regarded it as essential to the realization of Arab ambitions. Though Feisal was unable to express definite views without receiving authorization from his father, according to Joyce, he would accept a Jewish Palestine if doing so would influence the Allies to support his claim to Syria.[33] The meeting went well, and paved the way for the public support of Zionism offered by Feisal at the Peace Conference the following year.

In Jerusalem, Weizmann found his Moslem audiences less receptive, though he assured them that Palestine was large enough to accommodate all its communities and that Jewish settlement would not be undertaken at the expense of Moslems or Christians. He was

---

[*] This may have been the first indication that high-ranking British officials were thinking of restricting Zionism to those sections of Biblical Palestine that lay west of the Jordan river.

disquieted by the attitude of British administrative officials in Palestine: when Weizmann urged them to avow their government's Balfour Declaration policy openly and to explain it to the Moslem community, Ronald Storrs and his colleagues refused.

In his comments to the Foreign Office, Storrs took issue with Weizmann's contention that it was the business of the military administration to bring home to the Moslem population the seriousness of Britain's pro-Zionist intentions. That had already been done, he said, by Balfour in London and by the world's newspapers. What was needed was for the Zionist Commission to imagine itself in the position of non-Jewish inhabitants of the country and to recognize how very much reassurance they would need. "Palestine, up to now a Moslem country, has fallen into the hands of a Christian Power which on the eve of its conquest announces that a considerable portion of its land is to be handed over for colonisation purposes to a nowhere very popular people." It was not lost on the urbane Ronald Storrs that he was governor of Jerusalem in line of succession from Pontius Pilate; and as such he washed his hands of an issue for which he did not hold himself responsible. He insisted to the Foreign Office, however, that he spoke "as a convinced Zionist."[34]

Gilbert Clayton also advocated delay. His strategy, of which he gave an indication in early 1918, was not merely to postpone the Zionist issue but to link it to the issue of an Arab Syria, as Feisal also proposed to do. To the strongly pro-Zionist Leo Amery, Clayton explained that "the two most important points are not to make too much of a splash locally with Zionism until the Arabs have got a slice of cake themselves, i.e., Damascus, and to get the French to come out clearly ... disavowing any ideas of Colonial annexation and emphasizing their adherence to the idea of Arab autonomy."[35]

Neither Clayton nor Storrs addressed the question of whether, if they refused to admit in Jerusalem that their government had issued the Balfour Declaration in London, Arabs and Jews in Palestine would ever learn to trust the British any more than Moslems in Syria and Lebanon trusted the French. As it was, the Zionist leaders were given cause to worry that the Balfour Declaration policy proclaimed in London might be undermined in Palestine by Clayton, Storrs, and other officers on the spot.

V

In Baghdad and Basra, not much more than lip service was paid to the pro-Arab independence policies proclaimed by Sykes and the Foreign Office. Sir Percy Cox was obliged to leave on a lengthy tour and eventually to return to Persia; in his absence, his deputy, Captain

Arnold T. Wilson, acted in his place and then succeeded him as civil commissioner. Wilson, an officer in the Indian Army, believed neither in independence for the provinces he governed nor in a role for King Hussein of the far-off Hejaz in their affairs.

The most famous author of books about Arab lands of her day, Gertrude Bell, had come up to Baghdad with the Army of the Tigris and served as Wilson's assistant. She at first employed her great prestige and extensive network of family and social friendships to back up his policy. Not much of a political thinker, she was given to enthusiasms and, at the time, was enthusiastic about Wilson's views. In February 1918 she wrote to her old friend Charles Hardinge, Permanent Under-Secretary of the Foreign Office, that "amazing strides have been made towards ordered government . . . There's no important element against us . . . The stronger the hold we are able to keep here the better the inhabitants will be pleased. What they dread is any half measure . . ." She concluded that no one in Baghdad or Basra could conceive of an independent Arab government.[36]

This was a far cry from the proclamation drafted by Sir Mark Sykes on the liberation of Baghdad, calling for a renaissance of the Arab nation, such as was proposed by the Emir of Mecca in the Hussein-McMahon correspondence, and hinting that Hussein would become the leader of the Arab nation.

Elsewhere, too, Sykes's alliance politics were modified as British officials moved away from their wartime enthusiasm for the ruler of Mecca. While Sykes continued to champion Hussein's cause, British officials noted the deterioration of the King's position *vis-à-vis* his rival, Abdul Aziz Ibn Saud, lord of the Arabian district of Nejd, whom India had backed all along. Sykes had received a hint of this deterioration when he visited the Hejaz in the spring of 1917; Hussein had been surprisingly conciliatory in agreeing to cooperate with Britain in Mesopotamia and even with France in Syria, adding "but we do ask that Great Britain will help us with Ibn Saud."[37]*

---

* One of the great failures of Kitchener and his colleagues in the intelligence field had been their ignorance of the spectacular revival of the puritanical Wahhabi sect in Arabia which had begun under the sponsorship of Ibn Saud, and, in late 1912, gave birth to a warrior brotherhood: the fierce *Ikhwan*. Minutes of a Cabinet War Committee meeting on 16 December 1915, to hear testimony from Sir Mark Sykes on the Arab question, show Lord Kitchener asking, "Wahabism, does that still exist?" and Sykes answering, "I think it is a dying fire."[38]

Two years later—and a full five years after the Wahhabi warrior brotherhood began to form—Gilbert Clayton for the first time reported to Sykes that "we have indications of considerable revivalist movement on Wahhabi lines in Central Arabia, such as has in the past occurred when the prestige of Islam has fallen low. We are not yet in a position to appreciate the strength of this movement," but conditions "conduce to fostering it. This question is engaging our serious attention here . . . it may modify the whole situation considerably."[39]

In January 1918 King Hussein told an Arab Bureau officer, Major Kinahan Cornwallis, that he was thinking of proclaiming himself Caliph. Three years earlier this had been Lord Kitchener's plan, prompted by memoranda from Clayton and Storrs, and had been championed by the officers who later formed the Arab Bureau (see Chapter 22).

By January 1918, however, the Arab Bureau, which now held Hussein in low esteem, had come around to the opposite view. Cornwallis, attempting to discourage Hussein, pointed out to him that serious problems would arise if he attempted to assume the caliphate. On receipt of Cornwallis's news, the High Commissioner, Sir Reginald Wingate, sent off a dispatch to the Foreign Office saying that he hoped for an opportunity of "checking premature or ill-considered action" by Hussein.[40] This was the same General Wingate who on 17 November 1915 had induced an Arab religious leader to tell Hussein that he was "the right man to take over his rightful heritage and verify the hopes of his people—the Mohammedans and Arabs to recover their stolen Khalifate" and calling upon the Hashemite leader to establish "the Hashemite Arabian Khalifate."[41]

Kitchener's followers found it inconvenient to remember that once they and their chief had encouraged Hussein to claim the caliphate; erasing it from their minds, they would later ignore it in their books and edit it out of official documents. In memoirs published three decades later, Sir Ronald Storrs deleted the caliphate section from Kitchener's historic cable in 1914 to Hussein. T. E. Lawrence wrote that Kitchener and his followers had believed in Arab nationalism from the beginning—when in fact they did not believe in it at all. They believed instead in the potency of the caliphate; that Hussein could capture it for them; and that in the East nationalism was nothing while religion was everything.[*]

Indeed, in 1918 politics and the desire to rewrite history both dictated a shift in emphasis: Feisal, not Hussein, began to emerge as Cairo's preferred Arab leader, for Feisal showed a disposition, lacking in his father, to accept British counsel and guidance.

By the autumn of 1918, the armies commanded by Hussein's sons were reckoned by British sources to total only a few thousand trained troops. In public the British claimed that vast numbers of Arabs had flocked to the standard of the Hejazi princes; in private they had a

---

[*] If their purpose had been to raise a nationalist revolt, they would not have sought out Hussein, the Turkish-appointed guardian of the Holy Places, who employed Turkish troops to quell Arab discontent. They would have sought out a nationalist warlord. That indeed is the way Lawrence later told the story in his book *Seven Pillars of Wisdom*, portraying Feisal, rather than his father, as such a leader.

different story to tell. Secret British government documents filed in 1919 admit that "The followings quoted during the war were grossly exaggerated."[42] A report from the British Agency in Jeddah in 1919 pictured King Hussein as militarily inconsequential: his following was estimated at only 1,000 regulars, 2,500 irregulars, and possibly several thousand more from Bedouin tribes, and their fighting qualities were rated as "poor." According to the report, King Hussein "indulged in wild dreams of conquest," but the withdrawal of British support would leave him "at the mercy of Ibn Saud and the rising wave of WAHHABISM."[43]

An Arab Bureau report on the Hejaz revolt in 1918 stated that "The real importance of this revolt has only made itself felt in the course of the last few months and it is spreading from day to day. At the same time it must be said that 90% of the Sherif's troops are nothing more than robbers . . ." According to the report, Arabs rose up against the Turks only when British forces had already arrived, so that "In a word, the extent of the Sherif's revolt depends entirely on the ability of the British to advance."[44] Colonel Meinertzhagen, the head of Allenby's intelligence, wrote that "It is safe to say that Lawrence's Desert Campaign had not the slightest effect on the main theatre west of Jordan."[45]

But others disagreed. Sykes, continuing to stand by the alliance with Hussein and believing that Feisal and his brothers were making a significant contribution to the war effort, argued that in Arabia and elsewhere, by 1918 the Hejaz revolt was occupying the attention of 38,000 Ottoman troops.[46] The memoirs of the enemy commander, Liman von Sanders, show that in 1918 when his armies turned to flee, they found themselves painfully harassed by Arab Bedouins.[47] The tone of Gilbert Clayton's memoranda show that he believed Feisal and Lawrence were accomplishing important objectives on Allenby's right flank. Other evidence, too, suggests that the Arab forces in Transjordan succeeded in spreading disorder in Turkish-held areas.

Mired in politics then and ever since, the question of how much Feisal contributed to the Allied success remains unresolved; at the time it raised the question of whether Britain should back Hussein and Feisal against indigenous Syrian Arab leadership, and whether Britain should support Feisal against Hussein.

Within the Sherifian camp there were strains, as Feisal, physically cut off from the Hejaz and his family, moved into the British orbit. In cables that the British military authorities secretly intercepted and read, Hussein complained that "they have turned my son against me to live under *other countries*, who is rebellions & dishonest to his Father [original emphasis]."[48] He complained that "Living under the orders of a disobedient son and a traitor has burdened my shoulder with this misery." He threatened that "If Feisal still persists in destroying his good fortune his nation and his honour" it would be necessary to appoint a war council in his place.[49] Meanwhile, according to Arab Bureau reports from Cairo, Syrian spokesmen indicated that they would be willing to accept Feisal as their constitutional monarch, but only in his own right, and not if he acted as deputy or representative of Hussein.[50]

VI

Although British leaders from 1914 onward had professed faith in the leadership of Hussein within the Arab world, in 1917 and 1918 they felt driven to reassess the validity of that belief.

As Britain moved to complete her conquest of the Arabic-speaking world of the Middle East, British officials began to worry about the local opposition that they might encounter. Clayton's endeavors, beginning in 1914, to arrive at an understanding with separatist leaders from Baghdad and Damascus had foundered on their objection to being ruled by non-Moslems. Now that Damascus was on Britain's line of march the question was how Damascenes could be won over to the Allied cause and to the Allied scheme for the future of the Middle East. That Feisal had agreed to the Allied program might carry no weight with them.

In the summer of 1918 William Ormsby-Gore told the Zionist Political Committee in London that "The Syrian 'Intelligentzia' lawyers and traders constituted the most difficult and thorny problem of the Near East. They had no civilisation of their own, and they had absorbed all the vices of the Levant."[51]

Sir Mark Sykes seems to have started worrying about the Syrian problem the year before in the context of pledges he intended Britain to keep to her allies—and her allies to keep to her. His concern was that Syrians might not accept the Sykes-Picot Agreement and the terms outlined by Sir Henry McMahon to the Sherif Hussein. In 1917 he asked the Arab Bureau to set up a meeting for him with Syrian Arabs leaders in Cairo, apparently in order to arrive at an agreement with them that would be consistent with the secret accords with France and with the Hejaz—accords whose existence, however, he could not reveal to them. He claimed he had succeeded; in his own hand he noted that "The main difficulty was to manoeuvre the delegates into asking for what we were prepared to give them, without letting them know that any precise geographical agreement had been come to."[52] The "precise geographical agreement" must have meant the Damascus-Homs-Hama-Aleppo line that was to be the westward frontier of Arab independence in Syria under the agreement with al-Faruqi in 1915 and with France in 1916.

But reports arrived from various quarters that the Ottoman government might be planning to pre-empt Arab nationalism by granting autonomy to Syria immediately. That would leave Britain in the awkward position of sponsoring the claims of King Hussein as against an indigenous Arabic leadership in Damascus that threatened to be far more popular in the Syrian provinces.

Toward the end of 1917 Sykes cabled Clayton: "I am anxious about Arab movement. Letters indicate difficulty of combining Meccan Patriarchalism with Syrian Urban intelligensia." Quick as always to invent a new expedient, Sykes proposed to create an Arab executive committee to promote unity. Clayton must have said it could not be done, for Sykes responded: "Agree as to difficulty but military success should make this easier." Sykes said that Picot should be persuaded to reassure the Syrians that France was in favor of their eventual independence. The same arguments were to be used on Picot on behalf of the Arabs that had been used on him on behalf of Zionism: that it was better to give up something in the far-off Middle East than to risk losing the war, and with it a chance to regain Alsace and Lorraine—provinces closer to home.[53]

Sykes was arguing that Britain could honor all pledges, and accommodate the Syrians as well, if only reasonable concessions were made all around. Clayton, as always, pictured Britain's wartime commitments as embarrassments to be shed, and replied to Sykes that "There is no doubt a very real fear amongst Syrians of finding themselves under a Government in which patriarchalism of Mecca is predominant. They realize that reactionary principles from which Sherif of Mecca cannot break loose are incompatible with progress on modern lines." Proposing to move away from the alliance with Hussein, he said that Feisal as an individual might be acceptable as head of a Syrian confederation, but only with a spiritual, not a political, role for his father. No such plan, however, and no committee or announcement or propaganda would be of any effect, Clayton continued, if the basic problem were not addressed. And that problem, he hinted (though he did not put it in these words), was posed by the pledges Sykes had made to the French and to the Zionists. As against the probable Turkish maneuver of setting up an autonomous Syrian government, nothing would be of any avail, he argued, because of the general fear in the Arabic-speaking world that Britain planned to turn Syria over to France. This was compounded, he claimed, by the public pledge just made to Zionism. The only solution was to obtain from France a clear public announcement denying that she intended to annex any part of Syria.[54]

Another approach was urged by Osmond Walrond, a former member of Lord Milner's staff who knew Egypt from before the war and who had come out to serve in the Arab Bureau in Cairo. As Walrond saw it, Britain was neglecting the Arab secret societies, and accordingly he set out to cultivate their support. Walrond wrote to Clayton in the summer of 1918 to describe his conversations with members of these societies. He said that he had asked them to elect a small committee to represent them so that he could deal with them. They had elected a committee of seven members.[55] Apparently Walrond's intention was to repeat Sykes's maneuver of the year before with another group of Cairo Arabs suspicious of Hussein: arrange for them to accept a statement of Britain's plans for the Middle East so that they, like Hussein, would be tied into acceptance of those plans.

In mid-1918 Sir Mark Sykes accordingly addressed a declaration of British intentions to Walrond's committee of seven Syrians in answer to questions ostensibly raised by them. It was an official declaration, approved by Sykes's superiors at the Foreign Office, but did not break new ground. Like so much that came from the pen of Sir Mark Sykes, it restated the same intentions for the postwar Middle East but in different words. Outside the Arabian peninsula, the Arab world was to fall under varying degrees of European influence or control. In effect, Sykes's Declaration to the Seven—later to be a subject of much controversy—recognized complete Arab independence only within the Arabian peninsula, for it offered such recognition only to areas that had been independent before the war or that had been liberated by the Arabs by themselves as of the date of the declaration.

Sykes could go no further in assuaging Arab suspicions of French intentions in Syria and Lebanon without securing France's cooperation in issuing a joint pledge. In the autumn of 1918 the French government was finally persuaded to join the British Foreign Office in issuing a new statement of Allied intentions designed to allay Arab fears—and American suspicions. The Anglo-French declaration of 8 November 1918 was broadly phrased to suggest full support for the creation of indigenous governments in the Middle East; but it was designed to mislead, for, on French insistence, it did not refer specifically to Arab "independence."[56] French officials seemed as unlikely as their British counterparts to follow the idealistic path that Sir Mark Sykes—with an eye toward accommodating the views of Wilson and the Americans—had marked out for them.

THE BATTLE FOR SYRIA

I

As the summer of 1918 drew to a close, Sir Edmund Allenby gave the order to advance on Syria, and foresaw that Liman von Sanders would expect him to repeat the strategy he had employed in southern Palestine. In the Jerusalem campaign, Allenby had feinted at the coast but lunged eastward to deliver his attack in the interior. In attacking northern Palestine, he therefore did exactly the reverse: he feinted inland, while launching his main attack along the coast. His purpose was to achieve overwhelming local numerical superiority along the coast so as to break through the Turkish lines at the most favorable point for his Australian and New Zealand (ANZAC) cavalry.

Although he held an overall two-to-one advantage in effectives (69,000 against 36,000, according to his estimates), he boldly left much of his roughly 65-mile-long line undefended in order to concentrate the maximum number of troops on the coast; he relied on control of the air and on brilliantly effective intelligence operations to keep the enemy away from the gaps in his own defensive line.

By night the bulk of Allenby's forces silently moved west to concentrate in the olive and citrus groves of the lightly defended coastal plain, where they were camouflaged and remained undetected. By day small units marched east, and then returned to march east over and over again, raising great clouds of dust which persuaded the Turks that a vast army was on the march to attack inland. In the east, too, small British units threw up what appeared to be large camps, stabled with what appeared to be horses. East of the Jordan, British agents allowed it to be discovered that they were bargaining for large quantities of forage.

Deceived, Liman von Sanders concentrated his forces inland in eastern Palestine, and when the attack came his armies were caught off balance. So effective was Allenby's offensive that it was not until days after it had begun that the Ottoman commanders came to appreciate the real situation.

At 4:30 in the morning of 19 September 1918 nearly 400 British cannon suddenly opened fire on the surprised and outnumbered (45,000 against 8,000) Ottoman defenders of the coastal plain. Fifteen minutes later the infantry attack commenced. British, French, and Indian troops pushed the overwhelmed defenders aside, as the cavalry poured through the gaping hole in the Ottoman lines to win the battle of Megiddo—the "Armageddon" of the Bible.

At dawn, special bomber squadrons of the Royal Air Force attacked telephone and telegraph exchanges behind enemy lines, effectively cutting off all communications. Other R.A.F. warplanes guarded the skies over enemy airports, keeping German reconnaissance planes on the ground. Liman and his field commanders were cut off from information and from one another.

As Ottoman units reeled backward, they found their lines of retreat blocked by British units which had raced before and behind them to secure control of the key roads. The ANZAC cavalry galloped northward for thirty miles along the coastal plain, but then cut inland, threatening to cut off the Ottoman line of retreat toward Damascus. British military aircraft bombed and strafed the retreating Turks. Meanwhile the few units Allenby had deployed in the east finally attacked inland. In the predawn darkness of 23 September battalions of the Jewish Legion seized control of the crucial Umm esh Shert ford across the Jordan river. The Second Australian Light Horse Brigade went across it, and by evening the Ottoman forces east of the river found themselves enveloped in a giant pincer.

At Ma'an, in the south of Transjordan, above Aqaba, the Turkish garrison which had been beseiged by Feisal's forces ever since their arrival from Aqaba the year before, held out until Australian cavalry arrived to accept their surrender and protect them against the massacre threatened by the Arab besiegers. Further north, Feisal's Camel Corps disrupted the railroad lines upon which the main Turkish forces depended.

On 25 September Allenby ordered an advance on Damascus, while the remnant of the Ottoman forces broke and fled.[1] The occupation of the principal towns of the Syrian provinces was imminent; decisions about occupation policy were made rapidly. There is still controversy as to who made them and why.

II

In the summer Allenby had told London that, subject to his own supreme military authority, he would accept French advisers to deal with civil administration in areas of special interest to France, so long as London would tell him what areas these were and whether they were still defined by the Sykes-Picot Agreement.[2] Although the Cabinet and its Eastern Committee strongly favored discarding the Sykes-Picot Agreement, the Foreign Office reaffirmed the agreement by directing Allenby to follow its territorial outlines. Leo Amery, of the War Cabinet secretariat, bitterly blamed the political chiefs of the Foreign Office—Balfour and Cecil—for this.[3] Amery's colleague, Sir Mark Sykes, however, was the Foreign Office official directly responsible for policy in Syria and, presumably, the person who made or recommended the decision in the first instance.

On 25 September the War Office instructed Wingate in Cairo and Allenby at headquarters that if Syria were to fall within the sphere of any European power, that power was to be France.[4] The terms of that instruction left open the possibility that it might not fall within the sphere of a European power—that Feisal might achieve his independence. However, Allenby was instructed to employ French officers for all areas of civil (as distinct from military) administration. According to the War Office cables, if Allenby were to take Damascus, "it would be desirable that in conformity with Anglo-French agreement of 1916 he should if possible work through an Arab administration by means of a French liaison."[5]

Flags were to indicate the designated areas of temporary administration. The hoisting of Hussein's flag over Damascus and other important Syrian cities once they were captured was authorized, and indeed ordered, by the Foreign Office.[6] The flag was the black, white, green, and red one that Sykes had designed (see page 315) and it served two political purposes: it boosted Hussein's claim to leadership in Arab Syria,* and it reminded France that inland Syria was designated for at least nominal Arab independence.

At a conference in the Palestinian town of Jenin on 25 September, Allenby approved the plans of Australian General Harry Chauvel—who was in charge of the operation—for the advance on Damascus. Chauvel, according to his later notes, raised the issue of occupation policy. Damascus, he said, was a city of 300,000 people; it was too big to be handed over to a military governor and a mere handful of assistants. Allenby replied that Chauvel should retain the Ottoman governor and administration, and supply them with whatever extra military police they might need to keep order. Chauvel asked about rumors that the Arab movement was to have the government of Syria, but Allenby replied that any decision would have to wait until

---

* In early 1918 Gilbert Clayton had written to Sykes that "If Feisal makes good in a military sense he may well carry Syria with him" but that if he did not, nobody from Mecca would matter in Syrian politics.[7] The raising of the flag constituted a symbolic affirmation of Feisal's military success that could pave the way for his political leadership.

he came to Damascus himself. He added that, "if Feisal gives you any trouble, deal with him through Lawrence who will be your liaison officer."[8]

There was a flurry of cables between London, Paris, and the Middle East. Although Allenby had told Chauvel to keep the *Turkish* administration in Damascus in place for the time being, the Foreign Office told the French government that Allenby would deal with a provisional *Arab* administration in Damascus—in line with the Sykes-Picot Agreement—through a French liaison officer.[9] In turn, the French government agreed that the Allies should recognize the Arabs as a belligerent power—in other words, as an ally.[10] These communications between Britain and France show that the Foreign Office expected Allenby to replace the Turkish administration in Damascus with an Arab one sooner or later; but that it believed the Sykes-Picot arrangements would not come into play until then.

Armed with these agreements, the Foreign Office got the War Office to send Allenby new and important instructions, developing policy themes that had been hinted at before. The Syrian lands that Allenby was in process of occupying were to be treated as "allied territory enjoying the status of an independent state" rather than as occupied enemy territory. It was in this connection that the Foreign Office issued its much-discussed directive that "It would be desirable to mark the recognition and establishment of native Arab rule by some conspicuous or formal act such as the hoisting and saluting of the Arab flag at important centres."[11]

Sykes (if that is who it was) went on in the cable to outline a characteristically ingenious scheme. The existing agreement with France was that wherever in the Syrian provinces Britain established a military administration, France was entitled to have her officers exercise all civilian administration on behalf of the Allies. In the telegram of 1 October, Allenby was instructed to limit his area of military administration to the bare minimum, limiting the French role correspondingly. The Foreign Office also told him to reduce British military administration in Transjordan as well, so that the French could not say that Britain's action in inland Syria was part of a plot to reduce France's role there—which of course it was.

Wingate, who had read the cables, wrote to Allenby that "it will be very interesting to see how the Sherifian Flag and the French liaison is taken by all and sundry."[12] In effect, the Foreign Office had instructed Allenby to carry out the formal requirements of the Sykes-Picot Agreement, while (as advocated by Mark Sykes) revising the spirit of the agreement. This was a solution satisfactory neither to the French, who wanted more, nor to Feisal or the Arab Bureau, who wanted France to have nothing at all.

As required by the Sykes-Picot Agreement, France was to be given

direct control of the coastline. Inland Syria was to be independent—
not independent in name only, as envisaged by the agreement—but
substantively independent; but France would have her official liaison
officer, as required, and later would presumably have her official
adviser at Feisal's court. Syria's ruler, as indicated in the McMahon
correspondence, would be a Hashemite. The hoisting of Sykes's flag
over Damascus and the towns of Homs, Hama, and Aleppo thus
would symbolize the weaving together of all the strands of British
Middle Eastern policy along the lines that Sykes had always advocated.
He had said all along that he had shaped Britain's commitments to be
consistent with one another, and that all would fit within the formal
framework of the agreement that he had devised.

Meanwhile on 29 September it was decided at General Allenby's
field headquarters that Feisal's Arabs should be the only Allied
troops to enter and occupy Damascus—presumably to forestall resistance by a possibly hostile Moslem metropolis to a Christian
occupation.* Feisal was three days away, so in the meantime the
ANZAC cavalry units pursuing the fleeing Turks were instructed to
ride around, rather than through, Damascus.

But in the confusion of advance and retreat, the actors in the
drama of Damascus's liberation did not follow the script that Allenby
and Clayton had written for them. The Ottoman government did not
remain in the city; it fled with the retreating Turkish army at about
noon on 30 September, leaving disorder behind. Local Arab notables,
the Emir Abd el Kader and his brother Said, descendants of the
Algerian warrior who had fought the French a century before and
had been subsidized to live in exile, moved at some point into some
sort of control of the city. The Abd el Kader brothers, whom
Lawrence regarded as personal enemies and, perhaps, as supporters
of Hussein and Islam rather than of Feisal and nationalism,** claimed

---

* Evidence is scanty as to who made the decision and why. A report to the
Foreign Office from Allenby's chief political officer, General Gilbert Clayton,
suggests that Clayton must have feared there would be unrest in the city if the
Australians occupied it, presumably because Damascenes would guess that Britain
intended to turn them over to France. Clayton had expressed fears all along that
Britain—by allowing herself to be associated with France—might excite the hostility
of Syrian Arabs. Clayton later reported to the Foreign Office that "Our permitting
the occupation of Damascus by the Sherifians has allayed some of the suspicions of
French intentions."[13]

** Nobody knows for sure what the quarrel between Lawrence and the Abd el
Kaders was about, though a number of possibilities have been suggested. The Abd
el Kaders may have feared that Hussein was being duped by the British or that
Feisal was under Lawrence's influence; while Lawrence may have considered them
to be pan-Islam, anti-Christian chauvinists. Or Lawrence may have believed them
to be pro-French or pro-Turk. It has also been suggested that the quarrel was
mainly or entirely personal, and that perhaps the Abd el Kaders were about to reveal
damaging information about Lawrence's personal life.

to have raised the Hejaz flag on the afternoon of 30 September in the name of Hussein. Thus when the Arab flag was finally hoisted, it had nothing to do with the Foreign Office's plan; Damascene Arabs did it on their own.

At first light on the morning of 1 October, an Australian cavalry brigade that had been ordered to cut the Ottoman retreat along the Homs road north of Damascus, decided to go through Damascus to reach the Homs road, and entered the city; whereupon Said Abd el Kader, surrounded by notables, officially welcomed them. Thus the honor of being the first Allied troops to enter Damascus fell to the Australians, contrary to plan.

An hour later General Chauvel and his staff joined Major-General Sir George Barrow, the local divisional commander, a few miles south of the city. Lawrence was supposed to be staying with Barrow, and Chauvel wanted to see him in order to start making arrangements for preserving the existing civil administration of the city. To his chagrin, Chauvel discovered that Lawrence had slipped away early in the morning, without permission and without informing anyone, to follow the Fifth Cavalry Division into Damascus. Chauvel borrowed a car and drove into Damascus himself to find out what was happening.

By now the Allenby-Clayton plan for Feisal to liberate the city was in tatters. Feisal was still days away, while the British and Australians were in Damascus, either trying to move through the streets or hoping to find out what was going on. Chauvel, who had been ordered not to lead his men into the city, now followed them in instead.

T. E. Lawrence, Chauvel's A.W.O.L. staff liaison officer, had taken his favorite battered old Rolls-Royce armored car that morning and—with a fellow British officer, W. E. Stirling, and Nuri el-Sa'id, an ex-Ottoman officer who was a chief Feisal loyalist—had driven to the city and found that some of Feisal's tribal allies, who had arrived earlier, had accepted the Abd el Kaders as Damascus's governors. Executing a swift *coup d'état*, Nuri ordered the Abd el Kaders to withdraw and appointed his own pro-Feisal candidate as governor. Then an irate General Chauvel arrived, demanding explanations.

Lawrence, making excuses, said he had assumed Chauvel wanted him to scout out the situation, and claimed that he had been on the verge of returning to tender his report.

When Chauvel then asked Lawrence to bring the governor to him, Lawrence presented Nuri's candidate, claiming that he was the governor. Chauvel called that nonsense, pointing out that Nuri's candidate was obviously an Arab, while the Ottoman governor would have been a Turk. But Lawrence replied that the Ottoman governor had fled (which was true), and that the people had elected Nuri's candidate to take his place (which was false).

Taking Lawrence's word for it, Chauvel confirmed the appointment of Nuri's pro-Feisal candidate as governor. According to Chauvel's own account, he soon learned that Nuri's candidate was supported by only a small pro-Feisal clique, and that the population as a whole was disturbed by the appointment; but Chauvel did not see how he could change the appointment after having announced it. However, faced with serious disorders, he marched his British forces through the city on 2 October in an attempt to overawe opposition. This was exactly what Allenby and Clayton had hoped to avoid: the population aroused, Christian troops defiling through the streets of a great Moslem city to restore order, and Feisal's Arab troops—whose presence was meant to reassure local opinion—still nowhere in sight.

It was not until the morning of 3 October that Lawrence announced that Feisal and several hundred followers were about to arrive, and asked permission to stage a triumphal entry into the city for them. Later, Chauvel grumblingly wrote that "Seeing that he, Feisal, had had very little to do with the 'conquest' of Damascus, the suggested triumphal entry did not appeal to me very much but I thought it would not do harm and gave permission accordingly."[14]

It was arranged for 3:00 that afternoon, but General Allenby's schedule would not allow for it. Allenby had only a few hours to spend that afternoon in Damascus, and called on Feisal and Lawrence to attend him at the Hotel Victoria, where he had established himself. Allenby's visit was prompted by Chauvel's appointment of the pro-Feisal Arab to the governorship which, in turn, activated the Sykes-Picot Agreement and the inter-Allied agreement that Allenby would deal with an *Arab* administration in Syria through the French. Had Allenby's original orders been carried out—to retain a Turkish governor for the time being—this complication would have been postponed, but now it had to be faced. Allenby did not blame Chauvel, but indicated that what he had done had given rise to complications with the French which required a meeting with Feisal immediately.

Allenby, Chauvel, Feisal, and their respective chiefs of staff were present at the conference, as were officers of the British mission to the Hejaz, an officer of the Arab Bureau from Cairo, and Feisal's chief commander. Lawrence acted as interpreter.

At the meeting the British commander spelled out in specific detail for the Arabian prince the arrangements that had been agreed upon by Britain and France, and asserted his determination to enforce them until and unless they were modified at the Peace Conference. The terms were exactly those that Sir Mark Sykes and the Foreign Office had instructed him to uphold. Any hopes that Lawrence may have entertained, or inspired in Feisal, that Clayton and Allenby would help them connive at subverting the Foreign Office's policy were dashed that afternoon. Feisal's bitter disappointment was not that the Arab confederation would not include Palestine—he said he accepted that—but that it did not include the Lebanon (that is to say, the Lebanon, or "white," Mountains), and that Syria was not to be free of French control.

According to Chauvel's minutes of the meeting, Allenby (referred to as "the Chief") plainly told Feisal:

(a) That France was to be the Protecting Power over Syria.

(b) That he, Feisal, as representing his Father, King Hussein, was to have the Administration of Syria (less Palestine and the Lebanon Province) under French guidance and financial backing.

(c) That the Arab sphere would include the hinterland of Syria only and that he, Feisal, would not have anything to do with the Lebanon.

(d) That he was to have a French Liaison Officer at once, who would work for the present with Lawrence, who would be expected to give him every assistance.

Feisal objected very strongly. He said that he knew nothing of France in the matter; that he was prepared to have British Assistance; that he understood from the Adviser whom Allenby had sent him that the Arabs were to have the whole of Syria including the Lebanon but excluding Palestine; that a Country without a Port was no good to him; and that he declined to have a French Liaison Officer or to recognise French guidance in any way.

The Chief turned to Lawrence and said: "But did you not tell him that the French were to have the Protectorate over Syria?" Lawrence said: "No, Sir, I know nothing about it." The Chief then said: "But you knew definitely that he, Feisal, was to have nothing to do with the Lebanon." Lawrence said: "No, Sir, I did not."

After some further discussion, the Chief told Feisal that he, Sir Edmund Allenby, was Commander-in-Chief and that he, Feisal, was at the moment a Lieut.-General under his command and that he would have to obey orders. That he must accept the situation until the whole matter was settled at the conclusion of the War. Feisal accepted this decision and left with his entourage, except Lawrence.[15]

Neither Feisal nor Lawrence had been candid with the plain-spoken Allenby. The terms outlined to them were those of the Sykes-Picot Agreement, with which all of them were well acquainted. What Feisal meant in denying knowledge of those terms (Lawrence explained later in London) was that he had not been informed of them officially.[16] For himself, Lawrence had not even that excuse; he had simply lied.*

As Feisal left the meeting, Lawrence told Allenby that he was unwilling to serve alongside a French adviser to Feisal. Lawrence said that he had accumulated some leave time and would like to take it immediately and return to Britain. Allenby agreed. By all indications, he was not at all angry with Lawrence; far from it, for he encouraged Lawrence to go to London to argue his case to the Foreign Office in person.

Feisal, having withdrawn from the meeting, returned to lead his tardy and compromised triumphal entry into Damascus, riding at the head of between 300 and 600 mounted men. Perhaps with encouragement from Lawrence (who later denied it), Feisal then sent a commando force of a hundred of his followers to Beirut, which they entered unopposed and where they raised the Arab flag of the Hejaz on 5 October. The following day the alarmed French sent warships into Beirut harbor and landed a small contingent of troops. On 8 October Indian troops of Allenby's Egyptian Expeditionary Force entered the city. Allenby took command of the situation by ordering Feisal's force to lower the Arab flag and withdraw; when they did so, the French were left in control. Later François Georges Picot arrived to act as France's civil and political representative in the area, subject to the supreme authority of Allenby as commander-in-chief.

Clayton advised Feisal to rein back his followers in Lebanon; on 11 October, he wrote to Wingate that "I have told Feisal . . . that he will only prejudice his case before the Peace Conference if he tries to grab . . . It is not an easy problem. I hope that with a certain amount of give & take on both sides a modus vivendi will be reached . . ."[17]

The French armed forces in Beirut in fact proved too weak to affect the full annexationist program that the colonialist party in France desired, and French agents therefore pursued a fall-back position to provide for the possibility that their claim to the whole of Syria might fail.** The plan, conceived by French officers in the field, was to carve out of Syria an independent state that would include not only the Christian areas of Mount Lebanon but also a large area of predominantly Moslem territories, and which was to be ruled by Maronite Christians under French sponsorship.[19] Activities

---

* In Chapter 101 of *Seven Pillars of Wisdom*, he admitted that he had known of the agreement and that "Fortunately, I had earlier betrayed the treaty's existence to Feisal . . ."
   ** Some of the French troops were Armenian refugees who had been conscripted. Others were native troops from North Africa. The entire force has been described as "only 3,000 Armenians, 3,000 Africans 'and 800 Frenchmen who had been promised that they would not have to fight.' "[18]

on behalf of this plan further contributed to the fragmentation of political life that had already begun to cause unrest behind Allied lines.

Beneath the surface of Allenby's orderly arrangements of the chain of command, feuds, intrigues, and factionalism seethed in the wake of the disappearance of Ottoman authority. Bedouins clashed with city dwellers. Former enemies moved to take over Feisal's movement from within. Obscure quarrels were settled in dark places. In Damascus, Emir Abd el Kader was shot and killed by pro-Feisal police, supposedly while trying to escape when they came to arrest him.

The natural environment was even more out of control. The British cavalry had been afflicted by malaria as it passed through Turkish-held territories where sanitation had been neglected; after a fortnight of incubation, the disease struck down whole regiments as the conquest of the Syrian provinces was being completed. Malaria was followed by influenza that proved to be not just debilitating but massively fatal.

III

Allenby—from his headquarters in the Middle East—arranged a warm reception for Colonel Lawrence in London as he arrived to plead the case against France. At the end of October, Lawrence appeared before the Eastern Committee of the Cabinet and reported that Picot proposed to impose French advisers on Feisal, but that Feisal claimed the right to choose whatever advisers he wanted. Moreover, he wanted either British or—oddly, in view of the enmities that developed later—American Zionist Jewish advisers.[20]

Feisal, according to Lawrence, relied on the provisions of the Declaration to the Seven, the document in which Sir Mark Sykes outlined Allied intentions to anti-Feisal Syrian émigré leaders in Cairo. In Feisal's name, Lawrence misconstrued the declaration, claiming that it promised independence to the Arabs in any area they liberated themselves. (In context, it is clear that the declaration promised independence only in areas that had already been liberated by Arabs as of the date of the declaration in June 1918; areas in Ottoman hands as of that date were placed in a separate category.) Feisal himself misconstrued the declaration even further; reportedly, he claimed to have an agreement with the British and French according to which the first one to arrive at any city won the right to govern it.[21]

Lawrence began to maintain that Feisal's troops in fact had been the first to enter Damascus, declaring that 4,000 tribesmen associated with Feisal's cause had slipped into the city during the night of 30 September—1 October and thus had been the first Allied troops to arrive. But there was first-hand evidence that the 4,000 tribesmen were entirely imaginary. Nobody saw them there; and nobody saw them enter or leave—even though they would have had to pass through British lines to do so.[22]

In the Eastern Committee and in the Cabinet, Lawrence nonetheless found a sympathetic audience for his plea that French influence or control should not be introduced into the Moslem Arabic-speaking Middle East. He also found important allies in the press.

At the end of November 1918, *The Times* published several anonymous articles, written by Lawrence, providing a much exaggerated account of what had been accomplished by Feisal's forces and stating that the account came from an eyewitness correspondent. Lawrence's version of the facts began to be circulated in other periodicals as well, much to the annoyance of the Australian troops in Syria. The official "pool" news correspondent of the London newspapers with Allenby's Egyptian Expeditionary Force wrote that "An article was printed in an official paper circulated among the troops that the Arab Army was first in Damascus. The credit of winning Damascus and being the first in the city belongs to the Australian Light Horse, and General Chauvel was quick to have the error rectified."[23]

For personal as well as political reasons, Lawrence continued to maintain the pretense that Feisal's forces had liberated Damascus; and so great was his artistry that he succeeded in insinuating at least some of his version into the historical record. Yet he must have known that sooner or later his fraudulent claim would be exposed for what it was. In the 1920s, when the poet and novelist Robert Graves, a friend who was writing a biography of Lawrence, proposed to base his account of the liberation of Damascus on that supplied by Lawrence in his *Seven Pillars of Wisdom*, Lawrence cautioned him: "I was on thin ice when I wrote the Damascus chapter and anyone who copies me will be through it, if he is not careful. S.P. [*Seven Pillars*] is full of half-truth here."[24]

IV

Lawrence used his version of the Damascus campaign to attempt to persuade his government to jettison the Sykes-Picot Agreement, which almost all officials with whom he spoke wanted to disavow. Gilbert Clayton had written to Lawrence in 1917 that though Britain was bound in honor to the agreement, it would die of its own accord if ignored: "It is in fact dead and, if we wait quietly, this fact will soon be realized."[25] In 1918 Clayton told Picot that the agreement no longer could be applied because it was "completely out of date."[26]

The Eastern Committee hoped to rescind—rather than merely ignore—the Sykes-Picot Agreement, and had thought that the Foreign Office would arrange to modify or rescind it in the context of negotiations with respect to how the occupied territories were to be administered. The Foreign Office did no such thing, but took the position that Britain was absolutely bound by the agreement unless France agreed to change or cancel it. When Lord Curzon, the chairman of the Eastern Committee, learned the terms that had been worked out with France, he observed with some asperity that "The Foreign Office appeared now to be relying upon the Sykes-Picot Agreement from which the Committee had hitherto been doing their best to escape."[27]

Sir Mark Sykes, who had worked out the terms of the administrative arrangements with the French, persisted in believing that the Sykes-Picot Agreement met current needs. In the spring of 1917 he wrote to Percy Cox, chief political officer of the British administration in Mesopotamia, that one of its virtues was that it was framed in such a way as not to violate the principles that Woodrow Wilson's America and the new socialist Russia espoused with respect to national self-determination and nonannexation. "The idea of Arab nationalism may be absurd," he wrote, "but our Congress case will be good if we can say we are helping to develop a race on nationalist lines under our protection." Hussein may not give much help in the war physically, he continued, but he gives moral help that France ought to recognize, and "I think French will be ready to co-operate with us in a common policy towards the Arab speaking people."[28]

David Hogarth, head of the Arab Bureau, wrote to Gilbert Clayton at that time that nobody both took the Sykes-Picot Agreement seriously and supported it, except for Sir Mark Sykes.[29] This was a slight exaggeration, because officials of the Foreign Office, which Sykes joined, also took the pact seriously, but it was not far from the truth.

Lord Curzon stated that the Sykes-Picot Agreement was not only obsolete "but absolutely impracticable."[30] As chairman of the Eastern Committee, which was in charge of defining British *desiderata* for the postwar Middle East, he made it clear that Britain would like the French out of Syria altogether.[31] But a War Office representative told the committee that the only way to break the agreement was to operate behind "an Arab facade" in appealing to the United States to support Wilson's theories of self-determination.[32]

Curzon said that "When the Sykes-Picot Agreement was drawn up it was, no doubt, intended by its authors ... as a sort of fancy sketch to suit a situation that had not then arisen, and which it was thought extremely unlikely would ever arise; that, I suppose, must be the principal explanation of the gross ignorance with which the boundary lines in that agreement were drawn."[33]

Lloyd George also felt that the pact had been superseded by events, but then, he had been against it from the start. As was his wont with his favorites, he made excuses for Sykes, and rewrote history to absolve him from blame. He wrote, decades later, that

> It is inexplicable that a man of Sir Mark Sykes' fine intelligence should ever have appended his signature to such an arrangement. He was always ashamed of it, and he defended his action in agreeing to its terms by explaining that he was acting under definite instructions received from the Foreign Office. For that reason he hotly resented the constant and indelible reminder that his name was and always would be associated with a pact with which he had only a nominal personal responsibility and of which he thoroughly disapproved.[34]

In the opinion of Lloyd George, the Sykes-Picot Agreement "was a fatuous arrangement judged from any and every point of view."[35]

Even Sykes himself finally came to agree: on 3 March 1918 he wrote to Wingate and Clayton that the agreement had to be abandoned because of such events as the United States' entry into the war, Woodrow Wilson's Fourteen Points, the Bolshevik Revolution, and the publication by the Bolsheviks of the terms of the Sykes-Picot Agreement to an apparently indignant world.[36] On 18 June 1918 he told the Eastern Committee that, while the Sherifians had no right to be indignant about the Sykes-Picot Agreement, for he had fully informed Hussein of its terms, Britain should ask France to agree that the agreement no longer applied.[37] A month later he told the committee that "The Agreement of 1916 was dead, although the French refused to admit it. What was required now was some modification of, or substitute for, that Agreement."[38] When the French refused to agree to modify the agreement, however, he went ahead to negotiate terms for the administration of occupied territories on the basis that the agreement therefore remained in force.

On 5 October 1918 Leo Amery noted in his diary: "Talk with Sykes about what to do with the Sykes-Picot Agreement. He has evolved a new and most ingenious scheme by which the French are to clear out of the whole Arab region except the Lebanon" and in return get all of Kurdistan and Armenia "from Adana to Persia and the Caucasus."[39] But the French did not agree.

Picking up on Feisal's protest to Allenby "that a Country without a Port was no good to him" Sykes explored a possible compromise in which the Sykes-Picot Agreement would be modified by transferring one coastal port from the area of direct French control to the area in which Feisal would serve as ruler. General Allenby seemed hopeful about this approach. On 15 December he wrote to his wife that "Sykes is all for soothing the Arabs & giving them a port; & Picot is less Chauvinist than he was."[40] But nothing came of this approach either.

The French refused to waive any of their rights under the agreement; but there was a chorus of opinion from British officers serving in the field to the effect that it would be disastrous to attempt to enforce its terms.

The followers of the late Lord Kitchener, saying the same thing through many voices, as they so often did, had been arguing for some time that the Sykes-Picot Agreement had to be annulled in the interests of Jewish-Arab friendship in Palestine. Jewish-Arab friendship was a cause in which Sir Mark Sykes sincerely believed; whether his colleagues who raised the point shared his belief in it is doubtful.

Ronald Storrs, governor of Jerusalem, reported that the Arabs were ready to accept the Zionist program, but only under a British government for Palestine.[41] Gilbert Clayton reported that the Arab and Zionist causes were "interdependent," and that both of them could be satisfied and would cooperate, but only if the French could be made to agree that the Sykes-Picot Agreement "is no longer a practical instrument."[42] Chaim Weizmann assisted in the campaign by writing to Balfour along the same lines, and added that French intrigues aimed at securing exclusive commercial concessions were obscuring the cause of self-determination for Jews as well as for Arabs.[43] T. E. Lawrence told the Eastern Committee that "there would be no difficulty in reconciling Zionists and Arabs in Palestine and Syria, provided that the administration of Palestine remained in British hands."[44]

If the agreement were to be abrogated with respect to Palestine, there was no reason why it should not be abrogated with respect to Syria as well—though Prime Minister Lloyd George repeatedly asserted that Britain had no desire to take over Syria for herself, and British officers in the field made the same claim. They asserted that they wanted France to relinquish her claims, not in favor of Britain, but in favor of an independent Arab nation led by Feisal. This was sheer dishonesty, for the Arab Bureau officers did not believe that Arabs were capable of self-government. By an independent country ruled by Feisal they meant a country guided by themselves as agents of Britain.

David Hogarth, the head of the Arab Bureau who succeeded Clayton as chief political officer in the field, reported from newly liberated Damascus that Feisal's Arab administration was incompetent. He wrote that a European power *must* run things.[45] If France were to be excluded, it was evident which European power (in his view) would be obliged to assume that responsibility.

V

Nearly a fortnight after his interview with Feisal at the Hotel Victoria in Damascus, Sir Edmund Allenby returned to Damascus to be the dinner guest of Prince Feisal. He reported to his wife that "He gave me an excellent dinner; Arab dishes, but all good, served in the ordinary ways of civilization. Water to drink; but good, fresh, cool water; not tepid barley water!" Allenby added that "You would like Feisal. He is a keen, slim, highly strung man. He has beautiful hands, like a woman's; and his fingers are always moving nervously when he talks. But he is strong in will, and straight in principle." As to politics, "He is nervous about the peace settlement; but I tell him he must trust the Entente powers to treat him fairly."[46]

"Trust the Entente Powers": Feisal could not have thought that was a particularly firm foundation on which to base his future prospects. The Entente Powers did not even trust one another. The French did not believe that the British were sponsoring Jewish and Arab aspirations in good faith, while the British discussed how, rather than whether, to break their agreements with France. Neither Britain nor France planned to honor wartime commitments to Italy. Neither Britain nor France was disposed to carry out the idealistic program of Woodrow Wilson with which, when Washington was listening, they pretended to be in sympathy.

Feisal was aware that only the year before, British leaders had contemplated behind his back a compromise peace in which the Russian rather than the Ottoman Empire would have been partitioned—thus abandoning him and his father to the mercies of the Turks. He knew, too, that Britain and France had secretly agreed two years before to divide the Arab world between them, and that they had revealed details of their agreement to him only when they were forced to do so.

Trust was not a part of the atmosphere in which Feisal lived. He himself had corresponded with the Turks that year about his changing sides in the war. His father had held similar correspondence with the Turks. Neither of them had kept faith with Britain, and Feisal had not kept faith with his father either.

His only regular troops were deserters from the enemy camp, who might as easily desert him, in turn, if his star waned. The Bedouin tribes that were his allies were notoriously fickle, often changing sides in Arabia even on the field of battle itself; and they were bound to him principally by the gold that was Lawrence's, not his, to dispense. As for the Syrians, they accepted him only because he was placed over them by the British army.

Even his own body betrayed him; his worry-bead fingers gave him away. He was nervous—and had every reason to be.

PART VIII

THE SPOILS OF VICTORY

"The victor belongs to the spoils."
—F. Scott Fitzgerald

38

THE PARTING OF THE WAYS

I

Giddy with fatigue and caught up in the last hysterical convulsions of the war, the Ottoman and British empires launched themselves into far-off deserts and inland seas to fight a barely remembered series of final campaigns that produced no decisive result. Yet in the course of the military and political maneuvering two new developments arose that were to affect profoundly the future of the twentieth century. Western armies found themselves at war with Russia, their former ally; and oil became a crucial issue in the battle for the Middle East.

It all began because Enver Pasha, instead of attempting to deal with the losing situation in Syria, opened up a new theater of operations against a less formidable opponent. As a result, while the British were marching from success to success in the Arabic-speaking provinces of the Ottoman Empire, Ottoman forces to the north were marching from success to success in what used to be the Russian Empire. In the last half of 1918 Turkey and Britain were engaged in what appeared to be not so much one war as two parallel wars in which they pursued similar goals: to exclude their allies from a share in the winnings. Enver Pasha, like Lloyd George, was so captivated by the prospective spoils of victory that he could not bear to share them with other countries. The near-dictatorial Turkish leader, like his near-dictatorial British counterpart, therefore took the risk of endangering his alliances for the sake of imperial ambitions.

Lenin had it the wrong way around. Imperialism—defined as the quest for colonies—did not cause the war; the war engendered imperialism. Their staggering losses drove the belligerent powers to try to compensate by seeking new gains. The collapse of the Russian Empire answered the need for new worlds to conquer; its domains were there to be taken. Lord Milner worried that once Russia was out of the war Germany might be more difficult to defeat, and raised the possibility of a negotiated compromise peace in which Britain would be compensated by dividing the Russian rather than the Ottoman Empire. Germany, however, having smashed the Czar's Empire, was in no mood to share her winnings with the Entente Powers. The Germans continued to pursue their campaigns of war and subversion against Russia. Their postwar goals of aggrandizement grew more far-reaching as the wartime need for agricultural products and raw materials became more pressing; and as they pursued those goals, they collided with their Turkish allies.

Enver Pasha had dreamed of one day uniting all the Turkish-speaking peoples of Asia under Ottoman leadership, but this became his operational political program only when the disintegration of Petrograd's authority dangled that prospect in front of him. After the war, Winston Churchill, among others, fostered the legend that the Young Turks had been animated by pan-Turkish ("pan-Turanian") ideology all along and had brought Turkey into the war in order to pursue expansionist plans in Central Asia. The evidence now available is to the contrary: the demands the C.U.P. made of Germany in 1914 and through 1917 show that the Ottoman leaders were thinking in essentially defensive terms at that time, hoping at most to shore up their existing frontiers in order to win a more complete independence within them. It was only in 1917 that Enver seriously planned to expand the Ottoman Empire eastward. Vast territories, no longer held by the Czar, seemed there for the taking, and could compensate for what Britain had taken in the Arabic-speaking south.

A British Intelligence report on the movement to unite all the Turkish-speaking peoples, the Pan-Turanian Movement, prepared by the Department of Information in the autumn of 1917, estimated that outside the Ottoman Empire more than seventeen million people in Asia spoke one or more of the Turkic languages. According to the report, "Turkish-speaking Central Asia is one of the largest continuous language areas in the world—larger than the Great Russian area and almost as large as the English or Spanish-speaking area in America." While disdainful of pan-Turanianism as an ideology, the report pictured it as a dangerous instrument in the hands of the Young Turk leaders. "The whole population is Turkish; the whole population is Sunni; and the present possessor [i.e. Russia] is not an ancient Moslem State, but a recent Christian conqueror." Were the C.U.P. to create a Turkish-Islamic state there, in alliance with Persia and Afghanistan, India would be directly threatened. "It would create a vast anti-British hinterland behind the anti-British tribes on the North-Western frontier."[1]

Enver, though aware of these possibilities, made no precipitate move but allowed events to evolve favorably on their own. The overthrow of the Czar left a Russian army of half a million soldiers in northeastern Turkey, holding such major towns as Trebizond,

Erzerum, and Kars. The troops, initially at least, were not Bolshevik in sentiment, but suffered from war weariness. As discipline disintegrated, they deserted and returned to Russia. In agreement with the German General Staff, the Ottoman forces did not attack the thinning Russian lines but allowed the Russian army to dwindle to nothing of its own accord.

By the time the Bolsheviks seized power in Petrograd in the autumn of 1917, practically all that remained was a volunteer force from the Transcaucasian areas across the frontier and a few hundred Russian officers.[2] Still Enver held back, expecting the Bolsheviks to sue for peace, as they did several weeks later.

The Turkish military situation on the eastern frontier with Persia also improved of its own accord. British forces in the south of Persia had been operating behind the shield of Russian forces in the north, but could no longer do so with assurance. As revolutionary fervor took hold of the Russian troops, they became increasingly friendly to the Persian nationalists whom they had hitherto held in check. On 27 May 1917 the pro-Allied regime in Teheran collapsed, and on 6 June was replaced by a government of nationalist hue which approached Petrograd with a view toward reducing the Russian military presence.

High-ranking officials in the War Office in London and in the Government of India feared that Turkey might attack through Persia toward Afghanistan[3]—although the Chief of the Imperial General Staff did not share these views. The Cabinet wavered between making concessions to the new Persian regime or allowing relations to deteriorate; dangers were apparent either way.

As the authority of the Kerensky government in Petrograd evaporated, the Russian army in the north of Persia appeared to British officials to be increasingly unreliable. On 31 October 1917 an interdepartmental committee in Whitehall decided to put the anti-Bolshevik segments of the Russian army in northern Persia on the British payroll; but the Russians nonetheless proved unwilling to do Britain's bidding.

Once the Bolsheviks seized power in Petrograd the following week, matters rapidly came to a head. Within months, on 29 January 1918, Trotsky, as Soviet Commissar for External Affairs, renounced the Convention of 1907, which formed the basis of the Anglo-Russian occupation of Persia. Disclaiming responsibility for any anti-Bolshevik Russian troops remaining on Persian soil, he expressed the hope that the other foreign armies occupying Persian soil—the Turks and the British—would withdraw as well.

The British government feared that the Russian withdrawal would expose the Indian Army in Mesopotamia to an attack from behind by Ottoman armies wheeling through Persia; for despite the long conflict between the two empires in that area, Britain had come to rely on

Russia to hold the line against the Turks in northern Persia, and was uncertain what course to pursue when that protection was abruptly withdrawn.

II

In March 1918 Germany imposed crushing armistice terms on the defeated Russians. As soon as they had signed the armistice with Russia, the Ottoman and German empires began to dispute possession of the provinces that the Russian Empire had ruled adjoining the Turkish frontier. Christian Georgia and Armenia, and Moslem Azerbaijan—the three states collectively called Transcaucasia—were now independent. Germany urgently needed the agricultural and mineral wealth and the railroad system of Georgia, and even more so the oil wells of Azerbaijan, to sustain her war effort. Thinking ahead to the postwar world, German leaders also intended to use Transcaucasia as a spearhead into the markets of the Middle East.

The Ottoman leaders also looked to the commercial uses of the provinces across their frontier. They thought in terms of restoring the old trade route with Iran, and of reviving their Black Sea and Crimean commerce. Enver, above all, aimed at the creation of a new Turkish empire that stretched into Central Asia, to which Transcaucasia would be the link.

Convinced that Germany had disregarded Turkish interests when she negotiated the terms of the armistice with Russia, Enver proceeded to disregard German interests in Transcaucasia, and sent the flower of his remaining armies across the frontier to conquer Georgia and Armenia and to march on Azerbaijan. For the purpose he created a special army corps, detached from the regular Ottoman army which was permeated with German officers. His new "Army of Islam" contained no Germans: it consisted only of Ottoman troops and Azerbaijani Tartars. Its orders were to march on the Azerbaijani metropolis of Baku, which had been taken over by a local Soviet. Baku, an industrialized city of some 300,000 people on the shores of the Caspian Sea, was only half Moslem and quite unlike the surrounding Tartar hinterland. At the time it was the great oil-producing city of the Middle East.

By 1918 the military importance of oil began to be generally recognized.[*] Before the war, Churchill's Admiralty had switched to oil as

[*] Winston Churchill, who had recognized it before the war and had arranged at that time for the British government to purchase a majority shareholding in the Anglo-Persian Oil Company, aroused a great deal of opposition, especially within the Government of India, from British officials who did not see the need for it.[4]

fuel for the navy's ships and, during the war, the Allies came to rely heavily on fuel-consuming trucks for land transport. Tanks and aircraft had begun to come fully into their own in the last days of the war and they, too, consumed quantities of gas and oil. In 1918 Clemenceau's government in France and the U.S. Department of the Navy both came to recognize that oil had become of cardinal importance.

Germany, beset by shortages, had counted on replenishing her resources from the captured south and west of Russia, and controlled much of the economy of Georgia during 1918; but in Berlin the resources of Georgia were not regarded as sufficient. Enver's race to Baku, in Azerbaijan, threatened to deprive Germany of the oil she so desperately needed, and also threatened to wreck the armistice arrangement with Russia. The enraged heads of the German General Staff sent angry notes to Enver, which he disregarded.

The state secretary of the German Navy Department told the leaders of his country's Foreign Office and General Staff that it was absolutely crucial for Germany to get hold of Baku's oil and that the Ottoman attack on the city therefore had to be stopped.[5] The German leaders told the Russian ambassador in Berlin that they would take steps to stop the Ottoman advance if Russia gave assurances that she would supply at least some of Baku's oil to Germany. "Of course, we will agree," Lenin cabled to Stalin in reporting this development.[6]

Baku was also important strategically. As a major port it dominated Caspian shipping and would enable Enver to move his armies by sea, if he chose, to the eastern shore of the Caspian, where the Moslems of Turkestan could be expected to rally to his standard and where he would avail himself of the railroad network that the Russians had built there to enable them to reach Afghanistan and attack India.

The British, keenly aware of the danger, viewed Enver's progress with foreboding.

III

Two tiny British military missions in northern Persia watched these events from across the frontier with no clear idea of what role they should play in them.[7]

Major-General L. C. Dunsterville was appointed chief of the British mission to the Caucasus in early 1918. Had he ever reached Tiflis, the Transcaucasian capital, he would have served as British Representative there as well, where his objective would have been to help stiffen the resistance of the Russian army in Turkey against an Ottoman advance.

Dunsterville's convoy of forty-one Ford cars and vans traveled via Mesopotamia into Persia and headed toward a Persian port on the Caspian Sea then called Enzeli (later renamed Pahlevi) on the road to Transcaucasia. By the time the British arrived, most of Transcaucasia had fallen into Ottoman or German hands. A worried British government ordered Dunsterville to clear the road to Enzeli of a revolutionary band of Persian nationalists, allied to the Bolsheviks but also acting in the interests of the advancing Ottoman Army of Islam.

As Enver's forces approached Baku, the British government debated what role Dunsterville's tiny force should or could play in the unexpected battle for Central Asia in which Turks, Germans, Russians, and others were involved. The question also arose of what Major-General Wilfred Malleson's mission ought to be. General Malleson was an officer in the Military Intelligence branch of the Indian Army, who had served for years on the staff of Lord Kitchener. Simla had sent him out with six officers to Meshed, in eastern Persia, to watch over developments in the vast lands of Russian Turkestan that were believed to be Enver's next objective. Dunsterville was to watch over the lands to the west of the Caspian Sea, and Malleson was to watch over the lands to the east.

In Malleson's area of responsibility, there were several matters that concerned the British military leaders. One of these was the large store of cotton which might fall into enemy hands. Another was the presence of some 35,000 German and Austrian prisoners-of-war who might be released either by the Bolsheviks or by Enver's forces.

To the British leaders the intentions of the enemy forces at work west and east of the Caspian were obscured by the growing political fragmentation in those areas. Politically the Germans appeared not only to be hand-in-glove locally with the anti-Bolsheviks in Tiflis, but also to be involved with the Bolsheviks in Petrograd, while having fallen out with the Turks, who were their public allies but their secret enemies. Enver's allied force of Ottoman and Azerbaijani Moslem Turks and Tartars was on the march toward Baku, which was governed by a divided Soviet that reflected a division within the city itself. The Azerbaijani half of the population favored the Ottoman Empire, while the Armenians, fearing massacre, were in favor of anybody but the Turks. The Social Revolutionaries and other non-Bolshevik Russians feared British intervention, but in the end grew to fear Turkey more. Stepan Shaumian, the Bolshevik chairman of the Soviet, while leading the resistance to the Ottoman-Azerbaijani allies, even preferred Turkish rule to a British intervention and, in any event, had received direct orders from Lenin and Stalin not to accept British aid.

In Turkestan a Bolshevik-controlled Russian Soviet was in control of the oasis town of Tashkent, but its forces had been beaten by the native Turks of Bukhara, and had been obliged to recognize the Emir of Bukhara—whose domains had fallen under Russian sway during the Great Game in the nineteenth century—as once again an independent ruler. Rumors reaching London indicated that the newly independent khanates of Bukhara and Khiva might be entering into alliance with the Porte.[8]

As viewed from London, the chaos in Central Asia was a source of danger and promise. The danger was that it might permit an assault on India, and on the Indian Army in Persia and Mesopotamia, that could ignite flames impossible to extinguish. According to a General Staff memorandum:

> [Germany] will make use of the Pan-Turanian movement and of Mohammedan fanaticism to fan into a flame the ever glowing embers of a religious war, in order to let loose on India the pent-up tide of a Moslem invasion ... While Russia was healthy and while Persia was under control we were able to deal with this difficulty, but if German agents had free access to the lawless tribes of Afghanistan and the frontiers of India, bred as they have been on tales of the legendary wealth of loot which might be theirs, innumerable hordes of savage warriors could swarm into the plains, ravaging, murdering, destroying. The institutions built by long years of careful government would be swept away in a few short weeks and the attenuated garrison of the country would have to be largely reinforced from troops badly needed elsewhere. None but White[*] troops could be trusted.[9]

Since British policy-makers believed the Russian Bolshevik government was in the pay of imperial Germany, and were not aware of the extent to which the Porte and the Wilhelmstrasse had parted company, it appeared in 1918 that the Germans had taken control of northern Asia, were in process of taking over the center of Asia, and were preparing to mount an attack on British positions in southern Asia. It fitted in with the wartime view that Germany aimed at a world empire and with the fear that, when the war was over, all of Asia might be left as a vast slave colony in Germany's possession, and its wealth and raw materials would fuel German industry and allow it to dominate the globe.

Leo Amery proposed to Lloyd George that Britain should adopt a strategy to counter that threat. If Britain were to capture the center of Asia, then the partition of Russia between Germany and Britain, which Milner had proposed the year before, would in effect be

---

[*] "White troops": British rather than Indian soldiers of the Indian Army.

achieved. At the end of 1917 Amery noted in his diary that "The war is going East with a vengeance and we shall find ourselves fighting for the rest of it to decide where the Anglo-German boundary shall run across Asia." The French, looking to eastern Europe for their postwar gains, would fail, he predicted, "while we poor meek British will probably find our non-aggressive little Empire at the end of the war including Turkestan, Persia, and the Caucasus!"[10]

This represented yet a further enlargement of the vast section of the globe that Amery regarded as properly falling under British hegemony. Like Milner's other associates, his essential focus was on "the whole of the great semi-circle which runs from Cape Town to Cairo, thence through Palestine, Mesopotamia and Persia to India and so through Singapore to Australia and New Zealand." Within that area, he wrote to the Prime Minister of Australia in late 1917, "What we want ... is a British Monroe Doctrine which should keep that portion of the world free from future interference of ambitious powers ..."[11]

By June of 1918 Amery had come to feel (and to advise Lloyd George) that, if German expansion in Asia were not stopped, this "Southern British World" could not "go about its peaceful business without constant fear of German aggression." He wrote that "as soon as this 'little side show' in the West is over ... we shall have to take the war for the mastery of Asia in hand seriously."[12] This harked back to his view that British foreign policy was flawed by giving Britain's interests in Europe priority over her interests elsewhere. He wrote in 1917 that "The great danger to my mind is that the Foreign Office and the public ... take too European a point of view about peace terms, instead of looking at them from the perspective of an Empire which is distributed all over the world ..."[13] He also thought that they were taking too European a point of view about the war. He discerned fresh dangers in Asia.

He wrote to Smuts on 16 October 1917, warning that Enver would gain "some five million" Turks who dwelt in Transcaucasia and then would link up with the Turks of Turkestan.[14] Events early in the following year seemed to confirm this view.

Amery, like other British military and political leaders in the first half of 1918, was persuaded that the German and Ottoman conquest of Transcaucasia demonstrated that Germany was in process of executing the "Grand Design" outlined in John Buchan's *Greenmantle*. In Buchan's adventure novel, the Germans were planning a sweep through Islamic Asia to and across the Indian frontier to destroy the British Empire in the east and replace it with their own.[15] Thus in waging war as in making peace, according to Amery, British forces should be moved up to a defensive line running all the way across the former Russian Empire from the Urals in the west to Siberia in the east.[16]

Neither the War Office nor the Government of India was willing to make available the forces for such large schemes in distant places; and Amery went so far as to propose that Japan and the United States should be invited to associate themselves in the enterprise of occupying the Urals to Siberia line.[17] British and Allied military leaders also urged that Japan should be asked to send armies through Siberia and across Asia to join battle with Enver's forces west of the Caspian Sea.[18]

But Lloyd George and Lord Milner were so completely occupied with the war in Europe and Palestine that Amery could not attract their attention; and in the absence of their leadership, their subordinates failed to develop a coherent policy. Breathtakingly ambitious geopolitical goals were outlined by Amery and by general officers of the high command, but no resources were allocated and no strategy was put in motion to achieve them.

So, without guidance and without support, the tiny missions sent out by the British Government of India headed into the interior of Asia.

IV

Baku, the oil capital of Central Asia, was a focus of activity in the summer of 1918, as Bolshevik leaders fled the city. A new non-Bolshevik government was hastily formed, which called in the British. Dunsterville asked and received permission from his superiors to enter and defend Baku. His advance guard arrived in Baku 4 August, thwarting German hopes of obtaining Baku's oil, whereupon the Germans decided that Turkey was a lesser danger than Britain just as the Bolsheviks were reaching the opposite conclusion.[19] The Germans asked permission of the Bolshevik government to launch an attack on British-held Baku, either alone or in combination with Enver's Army of Islam. The Bolshevik government agreed to accept a German occupation of Baku, but not in combination with the Army of Islam; for even the British, according to Petrograd, were preferable to the Turks. But the German force in Georgia was too weak to spare troops in time for a campaign against Baku—and that left the Army of Islam and the British mission as the only contestants in the field.

Dunsterville's force amounted to about 900 officers and men according to one source, or about 1,400 according to another.[20] The Army of Islam was estimated to be ten or twenty times greater. When it attacked Baku, the British were on their own; local forces proved to be of little help. On 14 September Dunsterville evacuated his forces from the city and withdrew to Persia, having occupied the city—and deprived the enemy of oil—for six weeks. A British

Reuters' dispatch described the Baku evacuation as one of the "thrillingest chapters" of the war.[21]

At about the time that Dunsterville marched to the relief of Baku, General Malleson, also by invitation, marched to the relief of Turkestan, whose government had been formed by anti-Bolshevik Russian Mensheviks and Social Revolutionaries with the aid of railroad workers. The Turkestan government proclaimed its independence from the Bolshevik Russian authorities; and, in responding to its appeal, Malleson in effect was intervening in a Russian civil war—an act prompted by fears that Germany would get Turkestan's cotton supplies, and that the German and Austro-Hungarian prisoners-of-war would be freed.

The Turkish-speaking native population of Turkestan, while opposed to both the Bolshevik and the anti-Bolshevik Russian settlers, threw their support behind the latter when forced to choose between the two. It was expected that once Enver's Army of Islam arrived, they would support it.

There on the plains of Turkestan—in the middle of nowhere, as far as the western world was concerned—the confused armies clashed. On the battlefields of Dushak, Kaakha, and Merv, General Malleson's British-Indian forces fought alongside Enver's Turkish supporters against Soviet Russians aided by imperial German and Austro-Hungarian prisoners-of-war who had been released and armed by the Bolsheviks. Alliances had been reversed: it was now Britain and Turkey versus Russia and Germany.

General Malleson did not withdraw from Central Asia until April 1919, half a year after the war ended; and he withdrew only when the anti-Bolshevik White armies of General Denikin occupied the area. His intervention, which initially was aimed at stopping the progress of the Ottoman and German empires, in the end was directed against the Bolsheviks.[*] At the time the British authorities did not distinguish clearly among the three; all of them seemed to be ranged together on the enemy side in the world war.

The Government of India had also sent out a third mission, consisting of three officers who were unaware of the Dunsterville and Malleson forays into former Russian territory. They were sent to Kashgar in Chinese Turkestan to observe developments from across the border. Once there they decided to cross into Russian Turkestan

---

[*] Interventions elsewhere in the Russian Empire by British and Allied troops fall outside the scope of this volume. The Government of India did not coordinate its three missions, discussed above with the other interventions, nor did Simla send out the three missions in the context of some more general plan or pattern of intervention.

and to proceed to Tashkent—the seat of the local Soviet government—in an attempt to win the cooperation of the Bolshevik authorities in the matters of the prisoners-of-war and of the cotton. Only when they arrived in Tashkent did they learn that Malleson had intervened on behalf of the rival government.

Two of the three officers returned to Kashgar. The third, Colonel Frederick Marshman Bailey, decided to remain in Tashkent to represent British interests in the event that the local Bolshevik regime collapsed. When he learned that the local authorities were preparing to take measures against him, he disguised himself and disappeared. In hiding he took many identities, among them those of a Hungarian cook, a Rumanian coachman, and an Albanian butterfly collector. He remained undercover until 1920, gathering information as events unfolded. At the end he posed as an agent of Bolshevik Russian counterintelligence. Soviet authorities, greatly exaggerating, credited him with being the mastermind of vast intrigues against them.

London and Petrograd, having been wartime allies not long before, were now enemies. Between 1917 and 1918, the political world had turned upside down.

V

As Ottoman fortunes prospered in the east, they crumbled in the south and west. A secret report to David Lloyd George in 1918 indicated that Enver was talking of an Ottoman empire from the Adriatic to India; yet at other times he supposedly spoke of surrendering. Enver was reported to have predicted gloomily that "if the Germans won this War, Turkey would be Germany's vassal."[22]

Ludendorff, the presiding genius of the German General Staff, claimed that the Porte could not be trusted. The oil of Baku was essential to Germany, he stated, but the Turks had shown that they intended to keep all the resources of Transcaucasia for themselves.[23] In response to an inquiry from the Wilhelmstrasse to the General Staff, Ludendorff reported in September 1918 that the military authorities had been studying the consequences should Turkey betray Germany and go over to the Allied side.[24]

The close collaboration between Germany and Bolshevik Russia infuriated the Porte. Against a background of Turkish press criticism of German meddling in Transcaucasia, Talaat sent word to Berlin that if Germany continued to make arrangements with Russia—the "enemy of yesterday and the enemy of tomorrow"—at Turkey's expense, the Ottoman government might have to go its own way in the war.[25] On 7 September 1918 Talaat went to Berlin to argue for organizing the Turkish-speaking millions of Central Asia for a military crusade against Britain—and Russia.[26]

At the same time Britain, too, moved closer to war against Russia. Malleson remained in Central Asia, where the execution of a group of Bolshevik commissars by his anti-Bolshevik allies was blamed on Britain by the Petrograd government. On the other side of the Caspian, a sudden collapse of the Central Powers followed by the soon-to-be-discussed armistices of autumn 1918, led British forces to return through Baku to replace Ottoman and German troops in the independent republics of Transcaucasia. Thus the southern stretches of the former Russian Empire on both sides of the Caspian Sea appeared to be in the hands of anti-Bolshevik or separatist groups under British protection.

A significant observation was made by a British participant in the first battle between Malleson's force and the Bolsheviks in Central Asia. Both the anti-Bolshevik troops and the Bolshevik troops, he noted, were wearing the same uniforms. "At close quarters," he wrote, "it was difficult to distinguish friend from enemy."[27] By the autumn of 1918 that was true not merely in Central Asia but all across the Middle East.

39

BY THE SHORES OF TROY

I

In the summer of 1918 the Chief of the Imperial General Staff advised the Imperial War Cabinet in London that victory in Europe could not be won before the middle of 1919 and was far more likely to be won in the summer of 1920. Commanders in the field took a more hopeful view of the prospects for an early victory, but they had frequently been wrong in the past, and in London their cheerful predictions were viewed with considerable skepticism.

Ludendorff's powerful offensives of the spring and early summer, which had once again threatened Paris, had been stopped, and the Germans were falling back; but by September 1918 Ludendorff had established a strong defensive line and there was no reason to believe that he could not hold it for a long time. The war in the East, too, seemed likely to drag on, for Enver's forces driving toward the Caspian seemed poised to continue their offensive toward Persia, Afghanistan, or India.

Suddenly—and unexpectedly—an Allied breakthrough came in Bulgaria, where General Louis-Félix-François Franchet d'Esperey, the new French commander of the Allied forces in hitherto-neglected Salonika in Greece, launched a lightning offensive at the end of the summer. Bulgaria collapsed and, on 26 September 1918, asked for an armistice. The request should have been forwarded to the Supreme War Council of the Allies in Paris, but Franchet d'Esperey dared not chance the delay. He composed the terms of an armistice himself, and had it signed within a matter of days so that he could turn immediately to mount a devastating offensive on the Danube against the Germans and Austrians, thus successfully executing the "Eastern" strategy that Lloyd George had been advocating in vain ever since the war began.*

On 29 September Ludendorff, learning that a Bulgarian armistice

* But of course it can be argued that it would not have worked before 1918.

had been concluded that day, advised his government that Germany would therefore have to sue for an armistice too: he had no troops with which to make a stand on the new southeastern front—the Danube front—that Franchet d'Esperey had opened up.

The British Cabinet had not expected the enemy to collapse so soon or so suddenly, was not prepared for it, and did not entirely believe it. Armistice terms for the various enemy powers had not been drafted or even considered. A day after Franchet d'Esperey received the Bulgarian request for an armistice, the British Chief of the Imperial General Staff inquired "what our Foreign Office was going to do if Turkey followed suit."[1] Balfour, the Foreign Secretary, replied—with complete candor—that he did not know.

But the issue had to be faced immediately: it presented itself within a matter of days. Between 1 and 6 October both the government of the Ottoman Empire and several prominent individual Turkish leaders launched peace feelers. On the night of 3–4 October Germany, too, sent a note to President Wilson, inaugurating armistice negotiations that were to go on for several weeks, as fighting continued and as German troops successfully held on to a defensive line that ran through eastern France and Belgium.

On 1 October the British War Cabinet decided to convoke a meeting of the Supreme War Council of the Allies in order to address the question of peace terms for Turkey. At the same time, however, the War Cabinet decided to send two British Dreadnought-class battleships to the Aegean to strengthen Britain against France in the waters off Turkey.

The Cabinet was seized by a panicky fear that the war might come to an end before the British armed forces could occupy the vital Middle Eastern areas it hoped to dominate. Amery warned Smuts and the Chief of the Imperial General Staff that only actual possession of the Middle East before a cease-fire went into effect would enable the Cabinet to bring the region into the British orbit.[2] The armies of British India in Mesopotamia were still weeks away from strategically important and oil-rich Mosul; on 2 October its commander was advised by the War Office to "occupy as large a portion of the oil-bearing regions as possible."[3]

On 3 October the War Cabinet discussed at length the question of an armistice or peace agreement with the Ottoman Empire. The Prime Minister, who hoped to reduce France's and Italy's share in Britain's winnings in Ottoman Asia, argued that in all fairness her Allies were not entitled to what they had originally been promised. According to an extract from minutes of the meeting,

> The Prime Minister said he had been refreshing his memory about the Sykes-Picot Agreement, and had come to the conclusion that it was quite inapplicable to present circumstances,

and was altogether a most undesirable agreement from the British point of view. Having been concluded more than two years ago, it entirely overlooked the fact that our position in Turkey had been won by very large British forces, whereas our Allies had contributed but little to the result.[4]

It was specious reasoning, but Balfour, responding as though the Prime Minister were sincere in urging fair play, pointed out the fallacy in his reasoning.

Mr Balfour reminded the War Cabinet that the original idea had been that any territories that the Allies might acquire should be pooled and should not be regarded as the property of the nation which had won them. The theory had been that the fighting in one theatre of war, where there was little to gain, might be just as important a contribution to the cause of the Allies as much easier fighting in other theatres where great successes were achieved. He believed that some statement of this kind had been made.[5]

Bonar Law confirmed Balfour's recollection.

Lloyd George took another approach and argued that Britain and Turkey ought to conclude a peace agreement immediately, rather than a mere armistice. (It was evident that, with British armies in occupation of most of the Ottoman Empire, a peace treaty negotiated immediately was likely to favor Britain as the only power in a position to extract concessions from the Porte.)

Lloyd George argued that the Ottoman Empire was unlikely to accept a mere armistice without knowing what peace terms were to be imposed later. Suspicion of French and Italian ambitions, he said, would drive the Porte to refuse such an arrangement. Therefore Turkey would fight on. This, the Prime Minister continued, would be intolerable, for it meant that the British would have to fight on, too, for the sake of securing purely French and Italian ambitions; and that ought to be out of the question. He said that he would present the matter in this light to the French and Italian premiers in Paris, and he expressed confidence that they would let him have his way.

Nonetheless the Cabinet drafted the terms of a proposed armistice agreement, which the Prime Minister took with him to Paris to discuss with the other Allied heads of government toward the end of the first week in October. In Paris the Allies agreed on an armistice proposal based largely on the British draft and agreed that the armistice should be negotiated on behalf of the Allies by whichever power was approached by Turkey in the matter. However the Allied premiers dismissed out of hand Lloyd George's scheme for an immediate peace treaty.

A subject of increasing controversy between the Allied leaders was the question of who should exercise supreme military command in the several theaters of war against the Ottoman Empire. The French, who exercised supreme naval command in the Mediterranean, sought to displace the British commander of its Aegean wing, Vice-Admiral Somerset Arthur Gough-Calthorpe, who claimed that the French were "on the whole incapable of running a sound naval campaign."[6] The issue was not merely military; for whichever country held the command would be first off the mark in getting to the spoils of victory.

In Franchet d'Esperey's command, the eastern flank (which faced Turkey) had been led by a British general, George Francis Milne. Franchet d'Esperey, flushed with success in Bulgaria, now proposed to break up his British contingent, to entrust the eastern flank to a French commander and to prepare an eventual triumphal march into Constantinople, led by himself. Lloyd George vetoed the triumphal entry, and succeeded in getting Clemenceau to order General Milne to be reinstated as commander of Salonika's Turkish front. With the support of Marshal Foch, Lloyd George managed to change the Clemenceau-Franchet d'Esperey strategy of concentrating all land forces in the Balkan theater on the European campaign. Instead some forces were detached under General Milne to march on Constantinople in support of an Allied naval attack through the Dardanelles.

Lloyd George proposed, in a letter to Clemenceau dated 15 October, that a British admiral should lead the triumphal entry into Constantinople by sea. On 21 October Clemenceau replied, refusing to agree; his counterproposal was that the Allied fleet steaming up the straits to the Ottoman capital should be under French command. Clemenceau argued that since a British general had been given command of the Salonika campaign against Turkey, it was intolerable that a British officer should also be given command of the naval campaign. He pointed to the immense French investment in the Ottoman public debt as a significant national interest that required France to play a leading role in matters affecting Turkey.

II

In hiding, in a Greek home in Pera, the residential section of Constantinople, was Lieutenant-Colonel Stewart F. Newcombe. A British officer active in the Arab Revolt, he had been taken prisoner a year before while leading a daring diversionary attack during Allenby's Jerusalem campaign. On his third attempt, he had succeeded in escaping from Turkish captivity, and from 22 September

1918 he had been hiding in Pera, where he soon learned that there were Ottoman politicians who were in search of an immediate armistice.

Opinion in the Ottoman capital was at a turning point. Until mid-September, C.U.P. members by and large still believed in ultimate victory. Civilian members of the Cabinet had deferentially accepted Enver's assurances that all was going well. Later they claimed to have believed the War Minister when he explained that the apparent German retreat in France was actually a brilliant deception: a maneuver by the German General Staff to trap the unwary Allied armies and destroy them. Enver went so far as to ask Cabinet members not to give Berlin's game away, and to repeat in public—as though they believed it—that the Germans had been defeated and were retreating.[7]

Talaat, the Grand Vizier, was better informed, knew that the Germans really *were* suffering defeats, and therefore advocated a German-Turkish bid for a compromise peace; but not even he believed that it had to be done urgently, for Enver had misled him, too, into thinking that the military situation was satisfactory for the moment and that it offered some new grounds for hope.[8]

In September, Talaat went to Berlin and Sofia and learned something of the true situation from his allies there: on his way back he witnessed the collapse of the Bulgarian army and was officially notified that Bulgaria would seek a separate peace. Bulgaria was the land link to Germany; her defection—in Talaat's judgment—doomed Turkey to defeat. He returned determined to seek a peace agreement. In concert with the Germans, his government promptly went ahead to sound out the American government on the possibility of surrendering to the United States on the basis of Woodrow Wilson's Fourteen Points. Washington, not being at war with the Porte, inquired of Britain how to reply, but received no response from London; for whatever reason the British reply never reached Washington, which therefore was unable to respond to the Porte. In effect this meant that the benefit of the Fourteen Points was not available to the Ottoman Empire, for only a power that surrendered to the United States could expect American peace terms.

It was at this point that Newcombe, from his hiding place, took a hand in matters. Enver, who was determined to go on with the war, felt that by continuing to fight Turkey could win better terms; and pointed to Turkish successes in the Caucasus and on the Caspian as proof that he could win victories in the east that would force Britain to concede favorable peace terms in 1919. These were the arguments that Newcombe assailed. He drafted notes for the Young Turk leaders in which he attempted to prove that just the reverse was true: that Britain would grant more favorable terms in 1918 than in 1919.

Through his Turkish friends, Newcombe's notes were circulated at the Porte, and he reported later that they had produced a profound effect. According to his informants, the notes had caused a split in the C.U.P. leadership.[9]

Actually the split had been caused by the Cabinet's realization—brought about by the collapse of Bulgaria and by Germany's decision to sue for peace—that Enver had been deceiving it. Turkey's allies were not (as Enver had claimed) winning the war; they were facing destruction—and would leave the Ottoman Empire isolated, cut off from its supplies of fuel, ammunition, money, and possible re-inforcements, to face the victorious Allied Powers alone. Early in October the Finance Minister noted in his diary that "Enver Pasha's greatest guilt is that he never kept his friends informed of the situation. If he had said five or six months ago that we were in so difficult a situation, naturally we would have . . . made a favourable separate peace at that time. But he concealed everything, and . . . he deluded himself and brought the country to this state."[10]

On the morning of 1 October, soon after Talaat learned that Germany was about to sue for peace, he called his Cabinet together to tell its members that they must resign. The Ottoman Empire was forced to seek an armistice immediately, he told them, and the Allies would impose far harsher terms if they thought that he and his C.U.P. colleagues were still in control.[11] Enver and Djemal disagreed and argued that the Cabinet could secure better terms by holding on and holding out, but they were in the minority. Talaat prevailed, and informed the Sultan that he and his Cabinet intended to resign.

The new Sultan, Mehmed VI, who had succeeded to the throne several months earlier on the death of his brother, was provided with a new Grand Vizier and Cabinet only with the greatest difficulty. The Sultan preferred a neutral Cabinet, or perhaps one drawn from the ranks of the political opposition, but Talaat and the Young Turkey Party still controlled the Parliament, the police, and the army, and demanded representation in the Cabinet to keep watch on the new regime. It took a week to find a statesman approved by the Sultan yet prepared to agree to Talaat's terms. At last the distinguished Field Marshal Ahmet Izzet Pasha—a man believed to be acceptable to the Allies—formed a new Cabinet that included several members of the C.U.P. On 13 October Talaat and his ministers formally resigned. The next day Izzet Pasha drove through silent, gloomy crowds to the Porte to take office.

The Ottoman situation was more grave than the Allied Powers realized. The fall of Bulgaria had severed the land route to Austria and Germany, cutting off hope as well as supplies. Within Turkey itself half a million marauding deserters from the Ottoman army brought chaos in their wake. Though he did not weaken his position by disclosing it, the new Grand Vizier felt that it was not possible to go on with the war. Two days after taking office, Izzet Pasha attempted to send Colonel Newcombe to Greece—the nearest Allied army headquarters—to try to bring the war to an end, but no airplane could be found in which to fly him there.

The Porte therefore sent an emissary by sea: another British prisoner-of-war, General Charles Townshend. Townshend had surrendered to the Ottoman army at Kut in Mesopotamia in the spring of 1916, and had lived ever since under house arrest on an island off Constantinople. Entertained and lionized by the Ottoman leaders, he moved with relative freedom in the political society of the capital. Townshend became aware in the autumn of 1918 of rising peace sentiment and, like Newcombe, he decided to give events a push.[12]

When Townshend learned that the Talaat ministry had fallen, he arranged an interview with the new Grand Vizier, and on 17 October went to the Sublime Porte carrying some notes that he had sketched out to indicate the sort of peace terms that might be asked by Britain. His notes suggested that Britain would be willing to leave the Ottoman Empire in possession of Syria, Mesopotamia, and perhaps even the Caucasus, so long as these regions were allowed local autonomy within a restructured empire that would resemble a confederation of states.

Townshend offered to help Turkey obtain generous terms along these lines and offered to make immediate contact with the British authorities. The Grand Vizier told him that it was a crime for the Ottoman Empire to have made war on Britain, and that it was Enver's fault. He accepted Townshend's offer of help in securing honorable peace terms without letting Townshend suspect that he would accept whatever terms he could get.

That evening Townshend met with the Minister of the Marine, who was his best friend in the new ministry, and who set out Turkey's armistice terms, which were similar to those outlined in Townshend's notes. Arrangements were then made to send Townshend out of Turkey through the port of Smyrna. Under cover of darkness, he left Smyrna on a tugboat.

Early in the morning of 20 October, Townshend's tugboat reached the Greek island of Mitylene, where it encountered a motor vessel of the British navy. From Mitylene, Townshend wired the details of the Turkish position to the Foreign Office in London. At his request, a fast vessel then took him to the British naval commander in the Aegean, Admiral Calthorpe, whose headquarters were at the Greek island of Lemnos.

Townshend told London that the new Grand Vizier was willing to make peace on the basis of the sort of generous terms that he himself had sketched out in Constantinople. He gave London the impression that if such generous terms were not offered, the Ottoman Empire would continue to wage war. Above all, however, he indicated that the Porte wanted to deal with Britain rather than with the other Allies. (In fact—though Townshend did not know it—Izzet's first attempt had been to establish contact with France, but his emissary had not yet been able to get through to French headquarters.[13] For decades afterward the British continued to believe—as have most historians—that Turkey had insisted on surrendering to them rather than to the French.)

Calthorpe, on 20 October, also cabled the news to London. He stressed (according to the Prime Minister) "that the Turks particularly wanted to deal with us, not with the French."[14] At the same time Calthorpe attacked the French plan of taking command of the fleet that would stream toward Constantinople. According to Calthorpe's cable, "the effect of a Fleet under French command going up to Constantinople would be deplorable."[15] Of course no Allied fleet could enter the Dardanelles safely unless the forts on shore were turned over to the Allies. Calthorpe reported that Townshend said the Turks would make this concession, not to all of the Allied forces, but to Britain, if she would agree to protect them against whatever action might be taken by the German forces remaining in the vicinity. "General Townshend thinks that the Turks would be willing to send pleni-potentiaries now to treat for peace with British representatives and that they would allow the British to take over the Forts of the Dardanelles if they were assured of support against the Germans in Turkey and the Black Sea."[16]

The telegrams from Townshend and Calthorpe led to the longest British Cabinet meeting of the war. The Cabinet, still somewhat fearful that the war against Germany might drag on into 1919 or 1920, wanted to secure sea passage for the Royal Navy through the Dardanelles into the Black Sea, where the fleet could move to the Rumanian coast to play a significant role in the final stages of the war in Europe. The Cabinet agreed, if necessary, to dispense with the rest of the twenty-four terms of the Allied armistice proposal so long as the Turks ceased hostilities, turned over the Dardanelles forts, and did everything possible to ensure safe passage for the fleet through the straits and into the Black Sea.

The Cabinet authorized Calthorpe to negotiate an armistice rather than a peace agreement because the latter would require consultation with the Allies and thus would cause delays.[17] The Cabinet told him to accept no less than surrender of the Dardanelles forts and free passage through the straits. The Cabinet also instructed him to ask for the rest of the twenty-four terms and to secure the adoption of as many of them as possible, but to give way if the Turks would not agree to them.

The French Foreign Minister protested on the ground that France had not been consulted before the Cabinet gave Calthorpe authorization to negotiate and to depart from the armistice terms upon which the Allies had agreed. Clemenceau was furious. It was not that the French Premier had changed his opinions and now harbored designs on the Middle East; it was that he did not want France treated as though she were a subordinate or defeated country.[18] The Cabinet quickly sent Lord Milner to Paris to explain matters to Clemenceau, and for the moment the French were mollified.

A new cause of contention arose as soon as the French became aware of the British interpretation of the inter-Allied agreement as to who should conduct armistice negotiations. The agreement provided that the first member of the Alliance approached by Turkey for an armistice should conduct the negotiations. Britain, having been approached by the Turks through Townshend, interpreted the agreement to mean that she should not merely conduct the negotiations, but should conduct them alone.

The British government instructed Admiral Calthorpe to exclude the French from the negotiations should they attempt to participate in them. Perhaps the British were afraid that the French, if allowed to participate, would insist on making demands on Turkey that would delay or prevent the concluding of an armistice.[19] Or alternatively, it may have been (as many in France believed) an overt opening move in the British campaign to deny France the position that had been promised to her in the postwar Middle East.

III

The armistice conference opened at 9:30 in the morning on Sunday, 27 October 1918, aboard the *Agamemnon*, a British battleship at anchor off the port of Mudros on the Greek island of Lemnos. The small Ottoman delegation was headed by Townshend's friend Rauf Bey, the new Minister of the Marine. The British delegation was headed by Admiral Calthorpe.

Calthorpe showed the Ottoman delegation a letter he had received from Vice-Admiral Jean F. C. Amet, the senior French naval officer in the area, stating his government's desire that he should participate in the negotiations. He proposed to attend the meetings aboard the *Agamemnon* as the representative of Vice-Admiral Dominique M. Gauchet, the Allied naval commander-in-chief in the Mediterranean and, as such, Calthorpe's superior officer.

The Ottoman delegates explained that they were accredited only to the British, not to the French. Calthorpe replied that it would not have been desirable for the French to participate in any event. He refused to invite Admiral Amet aboard the *Agamemnon*.

The negotiations were conducted in the captain's after-day cabin on deck. In a seemingly open spirit, Calthorpe began by reading aloud and discussing the proposed armistice terms one at a time. As the Ottoman delegates did not at first see the document in its entirety, they did not immediately comprehend the cumulative effect of its twenty-four clauses. Moreover, Calthorpe assured them that Britain meant no harm and intended only to be helpful. He explained what he supposed to be the Allied purpose in framing the various clauses in such a way as to suggest that they provided remedies for contingencies so remote that it was unlikely they would ever have to be invoked. At the same time, he managed to suggest that there was not much give in the Allied position: that if the Turks wanted an armistice, they would have to accept the Allied draft more or less in its entirety.

Seeing no alternative, on the evening of 30 October the head of the Ottoman delegation, Rauf Bey, signed an armistice little changed from the original Allied draft. It provided that hostilities should cease as of noon the following day. The armistice was in fact a surrender which permitted the Allies to occupy strategic points in the Ottoman Empire should their security be threatened: in effect the Allies were free to occupy any territory they wanted.

When Rauf Bey and his fellow delegates returned to Constantinople, they claimed that the armistice did not constitute a surrender and pictured its terms as far more lenient than they actually were.[20] In doing so they sowed the seeds of later disillusion and discontent.

While the armistice negotiations were going on, Talaat convened a meeting of close political associates at Enver's villa to found an underground organization designed to protect those Young Turkey leaders who were to remain in the country from possible Allied reprisals, in case there should be any, and also to lay the ground for armed resistance to Allied terms should that prove necessary. Underground cells were organized in Constantinople and thereafter throughout the provinces.

For themselves, Enver, Talaat, and Djemal made arrangements (of which the Grand Vizier was aware) to escape;[21] and on 2 November the ex-rulers of Constantinople fled with their German allies. The following day, 3 November, the Grand Vizier went through the motions of demanding that the Germans return the fugitives, but Germany was disintegrating and the fugitives had disappeared.

IV

Clemenceau, the French Premier, was enraged at Britain's having made unilateral decisions at Mudros, and protested vehemently at a session of the Supreme War Council of the Allies at the Quai d'Orsay on 30 October. But Lloyd George, according to observers, gave back better than he got. Colonel House, Woodrow Wilson's emissary, said of the two prime ministers that "they bandied words like fish-wives, at least Lloyd George did."[22]

Lloyd George told Clemenceau and the others that

> except for Great Britain no one had contributed anything more than a handful of black troops to the expedition in Palestine ... The British had now some 500,000 men on Turkish soil. The British had captured three or four Turkish Armies and had incurred hundreds of thousands of casualties in the war with Turkey. The other governments had only put in a few nigger policemen to see that we did not steal the Holy Sepulchre! When, however, it came to signing an armistice, all this fuss was made.[23]

Balfour pointed out that Franchet d'Esperey had negotiated the Bulgarian armistice without consulting Britain, and that Calthorpe had been no less entitled to negotiate the Turkish armistice without consulting France. Clemenceau took counsel with his Foreign Minister and, in the end, agreed that as the Armistice of Mudros was already signed, there was nothing further to be done about it; he would consider the matter closed.

On 12 November 1918, almost two weeks after the Turkish armistice was signed and the day after the armistice on the western front, a squadron under the command of Admiral Calthorpe entered the straits of the Dardanelles, passing close to the ruined site of ancient Troy,* and steamed in triumph toward Constantinople— under the British flag.

V

One of the British Prime Minister's reasons for acting quickly in the Turkish matter was that he wanted to settle things before the United

---

* Three thousand years before, Troy had seen another wartime European alliance come to grief when Agamemnon, the leader of the alliance, did what Britain did aboard the *Agamemnon*: he withheld a victory prize that previously had been awarded to an ally.

States intervened. An entry for 6 October in the diary of Maurice Hankey, Secretary to the War Cabinet, records an unusually frank statement by the Prime Minister of what he intended to do.

Ll G took a very *intransigeant* attitude and wanted us to go back on the Sykes-Picot agreement, so as to get Palestine for us and to bring Mosul into the British zone, and even to keep the French out of Syria. He also had some subtle dodge for asking America to take Palestine and Syria, in order to render the French more anxious to give us Palestine, so that they might have an excuse of [for] keeping Syria. He was also very contemptuous of President Wilson and anxious to arrange the division of Turkey between France, Italy, and G.B. before speaking to America. He also thought it would attract less attention to our enormous gains in the war if we swallowed our share of Turkey now, and the German colonies later.[24]

Balfour took a much different point of view. When the French suggested doing what Lloyd George had in mind—settling matters before the Americans arrived—Balfour thought the suggestion little short of insane. "Their deliberate effort to exclude the Americans from any effective share in the world settlement is . . . neither in our interest nor in that of the French themselves . . . House is undoubtedly anxious to work with us as closely as he can and it would be fatal to give him the impression that we were settling or had the least desire to settle great questions behind his back."[25] Balfour believed that the stability of the peace settlement would require American participation. Unlike the Prime Minister, he was not only sincere in offering the United States the mandate for Palestine, but believed it vital that she should be made to accept it.

Leo Amery, of the War Office and the War Cabinet secretariat, who had become politically close to the Prime Minister, feared rather than hoped that the United States might accept such an offer if it were made. He wrote to the Zionist leader Dr Chaim Weizmann to ask him to work against a U.S. trusteeship, and secured a statement from Dr Weizmann that he agreed with Amery that Britain would be a better choice as the mandatory power.[26]

However, Maurice Hankey, Secretary to the War Cabinet and Amery's immediate superior, was in favor of a U.S. trusteeship as a way for Britain to secure the strategic benefit of excluding any potential enemy from Palestine without assuming the burden of doing so herself. He told Lloyd George that he wanted the United States to have Palestine "with the object of creating a buffer state to cover Egypt."[27] Implicit in his suggestion was the old Kitchener notion that Palestine was of no value in herself. Lloyd George, of course, disagreed.

VI

On 1 December 1918 Clemenceau met in London with Lloyd George at 10 Downing Street. It was a month after the armistices, and a couple of months before the peace conferences were to open in Paris. It was not until the end of December that the President of the United States was to visit London and outline his idealistic vision of the future; there was time to reach private agreements before then. The two prime ministers met alone and neither took notes. An account of what occurred was supplied in writing to the British Cabinet some eight months later by Balfour, who presumably had it from Lloyd George. Later it was confirmed in Lloyd George's memoirs of the peace treaties.

In the course of a conversation that began with European questions, the subject of the Middle East was raised. Clemenceau asked what modifications of the French claims were desired by Britain. Lloyd George replied: "Mosul."[*] Clemenceau said, "You shall have it. Anything else?" Lloyd George replied, "Palestine." Again Clemenceau said, "You shall have it."[28] A man of his word, Clemenceau kept to it through all the bitter wrangling of the peace conferences, despite the fact that there was no written confirmation of his concessions and even though the British did not recognize that he expected to receive compensation for them.[**]

Throughout his long political life, it had been Clemenceau's policy to defer to Britain in the Middle East in order to secure her support in Europe against Germany; and that is what the French Premier seems to have believed that he had accomplished on 1 December. Apparently Clemenceau believed—wrongly, as it turned out—that he had obtained at least the tacit agreement of Lloyd George to support France's claims in Europe in return for Clemenceau's express agreement to grant Britain's claims in the Middle East.

But in fact the two prime ministers had not even reached an agreement about the Middle East on 1 December. It transpired over the course of the next few months that Lloyd George had not presented all of his Middle Eastern claims when asked by Clemenceau to do so on 1 December; in addition to those he mentioned, he also wanted France to relinquish her claim to Syria.

---

[*] Mosul, commercial center of the oil-rich region that is now northern Iraq, had been promised to France in the Sykes-Picot negotiations (1916) by Sykes and Kitchener.

[**] In French political circles, it was believed that Lloyd George had given assurances in return—though it is not clear what they were supposed to have been.

In this Lloyd George was not pursuing a purely personal foreign policy; on 2 December—the day following the Lloyd George-Clemenceau meeting—Lord Curzon told the Eastern Committee of the Cabinet that he believed it was imperative to exclude France from Syria. Curzon, who was chairman of the committee—which the Cabinet had entrusted with the task of redefining Britain's goals in the Middle East—fell back on the logic of the Great Game in which he had earlier played so conspicuous a role. Former Viceroy of India and traveler along the then-expanding Russian frontier, he had believed earlier, and now had come to believe again, that Britain's strategic goal was to prevent any Great Power from cutting the road to India. There was no reason to believe that France, Britain's European partner, had any intention of interfering with Britain's road to the East. But possession of Syria would put France in a *position* to do so; and indeed would make France the only Great Power that could mount such a threat.

As the General Staff argued in a memorandum of 9 December 1918, "It is difficult to see how any arrangement could be more objectionable from the military point of view than the Sykes-Picot Agreement of 1916, by which an enterprising and ambitious foreign power is placed on interior lines with reference to our position in the Middle East."[29] That was Curzon's view, too.

Lord Curzon told the Eastern Committee that

> A good deal of my public life has been spent in connection with the political ambitions of France in almost every distant region where the French have sway. We have been brought, for reasons of national safety, into an alliance with the French, which I hope will last, but their national character is different from ours, and their political interests collide with ours in many cases. I am seriously afraid that the great power from whom we have most to fear in future is France.[30]

Curzon took an especially spacious view of the area from which France therefore had to be excluded in Asia. The Chief of the Imperial General Staff, Sir Henry Wilson, who saw things similarly, wrote that, "from the left bank of the Don to India is our interest and preserve."[31] Balfour was skeptical; the gateways to India, he remarked, were "getting further and further from India, and I do not know how far west they are going to be brought by the General Staff."[32]

The Prime Minister was not of a mind to ground his policies in any such geopolitical theory. So far as one can tell, Lloyd George was simply trying to keep as much captured territory as he could; in the Syria matter, he appears to have been merely an opportunist indulging in unsystematic overreaching.

VII

Support for the Prime Minister's objectives came from the Kitchener loyalists in the Middle East, who had been saying for more than a year that Britain had to have Palestine, using the pretext that she needed it in order to reconcile Arabs and Jews. A few months after the Armistice of Mudros, General Gilbert Clayton enlarged on this line of argument. In a memorandum that appears to have reached the Prime Minister's desk, he claimed that after some months of experience in occupation of former Ottoman territories, it had become clear to him that in practice the commitments made by Britain to France—not merely in Palestine, but also in Syria—had become incompatible with those made to Arabism and Zionism. Friction was bound to continue and to create dangers for Britain. A choice, he wrote, had to be made. Clayton argued that if Syria had to be given to France, then Britain should renounce interest in Palestine in favor of the United States or some other country willing to assume the burden. The better alternative, however, would be for Britain to take over the government both of Palestine and Syria, with due regard to both Jewish and Arab aspirations, and to reward France elsewhere, perhaps by giving her Constantinople.[33]

In the winter of 1919 the office of the Prime Minister distributed to the British press a confidential background memorandum purporting to show that Feisal's forces "materially assisted" General Allenby in the conquest of Syria and that they entered "the four great inland towns of Syria [Damascus, Homs, Hama, and Aleppo] ahead of General Allenby's other forces" and did so, according to the memorandum, not as foreign invaders from the Hejaz, but as a native force. "The great majority of the Arab troops who thus assisted in liberating Syria were natives of the province."[34] The tendency of the memorandum was to demonstrate that Arabic-speaking Syria had risen up and freed herself, and that it would be contrary to the principles professed by the western democracies to attempt to re-impose foreign rule.

Feisal's Arab corps in the Palestine and Syria campaigns was composed of approximately 3,500 men, but Lloyd George obtained from Feisal a public statement that the Arabs who at one time or another during the war had served or allied with him or his father numbered about 100,000; and in his argument against the French that is the figure the Prime Minister used. Lloyd George knew the figure to be wildly inflated ("Eastern arithmetic is proverbially romantic," he later wrote) and indeed he believed the Arab contribution to the conquest of Palestine and Syria "was almost insignificant."[35] As against the French, however, the Prime Minister argued that he was placed in a difficult position when asked by them to act against his other great ally, Feisal. Feisal and a large army of Syrians had liberated their own country, he claimed, and now administered it, under General Allenby, and Britain could hardly be expected to allow France to move against them. Britain was released from her alliance obligations to France (he was saying in effect) by her alliance obligations to Syria.

At the end of the winter of 1919, Allenby came to lunch with Lloyd George and his secretary, Frances Stevenson, and the latter noted in her diary that "D. [Lloyd George] was urging him to give the French the facts about Syria, that the French would not be tolerated there. I believe he did at a subsequent meeting between P.M. [the Prime Minister], Clemenceau & Winston. The French are very obstinate about Syria & are trying to take the line that the English want it for themselves." She noted that Lloyd George's comment about this was that "France is a poor winner. She does not take her victories well."[36]

Shortly before the Allenby lunch, Lord Milner had written from Paris to the Prime Minister to describe his conversations with Clemenceau. Milner wrote that he told the French Premier "quite frankly that, while we were dissatisfied with the Sykes-Picot scheme which he himself recognized the need of radically altering, we had no desire to play the French out of Syria or to get Syria for ourselves ... The Syrian difficulty was not our doing, but was due to the fact that the French had unfortunately fallen foul of the Arabs. This put us in a very awkward position ..." because the Arabs under Feisal "contributed materially to our victory."

Milner knew that he was not being frank with Clemenceau about British motives and intentions, for he added that "I have almost every other Government authority military and diplomatic against me. I am totally opposed to the idea of trying to diddle the French out of Syria."[37]

Of course Lloyd George claimed—as did Milner in conversation with Clemenceau—that he did not want Syria for Britain, and indeed would refuse a British mandate for it; he was supporting the Arab cause of Feisal. But the Arab cause was a mere façade behind which Britain expected to rule, for, as Clemenceau told Milner—who did not deny it—Feisal did what his British advisers told him to do.[38]

Milner pointed out to Lloyd George that Clemenceau was far more liberal on the Middle Eastern issue than were the government and bureaucracy behind him. It was implicit in Milner's observation that if the French Premier failed to obtain satisfactory terms, he might be replaced by someone with whom it would be far less easy to deal.

In the autumn of 1919 Alfred Mond, the industrialist of Imperial Chemicals whom Lloyd George had brought into his government as

Commissioner of Works, reported that Baron Edmund Rothschild had told him in Paris that French opinion would be alienated by Britain's favoring the Arabs against the French. Mond stressed the "enormous importance of keeping the Anglo-French Alliance intact."[39] But the Prime Minister seemed blind to the danger that he might place that alliance in jeopardy.

Even Sir Mark Sykes, who for years had labored to show that there was room for all to have a fair share in the future of the Middle East, returned from Syria in an apparently changed frame of mind (if Lloyd George's private comments soon afterward are to be believed—and perhaps they should not be). The Prime Minister said that Sykes

> was a worried, anxious man ... He was responsible for the agreement which is causing us all the trouble with the French. We call it the "Sykes-P." agreement. Sykes negotiated it for us with Picot, the Frenchman, who got the better of him. Sykes saw the difficulties in which he had placed us, and was very worried in consequence. I said something to him about the agreement, and at once saw how I had cut him. I am sorry. I wish I had said nothing. I blame myself. He did his best. I did not wish to emphasize his mistake or to make him more miserable.[40]

In a similar vein, T. E. Lawrence concluded that Sykes now wished "to atone" for his previous willingness to share the Middle East with Britain's ally.[41]

If so, Sykes had run out of time. He died in Paris on 16 February 1919, in his room at the Hôtel Lotti, a victim of the world-wide influenza pandemic of 1918–19,[*] whose outbreak was attributed by France to Spain, by Spain to France, by the United States to eastern Europe, by western Europe to America, and by Allenby's armies to the retreating Turks.[43]

---

[*] It killed more than twenty million people, overshadowing the eight and a half million killed in the war. It has been claimed that by 1919 every man, woman, and child on the planet had been infected by the disease.[42]

PART IX

THE TIDE GOES OUT

40

THE TICKING CLOCK

I

Victory in the First World War brought the British Empire to its zenith: with the addition of the territories it had occupied in the Middle East and elsewhere, it had become larger than it—or any other empire—had ever been before. Lloyd George, though his country was war-weary and tired of distant and expensive adventures, sought to hold on to as much as possible of what Britain had gained in the war. That was to be a chief objective in the negotiations he was about to begin with the other Allied and Associated Powers. But before turning to the Peace Conference, the Prime Minister chose to seek a mandate from the electorate.

On the night that the armistice with Germany was signed, the Prime Minister asked only two other politicians to dine with him and with the Chief of the Imperial General Staff, Sir Henry Wilson, at Downing Street. They were Winston Churchill and Churchill's best friend, the brilliant Attorney-General, F. E. Smith. In his diary, Sir Henry Wilson noted that "we discussed many things but principally the General Election!"[1]

With his keen eye for political advantage, the Prime Minister saw a chance to win at the polls by calling an election in the immediate flush of victory. With a renewed and secure parliamentary majority, he hoped to gain time to carry through his programs. He sought his new mandate when his popularity was at its height. At the end of 1918 he was still "the man who won the war." The leader of the Conservative Party spoke for many in saying that "He can be Prime Minister for life if he likes."[2]

The general election took place on 14 December 1918, though to allow time to receive soldiers' ballots, the votes were not counted until 28 December. Liberal Prime Minister Lloyd George and his political partner, the Conservative leader Andrew Bonar Law, led the governmental Coalition. Asquith's wing of the Liberals contested the elections; and Labour also dropped out of the Coalition to do so.

The Coalition scored an overwhelming victory. Even Lloyd George was stunned by its magnitude. Almost 85 percent of those who took their seats in the new House of Commons were his supporters. Asquith's Liberals were crushed by the Coalitionists and Asquith himself lost his seat, as did other prominent leaders of the prewar Liberal Party. The Asquith Liberals were overtaken by Labour, which for the first time could lay claim to be the official Opposition.

The nature of the electorate had been radically transformed by wartime legislation that for the first time gave the vote to women (from the age of thirty) and to all men (from the age of twenty-one). Twenty-one million people were eligible to vote in 1918, as compared with a mere seven and a half million before the war; and both the new working-class and women voters seemed to have radically different ideas about such issues as paying the bills for imperial expansion abroad.

For Lloyd George, a potentially disquieting feature of his spectacular triumph was that the electoral gains for the most part were made by Bonar Law's Conservatives rather than by his own Liberals. Indeed the Conservatives commanded a majority in the new House of Commons. Many of the Conservatives were new men, taking their seats in the House of Commons for the first time; and, of these, many were businessmen who tended toward the right wing of their party. Their political agenda was not the same as the Prime Minister's.

For the moment, however, the Prime Minister received full support from Andrew Bonar Law and therefore felt politically secure. Lloyd George had formed a close working partnership with the Conservative leader that suited both men well. Modest and shy, Bonar Law was happy to let the exuberant and colorful Prime Minister take the lead and the limelight. "I tell you we must never let the little man go," said Bonar Law to one of his lieutenants, in reference to the diminutive occupant of 10 Downing Street, "His way and ours lie side by side in the future."[3]

II

Winston Churchill, a 45-year-old politician trying to live down his past, was asked by Lloyd George to serve as Secretary of State for War and for Air in the postwar Cabinet. The Prime Minister tendered his offer of the two ministries ("Of course there will be but one salary!") on 9 January 1919.[4] Churchill accepted the offer the following day. As Minister of Munitions he had not been a member of the War Cabinet, so his entry into the War Office marked his return to the inner circles of government. Predictably, the appointment aroused violent opposition.

A Conservative newspaper commented that "we have watched his brilliant and erratic course in the confident expectation that sooner or later he would make a mess of anything he undertook. Character is destiny; there is some tragic flaw in Mr Churchill which determines him on every occasion in the wrong course . . . It is an appointment which makes us tremble for the future."[5]

Churchill, who had to overcome a reputation—deserved or not—for squandering the resources of the country, set out to show that he could be economical: he argued that ambitious policies ought to be scaled back if the resources to support them were not available. But when he suggested that Britain might lack the money and the manpower to back up Lloyd George's plans for Britain to replace the Ottoman Empire in the Middle East, the Prime Minister pointedly ignored him.

The Prime Minister claimed that Britain was entitled to play the dominant role in the Middle East, recalling that at one time or another two and a half million British troops had been sent there, and that a quarter of a million had been killed or wounded; while the French, Gallipoli apart, had suffered practically no casualties in the Middle East, and the Americans had not been there at all.[6] At the Peace Conference, Lloyd George argued that his claim was based on the 1,084,000 British and imperial troops occupying the Ottoman Empire.[7] In the occupation forces, as he pointed out, there were no non-British contingents of meaningful size.

During the war, according to the Secretary of the Cabinet, the Prime Minister had "never lost sight of the advantages he might hope to derive at the eventual peace conference from the acquisition of the territory of our enemies."[8] Lloyd George had said to a friend that "once we were in military possession it would make a great difference."[9]

What Winston Churchill insistently repeated was that this situation—the occupation of the Middle East by a million British soldiers—was only temporary; the troops demanded to be brought home. This was the first problem with which Churchill had to grapple as War Minister, and he contended that it imposed new priorities on the government as a whole.

On 10 January 1919, Churchill's first day in office as Secretary of State for War, the Chief of the Imperial General Staff urgently consulted him about a crisis in the ranks: soldiers had demonstrated, demanding immediate demobilization. Disorder was widespread, and Churchill feared that the unrest might lead to a Bolshevik uprising; later he wrote that such fears were valid at the time because "So many frightful things had happened, and such tremendous collapses of established structures had been witnessed, the nations had suffered so long, that a tremor, and indeed a spasm, shook the foundations of every State."[10] Churchill believed that the troops had to be brought home as fast as the railroads and troopships could bring them.

A fortnight later 5,000 British troops at Calais mutinied to demand demobilization, but Churchill was ahead of them with his solution, for he had already prepared a demobilization plan of evident fairness; and under his direction it was rapidly carried into effect throughout 1919.

But demobilization threatened to prejudice Britain's chances of imposing peace terms. Field Marshal Sir Douglas Haig, Commander-in-Chief of the British Expeditionary Force in Europe, told Churchill on 15 January 1919 that the existing British army "was rapidly disappearing," and unless an army of occupation was created, "the Germans would be in a position to negotiate another kind of peace."[11] The same would be true of the Turks. A few days later Churchill submitted a memorandum to the Prime Minister in which he argued that "Unless we are to be defrauded of the fruits of victory and ... to throw away all that we have won with so much cost and trouble, we must provide for a good many months to come Armies of Occupation for the enemy's territory. These armies must be strong enough to extract from the Germans, Turks and others" the terms demanded.[12]

To give the Prime Minister time to impose his peace terms, Churchill attempted to maintain armies of occupation with newly inducted troops, on the basis of Britain's first peacetime draft; but the Prime Minister, mindful of domestic political realities, ordered a reduction in the size of Churchill's armies. Later Churchill was obliged to promise that conscription would come to an end by March 1920. Though he warned the House of Commons, "Do not disband your army until you have got your terms,"[13] political considerations forced a demobilization so rapid that, by October 1919, Churchill admitted that "the Army had melted away."[14] Yet in the East, as will be seen presently, Britain had still not got her terms. In 1914 Churchill had been the Cabinet minister most keenly aware that the timetables of mobilization were driving the Great Powers into a world war; in 1919 he was the Cabinet minister most keenly aware that the timetables of demobilization were forcing the empire to abandon the field before victory had been secured.

He also saw that, in order for Britain to live within her means, the government urgently needed to cut expenses. Churchill promised the Commons that "I shall do my utmost to secure substantial reductions in military forces, for without those reductions good finance is impossible."[15] In fact in the years to come he slashed expenditures to a mere 17 percent of what they had been, from 604 million pounds in 1919 to 111 million pounds in 1922.[16]

Another problem, he argued, had to be faced: bringing the British troops home left the Middle East in the hands of Indian soldiers. British India, during the 1914 war, had sent more than a million troops overseas, many of them Moslem.[17] At the beginning of 1920 Churchill pointed out to the Cabinet the political consequences of the fact that these predominantly Moslem soldiers were the occupation troops who had been left in place, entrusted with the distasteful task of coercing fellow Moslems. Churchill wrote that "All our limited means of getting the Middle East to settle down quietly are comprised in the use of Indian troops. We must not do anything that will raise Indian sentiment against the use of these troops or affect their own loyalty."[18] Since Britain now had to rely on her Moslem troops, her policies in the Middle East would have to be modified so as not to offend Moslem sentiment; and he argued—though with little effect on the Prime Minister—that this pointed toward the need for a friendlier policy toward the Turks.

III

David Lloyd George, flowing with energy despite his arduous years of wartime leadership, formed his postwar Coalition government a week before his fifty-sixth birthday. The items on his immediate personal agenda were in the realm of foreign policy. He arranged to spend much of his time abroad, redrawing the political map of the world. To free himself to concentrate on foreign policy, he left the management of domestic policy and the House of Commons to Bonar Law.

But Bonar Law proved unequal to the task; he failed to win time for the Prime Minister to concentrate on reconstructing the world undisturbed. It was not only that the war in Ireland had resumed, but that the social and economic conflicts within Britain had moved out of the polling stations and into the streets and factories. Management and labor, each trying to maintain its wartime gains even though the economy was shrinking, turned to industrial warfare a month after the election. Violence broke out. The government took counsel with the army and naval chiefs of staff on measures to suppress what they—haunted by Bolshevism—feared might be a working-class revolution.

In 1920 and 1921 the British economy collapsed. Prices collapsed, exports slumped, companies went out of business, and the country was gripped by mass unemployment on a scale never known before. Politicians began to question whether Britain could afford foreign policy adventures in places like Palestine and Mesopotamia and began to question whether she could even afford measures that were designed to buy social peace at home. The Prime Minister had espoused a positive Liberal program of housing and social reform—in large part, it was in the hands of his principal parliamentary leader, Dr Christopher Addison—but he was driven to abandon the program, and Dr Addison, in the face of Tory attacks on government wastefulness. Yet it had always been Lloyd George's view that "the way to prevent the spread of the revolutionary spirit was to embark at once on large schemes of social progress."[19] In his view, to give up such schemes was to leave the door open for agitation and violence; yet that is what he did rather than abandon his imperial ambitions in the Middle East.

It was against this background of a disappearing army, a deteriorating economy, and a disintegrating society that the Prime Minister—a man who had worked miracles during the war—concentrated on redrawing the map of the Middle East and of the world, while Winston Churchill, unheeded, continued to warn that time was running out.

41

BETRAYAL

I

The specific terms of the Middle East agreement upon which the Prime Minister and his Allied colleagues finally settled proved to be less important than the process by which they were reached. One aspect of that process was that it took a long time, during which circumstances, as will be seen, were to change for the worse. Friendly foreign leaders were replaced by others less cooperative; quarrels developed between former allies; defeated enemies regrouped and revived; and the British army—it was Churchill's constant theme— was dwindling away and losing its ability to hold on to its conquests.

Another aspect of the negotiations that was to weaken the eventual settlement was the general sense that they were conducted in bad faith. The negotiations—to be described presently—were shaped by the Prime Minister's strategy of playing off the United States against Italy and France, while counting on the United States to protect Britain against possible future threats from Soviet Russia or from a revived and rearmed Germany. It was not until the 1918–19 nego-tiating season had given way to that of 1919–20 that Lloyd George discovered that the United States was not going to be Britain's—or anybody's—ally: she was going to withdraw from world affairs and "entangling alliances." As will be seen, Lloyd George was then obliged to reverse course, seeking a French alliance since an American one was unavailable; and that, in turn, required him to reverse the course of his anti-French policy in the Middle East. But by then the damage to the Anglo-French alliance had already been done.

In the end the British leaders felt a sense of having been betrayed by the Americans, while the Americans felt that the British had cynically betrayed the ideals for which the world war supposedly had been fought. As a result of Lloyd George's lack of scruple and Woodrow Wilson's lack of skill, the negotiation of a Middle Eastern settlement began badly and ended worse.

389

II

So determined was Woodrow Wilson to play a personal role in formulating the provisions of the peace treaties that he came to Europe to negotiate them himself—the first American president to leave the United States during his term of office. His unprecedented move made the Allies uneasy; as Clemenceau observed, he and his fellow prime ministers, as heads of government, would be outranked by the President who also served as head of state. By right of precedence, the President therefore would be entitled to chair the Peace Conference.

Suggestions were made in the press and elsewhere that Wilson should stay home to devote himself full time to winning support in the Senate and in the country for his peace terms, leaving his adviser, Edward House, to represent him in Europe. The President rejected such suggestions and, perhaps because of them, began to question the good faith of Colonel House. Crossing the ocean on the liner *George Washington* in December 1918, Wilson and his many American advisers arrived at Brest on Friday the 13th.

Everywhere he went, Wilson met with a tumultuous welcome. John Maynard Keynes wrote that "When President Wilson left Washington he enjoyed a prestige and a moral influence throughout the world unequalled in history."[1] Nothing, however, could have provided a better description of what was going to happen at the Peace Conference than Wilson's speeches about what was not going to happen. Peoples and provinces were indeed "bartered about from sovereignty to sovereignty as if they were chattels or pawns in a game." It was not the case that every settlement was "made in the interest and for the benefit of the population concerned"; on the contrary such settlements were made (though Wilson said they would not be) in order to provide an "adjustment or compromise of claims among rival states" seeking "exterior influence or mastery."* Not even his own country was prepared to follow the path that he had marked out.

In November 1918, at roughly the time the Armistice agreements were signed, the President's party had lost control of the United States Senate in the midterm elections. The Senate Foreign Relations Committee therefore passed into the hands of the President's adversaries. Even before the Peace Conference began, the President accordingly was on notice that he would face problems in securing ratification of whatever terms he might negotiate. Nothing in the President's unbending nature disposed him to make the concessions or to engage in the political deal-making that would have mitigated these political problems at home.

---

* For Wilson's speeches, see Chapter 31.

Abroad it became clear almost immediately that he had not thought
through how he was going to carry into effect the generous and
idealistic principles that he had articulated. He arrived in Europe
with many general opinions but without specific proposals for dealing
with the matters that were to be decided. In his memorable portrait
of Wilson, Keynes pointed to what followed: "As the President had
thought nothing out, the Council was generally working on the basis
of a French or British draft."[2] Lacking both detailed knowledge and
negotiating skills, Wilson was reduced to an obstructive role, often
refusing to be carried along by his colleagues, but unable to carry
them along with him.

House advised compromise—with the Allies abroad, and with the
Senate at home. Wilson spurned the advice, and turned against the
intimate friend who offered it. The President broke with House;
from mid-1919 on he refused to see him again.

III

Lloyd George's Middle Eastern strategy was to direct the Americans'
anti-imperialist ire against the claims presented by Italy and France,
distracting the President from areas in which he might make difficulties for Britain. Maurice Hankey, British Secretary to the Peace
Conference, recorded in his diary even before the conference convened that Lloyd George "means to try and get President Wilson
into German East Africa in order to ride him off Palestine."[3] In fact
much of the time no special effort was needed: European issues inevitably were given a high, and other issues a relatively low, priority.
The question of Russia and the fear that Bolshevik revolutions would
break out throughout Europe haunted the Peace Conference. The
other great question was the future of Germany. The future of the
Ottoman Empire ranked as a lesser issue and Wilson was too pre-
occupied to pay full attention to the Middle East. When Wilson did
turn to these matters, Lloyd George adroitly excluded from the conference agenda questions about the British-occupied areas of the
Middle East, placing them beyond the scope of the President's scrutiny. At the same time, the Prime Minister diverted the President's
anti-imperialist energies into critical scrutiny of the ambitions of
Britain's rivals in the Middle East—her wartime Allies.

IV

Italy had agreed to come into the war on the Allied side in return for
British and French promises of territorial gain that eventually included a share in the partition of the Ottoman Empire. The promise

of Turkish territory was embodied and defined in a treaty signed by Italy, Britain, and France, known as the Agreement of St Jean de Maurienne, concluded in the middle of 1917. By its terms, the agreement was subject to the assent of the Russians. Since the Russian government had been overthrown by the Bolsheviks, the agreement had never come into effect. The Italians claimed the territories nonetheless, asking for equal treatment. As one Italian senator put it, "If the others have nothing, we will demand nothing."[4]

Italy had been promised a portion of Anatolia—Asia Minor, as it was sometimes called—if she came into the war, but there were no Italian communities there for her to protect, and no other communities whose interests she purported to sponsor. Indeed, in terms of Woodrow Wilson's self-determination principles, there was no reason for Italy to occupy any part of Asia Minor at all. Prime Minister Emanuele Orlando seemed to recognize the difficulties of his case, but Italian public opinion was caught up in a gust of nationalist frenzy, as were Parliament and the Cabinet, as represented by Foreign Minister Baron Sidney Sonnino.[5] Orlando and Sonnino had reason to fear that a failure to persuade the Allies to honor wartime promises to Italy would undermine their political position at home, and felt driven to take action.

Starting in the middle of March 1919, Italian troops began a program of landing in southern Anatolia at Adalia (the present-day Antalya), supposedly to restore order, and then re-embarking. Eventually they stopped re-embarking, and after two months they had troops on a more or less permanent basis at Adalia and also, further up the coast, at Marmaris.[6] The Allies feared that, having landed, the Italians were about to march inland to occupy the entire section of Anatolia to which they claimed they were entitled.

Lloyd George pushed the United States into the lead on this question. Woodrow Wilson appealed to Italian public opinion to exert a moderating influence on Orlando's territorial demands in Europe and the Middle East; whereupon, on 24 April 1919, the Italian delegation left the Peace Conference to return home to seek domestic support. In the absence of the Italians, the United States, France, and Britain turned against them. Italy, though yesterday's ally, suddenly loomed as an imperialist aggressor posing threats to the peace; and as the Allies banded together against her, Clemenceau remarked: "What a beginning for the League of Nations!"[7]

On 2 May 1919, outraged by reports of Italian ships being sent to Smyrna, President Wilson offered to send in the American navy, and spoke of the possibility of the United States going to war against Italy in order to defeat aggression.[8] By 5 May, as Wilson and others told tales of atrocities they claimed were being committed by the Italians, the Allies were at fever pitch, and determined to reach a decision before the Italian delegation returned on 7 May. Following a suggestion by Lloyd George, they agreed to ask Greece, which was near at hand, to land troops at Smyrna, supposedly to keep order, but in fact to pre-empt the Italians. The Greeks landed their troops on 15 May.

Though intended by the Allies as a temporary measure directed solely against the Italians, the Greek landing assumed a different— and more permanent—character from the start. Maurice Hankey, head of the British secretariat at the Peace Conference, believed that the Smyrna enclave, where Greek troops had landed, ought to be detached from Turkey and incorporated into Greece.[9] In this view he was not alone; Lloyd George and Wilson were enchanted by Eleutherios Venizelos, the Greek Prime Minister, and were won over to his vision of Greece's historic mission.

Venizelos had established an astonishing hold over the imaginations of his fellow Allied leaders; but even had he not done so, his case was strong where Italy's was weak. His position was intrinsically appealing both to Wilson's sense of America's principles and to Lloyd George's sense of Britain's interests. Venizelos's claims to Anatolia, unlike Italy's, were based on population as well as history. Smyrna, the coastal metropolis, was a Greek city, and had been a center of Greek civilization since remotest antiquity. According to the then-current (1911) edition of the *Encyclopaedia Britannica*, of its population of 250,000, "fully a half is Greek." The *Britannica* added that "Modern Smyrna is in all but government a Christian town . . ." The notion of transferring its government from Moslem Turkey to Christian Greece appealed strongly to Lloyd George's Christian and Hellenist values. It appealed, too, to President Wilson's principles of self-determination.

Like Italy, Greece had been late in entering the war on the Allied side but, unlike Italy, Greece had been regarded by the British as a client and protégé since the early days of the Great Game. The British navy, at the battle of Navarino in 1827, had won the war for Greek independence, and the two countries had traditions of friendship for one another. Lloyd George saw Venizelos's Greece as Britain's natural ally.*

Italy and Greece had advanced conflicting claims: they eyed essentially the same areas of the expiring Ottoman Empire. In sending in Greek troops, Wilson and the Allied leaders intended to keep the Italians from seizing these areas before a decision could be reached as to who should have them. But the effect of doing so was to deny the

---

* It will be remembered that Venizelos offered to bring Greece into the Ottoman war as Britain's ally as far back as the summer of 1914. That was even before Turkey and Britain had definitely decided to go to war. See page 74.

Italian claim and to favor that of Greece. On the British side there
were those who were dismayed by this outcome, but it fitted with
Lloyd George's view of Britain's interests and principles.

Accomplishing many purposes at once, Lloyd George was able to
divert Woodrow Wilson's attention from Britain's designs to those of
Italy, by letting the American President take the lead in imposing
what was really Britain's policy in Smyrna. At the showdown with
the Italian leaders, Wilson castigated them for their "imperialist
ambitions."[10] Taking a friendlier line, Lloyd George instead appealed
to their nobility, in a speech of such eloquence that it moved
Orlando, the Italian Prime Minister, to tears. Orlando went to the
window and sobbed emotionally. Across the street, an observer who
caught sight of him asked, "What have they been doing to the poor
old gentleman?"[11]

What they were doing to him was presently made clear. On 19
June 1919, weakened by his failure to achieve Italy's territorial
ambitions at the Peace Conference, Orlando was obliged to resign as
Italy's Prime Minister.

V

Lloyd George's second diversionary project for Wilson was to turn
him against the French claim to Syria.

The American President was allowed to participate in the Ottoman
negotiations even though the United States had never joined in the
war against Turkey. Although Woodrow Wilson's Fourteen Points
were not applicable to the Ottoman settlement (unlike Germany,
Turkey had not been allowed to surrender on the basis that any of
the points would be applied), they were an expression of the political
philosophy with which he approached public issues. Lloyd George
recognized this; and when President Wilson turned to the Arabic-
speaking Ottoman provinces, the British Prime Minister shrewdly
diverted his attention from Britain's designs to those of France by
directing his attention to the French threat to Syrian independence—a threat that ran counter to Wilson's points and principles.

The British delegation did not go so far as to pretend to the
President or to the other delegates that Feisal had liberated
Damascus. General Allenby accurately informed the conferees that
"Shortly after the capture of Damascus, Feisal had been allowed to
occupy and administer the city."[12] The British did pretend, however,
that Feisal and his followers had played a substantial role in the
liberation of Syria. The British contended that Feisal had therefore
earned the right to serve as the ruler of a free Syria; and specifically

that he should be free to reject French advice and advisers if he chose to do so. As presented by Lloyd George, this was the issue of the dispute. According to the Prime Minister the parties to the dispute were Feisal's Syria and Clemenceau's France. Britain, he claimed, was a friend to both parties and therefore would not take sides.

Wilson was naturally disposed to support the Syrians' right to choose their own government and destiny. He also could not help but be favorably influenced by Feisal's willingness to cooperate in achieving a settlement. Feisal met with Felix Frankfurter, a representative of the American Zionist leader, Louis Brandeis; and, after the meeting, Frankfurter reported to Brandeis that "The Arab question has ceased to exist as a difficulty to the realisation of our programme before the Peace Conference."[13] Indeed, as Arab representative at the Peace Conference, Feisal told the conferees that he excluded Palestine from the area he claimed for Arab independence. Feisal's apparent reasonableness in dealing with Jewish claims contrasted sharply with Clemenceau's hard line in dealing with Arab claims to independence—claims that Clemenceau took to be a British-inspired sham.

The British said that they were ready to allow the French whatever influence over Feisal that they were able to exert. That, in the French view, was thoroughly dishonest, for Feisal, as everybody knew, refused to accept French direction or influence. It was evident that he was beholden to the British. He was on their payroll; his delegation's expenses were paid by Britain. At the Peace Conference he went everywhere with his British liaison officer, T. E. Lawrence, who was his friend, adviser, confidant, translator, and inseparable companion.

Recognizing that to accept Feisal as Syria's spokesman was in effect to concede Syria to Britain, the French produced Syrian leaders of their own. The most prominent of them had lived in France for many years, some of them under Quai d'Orsay sponsorship. They claimed that, despite similarities in language and religion, Syrians were not Arabs, and deserved a country of their own under French guidance.

Lloyd George counterattacked by linking British cooperation with France against Germany in Europe to resolution of the Syrian question. The German issue was of overriding importance to Clemenceau, as he had demonstrated at the end of 1918 when he conceded Palestine and Mosul to Lloyd George in order to cement the Anglo-French alliance.

Clemenceau had already gone almost to the limit of what was politically possible for him. When he accepted Feisal as leader of

Syria, subject to Feisal's meeting French terms, he went the whole way. In asking him to accept not merely Feisal but also full Arab independence, the British were asking him to go further and ruin himself politically; yet he needed Britain's help against Germany and, in coupling the issues, Lloyd George placed him in an agonizing position. During the course of their conferences the French Prime Minister often erupted into frustrated rage. Once he was driven to such anger that he offered Lloyd George the choice of sword or pistols.[14]

It was not as though he had not made his position plain. He had told one of Lloyd George's advisers that French political opinion would not permit the abandonment of claims to Syria: "he personally was not particularly concerned with the Near East," but France "always had played a great part there, and . . . French public opinion expected a settlement which was consonant with France's position. He could not . . . make any settlement which did not comply with this condition."[15] This was no exaggeration, as was demonstrated when officials of the French Foreign Ministry organized a press campaign against their own Prime Minister in *Le Temps* and *Le Journal des Débats*, alleging that he was giving away too much to the British.[16] But Lloyd George went on pushing for more concessions, and went on breaking what Clemenceau had regarded as firm British commitments to France. "I won't give way on anything any more," Clemenceau said, "Lloyd George is a cheat."[17]

It remains unclear why Lloyd George was so determined to exclude France from the Middle East. With respect to French claims to Syria, and to Cilicia, the adjacent area just to the north, Lloyd George's stated position was that British troops would have to remain in occupation in order to keep the peace between the French and Feisal's Arabs;[18] but it was a somewhat one-sided peace that Britain imposed. A small French force continued to occupy a narrow coastal area centered on Beirut. From Feisal's area, Arab units continued to mount hit-and-run guerrilla raids against the French. The presence of Allenby's British troops protected Feisal's area from French retaliation.

General Allenby warned that war might break out between the Arabs and the French. President Wilson appeared to take the warning seriously, and reacted by making a proposal that took Lloyd George and Clemenceau by surprise: a commission should be sent out to the Middle East to ascertain the wishes of its inhabitants. The proposal was viewed as childish by French and British career officials, who did not believe that public opinion, in the European or American sense, existed in the Middle East. For Lloyd George the proposal was dismaying because sending out a commission would take time. Nonetheless, the British Prime Minister tried to make the best of it by attempting to get the commission to focus exclusively on the claims of France—and the resistance to those claims by the Arabs whom France sought to rule.

The British, like the French, had staked out an enormous claim in the Middle East, but Lloyd George successfully kept the British claims from being scrutinized. When President Wilson's Commission of Inquiry went out to ascertain the wishes of the Middle Eastern peoples, it did not go to Mesopotamia, where British India had instituted direct rule. The British, who had declared Egypt a protectorate, also succeeded in securing American recognition for this extension of their rule, which had the additional effect of keeping Egypt off the agenda of the Peace Conference. In early 1919 Persia was also added to the British sphere as an informal protectorate; and that, too, was accomplished outside the Peace Conference by a Convention between the two countries signed on 19 August 1919. Britain's control of the Persian Gulf sheikhdoms, rounded out and regularized during the war, was not discussed or contested in Paris; nor was Britain's paramount position in Arabia, secured by alliances with Hussein and with Ibn Saud that made them her protégés. It had been agreed in advance between Lloyd George and Clemenceau that Palestine should be awarded to Britain, so that Syria was left as the only contested issue on the commission's agenda.

As the wrangling at the Peace Conference became more embittered, Clemenceau refused to send out French participants to the Commission; and Lloyd George, suddenly worried that he might have gone too far in estranging France, decided that the British participants in that case would not be sent along either. Thus the American commissioners—Henry King, the president of Oberlin College in Ohio, and Charles Crane, a Chicago businessman and contributor to the Democratic Party—proceeded on their mission alone.

The King-Crane Commission traveled to Syria and Palestine, where British officers were often in a position to determine who should testify and who should not. The French were enraged by the British manipulation and organization of witnesses and testimony. In the end it did not matter: the report of the commission was never considered, it played no official role, and its text was not made public until more than three years later. The King-Crane inquiry increased the animosity between France and Britain, and it aroused such false hopes among various groups of Arabs that Gertrude Bell, a specialist in Middle Eastern affairs, denounced it as a criminal deception.[19] Above all, its proceedings had taken too much time—and Lloyd George was running out of time.

VI

Britain had never gone ahead with the notion of an American Mandate for Palestine but had proposed that the United States should assume the League of Nations Mandates to occupy and govern portions of Anatolia, Constantinople, the Dardanelles, Armenia, and the Caucasus. In the end these narrowed down to Constantinople, the Dardanelles, and Armenia.

There were two reasons why Britain wanted the United States to assume these Mandates: it would implicate the United States in the Middle Eastern settlement so as to insure that she would help to support its terms; and it would station the United States in the front lines if Soviet Russia were ever to attack Turkey.

Wilson and the other Americans in Paris made it clear that it would be difficult to persuade Congress to accept the Mandates. Nonetheless the President undertook to try. That proved to be Lloyd George's undoing; long after it had become clear that Wilson was going to fail, the Prime Minister was obliged to wait for an official American response that seemed to be a long time coming.

On 29 June 1919, a bit more than six months after he had arrived in Europe for the Peace Conference, the President returned to the United States for the last time. Carrying his campaign directly to the people, Wilson collapsed from exhaustion, and went into a state of partial physical and political paralysis. In the Senate his program, including ratification of the Treaty of Versailles and American adherence to the League of Nations, went down to defeat, as the President committed one political blunder after another, driving even potential supporters to oppose him.

Wilson had lost control over the left side of his body, and his thinking, too, may well have been impaired. Despite his incapacity, he and his wife refused to turn over his authority to others. Years later—long after Wilson's death—Lloyd George wrote of his illness that "The only faculty that remained unimpaired to the end . . . was his abnormal stubbornness."[20]

From July to November of 1919, all Ottoman decisions were put off until it was learned what position the United States would take on assuming the Mandates for Constantinople and Armenia. But, after his partial physical recovery, President Wilson did not get around to proposing an American Mandate for Armenia until 24 May 1920. The Senate rejected his proposal the following week.

Maurice Hankey noted in his diary that "We cannot get on with the Turkish treaty until we know whether the Americans will accept a mandate in Turkey."[21] In his note he suggested the possibility that an incident might occur in Anatolia unless a treaty were concluded speedily. Lloyd George complained that Wilson had placed the Allies "in an impossible position."[22]

The breakdown of his American ally drove Lloyd George to make his peace with France and Italy; but the British Prime Minister found that he now had to contend with Allied leaders with whom it was far less easy to deal. The new Italian leaders were inclined to look for commercial rather than territorial concessions in Turkey; they therefore were disposed rather to oppose than to participate in Lloyd George's proposed partition of Turkey, especially as the new Italian Foreign Minister (1920–1), Count Carlo Sforza, was sympathetic to Turkish nationalism.

In France, Clemenceau had failed to obtain the presidency in 1920; and had thereupon resigned the premiership and retired from politics. Lloyd George ascribed Clemenceau's defeat in part to his willingness to make concessions to Britain in the Middle East.[23] Alexandre Millerand, who replaced Clemenceau as Premier, was not disposed to make such concessions.

When the Allies finally met at 10 Downing Street on 12 February 1920, to start drawing up an Ottoman treaty, Lord Curzon spoke for the Prime Minister as well as himself in saying that "The delay in negotiating the Treaty was exclusively due to the Powers having to await the decision of the United States."[24] It would have been more true to say that the delay was due to Lloyd George's attempt to play off the United States against Britain's wartime Allies.

VII

Woodrow Wilson had predicted that the peace would not endure if its terms were not basically fair to all sides. The terms that the Allies imposed on their defeated enemies after the First World War were perceived by many at the time, and have been perceived by many since, as a failure in that respect. Felix Frankfurter later recalled that "My months at the Paris Peace Conference in 1919 were probably the saddest of my life. The progressive disillusionment of the high hopes which Wilson's noble talk had engendered was not unlike the feelings that death of near ones brings."[25] Perhaps Wilson had pitched the world's hopes too high; when uprisings subsequently broke out in the Middle East, Maurice Hankey blamed them on Woodrow Wilson's Fourteen Points and his "impossible doctrine of self-determination."[26]

Over and above any specific decisions there was a general sense that something was fundamentally wrong with the Peace Conference itself. In a general sense, and for the public that judged the Allies by their wartime promises and expressed principles, it was the way in which decisions were made that constituted a betrayal. Decisions, by all accounts, including those of the participants, were made with little knowledge of, or concern for, the lands and peoples about which and whom the decisions were being made. This was true even of the peace terms imposed in Europe, and was even more so of those imposed by Europeans upon the distant and unfamiliar Middle East. Arthur Balfour watched Wilson, Lloyd George, and Clemenceau in conference—relying for expertise only on Maurice Hankey (who was forty-one when the Peace Conference convened, some thirty-five years younger than Balfour)—and pictured them as "These three all-powerful, all-ignorant men, sitting there and carving up continents, with only a child to lead them."[27] An Italian diplomat wrote that "A common sight at the Peace Conference in Paris was one or other of the world's statesmen, standing before a map and muttering to himself: 'Where is that damn'd . . .?' while he sought with extended forefinger for some town or river that he had never heard of before."[28] Lloyd George, who kept demanding that Britain should rule Palestine from (in the Biblical phrase) Dan to Beersheba, did not know where Dan was. He searched for it in a nineteenth-century Biblical atlas, but it was not until nearly a year after the armistice that General Allenby was able to report to him that Dan had been located and, as it was not where the Prime Minister wanted it to be, Britain asked for a boundary further north.

The impression was created, too, that most of the interested parties, in the Middle East as elsewhere, were being excluded from the deliberations. Instead of all the Allied Powers, only five of them met in the first instance to plan the negotiations. They were then superseded by the Council of Four: the leaders of the United States, Britain, France, and Italy. Disagreements and difficulties at home led Italy to withdraw; domestic politics led the United States to withdraw. Discussing the Middle East a year after the armistice, the French Foreign Minister told the British Foreign Minister, who agreed, that "there remained only two parties whose interests had seriously to be considered and reconciled, namely, Great Britain and France";[29] and together they went on to make the decisions about the Ottoman domains.

Yet there were dozens of other parties whose interests were at stake, and their numbers were swelled by the number of their spokesmen. In addition to two main rival delegations from Armenia, for example, there were some forty independent Armenian delegations at the Peace Conference. Ten thousand people came to Paris for the Peace Conference. The hordes of claimants in the background cast into bold relief the narrowness of the interests taken into account by the two governments that remained to make the decisions.

Moral claims and wartime promises were the stock-in-trade of those who came to plead a case. The texts of wartime pledges by Allied leaders, and especially by various British government officials, were scrutinized and compared, as indeed they still are by scholars, to see whether such pledges could be read in such a way as to be consistent with one another, and as though such pledges had given rise to rights that could be enforced in a court of law. The Constantinople Agreement (1915), the Treaty of London (1915), the Hussein-McMahon correspondence (1915–16), the Sykes-Picot Agreement (1916), the Agreement of St Jean de Maurienne (1917), the Balfour Declaration (1917), the Hogarth message (1918), the Declaration to the Seven (1918), and the Anglo-French Declaration (1918), as well as President Woodrow Wilson's Fourteen Points (8 January 1918), Four Principles (11 February 1918), Four Ends (4 July 1918), and Five Particulars (27 September 1918), were among the many statements that were presented by rival claimants to be honored as promissory notes or contracts at law.

David Lloyd George, who saw the negotiations as a bargaining rather than a judicial process, was proud of what he had been able to accomplish in the Middle Eastern settlement. He had made material gains for Britain. Referring to *assignats** the Prime Minister told an intimate friend: "Well, Wilson has gone back home with a bundle of assignats. I have returned with a pocket full of sovereigns in the shape of the German Colonies, Mesopotamia, etc. Everyone to his taste."[30] In all the Prime Minister had succeeded in adding nearly a million square miles to the British Empire.

He was not blind to the moral considerations at issue, but his interpretations of them were fiercely partisan. Writing to defend the peace treaties more than a decade later, Lloyd George claimed that "The Treaties of Paris constitute the greatest measure of national liberation of subject nations ever achieved by any war settlement on record . . . no peace settlement has ever emancipated as many subject nationalities from the grip of foreign tyranny as did that of 1919."[31]

He was particularly incensed by claims that he had not honored the pledges made to the Arabic-speaking peoples.

> The Allies redeemed the promises made in these declarations to the full. No race has done better out of the fidelity with which the Allies redeemed their promises to the oppressed races than the Arabs. Owing to the tremendous sacrifices of the Allied Nations, and more particularly of Britain and her Empire, the Arabs have already won independence in Iraq, Arabia, Syria, and Trans-Jordania, although most of the Arab races fought throughout the War for the Turkish oppressors.

He added in particular that "The Palestinian Arabs fought for Turkish rule."[32]

Perhaps he could have imposed his Middle Eastern settlement

---

* The worthless paper currency issued in France during the French Revolution.

more effectively if he had arrived at it at the end of 1918. But the
attempt to go back on Britain's wartime pledges had taken an immense amount of time and so had lost him that chance. By the
summer of 1920 it was too late for the Prime Minister to impose his
terms upon his wartime Allies and upon an increasingly troublesome
Middle East because—as Churchill had warned repcatedly—by then
he no longer had the troops to do so.

42

THE UNREAL WORLD OF THE
PEACE CONFERENCES

I

"Diplomacy by Conference" was a phrase, attributed to Maurice Hankey, that described Lloyd George's proceedings in the postwar years.[1] It became the standard description of the unreal world in which the Prime Minister lived. Divorcing himself as best he could from the other responsibilities of his office, he spent more than three years in attending international meetings aimed at shaping the post-war world. The meetings among the Allies began almost as soon as the armistices were signed, and developed into a way of life. Lloyd George, between 1919 and 1922, attended no fewer than thirty-three international conferences; and, even before they began, had engaged in informal meetings, such as those with Clemenceau and with Wilson in London at the end of 1918. The formal preliminaries to the Peace Conference began in Paris in January 1919, and shifted to other locations from time to time. At issue were the terms to be imposed upon the German, Austro-Hungarian, and Ottoman empires, and their ally, Bulgaria. The decisions about the Ottoman Empire were agreed upon for the most part at the First Conference of London (beginning in February 1920), were confirmed in the Italian Riviera resort town of San Remo (April 1920), and were embodied in a treaty signed at Sèvres, a residential suburb of Paris, on 10 August 1920.

With respect to the negotiation of the peace settlement in the Middle East, the decisive fact was that it took so much time. Of all the peace treaties, that with the Ottoman Empire was the last to be concluded. Beginning with the informal discussions between Lloyd George and Clemenceau after the armistice, it took sixteen months to reach agreement on substantive matters, and another four months to dispose of remaining issues and sign a treaty. In all, it took nearly two years to conclude the peace treaty with the Ottoman Empire; at the outset Lloyd George had predicted that it would take about a week.[2]

Because of the long delay, situations were allowed to develop, and decisions were required to be made, that in the end proved more important than the terms of the treaty itself. The Allied statesmen thought that they had determined the future of Arabic-speaking Asia by what they did at San Remo, and of the Turkish-speaking Ottoman Empire by what they did at Sèvres; but what they did *not* do in 1918 and 1919 proved to have more influence on the future of both.

At the outset Lloyd George had stated that it would be impossible for his country to support indefinitely its 1,084,000-man army of occupation in the Ottoman Empire.[3] Churchill and the General Staff, it will be recalled, had impressed upon him the need to reach a settlement while he still had the troops to enforce it. By the summer of 1919, some six months later, the British Cabinet was told that the army of occupation was down by more than two-thirds to 320,000 men.[4] As the army melted away, its commanders adhered to a timetable of withdrawal that imposed a series of deadlines upon the Prime Minister at the Peace Conference, as did the continuing drain of British financial resources.

In the north, along the Caucasus frontier with Russia, British troops had remained in place in the hope that the United States, Italy, or France could be persuaded to replace them and defend newly independent Armenia, Georgia, and Azerbaijan if Russia or Turkey should revive sufficiently to attack them. But Britain lacked the men and money to undertake the job, and was eventually forced to abandon her charges to their fate.

In ordering British forces to leave these formerly Russian territories, the Prime Minister disregarded the strong objections of Winston Churchill. For all his recent enthusiasm for retrenchment, Churchill was a firebrand on the communist issue and was prepared to send men and money into Russia to overthrow the Soviet regime. Even Maurice Hankey, who believed that "in the coming years Bolshevism was the greatest danger to Europe,"[5] described Churchill as "quite barmy in his enthusiasm for the anti-Bolsheviks";[6] Churchill was obsessively determined to keep British troops north of the Turkish frontier to help the Whites fight the Reds in the Russian Civil War. Lloyd George's political fears were of a different sort. The Prime Minister told Hankey that he was anxious to get all British troops out of all formerly Russian territories to keep them from becoming "restless"; by which he presumably meant that he wanted to keep them from being infected with the revolutionary virus.[7] Pursuant to his orders, British forces north of the Russian-Turkish frontier were evacuated in the summer of 1919.

To the south of the old Russian frontier, in mountain valleys where the present Turkish borders run with those of Syria, Iraq, and Iran, lay the area imprecisely known as Kurdistan, where British officials thought of sponsoring another of their protectorates. The area fell within the sphere promised to France in the Sykes-Picot Agreement, so the British envisaged a series of autonomous Kurdish states, to be advised by British political officers, which the French were to be asked to concede in the Wilsonian spirit of self-determination for the Kurdish people. The Kurds are an ancient mountain people who have never known unity, and whose energies have been channeled into violent quarrels with neighbors, especially Arabs and Armenians. A British attempt to organize them in 1919 resulted in three uprisings, as the Kurds turned against the British newcomers; soon afterward, British troops pulled back from Kurdistan, too.

II

Within Turkey, the British position continued to disintegrate. The British authorities still relied on the Armistice of Mudros. The brief armistice document dealt almost entirely with naval and military matters, requiring the Turkish authorities to demobilize all their armed forces except those required to maintain internal order. Ottoman troops piled up their weapons and munitions in dumps. British officers supervised the surrender, riding through the country-side in twos and threes. The armistice terms permitted the Ottoman authorities to remain in control of the Turkish-speaking remnant of their empire, subject to the Allies' right to occupy strategic points should a situation arise that threatened their security. In practice, British naval control of the seacoast, coupled with control of the communications and transportation systems, took the place of military occupation of Turkey.

The capital city, Constantinople, remained in theory unoccupied, although Allied forces were much in evidence. The British fleet was anchored there, and, in a triumphal ceremony, the French General Louis Franchet d'Esperey, the Allied commander in Ottoman Europe, rode into the city on a white charger.

The Ottoman government formed to negotiate the armistice was dismissed soon afterward by Mehmed VI, who had become Sultan in June 1918 and was chiefly concerned with retaining his throne. To this end, his policy was to seek favor with the Allies, and when Turkish politicians began to oppose Allied claims and proposals, the Sultan dissolved Parliament and ruled by decree. Soon afterward Mehmed appointed his brother-in-law to head the government as Grand Vizier, thus completing the change back from constitutional to personal rule.

The Sultan's government was not, however, unchallenged. Civilian and military networks of the Young Turkey Party operated throughout Anatolia, and the War Office—Enver's fiefdom—remained largely under their control.[8] They plotted against the new Sultan and his ministers, and hoped to force the Allies to offer milder peace terms.

Outside the capital city, all authority was on the wane. In the interior there was an upsurge of brigandage and communal strife. This breakdown of order throughout Asia Minor was a cause of concern to the Allies, especially when it resulted in threats to the safety of Christians. When Greek villages behind the Black Sea port of Samsun were attacked by Turkish Moslems, the Allies demanded that the Grand Vizier take action. Alarmed, the Grand Vizier consulted the Acting Minister of the Interior, who advised that there was no way to bring the situation under control from Constantinople—an officer would have to be sent into the field to deal with matters on the spot. The Acting Minister suggested the name of his friend, General Mustapha Kemal, the hero of Gallipoli, whose opposition to Enver had kept him from receiving the major command appointments during the war that were his due. The suggestion was adopted and Kemal succeeded in obtaining exceptionally broad civil and military powers as Inspector-General of the Ninth Army, covering most of Anatolia.

On the evening of 6 May 1919 he embarked for Samsun. It was the beginning of one of the great political voyages of the twentieth century. At midnight Wyndham Deedes—the British Intelligence expert on Ottoman affairs—sped to the Sublime Porte to warn the Grand Vizier not to let Kemal go, only to learn that he was too late.

Kemal had already set off for Samsun, and his purpose—as Wyndham Deedes seems to have divined—was to rally forces throughout Turkey to resist Allied peace terms if they proved too harsh. Those forces consisted in large part of Ottoman troops in the unoccupied center and east of Turkey, and—armed with the Sultan's commission and his own formidable skills—Kemal planned to put himself at their head.

III

In 1918−19 Turkey was dark—and cold. Fuel was scarce, and the lights of Constantinople were kept dim. Elsewhere, too, the lands that at the outset of the war had formed the Ottoman domains entered into a sort of twilight existence, defined in terms of international law by the Regulations annexed to the 1907 Hague Convention Respecting the Laws and Customs of War on Land. As the occupying power in most of these domains, Britain's obligation was essentially to keep things as they were under Ottoman law until some final determination as to their fate should be made.

Such a determination would take the form of a treaty of peace between the Ottoman Empire and its conquerors. On the Ottoman side, no difficulty suggested itself; the Sultan lived in the shadow of British warships and in fear of losing his throne, and presumably would sign almost any document the British naval commander placed in front of him. All that the Allies had to do was decide among themselves what terms they wanted to impose.

That situation changed fundamentally in May 1919 when President Wilson and Prime Minister Lloyd George decided to play the Greeks off against the Italians in Anatolia. The unintended effect of the decision was to arouse Greek hopes and Turkish fears that Greece had come back to Asia Minor to stay. Moslem Turkish hatred of the two large Christian populations in their midst—Greeks and Armenians—had always exerted a powerful force, and did so again even in Turkey's exhausted state. While the Allied statesmen were looking the other way, Ottoman soldiers in the interior of Anatolia regrouped and returned to seize their weapons from the dumps where they were deposited.

Within days after the news of the Greek landing at Smyrna became known, Inspector-General Mustapha Kemal was ordered to return to Constantinople—and disobeyed. Instead he met with three colleagues, at the ancient provincial capital city of Amasya, to draft a declaration of independence. Disregarding the Sultan's government as a captive of the Allies, Kemal attended a regional nationalist congress at Erzerum, in the east of Turkey, and then assembled a national congress at Sivas, in the interior of Anatolia, midway between Erzerum and Ankara. He won the allegiance of a number of army officers his own age and younger, many of whom, like himself, had been associated with the military wing of the C.U.P.; for the most part he carried with him the majors and colonels rather than the generals.[9] He also seems to have taken over leadership of the military and civilian resistance networks organized by the Young Turks, although he prudently disclaimed any connection with the officially disbanded C.U.P. Despite Kemal's strong secular bias, Moslem holy men proved to be his strongest adherents.

The Allied leaders knew little about Mustapha Kemal, the lean, tough-minded, hard-living officer in his late thirties who inspired and led the rebellion against them. Neither the British Foreign Office nor British Intelligence was even able to tell the Prime Minister whether Kemal was acting for or against the Sultan.

Unaware of what was happening in Turkey, the Allied leaders in Europe continued to meet in conferences that were intended to decide Turkey's fate. At a conference in London on 28 February 1920, the Allied leaders were amazed by the news that an army of 30,000 Turkish troops under Kemal's command had defeated a small French contingent at Marash in southern Anatolia. What surprised them—Lloyd George later claimed—was not so much the outcome of the battle (for the French were greatly outnumbered) but the revelation that Kemal's army of regulars existed. According to Lloyd George, this was the first that he and his colleagues had heard of such an army. "Our military intelligence had never been more thoroughly unintelligent," he later wrote in his memoirs, typically putting the blame on others.[10]

IV

As Kemal's revolt spread through Anatolia, a parallel movement developed in the Arabic-speaking south of the Ottoman Empire, where the token French presence along the seacoast at Beirut, Tripoli, Sidon, and Tyre presented a tempting target to Moslem militants in Damascus. The French intruders on the coast of Syria and Lebanon threatened to overthrow the delicate balance of Christian and Moslem religious communities, evoking a reaction not unlike that against the Greeks in Turkey.

Britain allowed inland Syria, like inland Anatolia, self-rule. In theory the Syrian administration was headed by Feisal, who was away at the Peace Conference. In practice it was administered by people over whom he had little control, and who feuded bitterly with one another. For more than a year after the Ottoman retreat, inland Syria—with its capital at Damascus—was administered, if somewhat chaotically, by Arabs, and the novel habit of independence, once contracted, was not one that they wished to surrender.

A British Intelligence chief warned the Foreign Secretary in London in 1919 that the Arab government in Damascus and Kemal's movement in Turkey were preparing to enter into an alliance.[11] But the Arab and Turkish movements were not as alike as he supposed: Kemal was a nationalist in the western sense of the word, while in Arab Damascus, though everybody now spoke the fashionable language of nationalism, it was not a native tongue. Of the Arabic-speaking leaders who governed from Damascus in 1919, most— perhaps four out of five—had not been adherents of an Arab national identity or of Arab independence as late as 1918.[12] The Syrians among them were mostly from landowning families, with a stake in maintaining the established order. An analysis of the occupational groups from which they were drawn[13] shows the leadership made up in large part of Ottoman soldiers and officials, many of them from Iraq and Palestine, who were out of a job. Most of them had remained loyal to Turkey during the war with Britain.

In the year since the Ottoman army had left Damascus, and under the noses of the distracted British, who were thinking about France, the Ottoman Arabs who had opposed them during the war had taken back control of the liberated province. The Ottoman Arabs, however, were fragmented along geographical lines in their current political concerns. Those from communities like Jerusalem denounced Zionism in Palestine; those from Baghdad complained of the British in Mesopotamia; and the Syrians wanted to expel the French from their seacoast and from Lebanon. Meanwhile, leaders of the traditional pro-Ottoman anti-Feisal ruling families were pitted against ambitious young militants seeking their political fortunes. Behind the rhetoric of the political parties and the renascent secret societies lay obscure family and local conflicts. It was a confused and confusing political situation, in which Feisal's position was secured essentially by the support of Britain, visibly represented by General Allenby's armies, and by the common Arab supposition that because of Feisal, Britain would oppose the colonialist designs of France.

In retrospect it can be seen that Britain entered 1919 with a period of grace of less than nine months in which to bluff France into backing down; by the summer of 1919 financial pressures and social unrest forced Lloyd George and the War Office to recognize that a timetable for British withdrawal from Syria could no longer be postponed. On 4 September 1919 the Prime Minister convened a conference of his advisers at the vacation house of his friend Lord Riddell, near Trouville on France's Normandy coast, to consider what should be done about the Middle East. Only a few days before Riddell had recorded in his diary that Lloyd George was "angry with the French for their attitude concerning Syria. He said that the Syrians would not have the French, and asked how the Allies could compel them to accept mandatories who were distasteful . . . His attitude to the French has changed greatly . . . He continually refers to their greed."[14] Yet he and his advisers saw no alternative but to abandon the field to the French.

On 13 September 1919 the British government announced that withdrawal would take place in November, leaving the French and Feisal to settle matters between themselves. According to the British leaders, they thereby honored their commitments both to France and to the Arabs. It was a disingenuous claim. The British had pretended that Feisal headed a great Arab army in Syria, but government officials were aware that this was a pretense without substance. For the British army to leave was to leave Feisal to the mercy of the French. To Kitchener's followers in Britain and the Middle East, this meant a betrayal of all they had worked for; while to the French, the nine-month attempt to face them down, even though it was abandoned, was unforgivable.

For Feisal, the nervous prince with the worry-bead fingers, the British announcement of withdrawal was another sudden turning in the labyrinth of deception through which he tried to wend his way. There was, however, a teasing, tantalizing possibility that briefly opened up before him. Clemenceau, willing as always to accommodate British preferences in the Middle East—if politically possible—was prepared to let Feisal be king of Syria (since that is what Britain wanted) if Feisal would meet him halfway. The French Premier agreed to enter once again into negotiations with the Arab leader, aimed at securing recognition of France's minimum terms: that France would rule a Greater Lebanon, and that Syria, though independent, would become a French client state. But these French terms placed Feisal in the middle, between colliding forces. The militant Arabs of Damascus who claimed to be his followers, but who had no particular attachment to him, were prepared to allow him to call himself their ruler only so long as he could keep the French out; while the French were prepared to let him rule only if he could succeed in bringing them in. Feisal, a stranger in the land of Syria, was in no position to do anything but mediate. All he could do was obtain concessions from Clemenceau and then try to obtain concessions from the Arab militants in Damascus.

Early in January 1920, Feisal and Clemenceau arrived at a secret accord—secret, because Clemenceau, seeking to become President of France, did not want his opponents to be able to claim he had been weak on Syria—permitting Feisal's Arab state its independence, but with exclusively French advisers. The accord was designed to lead to a French Mandate, but only of the loosest sort. Feisal then left for Damascus to see if he could persuade the Arab leadership there to accept its relatively mild terms; but his mission proved to be another blind turn in the political labyrinth for on 17 January Clemenceau, rejected in his bid for the presidency, gave up his political career. Alexandre Millerand, Clemenceau's successor as Premier, lacked his inclination to save Britain's face in the Middle East, and therefore saw no need either to allow Syria her independence or to let Feisal mount her throne.

V

At the beginning of 1920, with Britain no longer blocking French ambitions in Syria, the way was clear for the two Allies finally to formulate the terms they would impose upon the defeated Ottoman Empire. The terms upon which they then agreed were that the Arabic-speaking portions of the empire were to be detached and divided between the two European powers, with Palestine and Mesopotamia to be kept by Britain; Arabia was to remain independent under British-influenced monarchs, Egypt and the Gulf coast already having been taken by Britain; and Syria, including Lebanon, was to go to France. Palestine, including Transjordan; Syria, including Lebanon; and Iraq were all destined for eventual independence, if one believed the language of the League of Nations Mandates, pursuant to which the Allies awarded these territories to themselves. But France, in particular, regarded the pledge of independence as window-dressing, and approached Syria and Lebanon in an annexationist spirit.

Apart from the Dodecanese islands, most of the Aegean islands and European Turkey (eastern Thrace) were ceded to Greece. Smyrna, and the district of western Anatolia of which it was the leading city, were to be administered by Greece for five years, after which a plebiscite would be taken, presumably leading to incorporation of the area within the Kingdom of Greece. The Dardanelles, where the Royal Navy could make itself felt, were placed under international control, and along with Constantinople became hostages guaranteeing Turkey's good behavior in such matters as the treatment of Christian minorities. In eastern Anatolia, Armenia was granted independence, and Kurdistan was given autonomy. Turkish finances were placed under British, French, and Italian supervision. Within these limits, and subject to these restrictions, what little remained of Turkish-speaking Anatolia was to remain nominally independent under the Ottoman Sultan.

Such were the terms, agreed upon in London and San Remo in the first half of 1920, that were dictated to the Sultan's government—which reluctantly signed the treaty imposed upon it in August 1920, in the French suburban city of Sèvres. As only France's Poincaré seems to have noticed, it was an inauspicious choice for the site of a treaty upon which Europe intended to rely; Sèvres was known for its china, which was fragile and easily broken.

Lloyd George was the only one of the original Big Four who remained in his position when the final peace treaty was signed. He was also the only British Cabinet minister at the beginning of the First World War who remained in the Cabinet throughout the war until its conclusion. The only British politician to survive the war, he was the only Allied leader to survive the peace; but the Ottoman settlement, of which he was so proud, was to prove his undoing.

PART X

STORM OVER ASIA

43

THE TROUBLES BEGIN: 1919—1921

When the British armed forces occupied the Middle East at the end of the war, the region was passive. But soon troubles began. They began in Egypt, with demands for independence in 1918 followed by rioting in 1919. Next—though there was no immediately apparent connection—war broke out in 1919 in Afghanistan, on the Indian frontier. At about the same time, British policy in Arabia began to come apart. It was possible to believe that it was just bad luck that caused one thing after another to go wrong for Britain in the Middle East; and one could have continued to believe that when tribal disturbances brought disorder to Transjordan or, in the spring of 1920, when Arabs rioted against Jews in western Palestine, or in the summer of 1920, when Iraq flamed into revolt. An obvious explanation for the disorders, and arguably the correct one, was that, after the war, Britain's garrisons in the Middle East were so undermanned as to embolden Britain's local opponents everywhere to defy her.

The French, weakened in the Middle East, as were the British, by pressures to economize and demobilize, were similarly defied by Arab politicians, against whom they finally went to war in Syria. Russia, defeated in the war and crippled by revolutions and civil war, also faced Moslem revolts and independence movements in Central Asia, her domain in the Middle East. But both the French and Russians, instead of finding common cause with Britain, intrigued to undermine her position in the Middle East, thus confusing the issue by making it plausible to suppose that they were causing (rather than merely adding to) Britain's difficulties.

In retrospect, one sees Britain undergoing a time of troubles everywhere in the Middle East between 1919 and 1921; but it was not experienced that way, at least not in the beginning. Rioting in Egypt in 1919, for example, was seen as an Egyptian law and order problem that was then brought under control; it was not seen as a prelude to the riots that broke out in Palestine in the spring of the next year or to the revolt that spread in Iraq as spring gave way to summer. So the chapters that follow tell of the successive Middle

Eastern challenges to Britain—and to the French, to whom Britain had yielded Syria—roughly in the order that they occurred, and as though they amounted merely to one separate set of difficulties after another.

Though they were not perceived at the time as coming together to constitute one large overall event, the individual intrigues and revolts against British rule were believed by a great many British officials to be instigated by a single group of conspirators; and presently it will be seen who these were believed to be. Whether the disorders and uprisings in the Middle East were indeed planned and coordinated or, on the contrary, sporadic, was a principal question confronting the Lloyd George government as the extent of the challenge to British rule in the Middle East emerged in 1919 and 1920 and stood revealed to a disenchanted British public, press, and Parliament by 1921.

44

EGYPT: THE WINTER OF 1918—1919

The first postwar challenge to Britain's Middle Eastern position was in Egypt, the Arabic-speaking country that she had ruled "temporarily" for decades, and whose British administrators had persuaded themselves at the outset that the Arabic-speaking peoples preferred British rule to any other. But Britain had repeatedly promised Egypt her independence and it was not unreasonable for Egyptian politicians to have believed the pledges, and thus to suppose that once the war was brought to a successful conclusion, Britain might agree to some sort of timetable leading to eventual Egyptian independence.* At least one group of local politicians proposed to take Britain at her word. On 13 November 1918, two weeks after the Ottoman surrender aboard the *Agamemnon*, a delegation of out-of-office Egyptian political figures was granted an interview with Sir Reginald Wingate, the British High Commissioner in Cairo. The delegation had been formed and was led by Saad Zaghlul, a lawyer of about sixty, a former judge, administrator, Minister of Education, and Minister of Justice, and a leader of the Legislative Assembly, which the British had prorogued indefinitely at the beginning of the war. Zaghlul explained to Wingate that he had requested the interview in the expectation that martial law and the protectorate would soon be abolished, now that the war was over. Indicating that he expected Britain to keep her promise to grant Egypt independence, Zaghlul asked that Egypt should be heard by the Allies during their peace negotiations. He also asked to go to London to negotiate the promised changes in Egypt's political status.

Neither negotiations nor independence were what British officials had in mind at the time. A guide to their thinking was provided by

---

* When Britain went to war against the Ottoman Empire at the end of 1914, the Asquith government formally announced that Egypt had been released from Ottoman suzerainty and had become a British protectorate; but the British authorities also announced that the freedom and independence of Egypt were among the goals for which Britain was fighting.[1]

a British official's account, some time later, of the meeting with Zaghlul. "On Nov. 13 he paid a visit to the High Commissioner and expressed the desire to go to London to put forward a programme of complete autonomy, a proposal which was rejected as calculated to serve no good object."[2]

Receiving no encouragement from Wingate, Zaghlul began that same day to try to force the issue. Perhaps acting with the secret support of the new Egyptian Sultan, Ahmed Fuad,* he set out to organize a delegation that could win broad support from the groups and classes within Egypt whose interests he aspired to represent; which, in turn, drove rival political figures to form and head delegations of their own. On 17 November 1918 Wingate cabled the Foreign Secretary that Egyptian politicians were calling for a "programme of complete autonomy"; that he had warned them against agitation; but that the Sultan and his ministers did not feel strong enough to oppose nationalist demands.[3] Indeed the Sultan's ministers, not wanting to be viewed as Britain's nominees, claimed that they would refuse to lead a delegation abroad unless Zaghlul and his colleagues were also allowed to proceed to Europe. In the event, Britain did not allow any delegation to go either to London or to Paris during 1918.

In January 1919, as the opening date of the Peace Conference approached, Zaghlul and his Wafd ("Delegation") Party stepped up their activities. They were indignant to learn, on 12 January, that a delegation from Syria would be allowed to attend the Peace Conference. At a so-called General Congress of the Wafd held the next day in the home of one of its members, Zaghlul claimed the same right for Egypt, and spoke in favor of independence. Thereafter the British administration prevented Zaghlul from speaking in public; whereupon the Sultan's ministers resigned rather than lead a delegation to Europe while Zaghlul was being silenced. The British military authorities then arrested Zaghlul and three of his principal colleagues, and, on 9 March, deported them to Malta.

A wave of demonstrations and strikes swept the country. The British authorities were taken by surprise. The cables sent from Cairo to London at the time suggest that the Residency had little understanding of what had been happening in Egypt during the wartime years.[4] It was unaware of the implications of the profound social and economic changes brought about by the war: the new classes and ambitions that had emerged, the new interests, the new resentments, and the new sources of discord and disaffection.

The Residency did know, though, that there were many Egyptians

---

* Ahmed Fuad became Sultan of Egypt on the death of his brother in October 1917.

who would have been happy to see Britain lose the war against Turkey. Wingate, Clayton, and their associates, in arguing unsuccessfully that Britain ought to annex Egypt and rule the country directly, had pointed out some of the dangers that might arise if such people took control of Egypt's destinies. Lieutenant-Commander Hogarth of the Arab Bureau, in a memorandum of 22 July 1917 supporting Clayton's annexation proposal, had claimed that Egypt "is at present potentially an enemy country" and that the danger could be averted only by Britain's taking responsibility for the reorganization of Egyptian society.[5]

Within the murky world of Egyptian politics, the new Sultan, the Sultan's ministers, and such opposition leaders as Zaghlul, all were maneuvering, sometimes for and sometimes against one another, under the cover of their respective nationalist proposals, to win the support of the various disaffected groups within the Egyptian economy and Egyptian society. Yet of these currents, undermining the structure of the protectorate and threatening one day to sweep it away, the British authorities evinced little awareness. Zaghlul was seen as a mere disgruntled office-seeker, using his political demands as leverage to obtain a government job. According to the Residency in 1917, "He is now getting old and probably desires an income."[6] Yet within a week of his arrest and deportation, demonstrations in Cairo, Alexandria, and other towns spread to the Delta, led to violence, and were followed by massive strikes. Railroad lines were torn up in key places, in accord, ironically, with a British wartime plan to disrupt the country in the event of an Ottoman invasion. Transport workers struck. On 16 March 1919, a week after Zaghlul's deportation, Cairo's railroad and telegraph communications with both the Delta and Upper Egypt were cut, while foreign colonies were besieged. The flames of disorder raged out of control.

Widespread attacks on British military personnel culminated on 18 March in the murder of eight of them—two officers, five soldiers, and an inspector of prisons—on a train from Aswan to Cairo. The High Commissioner's administration reported that it retained "no means of regaining control in Upper Egypt, from whence there is practically no news."[7] According to a recent account, the upheaval "seemed likely for a moment to lead to a revolt on a scale unparalleled in the Eastern Empire since the Indian Mutiny."[8] These fears were exaggerated—but they were sincerely felt and widely held.

What the High Commissioner's office in the Residency found so shocking in the rebellion was its "Bolshevik tendency," and also that the "present movement in Egypt is national in the full sense of the word. It has now the sympathy of all classes and creeds ..."[9] Copts demonstrated alongside Moslems. Theological students demonstrated alongside students from the secular schools. Women, albeit only from the upper classes, demonstrated alongside men.[10] What especially unnerved the British authorities was the involvement of the peasantry in the countryside—the placid masses on whose inertia they had counted. Unnerving, too, was the subsequent discovery that the uprising was organized. Suddenly the British were faced with a local politician who appeared to have a national following— which surprised them and may have surprised him, too.

General Allenby, who was quickly sent out to deal with the situation, arrived in Cairo on 25 March and declared his intention of putting an end to the disturbances. On 7 April he announced Zaghlul's release. British troops gradually restored order in the spring and summer of 1919, but strikes and demonstrations continued.

At the end of 1919 London sent out a Commission of Inquiry under Lord Milner, which concluded that the British protectorate had indeed to be abolished and replaced by some new relationship, the nature of which Britain attempted to negotiate throughout 1920, 1921, and 1922.

The process proved to be frustrating, and deporting Zaghlul again proved to be of little help. The principal British fantasy about the Middle East—that it wanted to be governed by Britain, or with her assistance—ran up against a stone wall of reality. The Sultan and Egypt's other leaders refused to accept mere autonomy or even nominal independence; they demanded full and complete independence, which Britain—dependent upon the Suez Canal—would not grant. Though British officials tried to reach some kind of agreement with Egypt's leadership, they failed; and so in the years to come, Britain was obliged to maintain her armed presence and her hegemony in Egypt without the consent of the country's politicians.

On the other side of the Middle East, however, in Afghanistan, a real question arose as to whether Britain *could* preserve her hegemony without the consent of local leaders.

AFGHANISTAN: THE SPRING
OF 1919

Egypt, with its vital Suez Canal, was one of the key strategic positions on Britain's road to India; Afghanistan, with its mountain passes leading into the Indian plains, was another. Over the course of a century British armies had repeatedly been bloodied in the course of their efforts to prevent hostile forces from controlling the fierce mountain kingdom. The issue was believed by British statesmen to have been resolved satisfactorily in 1907, when Russia agreed that the kingdom should become a British protectorate.

On 19 February 1919, however, the Emir of Afghanistan was assassinated; and after a short period in which rival claimants maneuvered for the succession, his third son, 26-year-old Amanullah Khan, wrote to the Governor-General of India announcing his accession to the "free and independent Government of Afghanistan."[1] By the terms of Britain's agreement with Russia in 1907, Afghanistan was not, of course, fully free and independent, for Britain was entrusted with the conduct of her foreign relations. Yet on 19 April the new ruler went on to assert his complete independence in external as well as internal affairs.

Amanullah secretly planned an attack on British India—through the Khyber Pass—that was to coincide with an Indian nationalist uprising in Peshawar, the principal British garrison town near the frontier.[2] Amanullah believed that a nationwide Indian uprising would then occur.

Amanullah's army commander moved too soon, however, before the Peshawar uprising could be organized, and unwittingly alerted the British to their danger. On 3 May 1919 a detachment of Afghan troops crossed the frontier into British India at the top of the Khyber Pass. They seized control of a border village and a pumping station controlling the water supply to a nearby Indian military post. On 5 May the Governor-General of India telegraphed to London that it looked as though a war—the Third Afghan War—had started.

According to Amanullah, he had ordered his troops to the frontier

in response to the British repression of disturbances in India. Referring to the Amritsar Massacre,[*] and to the policy for which it stood,
Amanullah declared that in the name of Islam and of humanity, he
regarded the peoples of India as justified in rising up against British
rule, and that his own troops were at the frontier to keep disorder
from spreading.

The British were unsure of his intentions. They were aware that
during the war a German military mission had nearly persuaded the
Afghan government to launch an invasion of India, and they believed
that Enver's old pan-Turkish colleagues, and also the new Bolshevik
government in Russia, might influence the Afghan government in
dangerous ways. Alarming information reaching the British authorities in May, at the time Amanullah's troops crossed the border,
indicated that the Afghans planned a simultaneous attack on three
fronts, spearheaded by hordes of religious fanatics, responding to the
proclamation of a Holy War, and supported by regular troops in
coordination with frontier tribes;[3] while, at the same time, British
forces were to be immobilized by mass rioting within India.[4]

Believing that prompt action was necessary, British officers in the
border region attacked Afghan positions. Inconclusive combat took
place at scattered points along a wide front. For the British, the
unreliability of their native contingents proved only one of several
unsettling discoveries in a messy, unpopular, and unsatisfactory campaign. At a time when it could ill afford the money, the British
Government of India was obliged to increase its budget by an enormous sum of 14,750,000 pounds to cover the costs of the one-month
campaign.[5]

Although they succeeded in expelling the Afghan forces from
India and, by the end of May, had gained the upper hand, the
British forces were inadequate to the task of invading, subduing, and
occupying the Afghan kingdom. What won the day for them was the
use of airplanes, which the tribesmen, with their primitive weapons,
were unable to combat. In particular, it was the bombing of Afghan
cities by the Royal Air Force that unnerved Amanullah and led him
to ask for peace. Nonetheless, the outcome of the war, from the
Afghans' point of view, was better than a draw. They had withdrawn
from India but had regained their freedom within their own frontiers.

The Treaty of Rawalpindi, signed the morning of 8 August 1919,
brought the Third Afghan War to an end. In the treaty Britain
conceded the complete independence of Afghanistan, and relinquished control over Afghanistan's foreign relations—a control that

---

[*] On 11 April 1919 a small British military force in the Indian city of Amritsar,
the holy city of the Sikhs, opened fire on a group of people who had assembled in a
public park for a political meeting, killing 379 of them.

she had required in order to exclude hostile foreign powers, Russia chief among them, from the strategically important mountain kingdom. But soon after the conclusion of the Treaty of Rawalpindi, the Afghan government made use of its new independence by entering into a treaty with the Bolsheviks which, amongst other provisions, allowed the Russians to establish consulates within the kingdom. By 1921 the nervous British authorities were asking the Afghans to alter their agreement with the Bolsheviks, claiming that the Russians were setting up consulates at "places so remote from the sphere of Russia's legitimate interests that it was obvious that the consulates could serve no purpose but that of facilitating hostile intrigue on the Indian frontier."[6]

In 1921 the British entered into new negotiations with the Afghan regime. Urging liberal concessions, *The Times* correspondent wrote on 1 September 1921 that "the British Cabinet, despite the influence of Lord Curzon, whose great knowledge of the East is out of date," should be convinced that Afghan nationalism and independence had to be recognized, and that if they were, the Kabul regime would show friendship toward Britain.

But years of British tutelage had fostered not friendship but resentment. During the 1921 negotiations the British delegation was able to produce proof that the Afghans had joined in a plot against Britain; for British Intelligence had deciphered the Soviet code and had learned of plans for joint Afghan and Russian military action against the British Empire.[7] Despite liberal concessions by the British delegation, the Kabul regime continued to afford facilities to Bolshevik representatives and it was soon discovered that Russian agents were successfully intriguing with the warlike frontier tribes.[8]

Of course it could be argued that Afghanistan had always posed difficult problems and that the setback to British influence there was an isolated, exceptional event. But British policy in Arabia, too, was in tatters—and Arabia had seemed open to British influence and was ruled by monarchs who professed friendship for Britain. In the spring of 1919, while waging the Third Afghan War, Britain suddenly faced a losing situation in Arabia; and while there was no apparent connection between the two, or between either of the two and the situation in Egypt, the coincidence of difficulties on the western, eastern, and southern ends of Britain's Middle Eastern empire suggested that Britain might have overextended her imperial commitments.

ARABIA: THE SPRING OF 1919

Of all the Middle Eastern lands, Arabia seemed to be Britain's most natural preserve. Its long coastlines could be controlled easily by the Royal Navy. Two of its principal lords, Hussein in the west and Ibn Saud in the center and east, were British protégés supported by substantial regular subsidies from the British government. As of 1919 no rival European powers sought to intrude themselves into Arabian political affairs. The field had been left clear for Britain.

Yet the First World War was barely over before the Cabinet in London was forced to recognize that its policy in Arabia was in disarray. Its allies—Hussein, King of the Hejaz, and Ibn Saud, lord of Nejd—were at daggers drawn. Hussein complained that he was obliged to spend 12,000 pounds a month out of his British subsidy to defend against attacks from Ibn Saud, who himself received 5,000 pounds a month in subsidies.[1] The British representative who relayed Hussein's complaint characterized Britain's financing of both Ibn Saud and Hussein—when they were fighting one another—as absurd.[2] So was the bitter dispute that broke out within the British government over what to do about it—which paralyzed the process of making a decision, so that none was made. Instructions and ultimatums were drafted but not sent. Officials who made decisions were not told that other officials had cancelled those decisions. There were changes of mind from one day to the next.

The dispute centered around possession of the small urban oasis centers of Khurma and Turaba, located at the frontier where Hussein's hegemony left off and Ibn Saud's began. The stakes were larger than they seemed, in part because possession of Khurma and Turaba brought with it tribal allegiances that also involved substantial areas of grazing land, but mostly because the quarrel was about religion. In early 1918 the *Arab Bulletin* had recorded Hussein's complaints that his authority was being undermined by religious proselytizing conducted by Ibn Saud's adherents; for the Saudi claims on Khurma and Turaba derived from religious conversion.

Ibn Saud was the hereditary champion of the teachings of

Muhammad ibn Abdul Wahhab, an eighteenth-century religious leader whose alliance with the House of Saud in 1745 had been strengthened by frequent intermarriage between the two families. The Wahhabis (as their opponents called them) were severely puritanical reformers who were seen by their adversaries as fanatics. It was Ibn Saud's genius to discern how their energies could be harnessed for political ends.

At the end of 1912 a movement of religious revival had begun that was to change the nature of Arabian politics in Ibn Saud's favor. Tribesmen started selling their horses, camels, and other possessions in the market towns in order to settle in cooperative agricultural communities to live a strict Wahhabi religious life. The movement became known as the *Ikhwan*: the Brethren. Ibn Saud immediately put himself at the head of it,[3] which gave him an army of true Bedouins—the greatest warriors in Arabia. In the Brethren, both the authority of each tribe's sheikhs and the separation between tribes tended to diminish, while the authority of Ibn Saud grew.

It was the spread of this uncompromising puritanical faith into neighboring Hejaz that, in Hussein's view, threatened to undermine his authority. Hussein was an orthodox Sunni; to him the Wahhabis were doctrinal and political enemies. He sent expedition after unsuccessful expedition against Khurma and Turaba to recall them from their Wahhabi ways. The final expedition was mounted in the spring of 1919, in the flush of Allied victory over the Ottoman Empire. Led by Hussein's son Abdullah, the trained Hejazi army of 5,000 men brought along the modern equipment which the British had supplied during the war. On 21 May 1919 Abdullah's troops occupied Turaba, whereupon Ibn Saud set out from Riyadh to attack them. But the pitched battle for which both sides had prepared never took place. A Brethren force of 1,100 camel-riders, who had gone ahead of Ibn Saud's forces as scouts, came upon Abdullah's camp on the night of 25 May. Armed only with swords, spears, and antique rifles, they swooped down upon the sleeping Hejazi army and destroyed it. Abdullah, in his nightshirt, escaped; but his troops did not.[4]

The defeat of Hussein's forces was so complete that it brought Britain to his rescue. British airplanes were sent to the Hejaz; British warnings were sent to Ibn Saud.[5] Ever the diplomat, Ibn Saud avoided confrontation, made a show of deferring to Britain's desires, and claimed to be trying his best to restrain the hotheaded Brethren. Hussein provided a complete contrast, remaining obdurate; and it was only with difficulty that Britain forced him to accept a temporary armistice in August 1920. Thus it seemed that Cairo and London had backed the wrong side, especially as Ibn Saud went on to new victories, capturing the mountainous province of Asir in 1920, and overthrowing the rival Arabian House of Rashid at the end of 1921. Spearheaded by the Brethren, whose fighting men were estimated at 150,000,[6] Ibn Saud's forces went about rounding out their conquest of Arabia.

On 20 September 1920 a special Middle Eastern correspondent of *The Times* wrote that the Arab Bureau's old proposal that Hussein become Caliph of Islam—inspired by Lord Kitchener's suggestion in the autumn of 1914—was proving to be a disaster. He predicted that Ibn Saud would invade the Hejaz and capture it; in fact Ibn Saud did so, and drove Hussein into exile, four years later.

Against their will, the British were placed in an adversary position with respect to Ibn Saud by their need to shore up Hussein. British prestige was involved; as a Foreign Office official noted, "we shall look fools all over the East if our puppet is knocked off his perch as easily as this."[7] Yet the British could do little about it. As in Afghanistan, the physical character of the country was forbidding. Not even a demonstration use of force seemed practical; asked what targets along the Arabian coast the Royal Navy might bombard, officials along the Gulf coast replied that in fact there were none worth shelling.[8]

Thus on the southern as well as the western and eastern frontiers of their Middle Eastern empire, British officials in 1919 began to find themselves no longer in control of events for reasons that they could not immediately fathom; and no course of conduct was evident to them that could bring the local populations back into line.

But perhaps the most serious challenge they encountered was in Turkey—the heartland of the Ottoman Empire, which Britain supposedly had crushed in 1918.

TURKEY: JANUARY 1920

The fate of what remained of the Ottoman Empire was at the heart of the Middle Eastern question as the Allied Powers—throughout 1919, 1920, and 1921—continued to wrangle about the disposition of its Turkish-speaking center in Anatolia. Lloyd George changed his mind several times about what should be done. In early 1919 he favored a plan whereby the United States would take Constantinople and Armenia; Greece would take an enclave centered on Smyrna; and the rest of the country would be divided between France in the north and Italy in the south. A few months later he changed his mind completely and, falling in with the views of his Cabinet, declared that "the Allies had no more right to split up Turkey than Germany, in former days, had had to split up Poland."[1] The treaty that he proposed to impose upon the Sultan the following year nonetheless was harsh, and imposing its terms upon the Turkish government in 1920 proved more difficult than Lloyd George had supposed.

At the end of 1919, elections were held throughout the post-armistice Ottoman Empire for a new Turkish Chamber of Deputies; and Turkish nationalists won an overwhelming victory. Even before the Chamber convened, newly elected deputies converged on Angora (now Ankara), deep in the interior of the country and far from the sea and the guns of the British Navy, where Mustapha Kemal, the 38-year-old nationalist general, had moved his headquarters. There they subscribed to a Kemalist declaration of political principles that became known as the National Pact. The National Pact called for the creation of an independent Turkish Moslem nation-state. The pact's widespread appeal underscored a comment by the British naval commander in the Mediterranean to the effect that "the Greek occupation of Smyrna has stimulated a Turkish patriotism probably more real than any which the war was able to evoke."[2]

In mid-January 1920 the new Chamber of Deputies convened in Constantinople. On 28 January 1920, in secret session, the deputies

voted to adopt the National Pact; and on 17 February, they announced to the public that they had done so. While the leaders of
France and Britain were meeting in Europe to reach final agreement
on the terms of the peace settlement they meant to impose, the
Ottoman Chamber of Deputies, without being asked, had defined
the minimum terms they were prepared to accept. If the political
theme of the twentieth century is seen to be the ending of Europe's
rule over its neighboring continents, then the Ottoman Chamber's
declaration of independence signalled the dawn of the century.

French and British military leaders warned their prime ministers
that at least twenty-seven army divisions would be needed to impose
upon the rebellious Turks the terms on which the two prime ministers were resolved.[3] This was well beyond what the Allies could
field. The British Imperial General Staff urged Lloyd George to
reconsider his proposed peace terms, but he refused to do so. In
early 1920 hostilities commenced. Fighting erupted in Cilicia, the
southern Turkish-speaking area (adjoining Syria) that Britain had
allowed France to occupy. From February through April, Kemalist
forces inflicted repeated defeats on the French, capturing positions,
inflicting hundreds of casualties, and taking thousands of prisoners.
The French Premier, Millerand, caught between pressures for demobilization and pressures to protect French interests in Syria,
ordered his local commander to try to come to some agreement with
the Turkish nationalists.[4]

Lloyd George was opposed to conciliation; he met force with
force. In mid-March, Britain led an Allied military occupation of
Constantinople.[5] Allied troops moved in and replaced the Ottoman
police, declaring martial law and dissolving the Chamber of Deputies.
The Allied army of occupation promptly arrested 150 Ottoman
military and civil officials, including a substantial number of the
elected deputies, and deported them to Malta, where Zaghlul and his
Egyptian colleagues had been sent (but subsequently released) the
year before.[6] France and Italy hastened to assure Kemal that these
measures represented British policy, not their own.[7]

The occupation of the Sultan's capital at Constantinople did not
damage Mustapha Kemal. Contrary to what some British authorities
believed, he no longer acted for the Sultan—and an unintended
effect of the Allied occupation was to destroy whatever prestige or
legitimacy that remained to the Sultan's government and to transfer
it to Kemal's regime. This was illustrated the following month when
100 members of the Chamber of Deputies who remained free joined
in Angora with 190 others elected from what they termed resistance
groups to form a new Parliament.[8] They voted to create a government
of the Grand National Assembly, of which Mustapha Kemal
was elected president.[9] The Sultan was declared a prisoner of the

Allies, and his acts invalid. The Sultan's government, in occupied Constantinople, replied by branding the leaders in Angora as traitors. Kemal's Angora government prudently chose to leave its relationship to the Sultan's government ambiguous.

The conflict in Anatolia was clouded by the emergence of semi-autonomous warlords and outlaw bands, sometimes acting for themselves, sometimes acting in alliance with one or the other of the governments, or with the British, or with the Greeks, or with communists (Russian and otherwise). There were local rebellions, in some cases undertaken by great landholding families seeking to reassert their interests, but there were also marauding groups of nomads and refugees, Kurds, Circassians, and Tartars from the Crimea and Central Asia. Though groups such as the Green Army began as expressions of one or another political cause, they tended to degenerate into no more than glorified bandits.[10] Torn by anarchy and civil war, the Turkish-speaking Ottoman Empire came increasingly to resemble the lands that had been Czarist Russia, and which in 1918 had formed a vast indistinct battlefield on which Whites and Reds, bandits and warlords, foreign armies and indigenous independence movements engaged in a confusing and multisided conflict. The frontier between the two ancient empires was blurred by local uprisings and the movements of various armed groups; while the flow of Bolshevik agents and propaganda into Anatolia made it seem that an effective border between the two vast and confused ex-empires no longer existed.

The first decision of Kemal's new government in Angora was to send a mission to Russia, where it arrived in May 1920, possibly in pursuance of earlier agreements between Kemal's Nationalists and Lenin's Bolsheviks.[11] The working relationship that emerged, though with such difficulty that it was not solidified for nearly a year (in the treaty of 16 March 1921), was one that the British authorities misunderstood. The Russian Bolsheviks had given refuge and encouragement to Enver Pasha, the Ottoman Empire's exiled wartime leader; and the British wrongly assumed that Enver was behind the Angora government.[12] In fact Enver and Kemal were deadly rivals; when this became clear to them, the Russians flirted with the idea of using one against the other but, in the end, felt compelled to choose between them.

Wrong in believing that Kemal was secretly acting on behalf of the Sultan, and wrong, too, in suspecting that he was acting for Enver, the British were also wrong in suspecting that he was acting for the Bolsheviks. Kemal was in fact an implacable enemy of Russian Bolshevism, and as soon as he felt able, he suppressed the Russian-inspired Turkish Communist Party, killed its leaders, and killed or imprisoned its agents. As a result, many of the Russian leaders were disposed to treat Kemal as an enemy. The Kemalists were given the impression that it was only as a result of Stalin's powerful intervention, and over the objections of the Soviet Ministry of Foreign Affairs, that Russia agreed to deal with Angora at all.[13] Stalin, Commissar for Nationalities and for State Control, evidently put Russian national interests ahead of Bolshevik ideology, and recognized that Kemal might be able to inflict damage on the British. Damaging the British was one of Stalin's chief objectives, and the realistic—or cynical—Bolshevik was willing to support even Kemal in order to achieve his goal. So Soviet money and supplies began to pour over the Russo-Turkish frontier, in amounts still not known, to aid the anti-Bolshevik Nationalists. It was the first significant military aid that Soviet Russia had given to a foreign movement. But within the Bolshevik government, the resistance to supplying aid to Turkish anti-Bolsheviks must have been intense, for it took a year—from the spring of 1920 when the Turkish mission went to Russia to ask for support—to complete the arrangements.

Meanwhile, the possibility that Turkey would be thrown into the arms of the Soviets reinforced the views of Allied military officials, who believed that Lloyd George would be making a mistake in forcing the Sultan's government to sign a harsh treaty. On the British side as well as the French, it was the view of the admirals and generals most directly concerned that they did not have the manpower to impose terms on the rebellious Turks. Venizelos, the Greek Prime Minister, told the other Allied leaders that Greek forces could do it alone, but the British service chiefs did not share his confidence.

A close friend asked Lloyd George whether he still thought it wise to give Smyrna to the Greeks. "I have no doubt about it," replied the Prime Minister. "You must decide whom you are going to back. The Turks nearly brought about our defeat in the war. It was a near thing. You cannot trust them and they are a decadent race. The Greeks, on the other hand, are our friends, and they are a rising people . . . We must secure Constantinople and the Dardanelles. You cannot do that effectively without crushing the Turkish power." Referring to the doubts about his policy voiced by British military leaders, he said, "Of course the military are against the Greeks. They always have been. They favour the Turks. The military are confirmed Tories. It is the Tory policy to support the Turks."[14]

On the night of 14–15 June 1920, Kemal's Turkish Nationalist troops attacked a British battalion near Constantinople, posing a threat to the forces occupying the Ottoman capital, where the Allies held the Sultan as a virtual prisoner. Coming only a month after Kemal sent his mission to Russia (though a year before Russo-Turkish arrangements were concluded) and soon after the defeats the Nationalists had inflicted on the French in Cilicia, the Turkish attack caused alarm. The British commanding officer telegraphed for reinforcements. The Chief of the Imperial General Staff in London reluctantly recognized that the only troops available were Greek, and proposed to the Cabinet that a Greek division be requested to help defend Constantinople. Venizelos was willing to supply it, provided that the Allies also authorized Greece to advance from Smyrna. This would allow the Greek army to seize and occupy the substantial enclave that Venizelos proposed to annex. It would complete the transformation of Greek troops from a temporary policing force into a permanent army of occupation.

Lloyd George was more than willing. He had met with Venizelos earlier, had warned him that the other Allies would not help, had asked Greece to enforce the terms of the Treaty of Sèvres by herself, and had agreed with Venizelos that their military advisers exaggerated the difficulty of doing so.[15] On 20 June 1920 French Premier Millerand agreed with Lloyd George to authorize a limited Greek advance from Smyrna. On 22 June the Greeks launched a successful three-pronged attack which by early July had brought them all of Asia Minor as far as the Anatolian plateau. On the far side of the Dardanelles, meanwhile, Greek troops drove through eastern Thrace. Months before—in occupying Constantinople—the Allies had crushed resistance in the capital. Now the Greek army seemed to have crushed resistance outside the capital as well—if the existence of Kemal was ignored. "Turkey is no more," an exultant Lloyd George announced triumphantly.[16] On 10 August 1920 the Treaty of Sèvres was signed by representatives of the virtually captive Turkish Sultan and his helpless government.

The Treaty of Sèvres (see page 411) embodied almost all of the terms that Lloyd George and Venizelos most desired. While reducing the Ottoman state almost to a nonentity, it restored to Greece the coastal lands of Asia Minor that Greeks had settled nearly 3,000 years before. Like Arabs, Greeks were bound together by a common language and civilization rather than by political ties, so that what Greece accomplished in 1920 with British political backing was to extend her territorial frontier in Europe to her cultural frontier in Greek-speaking Asia. It was the Liberal dream of triumphant Hellenism and Christianity, promoted by Gladstone's political heir, David Lloyd George.

The problem, which seems to have struck Venizelos and Lloyd George almost immediately after the signing at Sèvres, was how to keep the terms of the treaty from being eventually overthrown. The British armed forces had already been demobilized, and there was considerable domestic political pressure in Greece, too, to demobilize immediately. Yet once the Allies departed from Turkey, Kemal might well descend from the Anatolian plateau to retake the coast and undo the treaty. In October 1920 Venizelos raised with Lloyd George the question of the other alternative: whether to send his army into the interior to destroy Kemal's Nationalists while Greece still had the armed forces to do so.[17] Like Napoleon amidst the burning ruins of Moscow, Venizelos and Lloyd George were challenged by an enemy who would neither stand and fight nor surrender. Indeed, Kemal's plan was to pursue the strategy the Russians had used successfully against Napoleon in the war of 1812: drawing the enemy forces into the interior, while wearing them down.

What Venizelos and Lloyd George would have decided to do can never be known for sure, for one of the most bizarre political accidents in modern history took the matter out of their hands. On 30 September 1920 the young Greek King, Alexander, while taking a walk in the grounds of his palace, was bitten by a monkey. A severe fever set in and, on 25 October, Alexander died. In a famous phrase, Winston Churchill later wrote that "It is perhaps no exaggeration to remark that a quarter of a million persons died of this monkey's bite"[18]—for it was his belief that if Alexander and Venizelos had continued to rule Greece, the tragic outcome of the war that Greece was to wage against Turkey in 1921 and 1922 would have been averted (see Chapter 60 below).

The immensely complicated question of succession to the throne arose at the same time as the Greek elections. The results were astonishing. Against almost all expectations the supposedly popular Venizelos was defeated. Brought back into power were the pro-German, anti-Allied leaders whom Venizelos and the French had deposed and exiled during the war.

Constantine I, Alexander's father, forced off the throne in 1917, was once again king. Back from French-imposed exile, Demetrios Gounaris, the bitter enemy of Venizelos and of the Allies, controlled the government. Constantine and his ministers were eager to press forward in Turkey. But for anyone on the Allied side who wanted to abandon the complexities of the Asia Minor involvement, the turnabout in Greece provided the perfect occasion for doing so. The French and the Italians took advantage of the situation by withdrawing their support from Greece and, by implication, from the Treaty of Sèvres. Both countries had been increasingly unhappy with Lloyd George's venturesome policy. France, in particular, had felt constrained only by a personal commitment to Venizelos, from which his defeat at the polls released her. Thereafter both Italy and France looked increasingly to a future Kemalist government of Turkey as a source of financial concessions and advantages.

In Britain, Churchill and the War Office argued in favor of concessions to Kemal in order to detach him from Bolshevik Russia. Indeed Churchill urged making a peace with Kemal that would re-create that "Turkish barrier to Russian ambitions" that had been the traditional British policy during the Great Game.[19] But Lloyd George resisted all such proposals.[20] Massive unemployment and other severe economic and social problems in Britain—as well as problems in Egypt, Afghanistan, Arabia, and elsewhere in the Middle East—still did not cause Lloyd George to conclude (as Churchill had concluded) that Britain could not afford to devote resources to coercing Turkey.

In an apparent effort to settle matters, however, the Allies convened a round-table conference in London to which a Kemalist delegation was invited. The conference was scheduled to meet in London, and its first full session fell on 21 February 1921. The new Greek government agreed to attend the conference, but before the conference convened the Greek army's high command ordered a probe of Kemal's defenses. Evidently thinking in terms of a military rather than a negotiated settlement, the Greek commander-in-chief sent forward a reconnaissance force toward the Kemalist lines in the interior. Moving over difficult, broken, high ground in harsh winter weather, the Greeks met and were repulsed by a Turkish force under the command of Kemal's colleague, Ismet, near a little village called Inonu. For the Turks the outcome was a portent of victories to come. The Greeks, however, came away from the engagement with the impression that they had tested the fighting qualities of the Turks and had found that the Turkish defenses were vulnerable.

At the London conference in February, little progress was made toward resolving the dispute about Anatolia's fate. The Greeks had made up their minds in advance that they were prepared to go to war in order to win a total victory. The Kemalist Turks, moreover, were not willing to let Greece retain the Smyrna enclave; yet any Greek government would have raised domestic political difficulties for itself by surrendering it. Venizelos—out of office, but still active—had already told Lloyd George that if King Constantine's government abandoned Smyrna, Venizelist leaders in Greek Anatolia would proclaim Smyrna an independent republic and would carry on the war against the Turks. "Hellenism," he wrote to the British Prime Minister, "is a force much broader than the confines of the Greek Kingdom, and ... if the latter does not wish or is unable to hold Smyrna with its surrounding district, it is possible for Hellenism in Turkey itself to undertake this duty, provided the allies, or to speak more precisely England, are disposed to support this task ..."[21] In guarded terms, Lloyd George indicated that he might be disposed to tender such support.[22]

The London conference achieved nothing; neither side was willing to compromise. The Kemalist delegation was encouraged, by the eagerness of France and Italy to negotiate separately with it, to believe that it need not moderate its demands. Similarly, the Greeks were encouraged to remain intransigent by the anti-Turkish enthusiasm of the British Prime Minister. Lloyd George was convinced that Venizelos had been profoundly right in observing that "the most important result for humanity of the great war was not the dissolution of the Austro-Hungarian Empire nor the limitation of the German, but the disappearance of the Turkish Empire."[23]

But victory over Ottoman resistance forces continued to elude the Prime Minister. In Turkey itself, Kemal still defied the Allies, while to the south—in Syria—Ottoman officers, officials, and notables centered in Damascus also proclaimed Arab defiance of the Allies.

48

SYRIA AND LEBANON: THE SPRING AND SUMMER OF 1920

I

The nominal ruler of Syria was Feisal, the prince from Mecca who had led the Arab striking force on the right flank of the Allied armies in the Palestine and Syrian campaigns. Pending negotiation of a peace settlement, General Allenby—commencing in the autumn of 1918—had allowed Feisal to administer Syria's affairs from the capital city of Damascus. Feisal himself spent much of 1919 in Europe negotiating with the Allies; he entrusted the administration of Syria to others.

As the metropolis of the Arabic-speaking areas that Britain had left provisionally independent, the ancient oasis town of Damascus was a center upon which discontented Arab political and military figures from many parts of the former Ottoman Empire converged.[1] Carelessly administered in Feisal's name by feuding rivals, it was in a state of continuous unrest throughout 1919 and 1920, as traditional ruling families battled against the ambitions of adventurous newcomers, while militants of the principal political clubs divided largely along regional lines.

A General Syrian Congress was called into being by Feisal and assembled 6 June 1919. Feisal, aware that he was a foreigner in Damascus and mindful of the principles proclaimed by Woodrow Wilson, summoned the congress to endorse the demands he planned to present at the Peace Conference and to prove to the conference that he was the authentic spokesman for the peoples of the Syrian provinces. Feisal had not yet recognized the necessity of placing control of the Syrian General Congress in the hands of men who would be prepared to endorse the extensive concessions that, in the nature of international politics, he would be obliged to make at the Peace Conference in Paris.

The old-guard traditional ruling families in Syria were among those whose loyalty to the Ottoman Empire had remained unshaken throughout the war. They had remained hostile to Feisal, the Allies,

435

and the militant Arab nationalist clubs; yet they won congressional seats in Damascus and in the other principal inland towns of Homs, Hama, and Aleppo. Nonetheless the radical nationalist clubs succeeded in winning control of the General Syrian Congress, in part by making deals with some elements in the conservative old-guard.[2]

Of the three main nationalist clubs, one—al-'Ahd, the organization of Arabic officers in the Ottoman army—was dominated by members from the Mesopotamian provinces, whose chief interest was in the future of their own provinces. Another, the Arab Club, was dominated by members from the Palestinian area and was set up as an anti-Zionist organization devoted to forcing Feisal to abandon his commitment to Zionism. Several members of the Executive Committee of the Arab Club occupied important positions in Feisal's administration, even though the Palestinians had largely remained pro-Ottoman and anti-Feisal throughout the war. Palestinians also achieved leadership positions in the broad-based Istiqlal Party, established by the third and most prominent of the nationalist clubs, al-Fatat.

The orientation of the General Syrian Congress was revealed as soon as it met in mid-1919, by its call for a completely independent Greater Syria that would include all of the area that is occupied today by Syria, Lebanon, Jordan, and Israel. To Feisal, who hoped for an American or British Mandatory regime and for American, British, and Zionist support against the demands of France, it appeared that matters were passing out of his control and that he would have to take steps "to take steam out of the Syrian Congress."[3] However, he was obliged to remove himself from the scene in order to attend negotiations with the Great Powers in Europe.

At the end of the negotiations in Europe in 1919, Feisal succeeded in reaching the secret understanding described earlier with the French Premier, Clemenceau. Their agreement allowed Feisal to reign over an independent Syria over which France would exercise only a loose trusteeship.[4] From the point of view of Clemenceau, these were generous terms: no other French politician would have agreed to let Arab Syria retain a certain measure of independence or offered to let the pro-British Feisal remain in Damascus—let alone as Syria's monarch. When Clemenceau fell from power in January 1920, the strong colonialist bloc in the newly elected French Parliament certainly might have balked at honoring such terms. Feisal's only hope was the French would feel themselves bound by the secret agreement once they learned of its existence—so long as the Syrian Arabs were willing to be bound by it too. But when Feisal returned from Europe to Syria on 14 January 1920, he found that Arab nationalists were unwilling to accept any role at all for France in guiding Syria's affairs. In vain, Feisal warned a committee of one of the Arab nationalist societies in Damascus that to reject his agreement with Clemenceau meant war with France; but the committee replied that "We are ready to declare war on both England and France."[5] Later in January, with militant Arab nationalists in control, the General Syrian Congress voted down the terms of the Feisal—Clemenceau agreement.

Unable to persuade the nationalists to follow his policy of conciliating France—unable, in other words, to lead the nationalists—Feisal seemingly changed course and began to talk as though he meant to follow them. In February he was reported to be speaking of winning full Arab independence from France "by the sword."[6] But this appears to have been mere demagoguery, designed to rival that of the nationalists in bidding for popular support. For under cover of his violent rhetoric, Feisal reached out to the only significant indigenous force that could be induced to support his policy of compromise with France: his former enemies, the conservative, traditional ruling families of Damascus and the inland towns, who had supported the Ottoman Empire in the world war against the Allies and Feisal. Feisal persuaded them to form a new political party—the National Party—which espoused in public the independence of a Greater Syria, but in private was prepared to accept the Feisal-Clemenceau agreement and a French presence. The National Party did not in fact insist on full and immediate independence for Syria and was also prepared to recognize a Jewish National Home in Palestine.[7*]

Rushing to head off the National Party by acting before it could organize its forces, the militant nationalist clubs called the General Congress back into session. The second Syrian General Congress convened in early March 1920, and immediately passed a resolution proclaiming Syria to be completely independent within her "natural" boundaries, including Lebanon and Palestine, under the kingship of Feisal as constitutional monarch.[8] At the same time an Arab delegation in Palestine confronted the British military governor with a resolution opposing Zionism and petitioning to become part of an independent Syria; while a group of Mesopotamians met to proclaim the independence of their provinces—Basra and Baghdad—under the kingship of Feisal's brother, Abdullah.[9] Thus early in 1920, within weeks after the Ottoman Chamber of Deputies in Constantinople had publicly defied the Allies and declared the independence of the Turkish-speaking part of the empire, the Arabic-speaking part seemed to be following the same course.

General Allenby, thoroughly alarmed, warned his superiors that if

---

* Arab opinion in Palestine and Syria regarded both as part of the same country, so that Zionism was also an issue in Damascus, although it was not the overriding issue that it was in Jerusalem, Jaffa, or Haifa.

Britain and France "persist in their attitude of declaring null and void the action of Feisal and Syrian Congress, I feel certain that war must ensue. If hostilities arise, the Arabs will regard both French and English as their enemies, and we shall be dragged by the French into a war which is against our own interests and for which we are ill-prepared."[10] Britain blamed France for this. Lord Curzon summoned the French ambassador to the Foreign Office to point out the mistakes France had made, and to place on record his opinion that the dire turn of events was entirely France's fault.[11]

The French and, even more so, the British were startled by the Damascus proclamations; and cautioned Feisal that grave consequences would follow any attempt to carry them into effect.[12] Yet, carried away by a congress that he could not control, Feisal not only allowed his followers to carry on guerrilla attacks against the French and Christians on the coast,[13] but moved to establish support for Kemalist Turkey, which was successfully inflicting defeats on the French in Cilicia, above the frontier. Feisal and his partisans denied France the use of the Aleppo railroad line, cutting off reinforcements by land and obliging the French to supply their beleaguered garrison in Cilicia by sea instead.[14]

But the Syrian nationalists failed to realize how much their position and Feisal's had depended on British support; their proclamations, attacking British claims to govern Mesopotamia and Palestine, effectively forced Britain back into the arms of France, and briefly restored the alliance of the two European powers in the Middle East. Even Lloyd George, whose initial reaction was glee at the news that France was being defied, saw no alternative but to reach agreement with the French. The policies of Lloyd George and the armies of Allenby had formed the shield behind which the Syrians had been allowed to indulge in provocative politics with impunity. Once the shield was withdrawn, the French government—as its colonialist group quickly saw—was free to act.

France's main concern was to detach the Syrians from their dangerous alliance with the forces of Kemalist Turkey. Robert de Caix, the leading propagandist of the colonialist society the Comité de l'Asie Française, who had become France's chief political representative in Syria, led a delegation to Angora on 20 May 1920 to negotiate an armistice with Kemal in person. He succeeded in patching up a temporary truce. This, together with an agreement with the British, paved the way for France to take military action.

On 27 May 1920 Paris ordered its commander in Beirut, General Gouraud, to prepare to take the field against Feisal. On Bastille Day 1920, General Gouraud, pushed by Paris, sent an ultimatum to Feisal, setting forth terms that he could not have expected the Arab leader to accept, including the disbanding of the Arab army. But Feisal, evidently losing his nerve, agreed to the French terms, whereupon the mobs of Damascus rioted against him. General Gouraud, under orders from Paris, took the position that the reply Feisal had sent him—abject though it was—was nonetheless unsatisfactory. Feisal rushed to send another, offering unconditional surrender, but Gouraud was prevailed upon by de Caix to reply that it was too late, and to order his troops to march on Damascus.

The French had few troops available for the campaign, and meanwhile the breakdown of their truce with Kemal suddenly exposed them to dangers on both sides: Kemal to the north, Feisal to the east. The French appeared to be trapped between enemies on two fronts, but they were in luck, for they met with no effective resistance from the Syrians. The largely Senegalese troops of France's Army of the Levant advanced through twisting gorges in which a competent opponent would have ambushed them; but unaccountably, Feisal's partisans waited until the Senegalese emerged before challenging them.[15] At that point, a French air squadron appeared overhead, and the defenders of Damascus panicked, turned, and fled, offering no resistance.[16] On 26 July 1920 the French occupied Damascus; on 27 July they ordered Feisal into exile; and on 28 July he left. The French Prime Minister proclaimed that Syria henceforth would be held by France: "The whole of it, and forever."[17]

The French authorities went ahead to divide Syria into sub-units. One of these, Great Lebanon, was the forerunner of the country today called Lebanon. The Great Lebanon proclaimed by General Gouraud on 1 August 1920 also corresponded roughly to the area of direct rule promised to France in the Sykes-Picot Agreement. In addition to the old Turkish canton of Lebanon—in which France's Maronite Christian protégés as well as their traditional enemies, the Druses, were centered—Great Lebanon included the coastal cities of Beirut, Tripoli, Sidon, and Tyre, as well as the long Bekaa valley which covered a considerable area in the interior of the country. None of these territorial additions—Beirut, Tripoli, Sidon, Tyre, or the Bekaa—had fallen within the canton of Lebanon, where Christian power was based; indeed they brought with them large Sunni and Shi'ite Moslem populations.

Whether this expansion of Lebanon—which was to lead to so much bloodshed in the 1970s and 1980s, as various groups attacked the leading position of the Maronite minority in what had become a predominantly Moslem country—was the result of Maronite Christian or of French political pressure cannot be determined.[18] Many hands pushed General Gouraud toward his decision. At the time its risks were not fully appreciated.

II

The ease with which the occupation of Damascus had been effected seemed to expose the pretensions of Feisal and Arab nationalism as shams that had been invented by Britain in order to cheat France out of her claim to Syria. Whenever there were local uprisings in Syria—and there were disturbances from time to time throughout the life of the French Mandate—it was natural for the French to blame them on the British, and they did so.[19] Lloyd George, who had lost France's good will by attempting to withhold Syria, did not regain that good will by changing his policy so as to let France have her.

Having withdrawn his troops in 1919, Lloyd George had in fact lost control of events in Syria at least as much as he had in the interior of Anatolia, in the deserts of Arabia, in the mountains of Afghanistan, and in the peasant villages of Egypt. In Syria the result was that the British were blamed on all sides. The French blamed them for putting Feisal up and the Arabs blamed them for letting Feisal down.

Arab partisans of Feisal in Palestine and Iraq now ranged themselves among Britain's enemies—which raised the question of why Britain was maintaining a presence in the Middle East. The British public had been told that one of Britain's goals was to support Feisal's Arab movement. But if Feisal's Arabs had become Britain's enemies, why should she continue to support them? Moreover, Feisal's supporters jeopardized Britain's relations with France—among other places, in British-held Palestine east of the Jordan river. Their activities seemed likely to goad France into an invasion of Transjordan, which would plunge Britain into an unwanted and dangerous international conflict. Relations between Britain and France were fragile enough as it was—especially in regard to Palestine, a land that France had coveted for herself—and the British feared that Feisal's partisans east of the Jordan might provide the French colonialist group with an excuse for sending troops across the border.

EASTERN PALESTINE
(TRANSJORDAN): 1920

At about the same time that it ordered the invasion, conquest, and occupation of Syria, the French government inaugurated a diplomatic and propaganda campaign designed to prevent neighboring Palestine from becoming "a Zionist state."[1] Since Britain was sponsoring Zionism in Palestine, the campaign took on an anti-British hue; but the French government was even more opposed to a Jewish than to a British Palestine, and feared that France's commercial and clerical interests in the Holy Land might be endangered by British-sponsored Zionism.

The language used by the Quai d'Orsay expressed refined, and that used in the press expressed crude, anti-Semitism.[2] But in June 1920—when the two European allies, Britain and France, entered into detailed negotiations to draw a frontier between Palestine and Syria-Lebanon ("Palestine" and "Syria" were both vague terms, and it was unclear at the time where one ended and the other started)— the hard stance taken by French negotiators expressed French self-interest. For the French pictured the frontier as between France and Britain in the Levant, and took an uncompromising position, urged on by a colonialist group that bitterly accused France's leaders of having abandoned too many of her claims and interests in Asia. The new chairman of the Commission of Foreign Affairs of the Chamber of Deputies, who also served as president of one of the principal French colonialist societies, the Comité de l'Orient, was as ready as was the popular press to brand compromise as treasonable. At stake in the negotiation of Palestine's frontiers were the valuable headwaters of the Jordan and Yarmuk rivers—which the French successfully insisted on obtaining for Syria-Lebanon.

The Oeuvre des Ecoles d'Orient, which represented French Catholic missionaries in the Middle East, pictured the Jewish National Home as "merely a means for the English to undermine our position."[3] It also claimed to discern a Jewish world conspiracy behind both Zionism and Bolshevism "seeking by all means at its disposal the destruction of the Christian world."[4] Robert de Caix, who managed France's political interests in Syria, agreed, claiming that "The revolutionary and prophetic spirit which is so often found among Jews has turned to Bolshevism" among the Zionists who were arriving in Palestine from eastern Europe.[5] Thus the French saw their position in Syria and Lebanon as being threatened by a movement that they believed to be at once British, Jewish, Zionist, and Bolshevik. According to the president of the Oeuvre des Ecoles d'Orient, it was not merely French national interests but also religious sensibilities that required action to be taken against the Protestant and Jewish positions in Palestine. "It is inadmissible," he said, "that the 'Country of Christ' should become the prey of Jewry and of Anglo-Saxon heresy. It must remain the inviolable inheritance of France and the Church. It would be a national infamy and an irreparable crime not to remove this sacred land from the brutal rapacity of our allies."[6]

At the time, the French government financed an anti-British political club called the Literary Society which had branches in Jerusalem and other Palestinian towns. However, in 1920, the immediate French threat to British interests was posed in the large, and largely unpopulated, area east of the Jordan called Transjordan, that was to form roughly 75 percent of the territory included in the British Mandate for Palestine. In terms of tribal life and structure, Transjordan was akin to Arabia; in historical terms, much of it was part of the land of the Bible, and it had also once formed part of the Roman province of Arabia. Since the autumn of 1918, when Allenby drove out the Turks, it had been essentially ungoverned, for the British military authorities had left it under Feisal's ineffective Damascus administration. This turned out to have been (from Britain's point of view) a mistake, for when the French supplanted Feisal and his ministers as rulers of Damascus, they put themselves in a position to claim this area as Feisal's successors.

Transjordan was a disordered area of tribal conflict. The British feared that the lawlessness of the area might be seized upon by the French as an excuse for occupying it to bring order and civilization. Arab enemies of French rule in Syria—claiming they were fighting to bring Feisal back to Damascus—had gathered and might mount raids from Transjordan against French Syria; and these could be used by the French as justification for mounting an invasion in retaliation.

The British administration, centered in western Palestine, proposed to send in British troops, but there were none to be had, for London opposed the venture; all that London would authorize was the sending in of a handful of civil administrators.[7]

A British officer serving in Transjordan, C. D. Brunton, reported to his superiors that people were saying the British would withdraw

from the country and that "no one seems satisfied with our occupation."[8] Captain Brunton predicted that it would take little to throw
the country into complete anarchy. He explained that

> the people here do not form a homogeneous political entity.
> There is a sharp line of division between the settled population
> and the Bedouin. The former wish settled government and
> protection from the extortions and violence of the latter. The
> Bedouin prefer anarchy to order as they live from extortions
> from the peasantry and rapine as well as from their flocks and
> herds. You cannot expect them to form a government for their
> common country.[9]

His immediate concern was that a representative of Feisal's
Hashemite family was raising passions against the French. On 9
September 1920 Brunton reported that the Hashemite representative
had proclaimed a Holy War against the French in Syria, had recruited
volunteers, and had released criminals from jail in the town of
Amman to join his movement.[10] Two days later, in a calmer mood,
he was able to report that the Hashemite representative had secured,
in all, only fifty volunteers.[11] But Brunton remained unhappy about
the British government's approach to governing Transjordan: "The
idea of controlling a country partially inhabited by predatory savages
by giving it Home Rule and a few British advisers may sound
attractive as an experiment," he wrote, but in practice it was not
working.[12]

Since Britain did not maintain an army in Transjordan, she could
not defend the territory if France were to invade it. To retain
Transjordan for herself, Britain would therefore have to avoid pro-
voking a French invasion. Arab raids on French positions in Syria—
if launched from Transjordan—could provoke such an invasion, and
therefore had to be stopped. The policy of F. R. Somerset, a British
official in Transjordan, was to stop the Arab tribes from launching
raids against French Syria by playing off one tribe against another.

Somerset's policy, if successful, would deprive France of a reason—
or an excuse—for invading undefended Transjordan. But what if
France were to attack the British trusteeship—not merely of Transjordan, but of the rest of Palestine as well—by other means: by
politics, propaganda, and subversion rather than armed invasion? As
of 1920, Arab nationalists hated France; but what if France should
turn them around and persuade them to hate Britain instead?
Somerset feared that France might launch a propaganda crusade for
a Greater Syria, to include Transjordan and western Palestine, on an
anti-Zionist platform[13] that would be popular with Arabs everywhere
in Palestine. France might promise the Arabs that if she were allowed
to take Palestine (including Transjordan) away from Britain, she

would put a stop to Zionism—and Arabs might rally behind France on the basis of such a program. Somerset's view, which was shared by a large section of British officialdom, was that Zionists were compromising the British cause, as well as their own, by making their ultimate intentions public. "It is the Jews and not us that everyone is against," he wrote. "If the Jews would keep their silly mouths shut they could buy up the whole country."[14] T. E. Lawrence took rather a different view: "He trusted that in four or five years, under the influence of a just policy, the opposition to Zionism would have decreased, if it had not entirely disappeared."[15]

But, for the moment, Arab opposition to Zionism was loud and lively, and was disturbing the peace of British-held Palestine.

50

PALESTINE—ARABS AND JEWS: 1920

In 1917–18, when General Allenby took Palestine away from the Turks, he established a British military administration for the country. Ever since then, throughout the military administration, there had run a strong streak of resentment at having been burdened by London with an unpopular and difficult-to-achieve policy: the creation of a Jewish homeland in Palestine pursuant to the Balfour Declaration. From the beginning, Gilbert Clayton, as chief political officer to General Allenby, and Ronald Storrs, as governor of Jerusalem, had avoided giving any sign that they proposed to support that policy. Both men privately professed to believe in Zionism, though Clayton in particular seemed to define it in its narrowest possible sense: the fostering of an expanded Jewish community in Palestine that could serve as a cultural and sentimental center for Jews throughout the world, but within a British administered, multinational Palestine that would not become a Jewish state. Other British officers serving in Palestine were unsympathetic to Zionism even in this limited sense, and sided with the Arabs, who opposed it altogether. As they saw it, London's policy of Zionism might have been expressly designed to stir up trouble, and must have been devised by far-off officials who did not have to live with and deal with local conditions.

To Zionist leaders, on the other hand, it appeared that the wavering stance or downright hostility of the British administration hampered their effort to secure Arab acceptance of the Balfour Declaration. They claimed that, had the Arab population of the country been made to feel that the Balfour Declaration was the unalterable policy of the British government and inevitably would be carried into effect, Arabs would have acquiesced—and might even have become receptive to its benefits. Dr Weizmann and his colleagues in the Zionist leadership stressed their desire to cooperate with the Arab communities; emphasized that the new Jewish immigrants would not be taking anything away from the existing inhabitants, but would buy, colonize, and cultivate land not then being used; and repeated that Jewish colonization would bring substantial economic benefits to the whole country, and indeed to the whole Arab Middle East.

Among the Arabic-speaking communities of Palestine, there was considerable disagreement on most issues, and perhaps even on Zionism. This was shown in February 1919, at a congress convened by the anti-Zionist Moslem-Christian Society. A majority of the thirty active politicians who attended the congress were able to paper over their differences by agreeing on a program calling for an Arab federation headed by Feisal and centered on Syria. There was some feeling, however, in favor of creating a separate Palestine, some pro-British feeling, some pro-French feeling, and enough discord so that five of the thirty delegates did not sign a resolution opposing Zionism. Much volatility in political views was demonstrated by the delegates and their colleagues during the course of the next couple of years, as those who had called for Feisal to become king turned against him, pro-British and anti-British factions changed sides, and the proponents of Greater Syria were forced, by the French conquest of Damascus, to restrict the focus of their views to the territory about to be embraced within Britain's Palestine Mandate.

Arab politics within Palestine were formed by the rivalry between the great urban families. Throughout the British occupation, the most conspicuous rivalry was that between the Jerusalem families of al-Husseini and al-Nashashibi. Al-Nashashibi family politics moved from anti-British to pro-British and pro-conciliation in 1920; and in the years immediately thereafter the Zionist leadership believed that it had arrived at a basis for mutual cooperation with the al-Nashashibi that might lead to Arab-Jewish harmony. The al-Husseini, however, who moved at the same time from supporters to opponents of the British, found themselves favored in the competition to lead the Arab communities of the area by the sympathy shown by the British local administration to the anti-Zionist cause. If even British officers argued that the Arabs should make no concessions, how could pro-conciliation Arab leaders persuade their followers that concessions had to be made?

Violence broke out late in 1919 when Bedouin tribes attacked Jewish settlements in the Upper Galilee, in the no-man's land between the British and French military administrations. Early in 1920, marauding Arabs entered the Zionist settlements and, in the ensuing gun-fighting, several settlers were killed, including the Russian-Jewish war hero, Captain Joseph Trumpeldor.

Thereafter rumors were rife of violence to come in Jerusalem that spring. In response Vladimir Jabotinsky—the Russian-Jewish journalist who had organized the Jewish regiment in Allenby's army—secured the agreement of other Zionist leaders to allow him to form a self-defense group, to be composed largely of veterans like himself of the Jewish Legion in the British army. Jabotinsky informed the British governor of Jerusalem that he was forming such a group; asked that his group be, in effect, deputized; and requested the British administration to issue arms to him. When the British refused, he bought arms from an Armenian gunrunner in the Old City.

The violence predicted for Jerusalem broke out on 4 April 1920. During the Moslem springtime festival of the Prophet Moses, fiery orators roused Arab mobs to what became three days of rioting against Jews, of whom some were killed and hundreds wounded.[1] No casualties were suffered in New Jerusalem, however, which was patrolled by Jabotinsky's forces. All of the casualties were suffered in the Old City of Jerusalem, which British army units prevented Jabotinsky's forces from entering.

Adding an especially ominous tinge to the bloodletting in the Old City was the cry of the rioting mobs that "The Government is with us!"[2] That the mobs were not unjustified in their cry became evident when the British military authorities meted out punishment. Only a few rioters were punished by serious court sentences; but Jabotinsky and his colleagues were swiftly brought before a closed court martial, charged with distributing arms to the self-defense group, and sentenced to fifteen years' hard labor in the fortress-prison of Acre.[3] These decisions caused an outcry that led the British government to order a court of inquiry into how the military were conducting the administration of Palestine.

The government's court of inquiry held hearings in Jerusalem, at which military officials claimed that Jews were at fault, saying they had provoked the Moslems, while Jewish witnesses charged that the British military government had encouraged the rioters. Richard Meinertzhagen, the head of Military Intelligence in Cairo, had been sent out to Palestine to report on whether London's pro-Zionist policy was being carried out, and when he testified in court that the Jewish witnesses were correct, the government was shocked into accepting the truth of their testimony.[4]

Meinertzhagen confided in his diary that "I am not sure that the world is not still too selfish to appreciate the worth of the merits of Zionist aims. The world is certainly too anti-semitic and too suspicious of jewish brains and money. In any case I find myself alone out here, among gentiles, in upholding Zionism ... And that is the irony of the whole situation, for I am also imbued with antisemitic feelings ..."[5] Suspecting that his fellow officers might have moved from sentiments to actions, he spied on them while he was in Palestine. Later, he reported to General Allenby that he had planted an agent within the military administration, and had learned that the

British colonel who served as chief of staff of the administration was conspiring with the Arab Mufti of Jerusalem to foment new anti-Jewish riots.[6]

Within weeks after the government had held its court of inquiry, London disbanded the military administration of Palestine and installed a civilian administration in its place. Lloyd George appointed Herbert Samuel to be its head, as the new High Commissioner. Samuel, a Jew and a leading Liberal, had been the first member of the British government—in 1914, when the war against Turkey began—to have proposed the creation of a British-sponsored Jewish homeland in Palestine. His appointment showed that the Prime Minister was unwavering in his Palestine policy; yet the violence which the military administration had encouraged caused others in London to have second thoughts about support for a Jewish homeland. Even Winston Churchill, who had been an enthusiastic pro-Zionist all his life, wrote, on 13 June 1920, to Lloyd George that "Palestine is costing us 6 millions a year to hold. The Zionist movement will cause continued friction with the Arabs. The French ... are opposed to the Zionist movement & will try to cushion the Arabs off on us as the real enemy. The Palestine venture ... will never yield any profit of a material kind."[7]

These doubts were intensified by spectacular uprisings in Iraq at about the same time, that drained Britain's resources, and which—coming after the riots in Egypt, the war in Afghanistan, the religious war in Arabia, the nationalist rebellion in Turkey, and the troubles with French Syria—suggested to many Englishmen that Britain should withdraw from the Middle East entirely.

MESOPOTAMIA (IRAQ): 1920

In the first heady days of Arab nationalism in Damascus after the war, it became apparent that one of the important regional differences between the various Arab activists was that those from the Mesopotamian provinces—the eastern half of the Arabic-speaking world—were for the most part military men. Although the Mesopotamian soldiers claimed to act in the name of Feisal and his brothers, most of them were former Ottoman officers who had remained loyal to the Sultan and the Young Turks until the very end of the war. Battlefield professionals and dedicated opponents of Britain, they could have been expected to constitute a more serious potential threat to British plans than did the politicians and orators of Damascus or Jerusalem.

At first the British administration in the Mesopotamian provinces did not see it that way. Tensions between the diverse populations of the area seemed to pose greater problems, and the lawlessness of groups such as the Kurds and the Bedouin tribes seemed to pose greater threats. Incoherence, communal strife, and habitual disorder—rather than organized nationalism—were perceived as the challenge. The talk of national self-government came mostly (according to the local British authorities) from ambitious intriguers of shady character who would subside into insignificance if only the Allied leaders would cease their unsettling Wilsonian propaganda.

At the close of the war, the temporary administration of the provinces was in the hands of Captain (later Colonel) Arnold Wilson of British India, who became civil commissioner. His famous assistant was Gertrude Bell, at that time the best-known British writer about Arab countries. She tended toward protectorate, he, toward direct rule, but in 1918 they were enough in agreement for him to forward with approval her memorandum arguing that the talk of self-determination before and at the Peace Conference was detrimental. She had previously written that "the people of Mesopotamia, having witnessed the successful termination of the war, had taken it for granted that the country would remain under British control and

were as a whole content to accept the decision of arms." The declarations in favor of national self-determination at the Peace Conference
by Woodrow Wilson and others "opened up other possibilities which
were regarded almost universally with anxiety, but gave opportunity
for political intrigue to the less stable and more fanatical elements."[1]

When, in line with the American principles being adopted—or at
least affected—in London, the Cabinet instructed Arnold Wilson to
ask the peoples of Mesopotamia what states or governments they
would like to see established in their area, Wilson's reply was that
there was no way of ascertaining public opinion.[2]

While he was prepared to administer the provinces of Basra and
Baghdad, and also the province of Mosul (which, with Clemenceau's
consent, Lloyd George had detached from the French sphere and
intended to withhold from Turkey), he did not believe that they
formed a coherent entity. Iraq (an Arab term that the British used
increasingly to denote the Mesopotamian lands) seemed to him too
splintered for that to be possible. Mosul's strategic importance made
it seem a necessary addition to Iraq, and the strong probability that
it contained valuable oilfields made it a desirable one, but it was part
of what was supposed to have been Kurdistan; and Arnold Wilson
argued that the warlike Kurds who had been brought under his
administration "numbering half a million will never accept an Arab
ruler."[3]

A fundamental problem, as Wilson saw it, was that the almost two
million Shi'ite Moslems in Mesopotamia would not accept domination by the minority Sunni Moslem community, yet "no form of
Government has yet been envisaged, which does not involve Sunni
domination."[4] The bitterness between the two communities was
highlighted when each produced a rival Arab nationalist society.[5]
Also to be considered was the large Jewish community, which dominated the commercial life of Baghdad, and the substantial Christian
community that included the Nestorian-Chaldaean refugees from
Turkey who had gathered in the area of Mosul.

* Seventy-five percent of the population of Iraq was tribal, Wilson
told London, "with no previous tradition of obedience to any government."[6] Along the same lines, Gertrude Bell wrote to her father that
"The provincial magnates are going strongly against an Arab Amir, I
think, and even against an Arab Govt. They say they don't want to
be rid of one tyranny in order to fall into the clutches of another."[7]

Unlike Arab nationalists, who were thinking in terms of political
unity on a large scale,* there were those who questioned whether
even attempting to unite the Mesopotamian provinces might not be
too ambitious to be practical. Gertrude Bell, working on her own
plans for a unified Iraq, was cautioned by an American missionary
that she was ignoring rooted historical realities in doing so. "You are

flying in the face of four millenniums of history if you try to draw a line around Iraq and call it a political entity! Assyria always looked to the west and east and north, and Babylonia to the south. They have never been an independent unit. You've got to take time to get them integrated, it must be done gradually. They have no conception of nationhood yet."[9]

A leading Arab political figure in Baghdad cautioned her along different lines. Speaking to her on 12 June 1920, he reproached her with the fact that, more than three years after occupying Baghdad in the war, Britain continued to talk about establishing an independent government but still did nothing about it. He contrasted this with the situation in Damascus, where the British had set up Feisal's independent administration as soon as they had arrived. Well aware that she was one of the British officials who were making plans for his government, he reminded her that "You said in your declaration that you would set up a native government drawing its authority from the initiative and free choice of the people concerned, yet you proceed to draw up a scheme without consulting anyone. It would have been easy for you to take one or two leading men in your councils and this would have removed the reproach which is levelled against your scheme ..."[10]

[Gertrude Bell discounted the danger of a native uprising.] Her chief, Arnold Wilson (against whom she intrigued), did not. He warned London that demobilization had left his armed forces dangerously undermanned. The military deployed only a tiny force of mobile troops to patrol an area of 170,000 square miles.[11] He pointed to the danger posed by Feisal's adherents; although Nuri el-Sa'id and other top Mesopotamian officers who had served in the Hejaz forces with Lawrence and the Allies had been forbidden to return home, as suspected potential troublemakers, a number of activists—many of whom had served with the enemy during the war—had slipped back into the country after the Damascus proclamations calling for Mesopotamian independence. There was also talk of agents sent by Kemalist Turkey.[12]

British nerves were on edge as vague rumors, constant unrest, and repeated killings took their toll. In the summer of 1919 three young British captains were murdered in Kurdistan. The Government of India sent out an experienced official to take their place in October 1919; a month later he, too, was killed.

---

* (*See page 450.*) Nuri el-Sa'id, the Mesopotamian officer who had served as one of the heads of Feisal's Allied army corps during the war, advocated the creation of a single government for Syria and Mesopotamia.[8] The Mesopotamian delegates associated with the Syrian General Congress in Damascus instead advocated splitting them between governments in Damascus and Baghdad.

At Christmas that year, Arnold Wilson sent to London to enlist the aid of Colonel Gerald Leachman, an officer whose feats of travel, adventure, and war in the eastern deserts had become legendary. Leachman arrived back in Mesopotamia, before the spring of 1920, to find that six British officers had been killed in the ten days before his return.[13] More was to come: the next month Leachman was able to rescue a party of British officers attacked by a raiding party in the desert but, in the early summer, he was unable to save two of his political officers who were abducted as hostages and later murdered. The desert was alive with Arab raiding parties and, in Leachman's opinion, the only way to deal with the disaffected tribes was "wholesale slaughter."[14]

In June the tribes suddenly rose in full revolt—a revolt that seems to have been triggered by the government's efforts to levy taxes. By 14 June the formerly complacent Gertrude Bell, going from one extreme to another, claimed to be living through a nationalist reign of terror.[15] She exaggerated, but in the Middle Euphrates, posts were indeed overrun, British officers killed, and communications cut.[16] For one reason or another—the revolts had a number of causes and the various rebels pursued different goals—virtually the whole area rose against Britain, and revolt then spread to the Lower Euphrates as well. A Holy War was proclaimed against Britain in the Shi'ite Moslem holy city of Karbalah.[17] On the northwestern frontier, Arab cavalry, initially led by one of Feisal's ex-officers, swept down on British outposts and massacred their defenders.

There was more bad news: Leachman, who left Baghdad on 11 August to attend a meeting with tribal allies at a station on the Euphrates, was tricked into sending away his armed escort—and then was shot in the back and killed by order of the tribal sheikh who was his host. "Arab Treachery" was the headline of the Reuters' report of the assassination; "Bad To Worse In Mesopotamia" was the headline of *The Times*.[18] The news of Leachman's killing led to further tribal uprisings against the British along the Euphrates. Fresh uprisings occurred north and west of Baghdad. By mid-August a group of insurgents felt confident enough to declare a provisional Arab government.[19]

In a leading article on 7 August 1920, *The Times* demanded to know "how much longer are valuable lives to be sacrificed in the vain endeavour to impose upon the Arab population an elaborate and expensive administration which they never asked for and do not want?" In a similar article on 10 August, *The Times* said that "We are spending sums in Mesopotamia and in Persia which may well reach a hundred million pounds this year" in support of what it termed "the foolish policy of the Government in the Middle East."

The Government of India poured in reinforcements of men and

supplies to restore order. The main population centers quickly were secured, but regaining control of the countryside took time. It was not until October that many of the cut-off Euphrates towns were relieved and not until February of 1921 that order was restored more or less completely. Before putting down the revolt Britain suffered nearly 2,000 casualties, including 450 dead.[20]

The British were confused as to the origins of the revolt. Arnold Wilson submitted a list of thirteen contributing factors, stressing, above all, the involvement of Feisal's supporters and Kemal's Turkey, perhaps supported, he claimed, by American Standard Oil interests.[21] An intelligence officer attached to the India Office produced a chart outlining the conspiracy, implicating Feisal but, even more so, the Turks, who (he asserted) continued to take orders via Moscow and Switzerland from Berlin.[22] His chart was circulated among Cabinet members in London.

The mysterious uprisings in Iraq threw the normally poised British Indian administration off balance. Sir Arnold Wilson told the Cabinet at the end of 1920 that "there was no real desire in Mesopotamia for an Arab government, that the Arabs would appreciate British rule."[23] If that were so, then the explosion in Mesopotamia could not be explained as an Arab independence movement. "What we are up against," said Wilson, "is anarchy plus fanaticism. There is little or no Nationalism."[24] The tribesmen, he said, were "out against all government as such" and had no notion what they were fighting for.[25] In mid-August he said that the "revolutionary movement has for some time past ceased to have any political aspect and has become entirely anarchic."[26]

It was not a satisfactory explanation, coming—as the Iraqi uprisings did—on top of troubles everywhere else in the Middle East. Why were the despised Turks, under Kemal's leadership, successfully continuing to defy the Allies? Why was Britain's protégé, King Hussein, losing the struggle for mastery in Arabia? Why did the Egyptians continue to refuse to negotiate—on any basis—for Britain's forces to remain in their country? Why were the Afghans conspiring with the Russians? Why did Feisal lose out to France and then allow his followers to strike out at Britain? Why did Arabs riot in Palestine and rebel in Iraq—all at a time when Britain's economy had collapsed and when the government's time, energy, and resources were needed to revive it?

In London there was no agreement about what had happened in the Middle East, but there was a strikingly large body of opinion that held that what had occurred was caused by outsiders, and that the disorders through the East were somehow linked with one another. Certain names continued to recur in the course of British speculations as to the origins of the disorders: Enver Pasha, Mustapha Kemal,

Feisal, Pan-Islam, the Germans, Standard Oil, the Jews, and the Bolsheviks.

With respect to the Bolsheviks, British suspicions in fact proved to be well founded. The Russians, looking for a chance to undermine the British position in Asia, decided that, by bringing pressure to bear on Britain elsewhere, they might enable the insurgency in Iraq to succeed. The area of British vulnerability they chose to exploit was in Persia, the political battlefield on which Britain and Russia had clashed so often in the course of the Great Game.

52

PERSIA (IRAN): 1920

When the First World War came to an end, the British Prime Minister's attention was too much occupied elsewhere for him to pay much attention to Persia, the Ottoman Empire's eastern neighbor, which was not, in any event, an area of the world in which he took much interest. By default the way was left open for George Curzon, chairman of the Eastern Committee of the Cabinet and, from 1919 onward, Foreign Minister, to take charge. Lord Curzon cared about Persia more than he cared about practically anywhere else.

Curzon's tendency was to exaggerate the importance of areas in which he was expert and there was no question that he was an expert on Persia. His journey in 1889 to that then little-known land was famous; and his book *Persia and the Persian Question* was judged to be the standard authority on the subject in the English language. His view, correspondingly, was that the magnitude of British interests in that country was immense.

From the nineteenth century, Lord Curzon brought with him a strategy of creating "a Moslem nexus of states" in the Middle East as a shield to ward off Russian expansion.[1] Russian expansionist designs had figured prominently in his expressed thoughts and in his writings when he explored Central Asia in the late nineteenth century, and had figured prominently in his politics when he became Viceroy of India early in the twentieth century. When the Bolshevik Revolution brought about Russia's withdrawal from her forward positions, Curzon proposed to take advantage of the situation by putting his British-sponsored Moslem nexus of states into place. In the nineteenth century the nexus would have been a line across the Middle East from the Ottoman Empire through the Persian Empire to the khanates and emirates of Central Asia and Afghanistan; but Curzon was in no position to reconstruct a line that long.

Driven to withdraw by Winston Churchill and his policy of radical retrenchment, British forces almost everywhere in Asia were being evacuated from positions that Lord Curzon wished to see maintained. Of the nexus, only Persia remained—but there Curzon retained his

solitary dominance of British policy. Edwin Montagu, a member of
the Cabinet's Eastern Committee, observed that the draft minutes of
a meeting of the committee, from which all members but Curzon
were absent, recorded that "the Committee agreed with the Chairman." "Surely you will not allow this to stand?" Montagu wrote to
Curzon; "the Committee consisted of the Chairman: and the Chairman, of course, not unnaturally, agreed with the Chairman."[2] Insofar
as Persia was concerned, that was the manner in which he proceeded,
taking policy entirely into his own hands and ignoring the reluctance
of his Cabinet colleagues to follow where he led.

"The integrity of Persia," he had written two decades earlier,
"must be registered as a cardinal precept of our Imperial creed."[3]
Safeguarding that integrity against future Russian encroachments
remained the principal object of his policy. The means at his disposal,
however, were few and slender.

The end of the world war found Britain (and British India) with
small forces in four areas of Persia. In the northeast and the northwest, there were the tiny military missions of Generals Malleson and
Dunsterville, whose adventures in Russia were followed earlier (see
Chapter 38). On the Gulf coast there were a few garrisons of Indian
troops. In the south there was a native force recruited during the war
and led by British officers, called the South Persia Rifles; but mu-
tinies and desertions, triggered before the armistice by a tribal revolt
against British rule, had brought its effectiveness into question.

These forces were insufficient to Lord Curzon's purposes, even
had there not been pressure from the War Office and from India to
make further reductions in troops and subsidies. Curzon therefore concentrated his energies on the organization of a new British-
supervised regime in Persia that could transform the sprawling,
anarchic, much-divided territory into an efficient, effective country
able to support and defend itself, and thus dispense with British
subsidies and troops.

The plan was embodied in a treaty between Britain and Persia that
Lord Curzon imposed upon the governments of both countries.
Flabby young Ahmed Shah, last of the fading Kadjar dynasty to sit
upon the throne of Persia, posed no problem: he was fearful for his
life and, in any event, received a regular subsidy from the British
government in return for maintaining a pro-British Prime Minister in
office. Under Lord Curzon's supervision, the British Minister in
Teheran negotiated a treaty with the Persian Prime Minister and two
of his colleagues—who demanded and received a secret payment of
130,000 pounds from the British in return for signing it.[4]

Curzon was proud of the Anglo-Persian Agreement of 9 August
1919. "A great triumph," he wrote, "and I have done it all alone."[5]
By the terms of the agreement, British officers were to construct a

national railway network; British experts would reorganize the national finances; a British loan would provide the wherewithal for accomplishing these projects; and British officials would supervise the collection of customs duties so as to ensure that the loan would be repaid.

According to Curzon, the agreement was designed to bolster Persian independence. He did not foresee that others would put a different construction upon it. He made no provision for the possibility that oil-conscious allies—France and the United States—might react against the apparent grant to Britain of a political monopoly. He seemed unaware, too, of the direction in which currents of opinion were flowing in Persia itself: he assumed that, as in times gone by, Persians feared Russian expansionism and would welcome protection against it. Persian fear of it instead seems to have disappeared when the Russian Empire collapsed in 1917. By 1919 Britain represented the only European threat to the autonomy of the interest groups—the local, provincial, and tribal leaderships in particular—that exercised such authority as still functioned in the chaotic Persian territory. As for public opinion: in the capital, Teheran, of the twenty-six newspapers and other periodicals published there at the time, twenty-five denounced the Anglo-Persian Agreement.[6]

A short time after execution of the agreement, it was discovered in London and Teheran that a provision in the Persian Constitution required that all treaties had to be ratified by the Majlis (as the legislature was called). The Majlis had not met since 1915 and had been ignored by both governments in arriving at the agreement.

In the closed world of traditional diplomacy it was not then regarded as honorable for a legislature to fail to ratify a treaty duly executed by the government; the requirement of ratification, accordingly, was regarded as a mere technicality and, as such, was easy for negotiators to overlook. Yet once the issue was raised it assumed importance. For Lord Curzon, it became important to demonstrate to his Cabinet colleagues and to critics in France and the United States that the agreement was a genuine expression of the will of the Persian nation, which only an affirmative vote of the Majlis (imperfectly representative though that body might be) could provide. But one Persian Prime Minister after another (for ministries in Teheran fell in rapid succession) delayed convoking the Majlis for fear that its members could not be controlled. As no move could be made to implement the agreement until it was ratified, Persia remained in disorder, vulnerable (British officials feared) to Bolshevik propaganda and agitation.

All along, the proclaimed policy of the Bolshevik regime with regard to Persia had provided an appealing contrast to that of Britain. At the beginning of 1918, the Soviet government renounced Russian political and military claims on Persia as inconsistent with Persia's sovereign rights. As the summer of 1919 began, the Soviet government also gave up all economic claims belonging to Russia or Russians in Persia, annulling all Persian debts to Russia, cancelling all Russian concessions in Persia, and surrendering all Russian property in Persia. Of course it could be pointed out that the Soviet government was surrendering claims it was too weak to enforce; in that sense, it was giving away nothing. Yet its surrender of economic claims in the summer of 1919 placed in stark relief the far-reaching economic concessions that Lord Curzon demanded and received for Britain in the Anglo-Persian Agreement signed that same summer. Freed, at least temporarily, from their fears of Russia, Persian nationalists allowed themselves to resent the strong measure of foreign control central to Lord Curzon's plan for their protection.

So nationalist opinion hardened. The winter of 1919–20 passed, and ratification of the Anglo-Persian Agreement drifted slowly, frustratingly, out of Curzon's grasp. Then, in the spring of the year, events took a new turn.

In August of 1918 Captain David T. Norris of the Royal Navy had organized a small British naval flotilla to control the Caspian Sea for General Dunsterville's military mission as it occupied and then retreated from Baku (see page 359). In the summer of 1919 the British government had turned the flotilla over to the White Russian forces of General Denikin for use in the Russian Civil War. When Denikin's forces collapsed, the remains of the flotilla, some eighteen vessels, manned by anti-Bolshevik Russians, found refuge in Enzeli, the Royal Navy's base and the principal Persian port on the Caspian Sea. There they were taken into custody by Persian officials and by the British and Indian garrison still in place. As of the spring of 1920 the British and Persian governments had not yet decided what to do with the flotilla, which still was of a size and strength sufficient to affect any contest for mastery of the Caspian.

At dawn on 18 May 1920, thirteen Soviet Russian warships launched a surprise attack on Enzeli. Under cover of a barrage from their ships, Soviet troops landed and cut off the British garrison in its camp at the tip of a peninsula. The trapped British commanding general, after vainly seeking instructions from his superiors in Teheran, accepted the terms dictated to him by the victorious Soviet commander: the British garrison surrendered both its military supplies and the Denikin flotilla to the Bolsheviks, and then retreated from Enzeli.

Within weeks a Persian Socialist Republic was proclaimed in Gilan, the province in which the port of Enzeli was located, and a Persian Communist Party was founded in the province to support it. Although Russians played a key role in these events, Soviet Russia was at pains to deny it. Moscow even denied having ordered the attack on Enzeli; according to Soviet spokesmen, it was undertaken by the local Russian naval commander on his own responsibility.

If there were a justification for the Anglo-Persian Agreement and for a commanding British presence in the country, it was shattered by the chain of events that began at Enzeli. Britain had undertaken to defend Persia against Russia and Bolshevism—but was visibly failing to do so. The retreat from Enzeli spurred the War Office to demand the withdrawal of the remaining British forces from Persia. As Winston Churchill wrote to George Curzon, there was something to be said for making peace with the Bolsheviks, and something to be said for making war on them, but nothing to be said for the current policy.[7] According to the new Prime Minister of Persia, the Anglo-Persian Agreement was "in suspense." The Prime Minister of Britain blamed his Foreign Secretary for what had occurred, saying that Curzon was almost entirely responsible for saddling Britain with responsibilities in Persia that should never have been assumed.[8]

At the end of the summer of 1920, the Russian Bolshevik representative, Lev Kamenev, came to London as chairman of a peace delegation charged with negotiating an end to the conflict between Russia and her former wartime allies. Kamenev was one of the half-dozen or so principal leaders of the Communist Party of the Soviet Union, and for many years had been one of the closest political associates of Lenin. In London, Kamenev seems to have become aware of the extent to which the British government had been thrown off balance by the uprisings in Iraq, and saw a chance for his government to exploit the situation in Persia in order to increase Britain's difficulties in Iraq. In a secret cable (decoded by British Intelligence) from London to the Soviet Foreign Minister in Moscow, Kamenev stated that "pressure on the British troops in North Persia will strengthen the position of the Mesopotamian insurgents." A revolution along a geographical line running from Enzeli in Persia to Baghdad in Iraq, he continued, "threatens the most vital interests of the British Empire and breaks the status quo in Asia."[9] Here was the linkage between one uprising and another, in which British officials believed with superstitious fervor; but, contrary to what they believed, only the events in northern Persia (and to some extent those in Afghanistan) were directly inspired by Soviet Russia.

In the autumn of 1920 a new British commander, Major-General Edmund Ironside, arrived to take charge of the situation in northern Persia. His views about what should be done were considerably at variance with those of Lord Curzon. An overwhelming figure, six feet, four inches tall and weighing 275 pounds, Ironside did not hesitate to impose his own policy.[10] Like Churchill, he thought it foolish to oppose the Bolsheviks if one were not allowed to engage in an all-out war to defeat them. The best that could be hoped for, in his opinion, was for Britain and Russia to withdraw their forces—if a Persian government could be left in place that could hold its own.

In the whole of northern Persia there was only one more-or-less indigenous force available to Ironside that was of some consequence— the Persian Cossack Division, which had been created in 1879 by the Russian Czar as a bodyguard for the Persian Shah. But it suffered from being Russian-inspired and Russian-led: its commander and a number of its commissioned and noncommissioned officers were Russian, and through the years it had been heavily subsidized by the Russian government. After the Russian revolutions, the British government had taken over the payment of the subsidy; yet in 1920 its commanding officer, a Russian colonel named Starosselski, refused nonetheless to comply with British demands and, though an anti-Bolshevik, insisted on upholding "Russian interests."[11]

General Ironside eyed the Persian Cossacks as a vehicle for the accomplishment of his program. The Persian element in it was large and the Russian group was small: 6,000 Persian soldiers and 237 Persian officers, versus 56 Russian officers and 66 noncommissioned officers.[12] The Russian commander, Starosselski, was in a vulnerable position: after scoring initial successes against the Persian Socialist Republic, he had failed dismally.

Ironside promptly arranged to have Starosselski dismissed; later he also arranged for Starosselski's replacement to be sent away. In their place, Ironside put Reza Khan, a tough, bullet-headed Persian colonel whom Ironside later described as "the most manly Persian" he had met.[13]

Aware of War Office plans to complete the evacuation of British forces from Persia in 1921, Ironside went about arranging for Reza Khan to rule the country as Britain departed. On 12 February 1921 Ironside told Reza Khan that the remaining British forces would not oppose him if he carried out a *coup d'état*, so long as he would agree—as he did—not to depose the British-subsidized monarch, Ahmed Shah.*

On 15 February Ironside met with the Shah but failed to persuade him to appoint Reza Khan to a position of power; so, on 21 February, Reza Khan marched into Teheran at the head of 3,000 Cossacks and seized power, installing himself as commander-in-chief of the armed forces. "So far so good," Ironside commented when he heard the news. "I fancy that all the people think that I engineered the coup d'état. I suppose I did, strictly speaking."[14]

---

* Nonetheless in 1925 Reza Khan placed himself on the throne as Reza Shah Pahlavi, deposing Ahmed Shah, who by then resided in Paris. In 1935 Reza Shah changed the name of his kingdom from Persia to Iran.

In fact, Ironside's role in these events was quite unknown, and remained unknown until discovered and revealed by an American scholar more than half a century later.[15] In London—where officials were unaware of Ironside's involvement—the course of events in Persia was greeted first with puzzlement and then with dismay. On 26 February 1921, only five days after achieving power, the new government in Teheran formally repudiated the Anglo-Persian Agreement. The same day it directed the Persian diplomatic representative in Moscow to sign a treaty (its first treaty since taking office) with Soviet Russia. The twin events of 26 February marked a revolution in Persia's position, as the country turned from British protection against Russia to Russian protection against Britain. These events occurred just as Russia also signed a treaty with Moslem Afghanistan, and only a month before the final conclusion of Russia's treaty with Kemalist Turkey. In Turkey, Persia, and Afghanistan—the three crucial countries that Britain had been disputing in the Great Game with Russia for more than a century—the new rulers had each negotiated a treaty with Moscow as his first move in foreign policy. Moreover, Kemalist Turkey's first treaty with an Islamic nation was concluded with Afghanistan; it was negotiated in Moscow with Russia's encouragement. All of Moscow's new Islamic protégés were joining hands under Russia's aegis against Britain. By their terms, the treaties were directed against imperialism, and their language left little doubt that it was British imperialism that they meant. Again, British officials were left with a sense that the many revolts against Britain in the East were linked together.

Lord Curzon, who in 1918 had said that "the great power from whom we have most to fear in future is France," claimed in 1920 that "the Russian menace in the East is incomparably greater than anything else that has happened in my time to the British Empire."[16] It was not that Russia was particularly powerful; war, revolution, and civil war had taken too great a toll for that to be true. Rather it was that the Bolsheviks were seen to be inspiring dangerous forces everywhere in the East. With Russian encouragement, Djemal Pasha, Enver's colleague in the Young Turk government, went out to Afghanistan in 1920 to serve as a military adviser; and his mission illuminated what the British government most feared. The C.U.P., the continued influence of Germany even in defeat, pan-Islam, Bolshevism, Russia—all had come together and were poised to swoop down upon the British Empire at its greatest points of vulnerability.

Thus the Soviets were supporting Persian nationalism against Britain. They were doing so because Kamenev believed that bringing pressure to bear on the British position in Persia might help rebel groups in neighboring Iraq to resist British rule in that country. Meanwhile Soviet-supported Turkish nationalism, led by Kemal and inspired (the British believed) by the Young Turkey movement, threatened to tear up the peace treaty that Lloyd George had imposed upon the Ottoman Empire. At the time Arab rioters in Egypt and Palestine had taken to the streets, and Ibn Saud in Arabia and Feisal in Syria had taken to the field with their armies, to contest the dispositions that Britain had made of their destinies. For Britain— flat on her back economically, and in no position to cope with foreign disturbances—the Middle Eastern troubles were overwhelming, and looked as though they had been purposefully incited by a dedicated enemy: Soviet Russia.

PART XI

RUSSIA RETURNS TO
THE MIDDLE EAST

UNMASKING BRITAIN'S ENEMIES

I

It was true that the Soviets encouraged Persian nationalism, supported Turkish nationalism, and sought to aid rebellion in Iraq; but the Russians had not inspired—and did not direct—any of these movements. The growing British conviction that Bolshevik Russia was involved in a far-reaching international conspiracy that had *incited* rebellion throughout the Middle East was a delusion. What had occurred was a series of uncoordinated uprisings, many of them spontaneous, that were rooted in individual, local circumstances. Although the Soviets tried to make use of these local movements, neither Bolshevism nor Bolsheviks played any significant role in them. Yet there was an edge of truth to the British perception that Britain had moved into conflict with the new Russian state and that the Bolsheviks—hoping to exploit local opposition to British rule— viewed the Middle East as a theater of operations in that conflict.

Among British and other Allied officials, it had been a common belief that aiding the German war effort was not a mere incidental effect of the Bolshevik *coup d'état*, but its driving purpose. The Germans, urged on by Alexander Helphand, had financed the Bolsheviks and had sent Lenin back to lead them. It may have been a matter of indifference to Lenin whether the achievement of his program helped or harmed either of the contending capitalist alliances; but to many Allied officials at the time, the evidence of German financial involvement demonstrated that helping Germany was Lenin's desire and his intention. Such officials therefore viewed Bolsheviks as enemy agents, and regarded the Bolsheviks' communist theories as mere camouflage, or propaganda, or as an irrelevance. In turn, this view of Bolshevism fitted in with suspicions that had been formed and harbored by British officials, especially in the Middle East, since long before the war—suspicions that placed German-inspired Bolshevism in the context of an older conspiracy theory: a pro-German international Jewish plot.

Confirmation that Jews were pro-German seemed to be provided by events in the Ottoman Empire in the early part of the twentieth century. As seen earlier (see pages 41–3), Gerald FitzMaurice had reported to his government that the Young Turks were tools in Jewish hands; and though FitzMaurice's report, as historians now know, was false, it was believed at the time to be true. When the C.U.P., once in power, moved the Ottoman Empire into the German orbit, its policy was seen as an example of the effectiveness of the Jewish alliance with Germany.

The Middle Eastern old hands who subscribed to this view—men like Wingate and Clayton—believed that Islam was a weapon that could be wielded at will by the Sultan-Caliph of Constantinople. When the supposedly Jewish Young Turks took control of the Sublime Porte, British officialdom therefore assumed that Islam, as well as the Ottoman Empire and the pan-Turkish movement, had passed into the hands of the German-Jewish combine.

It was in this context that the second Russian Revolution was seen by British officials as the latest manifestation of a bigger conspiracy. Jews were prominent among the Bolshevik leaders; so the Bolshevik seizure of power was viewed by many within the British government as not merely German-inspired but as Jewish-directed.

When the uprisings in the Middle East after the war occurred, it was natural for British officials to explain that they formed part of a sinister design woven by the long-time conspirators. Bolshevism and international finance, pan-Arabs and pan-Turks, Islam and Russia were pictured by British Intelligence as agents of international Jewry and Prussian Germany, the managing partners of the great conspiracy. In the mind of British officialdom, bitter enemies such as Enver and Kemal were playing on the same side; and so, they believed, were Arabs and Jews.

British officials of course were aware that significant numbers of Palestinian Arab Moslems, reacting against Zionist colonization, expressed violent anti-Jewish feelings; but this observation did not necessarily negate their view that Islam was controlled by Jewry. Islam, in the sense that Britons feared it, was the pull and power of the Caliph, whom they viewed as a pawn moved by Britain's adversaries—a view that, oddly, they continued to hold even after the Sultan-Caliph became their virtual prisoner in Constantinople. As they saw it, it was evident that Arabs could not govern themselves; so that the question came down to whether the Arabic-speaking Middle East should be governed by Germans and Jews, acting through the agency of Turks, or whether it should be governed by Britain. The appeal of British government, they felt, was that it was decent and honest; the appeal of Britain's adversaries was that Turkish government was Moslem government. Islam was thus being used, as was Bolshevism, and as were Turks and Russians, by a cabal of Jewish financiers and Prussian generals to the detriment of Britain.

While in the clear light of history this conspiracy theory seems absurd to the point of lunacy, it was believed either in whole or in part by large numbers of otherwise sane, well-balanced, and reasonably well-informed British officials. Moreover, it could be supported by one actual piece of evidence: the career of Alexander Helphand. Helphand *was* a Jew who conspired to help Germany and to destroy the Russian Empire. He *was* closely associated with the Young Turk regime in Constantinople. He *did* play a significant role in selecting Lenin and in sending him into Russia to foment a Bolshevik revolt with a view to helping Germany win the war. He *did* continue to weave his conspiratorial webs after the war. He was what Wingate and Clayton believed a Jew to be: rich, subversive, and pro-German.

Against this background, the trend of British Intelligence assessments in the immediate postwar years appears less irrational than would otherwise be the case. On 5 May 1919, only half a year after the armistices had brought hostilities in the First World War to an end, a British intelligence agent filed a report with the Arab Bureau based on extensive conversations with Young Turk leaders who had found safety in Switzerland. According to the Arab Bureau's intelligence operative, the Allied victory had not brought enemy anti-British agitation to an end. On the contrary, the work of the wartime Pan-Islamic Propaganda Bureau in Berlin was being continued in India, Egypt, Turkey, Persia, and elsewhere with the goal of inciting "The Revolt of Islam." "The Eastern enemies of Great Britain have united with avowed object of overthrowing British rule in the EAST," he reported. "They can rely upon the support of Germany and of the Russian Bolsheviks ..."[1] The intermediary between the Middle Eastern rebels and the Bolsheviks, the report continued, was Alexander Helphand.

The eruption of violence in Mesopotamia the following year elicited other intelligence reports along similar lines, notably from Major N. N. E. Bray, a special intelligence officer attached to the Political Department of the India Office. It was Bray whose chart of the alleged conspiracy was circulated to the Cabinet at the end of the summer of 1920 (see page 453). Bray argued that in Mesopotamia, "both the Nationalist and Pan-Islamist movements derive their inspiration from Berlin—through Switzerland and Moscow. The situation is further complicated with Italian, French and Bolshevist intrigues."[2]

Bray urged the government to track down the secret "comparatively small central organization" at the center of the far-reaching international conspiracy.[3] Since it did not exist, it was never found. Nonetheless the preponderant opinion within the government, at least for a time, was that the rebellions breaking out in Britain's

Middle Eastern domains were the result of coordinated hostile forces from outside. Within the Foreign Office there were several officials who argued that the source of the various Middle Eastern troubles was to be located within the Middle Eastern countries themselves; but these officials represented a minority point of view.

In fact there was an outside force linked to every one of the outbreaks of violence in the Middle East, but it was the one force whose presence remained invisible to British officialdom. It was Britain herself. In a region of the globe whose inhabitants were known especially to dislike foreigners, and in a predominantly Moslem world which could abide being ruled by almost anybody except non-Moslems, a foreign Christian country ought to have expected to encounter hostility when it attempted to impose its own rule. The shadows that accompanied the British rulers wherever they went in the Middle East were in fact their own.

What Britain faced in the Middle East was a long and perhaps endless series of individual and often spontaneous local rebellions against her authority. The rebellions were not directed *by* foreigners; they were directed *against* foreigners. Perhaps if the British Empire had maintained its million-man army of occupation in the Middle East, the region's inhabitants might have resigned themselves to the inevitability of British rule and to the uselessness of attempting to defy it; but once Britain had demobilized her army, the string of revolts in the Middle East became predictable. The agents of British policy in the Middle East, however, continued to blame their troubles—as Kitchener and his colleagues had blamed all their Middle Eastern failures since 1908—on the supposedly Jewish-controlled, German-influenced Young Turk leadership and its international ramifications, chief among which were Islam and now Bolshevism in a line that ran from Enver through Alexander Helphand to Lenin.

II

A sensationalist exposé was published in London for the first time in 1920 that purported to disclose the origins of this worldwide conspiracy. Entitled *The Jewish Peril*, the book was an English translation of the *Protocols of the Learned Elders of Zion*. A French translation was published in Paris at the same time. The *Protocols* purported to be a record of meetings held by Jews and Freemasons at the end of the nineteenth century in which they plotted to overthrow capitalism and Christianity and to establish a world state under their joint rule.

The *Protocols* had originally appeared in Russia, in a newspaper in 1903 and in book form in 1905, and had allegedly been discovered by Sergei Nilus, a Czarist official. They attracted little attention until the Russian revolutions of 1917, when it was widely remarked that many of the Bolshevik leaders were Jews and that communist doctrine bore a certain resemblance to that described in the *Protocols*. Therefore there were those in London and Paris in 1920 who accepted Nilus's revelations as genuine. As such, the *Protocols* explained—among other things—the mysterious revolts against Britain everywhere in the East.

It was not until the summer of 1921—a year after they appeared in London and Paris—that the *Protocols* were proven to be a forgery by Philip Graves, Constantinople correspondent of *The Times*, who revealed that they had been concocted by the Czarist secret police. The police had not even bothered to compose the forged documents themselves; they had plagiarized them, as Graves was informed by a White Russian refugee named Michael Raslovleff (whose name was not revealed until 1978). Raslovleff, who parted with the information only because of a "very urgent need of money," showed Graves that whole sections of the *Protocols* were paraphrased from a satire on Napoleon III written by a French lawyer and published in Geneva (1864) and Brussels (1865).[4] It was an obscure work, of which few copies were still in existence; Raslovleff showed Graves the copy he had bought from a former Russian secret police official, and *The Times* in London found a copy in the British Museum. Raslovleff said that if the work had not been so rare, somebody would have recognized the *Protocols* as a plagiarism immediately upon their publication. (Subsequently it has been learned that passages in the *Protocols* were plagiarized from other books as well, including a fantasy novel published at about the same time as the French satire.)

III

For the important body of British opinion represented by *The Times*, those responsible for Britain's setbacks in the Middle East were not foreign conspirators but British officials—British Arabophiles chief among them. Particularly alarmed by the uprisings in Iraq, a special Middle Eastern correspondent of *The Times* filed a dispatch, published on 20 September 1920, in which he wrote that "My conviction, based on careful study, is that the Arab Bureau at Cairo, the G.H.Q. at Cairo, and our Occupied Enemy Territories Administrations in Palestine and last year in Syria, bear a heavy load of responsibility for the present waste of British lives and money in Mesopotamia." He charged that "British Pan-Arab propaganda is one of the most serious existing dangers to the world's peace." Putting aside the few British officials who genuinely believed in Arab independence, he denounced the "extremely dangerous officials who have no great belief in the Arabs' own capacity for government, but an intense belief in our Imperial Mission" to run Arab affairs behind a façade of nominal Arab independence. He did not mention Wingate, Clayton, or Hogarth by name, but the description fitted them; and they, in his account, and not the Bolsheviks, were the cause of the disorders throughout the Middle East.

In a leading article the next day, *The Times* denounced the Arab Bureau's long-held belief in an Arab confederation of the Middle East presided over by King Hussein: "...the delusive dream of a huge Arabian Federation should no longer be entertained in any official quarter." A year later, on 27 September 1921, *The Times* rejected the Arab Bureau's old notion of a special British mission in the Moslem world. Discerning a common theme in the many Moslem Middle Eastern revolts against European Christian rule, *The Times* was of the opinion that "The problem is far too big for any one European nation to cope with alone ..."

The principal danger, as *The Times* pictured it, lay in British overcommitment. The principal challenge to the country, in its view, was at home and was economic. Britain needed to invest her money in renewing herself economically and socially, and was threatened in her very existence by a governmental disposition to squander money instead on Middle Eastern adventures. In an editorial published on 18 July 1921 *The Times* denounced the government for this, saying that "while they have spent nearly £150,000,000 since the Armistice upon semi-nomads in Mesopotamia they can find only £200,000 a year for the regeneration of our slums, and have had to forbid all expenditure under the Education Act of 1918."

But while *The Times* argued that the danger to Britain came from British officialdom, much of British officialdom continued to focus on the Soviet threat to the Middle East, and on the question of how to respond to that threat.

THE SOVIET CHALLENGE IN THE MIDDLE EAST

The heads of the three great departments of the British government charged with dealing with the Russian question in the Middle East—the Foreign Office, the War Office, and the India Office—disagreed among themselves about the nature of the Soviet challenge and about how to respond to it.

Lord Curzon, guardian of the flame of the Great Game who became Foreign Secretary in 1919, argued for a forward British military position in the Middle East to guard against Russia. He urged the British army to take up positions defending Transcaucasia (which had broken away from Russia) and northern Persia. He and the Permanent Under-Secretary at the Foreign Office, Lord Hardinge—both of them former viceroys of India—claimed that the loss of any one area in the Middle East to Russian aggression would, in turn, lead to the loss of the area behind it, in a domino reaction that might lead eventually to the loss of India.[1]

The Secretary of State for India, Edwin Montagu, and the Viceroy of India, Frederic John Napier Thesiger, 3rd Baron Chelmsford, disagreed. Montagu and Chelmsford believed that Bolshevik Russia posed a political rather than a military threat to Britain's position in the Middle East. They argued that Britain ought to be competing against Russia to win the support of nationalist forces throughout Islamic Asia. Instead, as they saw it, Britain was pursuing politics that might have been expressly designed to drive these forces into the arms of Moscow; and the presence of British armies might be expected to alienate these forces still further.

Montagu wrote to Curzon at the beginning of 1920 that "The danger of the Bolsheviks to Persia and to India" was largely the result of the British government's own policies, which he characterized as anti-Mohammedan. "We could have made Pan-Islamism friendly to Great Britain," he wrote, but instead "We are making it hostile."[2] India, of course, had opposed London's Middle Eastern policy ever since Lord Kitchener took charge of it in 1914; and what Montagu wrote in 1920 was consistent with the criticisms he had levelled all along against his government's pro-Arab and pro-Zionist policies and against the school of Kitchener view that Islam was a force managed and directed by Britain's enemies.

Chelmsford, in telegrams to Montagu at the beginning of 1921, put the matter in historical perspective by pointing out that until 1914 the British had been the "champions of Islam against the Russian Ogre."[3] Now, however, the harsh Treaty of Sèvres that Lloyd George had imposed on the helpless Ottoman Empire and the one-sided treaty that Curzon had imposed on the prostrate Persian Empire appeared to Indian Moslems as examples of "Britain's crushing of Islam."[4] In Russia, on the other hand, the war had brought into power a new regime that—at least in the Middle East—spoke the language of national independence. In the long run, according to the Viceroy, the "real defence" against Russian Bolshevik expansion in the Middle East lay not in installing forward military positions but in supporting a "nationalist spirit" among the Moslem peoples of the region whose basic religious tenets were hostile to Bolshevism and whose nationalism would lead them to oppose Russian advances.[5] It would be a mistake for Britain to maintain a military presence in the Middle East, he continued, or even a merely economic one, for it might lead native leaders to conclude that the real threat to their independence came from London.

Major-General Sir Edmund Ironside, during the time he served as commander of the British troops remaining in northern Persia, strongly believed that his troops should not be there. As he saw it, the rugged terrain on the Indian northwest frontier provided so effective a defensive line that a forward defense of India was unnecessary, while the long line of communications required in order to conduct a forward defense of India from Persia rendered such a strategy impractical.[6]

In the end the argument between the Foreign Office and the India Office was settled by the War Office. Sir Henry Wilson, Chief of the Imperial General Staff, decisively ruled against the Foreign Office on the grounds that he did not have the troops to carry out the forward policy in the Middle East that Lord Curzon advocated. In 1920 he submitted a paper to the Cabinet reporting that Britain had no reserves whatsoever with which to reinforce garrisons anywhere in the world should the need arise.[7] The only feasible policy, in his view, was to husband resources and to concentrate Britain's military forces in those areas of greatest importance and concern—and neither Persia nor the Caucasus frontier was among them.

Winston Churchill, the War Minister and Secretary for Air, argued in early 1920 that if troops *were* available for Persia and the Caucasus frontier, they should be used instead in Russia—to support the Czarist generals in their bid to unseat the Bolshevik government.[8]

Churchill took the new rulers of the Kremlin at their word: he pictured them as internationalists and revolutionaries. He believed that most of them were not Russian at all—that they were Jews. Churchill therefore did not believe that they pursued Russian goals, whether nationalist or imperialist. He failed to explain why their objectives in the Middle East were so uncannily similar to those of the czars.

Minutes of a 1920 conference of Cabinet ministers underlined the particular menace Churchill and some of his colleagues felt the Bolsheviks posed in Moslem Asia. "Every day they were making great strides towards the East, in the direction of Bokhara and Afghanistan. They were carrying out a regular, scientific, and comprehensive scheme of propaganda in Central Asia against the British."[9] The Chief of the Imperial General Staff warned the ministers that "the Caspian would fall into the hands of the Bolsheviks who could ... create disturbance in North Persia. The unrest would spread to Afghanistan, which was already very unsettled, and also to India which was reported to be in a more dangerous state to-day than it had been for the last thirty years."[10] Echoing these fears, Winston Churchill wrote to the Prime Minister asking "what are we to do if the Bolsheviks overrun Caucasia and join with the Turkish Nationalists; if they obtain the command of the Caspian and invade Northern Persia; if they dominate Turkestan and join with Afghanistan in menacing India from without and endeavouring to raise up a revolution within?"[11]

The British-subsidized White Russian campaign in the Russian Civil War that broke out between the Bolsheviks and their adversaries was seen by the public as Churchill's private war, and when the White armies faltered in late 1919, and then fell apart early in 1920, it was seen as yet another of his costly failures. The Prime Minister wrote to him that "I have found your mind so obsessed by Russia that I felt I had good ground for the apprehension that your abilities, energy, and courage were not devoted to the reduction of expenditure."[12] Speaking about Churchill and Russia a few months later, the Prime Minister was less restrained; the Chief of the Imperial General Staff noted in his diary that "He thinks Winston has gone mad ..."[13]

As a Liberal Prime Minister dependent on a right-wing Conservative majority in the House of Commons, Lloyd George nonetheless felt obliged to allow his War Minister to support the White Russians until it was plain that they had failed. But when the Whites collapsed, the Prime Minister felt free to seek an agreement with the Reds. He did not fear their imperial ambitions in the Middle East. For that matter he had not feared those of the czars.

In believing that an accommodation with Russia could be reached, the Prime Minister carried on the traditions of the Liberal Party to which he belonged. His former colleagues, Asquith and Grey, had believed the Russians to have legitimate grievances in the Middle East, such as lack of access to a warm water port, which, if satisfied, would leave them content not to advance any further. In the same vein, Lloyd George argued that the alleged Russian threat to India was a fantasy. Bolshevik Russia lacked the resources to pose such a threat, he believed, and even "When Russia was well equipped, the Russians could not cross the mountains."[14] He agreed that Bolshevik propaganda in India might be a danger, but observed that "you can't keep ideas out of a country by a military cordon."[15]

During 1920 and early 1921 Lloyd George engaged in the negotiation of a trade agreement with Moscow that was to give the Bolshevik regime *de facto* recognition and bring Russia back into the family of nations. He told Riddell that as a condition preliminary to negotiation he would insist that all Bolshevik propaganda abroad in Persia, Afghanistan, and elsewhere in the East should cease; and Riddell noted in his diary that "L.G. thinks Lenin will agree."[16] Quite the contrary proved to be true. The Soviet government, in a cable of instructions to its representative, indicated that "We can only agree to concrete concessions in the East at a political conference with England and on condition that we receive similar concessions from England also in the East. What these concessions are to consist of will be discussed when the time comes."[17] This hinted at continuing Russian imperial ambitions in the Middle East that were considerably more far-reaching than Lloyd George had supposed.

55

MOSCOW'S GOALS

I

While Britain's leaders were disagreeing with one another about the relationship between Bolshevik communism and Russian imperialism, the Bolshevik leaders themselves were debating the nature of that relationship, with all of its implications for their postwar policy in the Middle East.

Until the decade before the First World War, the Russian Empire had been expanding at the expense of its neighbors at a prodigious rate and for a long time. It has been calculated that, at the time, the Russian Empire had been conquering the territory of its neighbors at an average rate of 50 square miles a day for 400 years.[1] With the acquisition of foreign territories came foreign peoples. At the time of the first scientific census in 1897, most of the Russian Empire's subjects were not Russians. The Turkish-speaking peoples alone were more than 10 percent of the population, and Moslems were at least 14 percent.

Now, Lenin's Russia had to decide whether to try to reconquer the Moslem and other non-Russian peoples whom the czars had subjected to their rule. Lenin, for years, had argued that the non-Russian peoples should enjoy the right of self-determination. In theory he was a firm opponent of what he called Great Russian chauvinism. In 1915 he wrote that "We Great Russian workers must demand that our government should get out of Mongolia, Turkestan, and Persia . . ."[2]

In 1917 he overcame the resistance of his colleagues at the Seventh Social Democratic Congress and pushed through a resolution declaring that the non-Russian peoples of the Russian Empire should be free to secede.

The colleague whom he placed in charge of the nationalities issue was, however, of a different frame of mind. He was the Transcaucasian Bolshevik Joseph Dzhugashvili, who, after calling himself by many other aliases, had given himself the Russian name of Stalin.

475

Although for a time he outwardly deferred to Lenin's views on the nationalities question, Stalin did not share them; indeed he was fiercely at odds with Lenin over the nationalities issue and the constitution of the Soviet Union. Lenin's proposal was for each of the Soviet countries—Russia, the Ukraine, Georgia, and the various others—to be independent; they were to cooperate with one another as allies do, on the basis of treaties between them. Stalin's plan, on the other hand, was for the Ukraine, Georgia, and all the others to adhere to the Russian state—and Stalin prevailed. On 30 December 1922, the First Congress of Soviets of the Union of Soviet Socialist Republics approved the formation of a Soviet Union dominated by Russia.

II

How significant in practice were the differences between Lenin and Stalin?

Lenin argued that the European nations within the Russian Empire should be allowed independence—and, in that, he certainly disagreed with Stalin. There is some evidence, however, that he privately believed that the Middle Eastern nationalities should not be allowed independence until a much later date*—which was different from Stalin's belief that they should never be independent, but in the short run came to the same thing.

Although he was opposed to compelling non-Russians to submit to Russian rule, Lenin, like Stalin, had no qualms about compelling non-Bolsheviks to submit to Bolshevik rule—and here, too, Lenin's policy in practice did not appear as widely different from Stalin's as it did in theory. Under Lenin's leadership, Soviet Russia conquered non-Russian portions of the former Russian Empire and imposed local Bolshevik Soviet regimes upon them by force of arms. In each case a political police force, acting as a branch of Soviet Russia's secret police, was established by Lenin's government to help maintain the local Soviet regime. This was entirely in line with what Lenin had done in Russia: his was a minority regime that had seized power

---

* The Bashkir leader, Zeki Velidi Togan, wrote (years later) that in 1920 Lenin had told him that the problem in the colonial countries was that they lacked a proletariat. In communist theory the proletariat was to dictate and to lead, but the peasantry of the East did not have an industrial working class to do that for them. In effect this meant that the peoples of the East were not yet ready to exercise their right to be free. According to Togan, Lenin said that even after the socialist revolution had succeeded everywhere in the world, the former colonies of the European Great Powers would have to remain in tutelage to their former masters until such time as they developed an industrial working class of their own.[3]

by force and that held on to power by employing as many as a quarter of a million secret policemen.

But in Russian Central Asia, the Bolshevik minority consisted of Russians, while the non-Bolshevik majority consisted of natives; for Bolsheviks to rule non-Bolsheviks (which was Lenin's policy) was, in practice, for Russians to rule non-Russians (which was Stalin's policy).

III

In the beginning, the Bolshevik government promised the native populations of Central Asia their freedom. At the end of 1917, after seizing power in Petrograd, the Soviets issued an appeal for support, under the signatures of Lenin and Stalin, recognizing the Moslem population's right to "Organize your national life in complete freedom."[4]

Would the Bolshevik leaders nonetheless try to reconquer the Czar's Middle Eastern colonies? Their policy in this regard would offer London an important clue as to whether they were communist revolutionaries or Russian imperialists.

The Russian Middle East—Russian Turkestan*—was a colonial empire that the czars had carved out of the previously independent Moslem world. Like Algeria, Morocco, the Sudan, or a score of other tribal areas in Africa and Asia, it had been subdued by force of modern European arms. Like other such colonies, it found that its economy was exploited for the benefit of its European masters. Like them, too, it resented being settled by colonists from Europe; there was nobody that a Turkish-speaking Moslem hated more than a Russian who came to take possession of his soil.

Located deep in the heart of Eurasia, Turkestan is an area that remains little known to the outside world. The Russian-ruled part of it is about half the size of the continental United States: about one and a half million square miles. Vast mountain ranges on its eastern frontier block the moisture-laden clouds from the Pacific, so that most of its territory is an arid, largely unforested, plain. At the time of the First World War, about 20 to 25 percent of its population could be classified as nomads or semi-nomads, while the rest of its nearly ten million, largely Turkish-speaking, people lived in clusters around the fertile oasis towns.

The 1914 war and the revolutions of 1917 brought confusion and anarchy to Central Asia. In part this was due to the extent and

---

* Turkestan is used here in its broad geographic sense, rather than in its technical sense as the governor-generalate ruled from Tashkent under the czars.

topography of the country and to its mixed population. It was a frontier country, and, even in the best of times, tribal conflicts, as well as the opposition of the indigenous peoples to Russian colonization, kept the area in disorder. While Turkestan was remote from the war, it had been the scene of a tribal revolt against wartime measures; and it had suffered a breakdown in government as a result of the two revolutions in Petrograd. Social conflicts emerged, as a small urban middle class resisted an attempt by feudal leaders to reassert authority. Too many leaders and too many causes raised their banners and took to the field. Armies, armed bands, and raiding parties swept across the deserts and vast empty plains, appearing out of nowhere and as suddenly disappearing.

War and revolution had thrown up their human wreckage: refugees seeking a way out and adventurers seeking a way in. From the disbanded prisoner-of-war camps, Germans, Hungarians, Czechs, and soldiers of a dozen other nationalities streamed out in search of one goal or another. In the caravans and in the rickety railroad carriages that lurched across the treeless landscape of Central Asia were to be found an assortment of human types whose identities, missions, and motives were difficult to fathom; and the Soviet regime believed—or affected to believe—that foreign-inspired conspiracies were flourishing and ripening everywhere in the semi-tropical sunshine.

During the years of post-revolutionary chaos, new indigenous regimes proclaimed their existence throughout the region; and Moscow treated them as challenges to be overcome. At the end of 1917 Moslems in Central Asia set up a regime in Khokand, seat of what had once been a khanate in the western Fergana valley, in opposition to the Tashkent Soviet (which was composed of Russian settlers and did not include a single Moslem among its members). Lacking money and arms Khokand looked for allies but found none. Stalin curtly dismissed its claims to function as a regime. On 18 February 1918 the Red Army captured and sacked Khokand, destroying most of the city and massacring its inhabitants. From its ruins, however, arose a loosely organized movement of marauding guerrilla bands called Basmachis who plagued the Russians for years afterward.

During the next few years Soviet Russia destroyed one center of resistance after another. As the people of the Kazakh country learned in 1918, no support was to be obtained from the White Russians, for they, too, were opposed to native aspirations. The Kazakhs of the Central Asian plains had proclaimed their autonomy and asked the aid of the Czarist commander, Admiral Kolchak, in defending themselves against the Bolsheviks—only to find that he, too, was their enemy.

The most serious threat to Soviet ambitions was posed by the "Native States" of Khiva and Bukhara, two former Czarist protectorates in Central Asia. As frontier states neighboring on Persia, Afghanistan, and China, they enjoyed contact with the outside world and could serve as a focus of anti-Soviet alliances.

Moscow took advantage of internal strife in Khiva; the Red Army captured it on 13 September 1920, and installed a regime that allied itself with the Soviets. Thereafter Moscow ordered a series of liquidations of the Khivan leadership that paved the way for Khiva's eventual incorporation into the Soviet Union.

That left only Bukhara; and in dealing with the last bastion of native Turkish resistance, it occurred to the Soviets to make use of the Young Turkey leader Enver Pasha—whom British Intelligence had pictured as a member of the conspiracy directing the Bolshevik movement all along.

56

A DEATH IN BUKHARA

I

According to British Intelligence, the Young Turkey leaders were members of the German and Jewish conspiracy that controlled the Bolshevik regime. Yet from 1918 to 1922, as Britain's leaders tried to fathom the intentions of the Bolshevik leaders, so did the fugitive leaders of the Young Turks—who did not control the Bolsheviks or even know very much about them.

In November 1918, Enver Pasha, Djemal Pasha, and Talaat Bey escaped from the ruins of the Ottoman Empire with the aid of the retreating Germans and fled across the Black Sea toward Odessa. Eventually Enver and Talaat found their way to Berlin and there, in the late summer of 1919, they visited the Bolshevik representative Karl Radek in his jail cell. Radek had been one of the intermediaries between the German General Staff and Lenin in the Helphand-inspired funding of the Bolshevik Party. In 1919 he was imprisoned by the new German government in connection with the suppression of the communist uprising in Germany; but he was treated as a person of consequence and transacted political business from his cell.

The startling political proposal that Radek made to the Young Turk leaders was that Enver should proceed to Moscow to negotiate a pact between Russian Bolshevism and Turkish nationalism directed against Britain. Enver was a lifelong foe of Russia and no friend to Bolshevism; but Radek assured him that "in Soviet Russia everyone was welcome who would support the offensive against English imperialism."[1]

A close friend of Enver's in Berlin was General Hans von Seeckt, the brilliant creator and head of the new German army—the much-reduced and limited military force that the Allies permitted Germany to maintain pursuant to restrictions contained in the Treaty of Versailles. With his monocle and his rigid features, the 53-year-old von Seeckt was the prototype of the professional German officer to whom the Young Turks finally had turned for guidance during the war; and indeed during the final months of the war, von Seeckt had served as chief of staff of the Turkish army.

Von Seeckt now agreed to help Enver make the difficult and dangerous trip to Moscow across chaotic eastern Europe, where nationalist forces in Poland, Latvia, Estonia, Lithuania, and Hungary battled against communist revolutionaries or Russian Bolsheviks, as the Russian Civil War continued to rage. Enver gave von Seeckt a new appreciation of the possibilities afforded by the Bolsheviks for striking at the Allies. Karl Radek later wrote that Enver "was the first to explain to German military men that Soviet Russia is a new and growing world Power on which they must count if they really want to fight against the Entente."[2] These ideas, passed on by Enver to von Seeckt, bore fruit when von Seeckt, several years later, moved toward an alliance between the German military machine and Soviet Russia.

An officer on von Seeckt's staff arranged for Enver to be flown to Moscow in October 1919 in the company airplane of an aircraft manufacturer. But the arrangements miscarried; there was engine trouble, and the plane was forced to make an emergency landing in Lithuania. Enver carried false papers, and his true identity was not discovered; nonetheless, he was kept prisoner for two months in Lithuania—which, along with Latvia and Estonia, was at war with Soviet Russia—as a suspected spy. Once released, he returned to Berlin, and started out on a second effort to reach Moscow, this time being arrested and imprisoned in Latvia. According to his later account, he was questioned repeatedly by intelligence officers but succeeded in persuading them that his name was Altman and that he was "a Jewish German Communist of no importance."[3] By the summer of 1920 Enver finally reached Moscow, almost a year after first leaving Berlin.

His political odyssey away from anti-communism and anti-Russianism seemed to have been complete. Enver wrote from Moscow to von Seeckt on 26 August 1920 urging him to help the Soviets. He claimed that

> There is a party here which has real power, and Trotsky also belongs to this party, which is for an agreement with Germany. This party would be ready to recognize the old German frontier of 1914. And they see only one way out of the present world chaos—that is, cooperation with Germany and Turkey. In order to strengthen the position of this party and to win the whole Soviet Government for the cause, would it not be possible to give unofficial help, and if possible sell arms?[4]

At the same time Enver reported to von Seeckt that "The day before yesterday we concluded a Turkish-Russian treaty of friendship: under this the Russians will support us with gold and by all means."[5] (If the Bolshevik leaders really intended at the time to support Enver's bid to assume the leadership of the Turkish rebellion, however, they later changed their minds when they were made aware of the complexity of the Turkish political situation.)

II

On 1 September 1920 the Bolsheviks convened the "first congress of peoples of the east" in Baku, the capital of recently captured Moslem Azerbaijan. The congress brought together 1,891 delegates of various Asian peoples, of whom 235 delegates were Turks. The congress was sponsored by the Third (or Communist) International—the Comintern, as it was called—but a significant percentage of the delegates were not communists. Enver attended the congress as a guest of the Comintern, whose representatives at the congress were Karl Radek, Grigori Zinoviev, and the Hungarian Bela Kun. Zinoviev, the leader of the Communist International, acted as president of the congress.

Although Enver claimed to have been received by Lenin and was sponsored at the congress by Zinoviev, he was best known as the partner of imperial Germany and the killer of the Armenians; there was substantial opposition among the delegates to his being allowed to participate. A compromise was reached according to which a statement by Enver was read to the congress rather than delivered in person; even so it was punctuated by boos and protests. In his statement Enver claimed to represent a "union of the revolutionary organizations of Morocco, Algiers, Tunis, Tripoli, Egypt, Arabia, and Hindustan."[6] More to the point, he aspired to resume the leadership of Turkey; but Turkish delegates who supported Kemal made it plain to the Soviets that Moscow would antagonize them if it backed Enver.

Although the invitation to the congress had been phrased in the communist language of world revolution, Zinoviev, once at the congress, seemed to be calling on the assembled delegates for aid in a national struggle between Russia and Britain. In his opening address he cried out "Brothers, we summon you to a holy war, in the first place against English imperialism!"[7] Since many of those who were called upon to join in the crusade were non-communist or even anti-communist, the Comintern felt obliged to defend itself against the accusation that it was cynically using them as instruments of Soviet foreign policy. Karl Radek told the congress that "The eastern policy of the Soviet Government is thus no diplomatic manoeuvre, no pushing forward of the peoples of the east into the firing-line in order, by betraying them, to win advantages for the Soviet republic ... We are bound to you by a common destiny ..."[8] Enver's presence as the Comintern's guest belied this; that, at least, is what was said in European socialist circles within the next few weeks. The Comintern, according to a former colleague of Lenin's, had succumbed to a temptation "to regard the peoples of the east as pieces on the chessboard of the diplomatic war with the Entente."[9] A Social Democrat argued that at Baku the Bolsheviks had given up socialism in favor of power politics.[10]

A month after the Baku congress, Enver returned to Berlin. He began to purchase arms—perhaps on his own behalf, for he hoped to return to Anatolia to push Kemal aside and assume command of the forces resisting the Allies. He still retained support among former C.U.P. militants, and he also controlled an organization on the Transcaucasian frontier; his hopes of returning to power within Turkey were not entirely unrealistic.

Throwing its support behind Enver was an alternative with which Moscow could eventually threaten Mustapha Kemal, if and when it became necessary to do so; but for the moment the Bolsheviks had nothing for Enver to do.* As will be seen presently, it was to be a year before the Soviets found a mission on which to send him—a mission to Bukhara in turbulent Turkestan.

Awaiting an assignment, Enver settled in Moscow in 1921 as a guest of the Soviet government. A picturesque figure in the streets of the Russian capital, he attracted attention by wearing an enormous tarboosh that offset his tiny stature. He became the social lion of Moscow, according to the American writer Louise Bryant, who lived next door to him for half a year and saw him every day. She wrote

---

* However, his colleague Djemal Pasha proved to be of immediate use. In 1920, at the suggestion (or at any rate with the encouragement) of Moscow, Djemal went to Afghanistan, where he helped to dispel Afghan suspicions of Russia. Reportedly, in a letter to Lenin at the end of 1920, the Afghan monarch remarked that "His Highness Jemal Pasha has told us of all the noble ideas and intentions of the Soviet republic in regard to the liberation of the whole eastern world ..."[11] As adviser to the monarch, Amanullah Khan, Djemal helped draft a new constitution and worked on reorganizing the army. Djemal told a Moslem colleague that his purpose in reorganizing and strengthening the Afghan army was to add to the Soviet threat against India.[12] In addition to his work with the army, the Turkish leader also founded an organization called the Islamic Revolutionary League, devoted to freeing India from British rule. His intrigues with the warlike frontier tribes helped to keep them in a state of anti-British ferment. Over and above these activities, Djemal's mere presence in Kabul, overlooking the troubled Indian Empire from a strategic location about which the British were especially nervous, caused anxiety and concern in Simla and Whitehall.

that he "certainly has charm, in spite of his very obvious opportun-
ism, ... cruelty ... and lack of conscience."[13] She sensed that,
despite all the lionizing, he was bored.[14]

Enver's star was on the wane in Moscow, because that of his
rival—Mustapha Kemal—was on the rise. The working arrangement that the Kremlin arrived at with Mustapha Kemal's Turkish
Nationalist government allowed Soviet Russia to crush Georgia,
Armenia, and Azerbaijan. Kemal's overt anti-communism—on
28 January 1921 Kemalists killed seventeen Turkish communist
leaders by drowning them in the Black Sea—was not allowed by
Lenin or Stalin to stand in the way of agreement. In entering into a
series of interlocking pacts with the anti-communist nationalist
Moslem leaders of Turkey, Persia, and Afghanistan, Moscow seemed
to be traveling along the path marked out at the Baku congress:
abandoning revolutionary goals in favor of pursuing traditional
Russian objectives in the Great Game. The Soviets encouraged
revolutionary Kemalist Turkey to enter into a pact of her own, in
Moscow, with traditionalist Afghanistan, the purpose of which (as
indicated in Article Two) was to join hands in opposing aggression
and exploitation by the British Empire.

In the summer of 1921 Mustapha Kemal won the first in a series
of stunning successes against the British-backed Greek army. The
tide was running with him and, in the autumn, the Soviets moved
further toward alliance with him. Enver saw himself losing out to
Kemal.

In the summer of 1921, the Soviets, at Enver's request, provided
him with transportation to the Caucasus. Enver assured the Soviet
Foreign Minister that he was not going there to work against Kemal,
but broke his word. On arrival in Transcaucasia, he established
himself in Batum, in Georgia, on the Turkish frontier. There he
held a congress of supporters, and tried to cross into Turkey; but the
Soviet authorities forcibly detained him. Enver's continued presence
on the Turkish frontier became an embarrassment to the Soviet
leaders, who sent Enver away; either at their request or his, he was
entrusted with a mission to Central Asia.

In Central Asia, Moscow was attempting to complete its reconquest of the native Turkish-speaking Moslem populations, and
asked Enver to help.

Enver's mission was contrary to everything for which he had stood
in politics: his goal had been to liberate the Turkish-speaking peoples
from Russian rule. The mission also ran contrary to what the
Bolsheviks had preached before coming to power: they had claimed
that they were in favor of allowing the non-Russian peoples of the
Russian Empire freely to go their own way. Coming after the Russian

reconquest of Georgia, Armenia, and Azerbaijan, and after the un-
veiling of Moscow's alliance with anti-communist leaders of Islam,
the Soviet instructions to Enver raised the question of whether the
Bolsheviks had subordinated, postponed, or even abandoned
altogether the revolutionary ideals they had once espoused. Enver
undoubtedly had his own views about this, but he hid them from his
Bolshevik hosts as he set out for Bukhara in Central Asia.

III

By the summer of 1920—a year before Enver was sent there—
Bukhara was the last remaining bastion of Turkic independence in
Central Asia. Occupying about 85,000 square miles on the right bank
of the Oxus river, in the southeast corner of Russian Turkestan, back
against the mountainous southern and eastern frontiers that run with
Afghanistan and China, its population of roughly two and a half to
three million raised it above the level of its sparsely populated Turkish
neighbors. The structure of its Russian protectorate had melted away
during the revolutions of 1917, and its emir, Abdul Said Mir Alim
Khan, last of the Mangit line, reasserted the independence of Bukhara
and the autocratic powers that had been exercised by his ancestors.
The Soviets heard rumors of British complicity in the Emir's defiance
of their authority; and in fact British India did send a hundred camel
loads of supplies to aid the emirate. Bolshevik Russia attacked
Bukhara in 1918, but the Emir's tiny army, officially numbered at
11,000 men, was able to win the brief war.

At the time of the Bolshevik attack, Bukhara was still wealthy and
well supplied. The emirate had always been known for the fertility of
its oases, and its capital city—also called Bukhara—remained the
most important trading town in Central Asia. In the city's seven-mile
honeycomb of covered bazaars, business (according to at least one
traveler's report) went on as usual.[15] There was a lively traffic in the
products of craftsmen, in precious metals, jewels, rugs, leather, silks,
currencies, and all manner of food-stuffs. A center of the commerce
in rare manuscripts and libraries in many oriental languages, Bukhara
continued to be the principal book market in Central Asia.

But after his victory over the Bolsheviks in 1918, the Emir brought
this commercial prosperity to an end by cutting off all trade with
Russia. At the same time he allowed irrigation projects to be discon-
tinued. By the summer of 1920 Bukhara's economic situation was
grave and the country was unable to feed itself.[16] Popular discontent
and social strife erupted as a Young Bukhara movement (which was
opposed to Soviet intervention) and a smaller Communist Party

(which welcomed it) protested against the unenlightened policies and medieval ways of the ruler. The Emir, in some ways, had indeed brought back the Middle Ages. The twelfth-century Kalyan Minaret, or Tower of Death, from the top of which condemned criminals were thrown, was back in use. From his palaces, among his boy and girl harems, the Emir ruled in as arbitrary a way as had any of his ancestors.

Taking advantage of the Emir's unpopularity, the Red Army intervened. In the summer of 1920 the Red Army attacked again, and Russian troops under the command of Mikhail Frunze bombarded Bukhara. As the Young Bukharans launched an uprising in the city, the Red Army, with its airplanes and armored vehicles, moved forward on 2 September, bringing Bukhara's medieval regime to an end; the library, containing possibly the greatest collection of Moslem manuscripts in the world, went up in flames.

The Emir, alerted by a telephone call to his palace, fled, along with his harems and three wagon-loads of gold and precious stones from his treasury. A story was told later that, at points along the way, he left one or another of his favorite dancing boys, in the hopes of diverting and thus slowing his pursuers. His initial stopping point was the hill country of the east. From there he sought, and found, sanctuary across the frontier in Afghanistan.

After capturing the city of Bukhara, Soviet Russia recognized the absolute independence of a Bukharan People's Republic; but the recognition was in form only. Frunze's troops remained, and imposed requisitions on the country. Soviet interference in Bukhara's affairs pointed toward its eventual incorporation into Soviet Russia. Leaders of the Young Bukhara movement resisted the trend toward Russian control and attempted to assert their independence.

In the hills of eastern Bukhara, Basmachi groups loyal to the Emir began to harass the Russian conquerors. As yet no real links had been forged between the various Basmachi groups; nonetheless the Basmachis posed a challenge to Soviet rule that, even by the end of 1921, the Red Army had been unable to crush.

IV

Enver Pasha reached Bukhara on 8 November 1921, entrusted by the Russians with a role in the pacification of Turkestan.

As he approached the city through gardens of fruit trees, melons, grapevines, roses, poppies, and tobacco plants, he entered the Eden of his pan-Turkish ideology: the historic homeland of the Turkish peoples. Surrounded by eight miles of high crenellated stone walls, with 11 gates and 181 watch-towers, centuries-old Bukhara was an architectural embodiment of the Moslem past in which he gloried.

Once the holiest city of Central Asia, its 360 mosques reflected his faith—a faith shared by its inhabitants, whose men lived their religion and whose women wore the veil. The men of Bukhara wore turbans and the traditional striped robes called *khalats*, while Enver arrived with his European-cut military tunic; but between him and them there was a bond of brotherhood.

Enver's affinities extended even to the new government of Bukhara. The Young Bukhara Party was not dissimilar to the Young Turks whom Enver had led in Constantinople; and reformist leaders like Zeki Velidi Togan of Bashkiria had congregated there. When Enver left the city, only three days after entering it, he took with him the key figures in the government: its Chairman, and its Commissars of War and Interior. The story he told the Russians was that they were going hunting. In fact they made their way to the hill country of eastern Bukhara, where Enver made contact with partisans of the Emir. There, appointed commander-in-chief by the Emir, he assumed the leadership of the Basmachi war for independence from Russia.

With the support both of the Emir and of the Young Bukhara leaders, he was in a position to bring all factions together. His envoys sought out Basmachi bands throughout Turkestan to unify them under his banner. His proclaimed goal was the creation of an independent Moslem state in Central Asia. As always he stressed the unity of the Moslem peoples. His strong Islamic message won him the support of the mullahs, who rallied strongly to his cause, and of his important neighbor, the Moslem Emir of Afghanistan.

However Enver's personal weaknesses reasserted themselves. He was a vain, strutting man who loved uniforms, medals, and titles. For use in stamping official documents, he ordered a golden seal that described him as "Commander-in-Chief of all the Armies of Islam, Son-in-Law of the Caliph and Representative of the Prophet."[17] Soon he was calling himself Emir of Turkestan, a practice not conducive to good relations with the Emir whose cause he served. At some point in the first half of 1922, the Emir of Bukhara broke off relations with him, depriving him of troops and much-needed financial support. The Emir of Afghanistan also failed to march to his aid.

Enver's revolt scored some initial successes. He launched a daring raid on the city of Bukhara which unnerved his opponents. But the extent of his successes remains a subject of dispute. According to some accounts, he came to control most of the territory of Bukhara. According to others, Enver was merely one of a number of chiefs, who led a band of no more than 3,000 followers (out of an estimated 16,000 Basmachis roaming the country).[18] What is clear is that, however effective or ineffective, his activities were a cause of deep concern to the Kremlin.

In the late spring of 1922, Enver wrote to the government of

Soviet Russia asking it to withdraw Russian troops and to recognize the independence of his Moslem state in Turkestan. In return he offered peace and friendship. Moscow refused his offer.

The Red Army, assisted by the secret police, launched a campaign of pacification in the summer of 1922. In this they were aided by Enver's weaknesses. As a general he continued to be God's gift to the other side. As a politician, he was equally maladroit: he alienated the other Basmachi leaders, many of whom turned against him. By mid-summer, the Russians had reduced his following to a tiny band of fugitives.

Russian agents and patrols searched the narrow mountain ravines for traces of him, and eventually tracked him down to his lair in the hills, where Red Army troops quietly surrounded his forces. Before dawn on 4 August 1922, the Soviet soldiers attacked. Enver's men were cut down.

There are several accounts of how Enver died.[19] According to the most persuasive of them, when the Russians attacked he gripped his pocket Koran and, as always, charged straight ahead. Later his decapitated body was found on the field of battle. His Koran was taken from his lifeless fingers and was filed in the archives of the Soviet secret police.

V

Soviet Russia's liquidation of the last of the Turkish independence movements in Central Asia completed the process by which the Bolshevik authorities revealed that they would not keep their promise to allow non-Russian peoples to secede from Russian rule. It was now evident that they intended to retain the empire and the frontiers achieved by the czars.

Sir Percy Cox, who had recently returned to London from the Middle East, told the Cabinet in the summer of 1920 that the Bolsheviks would hold to the old Russian imperial frontier—but that they were not anxious to send their armies across it in search of new conquests.[20] Winston Churchill was conspicuous among those in London who believed that Cox was wrong; but events at the time shed little light on the matter one way or the other. Certainly the Kremlin was active in subverting the British Empire in the Middle East, but there is as little agreement today as there was during the Lloyd George administration as to the long-run intentions with which the Kremlin did so.

Enver Pasha's postwar adventures did, however, shed light on a number of other issues that British officials had raised during and just after the First World War about the opposition they faced in the

Middle East. British officials had conceived of Enver as the sinister and potent figure who sustained Mustapha Kemal in his opposition to the Allies; but events had shown that Enver and Kemal were deadly rivals, and that it was Kemal—not Enver—who commanded the more powerful following within Turkey, and who therefore could obtain arms from Soviet Russia. British officials had also pictured Enver as a creature of the German military machine, but, while he could call on personal friends like von Seeckt for favors, in his Russian years he acted entirely on his own; and as Enver fought his last campaign in 1922, von Seeckt's new German army was secretly working with the Bolsheviks, not with Enver.

For years Enver had threatened Britain and Russia with a pan-Turk uprising, but when he finally issued his call to revolt there was no appreciable response to it. Even within the guerrilla bands that he led, the Moslem religion rather than feelings of Turkishness provided the unifying bond. Pan-Islam, about which British officials continued to write with alarm, was also revealed as an empty slogan by the Bukharan campaign: the clannish peoples of the Middle East were not given to wider loyalties, and not one Moslem land—not even friendly Afghanistan—marched to Enver's aid. It was true that in various parts of Turkestan, Moslem natives reacted against Russian settlers, even as in Palestine Moslems reacted against Jewish settlers, but each group of Moslems responded locally and only for itself: throughout the Middle East, Moslems were acting alike rather than acting together.

When Enver journeyed to Moscow, the British view was that he and his new Russian associates were elements of a long-standing political combination, and that they would work toward the same political goals. In fact their goals were far apart. Enver and the Bolsheviks tried to use each other, but neither succeeded. The Bolsheviks proved adept at swiftly picking up anyone they thought might do them good—and at quickly discarding them when their usefulness was at an end. London continually misunderstood, and interpreted as long-term combinations, these emphemeral tactical alliances into which the Kremlin entered with such cynical ease. It might have amused Enver, in the last minutes before his head was cut off by the Russians, to know that British Intelligence had marked him down as Moscow's man.

Enver's adventures—had British Intelligence known the full story of them at the time—would have shown the British that they were mistaken in their several views of who was in charge of Bolshevik Russia. A prevalent British view was that the Bolsheviks were run from Berlin by the German generals; but when Enver arrived in Berlin in 1919 he found that the German army was out of touch with Russia and took no interest in the new rulers of the Kremlin. It was

Enver who suggested that the German army might profit from establishing a relationship with the Bolshevik regime, not vice versa; and
it was a suggestion that von Seeckt did not begin to implement until
1921.

Indeed what Enver found was that Lenin and his colleagues were
men who set their own agenda: that, above all, is where British
Intelligence officers were wrong about them. The men in the Kremlin
were engaged in giving orders, not in taking them. They were not
arms of somebody else's conspiracies; when it came to conspiracies,
they wove their own. Winston Churchill, who had correctly observed
as much, then spoiled his analysis by going on to claim that the
Soviet leaders were neither Russian nor pro-Russian. Along with so
many other British fantasies about the forces at work against them in
the Middle East, it was a theory that ought to have died with Enver
Pasha at Bukhara.

PART XII

THE MIDDLE EASTERN SETTLEMENT OF 1922

WINSTON CHURCHILL TAKES CHARGE

I

Russia, then, troubled after the war by the appearance of independence movements in Moslem Asia on her southern frontier, crushed them, and while doing so defined herself by charting her future relationship with the non-Russian peoples of what had once been the empire of the czars. So far as she was able, she would bring them under the rule of the Russian state—a policy formally adopted on 30 December 1922, when the First Congress of Soviets of the Union of Soviet Socialist Republics approved the formation of the Soviet Union.

France, too, was troubled after the war by the appearance of independence movements in the areas of the Moslem Middle East she sought to control, and crushed them, as seen earlier, in 1920. Clemenceau had wanted to preserve France's position as a power in Europe, and had always pictured the pursuit of overseas empire as a dangerous distraction; but his successors, by invading Syria, defined France's role in postwar world politics in other, more ambitious and less realistic, terms. France's occupation of Syria and Lebanon was formally validated by a League of Nations Mandate on 24 July 1922.

At the outset of the First World War, the three Allies had agreed to partition the postwar Middle East between them; but, in the postwar years, having lost unity of purpose, each went its own way in overcoming postwar disturbances in Moslem Asia, and each defined its own vision of its political destiny in doing so. Each followed its own road to 1922—for Britain's position in her sphere in the Middle East, like Russia's and France's, was formally embodied in documents promulgated in that year.

Of the three Allies, Britain faced the most widespread challenges across the face of the Middle East after the war. She met the challenges while in the grip of an economic crisis and at a time of profound social and political change at home. Middle Eastern policy on the road to 1922 was to severely test Britain's most colorful and creative politicians, Lloyd George and Churchill. For, as a result of the postwar troubles recounted earlier, everywhere from Egypt to Afghanistan, Britain's Middle East policy was in tatters—just as Winston Churchill had said all along that it would be—in the face of native resistance, communal strife, and local disorders.

II

Ever since the end of the war, Churchill—inside the government— had been the most severe critic of the Prime Minister's Middle Eastern policy, warning that peacetime Britain did not have the troops and that Parliament would refuse to spend the money to coerce the Middle East. He argued that Britain should therefore settle for terms that the Turks were willing to accept. On 25 October 1919 he presciently expressed concern that Greece might ruin herself in her Smyrna venture, and that Britain's alliance with France might be injured by a French invasion of Syria with hordes of Algerian troops. He worried about the Italians "disturbing the Turkish World" and about "the Jews, whom we are pledged to introduce into Palestine and who take it for granted that the local population will be cleared out to suit their convenience." Arguing that Allied policy in the Middle East ought to be completely reversed, he urged that the Ottoman Empire be restored to its prewar frontiers and suggested that the European powers renounce their claims to Syria, Palestine, and other such territories. "Instead of dividing up the Empire into separate territorial spheres of exploitation," he argued, "we should combine to preserve the integrity of the Turkish Empire as it existed before the war but should subject that Empire to a strict form of international control . . ."[1]

Keenly aware of the purposes served by Britain's Middle Eastern strategy during the nineteenth century, Churchill maintained that a similar strategy should be adopted by the Lloyd George government. "We ought to come to terms with Mustapha Kemal and arrive at a good peace with Turkey," he argued, in a memorandum to the Cabinet on 23 November 1920, so as to stop estranging "powerful, durable and necessary Turkish and Mohammedan forces. We should thus re-create that Turkish barrier to Russian ambitions which has always been of the utmost importance to us."[2]

In a letter to the Prime Minister written shortly thereafter, Churchill underlined his deep resentment at being obliged as War Minister to ask Parliament for vast sums to subdue the Middle East when it was only Lloyd George's "vendetta against the Turks" that made the expenditure necessary. He wrote that "We seem to be becoming the most Anti Turk & the most pro-Bolshevik power in the

world: whereas in my judgement we ought to be the exact opposite."
Pointing out that it was only because of the support of the Conservative Party that the government remained in office, he reminded the Prime Minister that the Conservatives were associated with the traditional nineteenth-century policy of supporting Turkey against Russia.

> All yr great success & overwhelming personal power have come from a junction between yr Liberal followers & the Conservative party ... But surely at this time—when we Coalition Liberals are vy weak in the Constituencies—it is adding to our difficulties to pursue policies towards the Turks & the Bolsheviks both of wh are fundamentally opposed to Conservatism [*sic*] instincts & traditions.[3]

Moving from domestic to foreign policy, Churchill wrote his most broadly reasoned criticism of British Middle Eastern policy some twelve days later in a memorandum to the Cabinet maintaining that "The unfortunate course of affairs has led to our being simultaneously out of sympathy with all the four Powers exercising local influence" in the Middle East: Russians, Greeks, Turks, and Arabs. A successful policy would consist rather in "dividing up the local Powers so that if we have some opponents we have also at any rate some friends. This is what we have always done in the whole of our past history. When Russia was our enemy the Turk was our friend: when Turkey was our enemy Russia was our friend."[4] According to Churchill's analysis, Lenin's Russia would not, and King Constantine's Greece could not, help Britain to achieve her goals; the only practicable course, he argued, was to ally with Turks and Arabs.

Sir Henry Wilson, Chief of the Imperial General Staff, noted approvingly in his diary that Churchill had "written a good paper for the Cabinet showing that we are now hated by the Bolsheviks, Turks, Greeks, & Arabs & this *must* be bad policy & that we ought to make friends with Turks & Arabs & enemies with Bolsheviks & ignore Greeks. This has been my view all along."[5]

On an administrative level, Churchill charged (as had Sir Mark Sykes in the early days of the world war) that Britain's Middle Eastern policy was rendered incoherent by the number of government departments running their separate territories and operations. This impeded progress toward curbing costs, he repeatedly told the Cabinet Finance Committee. On 31 December 1920, at Churchill's suggestion, the Cabinet decided to set up a special Middle East Department within the Colonial Office to be in charge of the troubled mandated territories, Palestine (including Transjordan), and Iraq.

Lord Milner, the Colonial Secretary, in failing health and spirits, was unwilling to assume such heavy new responsibilities and promptly resigned from the government. On 1 January 1921, Lloyd George offered the Colonial Ministry to Churchill who, after some hesitation, agreed to accept it. It was arranged that Milner should hand over the ministry on 7 February; but Churchill immediately began involving himself in Middle East departmental arrangements and affairs.

Churchill at once began trying to expand the powers of his new ministry, seeking military as well as full civil powers and attempting to bring all of Arabia within the ambit of his department. He also expressed decided views about the future of Egypt. The Foreign Secretary, Lord Curzon, protested repeatedly at Churchill's encroachments on his perogatives. Curzon complained that "Winston ... wants to grab everything in his new Dept & to be a sort of Asiatic Foreign Secretary."[6] A War Office official claimed that Churchill's idea was to set up "a sort of War Office of his own."[7]

The Prime Minister, at Churchill's suggestion, appointed a special interdepartmental committee under the chairmanship of Sir James Masterson Smith (a career official who had served under Churchill) to consider—and, Churchill hoped, to expand—the powers of the Colonial Office's new Middle East Department.

Churchill, who no longer spoke of restoring the Ottoman Empire, approached his new responsibilities with an open mind and with an evident desire to obtain guidance from the government's ablest officials in a program aimed at cutting costs while trying to keep commitments.

III

By 1921 the Government of India, under the influence of Gertrude Bell in Baghdad, had come over to the views of Cairo. India, like Cairo, now believed in protectorate rather than direct government, and supported the sons of King Hussein as Britain's candidates for Arab leadership. This brought an end to the long civil war within British ranks and Churchill's luck was that Britain's Middle East old hands now spoke with one voice; unlike previous ministers, he would not be caught in an official crossfire.

Churchill drew on the resources of other ministries to recruit an experienced and well-balanced staff to deal with his new Middle Eastern responsibilities. In the interim, while his staff was being assembled, Churchill relied upon the information, advice, and professional guidance of Sir Arthur Hirtzel, Assistant Under-Secretary of State for India, a career official who had served in the India Office since 1894. Hirtzel declined Churchill's offer to head the new Middle East Department; in his place he sent another career official, John

Evelyn Shuckburgh, who had worked under him and who had served in the India Office since 1900. Hirtzel wrote to Churchill that Shuckburgh was "really first-rate—level headed, always cool, very accurate & unsparing of himself: his only fault perhaps a tendency to excessive caution."[8]

Churchill chose Hubert Winthrop Young of the Foreign Office to be Shuckburgh's assistant. An army major during the war, Young had been in charge of transport and supplies for Feisal's Arab forces. His appointment, and Shuckburgh's, were endorsed in warm terms by the Masterson Smith committee. The committee found Shuckburgh to be "the best man" for the job and Young's services to be "essential."[9] The committee expressed strong reservations, however, about another appointment Churchill proposed to make: T. E. Lawrence, who was to be an adviser on Arab affairs. The committee cautioned Churchill that Lawrence was "not the kind of man to fit easily into any official machine."[10]

Lawrence indeed had earned a reputation for insubordination and for going over the heads of his official superiors to higher authorities. He was also the leading public critic of British policy toward the Arabs of Mesopotamia—a policy of which Churchill was now in charge. In the summer of 1920 Lawrence had written of Iraq in the *Sunday Times* that

> Our government is worse than the old Turkish system. They kept fourteen thousand local conscripts embodied, and killed a yearly average of two hundred Arabs in maintaining peace. We keep ninety thousand men, with aeroplanes, armoured cars, gunboats and armoured trains. We have killed about ten thousand Arabs in this rising this summer. We cannot hope to maintain such an average: it is a poor country, sparsely peopled ...[11]

Lawrence, a one-time junior officer in the Arab Bureau in Cairo, had by now become a celebrity, due to the efforts of an American named Lowell Thomas. Thomas, a 25-year-old fledgling showman from Ohio who until then had knocked about North America in search of fame, fortune, and adventure, had been working at a part-time job teaching public speaking at Princeton when, at the end of 1917, he raised enough money to go to England and then to send himself and a cameraman to the Middle East war front in search of a salable story with romance and local color. There he found Lawrence, wearing Arab robes, and decided to make him the hero of a colorful story he was about to write—a story about the Arab followers of Hussein and Feisal and the role they had played in the war against Turkey. The story was to form the basis of a show, in which—sacrificing truth to entertainment values—Thomas would picture Lawrence as the inspirer and leader of an Arab revolt that destroyed the Turkish Empire.

Thomas's show was a lecture with photos. It was entitled *The Last Crusade* and Thomas opened it at the Century Theater in New York in March 1919, with the backing of the New York *Globe*. A few weeks later he moved it to the old Madison Square Garden, a vast auditorium in which to accommodate the crowds that Thomas hoped to attract. An English impresario then arranged to bring the show to London, where it played to the largest halls: the Royal Opera House at Covent Garden and the Albert Hall.

It was a masterpiece of ballyhoo and it set show business records. It played in London for six months and was seen there by perhaps a million people. Thomas then took the show on a road tour around the world. It made young Lowell Thomas rich and famous; and it converted "Lawrence of Arabia" into a world hero.[*]

Lawrence, though embarrassed by the crudeness of Thomas's account, gloried in its bright glow. When *The Last Crusade* played in London, Lawrence frequently came up from Oxford to see it: Thomas's wife spied him in the audience on at least five different occasions, causing him to "flush crimson, laugh in confusion, and hurry away."[15]

The public believed Thomas's account; so that when Lawrence became an adviser to Winston Churchill, his appointment over-shadowed all others. His reputation grew. He passed off his fantasies as history,[16] and, in the years to come, Lawrence was to claim far more credit for his share in Churchill's achievements as Colonial Secretary than was his due.

But Lawrence's indirect influence on policy was considerable, for his account of the Arab uprising was believed by Churchill, who lacked personal knowledge of the matter, not having been involved in Middle Eastern affairs during the war after 1916. Unaware of the

---

[*] A few years later Thomas wrote a book called *With Lawrence in Arabia*, based on the show, repeating the story he had told to his mass audiences of millions around the world. It was an immensely readable, high-spirited write-up of Lawrence's service career—much of it untrue—that made its points through hyperbole. The *Arab Bulletin*, which appeared in twenty-six copies, in Thomas's account appeared in only four.[12] Feisal's corps of 3,500 men, added to the several thousands serving under Feisal's brothers during the war, when added up by Lowell Thomas produced an Arab army of 200,000.[13]

Pushing Kitchener, Wingate, Clayton, Hogarth, Dawnay, Joyce, Young, and other important British officials into the shade, Thomas showed young T. E. Lawrence single-handedly igniting and leading the Hejaz revolt. Thomas placed Lawrence in the Arabia desert fomenting the Hejaz revolt in February 1916;[14] in fact, Lawrence had a desk job in Cairo at that time, and visited Arabia for the first time the following October.

extent to which Lawrence and Lloyd George's staff had exaggerated the role of Feisal's Arabs in winning the war, Churchill was prepared to accept Lawrence's thesis that Britain owed a great deal to Feisal and his followers.

IV

Since 1918 many of Britain's leaders had entirely reversed their views about the Middle East. In the heady days when the war was being brought to a triumphant conclusion, it had seemed important to seize and to hold on to every corner of the Middle East that offered strategic advantage; but, after 1919, Parliament and the press clamored for withdrawal from these remote positions that cost so much to maintain.[*]

Churchill responded to the changed political mood from the day that he took over the War and Air Ministries at the beginning of 1919;[**] and when he moved to the Colonial Office at the beginning of 1921, he once more made cost cutting his top priority. As Colonial Secretary, Churchill announced "that everything else that happens in the Middle East is secondary to the reduction in expense";[19] he tested all proposals and programs against that one overriding criterion. The final figures provide the measure of his success: by September 1922, Churchill had eliminated 75 percent of Britain's Middle Eastern expenditures, reducing them from forty-five million pounds to eleven million pounds per annum.[20]

Churchill favored conciliating France—in order to save the money it would cost to oppose her—and he inclined toward installing Feisal and his brothers—the Sherifians, or Hashemites—as local rulers of

---

[*] Sir Hugh Trenchard, the head of the Royal Air Force, wrote to the R.A.F. Middle East commander on 5 September 1919 that "I am afraid from your many telegrams that you have not got the atmosphere that is reigning here. That atmosphere is, economy at all cost . . ."[17]

[**] His program was to cut commitments ruthlessly in order to cut costs. Indeed he cut the military budget so radically that his top professional army adviser took alarm. The Chief of the Imperial General Staff confided to his diary the following year that Churchill's program "consists in arbitrary reduction of garrisons for financial reasons wholly regardless of whether or not the residue are liable to be scuppered." He concluded that "Winston . . . is playing the fool & heading straight for disasters."[18] Actually, Churchill was doing no more than keeping in tune with the political temper of his times in insisting on cutting expenses, cost what it might in non-money terms. Churchill put financial considerations above all others, except when it came to dealing with Bolshevik Russia—the one area where Churchill, by his opinions and conduct, reminded the political world of his past excesses and extravagances.

much of the Arab world because to do so would provide Britain with an economical strategy: it would enable "His Majesty's Government to bring pressure to bear on one Arab sphere in order to obtain their own ends in another."[21] By applying pressure on just one member of the family, he believed, Britain could extract concessions from all of them; if each member of the family ruled a kingdom, Britain would need to threaten only one kingdom in order to bring all the Arab kingdoms back into line.

From time to time he considered partial or complete withdrawal from the Middle East and, on 8 January 1921, he cabled the British High Commissioner in Mesopotamia that unless the country could be governed more cheaply Britain would have to withdraw from it to a coastal enclave.[22] At another point, taking up what he believed to be a suggestion of Lloyd George's, he proposed to abandon Palestine and Mesopotamia altogether by giving them to the United States.[23]

When he accepted appointment to the Colonial Office, Churchill wrote to the Prime Minister that "I feel some misgivings about the political consequences to myself of taking on my shoulders the burden & the odium of the Mesopotamia entanglement ..."[24] He was wary of being blamed, as he had been over the Dardanelles expedition, for the failure of a policy that had been initiated by others. On the other hand, it ran counter to his nature to order a retreat under fire; his inclination was to remain in Palestine and Mesopotamia because to do otherwise would be to default on commitments that, wisely or unwisely, Britain had already made.

Churchill, when he took office as Colonial Secretary, brought with him a broad strategic concept of how to hold down the Middle East inexpensively. While he was still Secretary of Air and War, Churchill had proposed to cut Middle East costs by governing Mesopotamia by means of airplanes* and armored cars. A few well-protected air bases (he wrote at the time) would enable the Royal Air Force "to operate in every part of the protectorate and to enforce control, now here, now there, without the need of maintaining long lines of communications eating up troops and money."[25]

Churchill recognized that this strategy would not defend Mesopotamia against invasion; its sole purpose was "maintaining internal security."[26] Churchill's diagnosis of Britain's troubles in the Middle East therefore must have been that the disturbances were caused locally. In proposing to adopt a military posture that would be of little use against Russians, resurgent Germans, or Turks, he

---

* As Secretary for Air since 1919, Churchill—in collaboration with Sir Hugh Trenchard, Chief of the Air Staff and father of the Royal Air Force—had played a leading role in exploring the revolutionary implications of air power for postwar British policy.

implicitly acknowledged that the threat to Britain in Mesopotamia did not come from them.*

Churchill's strategy implied an old-fashioned concept of empire much at variance with the idealistic vision of Smuts, Amery, Hogarth, and T. E. Lawrence that in part had inspired wartime Britain to seek control of Arab Asia. Lawrence still clung to the vision of a free Arab Middle Eastern Dominion voluntarily joining the British Commonwealth as an equal partner. In a much-quoted phrase, he wrote in 1919 that "My own ambition is that the Arabs should be our first brown dominion, and not our last brown colony."[27] Churchill's strategy, which was aimed at putting down native revolt, suggested that Britain would rule her Arab subjects by coercion rather than consent. It harked back to his experiences in Kitchener's Sudan campaign, and the ease with which modern European weapons could subdue natives armed only with traditional weapons.

In imposing his strategy, he was guided by a more recent experience: the catastrophe at the Dardanelles, where his policies had been undermined by his departmental subordinates in London and by his officers in the field. It led Churchill to go to considerable trouble to make his chief officials feel that his program originated with them—a precaution all the more prudent given the strong opposition from the War Office and the High Commissioner in Mesopotamia to the replacement of troops by airplanes.

To Sir Percy Cox, British High Commissioner in Mesopotamia, Churchill cabled on 7 February 1921 that "The questions at issue cannot be settled by interchange of telegrams. I cannot ... find time to visit Mesopotamia. I propose therefore a conference in Egypt beginning during first or second week of March ... Conference would take a week ... I shall be accompanied by principal officers of new Middle Eastern Department of Colonial Office."[28]

Churchill then summoned his field officers from Palestine and the Persian Gulf to attend him at the conference. On 18 February 1921 he sent his own notes on Mesopotamia to John Shuckburgh, and entrusted him with the pivotal responsibility for establishing a conference agenda for Mesopotamia and for Palestine.

V

Egypt, which Churchill chose as the meeting place, was geographically convenient but inconvenient politically: the Egyptians knew

---

* Churchill was in constant fear that Lloyd George's anti-Turkish policies would bring about a Turkish attack in Iraq, which British forces were not equipped to meet.

that Churchill felt that Egypt should not be granted independence. On 21 February 1921 he wrote to his wife that "The people in Egypt are getting rather excited at my coming, as they seem to think it has something to do with them. This is, of course, all wrong. I have no mission to Egypt and have no authority to deal with any Egyptian question. I shall have to make this quite clear or we shall be pestered with demonstrations and delegations."[29]

Allenby, now British High Commissioner in Egypt, issued an official denial that Churchill was coming to consult about Egyptian affairs. The Foreign Secretary, Lord Curzon, wrote Churchill a confidential letter on 24 February urging him to transfer the venue of the conference to Jerusalem. Curzon claimed that Churchill's presence in Cairo might compromise the efforts of Allenby and the Egyptian government to reach agreement at a critical moment.[30] Churchill, however, declined to alter his arrangements.

Thus the Cairo Conference went forward as planned, but its location brought into sharp contrast the policies pursued by Churchill and those advocated by Allenby: Churchill was planning to hold the line against Arab nationalism and Allenby was not. Against the weight of Cabinet opinion, against the wishes of the Prime Minister and of Churchill, Allenby—in line with the recommendations made earlier by Lord Milner—persisted in his efforts to give Egypt a measure of independence by bringing the British protectorate in Egypt to an end.

By the threat of resignation he eventually prevailed and, on 28 February 1922, the British government unilaterally issued the so-called Allenby Declaration conceding formal independence to Egypt (subject to far-reaching reservations which, among other things, enabled Britain to supervise Egyptian foreign policy and to make unrestricted use of Egyptian territory for military movements). Allenby would have preferred a treaty to a unilateral declaration, but no Egyptian government would agree to sign a document that reserved so many powers to Britain.

Churchill apparently feared that Allenby's concession of even nominal Egyptian independence would undercut his own policy, in other Arabic-speaking countries, of continuing to withhold it. By an accident of geography, in 1921, both Allenby's and Churchill's contrary policies were elaborated in the city of Cairo; and in fact there was a substantive similarity between them, for both represented unilateral British decisions about how the Arab world should be run—and Arab leaders did not agree to either one of them.

VI

The Cairo Conference formally convened at the Semiramis Hotel on the morning of Saturday, 12 March 1921. During the following days some forty or fifty sessions were held. According to one count there were forty officials in attendance; "Everybody Middle East is here ...," wrote T. E. Lawrence to his oldest brother.[31]

The initial—and principal—conference topic was how to cut the costs of occupying Mesopotamia. Two committees, one political and one military, were established to consider the matter. Both committees worked on the basis of agendas that Churchill and his staff had drafted on board ship on their way over. The committees devoted their first four days to arriving at a plan for Mesopotamia.

Churchill and his staff had skillfully anticipated the advice that might be tendered by officers in the field. Gertrude Bell, who came in from Baghdad with her chief, Sir Percy Cox, wrote afterward that "Mr. Churchill was admirable, most ready to meet everyone half-way and masterly alike in guiding a big political meeting and in conducting the small committees in which we broke up. Not the least favourable circumstance was that Sir Percy and I, coming out with a definite programme, found when we came to open our packet that it coincided exactly" with what Churchill proposed.[32]

On the evening of 15 March Churchill dispatched a telegram, which arrived in London the following day, reporting to the Prime Minister that "All authorities ... have reached agreement on all the points, both political and military."[33] In itself this was a considerable achievement.

Essentially there were four elements in the Cairo Conference plan. Feisal was to be offered the throne of Mesopotamia, but every effort would be made to make it appear that the offer came from the indigenous population rather than from Britain. In maintaining a British presence in the country, the military would shift to Churchill's airforce-based strategy; but—as the head of the Royal Air Force, Sir Hugh Trenchard, estimated that the strategy would require about a year to implement—Britain would have to rely all the more heavily on Feisal to keep the country quiet in the interim. Although British experts disagreed intensely among themselves as to whether the Kurdish* areas in the northwest should be absorbed into the new state of Iraq, or instead should become an independent Kurdistan, it was agreed that for the time being they should continue to form a separate entity within the jurisdiction of the British High Commissioner in Mesopotamia. In addition to the Kurds, there were

---

* The Kurds are a scattered, tribal people who inhabit the plateaus and mountains where Iraq, Iran, Russian Armenia, and Turkey now overlap. They are mostly Sunni Moslems, speak a language of the Iranian group, and are believed to be of Indo-European descent. There were perhaps two and a half million of them in 1921; there are no reliable figures. There may be seven million of them today. They continue to fight for autonomy and are a subject of current concern to the governments of Iraq and Turkey.

other groups whose identity was distinct and whose needs posed problems. In the northwest particularly there were small groups with no place to go, among them the Assyrian (or Nestorian) Christian refugees, driven from their homes in Turkey during the war because of their pro-Allied sympathies; and about these homeless groups, struggling for survival, the Cairo conferees felt that there was little that could be done.

Having opted for a Hashemite solution in Iraq, the conference did the same—though on a temporary basis—for Transjordan. Disorder was endemic in that territory, and the Chief of the Imperial General Staff was of the view that Britain could not hold onto it without sending in two more battalions "which of course we have not got."[34] Even as the conference was taking place in Cairo, alarming news was received that Feisal's brother Abdullah, accompanied by 30 officers and 200 Bedouins, had arrived in the Transjordan city of Amman, apparently *en route* to Syria to attack Damascus. Abdullah claimed that he had come to Amman for a change of air in order to regain his health after an attack of jaundice. Nobody believed his explanation.

Churchill's solution was, in effect, to buy off Abdullah: to offer him a position in Transjordan if he would refrain from attacking French Syria. (It will be recalled that Britain feared that if Arabs from the territory of British Palestine were to attack the French in Syria, France would retaliate by invading British Palestine.) The position Churchill thought of offering Abdullah was temporary governor, charged with restoring order. In proposing to make use of Abdullah to restore order east of the Jordan, Churchill hoped to accomplish other objectives too. Churchill brought with him to the Cairo Conference a memorandum that his staff had prepared at the end of February that dealt with the claims of Arabs and Jews to Palestine. The memorandum, prepared by Shuckburgh, Young, and Lawrence, construed the geographical terms employed in the McMahon–Hussein correspondence of 1915 as meaning that the area of Arab independence was to stretch no further west than the Jordan river. Since the Balfour Declaration contained no geographical definition, Churchill's advisers concluded that Britain could fully reconcile and fulfill her wartime pledges* by establishing a Jewish National Home in Palestine west of the Jordan and a separate Arab

---

* Thus Churchill's aides accepted the view that meaningful pledges *had* been made to Hussein's Arabs during the war. This was an important about-face for British officialdom; McMahon, Clayton, and other wartime officials who had been involved in making the supposed promises to Hussein believed at the time that they were phrasing the promises in such a way that Britain was not committed to anything. In their view the pledges were meaningless.

entity in Palestine east of the Jordan.[35] Abdullah, if installed in authority in Transjordan, could preside over the creation of such an Arab entity.

Several important objections to Churchill's Transjordan scheme were voiced at the Cairo Conference. Sir Herbert Samuel, the High Commissioner for Palestine, and his Chief Secretary, Wyndham Deedes, pointed out that since Transjordan had been included by the League of Nations in the territory of Palestine (for which the League was offering Britain a Mandate), it was not open to Britain unilaterally to separate it from the rest of Palestine. What Samuel feared was that a separate Arab Transjordan could serve as a base for anti-Zionist agitation aimed at western Palestine.[36] A parallel fear was expressed by Lloyd George, who worried that the French—to whom Feisal was *persona non grata*—would regard British patronage of two Hashemite brothers—one in Mesopotamia, and the other in Transjordan, both on their Syrian doorstep—as a provocation. On 22 March the Prime Minister sent a telegram to Churchill, in which he remarked: "Cabinet ... discussed your proposals for Transjordania, as to which considerable misgivings were entertained. It was felt that almost simultaneous installation of the two brothers in regions contiguous to French sphere of influence would be regarded with great suspicion by them and would be interpreted as a menace to their position in Syria, deliberately plotted by ourselves."[37]

The Prime Minister appreciated the reasons that had led Churchill to propose "an Arab rather than a Palestinian solution" to the problem of Transjordan,[38] but feared that any attempt to establish a separate Arab entity east of the Jordan might involve Britain in costly new engagements and entanglements.

Churchill succeeded in persuading the Cabinet that without sending at least a small British military force into Transjordan, no government could be established there at all. He indicated that Abdullah would not be expected to stay in the country for more than a few months, but that on a trial basis Abdullah could help establish order and then help choose a local person to serve as governor. Churchill agreed to accept Lloyd George's compromise concept of Transjordan: "while preserving Arab character of area and administration to treat it as Arab province or adjunct of Palestine."[39]

In Churchill's view, Abdullah would help to restrain both the anti-French and the anti-Zionist movements that otherwise might establish their headquarters east of the Jordan. The Hashemite solution, in his view, would help to solve these problems rather than (as critics had suggested) to create them. According to T. E. Lawrence, Abdullah made an ideal British agent in the area, because he was "a person who was not too powerful, and who was not an inhabitant of

Trans-Jordania, but who relied upon His Majesty's Government for the retention of his office."[40]

A final problem was the reaction of the rival House of Saud to the proposed elevation of the House of Hashem to new honors. Churchill's proposed solution was to raise Ibn Saud's subsidy to 100,000 pounds a year.[41]

On 22 March the Cairo Conference came to an end and, at midnight on 23 March, Churchill left Cairo by train for Palestine. Once arrived, he met four times in Jerusalem with Abdullah and arrived at an agreement with him. Abdullah's "attitude was moderate, friendly, and statesmanlike," wrote Churchill in a memorandum to the Cabinet. To Arab anti-Zionist demonstrators, Abdullah "maintained an absolutely correct attitude, reproved the demonstrators, stated that the British were his friends, and that the British Government would keep their promises to Jews and Arabs alike."[42] Abdullah agreed to govern Transjordan for six months, with the advice of a British chief political officer and with a British financial subsidy, but without British troops. He agreed also to help establish the air bases upon which, in Churchill's plan, British control would ultimately be centered.

Britain's immediate hopes of pacifying Transjordan rested as heavily upon Abdullah as her hopes of pacifying Iraq depended upon Feisal. From Cap d'Ail on the French Riviera, where he stopped on the way home, Churchill wrote to Lord Curzon that "Abdullah turned around completely under our treatment of the Arab problem. I hope he won't get his throat cut by his own followers. He is a most polished & agreeable person."[43]

Upon his return to London, Churchill secured the support both of the Cabinet and of the Commons for his Middle East policy. Since at Cairo he had secured the support of Britain's officers in the field, the Colonial Secretary had his own country's leadership behind him—at least temporarily—as he attempted to impose his new design on the Middle East. But *The Times*, observing on 15 June 1921 that there was "a disconcerting air of topsy-turvydom about his structure," presciently pointed out that his ingenious attempt to reconcile rival claims and to validate claims without having the resources to do so had led him to assume contingent liabilities on Britain's behalf that could not be redeemed if they were ever presented for payment.

Meanwhile, as the Cairo Conference drew to a close, British officials prepared to stage-manage the selection of Feisal as monarch of the about-to-be-created state of Iraq, planning to remain behind the scenes and make it appear that Feisal had been freely and spontaneously chosen by the peoples of Iraq. They had received assurances that Feisal was prepared to be cooperative.

VII

Before he took office as Colonial Secretary, Churchill had taken advantage of the close relationship between T. E. Lawrence and Feisal to sound out Feisal's views. Lawrence had reported to Churchill's Private Secretary in mid-January that Feisal was prepared to enter into discussions with Britain without any reference to French-occupied Syria; and that Feisal also agreed to abandon all his father's claims to Palestine. Lawrence wrote that "The advantage of his taking this new ground of discussion is that all questions of pledges & promises, fulfilled or broken, are set aside. You begin a new discussion on the actual positions today & the best way of doing something constructive with them."[44]

At the Cairo Conference, Lawrence, Cox, Gertrude Bell, and others in the Political Committee had established a timetable for Feisal's candidacy for the throne of Iraq. Their plan was for Feisal to travel to Mecca, and from there to send telegrams to leading personalities in Iraq. In his cable Feisal was to say he had been urged by friends to come to Iraq and that, after discussing the matter with his father and brothers, he had decided to offer his services to the people of Iraq.

When the Cairo Conference disbanded, Lawrence sent an urgent message to Feisal, who was in London. "Things have gone exactly as hoped. Please start for Mecca at once by quickest possible route ... I will meet you on the way and explain the details. Say only you are going to see your father, and on no account put anything in press."[45]

At about the same time, Sir Percy Cox received a disquieting message from the officer he had left in charge of Baghdad. "Since your departure the situation has changed considerably," ran the message. Sayyid Talib, the dominant local political leader of Basra, had reached an agreement with the Naqib, the elderly leading notable of Baghdad, by the terms of which the former would support the candidacy of the latter in return for a chance at the succession. The two "put forward the claims of an Iraqi ruler for Iraq. There are indications that this claim receives a considerable measure of support, and there is I think no question but that Feisal's candidature will be strongly resisted ..."[46] Cox hurried back to Baghdad to persuade rival candidates to withdraw from the contest—among them, Ibn Saud, who objected to a Hashemite candidacy, but was mollified by cash and other British favors.

Meanwhile Sayyid Talib toured the country, meeting with tribal leaders and speaking in public, affirming the need for cooperation with Britain but proclaiming as his slogan, "Iraq for the Iraqis!"[47]

British intelligence officers reported with alarm that Talib was meeting with "a magnificent reception everywhere."[48]

Sayyid Talib had a long-standing invitation to take tea with Sir Percy Cox at the Residency in Baghdad in mid-April. When he arrived, he found that Cox had excused himself, leaving Lady Cox to entertain the guests. As he left the Residency after the tea party, Talib was arrested by one of his fellow guests, by order of Sir Percy Cox, his absent host. Talib was then deported to the island of Ceylon in the Indian Ocean. The day following Talib's arrest, Sir Percy Cox announced in a communiqué that he had ordered the deportation to preserve law and order in the face of Talib's threat to incite violence.*

Nonetheless resistance to Feisal's candidacy persisted, though it took other forms. Proposals were made in favor of a republic, in favor of a Turkish ruler, in favor of leaving the province of Basra separate from the province of Baghdad, and in favor of leaving matters as they were, under the administration of Sir Percy Cox as High Commissioner.

Guided (at his own request) by British advisers, Feisal meanwhile journeyed from London to the Hejaz, where he settled matters with his father, and thence onward at British expense to Basra, where he disembarked on 24 June. While aboard ship he received the welcome news that the official native leadership—the Council of Ministers in Baghdad, presided over by the Naqib—had invited him to be a guest of the nation.

In public the British government continued to maintain the official fiction that it was neutral and impartial; privately, Cox told Feisal to go out and campaign for popular support so that Britain could claim to have accepted the people's verdict.[49]

On 11 July the Council of Ministers unanimously adopted a resolution declaring Feisal to be the constitutional monarch of Iraq. On 16 July the Council authorized a plebiscite to ratify its choice. On 18 August the Ministry of the Interior announced that Feisal had won an overwhelming victory in the yes-or-no plebiscite. On 23 August Feisal's coronation was celebrated; and in official usage Iraq ("well-rooted country") replaced Mesopotamia as the name of his new kingdom.

Even before his coronation, however, Feisal began to trouble the British by insisting on formal independence and objecting to the

---

* It is questionable whether he ever uttered such a threat. What happened is this: at a private dinner party he gave for the correspondent of the *Daily Telegraph*, Talib said something to the effect that if Britain were not fair and impartial in dealing with the rival candidacies, the tribes might again rise in revolt. Accounts of the actual words he used differ. Cox received his account from Gertrude Bell, who was not present at the dinner herself.

29 The Union Jack is hoisted above Basra in January 1915

30 A street scene in Baghdad, which British troops entered
in March 1917

31 The reading of General Allenby's proclamation of martial law
in Jerusalem in December 1917

32 Australian Light Horse entering Damascus in 1918

33 General Allenby's official entry into Aleppo in March 1919

34 Ottoman soldiers surrender in November 1918

36 Admiral Calthorpe's flagship off Constantinople in December 1918

35 British sentry before the imperial palace in Constantinople
in April 1920

37 Woodrow Wilson

38 Lloyd George (right)

39 The Sultan's representative reluctantly signs the Treaty of Sèvres, 1920

40 British bluejackets on the march in Constantinople, 1920

41 A street in the French quarter of Smyrna after the city's fall, 1922

42 French troops enter Damascus, deposing King Feisal and bringing an end to Syria's brief independence, 1920

43 A peasant in a Turkish field with unburied bodies of Greek soldiers, 1922

44 Mustapha Kemal of Turkey

45 Reza Khan of Persia (Iran)

46 Amanullah Khan of Afghanistan (left), shown with members of his suite

47 King Fuad of Egypt (left) in his palace garden, Cairo

48 Zaghlul Pasha addressing his supporters: the rivalry between the palace and Zaghlul's Wafd Party was to be a principal feature of Egyptian politics after the First World War

49 Sons of King Hussein of the Hejaz (seated, left to right): Feisal, King of Iraq; Abdullah, Emir of Transjordan and later King of Jordan; and Ali, briefly King of the Hejaz before its capture by Ibn Saud

50 Ibn Saud with Sir Percy Cox and Gertrude Bell. A powerful enemy of King Hussein and his family, Ibn Saud nonetheless remained on friendly terms with the British who protected Transjordan and Iraq against attacks by his followers

League of Nations Mandate, which was a trusteeship; he proposed that relations between Iraq and Britain should instead be defined by a treaty between the two countries. The British claimed that they had no legal right to alter the status of Iraq without authorization from the League of Nations; but consented to negotiate a treaty so long as it referred to the Mandate. Feisal objected to including any such reference in the treaty. Negotiations that often caused anger and anguish in London went on for more than a year.

In the late summer of 1922, Churchill wrote to Lloyd George that "Feisal is playing a very low & treacherous game with us."[50] Churchill told the Prime Minister that he and his Cabinet colleagues ought to meet to discuss whether to depose Feisal or whether to evacuate Iraq. A few days later, at a conference of Cabinet ministers, Churchill reported that

> King Feisal had been making great difficulties and confusing the situation in Iraq. He had made objections to the Mandate but had stated his willingness to agree to a Treaty. He was not, however, prepared to recognize the mandatory basis as he thought that the mandatory system was a slur on Iraq. No argument had been of any effect with him. He had recently taken up the Extremists who now regarded him as their patron.[51]

Shortly afterward Churchill wrote to the Prime Minister that "I am deeply concerned about Iraq. The task you have given me is becoming really impossible." He wrote that there was "scarcely a single newspaper—Tory, Liberal, or Labour"—that was not "consistently hostile" to Britain's remaining in Iraq. He added that "in my own heart I do not see what we are getting out of it."[52] He proposed to send Feisal an ultimatum; if it were not accepted, "I would actually clear out."[53]

The Prime Minister replied that "On general principles, I am against a policy of scuttle, in Iraq as elsewhere . . ."[54] He referred, too, to the widely held belief that large reserves of oil might be discovered in the area: "If we leave we may find a year or two after we departed that we have handed over to the French and Americans some of the richest oilfields in the world . . ."[55]

Sir Percy Cox therefore persevered in his negotiations. After several dramatic political crises had run their course he succeeded in concluding a treaty, on 10 October 1922, that incorporated many of the substantive terms of the Mandate. The treaty was to last for twenty years but, as a result of opposition in Iraq, a half year later it was amended so as to reduce its term from twenty years to four years. Even so, Iraqi agitation for fuller independence continued, while in London *The Times* complained that the treaty was unfair to Britain because it imposed too heavy a burden of obligations.

Indeed, Britain was called upon immediately to shield Iraq from the growing power of Ibn Saud. The Arabian monarch, a dynastic enemy of the Hashemites, threatened Feisal as well as his brother Abdullah; and the British government felt obliged to protect them both. At the end of 1922, in a meeting at a port called 'Uqair, Sir Percy Cox imposed upon Ibn Saud an agreement defining the Saudi kingdom's frontiers with Kuwait and Iraq.

Despite their need for British protection, Iraqi politicians moved to assert themselves. The Anglo-Iraqi Treaty of 1922, like the Allenby Declaration of formal independence for Egypt the same year, marked a change in the political atmosphere of the Arab East.* Neither Iraq nor Egypt was granted more than limited autonomy, yet both had been recognized as entities possessing the attributes of statehood. In both countries, political leaders agitated for independence, while British-appointed monarchs could only maintain their position by doing the same.

VIII

Like Iraq, Transjordan continued to be a subject of concern at the Colonial Office. But where Feisal seemed too independent, Abdullah seemed too inactive; the Hashemite solution to Transjordan's problems was not taking hold.

One reason for employing Abdullah in Britain's service had been the argument that it would restrain him from attacking French Syria. T. E. Lawrence later claimed to have reassured Churchill that "I know Abdullah: you won't have a shot fired."[58] The shrewd and indolent Arabian prince was usually not inclined to engage in risky trials of strength. Indeed, within weeks of Abdullah's employment as temporary governor, British observers began to conclude that he was

---

* A sign of the times was a proposal by Sir Percy Cox early in 1922 to send the excavated antiques of Samarra, an ancient town on the Tigris river, to the British Museum before a native government could take office in Iraq.[56] For more than a century, European consuls, travelers, and archaeologists had been taking back with them ancient objects, structures, and works of art from Middle Eastern sites without hindrance. Suddenly, in 1922, Cox feared this situation was coming to an end in Iraq. Similarly, and at roughly the same time, when Howard Carter, in the Valley of the Kings in Egypt, made the archaeological find of the century in locating the tomb of King Tutankhamun, he did what archaeologists had not been driven to do before. On the night of 26 November 1922, Carter and his associates entered the tomb secretly and took their selection of objects in it for themselves. They then resealed it and staged what they claimed was their first entry into the tomb for the benefit of the authorities of the new Egyptian kingdom the following day. From 27 November onward there was an official of the Egyptian Service of Antiquities on guard at all times and no further portions of the King Tut treasure could be removed by the foreigners.[57]

too weak to govern. In April, Abdullah's authority was challenged when delegates he had sent to mediate an intertribal dispute were murdered; instead of crushing the revolt, Abdullah appealed to the British High Commissioner to do it for him. The High Commissioner responded by authorizing the use of British airplanes and armored cars, but it had been precisely in order to obviate the need for using British armed forces that Abdullah had been installed in Amman.

At about the same time, France's ambassador in London protested that Abdullah's presence in Transjordan acted as an incitement to violence against the French in Syria. The British contention was that, on the contrary, Abdullah would prevent such violence. Soon it appeared that he was unable or unwilling even to do this. In late June, four men ambushed and attempted to assassinate General Henri Gouraud, the French conqueror and governor of Syria. "It is on the Transjordanians that suspicion falls," Churchill was informed by his High Commissioner in Palestine.[59] The French authorities lodged a protest against the failure of Britain and Abdullah to prevent such attacks. They protested further when the alleged assassins were observed moving about freely in Transjordan.

The British High Commissioner was unhappy with the results of the Abdullah experiment, and told Churchill so in June. He reported to Churchill that one of the many causes of popular discontent was that native Transjordanians looked upon Abdullah's Syrian associates as wasteful and incompetent.[60] At the same time, the commanding general of the British army in Egypt and Palestine wrote that "in Trans-Jordania Abdulla is a fraud ... If anything is to be made of him he must be given a good strong Englishman who will run him entirely and British troops to back him up."[61] A bit later Hubert Young told Shuckburgh that "What we have got to face is either continued expenditure on Abdullah, whose influence has gone down almost to vanishing point, and who is no longer a substitute for even a section of Infantry, or to take our courage in both hands and send a small force over, if only temporarily ..."[62]

Practically alone in the British government at the time, T. E. Lawrence continued to discern uses—albeit temporary ones—for Abdullah in Transjordan. "His total cost is less than a battalion; his regime prejudices us in no way, whatever eventual solution we wish to carry out, provided that it is not too popular and not too efficient."[63] As the British government still could not decide whether to detach Transjordan permanently from Palestine—either by establishing it as a separate entity, or by allowing King Hussein to annex it to the Hejaz—the notion that Abdullah's temporary regime would postpone the day of decision was an attractive one. However, Lawrence's claim that the Abdullah solution cost the least money was the argument best calculated to appeal to Winston Churchill.

Abdullah demonstrated that he intended to be helpful to Britain by signing an Anglo-Hashemite treaty that Lawrence brought out with him to the Middle East. Lawrence came as Churchill's plenipotentiary, and had spent months in the Hejaz attempting to persuade King Hussein to sign the treaty. The treaty was to be a comprehensive settlement of all the claims advanced by Hussein for himself and the Arabs ever since the early days of the First World War. Its terms included confirmation that Britain recognized him as King of the Hejaz and would pay him an annual subsidy of 100,000 pounds; but he, in turn, was required to recognize the French Mandate for Syria and the British Mandate for Palestine. At times Hussein said he would sign the treaty, but then he would change his mind. At one point, according to Lawrence, Hussein demanded "recognition of his supremacy over all Arab rulers everywhere."[64] Lawrence believed that the old man of Mecca had become impossible to deal with. He secured Abdullah's signature on the treaty; in view of Hussein's rejection of it the signed document was rendered meaningless, but Lawrence seems to have appreciated Abdullah's attempt to be helpful.

After a few months as governor of Transjordan, Abdullah began to change his mind about future plans. At the beginning he had allowed the British to understand that he intended to stay in Transjordan only for a short time because the territory was relatively unimportant to him in view of his large ambitions elsewhere. In any event, T. E. Lawrence was sure he could talk Abdullah into leaving when the time came. In October 1921, however, Lawrence reported that Abdullah intended to stay on. Abdullah aspired to ascend the throne of Syria and, apparently, new developments had encouraged him to believe that within a short time France might be ready to negotiate a reconciliation that would allow him to achieve his goal; so his inclination was to remain in the vicinity.

At the same time, the need to replace Abdullah by a more effective ruler seemed to become less urgent. H. St John Philby, a forceful British figure—one of the great explorers of Arabia—became the new official adviser to Abdullah; and, even more important, Lawrence's friend Colonel F. G. Peake began whipping into shape a Bedouin force of regular troops under British command, which later—under his successor, John Glubb—became the formidable Arab Legion. The law and order situation seemed to be improving along the lines Lawrence had advocated, that is to say, without spending a significant amount of additional money. Lawrence began to believe it might be a good idea for Abdullah to stay on after all.

But to maintain Abdullah—an Arabian—as ruler of Transjordan, and to maintain Transjordan as an Arab preserve, in which Jews could not settle to build their homeland, was to depart from the Balfour Declaration policy of fostering a Jewish National Home. If the British were indeed planning to make Palestine into a Jewish country, it was hardly auspicious to begin by forbidding Jews to settle in 75 percent of the country or by handing over local administration, not to a Jew, but to an Arabian. The Balfour Declaration policy was embodied in the League of Nations Mandate entrusting Palestine to Britain, and in 1921–2 the Mandate—commissioning Britain as trustee of Palestine with the mission of creating a Jewish National Home while protecting the rights of non-Jews as well—was in the process of being offered by the League of Nations to the British Parliament for acceptance. Since Churchill's temporary decision *not* to encourage—or even allow—the building of a Jewish National Home in eastern Palestine ran counter to the provisions of the Mandate, he decided to change the terms of the Mandate, which was redrafted to provide that Britain was not obliged to pursue the Balfour Declaration policy east of the Jordan river.

The Zionist leaders worried that shrinking their eastern frontiers would cripple their program, the more so because, in negotiating with France to fix a boundary between Palestine and Syria-Lebanon, Britain had also surrendered territory on their northern frontier. Chaim Weizmann wrote to Churchill early in 1921 that the agreement with France "cut Palestine off from access to the Litani, deprived her of possession of the Upper Jordan and the Yarmuk and took from her the fertile plains east of Lake Tiberias which had heretofor been regarded as one of the most promising outlets for Jewish settlement on a large scale." Turning to Transjordan, he wrote "that the fields of Gilead, Moab and Edom, with the rivers Arnon and Jabbok . . . are historically and geographically and economically linked to Palestine, and that it is upon these fields, now that the rich plains of the north have been taken from Palestine and given to France, that the success of the Jewish National Home must largely rest."[65] Justice Brandeis, the leader of American Zionism, sent a cabled message to Balfour toward the end of 1921 making the same point, deploring the loss of the waters of the Litani river (in what is now Lebanon) and calling attention to the economic importance of the Transjordan plains.[66]

Yet the Zionist leaders did not campaign strongly against the administrative separation of Transjordan; they regarded it—not without reason—as a merely provisional measure. So did the Colonial Office. Views of the leading officials differed, but Shuckburgh summarized the agreement he and his colleagues had reached by saying that it had been decided not to allow Zionism in Transjordan for the present but also not to bar the door against it for all time.[67]

Churchill had not foreseen that by leaving Abdullah in Transjordan he would embroil Britain in the fierce Arabian religious war between the House of Saud and the House of Hashem; but, in 1922, only about a year after Abdullah's arrival, the fanatical Wahhabi

Brethren, the spearhead of Ibn Saud, rode across the undefined desert frontier to attack Abdullah. An estimated 3,000 to 4,000 Brethren raiders came within an hour's camel ride of Amman (now the capital of Jordan) before being crushed by British airplanes and armored cars.* In succeeding years Britain was drawn into playing a far more direct role in governing and defending Transjordan than Churchill had intended and British officials soon came to look upon Abdullah as a problem rather than as a solution.

Nevertheless the Colonial Office's temporary and merely administrative set of arrangements for Transjordan in time hardened into an enduring political reality. The Arabian prince with his foreign retinue settled in Amman and became a permanent new factor in the complex politics of the Palestine Mandatory regime. The recurring suggestion that Palestine be partitioned between Arabs and Jews ran up against the problem that 75 percent of the country had already been given to an Arab dynasty that was not Palestinian. The newly created province of Transjordan, later to become the independent state of Jordan, gradually drifted into existence as an entity separate from the rest of Palestine; indeed, today it is often forgotten that Jordan was ever part of Palestine.

---

* By sheltering and shielding Abdullah, Britain in effect partitioned the world of desert Arabians between the two contending royal houses, with the Jordanian frontier marking a dividing line. The only two countries whose names in 1988 still designate them as family property are the Kingdom of *Saudi* Arabia and the *Hashemite* Kingdom of Jordan; the international border between them still divides the two Arabian royal houses.

CHURCHILL AND THE
QUESTION OF PALESTINE

I

As Colonial Secretary in 1921—2, Churchill encountered even greater difficulty in dealing with the vexing problems of Palestine west of the Jordan river than with those of Transjordan and Iraq. The issue in Palestine was Zionism, and so intense were the passions it aroused that it was not always easy to remember what was really at issue. The Zionists pictured Palestine—correctly, as we now know—as a country that could support at least five or ten times more people than lived there at the time; so that without displacing any of the perhaps 600,000 Arab inhabitants, there was room to bring in millions of Jewish settlers.

At the time nothing like that many Jews were prepared to settle as pioneers in Palestine, but Zionists hoped and Arabs feared that they would do so, and the unrestricted right of Jews to enter the country became the central issue in Palestinian politics. Friends of Zionism claimed—and later demonstrated—that Jewish enterprise could enrich the country, but impoverished Arab peasant farmers were persuaded that they were being asked to share what little they possessed with foreigners.

As seen earlier, there had been Arab anti-Zionist riots in Palestine a year before Churchill became Colonial Secretary in February 1921. Not long after he attempted to solve the problems of the Middle East at the Cairo Conference that March, Palestine erupted again. In Jaffa, on May Day 1921, rioting broke out, beginning with looting, but going on to murder: during the first day the Arab mobs killed thirty-five Jews. In the course of a blood-soaked week, fighting spread to the entire country as Arabs besieged Jewish farm colonies outside the principal towns. The original Arab riots in Jaffa were an explosion of anger against a small group of Jewish communists who marched through the center of town to rival an earlier demonstration by a larger group of Jewish socialists. Thus the impression gained ground amongst the British that the disorders were Bolshevik in origin. Captain C. D. Brunton, who had served in the military administration for some time, claimed that the riots had been caused by "Bolshevist Jews" and argued that "the outbreaks of today may become a revolution tomorrow."[1]

The High Commissioner, Sir Herbert Samuel, responded to the Arab attacks by temporarily suspending Jewish immigration into Palestine. Zionist leaders feared that by rewarding Arab violence, Samuel had guaranteed that it would be renewed and that the history of the British Mandate for Palestine would be a stormy one.

Samuel's administration was slow to restore order; on 10 August 1921 *The Times* reported that "Public security, particularly in the north, is for all practical purposes, non-existent. Raids take place almost daily from Transjordania ..." *The Times* correspondent claimed that "neither Jews nor Arabs have any confidence in the authorities." He added that "The older inhabitants say that public security was far better maintained under the Turks."

Although Arab riots seemed likely to recur, Zionist leaders continued to seek accommodation with the Arabs and to express confidence that most Arabs were in favor of peace and cooperation.[*]

II

As Churchill recognized, one of his greatest problems in quelling the Arab riots while going ahead with a pro-Zionist program was that the British forces upon whom he relied were unwilling to enforce his policy.

The anti-Zionist case was easy for the British in Palestine to understand: Arabs had lived in the country for ages and did not want their life and landscape changed. British soldiers and officials worked every day among Arabs who told them so. Of course Jews lived in Palestine too, and their connection with the land was even more long-standing; but much of the case for Zionism, strong though it was, was not entirely tangible: it was partly historical, partly theoretical, and partly visionary (in the sense that it was only in the future that Jewish enterprise would bring a much higher standard of living

---

[*] Opening the Twelfth Zionist Congress in the summer of 1921, Nahum Sokolow said that Jews "were determined to work in peace with the Arab nation." Stressing the historical links between the two peoples, he argued that by cooperating they could "create a new life of the highest perfection for the people of the East" and that "Their interests were identical ..." Dismissing the recent Arab riots as the work of a small group of criminals, he assured the Arab community that Jews "were not going to the Holy Land in a spirit of mastery. By industry and peace and modesty they would open up new sources of production which would be a blessing to themselves and to the whole East."[2]

to all the peoples of the country). The Zionist case was also based on the suffering of Jews in such places as Russia and Poland; but members of the British Palestine administration had never witnessed that suffering and were not necessarily aware of it.

According to Vladimir Jabotinsky, the militant Zionist who had founded the Jewish Legion in Allenby's army, the British military found Zionism to be a "fancy" theory, far-reaching and aiming to repair the world's ills, and therefore unsound. According to Jabotinsky, such fancy schemes for improving the world ran counter to all the instincts of the average Englishman of the ruling classes.[3]

Jabotinsky pointed out, too, that the administration was staffed by professional Arabists. These were people (he wrote) so attracted to the Arab world (as they conceived it to be) that they underwent the discipline of learning the Arab language and qualifying themselves for the Civil Service, and were willing to leave Britain to spend their professional lives in the Arab Middle East; and it was natural that they would not want to see the Arab character of Palestine changed.

Jabotinsky touched on, but did not stress, what may have been the principal reason for British opposition to the Balfour Declaration policy: it caused trouble. It was unpopular with the Arabs who constituted the bulk of the population, while the job of the British colonial administration was to keep the population quiet and satisfied. British civil and military personnel in Palestine had reason to believe that they could have enjoyed an easy and peaceful tour of duty in a contented country, if it were not for London's policy, adopted for reasons not readily grasped, that excited communal tension and violence and exposed the local British administration to difficulty and even danger.

However disaffection in the British ranks led ironically to an increase in the difficulty and danger, by encouraging Arab resistance and intransigence at a time when London was not yet prepared to yield. A particular episode that was to have lasting consequences was the intervention of the Palestine administration in the selection of a new religious leader for the Moslem community.

The episode began with the death, on 21 March 1921, of the Mufti of Jerusalem. A mufti was an official who expounded the Moslem religious laws, and the Mufti of Jerusalem was the chief such jurist in his province. The British administration—bestowing a title apparently of its own invention—also designated him as the Grand Mufti and as the leader of the Moslem community in Palestine.[4] According to the Ottoman law, which the British incorporated into their own, the government was to select the new Grand Mufti from among three candidates nominated by a Moslem electoral college.

Although he was not among the three candidates nominated, Amin al-Husseini, a political agitator in his mid-twenties who had been sentenced to ten years' imprisonment (though later pardoned) for his leadership role in the 1920 riots, was named as the new Grand Mufti as a result of an intrigue by a violently anti-Zionist official named Ernest T. Richmond, a member of the British High Commissioner's secretariat.

Richmond was an architect who had served before the war in the Egyptian Public Works Administration and owed his job in Palestine to Ronald Storrs, a close friend with whom he shared a house for a time in Jerusalem. In the Palestine administration he served as a liaison with the Moslem community, acting (according to General Gilbert Clayton) "as to some extent the counterpart of the Zionist Organisation."[5] According to an official of the Colonial Office in London, Richmond was "a declared enemy of the Zionist policy" of the British government.[6] He crusaded against that policy, and several years later—in 1924—wrote to the British High Commissioner in Palestine that in pursuing Zionism, the High Commissioner and his officials, the Middle East Department of the Colonial Office in London, and the Zionist Commission in Palestine "are dominated and inspired by a spirit which I can only regard as evil."[7]

When he secured the position of Grand Mufti and leader of the Palestinian Moslems for Amin al-Husseini in 1921, Richmond must have believed that he was striking a blow against Zionism. As time would show, he had struck a crueler, more destructive blow against Palestinian Arabs, whom the Grand Mufti was to lead into a bloody blind alley. An all-or-nothing adventurer, the Grand Mufti placed Arab lands and lives at risk by raising the stakes of the Arab-Jewish conflict such that one or another—Jews or Arabs—would be driven out or destroyed. Eventually the Grand Mufti's road was to lead him to Nazi Germany and alliance with Adolph Hitler. While Amin al-Husseini did not control Arab Palestine—he had many rivals for leadership—his position as Grand Mufti gave him an advantage in the contest for the allegiance of the deeply divided Arab communities in Palestine.

Whether Palestinian Moslems would have followed other leaders had the British administration used its power and influence in other ways can never be known; but to the extent that Richmond's anti-Zionist initiative had an effect, it was not helpful to the Arab cause— or to that of Churchill and the British government in attempting to bring peace and progress to troubled Palestine.

III

Churchill approached the complex, emotion-laden and muddled question of Palestine with a simple, rational, and clear program. He believed in trying the Zionist experiment, and thought that it would benefit everyone. When he visited Palestine after the Cairo Conference, he told a Palestinian Arab delegation on 30 March 1921 that

> it is manifestly right that the scattered Jews should have a national centre and a national home to be re-united and where else but in Palestine with which for 3,000 years they have been intimately and profoundly associated? We think it will be good for the world, good for the Jews, good for the British Empire, but also good for the Arabs who dwell in Palestine and we intend it to be so; . . . they shall share in the benefits and progress of Zionism.[8]

Churchill had always shown sympathy for Jewish aspirations and for the plight of Jews persecuted by the czars. Like Balfour, he felt that the persecution of Jews in Russia and elsewhere had created a problem for the entire world, which the creation of a Jewish homeland in Palestine would solve.

In Churchill's view, there were three kinds of politically active Jews: those who participated in the political life of the country in which they lived; those who turned to the violent and subversive international creed of Bolshevism; and those who followed Dr Chaim Weizmann along the path of Zionism. For the majority of the world's Jews, who had grown up in countries such as Russia which refused them full and equal citizenship, the question (as he saw it) was whether they would become Bolsheviks or Zionists. An ardent patriot himself, he considered Jewish nationalism a healthy phenomenon that ought to be encouraged.

> If, as may well happen, there should be created in our own lifetime by the banks of the Jordan a Jewish State under the protection of the British Crown which might comprise three or four millions of Jews, an event will have occurred in this history of the world which would from every point of view be beneficial and would be especially in harmony with the truest interests of the British Empire.[9]

So Churchill had written—before taking office as Colonial Secretary—early in 1920.

Churchill was not unmindful of the opposition to Zionism among Palestinian Arabs, but he believed that it could be overcome by a program that combined basic firmness with attractive inducements and compromises. As Colonial Minister, he attempted to appease Palestinian Arab sentiment by scaling down Britain's support of Zionism. As indicated earlier, he decided that Zionism was to be tried first only in the quarter of Palestine that lay west of the Jordan river, and nothing was to be decided for the moment about extending it later into the other three-quarters of the country—Transjordan. Moreover, Churchill attempted to redefine the British commitment: he proposed to establish a Jewish National Home *in* Palestine rather than attempt to make Palestine herself into a Jewish entity, and he claimed that that was what the language of the Balfour Declaration meant. (In a private conversation at Balfour's house in the summer of 1921, both Balfour and the Prime Minister contradicted him and told Churchill that "by the Declaration they always meant an eventual Jewish State.")[10]

Churchill further attempted to allay Arab suspicions by demonstrating that their economic fears were groundless. Jewish immigrants, he argued repeatedly, would not seize Arab jobs or Arab land. On the contrary, he said, Jewish immigrants would create new jobs and new wealth that would benefit the whole community.

In June 1921 Churchill told the House of Commons that "There really is nothing for the Arabs to be frightened about ... No Jew will be brought in beyond the number who can be provided for by the expanding wealth and development of the resources of the country."[11] In August he repeated to an Arab delegation that had come to London that

> I have told you again and again that the Jews will not be allowed to come into the country except insofar as they build up the means for their livelihood ... They cannot take any man's lands. They cannot dispossess any man of his rights or his property ... If they like to buy people's land and people like to sell it to them, and if they like to develop and cultivate regions now barren and make them fertile, then they have the right ... [to do so].[12]

"There is room for all ...," he told them.[13] "No one has harmed you ... The Jews have a far more difficult task than you. You only have to enjoy your own possession; but they have to try to create out of the wilderness, out of the barren places, a livelihood for the people they bring in."[14]

In the same statement he complained to the Arabs that it was not fair of them to refuse to negotiate: "it is not fair to come to a discussion thinking that one side has to give nothing and the other side has to give large and important concessions, and without any security that these concessions will be a means of peace."

IV

Churchill had spent a lifetime immersed in the political culture of Europe, in which it was normal when putting forth a proposal to take account of the needs and desires of all interested parties, including adversaries. Thus when Kitchener, Clayton, and Storrs in 1914–15 contemplated excluding France from the postwar Arab Middle East, they noted that Britain would have to compensate France for doing so by seeing that she obtained territorial gains elsewhere in the world; and while this may not have been a realistic appreciation of what France would accept, it was a realistic recognition that if Britain made territorial gains France would insist on matching them.

Similarly, in postwar Turkey, Kemal—a statesman with a European cast of mind—formulated territorial demands for Turkish nationalism not merely on the basis of his appreciation of what Turkey needed but also on his understanding of what Turkey's neighbors could accept.

This was the sort of statesmanship to which Churchill was accustomed; but he did not find it in the Palestinian Arab delegation in London, which did no more than repeat its demands. Palestine was and is an area of complex and competing claims, but the Arab delegation took account of no claims, fears, needs, or dreams other than its own. Unlike the Zionist leaders, who sought to compensate Arab nationalism by supporting Arab versus French claims to Syria, who envisaged areas of Arab autonomy within Palestine, and who planned economic and other benefits for Arabs who chose to live within the confines of the Jewish homeland, the Arab leaders made no effort to accommodate Jewish aspirations or to take account of Jewish needs.

Dealing with Middle Easterners such as these was far more frustrating than had been imagined in wartime London when the prospect of administering the postwar Middle East was first raised. In Churchill's eyes, the members of the Arab delegation were not doing what politicians are supposed to do: they were not aiming to reach an agreement—any agreement. Apparently unwilling to offer even 1 percent in order to get 99 percent, they offered no incentive to the other side to make concessions. Churchill remonstrated with the Arab leaders—to no effect.

V

The Arab delegation to London, which was headed by Musa Kazim Pasha al-Husseini,* president of the Arab Executive, apparently refused to understand what Churchill was saying. Members of the delegation would ask a question, and then when Churchill had answered it, would ask the same question again, as though they had

---

* Not to be confused with his relative, the youthful Grand Mufti.

not heard Churchill's reply. Churchill showed signs of frustration and anger at this tactic, but continued to repeat his answers in the evident hope of finally making himself understood. It was in this spirit that he repeated that land was not being taken away from Arabs; that Arabs sold land to Jews only if they chose to do so.

In the Middle East, things rarely were what they seemed to be, and the land issue in Palestine was a case in point. The Arab delegation to London did in fact understand what Churchill meant about Arabs wanting to sell land to Jews, for Musa Kazim Pasha, the president of the delegation, was himself one of those who had sold land to the Jewish settlers.[15] So had other members of the Arab delegations that he brought with him to London in 1921–2 and in succeeding years.

Prince Feisal and Dr Chaim Weizmann had agreed in 1918 that there was no scarcity of land in Palestine: the problem, rather, was that so much of it was controlled by a small group of Arab landowners and usurers.[16] The great mass of the peasantry struggled to eke out a bare living from low-yielding, much-eroded, poorly irrigated plots, while large holdings of fertile lands were being accumulated by influential families of absentee landlords.

The Zionist plan, as outlined by Weizmann to Feisal in 1918, was to avoid encroaching on land being worked by the Arab peasantry and instead to reclaim unused, uncultivated land, and by the use of scientific agricultural methods to restore its fertility. The large Arab landholders, however, turned out to be eager to sell the Jewish settlers their fertile lands, too—at very considerable profits.* Indeed Jewish purchasers bid land prices up so that, not untypically, an Arab family of Beirut sold plots of land in the Jezreel valley to Jewish settlers in 1921 at prices ranging from forty to eighty times the original purchase price.[17] Far from being forced by Jews to sell, Arabs offered so much land to Jews that the only limiting factor on purchases became money: the Jewish settlers did not have enough money to buy all the land that Arabs offered to them.[18]

Not merely non-Palestinian Arabs but the Palestinian Arab leadership class itself was deeply implicated in these land sales that it publicly denounced. Either personally or through their families, at

---

* For a variety of reasons, the economic yield on Palestinian agricultural landholdings had sunk to low levels during the First World War and just afterward, and the Arab propertied classes were enabled to maintain their level of income only because of the bonanza provided by Jews purchasing land at inflated prices. Jewish settlement was a boon to wealthy Arabs, whatever they said in public to the contrary, and their claim that Jews were forcing them to sell was fraudulent. The genuine grievance was that of the impoverished Arab peasantry. As socialists, the Jewish farmers were opposed to the exploitation of others and therefore did all their own work; when Jews bought Arab farms the Arab farm laborers therefore lost their jobs.

least a quarter of the elected official leadership of the Arab Palestinian community sold land to Jewish settlers between 1920 and 1928.[19]

The Zionist leadership may have been misled by such dealings into underestimating the depth of real local opposition to Jewish settlement. The British government, on the other hand, misjudged not merely the depth but also the nature of the Arab response: in treating the land issue as if it were valid rather than the fraud it was, Churchill and his colleagues either misunderstood or pretended to misunderstand the real basis of Arab opposition to Zionism. Arab opposition to Jewish settlement was rooted in emotion, in religion, in xenophobia, in the complex of feelings that tend to overcome people when newcomers flood in to change their neighborhood. The Arabs of Palestine were defending a threatened way of life. The Arab delegations that went to see Winston Churchill did not articulate this real basis for their objection to Zionism. Instead they argued that the country could not sustain more inhabitants; and Churchill took them at their word. He accepted their statement that they were objecting on economic grounds; and then he went ahead to prove that their economic fears were unjustified.

VI

In a decision that had lasting impact—and that showed that Arab economic fears were unjustified—Churchill in 1922 approved a concession for hydro-electric schemes in the Auja and Jordan river valleys to Pinhas Rutenberg, a Jewish engineer from Russia. This put into motion a far-reaching plan to provide power and irrigation that would make possible the reclamation of the land and its economic development along twentieth-century lines. It was the first giant step along the road toward proving the Zionist claim that Palestine could support a population of millions and not—as Arab spokesmen claimed—merely of hundreds of thousands.

Churchill was especially impressed by the fact that the scheme was put forward and financed on a noncommercial basis, and was moved to tell the House of Commons that only Zionists were willing to undertake such a project on such a basis.

I am told that the Arabs would have done it for themselves. Who is going to believe that? Left to themselves, the Arabs of Palestine would not in a thousand years have taken effective steps toward the irrigation and electrification of Palestine. They would have been quite content to dwell—a handful of philosophic people—in the wasted sun-scorched plains, letting the waters of the Jordan continue to flow unbridled and unharnessed into the Dead Sea.[20]

Churchill continued to warn the Arabs—as he did from the very beginning—that they had better make the best of it because Britain was going to carry through on her commitments in any event. In the summer of 1921 he had told the recalcitrant Palestinian Arab delegation in London that "The British Government mean to carry out the Balfour Declaration. I have told you so again and again. I told you so at Jerusalem. I told you so at the House of Commons the other day. I tell you so now. They mean to carry out the Balfour Declaration. They do."[21]

But, in Palestine, officers of the British administration encouraged Arab leaders to believe otherwise. Churchill gloomily estimated that 90 percent of the British army in Palestine was arrayed against the Balfour Declaration policy.[22] On 29 October 1921 General W. N. Congreve, the commander of the British armies in Egypt and Palestine, sent a circular to all troops stating that, while "the Army officially is supposed to have no politics," it did have sympathies, and "In the case of Palestine these sympathies are rather obviously with the Arabs, who have hitherto appeared to the disinterested observer to have been the victims of an unjust policy forced upon them by the British Government." Pointing to Churchill's much narrowed interpretation of the Balfour Declaration, Congreve expressed confidence that "The British Government would never give any support to the more grasping policy of the Zionist Extremist, which aims at the Establishment of a Jewish Palestine in which Arabs would be merely tolerated."[23] In passing the circular on to Churchill, John Shuckburgh noted "It is unfortunately the case that the army in Palestine is largely anti-Zionist and will probably remain so whatever may be said to it."[24]

Shuckburgh's deputy, Hubert Young, wrote a memorandum in the summer of 1921 that Churchill circulated to the Cabinet, advocating "the removal of all anti-Zionist civil officials, however highly placed."[25] This did not get at the problem of military officials, however; and even the presence of Sir Herbert Samuel and Wyndham Deedes at the head of the civil administration did not seem to affect the political orientation of officials lower down.

In the Jewish community, too, there were those who despaired of obtaining support from the British authorities. Vladimir Jabotinsky, founder of the Jewish Legion, argued that Jews were going to have to protect themselves because the police and the army were not going to do the job. On 27 March 1922 the Near Eastern correspondent of *The Times* reported that "certain of the more extreme Zionists have committed the criminal error of smuggling arms into the country and forming a secret defence force called the 'Hagana'."

In turn, as time wore on, influential figures in Britain began to wonder whether their country could afford to continue occupying

Palestine in support of a Zionist program that had come to seem so difficult of realization. *The Times* had been an enthusiastic backer of the Balfour Declaration policy, which it had termed (on 27 April 1920) "the only sound policy the Allies could adopt toward the Jewish people," but its ardor waned as the difficulties multiplied. In the spring of 1922, *The Times* ran a six-part series of articles by Philip Graves, who had served in the Arab Bureau during the war, to explain Britain's growing unpopularity in Palestine; and Graves blamed Palestine's Jews for being rioted against rather more than he blamed the army for sympathizing with the rioters. He argued that the British army was war-weary. So, in fact, was the British public.

In the issue of 11 April 1922, in which the Graves series was concluded, *The Times* ran a leading article from the point of view of "the British taxpayer," in which it recalled the value of the Zionist experiment in Palestine, but wondered whether Britain could afford to continue supporting it. "It is an interesting experiment, but the question is whether we have counted the cost."

Thus the Colonial Secretary found that his government's Palestine policy was being undermined in Britain herself, where it had formerly enjoyed wide support. On 21 June 1922 a motion was introduced in the House of Lords declaring that the Palestine Mandate (which embodied the policy of the Balfour Declaration) was unacceptable; it was carried by sixty votes to twenty-nine. The nonbinding House of Lords motion served to focus attention on the Colonial Office debate in the House of Commons, which took place on the evening of 4 July. Churchill was attacked by a number of speakers for attempting to carry the Balfour Declaration into effect. Many of those who attacked Churchill had formerly supported the Balfour Declaration, and he used their earlier statements against them with telling effect. Churchill read out a dozen statements supporting the Balfour Declaration that had been made at the time of its issuance. He told the House that he could prolong the list by reading out many more such statements. He told his opponents that, having supported the making of a national commitment, they had no right to turn around and attack him for endeavoring to fulfill that commitment.[26]

As he did on a number of other occasions, Churchill spoke warmly of the need for Britain to honor her pledges. He told the House that the Balfour Declaration had been issued "not only on the merits, though I think the merits are considerable," but because it was believed at the time that Jewish support "would be a definite palpable advantage" in Britain's struggle to win the war.[27] He pointed out that he had not been a member of the War Cabinet at the time and had played no role in the deliberations from which the Balfour Declaration had emerged. However, like other Members of Parliament (he continued), he had loyally supported the policy of the War Cabinet and therefore accepted responsibility for fulfilling the commitments made by the War Cabinet on Britain's behalf as those obligations came due.

Churchill's speech ran the gamut of issues on which he had been challenged, including the Rutenberg concession, which had given rise to considerable opposition. He claimed that he had cut the cost of administering Palestine from eight million pounds in 1920 to four million in 1921 and to an estimated two million in 1922; and that as a result of the Rutenberg development program, it eventually would be possible for the British government to recoup these moneys that it had spent.[28]

Churchill's speech was a brilliant success. The vote in favor of the government's Palestine policy was 292 to 35 and Churchill cabled Deedes in Jerusalem that the vote in the Commons "has directly reversed House of Lords resolution."[29] Britain, in other words, would agree to accept the Palestine Mandate from the League of Nations.

The Executive of the Palestine Arab Congress then sent a telegram to the Colonial Secretary rejecting the terms of the League of Nations Mandate and also rejecting the governmental White Paper in which Churchill had spelled out his government's much-reduced scale of commitment to Zionism. With whatever reluctance, on behalf of the Zionist organization, Dr Chaim Weizmann accepted those much-reduced terms, hoping that they might provide a framework within which a Jewish majority might develop in Palestine and might then achieve self-government. Weizmann accepted the best terms he could get from Churchill, hoping that, with time, the terms could be improved; the Arab Executive refused to accept the best terms it could get from Churchill, hoping that, with time, it could dictate its own terms.

On 22 July the League of Nations formally and finally approved the rewritten Palestine Mandate, directing Britain to carry the re-defined Balfour Declaration policy into effect west of the Jordan river.

VII

Two influential Zionist leaders, David Ben-Gurion and Vladimir Jabotinsky, considered the significance of the Arab opposition and British reactions to it and arrived (as they often did) at opposite conclusions.

Ben-Gurion, a Polish-born leader of the Labor Zionist movement, had settled in Palestine as a farmer in 1906, at the age of twenty. Though a supporter of the Ottoman Empire at the outset of the First

World War, he had eventually enlisted in the British army. He was a socialist who believed that only a willingness to work confers a right to occupy a country, and that Jews and Arabs had an equal right to live and work in Palestine. In his interpretation, the Arab riots of 1920 and 1921 were the acts of "wildmen" who had been misled by the British administration into believing that violence would pay.[30] As a labor union leader, his declared policy was to organize the Arab workers, for he claimed that Arab and Jewish workers and farmers had interests in common—as against employers and landlords—and his object was to show Arabs that this was so. He envisaged a Palestine in which both the Arab and Jewish communities would enjoy autonomy.

To Ben-Gurion the 1920 and 1921 riots showed that Zionists had not made clear enough to the Arabs that their religious and civil rights would never be infringed.[31] As he so often did, he saw the solution in terms of educating and communicating. While he had foreseen from the beginning the possibility that Arabs might not agree to Jewish immigration and settlement, he did not dwell on that possibility or allow himself to believe it would actually occur. Some historians now believe that he was not entirely candid when he professed to believe in Arab-Jewish cooperation,[32] but a more persuasive interpretation is that he was the sort of person who believes it does no good to think about what might go wrong; he was a "constructivist," whose tendency was to believe that if you create and work, the future will take care of itself. He believed that the benefits of Jewish labor and creativity would flow to the Arabs of Palestine as well, and his policy continued to be cooperation both with the Arabs and the British administration.

On the other hand, Jabotinsky, the Russian-born journalist who had founded Allenby's Jewish Legion, believed that Arabs would never stand by peacefully and allow Jews to become a majority in Palestine; that an "iron wall" of military force would have to protect the Jewish settlers as they built their community into a majority; that the British had shown they could not be relied upon to provide that protection; and that Jews therefore would have to form their own army to protect themselves.[33] It was an almost hopeless assessment, and Jabotinsky found himself in the minority in accepting it.

It was a paradox that Ben-Gurion, who at the outset of the First World War had tried to create a Jewish army to fight for the Ottoman Empire, now relied upon the British government, while Jabotinsky, who had raised a Jewish regiment to fight for Britain, had lost that faith.

In the years to come, Ben-Gurion was to emerge as the leader of the mainstream within the Zionist movement, while Jabotinsky led the opposition to the official Zionist leadership throughout the 1920s and then—in the late 1930s—seceded to found his own rival Zionist-Revisionist organization, denouncing Churchill's decision in 1922 to remove Transjordan from the territory of the Jewish National Home and demanding the establishment of a Jewish state on both sides of the Jordan. The schism persists to this day in the politics of the state of Israel, in which the Labor Party claims the heritage of Ben-Gurion and the Herut Party, that of Jabotinsky.

What also persists in Israel, especially in Herut ranks, is the view that Jordan either is or should be an Arab Palestinian state: that Churchill's separation of Transjordania (as it was then called) from the rest of the Palestine Mandate in 1922 was not legitimate.

VIII

The Arabic-speaking section of the Ottoman Empire had now been politically redesigned. The Turks no longer ruled it. In the east, Kurdish, Sunni, Shi'ite, and Jewish populations had been combined into a new Mesopotamian country named Iraq, under the rule of an Arabian prince; it looked like an independent country, but Britain regarded it as a British protectorate. Syria and a greatly enlarged Lebanon were ruled by France. A new Arab entity that was to become Jordan had been carved out of Palestine; and west of the Jordan river was a Palestine that was to contain a Jewish National Home. It was far from the restored Ottoman Empire Churchill had once espoused.

Churchill had, however, achieved the principal objectives that he had set for himself in the Middle East when he became Colonial Secretary. His overriding goal had been to cut costs, and he had done so drastically. Moreover, he believed that he had created a system that could be operated economically in the future. His line of air bases stretching from Egypt to Iraq allowed him to keep the Middle Eastern countries under control with a minimum of expense.

His other goal had been to demonstrate that Britain kept her pledges. He had not fully achieved this with respect to Zionism, but he had done so in regard to whatever might have been owing to the dynasty of King Hussein. T. E. Lawrence, formerly the government's severest British critic on this score, judged that he had more than done so. At the end of 1922, referring back to the wartime correspondence between Hussein and Sir Henry McMahon, then British High Commissioner in Egypt, concerning the frontiers of Arab independence, Lawrence wrote that "He (Churchill) executed the whole McMahon undertaking (called a treaty by some who have not seen it) for Palestine, for Transjordania and for Arabia. In Mesopotamia he went far beyond its provisions ... I do not wish to make long explanations, but must put on record my conviction that England is out of the Arab affair with clean hands."[34]

But it was not the Arab affair that was Churchill's principal concern in the Middle East, even though it was his principal responsibility. His main concern was for the Turkish-speaking remnant of the Ottoman Empire; Lloyd George's policy in that area was—in Churchill's view—dangerously wrong, and threatened to bring down in ruin the entire British position in the Middle East.

59

THE ALLIANCES COME APART

I

Churchill's misgivings about Lloyd George's Turkish policy went unheeded, for the Prime Minister, in the pride of his position, of his victories, of his record of having been proven right when all the experts around him had said he was wrong, did not pay due attention to the opinions of his colleagues. Lloyd George played a lone and lordly hand, without accommodating the diverse political groupings at home and abroad from whom his power stemmed.

For years Lloyd George had been the star of a solar system of coalitions. As head of a parliamentary coalition of Conservatives and his own group of Liberals, he continued to command the support of a majority in the House of Commons, which sustained him in office as leader of a coalition Cabinet. As Prime Minister of Britain he also exercised leadership of a diverse coalition that included the empire and the self-governing Dominions of Canada, Newfoundland, South Africa, Australia, and New Zealand—a coalition that had joined the continental European Allies to oppose the Central Powers in the First World War. As of 1921, Lloyd George was the sole leader of the wartime alliance who still remained in office. It was in the still unsubdued domains of the Ottoman Empire that this system of coalitions started to come apart.

Russia had been the first of the European Allies to withdraw from the wartime coalition—and then to fight against it. Even before the war ended the new Bolshevik regime had moved into conflict with Russia's former Allies all along a southern tier in the Middle East and Central Asia.

Conversely, the Soviet government moved into a working alliance with a wartime enemy, Turkey, in the years immediately following the armistices, collaborating both with Enver Pasha and with Mustapha Kemal. It supplied arms and money that helped Kemal continue his struggle against the Allies. In 1921 the Soviet governments of Russia and its satellite regimes entered into comprehensive agreements with Kemal's Turkish regime, establishing a frontier and a working relationship between them.

In 1921, too, Soviet Russia also moved into a working relationship with another of the former enemy states. Acting upon Enver Pasha's suggestion, the leaders of the new German army entered into a secret partnership with the Soviet regime. The head of the army, Enver's friend General von Seeckt, established "Special Branch R" in the War Ministry to administer the relationship, which encompassed war production, military training, and the development of new weaponry. German officers were permitted to study weapons forbidden to them by the victorious Allies—tanks and airplanes, in particular—on Russian soil.[1] German industrial enterprises established factories in Russia to manufacture poison gas, explosive shells, and military aircraft. The German army established training academies for its tank commanders and fighter pilots on Soviet territory. At the same time, Soviet Russia sent officers to Germany to be schooled in the methods that had been developed by the feared and admired German General Staff. These clandestine arrangements were sanctioned by the German government in secret provisions of the Treaty of Rapallo* in 1922. It was symbolic of the new state of affairs that General Hans von Seeckt, who served in Constantinople as chief of staff of the Ottoman army at the end of the war, and who had served as head of the German army since 1919, was reporting to the Russian General Staff on the military situation in the Dardanelles in 1922. It was a measure of how far Russia had traveled since her 1914 war against Germany and Turkey; all three nations were now ranged together against Britain.

II

Italy was the next to change sides. As soon as the armistice was signed, she began to show sympathy for the plight of the Ottoman Empire, influenced perhaps by the tradition of comradeship between nationalist movements that stemmed from the teachings of the nineteenth-century Italian patriot Giuseppe Mazzini, as well as a desire to preserve and expand the prewar Italian economic presence in Turkey. Count Carlo Sforza, who was appointed Italian High Commissioner in Constantinople at the end of 1918, was a practical statesman of wide and humane principles who immediately took the initiative in establishing a working relationship with Mustapha Kemal and in encouraging the Turks to resist the more extreme demands of

---

* An agreement between Russia and Germany on 16 April 1922, that provided for the building up of political and consular contacts between the two countries.

the Allies. The Italians made no secret of this opposition within Allied councils to the peace terms proposed by Britain and France. In 1920, when the Sultan, forced by Britain and France, was on the verge of signing the Treaty of Sèvres, a high-ranking official of the British War Office reported that Italy was moving to support Kemal, who rejected the treaty. A month before the Treaty of Sèvres was signed, Lord Curzon reproached Count Sforza with the "unloyal attitude" of Italy in the Middle East.[2]

From the time of the armistice onward, the divergence between Italy's goals in the Middle East and those of her Allies widened. As a practical matter there was little incentive for her to support their program, especially after they sent the Greek army into the Smyrna enclave to pre-empt the Italian claim. To successive Italian governments, Allied policy seemed designed chiefly to profit Greece—a purpose that Rome had no interest in serving. Especially after Count Sforza became Foreign Minister in 1920, Italy treated Greece as a rival whose gains had to be matched rather than an ally whose claims had to be supported. In asserting her own claims, Italy received no help from the Allies. A clash with Kemalist forces at Konya in central Anatolia left the Italian authorities with the feeling that in their sector of occupied Turkey they would be left to face a Kemalist advance by themselves—and that they might be beaten. Deteriorating economic, financial, and social conditions at home finally led Italy to abandon her claims to Turkish territory and evacuate her forces from Anatolia: her hope was that Kemal's Angora regime would reward her for doing so by agreeing to economic concessions. Sforza entered into a secret accord with the Kemalists whereby Italy would supply them with substantial shipments of military equipment if such concessions were forthcoming.

As Foreign Minister, Count Sforza continued to press the British and French governments for revision of the Treaty of Sèvres and warned Lord Curzon that unless the Allies succeeded in coming to an understanding with Kemal, the Angora regime would be driven into alliance with Moscow—a possibility, he said, fraught with peril.[3] For a number of reasons, then, the Italian government continued to dissent from the policy embodied in the Treaty of Sèvres, yet made no overt move to oppose it, not daring to risk an open confrontation with Britain.

Within Italy there were demands for a more forceful approach to the realization of the country's ambitions. The rapt enthusiasm that had greeted Gabriele D'Annunzio's seizure of the Dalmatian port of Fiume in 1919—the famous author and nationalist had led his supporters to take over the town—showed the wellsprings of sentiment that were there to be tapped. Benito Mussolini used his newspaper, the *Popolo d'Italia*, to exploit the bitterness of those who felt cheated out of the rewards of victory. An agitator who, in turn, had advocated the extreme positions of almost all sections of the left and the right—in his own words, "an adventurer for all roads"—he charged that Italy was being cheated out of the "booty" in the Middle East.[4] Proclaiming a "great imperial destiny" for his country, he asserted that it had a right to become the dominant power in the Mediterranean.[5] The Great Power that stood in the way, according to him, was Britain; Mussolini proposed to help insurgent forces in Egypt, India, and Ireland.

When Mussolini, supported by his political followers, known as *fascisti*, became Prime Minister of Italy in 1922, Italy's local disagreements with Britain about territorial claims in Turkey and the eastern Mediterranean evolved into a more general and permanent estrangement. Mussolini's political program called for Britain to be chased out of the Mediterranean altogether.[6] Under his leadership, Italy, like Russia, moved from ally to enemy of the British Empire.

III

The United States withdrew from the Allied coalition in 1919–20, when the Senate rejected the Treaty of Versailles and membership in the League of Nations and refused to accept a Mandate to govern Armenia. In reply to a note from the French ambassador, the Secretary of State, on behalf of President Wilson, set forth the new American position in a note of 24 March 1920: the United States would not send a representative to the Peace Conference and would not participate in or sign the peace treaty with the Ottoman Empire, but it expected the peace treaty to take account of American views. In addition to President Wilson's views on specific Middle Eastern matters mentioned in the note, the United States insisted on an Open Door policy,* on nondiscrimination against nonsignatories of the treaty, and on the maintenance of existing American rights in the area.

In 1919 the Department of State commenced a program of legally asserting American rights in the occupied Ottoman territories, including not only those deriving from the Capitulation agreements governing the rights and privileges of Americans in Turkey, but also freedom of navigation of the Dardanelles, protection of American missionary colleges and endeavors, and adequate opportunity to carry out archaeological activities and commercial activities. The most conspicuous interests asserted by the United States were those of

---

* Which is to say that markets in the region were to be fully open to American businessmen.

American oil companies. It was these that brought the United States and Britain into collision.

The oil issue was raised for the first time on behalf of the Standard Oil Company of New York ("Socony"), which had been engaged in oil exploration in the Middle East before the war and held (from the Ottoman regime) concessions—that is to say, exclusive licenses to explore for oil in designated areas—in Palestine and Syria. It held no concessions in Iraq, however, and wanted to establish concessions there because it was the principal supplier of petroleum products in the area; the company's marketing strategy called for it to obtain supplies for its marketing organization at or near the point of sales.

In September 1919 Socony sent two geologists to prospect for oil in Iraq. One of them incautiously sent a letter to his wife telling her "I am going to the biggest remaining oil possibilities in the world" and "the pie is so very big" that whatever had to be done should be done to "gain us the rights which properly belong to American Citizens."[7] The letter was intercepted in Allied-occupied Constantinople by British censors, who forwarded a copy of it to the British government in London. London immediately sent orders to Sir Arnold Wilson, High Commissioner in Iraq, to forbid the geologists to prospect. At Socony's request the Department of State protested, but Lord Curzon, the Foreign Secretary, put the Americans off with a plausible but not entirely true tale: wartime restrictions applicable to all nationalities forbade such activities until peace was concluded.

The Standard Oil Company of New Jersey was the next to enter the picture. In 1910 its head geologist had concluded that there was oil potential in Iraq; but until after the war, New Jersey Standard did nothing about it. In February 1919 the company's president suggested to the board of directors that an effort be made to look for oil in Iraq; and a month later the company's head of foreign production was sent to Paris to take up the question with the American delegation to the Peace Conference.

Later the chairman of the board of New Jersey Standard, A. C. Bedford, went to Europe to deal with the matter personally. The various wartime arrangements negotiated between Britain and France to share the postwar oil wealth of the Middle East remained secret— the American government had been put off with false assurances that nothing had been decided upon that excluded the United States' interests—and these were matters that he looked into. On 27 April 1920, at the Conference of San Remo, Britain and France finally concluded a secret oil bargain, agreeing in effect to monopolize the whole future output of Middle Eastern oil between them. Bedford obtained a copy of the agreement from a member of the French delegation, and turned it over to the American embassy.

In view of the magnitude of the proposed Anglo-French monopoly, the American government looked upon the San Remo agreement as harmful, not merely to one or more American companies, but to the United States' interests as a nation. The war had focused attention for the first time on the vital military and naval importance of petroleum, and in the aftermath of the war the United States had undergone an oil-scarcity scare. The price of crude oil rose, and fears were expressed widely that domestic oil reserves were being depleted. The economic adviser to the Department of State wrote that "It is economically essential ... to obtain assured foreign supplies of petroleum" in order to assure supplies of bunker oil to the merchant marine and the navy, and in order to perpetuate the United States' position as the world's leading oil and oil products supplier.[8]

In the summer of 1920, the San Remo agreement was made public and the United States—able finally to acknowledge that it knew of the agreement—protested. Foreign Secretary Curzon replied that Britain controlled only 4.5 percent of world oil production while the United States controlled 80 percent—and that the United States excluded non-American interests from areas under its control.[9] Secretary of State Bainbridge Colby countered that the United States possessed only one-twelfth of the world's known oil reserves, that demand for petroleum exceeded supply, and that only unhampered development of existing resources could meet the growing need for oil.[10]

Conscious of having estranged the United States, British officials suspected that American oil interests were behind the anti-British insurrection in Iraq and the Kemalist movement in Turkey. Allegedly an insurrectionary leader arrested by British security officers in Iraq was found to have in his possession a letter from one of the Standard Oil companies showing that American funds were being dispensed by the American consul in Baghdad to the Shi'ite rebels centered in the holy city of Karbala.[11]

The American consul in Baghdad was indeed opposed to British rule in Iraq, but Washington was not. Quite the reverse was true: both the Department of State and the oil companies were in favor of British hegemony in the area. The oil companies were prepared to engage in exploration, development, and production only in areas governed by what they regarded as stable and responsible regimes. The president of New Jersey Standard reported to the State Department that Iraq was a collection of warring tribes; according to him an Iraqi government dominated by Britain offered the only hope of law and order.[12] Allen Dulles, chief of the Near Eastern Affairs Division of the Department of State, was one of the many officials who expressed dismay at the thought that Britain and France might relinquish control of their Middle Eastern conquests, and who expressed fear for the fate of American interests should they do so.[13]

Dulles reported that Guy Wellman, attorney for the American oil companies that were seeking a share in Iraqi development, was of the opinion that his clients would be much better off negotiating a partnership with British interests rather than attempting to operate on their own.[14]

A solution to the conflict between Britain and America began to emerge in the summer of 1920 when geologists advised the British government that oil prospects in Iraq were more speculative than had been supposed.[15] At the same time the Foreign Office was advised that the prospects—if they did materialize—were so vast that Britain lacked the capital resources to develop them by herself and would have to invite American participation.[16] For these, and for political reasons, Sir John Cadman, an important figure in the British oil industry, was delegated to go to the United States to initiate discussions. On 22 June 1922 A. C. Bedford of the Standard Oil Company of New Jersey called on the Department of State to report that on behalf of seven American oil companies he proposed to negotiate a participation in the British-owned concessionary corporation in Iraq. The Department of State responded that it had no objection to his doing so, provided no qualified American oil companies that wished to participate were excluded. Negotiations thereupon went forward.[*]

Thus the dispute with the United States was resolved. But the burden of imposing European control over the Middle East was left by America to Britain, unaided.

IV

France, Britain's closest major ally, was the last to desert the alliance. The long quarrel about whether the Sykes-Picot Agreement would be honored had taken its toll, as had Britain's sponsorship of the Hashemite family's political claims. With the retirement of Clemenceau, Aristide Briand, a veteran left-wing politician who had served several times as Premier, was regarded as the leader of those who were loyal to the British alliance; yet, when he became Premier again in January 1921, the rupture between the two countries finally occurred.

It occurred because Briand saw no way to maintain his country's position in Cilicia, the southern province of Turkey which then was still occupied by France. France's 80,000 occupation troops were a

---

[*] The final accord, the so-called Red Line agreement, was not reached until 31 July 1928.

drain on resources that could no longer be afforded; the French Parliament was unwilling to continue paying for them. Cilicia proved to be an awkward location for a French army to occupy, caught as it was between Kemalist Turks and troublesome Syria. In the spring of 1921, Premier Briand therefore sent the Turkophile Senator Henri Franklin-Bouillon on a mission to Angora to negotiate a way out. Franklin-Bouillon, a former president of the Foreign Affairs Commission of the Chamber of Deputies, was a leader of the colonialist group and strongly believed in the importance of Turkey as a Moslem ally.

On his second mission to Angora, in the autumn of 1921, Franklin-Bouillon succeeded in arriving at an agreement. It brought the war between France and Turkey to an end, and effectively recognized the Nationalist Angora regime as the legitimate government of Turkey. For the Nationalists, the Angora Accord was the greatest of diplomatic triumphs. According to Mustapha Kemal, it "proved to the whole world" that the Treaty of Sèvres was now "merely a rag."[17] The British saw it as a betrayal: it was a separate peace, and it freed the Turks to attack Britain's clients—Greece and Iraq. As the British suspected, the French also turned over to the Angora regime quantities of military supplies.[18] Thus Turks supplied by France were at war with Greeks backed by Britain and the former Entente Powers found themselves ranged on opposite sides of the Ottoman war that they had entered together as allies in 1914.

On 26 October 1921, in a memorandum to the Cabinet alerting them to news of the aid France would provide the Kemalists, Churchill commented that "It seems scarcely possible to credit this information, which, if true, would unquestionably convict the French government of what in the most diplomatic application of the phrase could only be deemed an 'unfriendly act'."[19] It should be understood that, according to a standard reference book, in the diplomatic lexicon "When a State wishes to warn other States that certain actions on their part might lead to war, it is usual to state that such action 'would be regarded as an unfriendly act'."[20] Thus Churchill was making a very strong statement indeed; his words implied that the Angora Accord might lead to a war between France and Britain.

Churchill had feared for some time that Nationalist Turkey would turn east to attack Feisal's fragile regime in Iraq, and believed that France—by allowing Turkey to use the Baghdad Railway section in Cilicia—was now about to facilitate such a move. According to Churchill's memorandum, "clearly the French are negotiating, through M Franklin-Bouillon, a treaty designed not merely to safeguard French interests in Turkey, but to secure those interests wherever necessary at the expense of Great Britain. They apparently believe that we have a similar anti-French arrangement with the Greeks. They are, of course, very angry about King Feisal" having been placed by Britain on the throne of Iraq.[21] According to Churchill, France would have liked nothing better than to have seen the collapse of Feisal and of British policy in the area, which also would have meant the destruction of his own handiwork.

Premier Briand failed to appreciate how strongly the Angora Accord would affect British policy in Europe. In 1921 Briand turned to Britain to guarantee France against a revival of the German challenge, having become aware that the American government was fundamentally out of sympathy with the whole trend of postwar French policy regarding Germany.[*] Fearful that France might be isolated, he approached Lloyd George and Curzon with a proposal for a bilateral alliance between Britain and France to provide the latter with security against Germany. The British leaders refused to consider forming such an alliance unless France resolved the quarrel in the Middle East stemming from the Angora Accord. Following the British refusal, the Briand government fell.

Former President Raymond Poincaré took office as the new Premier. He represented the opposite pole from Briand; he was not a great friend of Britain. His diplomacy proposed doing without Britain and instead going it alone as a Great Power by creating a network of alliances with less powerful countries in central and eastern Europe that included Poland, Rumania, Yugoslavia, and Czechoslavakia. It estranged Britain further, by suggesting to Britain's leaders that France aimed at establishing hegemony on the continent of Europe, as she had done under Louis XIV and Napoleon. The prospect of an alliance between Britain and France died in June 1922, when Britain suspended the negotiations; and the breach between the two countries widened thereafter.

V

To some extent the diplomatic isolation of Britain was the result of Mustapha Kemal's adroit diplomacy. The Angora regime had deliberately played off one ally against another.

Fundamentally, however, it was Britain's decision to impose

---

[*] In the immediate aftermath of the armistice, Marshal Foch had counted on moving the French boundary with Germany to the Rhine, so that natural frontiers would provide France with security. In the face of Woodrow Wilson and his Fourteen Points, France had been obliged to surrender this claim in return for a treaty of guarantee by her principal Allies. The treaty never took effect; it was rejected by the U.S. Senate on 19 November 1919. Moreover, the likelihood that France in fact could look to the United States for future support began to dim.

European rule on the former Ottoman Empire that led to the break-up of the alliance or—to the extent that there were other contributing factors—at any rate caused the break-up to lead in such dangerous directions. It is here that the contrast between Britain's Middle Eastern policy before and after 1914 can be glimpsed most vividly.

It was not merely that in the nineteenth century Britain had often kept conflict from flaring up between the European powers by securing mutual agreement that none of them would encroach on the Middle East. It was also the process by which she did so that contributed to the maintenance of international stability. The frequent reference of issues to the concert of the powers of Europe, and the habit of multilateral consultation and cooperation that it bred, helped to make world politics more civilized. In that sense the Middle Eastern question, despite its inherent divisiveness, contributed to international harmony.

But once the Asquith government agreed to Russian territorial demands in 1915, the Middle East became a source of discord. If the Czar were to control the Turkish-speaking northern part of the Ottoman Empire, then Britain—according to Lord Kitchener—would have to assume hegemony in the Arabic-speaking south. In turn, that brought into play French claims to Syria and Palestine. Thus one claim led to another, each power believing the others to be over-reaching. Even if Britain, after the war, had immediately partitioned the Ottoman Empire among the Allies, along the hard-bargained lines of the pledges she had made to them, there would have been some risk of future conflict among them if any of them pursued future expansionist designs. But conflict was made inevitable when, instead, Lloyd George attempted not merely to renege on the pledges but to take everything for the British Empire. It was worse still that he tried to do so without having the resources to back up his move.

Alliances tend to break up at the end of a war. Moreover, the partners with whom Britain had worked toward international harmony before the war were losing control of world politics. Yet it was the Middle Eastern question at the end of the war that led to the first clashes between Britain and her former allies, Russia, Italy, France, and the United States. It was bitterness engendered by Middle Eastern policy that hampered British efforts to find common ground with her former allies on policy elsewhere in the world, and that eventually led to the alliances falling apart.

60

A GREEK TRAGEDY

I

Lloyd George had been too proud in 1919 and 1920 to remember that his power derived from alliances and coalitions over which he presided, but which he did not control. Events now provided him with a reminder, and in 1921, as his foreign alliances fell apart, the Prime Minister found himself increasingly isolated within his own government in his war policy against Turkey. Bonar Law, after the change in monarch and government in Greece, in which the pro-Allied Venizelos was overthrown, was in favor of coming to terms with the Turks. Bonar Law could not be ignored; he led the party with a majority of seats in Parliament, and had he remained in the government he might have succeeded in forcing a change in policy. His supporters were pro-Turk and, so long as he served in the government, he reminded Lloyd George of their views. But Bonar Law retired from public life in the winter of 1921 due to ill health, depriving the Prime Minister of a political partner who could keep him in line. With Bonar Law's departure, the Prime Minister drifted increasingly out of touch with sentiment in the House of Commons. Aware that Cabinet colleagues, the Foreign Office, and the War Office were also opposed to his Greek-Turkish policy, he disregarded their views.

As the London Conference adjourned in March 1921—the conference at which the Allies, the Greeks, and the Kemalists failed to arrive at any agreement—Lloyd George sent Maurice Hankey round to Claridge's Hotel to tell the Greek leaders, who were staying there, that if they felt impelled to attack Kemal's forces, he would not stand in their way.[1] The Greek government took this as permission to resume the war, and launched a new offensive on 23 March 1921. Despite faulty staff work and stiff opposition, the Greek army moved up from the plain to the plateau.

Arnold Toynbee, the historian and scholar of international relations, accompanied the Greek army as a reporter for the *Manchester Guardian*. He reported that as his vehicle moved up from the plain "I began to realise on how narrow a margin the Greeks had gambled for a military decision in Anatolia, and how adverse were the circumstances under which they were playing for victory over Kemal."[2] At the end of the week, the Greeks were repulsed by Kemal's General Ismet at the village of Inonu and retreated.

The Greek government blamed its military commanders and on 7 April Gounaris—now Prime Minister—and his colleagues met with Ioannis Metaxas, Greece's outstanding military figure, to ask Metaxas to lead the next offensive in Anatolia. Metaxas refused and told the politicians that the war in Turkey could not be won. The Turks had developed a national feeling, he said, "And they mean to fight for their freedom and independence ... They realize that Asia Minor is their country and that we are invaders. For them, for their national feelings, the historical rights on which we base our claims have no influence. Whether they are right or wrong is another question. What matters is how they feel."[3]

The politicians told Metaxas that it would now be politically impossible for their regime to abandon the war: with eyes open to the risk they would run, they felt compelled to gamble everything on the success of one last offensive, scheduled for the summer.

On 22 June the Allies sent a message to the Greek government offering mediation in the war, but Greece replied with a polite refusal. Preparations for an offensive were so far along, wrote the Greeks, that it would be impractical to call them off.

King Constantine and Gounaris had left themselves with no option but to launch their crusade, and Lloyd George's fortunes rode with them. The British leader could do no more than watch and wait as foreign armies clashed in the obscure interior of Asia Minor. His secretary and mistress noted that he

> has had a great fight in the Cabinet to back the Greeks (not in the field but morally) and he and Balfour are the only pro-Greeks there ... [He] has got his way, but he is much afraid lest the Greek attack should be a failure, and he should have proved to have been wrong. He says his political reputation depends a great deal on what happens in Asia Minor ... [I]f the Greeks succeed the Treaty of Versailles is vindicated, and the Turkish rule is at an end. A new Greek Empire will be founded, friendly to Britain, and it will help all our interests in the East. He is perfectly convinced that he is right over this, and is willing to stake everything on it.[4]

On 10 July 1921 the Greek army launched a brilliantly successful three-pronged offensive. The Greek commanders had learned from the mistakes committed in January and in March, and did not repeat them. The offensive was crowned with the capture of Eskishehir, a rail center considered to be the strategic key to western Anatolia.

Lloyd George, jubilant, unleashed his powers of rhetoric and wit against his opponents. To his War Minister he wrote:

> I hear from Greek quarters that Eski Shehir has been captured and that the Turkish Army is in full retreat. Which ever way you look at the matter this is news of the first importance. The future of the East will very largely be determined by this struggle, and yet as far as I can see, the War Office have not taken the slightest trouble to find out what has happened . . . The Staff have displayed the most amazing slovenliness in this matter. Their information about the respective strength and quality of the two Armies turned out to be hopelessly wrong when the facts were investigated, at the instance of the despised politicians.

The Prime Minister saved his best salvo for last: "Have you no Department which is known as the Intelligence Department in your Office? You might find out what it is doing. It appears in the Estimates at quite a substantial figure, but when it comes to information it is not visible."[5]

Near Eskishehir the overwhelmed Turkish commander, General Ismet, could not bring himself to retreat. Kemal took the burden from his shoulders. "Pasha is coming," Ismet, relieved, told a companion, as a grey-faced Mustapha Kemal arrived to take personal responsibility for ordering the retreat.[6] Kemal acknowledged that his people would feel a "moral shock" when they learned that he was going to abandon western Anatolia to the enemy.[7] In the event, there was an uproar in the National Assembly, as political enemies, personal rivals, Enver's followers, and defeatists joined hands against him. After a time, Kemal called the National Assembly into secret session, and proposed a Roman course of action: the delegates should elect him dictator for a period of three months, and that should he then fail as supreme commander, the blame would fall entirely on him. The proposal brought together those who believed in victory and those who were certain of defeat, and was adopted.

Kemal pulled his forces back to within fifty miles of his capital at Angora, and deployed them behind a great bend in the Sakarya river. In the time available to him he requisitioned resources from the entire population, commandeering 40 percent of household food, cloth, and leather supplies, confiscating horses, and preparing for total war. He ordered his troops to entrench in the ridges and hills that rose steeply up from the near bank of the river toward Angora. By mid-August his army had dug into this powerful natural defensive position, circling Angora for sixty miles behind the loop in the Sakarya, dominating from high ground the passage of the river.

On 14 August 1921 the Greek army started its triumphal march on Angora. At staff headquarters, the chief of the supply bureau had warned that the Greek army's long line of communications and transportation would break down if it advanced beyond the Sakarya river; but his colleagues concluded that there was no cause for concern in as much as they did not intend to advance much further than that.[8] The Greek commanders believed that they had beaten the enemy and were now about to finish him off. They invited the British liaison officers who accompanied them to attend a victory celebration in Angora after the battle.

The advancing Greek army made first contact with the enemy on 23 August and attacked all along the line on 26 August. Crossing the river, the Greek infantry fought its way foot-by-foot up toward the heights, driving the enemy from one ridge-top line of entrenchments to another above it. The savage combat went on for days and then for weeks, with the Greeks gaining ground on the average of a mile a day. Eventually they gained control of the key heights, but victory eluded them; they were cut off from their supplies of food and ammunition by Turkish cavalry raids, and succumbed to exhaustion. Unable to continue fighting, the Greeks descended from the heights and crossed back over the Sakarya river on 14 September and re-treated back to Eskishehir, where they had started their march a month before. The campaign was over.

In Angora the grateful National Assembly promoted Mustapha Kemal to the rank of field marshal and endowed him with the title of "Ghazi"—the Turkish Moslem equivalent of "warrior for the Faith" or "Crusader."

II

Between the summer of 1921 and the summer of 1922, a lull prevailed on the battlefield, during which Prime Minister Gounaris and his Foreign Minister journeyed west to seek aid from the Allies. On the continent of Europe they met with little sympathy. In London they sat in the ambassadors' waiting room at the Foreign Office, hat in hand, waiting for Lord Curzon somehow to solve their problems. Lloyd George told them "Personally I am a friend of Greece, but . . . all my colleagues are against me. And I cannot be of any use to you. It is impossible, impossible."[9]

The British Prime Minister no longer had anything to offer the Greeks, but exhorted them to fight on nonetheless. His policy (such as it was) was for Greece to stay the course in the hope that things would change for the better. In the spring of 1922 he told Venizelos (who was in London as a private citizen and had come to see him in the House of Commons) that, when King Constantine eventually disappeared from the scene, public opinion in the Allied countries would swing back toward support of Greece. "Meanwhile Greece must stick to her policy," said Lloyd George, adding that, "this was the testing time of the Greek nation, and that if they persevered now their future was assured ... Greece must go through the wilderness, she must live on manna picked up from the stones, she must struggle through the stern trial of the present time." He said that he "would never shake hands with a Greek again who went back upon his country's aims in Smyrna."[10]

Lloyd George found himself increasingly isolated, even within his own government, and the Foreign Secretary, Lord Curzon, took effective control of British efforts to resolve the crisis; in collaboration with the Allies, he moved toward an accommodation with Nationalist Turkey.

Fearing that the Allies were about to betray him that summer, King Constantine withdrew three regiments and two battalions from the Greek army in Anatolia and sent them to Thrace, the European province of Turkey opposite Constantinople. His government then announced that Greece would occupy Constantinople in order to bring the war to an end. His desperate calculation was that this threat would impel the Allies to take some action to resolve the Greek-Turkish conflict, presumably in a manner favorable to Greece. He gambled that, at the very least, the Allies would consent to let his forces in Thrace pass through Constantinople to link up with and rejoin his weakened armies defending the Anatolian coast. But, instead, the Allied army of occupation in Constantinople barred the road to the Greeks.

Constantine's withdrawal of the Greek units from the Anatolian coast meanwhile prompted Kemal to hasten an attack on the weakened and overextended Greek defensive line there. Massing his forces in great secrecy, he launched an attack on the southern front at dawn on 26 August. After two days of fierce fighting the Greeks retreated in disorder. The commander-in-chief of the Greek army in Asia Minor "was almost universally said to be mad" (according to a British report from Athens) and later was termed a "mental case" by Lloyd George; whether or not these were exaggerations, he was incapable of coping with the situation.[11] On 4 September the Greek government appointed a new commander-in-chief in his place, but so complete had been the breakdown in communications that it did not know that the general it now placed in supreme command was already a prisoner in Turkish hands; he is said to have heard the news of his appointment from Kemal.[12]

Lord Riddell was with Lloyd George on Sunday, 3 September,

when the Prime Minister received a communication from friends of Greece

> begging L. G. to do something for the Greeks. He explained ...
> at length the impossibility [of doing anything] and strongly
> criticised the action of King Constantine, who, he said, was
> responsible for what had happened. Among other things he had
> appointed a most inefficient and unsuitable general. L.G.
> further said that as far as he could make out, he, Balfour, and
> Curzon were the only three people in the country who were in
> favour of the Greeks. He deplored the situation, but could do
> nothing.[13]

Greece assembled a fleet to evacuate her army from Asia Minor, and along the coast throngs of soldiers headed toward the ships in hopes of finding passage. The mass attempt at escape was a race against time: against the coming September rains and against the advancing, vengeful Turkish army.

The ancient Greek community of Asia Minor was seized with dread. The Archbishop of Smyrna wrote to Venizelos on 7 September that

> Hellenism in Asia Minor, the Greek state and the entire Greek
> Nation are descending now to a Hell from which no power will
> be able to raise them up and save them ... I have judged it
> necessary ... out of the flames of catastrophe in which the
> Greek people of Asia Minor are suffering—and it is a real ques-
> tion whether when Your Excellency reads this letter of mine we
> shall still be alive, destined as we are ... for sacrifice and
> martyrdom ... to direct this last appeal to you.[14]

Appeals, however, were in vain. Venizelos was powerless to give aid, and two days later the archbishop was sent to the martyred death that he foresaw: the local Turkish commander turned him over to a mob of several hundred knife-wielding Moslems who took him to a barber's shop and mutilated him before killing him.*

All-consuming religious and national tensions met their rendezvous with history in Smyrna, the greatest city of Asia Minor, at summer's end in 1922. Hatred ignited into flame in the Armenian quarter of

---

* Since the beginning of the war the atrocities between the Moslem and Christian communities had escalated. When the Greek army first landed in Smyrna in 1919, soldiers butchered unarmed Turks. Arnold Toynbee reported that in visiting Greek villages that had been destroyed by the Turks, he noticed that the houses had been burned to the ground one by one, deliberately; it appeared that the Turks had savored the doing of it.[15] King Constantine claimed that Greek corpses had been skinned by the other side.[16] Toynbee charged that in the 1921 campaign the Greek army deliberately drove whole villages of Turkish civilians from their homes.[17]

the city on Wednesday, 13 September. Later the fires spread—or were spread—to the Greek and European quarters. Between 50 and 75 percent of the ancient metropolis was destroyed; the Turkish quarter, however, remained untouched. Hundreds of thousands of people had lived in the Christian city, and it proved impossible to calculate how many of them died in its final agony. A correspondent of the Chicago *Daily News* was the first to pound out the story on his portable typewriter amidst the ruins: "Except for the squalid Turkish quarter, Smyrna has ceased to exist. The problem of the minorities is here solved for all time. No doubt remains as to the origin of the fire . . . The torch was applied by Turkish regular soldiers."[18] Pro-Turkish scholars to this day continue to deny this widely believed accusation.[19]

American, French, British, and Italian naval vessels evacuated their respective nationals from the burning quay. At first the Americans and the British refused to aid anyone else, while the Italians accepted on board anyone who could reach their ships and the French accepted anyone who said he was French—so long as he could say it in French. Eventually, though, the British and Americans came to the aid of refugees without regard to nationality. In the next few weeks Greece and the Allies, in response to a threat by Kemal to treat all Greek and Armenian men of military age as prisoners-of-war, organized the evacuation of masses of civilians as Greece completed her military evacuation as well.

By the end of 1922 about 1,500,000 Greeks had fled or been driven out of Turkey. Ernest Hemingway,* then a war correspondent for the Toronto *Star*, wrote that he had watched a procession of destitute Greek refugees that was some twenty miles long and that he could not get it out of his mind. His Croatian landlady, who was more familiar with such sights, quoted a Turkish proverb to him: "It is not only the fault of the axe but of the tree as well."[20] It was an easy saying, and in the weeks to come it was followed by a number of others, equally easy, as Allied statesmen searched their consciences and discovered, each in his own way, that blame for the catastrophe should be placed on somebody else.

In Britain, it was common to blame France, Italy, and Bolshevik Russia, but, above all, the United States. As the British ambassador in Washington explained to the American Secretary of State in October, the Allies had agreed to partition the Middle East in the novel and time-consuming form of receiving Mandates from the League of Nations—and had done so solely in order to please the

---

*The atrocities at Smyrna provided him with the background for "On the Quai at Smyrna," one of the memorable stories in his first collection, *The Fifth Column and the First Forty-Nine Stories*.

United States, which then had withdrawn from the Middle East peace process entirely. The United States had also agreed to accept Mandates to occupy and safeguard Constantinople, the Dardanelles, and Armenia, and then had gone back on her word two years later. By implication, the ambassador indicated that the Allies could have imposed their own kind of settlement in 1919 and would then have had done with it; but to accommodate and secure the cooperation of the United States, Britain had waited for years, and had assumed novel responsibilities, and now was left entirely on her own to carry the heavy burden of having to defend the American idea of Mandates.[21]

Secretary of State Charles Evans Hughes replied that

> he would say that he could not for a moment assent to the view that this Government was in any way responsible for the existing conditions ... The United States had not sought to parcel out spheres of influence ... had not engaged in intrigues at Constantinople ... was not responsible for the catastrophe of the Greek armies during the last year and a half ... diplomacy in Europe for the last year and a half was responsible for the late disaster.[22]

Behind the mutual recrimination was the fundamental shift in American foreign policy that occurred when President Woodrow Wilson was replaced by Warren Gamaliel Harding. A principal object of President Wilson's Middle Eastern policy had been to support Christianity and, in particular, American missionary colleges and missionary activities; but President Harding did not share these interests. When the Turks advanced on Smyrna, such American church groups as the conference of the Methodist Episcopal Church called for the American government to send troops to stop the massacre of Christians; but President Harding told Secretary of State Hughes, "Frankly, it is difficult for me to be consistently patient with our good friends of the Church who are properly and earnestly zealous in promoting peace until it comes to making warfare on someone of the contending religion ..."[23]

The other principal object of Woodrow Wilson's Middle Eastern policy had been to ensure that the peoples of the region were ruled by governments of their choice. President Harding did not share these concerns either. He limited his administration's efforts to the protection of American interests. In the Middle East, that mostly meant the protection of American commercial interests which were primarily oil interests. In Turkey the Kemalist government was prepared to grant oil concessions to an American group, and seemed likely to be able to provide the internal security and stable business environment that oil companies require. Turkish willingness to open the door to American companies was welcomed by the Department of State and may well have colored its perception of the Kemalist regime.

The plight of Greek, Armenian, and other Christians in the wake of Smyrna's destruction was addressed by the Secretary of State in a speech he delivered in Boston in October. "While nothing can excuse in the slightest degree or palliate the barbaric cruelty of the Turks," he said, "no just appraisement can be made of the situation which fails to take account of the incursion of the Greek army into Anatolia, of the war there waged, and of the terrible incidents of the retreat of that army, in the burning of towns, and general devastation and cruelties." Having noted that atrocities had been committed by both sides, the Secretary of State rejected the contention that the United States should have intervened. He pointed out that the entire situation was the result of a war to which the United States had not been a party; if the Allies, who were closely connected to the situation, did not choose to intervene, it certainly was no responsibility of America's to do so. He told his audience that the United States quite properly had limited its efforts to the protection of American interests in Turkey.[24]

III

Constantinople and European Turkey—eastern Thrace—were the next and final objectives on Kemal's line of march. The supposedly neutral Allied army of occupation stood between him and his objectives. As the Nationalist Turkish armies advanced to their positions, the Allies panicked. Hitherto the war had been far away from them; but if Kemal attacked, they themselves would have to fight.

In Britain the news was startling for the same reason. As late as 4 September, *The Times* had reported that "The Greek Army unquestionably sustained a reverse, but its extent is unduly exaggerated." But on 5 September, a headline read "GREEK ARMY'S DEFEAT"; on 6 September, a headline read "A GRAVE SITUATION"; and from mid-September on, the headlines "NEAR EAST PERIL" and "NEAR EAST CRISIS" appeared with terribly insistent regularity. Photos of burning Smyrna took the place of society weddings, theater openings, and golf championships. Britons, four years after the armistice, were shocked to be suddenly told that they might have to fight a war to defend far-off Constantinople. It was the last thing in the world that most Britons wanted to do, and an immediate inclination was to get rid of the government that had got them into such a situation.

But Constantinople and the Dardanelles, because of their world importance for shipping, and eastern Thrace, because it is in Europe, were positions that occupied a special status in the minds of British leaders. Winston Churchill, hitherto pro-Turkish, again came to the rescue of Lloyd George's policy and told the Cabinet in September that "The line of deep water separating Asia from Europe was a line of great significance, and we must make that line secure by every means within our power. If the Turks take the Gallipoli Peninsula and Constantinople, we shall have lost the whole fruits of our victory . . ."[25] Lloyd George voiced his strong agreement, saying that "In no circumstances could we allow the Gallipoli Peninsula to be held by the Turks. It was the most important strategic position in the world, and the closing of the Straits had prolonged the war by two years. It was inconceivable that we should allow the Turks to gain possession of the Gallipoli Peninsula and we should fight to prevent their doing so."[26]

By mid-September the last Greek troops standing between the Turks and the Allies had disappeared and a direct armed clash seemed imminent. The Cabinet met in a series of emergency sessions commencing 15 September, when Churchill told his colleagues that "The misfortunes of the Allies were probably due to the fact that owing to the delay on the part of America in declaring their position, their armies had apparently melted away." Armies were needed, in his view, for he "was wholly opposed to any attempt to carry out a bluff without force."[27] He stressed the necessity of securing support from the Dominions* and from France in reinforcing the British troops facing Kemal's armies.

On 15 September 1922 the Cabinet instructed Winston Churchill to draft—for Lloyd George's signature—a telegram to the Dominions informing them of the British decision to defend the Neutral Zone in Turkey and asking for their military aid. Shortly before midnight the telegram, in cipher, was sent to each of the Dominion prime ministers.

The Cabinet decided that the public also ought to be informed of the seriousness of the situation; and to this end Churchill and Lloyd George prepared a press release on 16 September that appeared that

---

* The need for securing support from the Dominions arose from the change in their position that had come about after—and as a result of—the First World War. At the Peace Conference in Paris in 1919, Jan Christian Smuts of South Africa, Prime Minister Robert Borden of Canada, and Prime Minister William Hughes of Australia successfully asserted the claim of their Dominions to be seated as sovereign nations on a plane of equality with Britain and the other Allies. When, at that time, Britain offered France a treaty of guarantee, Smuts and South African Prime Minister Louis Botha had wrung from Lloyd George a concession that such a treaty would not be binding upon them. They wrote that, from then on, it would be theoretically possible for Britain to go to war while one or more Dominions remained neutral.[28] In 1922 the theoretical possibility was put to the test.

evening in the newspapers. No members of the Cabinet other than Lloyd George and Churchill had seen it prior to publication. The communiqué expressed the desire of the British government to convene a peace conference with Turkey, but stated that no such conference could convene under the gun of Turkish threats. It expressed fear of what the Moslem world might do if comparatively weak Moslem Turkey could be seen to have inflicted a major defeat on the Allies; presumably the rest of the Moslem world would be encouraged to throw off colonial rule. The communiqué made reference to British consultations with France, Italy, and the Dominions with a view toward taking common military action to avert the Kemalist threat.[29]

The belligerent tone of the communiqué alarmed public opinion in Britain. The *Daily Mail* ran a banner headline: "STOP THIS NEW WAR!"[30] The communiqué also caused alarm abroad. Furious that the British government appeared to be speaking for him, French Premier Poincaré ordered his troops to be withdrawn from the front line of the Neutral Zone; the Italians followed forthwith, and the British forces were left alone to face the enemy.

The Dominion prime ministers were also offended. The communiqué—which was of course written in plain English—was published in Canadian, Australian, and New Zealand newspapers before the prime ministers had a chance to decode the ciphered cables they had received. It suggested that Churchill and Lloyd George were trying to rush them into something without giving them time to think. In reply, Canada and Australia refused to send troops. A revolution had occurred in the constitution of the British Empire: it was the first time that British Dominions had ever refused to follow the mother country into war. South Africa remained silent. Only New Zealand and Newfoundland responded favorably.

On 22 September Lloyd George called upon Churchill to take charge as chairman of a Cabinet Committee to oversee military movements in Turkey.[31] Churchill's brilliant friend, F. E. Smith, now Lord Birkenhead and serving as Lord Chancellor, had previously been critical of Churchill for changing over to an anti-Turkish position, but at the end of September joined Lloyd George and Churchill as a leader of the belligerent faction. It was a question of prestige, Birkenhead felt; Britain must never be seen to give in to force.[32]

In Britain the press campaign against the war continued. Public protest meetings were held. Trade union delegates went to Downing Street to deliver their protest to the Prime Minister personally.

The Foreign Secretary, Lord Curzon, crossed over to Paris to attempt to concert a strategy with the Allies. On 23 September he finally agreed with Poincaré and Sforza on a common program that yielded to all of Kemal's demands—eastern Thrace, Constantinople, and the Dardanelles—so long as appearances could be preserved; it was to appear to be a negotiated settlement rather than a surrender. It was not a happy meeting for the British Foreign Secretary; after being exposed to Poincaré's bitter denunciations, Curzon broke down and retired to the next room in tears.

Meanwhile, the British and Turkish armies confronted one another at Chanak (today called Canakkale), a coastal town on the Asiatic side of the Dardanelles that today serves as the point of departure for tours to the ruins of Troy. The French and Italian contingents having retired to their tents, a small British contingent stood guard behind barbed wire, with orders not to fire unless fired upon. The first detachment of Turkish troops advanced to the British line on 23 September. The Turks did not open fire, but stood their ground and refused to withdraw. A few days later more Turkish troops arrived. By the end of September, there were 4,500 Turks in the Neutral Zone, talking through the barbed wire to the British, and holding their rifles butt-forward to demonstrate that they would not be the first to fire. It was an eerie and unnerving confrontation. On 29 September British Intelligence reported to the Cabinet that Kemal, pushed on by Soviet Russia, planned to attack the next day. The report, though false, was believed. With the approval of the Cabinet, the chiefs of the military services drafted a stern ultimatum for the local British commander to deliver to Kemal, threatening to open fire.

The local British commander, disregarding the instructions from London—which could have led Britain into war—did not deliver the ultimatum. Instead he reached an agreement with Kemal to negotiate an armistice—and so brought the crisis to an end. For many reasons—including fear of what Lloyd George and Churchill in their recklessness might do—Kemal was prepared to accept a formula that allowed the Allies to save face by postponing Turkey's occupation of some of the territories she was eventually to occupy. Had Kemal invaded Europe it would have meant war. The belligerent posture of the British leaders appeared to have stopped him. Given the actual weakness of their position, this represented a brilliant triumph for Lloyd George and Churchill.

After much hard bargaining, negotiations for an armistice were concluded at the coastal town of Mudanya on the morning of 11 October, to come into effect at midnight, 14 October. Significant substantive issues remained; consideration of them was put off until a peace conference could convene. Essentially, Kemal obtained the terms he had outlined in the National Pact and had adhered to ever since: an independent Turkish nation-state to be established in Anatolia and eastern Thrace. Before long, Kemal's Turkey took physical possession of Constantinople, the Dardanelles, and eastern Thrace from the departing Allies.

In November 1922, the Kemalist National Assembly deposed the Sultan. The Sultan fled from Constantinople into exile. Thus in 1922 the centuries-old Ottoman Empire came to an end; and Turkey, which for 500 years had dominated the Middle East, departed from Middle Eastern history to seek to make herself European.

IV

Two aspects of the crisis and of the armistice negotiations made an especially marked impression in Britain. One was that the French representative at the armistice conference had played an adversary role by urging the Turks to resist British demands. This proved to be the climax of a line of French conduct throughout the Turkish crisis that was regarded in Britain as treacherous. Just as Britain's Middle Eastern policy had led France to re-evaluate and eventually to repudiate her alliance with Britain, so now France's policy caused the leaders of the British Empire to look at France through new and apprehensive eyes. A short time later the Prime Minister of South Africa wrote to the then Prime Minister of Britain that "France is once more the leader of the Continent with all the bad old instincts fully alive in her ... The French are out for world power; they have played the most dangerous anti-ally game with Kemal; and inevitably in the course of their ambitions they must come to realise that the British Empire is the only remaining enemy."[33]

Another unnerving aspect of the crisis was the apparently reckless conduct of the inner group in the Cabinet: Lloyd George, Birkenhead, Churchill, Chancellor of the Exchequer Sir Robert Horne, and the Conservative leader Austen Chamberlain. Not merely to the public and to the press, but also to their political colleagues, they gave the impression of being anxious to provoke another war. The First Lord of the Admiralty said that he had the feeling that "L.G., Winston, Birkenhead, Horne, and even Austen positively *want* hostilities to break out."[34] Maurice Hankey, Secretary to the Cabinet, recorded in his diary on 17 October 1922, that Winston Churchill "quite frankly regretted that the Turks had not attacked us"; Lloyd George agreed with Churchill about this, Hankey believed.[35]

Attacking the Cabinet ministers as "Rash and vacillating and incapable," *The Times* on 2 October had warned that "if this country once begins to suspect them, or any among them, of any disposition to make political capital at home out of a course which would land us in war, it will never forgive them."

Stanley Baldwin, a junior Conservative member of the government who privately had come to view the Prime Minister as "demoniacal," confided to his wife that "he had found out that ... L.G. had been all for war and had schemed to make this country go to war with Turkey so that they should have a 'Christian' ... war v. the Mahomedan ... On the strength of that they would call a General Election at once ... which, they calculated, would return them to office for another period of years."[36] Bonar Law expressed the opposite fear: that the Prime Minister would make peace in order to win the elections, but that once he had been re-elected he would go back to making war.[37]

Lloyd George's friend Lord Riddell told the Prime Minister "that the country will not stand for a fresh war." "I disagree," said the Prime Minister. "The country will willingly support our action regarding the Straits by force of arms if need be."[38] Decades later, writing of the Chanak crisis in his memoirs, Lloyd George avowed that "I certainly meant to fight and I was certain we should win."[39]

V

As the Chanak crisis moved toward its denouement, a military revolution broke out in Greece, launched by a triumvirate of officers in the field: two army colonels and a naval captain. There was much confusion but, in the end, no resistance. The government resigned on 26 September. King Constantine abdicated the following morning; his son mounted the throne as George II that afternoon. The main body of revolutionary troops marched into Athens on 28 September.

The triumvirate of revolutionary officers assumed authority, and at once ordered the arrest of the leaders of the previous government. Gounaris and several other ex-ministers were brought before a military court martial on 13 November, despite protests from the British government. The lengthy charges, though clothed in legalistic language, were of little legal validity. Essentially, they amounted to a political indictment of Gounaris and his associates for having brought about a national catastrophe.

At dawn on 28 November the president of the court martial announced its verdict. All eight of the accused persons were convicted of high treason. Two of them were sentenced to life imprisonment. The other six, including former Prime Minister Gounaris, were sentenced to death. The six condemned men, within hours, were driven to an execution ground east of Athens, in the shadow of Mount Hymettus. Small burial holes had already been dug at intervals of twelve metres. In front of each of the condemned men, at a distance of fifteen paces, stood a firing squad of five soldiers. The execution took place before noon. Having refused to wear bandages, Gounaris and his associates went to their death with their eyes open.[40]

VI

On 8 October 1922 Andrew Bonar Law, the retired leader of the Unionist–Conservative Party, wrote a letter to *The Times* and the *Daily Express*—published the next day—in which he appeared to express support for the strong stand the Lloyd George government had taken against Turkey at Chanak. On the other hand, he pointed out that the interests that Britain appeared to be defending, such as the freedom of the Dardanelles and the prevention of future massacres of Christians, were not uniquely British interests but world interests. Therefore, he wrote, "It is not ... right that the burden of taking action should fall on the British Empire alone." He claimed that "We are at the Straits and in Constantinople" not by our own action alone, but by the will of the Allied Powers which won the war, and America is one of those Powers."

In much-quoted sentences, Bonar Law argued that if the United States and the Allies were not prepared to share the burden of responsibility, Britain should put it down. "We cannot alone act as the policeman of the world. The financial and social conditions of this country make that impossible." He proposed to warn France that Britain might walk away from enforcing the settlement with Germany, and might imitate the United States in retiring into an exclusive concern with her own national interests, if France failed to recognize that a stand had to be taken in Asia as well as in Europe.[41]

Read as a whole, Bonar Law's letter did not call into question the policy pursued until then by the government; it merely offered advice for the future. Its isolationist tone, however, and the sentence about not being the world's policeman—which was often quoted out of context—struck a responsive chord in the ranks of those who found Lloyd George's policies dangerous and overly ambitious. Moreover, Bonar Law's willingness to take a public stand suggested that, with his health apparently restored, he might be persuaded to re-enter politics—which threatened to alter the delicate balance of forces within the Conservative Party and endanger the Coalition.

Bonar Law had chosen his foreign policy issue shrewdly. Tory sentiment was traditionally pro-Turk and had been alienated by the Prime Minister's pro-Greek crusade. "*A good understanding with Turkey was our old policy* and it is essential ..." (original emphasis), wrote the chief of the recalcitrant Tories on 2 October.[42] It was yet another instance in which rank-and-file Conservatives found that their principles and prejudices were being disregarded by the Coalition government. Coming after the concession of independence to Ireland and after the recognition of Bolshevik Russia, Lloyd George's anti-Turkish policy threatened to be one instance too many. The Prime Minister had dissipated his credit with them. He had done so at a time when the collapse of the economy, mass unemployment, a slump in exports, scandals concerning the sales of honors and titles to political contributors, and a series of foreign policy fiascos culminating in the Chanak crisis had left him a much diminished electoral asset. The Conservatives no longer felt compelled to follow him in order to survive at the polls.

The Prime Minister viewed matters differently. His government's firmness at Chanak had brought Turkey's armies to a halt; it was, in his view, a personal triumph for him and for Churchill, and he mistakenly believed that the electorate recognized it as such. On this erroneous assumption he proposed to call a snap election in the flush of victory, as he had done at the end of 1918 after the First World War had been won.

Austen Chamberlain and Lord Birkenhead, the Conservative leaders in the government, agreed to join with Lloyd George in fighting the elections once again on a coalition basis. To defend that decision, Chamberlain, as leader of the party, summoned the Conservative members of the House of Commons and of the government to a meeting the morning of Thursday, 19 October, at the Carlton, the leading Tory club.

Bonar Law was the person best placed to oppose Chamberlain, bring down the Coalition, and replace Lloyd George as Prime Minister. He hesitated; yet there was a strong press campaign urging him on, led by *The Times* and by the Beaverbrook newspapers.

Lord Beaverbrook was Bonar Law's most intimate political friend. He was largely responsible for having created the Lloyd George Coalition government during the war; now he acted to bring it down. On 11 October Beaverbrook wrote to an American friend that

> We are now in the throes of a political crisis. The failure of the Prime Minister's Greek policy had resulted in a complete collapse of his prestige with the Conservatives ... The immediate future will decide whether the Conservative Party is to remain intact, or whether the Prime Minister is strong enough to split it. It will have been a great achievement to have smashed two parties in one short administration. Yet that is what he can claim if he succeeds in destroying the Tories.[43]

Beaverbrook succeeded in overcoming Bonar Law's doubts and in making sure that the former Tory leader actually attended the decisive meeting at the Carlton Club. At the meeting, Law spoke against the

Coalition, and though he spoke badly his intervention proved decisive. By an overwhelming vote of 187 to 87, the caucus decided to contest the coming elections on a straight party basis.

Upon receiving the news, David Lloyd George immediately tendered his resignation to King George. Soon afterward Andrew Bonar Law took office as Prime Minister and called elections for 15 November.

The popular vote on 15 November was close, but in the winner-take-all British parliamentary system the results were a triumph for the Conservatives, who won a majority of seats in the new House of Commons. Lloyd George was repudiated; neither he nor Asquith commanded a large enough following to qualify even as Leader of the Opposition, for Labour had beaten the Liberals to take second place.

During the electoral campaign, the Beaverbrook press mounted a fierce attack on the Middle Eastern policy of the Coalition government, and demanded that Britain withdraw from her new acquisitions: Iraq, Palestine, and Transjordan. Although Beaverbrook's crusade was in fact launched without Bonar Law's sanction, it seemed to implicate the new administration in a blanket condemnation of Britain's postwar policy in the Middle East. It also called into question Britain's commitment to continue to support Arab and Jewish aspirations there.

As a result, during the election campaign the Colonial Secretary Winston Churchill was drawn into public controversy with Lord Curzon (who had deserted to Bonar Law) over the record of the past few years in the Middle East. Churchill charged that Curzon was "as responsible as any man alive for the promises that were given to the Jews and to the Arabs."[44] T. E. Lawrence wrote to the editor of the *Daily Express* in support of his former chief that "If we get out of the Middle East Mandates with credit, it will be by Winston's bridge. The man's as brave as six, as good-humoured, shrewd, self-confident, & considerate as a statesman can be: & several times I've seen him chuck the statesmanlike course & do the honest thing instead."[45]

In the general ruin of Coalition fortunes, Churchill was defeated for re-election in his constituency of Dundee. T. E. Lawrence wrote "I'm more sorry about Winston than I can say. I hope the Press Comment is not too malevolent. It's sure to have hurt him though. What bloody shits the Dundeans must be."[46]

Alone among the Coalition Liberal leaders, David Lloyd George retained his parliamentary seat; but he never held Cabinet office again. Like Lord Kitchener and Winston Churchill at the Dardanelles, he saw his political position ruined by the Middle East. For nearly a quarter of a century after 1922 the once all-powerful minister who had presided over the destinies of the world lingered on in political impotence and isolation, feared and mistrusted by men of lesser abilities, and looked down upon by them for having conducted a morally shabby administration. In part due to his own flaws, he was denied a chance to apply his fertile genius to the political challenges of the Great Depression, the appeasement years, and the Second World War. His political deviousness and his moral and financial laxness were never forgotten. It was not sufficiently remembered that single-handed he had kept Britain from losing the First World War, and that his colleagues had once claimed that they were content to let him be Prime Minister for life. He died in 1945.

In his later years Lloyd George devoted himself to re-fighting the old battles in his highly slanted, far from factual, but beautifully written memoirs. As he presented it, his last, lost crusade in the Middle East was intended to make the world a fundamentally better place. Of the decision reached at the Carlton Club, he wrote: "So the Government fell, and with it went first the liberation of Armenia and Asiatic Greece, and in the sequel the League of Nations and all the projects for substituting conciliation for armaments."[47]*

---

* Lloyd George and the Coalition Conservatives fell from power because they had failed to pay attention to political sentiment amongst the Parliamentary rank and file. To make sure that on their side there would be no such failure again, the Conservatives thereafter established an organization of backbench Members of Parliament to make their views known to the leadership. It exists to this day, and is called the 1922 Committee.

THE SETTLEMENT OF THE
MIDDLE EASTERN QUESTION

I

East of Suez, Lloyd George and his colleagues were the authors of a major chapter in history. The establishment of Allied control in the Middle East marked the climax of Europe's conquest of the rest of the world. It was the last chapter in a tale of high adventure—of sailors daring to cross uncharted oceans, of explorers tracking rivers to their source, and of small bands of soldiers marching into the interior of unknown continents to do battle with the vast armies of remote empires. The venture had begun centuries before, in the wake of Columbus's galleons, as Europeans streamed forth to subjugate and colonize the lands they had discovered in the Americas and in the waters to the east and west of them. It continued through the nineteenth century, as Britain assumed the empire of India, and as the Great Powers divided the continent of Africa between them. By the dawn of the twentieth century, East Asia apart, the Middle East was the only native bastion that the Europeans had not yet stormed; and, at the end of the First World War, Lloyd George was able to proudly point out that his armies had finally stormed it.

For at least a century before the 1914 war, Europeans had regarded it as axiomatic that someday the Middle East would be occupied by one or more of the Great Powers. Their great fear was that disputes about their respective shares might lead the European powers to fight ruinous wars against one another.

For the government of Britain, therefore, the settlements arrived at by 1922 were a doubly crowning achievement. Britain had won a far larger share of the Middle East (and Britain's rival, Russia, a much smaller one) than had seemed possible beforehand; but even more important, the powers seemed prepared to accept the territorial division that had emerged in the early 1920s without further recourse to arms.

Thus the troubling and potentially explosive Middle Eastern Question, as it had existed in world politics since the time of Bonaparte's

Egyptian expedition, was successfully settled by the postwar arrangements arrived at by 1922. A major issue that had been at stake was where Russia's political frontier in the Middle East would be drawn. By 1922 the question was solved: the Russian frontier was finally drawn to run with a northern tier of states that stretched from Turkey to Iran to Afghanistan—countries that maneuvered to remain independent both of Russia and the West, along a line that continued to hold firm for decades. The other great issue at stake since Napoleonic times had been what would eventually become of the Ottoman Empire—an issue that was resolved in 1922 by the termination of the Ottoman Sultanate and the partition of its Middle Eastern domains between Turkey, France, and Britain. Such was the settlement of 1922.

II

The settlement of 1922 was not a single act or agreement or document; rather, it was the design that emerged from many separate acts and agreements and documents that date mostly from that year.

Russia's territorial frontier in the Middle East was established by the draft constitution of the U.S.S.R. promulgated at the end of 1922, while her political frontier emerged from the treaties she signed with Turkey, Persia, and Afghanistan, and, to some extent, from the trade agreement she signed with Britain in 1921.

The deposing of the Ottoman Sultan and the establishment of a Turkish national state (confined to the Turkish-speaking portion of the dissolved empire) were effected by unanimous votes of the Turkish Grand National Assembly on 1 and 2 November 1922. Turkey's eventual frontiers in large part grew out of the armistice she signed with the Allies in the autumn of 1922, followed by a peace treaty with the Allies signed at the Swiss city of Lausanne the following year.[*]

The rest of the former Ottoman domains in the Middle East were partitioned between Britain and France by such documents as France's League of Nations Mandate to rule Syria and Lebanon (1922), Britain's League of Nations Mandate to rule Palestine including Transjordan (1922), and the treaty of 1922 with Iraq which Britain intended to serve as an affirmation of a Mandate to rule that newly created country.

Within her own sphere of influence in the Middle East, Britain made her dispositions in acts and documents that also, for the most

---

[*] Some frontier questions remained unresolved. Turkey's frontier with Syria, for example, was established only at the end of the 1930s.

part, date from 1922. She placed Fuad I on the throne of Egypt in that year, and made Egypt a nominally independent protectorate by the terms of the Allenby Declaration of 1922. She established a protectorate in Iraq by her treaty that year with that country: a country that she had created and upon whose throne she had placed her own nominee, Feisal. By the terms of the Palestine Mandate of 1922 and Churchill's White Paper for Palestine in 1922, Transjordan was set on the road to a political existence separate from that of Palestine—Abdullah, appointed by Britain, was to permanently preside over the new entity by a decision made in 1922—while west of the Jordan, Jews were promised a National Home and non-Jews were promised full rights. Independence or autonomy for the Kurds, which had been on the agenda in 1921, somehow disappeared from the agenda in 1922, so there was to be no Kurdistan: it was a nondecision of 1922 that was, in effect, a decision. In 1922, too, Britain imposed frontier agreements upon Ibn Saud that established boundaries between Saudi Arabia, Iraq, and Kuwait.

Thus Britain—like France in her sphere of the Middle East, and Russia in hers—established states, appointed persons to govern them, and drew frontiers between them; and did so mostly in and around 1922. As they had long intended to do, the European powers had taken the political destinies of the Middle Eastern peoples in their hands—and they did so by the terms of what I have called the settlement of 1922.

III

Everywhere else in the world—everywhere outside of Asia—European occupation had resulted in the destruction of native political structures and their replacement by new ones of European design. The Americas, Australia, New Zealand, and Africa were no longer divided in terms of tribes; they were divided, as Europe was, into countries. Governmental administration of most of the planet was conducted in a European mode, according to European precepts, and in accordance with European concepts.

Still, there was some reason to question whether European occupation would produce quite so deep or lasting an impression in the Middle East as it had elsewhere. It was not only that the Middle East was a region of proud and ancient civilizations, with beliefs deeply rooted in the past, but also that the changes Europe proposed to introduce were so profound that generations would have to pass before the changes could take root. These matters take time. Ancient Rome shaped Europe, and renascent Europe shaped the Americas, but in both cases it was the work of centuries; and in 1922 western

Europe was in no mood—and in no condition—to embark on an undertaking of such magnitude.

The long-expected European imperial adventure in the Middle East had therefore begun too late; Europeans could no longer pursue it either with adequate resources or with a whole heart. Europe itself, its *antebellum* world swept away in the cataclysm of 1914—18, was changing more rapidly in weeks or months than it had before in decades or centuries, and to a growing number of Europeans, imperialism seemed out of place in the modern age.

In the first years of the war it had still sounded acceptable openly to avow an intention to annex new colonies; but as Wilson's America and Lenin's Russia, with their anti-imperialist rhetoric, challenged old Europe, minds and political vocabularies began to change. Sir Mark Sykes, ever sensitive to shifts in the current of opinion, recognized in 1917 that the imperial concepts he and Picot had employed only a year before in their Middle East pact already belonged to a bygone era.

By the time that the war came to an end, British society was generally inclined to reject the idealistic case for imperialism (that it would extend the benefits of advanced civilization to a backward region) as quixotic, and the practical case for it (that it would be of benefit to Britain to expand her empire) as untrue. Viewing imperialism as a costly drain on a society that needed to invest all of its remaining resources in rebuilding itself, the bulk of the British press, public, and Parliament agreed to let the government commit itself to a presence in the Arab Middle East only because Winston Churchill's ingenious strategy made it seem possible to control the region inexpensively.

Thus the belief, widely shared by British officials during and after the First World War, that Britain had come to the Middle East to stay—at least long enough to re-shape the region in line with European political interests, ideas, and ideals—was based on the fragile assumption that Churchill's aircraft-and-armored-car strategy could hold local opposition at bay indefinitely. In turn, that assumption was another expression of the underestimation of the Middle East that had typified British policy all along. It had shown itself when Grey disdained the offer of an Ottoman alliance in 1911; when Asquith in 1914 regarded Ottoman entry in the war as being of no great concern; and when Kitchener, in 1915, sent his armies to their doom against an entrenched and forewarned foe at Gallipoli in an attack the British government knew would be suicidal if the defending troops were of European quality—Kitchener's fatal assumption being that they were not.

In 1922 the British government had arrived at a political compromise with British society, by the terms of which Britain could assert her mastery in the Middle East so long as she could do so at little cost. To British officials who underestimated the difficulties Britain would encounter in governing the region—who, indeed, had no conception of the magnitude of what they had undertaken—that meant Britain was in the Middle East to stay. In retrospect, however, it was an early indication that Britain was likely to leave.

IV

From a British point of view, the settlement of 1922 had become largely out of date by the time it was effected. It embodied much of the program for the postwar Middle East that the British government had formulated (mostly through the agency of Sir Mark Sykes) between 1915 and 1917. But the British government had changed, British official thinking had changed, and in 1922 the arrangements arrived at in the Middle East did not accurately reflect what the government of the day would have wished.

Giving France a League of Nations Mandate in 1922 to rule Syria (including Lebanon) was a case in point. In 1915 and 1916 Foreign Secretary Sir Edward Grey and the British negotiator Sir Mark Sykes had viewed with sympathy France's claim to Syria—and had accepted it. But in 1922 Britain's Prime Minister, Foreign Secretary, and officials in the field were all men who had said for years that to allow France to occupy Syria was to invite disaster.

Even within its own sphere in the Middle East, the British government was unhappy about the dispositions it was making in 1922. In 1914, 1915, and 1916, Lord Kitchener and his lieutenants had chosen to sponsor the Hashemites—Hussein of Mecca and his sons—as leaders of the postwar Arab Middle East. By 1918 British officials had come to regard Hussein as a burden, who was involving them in a losing conflict with Ibn Saud. By 1922 British politicians and officials had come to view Hussein's son Feisal as treacherous, and Hussein's son Abdullah as lazy and ineffective. Yet, in Iraq and Transjordan, Feisal and Abdullah were the rulers whom Britain had installed; Britain had committed herself to the Hashemite cause.

Palestine was another case in point: in 1922 Britain accepted a League of Nations Mandate to carry out a Zionist program that she had vigorously espoused in 1917—but for which she had lost all enthusiasm in the early 1920s.

It was no wonder, then, that in the years to come British officials were to govern the Middle East with no great sense of direction or conviction. It was a consequence of a peculiarity of the settlement of 1922: having destroyed the old order in the region, and having deployed troops, armored cars, and military aircraft everywhere from Egypt to Iraq, *British policy-makers imposed a settlement upon the Middle East in 1922 in which, for the most part, they themselves no longer believed.*

V

The Middle East became what it is today both because the European powers undertook to re-shape it and because Britain and France failed to ensure that the dynasties, the states, and the political system that they established would permanently endure. During and after the First World War, Britain and her Allies destroyed the old order in the region irrevocably; they smashed Turkish rule of the Arabic-speaking Middle East beyond repair.* To take its place, they created countries, nominated rulers, delineated frontiers, and introduced a state system of the sort that exists everywhere else; but they did not quell all significant local opposition to those decisions.

As a result the events of 1914–22, while bringing to an end Europe's Middle Eastern Question, gave birth to a Middle Eastern Question in the Middle East itself. The settlement of 1922 (as it is called here, even though some of the arrangements were arrived at a bit earlier or a bit later) resolved, as far as Europeans were concerned, the question of what—as well as who—should replace the Ottoman Empire; yet even today there are powerful local forces within the Middle East that remain unreconciled to these arrangements—and may well overthrow them.

Some of the disputes, like those elsewhere in the world, are about rulers or frontiers, but what is typical of the Middle East is that more fundamental claims are also advanced, drawing into question not merely the dimensions and boundaries, but the right to exist, of countries that immediately or eventually emerged from the British and French decisions of the early 1920s: Iraq, Israel, Jordan, and Lebanon. So at this point in the twentieth century, the Middle East is the region of the world in which wars of national survival are still being fought with some frequency.

The disputes go deeper still: beneath such apparently insoluble, but specific, issues as the political future of the Kurds or the political destiny of the Palestinian Arabs, lies the more general question of whether the transplanted modern system of politics

---

* Which is not to deny that the Turks also played a role in the destruction of their empire, and that, in any event, there were forces within the Middle East making for change.

invented in Europe—characterized, among other things, by the division of the earth into independent secular states based on national citizenship—will survive in the foreign soil of the Middle East.

In the rest of the world European political assumptions are so taken for granted that nobody thinks about them anymore; but at least one of these assumptions, the modern belief in secular civil government, is an alien creed in a region most of whose inhabitants, for more than a thousand years, have avowed faith in a Holy Law that governs all of life, including government and politics.

European statesmen of the First World War era did—to some extent—recognize the problem and its significance. As soon as they began to plan their annexation of the Middle East, Allied leaders recognized that Islam's hold on the region was the main feature of the political landscape with which they would have to contend. Lord Kitchener, it will be remembered, initiated in 1914 a policy designed to bring the Moslem faith under Britain's sway. When it looked as though that might not work—for the Sherif Hussein's call to the Faithful in 1916 fell on deaf ears—Kitchener's associates proposed instead to sponsor other loyalties (to a federation of Arabic-speaking peoples, or to the family of King Hussein, or to about-to-be-created countries such as Iraq) as a rival to pan-Islam. Indeed they framed the postwar Middle East settlement with that object (among others) in view.

However, European officials at the time had little understanding of Islam. They were too easily persuaded that Moslem opposition to the politics of modernization—of Europeanization—was vanishing. Had they been able to look ahead to the last half of the twentieth century, they would have been astonished by the fervor of the Wahhabi faith in Saudi Arabia, by the passion of religious belief in warring Afghanistan, by the continuing vitality of the Moslem Brotherhood in Egypt, Syria, and elsewhere in the Sunni world, and by the recent Khomeini upheaval in Shi'ite Iran.

Continuing local opposition, whether on religious grounds or others, to the settlement of 1922 or to the fundamental assumptions upon which it was based, explains the characteristic feature of the region's politics: that in the Middle East there is no sense of *legitimacy*—no agreement on rules of the game—and no belief, universally shared in the region, that within whatever boundaries, the entities that call themselves countries or the men who claim to be rulers are entitled to recognition as such. In that sense, successors to the Ottoman sultans have not yet been permanently installed, even though—between 1919 and 1922—installing them was what the Allies believed themselves to be doing.

It may be that one day the challenges to the 1922 settlement—to the existence of Jordan, Israel, Iraq, and Lebanon, for example, or to the institution of secular national governments in the Middle

East—will be withdrawn. But if they continue in full force, then the twentieth-century Middle East will eventually be seen to be in a situation similar to Europe's in the fifth century AD, when the collapse of the Roman Empire's authority in the West threw its subjects into a crisis of civilization that obliged them to work out a new political system of their own. The European experience suggests what the dimensions of such a radical crisis of political civilization might be.

It took Europe a millennium and a half to resolve its post-Roman crisis of social and political identity: nearly a thousand years to settle on the nation-state form of political organization, and nearly five hundred years more to determine which nations were entitled to be states. Whether civilization would survive the raids and conflicts of rival warrior bands; whether church or state, pope or emperor, would rule; whether Catholic or Protestant would prevail in Christendom; whether dynastic empire, national state, or city-state would command fealty; and whether, for example, a townsman of Dijon belonged to the Burgundian or to the French nation, were issues painfully worked out through ages of searching and strife, during which the losers—the Albigensians of southern France, for example—were often annihilated. It was only at the end of the nineteenth century, with the creation of Germany and Italy, that an accepted map of western Europe finally emerged, some 1,500 years after the old Roman map started to become obsolete.

The continuing crisis in the Middle East in our time may prove to be nowhere near so profound or so long-lasting. But its issue is the same: how diverse peoples are to regroup to create new political identities for themselves after the collapse of an ages-old imperial order to which they had grown accustomed. The Allies proposed a post-Ottoman design for the region in the early 1920s. The continuing question is whether the peoples of the region will accept it.

The settlement of 1922, therefore, does not belong entirely or even mostly to the past; it is at the very heart of current wars, conflicts, and politics in the Middle East, for the questions that Kitchener, Lloyd George, and Churchill opened up are even now being contested by force of arms, year after year, in the ruined streets of Beirut, along the banks of the slow-moving Tigris—Euphrates, and by the waters of the Biblical Jordan.

VI

British politicians and officials of the early 1920s did not foresee the problematical future of the 1922 settlement. They did not even foresee the immediate political future of those personally involved in it—among them, Winston Churchill, a principal architect of the settlement—although these were matters closer at hand, and with which they were more intimately familiar than the politics of the Middle East.

In 1922 it was almost universally agreed in Britain that Churchill was politically finished. Churchill, who had lost his seat in the Cabinet in October and his seat in the Commons in November, appeared crushed. While he did not doubt that he could re-enter Parliament at some point, it seemed unlikely that he would ever again be invited to serve in a government—at least in any major capacity.

A dinner companion of Churchill's at the end of November later remembered that "Winston was so down in the dumps he could scarcely speak the whole evening. He thought his world had come to an end—at least his political world. I thought his career was over."[1]

The new Parliament assembled on 27 November 1922, but Churchill was not a member of it, so there was nothing to keep him in Britain. At the beginning of December, he sailed for the Mediterranean. It was only a decade since, in the early summer of his career, he had cruised the Mediterranean aboard *Enchantress* with young Violet Asquith and her father; but that earlier cruise had taken place, politically speaking, in another century—indeed, in another world.

Once he had arrived in the south of France, Churchill settled in a rented villa near Cannes and resumed work on his war memoirs—a project that he had commenced earlier. He was far enough along with it so that he believed the opening sections would be ready for newspaper serialization in about a month. It was to be a work in many volumes.

In the course of composing his memoirs, he reflected on the unaccountable run of bad luck he had encountered in all that touched and concerned the Turkish East. He recalled the accidents, confusions, and blunders that had allowed the *Goeben* to reach Constantinople and help push the Ottoman Empire into the war—a war for which he, Churchill, had been personally blamed. He reflected on the almost unbelievable behavior of his admirals at the Dardanelles in fleeing the Narrows—the day before they might have won the Turkish war, and earned him the laurels of victory, instead of disgrace and dismissal. He told his readers how a monkey bit the King of Greece and caused the renewed Turkish war that brought down the Lloyd George government—and himself with it.

Once he had completed and published the first volume of these memoirs, Churchill returned to Britain, in the middle of 1923, to the apparently hopeless political wars. In the late autumn he stood for Parliament once again, was continuously heckled about the wartime Dardanelles failure, and was defeated by the Labour candidate. In late winter he stood for election again, in another constituency, and was again defeated, this time by a Conservative.

But Churchill's situation was changing. In late 1924 he returned to Parliament; and the political world was astounded to hear that Winston Churchill—far from being politically finished—had become Chancellor of the Exchequer, a position usually deemed to be the second most important in the Cabinet.

The clouds began to part, and a former colleague on the Liberal benches, George Lambert, writing to congratulate him on the new appointment, foresaw an even more astonishing eventuality. "Winston my boy," he wrote, "I have got a fair instinct for politics. I think I shall live to see you Prime Minister."[2]

NOTES

CHAPTER 1

1 Violet Bonham Carter, *Winston Churchill as I Knew Him* (London: Eyre & Spottiswoode and Collins, 1965), p. 263.
2 Ibid., p. 264.
3 Ibid., p. 262.
4 Ibid.

CHAPTER 2

1 For a fuller discussion, with citations, see David Fromkin, "The Great Game in Asia," *Foreign Affairs* (spring 1980), p. 936. Also see Edward Ingram, *Commitment to Empire: Prophecies of the Great Game in Asia 1797–1800* (Oxford: Clarendon Press, 1981); and Edward Ingram, *The Beginnings of the Great Game in Asia 1828–1834* (Oxford: Clarendon Press, 1979).
2 George N. Curzon, *Persia and the Persian Question* (London: Frank Cass, 1966), Vol. 1, pp. 3–4.
3 G. D. Clayton, *Britain and the Eastern Question: Missolonghi to Gallipoli* (London: University of London Press, 1971), p. 139.
4 J. W. Kaye, according to H. W. C. Davis, "The Great Game in Asia, 1800–1844", *Raleigh Lecture on History* (London: British Academy, 1926), pp. 3–4.
5 Marian Kent, *Oil and Empire: British Policy and Mesopotamian Oil, 1900–1920* (London: Macmillan Press for the London School of Economics, 1976), p. 6, and app. 8.
6 Quoted in Arthur Swinson, *North-West Frontier: People and Events, 1839–1947* (London: Hutchinson, 1967), p. 142.
7 M. S. Anderson, *The Eastern Question, 1774–1923: A Study in International Relations* (London and Basingstoke: Macmillan Press, 1966), p. 224.
8 Lady Gwendolen Cecil, *Life of Robert Marquis of Salisbury* (London: Hodder & Stoughton, 1921), Vol. 2, p. 326.
9 Paul Kennedy, *The Realities behind Diplomacy: Background Influences on British External Policy, 1865–1980* (Glasgow: Fontana, 1981), p. 20; Paul Kennedy, "A Historian of Imperial Decline Looks at America," *International Herald Tribune*, 3 November 1982, p. 6.
10 P. L. Cottrell, *British Overseas Investment in the Nineteenth Century* (London: Macmillan Press, 1975), p. 9.
11 Walter Bagehot, *The Collected Works* (London: *The Economist*, 1974), Vol. 8, p. 306.
12 Viscount Grey of Falloden, *Twenty-Five Years, 1892–1916* (London: Hodder & Stoughton, 1925), Vol. 1, p. 152.

CHAPTER 3

1 Thirty million: Charles Issawi, *The Economic History of Turkey: 1800–1914* (Chicago and London: University of Chicago Press, 1980), p. 1. Fifty million: George Lenczowski, *The Middle East in World Affairs*, 4th edn (Ithaca and London: Cornell University Press, 1980), p. 28.

2 *The Arab War: Confidential Information for General Headquarters from Gertrude Bell, Being Despatches Reprinted from the Secret "Arab Bulletin"* (Great Britain: The Golden Cockerel Press, n.d.), p. 9.

3 Issawi, *Economic History of Turkey*, p. 353.

4 *Encyclopaedia Britannica*, 11th edn, s.v. "Constantinople."

5 Bernard Lewis, *The Emergence of Modern Turkey*, 2nd edn (London, Oxford, and New York: Oxford University Press, 1968), p. 228.

6 John Presland (pseudonym for Gladys Skelton), *Deedes Bey: A Study of Sir Wyndham Deedes 1883–1923* (London: Macmillan, 1942), p. 19.

7 Margaret FitzHerbert, *The Man Who Was Greenmantle: A Biography of Aubrey Herbert* (London: John Murray, 1983), p. 83.

8 Elie Kedourie, *Arabic Political Memoirs and Other Studies* (London: Frank Cass, 1974), p. 244.

9 Ibid., p. 260.

10 Ibid., p. 257.

11 Ibid., p. 261.

12 Ibid., p. 255.

13 For accounts of the origins and internal workings of the Young Turkey movement, see Feroz Ahmad, *The Young Turks: The Committee of Union and Progress in Turkish Politics 1908–1914* (Oxford: Clarendon Press, 1969); and Ernest Edmondson Ramsaur, Jr, *The Young Turks: Prelude to the Revolution of 1908* (Princeton: Princeton University Press, 1957).

14 John Buchan, *Greenmantle* (New York: Grosset & Dunlap, 1916), ch. 1; Lewis, *Modern Turkey*, pp. 207–8, n. 4.

CHAPTER 4

1 Charles Issawi, *The Economic History of Turkey: 1800–1914* (Chicago and London: University of Chicago Press, 1980), p. 151.

2 Ibid.

3 Ibid.

4 Ibid., pp. 146–7 and 152–77.

5 Ibid., p. 147.

6 Ibid., p. 177.

7 Ibid., p. 178.

8 Harry N. Howard, *The Partition of Turkey: A Diplomatic History 1913–1923* (New York: Howard Fertig, 1966), pp. 47 *et seq.*

9 Sir Mark Sykes, *The Caliphs' Last Heritage: A Short History of the Turkish Empire* (London: Macmillan, 1915), p. 2.

10 Ahmed Djemal Pasha, *Memories of a Turkish Statesman: 1913–1919* (New York: George H. Doran, 1922), p. 108.

11 Martin Gilbert, *Winston S. Churchill*, Vol. 3: *1914–1916, The Challenge of War* (Boston: Houghton Mifflin, 1971), p. 189.

12 Ibid., p. 190.

13 Ulrich Trumpener, *Germany and the Ottoman Empire: 1914–1918* (Princeton: Princeton University Press, 1968), p. 20.

14 Ibid., p. 19.

15 Ibid.

CHAPTER 5

1 Ted Morgan, *Churchill: Young Man in a Hurry, 1874–1915* (New York: Simon & Schuster, 1982), p. 314.
2 Violet Bonham Carter, *Winston Churchill as I Knew Him* (London: Eyre & Spottiswoode and Collins, 1965), p. 262.

CHAPTER 6

1 Martin Gilbert, *Winston S. Churchill*, Vol. 3: *1914–1916, The Challenge of War* (Boston: Houghton Mifflin, 1971), pp. 179–80.
2 Ibid., opposite p. 156.
3 Richard Hough, *The Great War at Sea: 1914–1918* (Oxford and New York: Oxford University Press, 1983), p. 71.
4 Lord Kinross, *Ataturk: A Biography of Mustafa Kemal, Father of Modern Turkey* (New York: William Morrow, 1965), p. 79; Stanford J. Shaw and Ezel Kural Shaw, *History of the Ottoman Empire and Modern Turkey*, Vol. 2: *Reform, Revolution, and Republic: The Rise of Modern Turkey, 1808–1975* (Cambridge: Cambridge University Press, 1977), p. 311.
5 Winston S. Churchill, *The World Crisis: 1911–1914* (London: Thornton Butterworth, 1923), pp. 208–9.
6 Martin Gilbert, *Winston S. Churchill: Companion Volume*, Vol. 3, Part 1: *July 1914–April 1915* (Boston: Houghton Mifflin, 1973), pp. 1–2.
7 Ibid., p. 3.
8 Ibid., pp. 2–3.
9 Ibid., p. 5.
10 Ibid.
11 Ibid., p. 10.
12 Ibid., p. 9.
13 Ibid., p. 16.
14 Ibid.
15 Ibid., p. 19.
16 Ulrich Trumpener, *Germany and the Ottoman Empire: 1914–1918* (Princeton: Princeton University Press, 1968), p. 15.
17 Ibid., pp. 19–20.
18 Ibid., p. 16.
19 J. A. S. Grenville, *The Major International Treaties 1914–1973: A History and Guide with Texts* (New York: Stein & Day, 1975), p. 24; Harry N. Howard, *The Partition of Turkey: A Diplomatic History 1913–1923* (New York: Howard Fertig, 1966), p. 49.
20 Trumpener, *Ottoman Empire*, pp. 14, 22.
21 Trumpener, *Ottoman Empire*.
22 Gilbert, *Churchill: Companion Volume*, p. 36.
23 Y. T. Kurat, "How Turkey Drifted into World War I," in K. C. Bourne and D. C. Watt (eds), *Studies in International History* (London: Longman, 1967), p. 299.

CHAPTER 7

1 The account in the text follows that in Ulrich Trumpener, *Germany and the Ottoman Empire: 1914–1918* (Princeton: Princeton University Press, 1968).
2 Violet Bonham Carter, *Winston Churchill as I Knew Him* (London: Eyre & Spottiswoode and Collins, 1965), pp. 321–2.
3 Martin Gilbert, *Winston S. Churchill: Companion Volume*, Vol. 3, Part 1: *July 1914–April 1915* (Boston: Houghton Mifflin, 1973), p. 73.

4   Ibid.
5   Stanford J. Shaw and Ezel Kural Shaw, *History of the Ottoman Empire and Modern Turkey*, Vol. 2: *Reform, Revolution and Republic: The Rise of Modern Turkey, 1808–1975* (Cambridge: Cambridge University Press, 1977), p. 312.
6   Ibid., p. 311.
7   H. H. Asquith, *Letters to Venetia Stanley*, ed. by Michael and Eleanor Brock (Oxford and New York: Oxford University Press, 1982), p. 168.
8   Ibid., p. 171.
9   John Presland (pseudonym for Gladys Skelton), *Deedes Bey: A Study of Sir Wyndham Deedes 1883–1923* (London: Macmillan, 1942), pp. 138–9.
10 Gilbert, *Churchill: Companion Volume*, p. 58.
11 Harry N. Howard, *The Partition of Turkey: A Diplomatic History 1913–1923* (New York: Howard Fertig, 1966), p. 49.
12 Martin Gilbert, *Winston S. Churchill*, Vol. 3: *1914–1916, The Challenge of War* (Boston: Houghton Mifflin, 1971), p. 210.
13 Trumpener, *Ottoman Empire*, p. 31.
14 Ibid., p. 33.
15 Ibid.
16 Ibid.
17 Ibid., p. 32.
18 Viscount Grey of Falloden, *Twenty-Five Years, 1892–1916* (London: Hodder & Stoughton, 1925), Vol. 2, p. 164.
19 Joseph Heller, *British Policy Towards the Ottoman Empire: 1908–1914* (London: Frank Cass, 1983).
20 Trumpener, *Ottoman Empire*, p. 48.
21 Harry N. Howard, *Turkey, the Straits and U.S. Policy* (Baltimore and London: The Johns Hopkins University Press, 1974), p. 27, n. 2.
22 Trumpener, *Ottoman Empire*, p. 58.
23 Gilbert, *Churchill: The Challenge of War*, p. 216.
24 Shaw and Shaw, *Ottoman Empire*, p. 312.
25 Asquith, *Letters*, p. 309.
26 Martin Gilbert, *Winston S. Churchill*, Vol. 4: *1916–1922, The Stricken World* (Boston: Houghton Mifflin, 1975), pp. 752–3.
27 Asquith, *Letters*, pp. 165–6.
28 Ibid., p. 186.
29 Gilbert, *The Challenge of War*, p. 210.
30 Grey, *Twenty-Five Years*, p. 167.
31 Asquith, *Letters*, p. 402.
32 Christopher Sykes, *Two Studies in Virtue* (London: Collins, 1953), p. 205.

CHAPTER 8

1   Martin Gilbert, *Winston S. Churchill*, Vol. 3: *1914–1916, The Challenge of War* (Boston: Houghton Mifflin, 1971), p. 12.
2   George H. Cassar, *Kitchener: Architect of Victory* (London: William Kimber, 1977), p. 172.
3   H. H. Asquith, *Letters to Venetia Stanley*, ed. by Michael and Eleanor Brock (Oxford and New York: Oxford University Press, 1982), p. 157.
4   *Lord Riddell's War Diary 1914–1918* (London: Ivor Nicholson & Watson, 1933), p. 48; Cassar, *Kitchener*, p. 193.
5   Violet Bonham Carter, *Winston Churchill as I Knew Him* (London: Eyre & Spottiswoode and Collins, 1965), p. 316.
6   Lord Beaverbrook, *Politicians and the War 1914–1916* (London: Oldbourne Book Co., 1960), p. 172.

7   Duff Cooper, *Old Men Forget* (New York: E. P. Dutton, 1954), p. 54.
8   G. W. Steevens, *With Kitchener to Khartum* (New York: Dodd, Mead, 1900), p. 46.
9   Ibid., p. 48.
10 Ibid., p. 45.
11 *Encyclopaedia Britannica*, 12th edn, s.v. "Kitchener."
12 Cassar, *Kitchener*, p. 196.
13 Elie Kedourie, *In the Anglo-Arab Labyrinth: The McMahon-Husayn Correspondence and its Interpreters 1914–1939* (Cambridge: Cambridge University Press, 1976), pp. 12–13; L. Hirszowicz, "The Sultan and the Khedive, 1892–1908," *Middle Eastern Studies* (October 1972); Jukka Nevakivi, "Lord Kitchener and the Partition of the Ottoman Empire, 1915–1916," in K. C. Bourne and D. C. Watt (eds), *Studies in International History* (London: Longman, 1967), p. 318.
14 Lord Edward Cecil, *The Leisure of an Egyptian Official* (London: Hodder & Stoughton, 1921), p. 187.
15 *The Memoirs of Sir Ronald Storrs* (New York: G. P. Putnam's Sons, 1937), p. 206.
16 Kedourie, *Anglo-Arab Labyrinth*, p. 29.
17 Sir Mark Sykes, *The Caliphs' Last Heritage: A Short History of the Turkish Empire* (London: Macmillan, 1915).
18 *Encyclopaedia Britannica*, 11th edn, s.v. "Turkey"; Lord Eversley, *The Turkish Empire, from 1288 to 1914* (New York: Howard Fertig, 1969), p. 6.
19 *Arab Bulletin*, no. 47, 11 April 1917.
20 H. V. F. Winstone, *The Illicit Adventure* (London: Jonathan Cape, 1982), pp. 107–9 and 220–1.

CHAPTER 9

1   *Lord Riddell's War Diary 1914–1918* (London: Ivor Nicholson & Watson, 1933), p. 75.
2   G. W. Steevens, *With Kitchener to Khartum* (New York: Dodd, Mead, 1900), pp. 64–5.
3   University of Durham. Sudan Archive. Gilbert Clayton Papers. 469/8.
4   Ibid.
5   *War Memoirs of David Lloyd George*, Vol. 3: *1916–1917* (Boston: Little, Brown, 1934), pp. 304–5.
6   Kew. Public Record Office. Kitchener Papers. 30/57 45. Document 0045.
7   University of Durham. Sudan Archive. Gilbert Clayton Papers. 470/4.
8   Kew. Public Record Office. Kitchener Papers. 30/57 45. Document 0071.
9   Ibid. Document 0073.
10 University of Durham. Sudan Archive. Clayton Key Papers. G//S 513. File 1.
11 Kew. Public Record Office. Kitchener Papers. 30/57 47. Document QQ16.
12 Ibid. Document QQ15.
13 Christopher M. Andrew and A. S. Kanya-Forstner, *The Climax of French Imperial Expansion: 1914–1924* (Stanford: Stanford University Press, 1981), p. 68.
14 Ibid., p. 69.
15 Ibid., p. 40.
16 Ibid., pp. 69–70.

CHAPTER 10

1   *Encyclopaedia Britannica*, 12th edn, s.v. "World War."
2   John Buchan, *Greenmantle* (New York: Grosset & Dunlap, 1916), p. 17.

3 C. Ernest Dawn, *From Ottomanism to Arabism: Essays on the Origins of Arab Nationalism* (Urbana, Chicago, and London: University of Illinois Press, 1973), pp. 54–68.
4 The account in the text follows that in Elie Kedourie, *In the Anglo-Arab Labyrinth: The McMahon-Husayn Correspondence and its Interpreters 1914–1939* (Cambridge: Cambridge University Press, 1976), pp. 4–11.
5 Majid Khadduri, "Aziz 'Ali Al-Misri and the Arab Nationalist Movement," in Albert Hourani (ed.), *Middle Eastern Affairs: Number Four*, St Antony's Papers, no. 17 (London: Oxford University Press, 1965), pp. 140–3.
6 H. V. F. Winstone, *The Illicit Adventure* (London: Jonathan Cape, 1982), p. 380.
7 Kedourie, *Anglo-Arab Labyrinth*, pp. 13–14.
8 Ibid., p. 25.
9 Ibid., p. 17.
10 Zeine N. Zeine, *The Emergence of Arab Nationalism with a Background Study of Arab-Turkish Relations in the Near East* (Beirut: Khayats, 1966).
11 Dawn, *Ottomanism*, p. 152.
12 Albert Hourani, *The Emergence of the Modern Middle East* (Berkeley, Los Angeles and London: University of California Press, 1981), pp. 193–215; Dawn, *Ottomanism*; Zeine N. Zeine, *Arab Nationalism*, pp. 39–59.
13 George Antonius, *The Arab Awakening: The Story of the Arab National Movement* (New York: Capricorn Books, 1965), p. 133; Kedourie, *Anglo-Arab Labyrinth*, p. 19.
14 University of Durham. Sudan Archive. Gilbert Clayton Papers. 469/8.
15 Kedourie, *Anglo-Arab Labyrinth*, p. 22.
16 Ibid., pp. 17–18.
17 Kew. Public Record Office. Kitchener Papers. 30/57 47. Document QQ38.

CHAPTER 11

1 Elie Kedourie, *In the Anglo-Arab Labyrinth: The McMahon-Husayn Correspondence and its Interpreters 1914–1939* (Cambridge: Cambridge University Press, 1976), p. 30.
2 Briton Cooper Busch, *Britain, India, and the Arabs, 1914–1921* (Berkeley and London: University of California Press, 1971), p. 62.
3 Kedourie, *Anglo-Arab Labyrinth*, p. 30.
4 Busch, *Britain, India, and the Arabs*, p. 62.
5 Kedourie, *Anglo-Arab Labyrinth*, p. 120.
6 Ibid., p. 30.
7 H. V. F. Winstone, *Captain Shakespear* (London: Jonathan Cape, 1976).
8 Busch, *Britain, India, and the Arabs*, p. 60.
9 Ibid., p. 11.
10 Kedourie, *Anglo-Arab Labyrinth*, p. 52.
11 Ibid., pp. 47–51.
12 Ulrich Trumpener, *Germany and the Ottoman Empire: 1914–1918* (Princeton: Princeton University Press, 1968), p. 117.
13 Fritz Fischer, *Germany's Aims in the First World War* (New York: W. W. Norton, 1967), p. 126.
14 Trumpener, *Ottoman Empire*, p. 118.
15 Kedourie, *Anglo-Arab Labyrinth*, p. 76.
16 C. J. Lowe and M. L. Dockrill, *The Mirage of Power*, Vol. 3: *The Documents, British Foreign Policy 1902–1922* (London and Boston: Routledge & Kegan Paul, 1972), p. 538.

17 University of Durham. Sudan Archive. Clayton Key Papers. G//S 513. File 1.
18 Kew. Public Record Office. Kitchener Papers. 30/57 45. Document 0074.

CHAPTER 12

1 C. Ernest Dawn, *From Ottomanism to Arabism: Essays on the Origins of Arab Nationalism* (Urbana, Chicago, and London: University of Illinois Press, 1973), p. 14, nn. 42 and 43.
2 Kew. Public Record Office. Kitchener Papers. 30/57 47.
3 Ibid. Document QQ15.

CHAPTER 13

1 The text material on the Caucasus campaign follows the first-hand account supplied by Major Franz Carl Endres in the *Encyclopaedia Britannica*, 12th edn, s.v. "Turkish Campaigns."
2 90,000 effectives, according to Endres, ibid. The current *Encyclopaedia Britannica*, 15th edn. s.v. "World Wars," uses the figure 180,000.
3 Ibid.
4 Ahmed Emin, *Turkey in the World War* (New Haven: Yale University Press, 1930), p. 88.
5 Frank G. Weber, *Eagles on the Crescent: Germany, Austria, and the Diplomacy of the Turkish Alliance 1914–1918* (Ithaca and London: Cornell University Press, 1970), p. 98; C. R. M. F. Cruttwell, *A History of the Great War*, 2nd edn (Oxford: Clarendon Press, 1936), p. 351.
6 Margaret FitzHerbert, *The Man Who Was Greenmantle: A Biography of Aubrey Herbert* (London: John Murray, 1983), p. 147.
7 H. H. Asquith, *Letters to Venetia Stanley*, ed. by Michael and Eleanor Brock (Oxford and New York: Oxford University Press, 1982), p. 414.
8 The statistics that follow are taken from Charles Issawi, *The Economic History of Turkey: 1800–1914* (Chicago and London: University of Chicago Press, 1980), pp. 366 *et seq.*
9 Emin, *Turkey*, p. 92.

CHAPTER 14

1 Lord Beaverbrook, *Men and Power 1917–1918* (London: Hutchinson, 1956), p. xvii.
2 Walter Hines Page, quoted in Kenneth O. Morgan, *Lloyd George* (London: Weidenfeld & Nicolson, 1974), p. 13.
3 A. J. P. Taylor, *English History 1914–1945* (Oxford: Clarendon Press, 1965), p. 74.
4 Martin Gilbert, *Winston S. Churchill*, Vol. 3: *1914–1916, The Challenge of War* (Boston: Houghton Mifflin, 1971), p. 230.
5 Zara C. Steiner, *Britain and the Origins of the First World War* (London and Basingstoke: Macmillan, 1977).
6 *The Autobiography of Bertrand Russell* (London: Unwin Paperbacks, 1978), p. 239.
7 H. H. Asquith, *Letters to Venetia Stanley*, ed. by Michael and Eleanor Brock (Oxford and New York: Oxford University Press, 1982), p. 266.
8 Gilbert, *Churchill: The Challenge of War*, p. 226; John Grigg, *Lloyd George: From Peace to War 1912–1916* (London: Methuen, 1985), p. 194.
9 Lord Beaverbrook, *Politicians and the War 1914–1916* (London: Oldbourne, 1960), p. 175.
10 Gilbert, *Churchill: The Challenge of War*, pp. 328–9.

CHAPTER 15

1 Martin Gilbert, *Winston S. Churchill*, Vol. 3: *1914–1916, The Challenge of War* (Boston: Houghton Mifflin, 1971), p. 234.
2 Martin Gilbert, *Winston S. Churchill: Companion Volume*, Vol. 3, Part 1: *July 1914–April 1915* (Boston: Houghton Mifflin, 1973), p. 380.
3 H. H. Asquith, *Letters to Venetia Stanley*, ed. by Michael and Eleanor Brock (Oxford and New York: Oxford University Press, 1982), p. 374.
4 Gilbert, *Churchill: Companion Volume*, p. 500.
5 Asquith, *Letters*, p. 429.
6 Gilbert, *Churchill: The Challenge of War*, p. 287.
7 Ibid., pp. 296–7.
8 Ibid., p. 288.
9 Violet Bonham Carter, *Winston Churchill as I Knew Him* (London: Eyre & Spottiswoode and Collins, 1965), pp. 359–60.
10 Ibid., p. 359.
11 Gilbert, *Churchill: Companion Volume*, pp. 558–9.
12 Alan Moorehead, *Gallipoli* (New York: Ballentine Books, 1956), p. 59.
13 Ulrich Trumpener, *Germany and the Ottoman Empire 1914–1918* (Princeton: Princeton University Press, 1968), p. 142.
14 Ibid., p. 146.
15 L. S. Stavrianos, *The Balkans since 1453* (New York: Rinehart, 1958), p. 560.
16 Bonham Carter, *Churchill*, p. 368.
17 Ibid., p. 369.
18 Ibid., p. 361.
19 Gilbert, *Churchill: Companion Volume*, p. 625.
20 Bonham Carter, *Churchill*, p. 368.
21 Gilbert, *Churchill: The Challenge of War*, p. 315.
22 Ibid., p. 326.
23 Bonham Carter, *Churchill*, pp. 365–6.

CHAPTER 16

1 Christopher M. Andrew and A. S. Kanya-Forstner, *The Climax of French Imperial Expansion: 1914–1924* (Stanford: Stanford University Press, 1981), p. 73.
2 Viscount Grey of Falloden, *Twenty-Five Years, 1892–1916* (London: Hodder & Stoughton, 1925), Vol. 2, pp. 180–1.
3 H. H. Asquith, *Letters to Venetia Stanley*, ed. by Michael and Eleanor Brock (Oxford and New York: Oxford University Press, 1982), p. 300.
4 Ibid., p. 463.
5 Martin Gilbert, *Winston S. Churchill*, Vol. 3: *1914–1916, The Challenge of War* (Boston: Houghton Mifflin, 1971), p. 320.
6 Ibid.
7 Asquith, *Letters*, p. 183, n. 5.
8 Gilbert, *Churchill: The Challenge of War*, p. 320.
9 Elie Kedourie, *In the Anglo-Arab Labyrinth: The McMahon-Husayn Correspondence and its Interpreters 1914–1939* (Cambridge: Cambridge University Press, 1976), pp. 22–3.
10 David Lloyd George, *Memoirs of the Peace Conference* (New Haven: Yale University Press, 1939), Vol. 2, p. 669.
11 Gilbert, *Churchill: The Challenge of War*, p. 349.
12 Briton Cooper Busch, *Britain, India, and the Arabs, 1914–1921* (Berkeley and London: University of California Press, 1971), pp. 40–2.
13 Asquith, *Letters*, p. 510.

14 Ibid., p. 469.
15 Martin Gilbert, *Winston S. Churchill: Companion Volume*, Vol. 3, Part 1: *July 1914—April 1915* (Boston: Houghton Mifflin, 1973), p. 716.
16 Kew. Public Record Office. Kitchener Papers. 30/57 45. Document 0073.
17 Ibid. 30/57. Document QQ18.
18 Kedourie, *Anglo-Arab Labyrinth*, p. 33.
19 Ibid., pp. 49—50.
20 Ibid., p. 34.
21 H. V. F. Winstone, *Gertrude Bell* (London: Jonathan Cape, 1978), p. 165.
22 Marian Kent, "Asiatic Turkey, 1914—1916," in F. H. Hinsley (ed.), *British Foreign Policy under Sir Edward Grey* (Cambridge: Cambridge University Press, 1977), p. 445.
23 Kedourie, *Anglo-Arab Labyrinth*, p. 43.
24 Ibid., p. 41.
25 C. J. Lowe and M. L. Dockrill, *The Mirage of Power*, Vol. 3: *The Documents, British Foreign Policy 1902—1922* (London and Boston: Routledge & Kegan Paul, 1972), pp. 524—5.

CHAPTER 17

1 Martin Gilbert, *Winston S. Churchill: Companion Volume*, Vol. 3, Part 1: *July 1914—April 1915* (Boston: Houghton Mifflin, 1973), pp. 52—3.
2 Roger Adelson, *Mark Sykes: Portrait of an Amateur* (London: Jonathan Cape, 1975), p. 180.
3 Ibid., p. 182.
4 Margaret FitzHerbert, *The Man Who Was Greenmantle: A Biography of Aubrey Herbert* (London: John Murray, 1983), pp. 147—9.

CHAPTER 18

1 Martin Gilbert, *Winston S. Churchill*, Vol. 3: *1914—1916, The Challenge of War* (Boston: Houghton Mifflin, 1971), p. 343.
2 Ibid.
3 Martin Gilbert, *Winston S. Churchill: Companion Volume*, Vol. 3, Part 1: *July 1914—April 1915* (Boston: Houghton Mifflin, 1973), p. 703.
4 Gilbert, *Churchill: The Challenge of War*, p. 358.
5 Stephen Roskill, *Hankey: Man of Secrets*, Vol. 1: *1877—1918* (London: Collins, 1970), p. 159.
6 Gilbert, *Churchill: The Challenge of War*, p. 359.
7 Ibid., p. 371.
8 H. H. Asquith, *Letters to Venetia Stanley*, ed. by Michael and Eleanor Brock (Oxford and New York: Oxford University Press, 1982), p. 488.
9 Gilbert, *Churchill: The Challenge of War*, p. 375.
10 Gilbert, *Churchill: Companion Volume*, p. 731.

CHAPTER 19

1 Martin Gilbert, *Winston S. Churchill: Companion Volume*, Vol. 3, Part 1, *July 1914—April 1915* (Boston: Houghton Mifflin, 1973), p. 582.
2 Sir Ian Hamilton, *Gallipoli Diary*, Vol. 1 (London: Edward Arnold, 1920), p. 5.
3 Ibid., p. 25.
4 Martin Gilbert, *Winston S. Churchill*, Vol. 3: *1914—1916, The Challenge of War* (Boston: Houghton Mifflin, 1971), p. 294.
5 John Grigg, *Lloyd George: From Peace to War 1912—1916* (London: Methuen, 1985), p. 211.

6   Compton Mackenzie, *My Life and Times, Octave Five, 1915–1923* (London: Chatto & Windus, 1966), p. 269

CHAPTER 20

1   Martin Gilbert, *Winston S. Churchill*, Vol. 3: *1914–1916, The Challenge of War* (Boston: Houghton Mifflin, 1971), p. 450.
2   Margaret FitzHerbert, *The Man Who Was Greenmantle: A Biography of Aubrey Herbert* (London: John Murray, 1983), p. 151.
3   Ibid., p. 155.
4   *Lord Riddell's War Diary 1914–1918* (London: Ivor Nicholson & Watson, 1933), p. 94.
5   Ibid., p. 109.
6   Gilbert, *Churchill: The Challenge of War*, p. 476.
7   Riddell, *Diary*, p. 89.
8   Gilbert, *Churchill: The Challenge of War*, p. 440.

CHAPTER 21

1   Martin Gilbert, *Winston S. Churchill*, Vol. 3: *1914–1916, The Challenge of War* (Boston: Houghton Mifflin, 1971), p. 529.
2   H. Montgomery Hyde, *Carson* (London: William Heinemann, 1953), p. 393.
3   Martin Gilbert, *Winston S. Churchill: Companion Volume*, Vol. 3, Part 2: *May 1915–December 1916* (Boston: Houghton Mifflin, 1973), p. 1158.
4   Gilbert, *Churchill: The Challenge of War*, p. 549.
5   John Presland (pseudonym for Gladys Skelton), *Deedes Bey: A Study of Sir Wyndham Deedes 1883–1923* (London: Macmillan, 1942), p. 226.
6   Ibid., p. 231.

CHAPTER 22

1   Roger Adelson, *Mark Sykes: Portrait of an Amateur* (London: Jonathan Cape, 1975), p. 187.
2   Briton Cooper Busch, *Britain, India, and the Arabs*, 1914–1921 (Berkeley, Los Angeles, and London: University of California Press, 1971), p. 69.
3   Adelson, *Sykes*, p. 192.
4   C. J. Lowe and M. L. Dockrill, *The Mirage of Power*, Vol. 2: *British Foreign Policy 1914–1922* (London and Boston: Routledge & Kegan Paul, 1972), p. 209.
5   H. V. F. Winstone, *Gertrude Bell* (London: Jonathan Cape, 1978), p. 162.

CHAPTER 23

1   Roger Adelson, *Mark Sykes: Portrait of an Amateur* (London: Jonathan Cape, 1975), p. 187.
2   Ibid., p. 189.
3   *Secret Despatches from Arabia by T. E. Lawrence* (The Golden Cockerel Press), p. 69.
4   C. Ernest Dawn, *From Ottomanism to Arabism: Essays on the Origins of Arab Nationalism* (Urbana, Chicago and London: University of Illinois Press, 1973), p. 30.
5   Elie Kedourie, *In the Anglo-Arab Labyrinth: The McMahon-Husayn Correspondence and its Interpreters 1914–1939* (Cambridge: Cambridge University Press, 1976), p. 75.
6   Ibid., p. 77.

7   Ibid., p. 78.
8   Elie Kedourie, *The Chatham House Version and Other Middle Eastern Studies* (London: Weidenfeld & Nicolson, 1970), p. 14.
9   Kew. Public Record Office. Kitchener Papers. 30/57 48. Document RR 26.
10 London. House of Lords Record Office. Beaverbrook Collection. Lloyd George Papers. F—205—3. Document 17.
11 Karl Baedeker, *Palestine and Syria: With Routes through Mesopotamia and Babylon and the Island of Cyprus: Handbook for Travellers*, 5th edn, remodelled and augmented (Leipzig: Karl Baedeker, 1912), p. 157.
12 Kew. Public Record Office. Kitchener Papers. 30/57 47. Document QQ46.
13 These and similar quotations are assembled in Elie Kedourie, *England and the Middle East: The Destruction of the Ottoman Empire, 1914—1921* (Hassocks, Sussex: Harvester Press, 1978), p. 69.
14 Ibid.
15 Adelson, *Sykes*, p. 189.
16 Kedourie, *Chatham House*, p. 15.
17 Sherif Hussein's second note to Sir Henry McMahon, 9 September 1915.
18 John Presland (pseudonym for Gladys Skelton), *Deedes Bey: A Study of Sir Wyndham Deedes 1883—1923* (London: Macmillan, 1942), pp. 244—5.
19 University of Durham. Sudan Archive. Gilbert Clayton Papers. 470/2.
20 Ronald Sanders, *The High Walls of Jerusalem: A History of the Balfour Declaration and the Birth of the British Mandate for Palestine* (New York: Holt, Rinehart & Winston, 1983), p. 253.
21 Dawn, *Ottomanism*, p. 115.
22 Kedourie, *Anglo-Arab Labyrinth*, p. 108.
23 Presland, *Deedes Bey*, p. 247.
24 Kedourie, *Anglo-Arab Labyrinth*, pp. 119—20.
25 Ibid., p. 121.
26 Kew. Public Record Office. Kitchener Papers. 30/57 48. Document RR8.

CHAPTER 24

1   Roger Adelson, *Mark Sykes: Portrait of an Amateur* (London: Jonathan Cape, 1975), pp. 196—7.
2   Ibid., p. 199.
3   Jukka Nevakivi, "Lord Kitchener and the Partition of the Ottoman Empire, 1915—1916," in K. Bourne and D. C. Watt (eds), *Studies in International History* (London: Longman, 1967), p. 328; Philip Magnus, *Kitchener: Portrait of an Imperialist* (Harmondsworth: Penguin, 1968), pp. 374—5.
4   Oxford. St Antony's College. Middle East Centre. Mark Sykes Papers. DS 42.1.
5   Christopher M. Andrew and A. S. Kanya-Forstner, *The Climax of French Imperial Expansion: 1914—1924* (Stanford: Stanford University Press, 1981), p. 66.
6   Ibid., p. 75.
7   Ibid., pp. 75—7; St Antony's College. Middle East Centre. Mark Sykes Papers. DR 588.25. Extrait de la "Revue Hebdomadaire." Etienne Flandin, "Nos droits en Syrie et en Palestine."
8   Andrew and Kanya-Forstner, *French Imperial Expansion*, p. 89.
9   Marian Kent, *Oil and Empire: British Policy and Mesopotamian Oil, 1900—1920* (London and Basingstoke: Macmillan Press for the London School of Economics, 1976), p. 122.
10 Andrew and Kanya-Forstner, *French Imperial Expansion*, p. 93.
11 Ibid., p. 96.

12 Oxford. St Antony's College. Middle East Centre. Mark Sykes Papers. DS 42.1.
13 Adelson, *Sykes*, p. 200.
14 Oxford. St Antony's College. Middle East Centre. Hubert Young Papers. Notes for Lecture at Military Staff College.
15 Margaret FitzHerbert, *The Man Who Was Greenmantle: A Biography of Aubrey Herbert* (London: John Murray, 1983), p. 173.
16 Adelson, *Sykes*, pp. 202 *et seq.*
17 Andrew and Kanya-Forstner, *French Imperial Expansion*, p. 101.
18 C. J. Lowe and M. L. Dockrill, *The Mirage of Power*, Vol. 2: *British Foreign Policy 1914–1922* (London and Boston: Routledge & Kegan Paul, 1972), pp. 228–9.
19 Ibid.; Adelson, *Sykes*, pp. 202, *et seq.*
20 Adelson, *Sykes*, pp. 202 *et seq.*
21 Ronald Sanders, *The High Walls of Jerusalem: A History of the Balfour Declaration and the Birth of the British Mandate for Palestine* (New York: Holt, Rinehart & Winston, 1983), p. 334.
22 Adelson, *Sykes*, p. 226.
23 Kent, *Oil and Empire*, p. 123.
24 Ibid.

CHAPTER 25

1 The account in the text follows Russell Braddon, *The Siege* (New York: Viking Press, 1969), and standard reference works. For Aubrey Herbert's role, see Margaret FitzHerbert, *The Man Who Was Greenmantle: A Biography of Aubrey Herbert* (London: John Murray, 1983), pp. 169 *et seq.*

CHAPTER 26

1 Frank G. Weber, *Eagles on the Crescent: Germany, Austria, and the Diplomacy of the Turkish Alliance 1914–1918* (Ithaca and London: Cornell University Press, 1970), pp. 100–6.
2 Oxford. St Antony's College. Middle East Centre. Mark Sykes Papers. DR 588.25.
3 Sukru Elekdag, ambassador of the Turkish Republic, letter to the editor, *New York Times*, 11 May 1983, p. 22.
4 Stanford J. Shaw and Ezel Kural Shaw, *History of the Ottoman Empire and Modern Turkey*, Vol. 2: *Reform, Revolution, and Republic: The Rise of Modern Turkey, 1808–1975* (Cambridge: Cambridge University Press, 1977), pp. 314 *et seq.*
5 Ulrich Trumpener, *Germany and the Ottoman Empire 1914–1918* (Princeton: Princeton University Press, 1968), p. 203.
6 Ibid., p. 208.
7 Ibid., pp. 208–9.
8 Ibid., pp. 209–10.
9 Ibid., p. 212.
10 Ibid., pp. 213–16.
11 Ibid., p. 213.
12 Ibid., p. 213.
13 Ibid., p. 225.
14 Sukru Elekdag, "Armenians vs. Turks: The View from Istanbul," *Wall Street Journal*, 21 September 1983, p. 33.
15 Firuz Kazemzadeh, *The Struggle for Transcaucasia (1917–1921)* (New York: Philosophical Library, and Oxford: George Ronald, 1951), pp. 27–30.

CHAPTER 27

1 H. Montgomery Hyde, *Carson* (London: William Heinemann, 1953), p. 390.
2 Trevor Royle, *The Kitchener Enigma* (London: Michael Joseph, 1985), pp. 355 *et seq.*
3 Ibid., p. 373.
4 "Exposed: The Blunder that Killed Lord Kitchener," *The Sunday Times*, 22 September 1985, p. 13. See also George H. Cassar, *Kitchener: Architect of Victory* (London: William Kimber, 1977), p. 478. But another survivor claimed that Kitchener was not wearing an overcoat; see Philip Warner, *Kitchener: The Man Behind the Legend* (London: Hamish Hamilton, 1985), p. 199.

CHAPTER 28

1 John Presland (pseudonym for Gladys Skelton), *Deedes Bey: A Study of Sir Wyndham Deedes 1883–1923* (London: Macmillan, 1942), p. 263.
2 C. Ernest Dawn, *From Ottomanism to Arabism: Essays on the Origins of Arab Nationalism* (Urbana, Chicago and London: University of Illinois Press, 1973), p. 33.
3 Kew. Public Record Office. Kitchener Papers. Foreign Office 882. Vol. 19. AB/16/5.
4 Oxford. St Antony's College. Middle East Centre. Mark Sykes Papers. DR 588 (DS 244.4).
5 University of Durham. Sudan Archive. Gilbert Clayton Papers. 470/4.
6 Majid Khadduri, "Aziz 'Ali Al-Misri and the Arab Nationalist Movement," in Albert Hourani (ed.), *Middle Eastern Affairs: Number Four*, St Antony's Papers, no. 17 (London: Oxford University Press, 1965), pp. 140–63, and pp. 154–5.
7 George Antonius, *The Arab Awakening: The Story of the Arab National Movement* (New York: Capricorn Books, 1965), p. 153.
8 Dawn, *Ottomanism*, p. 47.
9 *The Memoirs of Sir Ronald Storrs* (New York: G. P. Putnam's Sons, 1937), p. 167.
10 Ibid., p. 168.
11 Ibid., p. 167.
12 Elie Kedourie, *In the Anglo-Arab Labyrinth: The McMahon-Husayn Correspondence and its Interpreters 1914–1939* (Cambridge: Cambridge University Press, 1976), p. 201.
13 Oxford. St Antony's College. Middle East Centre. Mark Sykes Papers. DR 588 (DS 244.4).
14 Ibid.
15 Bernard Lewis, *The Middle East and the West* (New York and London: Harper Torchbooks), p. 9.
16 The account of Brémond's activities is based on General Ed. Brémond, *Le Hedjaz dans la guerre mondiale* (Paris: Payot, 1931).
17 Major Sir Hubert Young, *The Independent Arab* (London: John Murray, 1933).
18 Desmond Stewart, *T. E. Lawrence* (New York and London: Harper & Row, 1977), p. 148.
19 The account of Lawrence's activities that follows is based principally on Stewart, *Lawrence*; Young, *The Independent Arab*; and Lawrence's writings.
20 *The Diaries of Parker Pasha*, ed. by H. V. F. Winstone (London and New York: Quartet Books, 1983), p. 158.
21 Oxford. St Antony's College. Middle East Centre. T. E. Lawrence Papers. DS 244.4.
22 London. Imperial War Museum. T. E. Lawrence Papers. 69/48/2.

CHAPTER 29

1 Robert Blake, *The Unknown Prime Minister: The Life and Times of Andrew Bonar Law 1858–1918* (London: Eyre & Spottiswoode, 1955), p. 290.
2 Milner's responsibility for the war is emphasized in Thomas Pakenham, *The Boer War* (New York: Random House, 1979).
3 Norman Stone, *Europe Transformed 1878–1919* (London: Fontana Paperbacks, 1983), p. 366.
4 A. J. P. Taylor, *The First World War: An Illustrated History* (London: Hamish Hamilton, 1963), p. 103.
5 Kenneth O. Morgan, *Lloyd George* (London: Weidenfeld & Nicolson, 1974), p. 92.
6 Blake, *The Unknown Prime Minister*, p. 294.
7 Ibid., p. 297.
8 *Lord Riddell's War Diary 1914–1918* (London: Ivor Nicholson & Watson, 1933), p. 334.
9 A. J. P. Taylor, *English History 1914–1945* (Oxford: Clarendon Press, 1965), p. 73.
10 Stephen Roskill, *Hankey: Man of Secrets*, Vol. 1: *1877–1918* (London: Collins, 1970), p. 339.
11 Terence H. O'Brien, *Milner* (London: Constable, 1979), p. 79.
12 John Grigg, *Lloyd George: From Peace to War 1912–1916* (London: Methuen, 1985), p. 489.
13 Roskill, *Hankey*, pp. 422–3.
14 Ibid., p. 436.
15 Ibid., p. 458.
16 Theodore Zeldin, *France 1848–1945*, Vol. 1: *Ambition, Love and Politics* (Oxford: Clarendon Press, 1973), pp. 698 *et seq.*
17 David Robin Watson, *Georges Clemenceau: A Political Biography* (London: Eyre Methuen, 1974), p. 269.
18 Ibid., p. 90.
19 Winston S. Churchill, *Great Contemporaries* (London: Fontana, 1959), pp. 248–9.
20 Watson, *Clemenceau*, p. 127.
21 Zeldin, *France*, p. 703.
22 Watson, *Clemenceau*, p. 28.
23 Roskill, *Hankey*, p. 466.

CHAPTER 30

1 *Encyclopaedia Britannica*, 12th edn, s.v. "Turkish Campaigns (I)," an article written by Major Franz Carl Endres.
2 Quoted in Y. T. Kurat, "How Turkey Drifted into World War I," in K. C. Bourne and D. C. Watt (eds), *Studies in International History* (London: Longman, 1967), pp. 291–315 at p. 294.
3 Harvey A. De Weerd, "Churchill, Lloyd George, Clemenceau: The Emergence of the Civilian," in Edward Meade Earle (ed.), *Makers of Modern Strategy: Military Thought from Machiavelli to Hitler* (Princeton: Princeton University Press, 1943), pp. 287–305 at pp. 290–1; James T. Shotwell, *The Great Decision* (New York: Macmillan, 1944), pp. 8–9.
4 A. J. P. Taylor, *English History 1914–1945* (Oxford: Clarendon Press, 1965), p. 34.
5 Sheila Fitzpatrick, *The Russian Revolution* (Oxford and New York: Oxford University Press, 1982), p. 10; Alec Nove, *An Economic History of the U. S. S. R.* (Harmondsworth: Penguin, 1982), pp. 20–5; *Encyclopaedia Britannica*, 11th edn, s.v. "Russia."

6 Hugh Seton-Watson, *The Russian Empire 1801–1917* (Oxford: Clarendon Press, 1967), pp. 704–5.
7 Norman Stone, *The Eastern Front 1914–1917* (London: Hodder & Stoughton, 1975), p. 288; Michael Kettle, *The Allies and the Russian Collapse March 1917–March 1918* (London: André Deutsch, 1981), p. 98.
8 Gordon A. Craig, *Germany 1866–1945* (Oxford and New York: Oxford University Press, 1978), p. 375.
9 Ulrich Trumpener, *Germany and the Ottoman Empire 1914–1918* (Princeton: Princeton University Press, 1968), p. 153.
10 Bertram D. Wolfe, *Three Who Made a Revolution: A Biographical History,* 4th rev. edn (New York: Dell, Delta Books, 1964), pp. 620 *et seq.*; Edmund Wilson, *To the Finland Station: A Study in the Writing and Acting of History* (Garden City, NY: Doubleday Anchor Books, 1953), pp. 445 *et seq.*
11 The account that follows is based on Z. A. B. Zeman and W. B. Scharlau, *The Merchant of Revolution: The Life of Alexander Israel Helphand (Parvus) 1867–1924* (London: Oxford University Press, 1965); and on the documents from the German archives reproduced in Z. A. B. Zeman (ed.), *Germany and the Revolution in Russia 1915–1918* (London: Oxford University Press, 1958).
12 Zeman and Scharlau, *The Merchant of Revolution*, p. 136.
13 Zeman (ed.), *Germany*, p. 1.
14 Zeman and Scharlau, *The Merchant of Revolution*, p. 155.
15 Ibid., p. 154.
16 Ibid., pp. 156–7.
17 Ibid., p. 158.
18 Leonard Schapiro, *The Russian Revolutions of 1917: The Origins of Modern Communism* (New York: Basic Books, 1984), p. 95.
19 Kettle, *The Russian Collapse*, pp. 13–35.
20 Norman Stone, *Europe Transformed 1878–1919* (London: Fontana, 1983), p. 371.
21 Edward Hallett Carr, *The Bolshevik Revolution 1917–1923*, Vol. 1 (New York: Macmillan, 1951), p. 70.
22 Zeman (ed.), *Germany*, pp. 35–6.
23 *Lord Riddell's War Diary 1914–1918* (London: Ivor Nicholson & Watson, 1933), p. 82.
24 Taylor, *English History*, pp. 94–5.

CHAPTER 31

1 Arthur S. Link, *Wilson: Campaigns for Progressivism and Peace, 1916–1917* (Princeton: Princeton University Press, 1965), pp. 179–80.
2 Ibid., pp. 201–3.
3 Charles Seymour, *The Intimate Papers of Colonel House*, Vol. 3 (Boston: Houghton Mifflin, 1928), p. 51.
4 John Maynard Keynes, *The Economic Consequences of the Peace* (New York: Harcourt, Brace & Howe, 1920), p. 42.
5 *War Memoirs of David Lloyd George*, Vol. 3: *1916–1917* (Boston: Little, Brown, 1934), p. 64.
6 *The Papers of Woodrow Wilson*, ed. by Arthur S. Link *et al.*, Vol. 41: *January 24–April 6, 1917* (Princeton: Princeton University Press, 1983), p. 438.
7 Ibid., p. 462.
8 Ibid., p. 520.
9 Ibid., p. 525.
10 Ibid.
11 Seymour, *Papers of Colonel House*, Vol. 3, p. 45.

12 Ronald Steel, *Walter Lippmann, and the American Century* (Boston and Toronto: Little Brown and Company, 1980), p. 133.
13 Seymour, *Papers of Colonel House*, Vol. 3, p. 323.
14 Ibid.
15 Seymour, *Papers of Colonel House*, Vol. 2, p. 415.
16 Steel, *Lippmann*, p. 136.
17 Laurence Evans, *United States Policy and the Partition of Turkey, 1914–1924* (Baltimore: The Johns Hopkins University Press, 1965), p. 39.
18 Ibid., pp. 40–2.
19 Lawrence E. Gelfand, *The Inquiry: American Preparation for Peace, 1917–1919* (New Haven: Yale University Press, 1963), p. 47.
20 Ibid., p. 273.
21 Ibid., pp. 60–2.
22 Ibid., pp. 240–50.
23 Ibid., pp. 250–52.
24 Seymour, *Papers of Colonel House*, Vol. 3, p. 39.
25 Wilson, *Papers*, Vol. 41, pp. 537–8.
26 Gelfand, *The Inquiry*, p. 173.

CHAPTER 32

 1 Roger Adelson, *Mark Sykes: Portrait of an Amateur* (London: Jonathan Cape, 1975), p. 222.
 2 Lord Beaverbrook, *Men and Power 1917–1918* (London: Hutchinson, 1956), p. 47.
 3 Ibid., p. 48.
 4 *War Memoirs of David Lloyd George*, Vol. 4: *1917* (Boston: Little, Brown, 1934), p. 68.
 5 Ibid., p. 66.
 6 Ibid., p. 432.
 7 Ibid., pp. 573–4.
 8 Martin Gilbert, *Winston S. Churchill: Companion Volume*, Vol. 4, Part 1: *January 1917–June 1919* (Boston: Houghton Mifflin, 1978), p. 59.
 9 Beaverbrook, *Men and Power*, p. 141.
10 Martin Gilbert, *Winston S. Churchill*, Vol. 4: *1916–1922, The Stricken World* (Boston: Houghton Mifflin, 1975), p. 18.
11 Gilbert, *Churchill: Companion Volume*, p. 99.
12 Gilbert, *Churchill*: Vol. 4, p. 30.
13 Gilbert, *Churchill: Companion Volume*, p. 101.
14 Ibid., p. 108.
15 London. House of Lords Record Office. Beaverbrook Collection. Lloyd George Papers. F–6–1. Documents 1 through 16 (b).
16 Gilbert, *Churchill: Companion Volume*, p. 60.
17 Elie Kedourie, *In the Anglo-Arab Labyrinth: The McMahon-Husayn Correspondence and its Interpreters 1914–1939* (Cambridge: Cambridge University Press, 1976), p. 159.
18 David Lloyd George, *Memoirs of the Peace Conference* (New Haven: Yale University Press, 1939), Vol. 2, p. 721.
19 Ibid., p. 722.
20 Barbara W. Tuchman, *Bible and Sword: England and Palestine from the Bronze Age to Balfour* (New York: Funk & Wagnalls, 1956), p. 121.
21 Ronald Sanders, *The High Walls of Jerusalem: A History of the Balfour Declaration and the Birth of the British Mandate for Palestine* (New York: Holt, Rinehart & Winston, 1983), p. 5.

22 Sir Charles Webster, *The Foreign Policy of Palmerston, 1830–1841: Britain, the Liberal Movement and the Eastern Question* (New York: Humanities Press, 1969), Vol. 2, p. 761. See also Leonard Stein, *The Balfour Declaration* (London: Valentine Mitchell, 1961), pp. 5–9, and Tuchman, *Bible and Sword*, pp. 80–224.

23 H. H. Asquith, *Letters to Venetia Stanley*, ed. by Michael and Eleanor Brock (Oxford and New York: Oxford University Press, 1982), p. 406.

24 Ibid., p. 477.

25 Ibid.

26 Ibid.

27 Ibid., pp. 477–8.

28 Isaiah Friedman, *The Question of Palestine, 1914–1918, British-Jewish-Arab Relations* (London: Routledge & Kegan Paul, 1973), p. 129.

29 Alex Bein, *Theodore Herzl: A Biography*, trans. by Maurice Samuel (Philadelphia: Jewish Publication Society of America, 1941), pp. 411 *et seq.*

30 London. House of Lords Record Office. Beaverbrook Collection. Lloyd George Papers. G–33–1. Documents 14 through 16.

CHAPTER 33

1 Isaiah Friedman, *The Question of Palestine, 1914–1918, British-Jewish-Arab Relations* (London: Routledge & Kegan Paul, 1973), p. 123.

2 Vladimir Jabotinsky, *The Story of the Jewish Legion*, trans. by Samuel Katz (New York: Bernard Ackerman, 1945), p. 31.

3 Joseph B. Schechtman, *Rebel and Statesman: The Vladimir Jabotinsky Story, the Early Years* (New York: Thomas Yoseloff, 1956), pp. 204–7 assigns the major share of the credit to Trumpeldor.

4 Jabotinsky, *The Jewish Legion*, p. 66.

5 Rehovot, Israel. Weizmann Archives. Memorandum of 7 February 1917 meeting; Roger Adelson, *Mark Sykes: Portrait of an Amateur* (London: Jonathan Cape, 1975), p. 226.

6 L. S. Amery, *My Political Life*, Vol. 2: *War and Peace: 1914–1929* (London: Hutchinson, 1953), p. 115.

7 George Antonius, *The Arab Awakening: The Story of the Arab National Movement* (New York: Capricorn Books, 1965), p. 412.

8 *The Leo Amery Diaries*, Vol 1: *1896–1929*, ed. by John Barnes and David Nicholson (London: Hutchinson, 1980), p. 137.

9 W. K. Hancock, *Smuts: The Sanguine Years, 1870–1919* (Cambridge: Cambridge University Press, 1962), p. 426.

10 Lord Beaverbrook, *Men and Power 1917–1918* (London: Hutchinson, 1956), pp. xxiv–xxv; A. J. P. Taylor, *English History 1914–1945* (Oxford: Clarendon Press, 1965), p. 82.

11 *War Memoirs of Lloyd George*, Vol. 4: *1917* (Boston, Little, Brown, 1934), p. 90.

12 Ibid., pp. 66–7.

13 *Selections from the Smuts Papers*, Vol. 3: *June 1910–November 1918*, ed. by W. K. Hancock and Jean Van Der Poel (Cambridge: Cambridge University Press, 1966), p. 465.

14 Ibid., p. 500.

15 Hancock, *Smuts*, pp. 434–5.

16 *Selections from the Smuts Papers*, Vol. 5: *September 1919–November 1934*, ed. by Jean Van Der Poel (Cambridge: Cambridge University Press, 1973), p. 25.

17 Ibid., p. 18.

18 Hancock, *Smuts*, pp. 434−5.
19 *The Smuts Papers*, Vol. 4: *November 1918−August 1919*, ed. by W. K. Hancock and Jean Van Der Poel (Cambridge: Cambridge University Press, 1966), pp. 26−7.
20 Amery, *My Political Life*, p. 116.

CHAPTER 34

1 Rehovot, Israel. Weizmann Archives. Sacher letter, 2 February 1917; Scott letter, 3 February 1917; Weizmann letter, 3 February 1917.
2 Rehovot, Israel. Weizmann Archives. Memorandum of 7 February 1917 meeting.
3 Ibid.
4 Rehovot, Israel. Weizmann Archives. Notes of 8 February 1918 meeting.
5 Ronald Sanders, *The High Walls of Jerusalem: A History of the Balfour Declaration and the Birth of the British Mandate for Palestine* (New York: Holt, Rinehart & Winston, 1983), p. 466.
6 Roger Adelson, *Mark Sykes: Portrait of an Amateur* (London: Jonathan Cape, 1975), p. 225.
7 Christopher M. Andrew and A. S. Kanya-Forstner, *The Climax of French Imperial Expansion: 1914−1924* (Stanford: Stanford University Press, 1981), p. 124.
8 Adelson, *Sykes*, p. 225.
9 Sanders, *The High Walls of Jerusalem*, p. 493.
10 Rehovot, Israel. Weizmann Archives. Sledmere Papers. Notes of conference held at 10 Downing St, 3 April 1917.
11 Ibid.
12 Ibid.
13 Adelson, *Sykes*, p. 227.
14 Oxford. St Antony's College. Middle East Centre. Mark Sykes Papers. DS 149.
15 Ibid. DS 149 (DR 588.25).
16 Kingston upon Hull. University of Hull. Brynmor Jones Library. Mark Sykes Papers. DDSY(2). 12−7.
17 Oxford. St Antony's College. Middle East Centre. Mark Sykes Papers. DS 149; Adelson, *Sykes*, p. 229.
18 Adelson, *Sykes*, p. 231.
19 Oxford. St Antony's College. Middle East Centre. Mark Sykes Papers. DR 588.25.
20 Ibid. DR 588.25 (DS 42.1).
21 Adelson, *Sykes*, p. 229.
22 Rehovot, Israel. Weizmann Archives. Sledmere Papers. 14 August 1917.
23 *The Leo Amery Diaries*, Vol. 1: *1896−1929*, ed. by John Barnes and David Nicholson (London: Hutchinson, 1980), p. 170.
24 Kenneth Rose, *The Later Cecils* (New York and London: Harper & Row, 1975), p. 153.
25 Philip Guedalla, *Men of Affairs* (London: Hodder & Stoughton, n. d.), p. 193.
26 Oxford. St Antony's College. Middle East Centre. Mark Sykes Papers. DR 588.25.
27 Andrew and Kanya-Forstner, *French Imperial Expansion*, p. 129.
28 Sanders, *The High Walls of Jerusalem*, p. 534.
29 Martin Gilbert, *Winston S. Churchill: Companion Volume*, Vol. 4, Part 1: *January 1917−June 1919* (Boston: Houghton Mifflin, 1978), p. 107.
30 David Lloyd George, *Memoirs of the Peace Conference* (New Haven: Yale University Press, 1939), Vol. 2, p. 733.

31 There were 130,000 purchasers of the shekel that signified adherence, according to Leonard Stein, *The Balfour Declaration* (London: Valentine Mitchell, 1961), p. 66. The world Jewish population was estimated to be 11,500,000 by the American Jewish Year-Book for 1909–10. *Encyclopaedia Britannica*, 11th edn., s.v. "Jews."

32 Isiah Friedman, *The Question of Palestine, 1914–1918, British-Jewish-Arab Relations* (London: Routledge & Kegan Paul, 1973), p. 178.

33 Walter Laqueur, *A History of Zionism* (New York: Holt, Rinehart & Winston, 1972), p. 184.

34 Rehovot, Israel. Weizmann Archives. Sir R. Graham letter to General Wingate, 21 September 1917.

35 *Amery Diaries*, p. 170.

36 Stein, *Balfour Declaration*, p. 529; Laqueur, *Zionism*, p. 181.

37 *Trial and Error: The Autobiography of Chaim Weizmann* (New York: Harper, 1949), p. 179.

38 London. House of Lords Record Office. Beaverbrook Collection. Lloyd George Papers. F–3–2–34.

39 Ibid.

40 Weizmann, *Trial and Error*, p. 208.

41 Lloyd George, *Peace Conference*, Vol. 2, p. 669.

42 Ibid., Vol. 3, p. 737.

43 Oxford. St Antony's College. Middle East Centre. Balfour Declaration.

44 Ibid.

45 Lloyd George, *Peace Conference*, Vol. 2, p. 723.

46 Ibid., p. 737.

47 Ezekiel Rabinowitz, *Justice Louis D. Brandeis: The Zionist Chapter of His Life* (New York: Philosophical Library, 1968), p. 6.

48 Michael E. Parrish, *Felix Frankfurter and His Times—The Reform Years* (New York: Free Press, and London: Collier Macmillan, 1982), p. 135.

49 Leonard Baker, *Brandeis and Frankfurter: A Dual Biography* (New York: Harper & Row, 1984), p. 74.

50 Ibid.

51 Rabinowitz, *Brandeis*, p. 4.

52 Alpheus Thomas Mason, *Brandeis: A Free Man's Life* (New York: Viking Press, 1946), p.446.

53 *Letters of Louis D. Brandeis*, Vol. 4: *(1916–1921) : Mr. Justice Brandeis*, ed. by Melvin I. Urofsky and David W. Levy (Albany: State University of New York Press, 1975), p. 355.

54 *Amery Diaries*, p. 189.

55 *Selections from the Smuts Papers*, Vol. 3: *June 1910–November 1918*, ed. by W. K. Hancock and Jean Van Der Poel (Cambridge: Cambridge University Press, 1966), p. 503.

CHAPTER 35

1 Briton Cooper Busch, *Britain, India, and the Arabs, 1914–1921* (Berkeley and London: University of California Press, 1971), p. 121.

2 Ibid., pp. 139–40.

3 Desmond Stewart, *T. E. Lawrence* (New York and London: Harper & Row, 1977), pp. 166–8.

4 Kew. Public Record Office. Arab Bureau Papers. Foreign Office 882. Vol. 18. Document TU/17/3.

5 Oxford. St Antony's College. Middle East Centre. Allenby Papers. DS 244.4.

6 *War Memoirs of David Lloyd George*, Vol. 6: *1918* (Boston: Little, Brown, 1937), p. 203.

7 General Ed. Brémond, *Le Hedjaz dans la guerre mondiale* (Paris: Payot, 1931), p. 9.
8 David Holden and Richard Johns, *The House of Saud: The Rise and Fall of the Most Powerful Dynasty in the Arab World* (New York: Holt, Rinehart & Winston, 1981), p. 53.
9 Oxford. St Antony's College. Middle East Centre. William Yale Papers. DS 149, DS 244.4, DS 126.1.
10 *War Memoirs of David Lloyd George*, Vol. 4: *1917* (Boston: Little, Brown, 1934), p. 98.
11 Ibid., p. 573.

CHAPTER 36
1 Oxford. St Antony's College. Middle East Centre. Mark Sykes Papers. DR 588.25.
2 Ibid. (DR 588.25) DS 42.1.
3 Ibid. Sir Gilbert F. Clayton Letter 3−8−16. DT 107.2 CG (DS 42.1).
4 Rehovot, Israel. Weizmann Archives. Clayton to Deedes, 6 September 1917.
5 Oxford. St Antony's College. Middle East Centre. Mark Sykes papers. (DR 588.25) DS 42.1.
6 Ibid. (DR 588.25) DS 149.
7 Ibid. (DR 588.25) DT 82.97.
8 Kew. Public Record Office. War Cabinet, Middle East Committee. CAB 27/23, p. 154.
9 *Trial and Error: The Autobiography of Chaim Weizmann* (New York: Harper 1949), p. 181.
10 Roger Adelson, *Mark Sykes: Portrait of an Amateur* (London: Jonathan Cape, 1975), p. 264.
11 Kingston upon Hull. University of Hull. Brynmor Jones Library. Mark Sykes Papers. 11−61.
12 Rehovot, Israel. Weizmann Archives. Clayton to Sykes, 15 December 1917.
13 Ibid. Sykes to Clayton, 14 November 1917.
14 Ibid. Sykes to Clayton, 1 December 1917.
15 Ibid. Sykes to Picot, 12 December 1917.
16 Oxford. St Antony's College. Middle East Centre. Mark Sykes Papers. DS 42.1. DR 588.25.
17 Ibid. (DS 149) DS 161.
18 Rehovot, Israel. Weizmann Archives. Clayton to Sykes, 15 December 1917.
19 Ibid. Wingate to Allenby, 16 December 1917.
20 Oxford. St Antony's College. Middle East Centre. William Yale Papers. DS 125.52, DS 126.1, DS 151.92.
21 Kew. Public Record Office. Arab Bureau Papers. Foreign Office 882. Vol. 17. Document 19A, pp. 4−5.
22 Ibid. Vol. 24. Document 36757.
23 Rehovot, Israel. Weizmann Archives. Deedes to Foreign Office, 19 November 1917.
24 Oxford. St Antony's College. Middle East Centre. Mark Sykes Papers. (DS 125) DS 125.3.01.
25 Ibid. DS 125.
26 Durham. University of Durham. Sudan Archive. Clayton Key Papers. G//S 513. File 1.
27 Oxford. St Antony's College. Middle East Centre. Mark Sykes Papers. (DS 125) DS 149.
28 Kingston upon Hull. University of Hull. Brynmor Jones Library. Mark Sykes Papers. 11−101.

29 Kew. Public Record Office. War Cabinet, Middle East Committee. CAB 27/23, p. 132.

30 Oxford. St Antony's College. Middle East Centre. Feisal Papers. B−31.

31 *The Letters and Papers of Chaim Weizmann*, Vol. 8, Series A: *November 1917−October 1918*, ed. by Dvorah Barzilay and Barnet Litvinoff (Jerusalem: Israel University Press, 1977), p. 210.

32 Reprinted in *Palestine Papers 1917−1922 Seeds of Conflict*, compiled and annotated by Doreen Ingrams (London: John Murray, 1972), p. 33.

33 Ibid., p. 37; Kew. Public Record Office. Arab Bureau Papers. Foreign Office 882. Vol. 24. Document 105824.

34 Kew. Public Record Office. Arab Bureau Papers. Foreign Office 882. Vol. 24. Document 92392; Ingrams, *Palestine Papers*, pp. 24−6.

35 *The Leo Amery Diaries*, Vol. 1: *1896−1929*, ed. by John Barnes and David Nicholson (London: Hutchinson, 1980), p. 206.

36 Briton Cooper Busch, *Britain, India, and the Arabs, 1914−1921* (Berkeley and London: University of California Press, 1971), p. 156; H. V. F. Winstone, *Gertrude Bell* (London: Jonathan Cape, 1978), p. 202.

37 Oxford. St Antony's College. Middle East Centre. Mark Sykes Papers. DR 588.25.

38 Ibid. DR 588.

39 Ibid. (DR 588.25) DS 149.

40 Kew. Public Record Office. War Cabinet, Middle East Committee. CAB 27/23, pp. 127−8.

41 Kew. Public Record Office. Arab Bureau Papers. Foreign Office 882. Vol. 18. (TU/15/5 (6).

42 Ibid. Vol. 20. M1/19/3.

43 Ibid. Vol. 20. HM/19/1.

44 Ibid. Vol. 17. Document 26.

45 Colonel R. Meinertzhagen, *Middle East Diary 1917−1956* (London: Cresset Press, 1959), p. 28.

46 Oxford. St Antony's College. Middle East Centre. Mark Sykes Papers. DR 588.

47 Liman von Sanders, *Five Years in Turkey* (Annapolis: United States Naval Institute, 1927), pp. 306−20.

48 Oxford. St Antony's College. Middle East Centre. Feisal Papers. 0−14.

49 Durham. University of Durham. Sudan Archive. Reginald Wingate Papers. 149/7/1−109.

50 Kew. Public Record Office. Arab Bureau Papers. Foreign Office 882. Vol. 17. Document 33.

51 Ingrams, *Palestine Papers*, p. 33.

52 Oxford. St Antony's College. Middle East Centre. Mark Sykes Papers. DS 588.25.

53 Ibid. DR 588.25.

54 Ibid.

55 Kew. Public Record Office. Arab Bureau Papers. Foreign Office 882. Vol. 17, pp. 97−103.

56 Christopher M. Andrew and A. S. Kanya-Forstner, *The Climax of French Imperial Expansion: 1914−1924* (Stanford: Stanford University Press, 1981), p. 162.

CHAPTER 37

1 The account in the text owes much to the lively narrative of Howard M. Sachar, *The Emergence of the Middle East: 1914−1924* (New York: Alfred A.

Knopf, 1969) at pp. 238 *et seq.* as well as to the eyewitness account in the *Encyclopaedia Britannica*, 12th edn, s.v. "Turkish Campaigns."

2 Kew. Public Record Office. Arab Bureau Papers. Foreign Office 883. Vol. 17, pp. 104–5.

3 *The Leo Amery Diaries*, Vol. 1: *1896–1929*, ed. by John Barnes and David Nicholson (London: Hutchinson, 1980), p. 241.

4 Oxford. Bodleian Library. Milner Papers. Palestine. 140/64.

5 Ibid. 140/54.

6 Ibid. 140/56.

7 Kew. Public Record Office. Arab Bureau Papers. Foreign Office 882. Vol. 24. Document 36757.

8 Oxford. St Antony's College. Middle East Centre. Allenby Papers. DS 244.4.

9 Durham. University of Durham. Sudan Archive. Reginald Wingate Papers. 149/9/1–158.

10 Ibid. 150/1/1–105.

11 Oxford. Bodleian Library. Milner Papers. Palestine. 140/64.

12 Durham. University of Durham. Sudan Archive. Reginald Wingate Papers. 150/1/1–105.

13 Kew. Public Record Office. Arab Bureau Papers. Foreign Office 882. Vol. 17, pp. 119–20.

14 Oxford. St Antony's College. Middle East Centre. Allenby Papers. DS 244.4.

15 Ibid.

16 Kew. Public Record Office. War Cabinet, Eastern Committee. CAB 27/24, pp. 148–52.

17 Durham. University of Durham. Sudan Archive. Reginald Wingate Papers. 150/2/1–112.

18 Christopher M. Andrew and A. S. Kanya-Forstner, *The Climax of French Imperial Expansion: 1914–1924* (Stanford: Stanford University Press, 1981), p. 11.

19 Ibid., p. 161.

20 Kew. Public Record Office. War Cabinet, Eastern Committee. CAB 27/24, pp. 148–52.

21 Jukka Nevakivi, *Britain, France and the Arab Middle East 1914–1920* (London: Athlone Press, 1969), p. 72, n. 3.

22 Oxford. St Antony's College. Middle East Centre. Allenby Papers. DS 244.4.

23 W. T. Massey, *Allenby's Final Triumph* (New York: E. P. Dutton, 1920), pp. 18–19.

24 *T. E. Lawrence to His Biographer, Robert Graves* (New York: Doubleday, Doran, 1938), p. 104.

25 Durham. University of Durham. Sudan Archive. Clayton Key Papers. G//S 513. File 1.

26 Oxford. Bodleian Library. Milner Papers. Palestine. 140/21–22.

27 Nevakivi, *Britain, France and the Arab Middle East*, p. 74.

28 Oxford. St Antony's College. Middle East Centre. Mark Sykes Papers. DR 588.25 (DS 42.1).

29 Oxford. St Antony's College. Middle East Centre. David Hogarth Papers. 30 (ii).

30 Kew. Public Record Office. War Cabinet, Eastern Committee. CAB 27/24, p. 186.

31 Ibid., p. 187.

32 Ibid., p. 169.

33 David Lloyd George, *Memoirs of the Peace Conference* (New Haven: Yale University Press, 1939), Vol. 2, pp. 664–5.

34 Ibid., p. 665.

35   *War Memoirs of David Lloyd George*, Vol. 4: *1917* (Boston: Little, Brown, 1934), p. 86.

36   *The Letters and Papers of Chaim Weizmann*, Vol. 8, Series A: *November 1917–October 1918*, ed. by Dvorah Barzilay and Barnet Litvinoff (Jerusalem: Israel University Press, 1977), p. 230.

37   Kew. Public Record Office. War Cabinet, Eastern Committee. CAB 27/24. Minutes of 18 June 1918 meeting.

38   Ibid. Minutes of 18 July 1918 meeting.

39   *The Amery Diaries*, p. 237.

40   London. King's College. Liddell Hart Centre for Military Archives. Allenby Papers. 1–9–21.

41   Kew. Public Record Office. Arab Bureau Papers. Foreign Office 882. Vol. 24. Document 92392.

42   Ibid. Document 123904.

43   Ibid. Document 138908.

44   Kew. Public Record Office. War Cabinet, Eastern Committee. CAB 27/24, pp. 153–61.

45   Durham. University of Durham. Sudan Archive. Reginald Wingate Papers. 150/10/1–137.

46   London. King's College. Liddell Hart Centre for Military Archives. Allenby Papers. 1–9–15.

CHAPTER 38

1   Kew. Public Record Office. Arab Bureau Papers. Foreign Office 882. Vol. 18. Document TU/17/17.

2   Ulrich Trumpener, *Germany and the Ottoman Empire: 1914–1918* (Princeton: Princeton University Press, 1968), p. 167.

3   Frederick Stanwood, *War, Revolution and British Imperialism in Central Asia* (London: Ithaca Press, 1983), pp. 32–3.

4   Marian Kent, *Oil and Empire: British Policy and Mesopotamian Oil 1900–1920* (London and Basingstoke: Macmillan Press for the London School of Economics, 1976), p. 118.

5   Trumpener, *Ottoman Empire*, p. 186.

6   Firuz Kazemzadeh, *The Struggle for Transcaucasia (1917–1921)* (New York: Philosophical Library and Oxford: George Ronald, 1951), p. 135.

7   The account that follows is in large part based on C. H. Ellis, *The Transcaspian Episode: 1918–1919* (London: Hutchinson, 1963); and Richard H. Ullman, *Anglo-Soviet Relations, 1917–1921: Intervention and the War* (Princeton: Princeton University Press, 1961).

8   Stanwood, *Central Asia*, p. 134.

9   Ullman, *Anglo-Soviet Relations*, p. 304.

10   *The Leo Amery Diaries*, Vol. 1: *1896–1929*, ed. by John Barnes and David Nicholson (London: Hutchinson, 1980), p. 188.

11   Ibid., p. 173.

12   Stanwood, *Central Asia*, p. 139.

13   *The Amery Diaries*, p. 173.

14   Ibid., pp. 175–6.

15   Ibid., p. 194.

16   Stanwood, *Central Asia*, pp. 146–7.

17   Ibid.

18   Ullman, *Anglo-Soviet Relations*, pp. 304–5.

19   Trumpener, *Ottoman Empire*, pp. 188–91.

20 Ellis, *Transcaspian Episode*, p. 39; Kazemzadeh, *Transcaucasia*, pp. 135 *et seq*.

21 Durham. University of Durham. Sudan Archive. Reginald Wingate Papers. 149/8/1—93.

22 London. House of Lords Record Office. Beaverbrook Collection. Lloyd George Papers. F—6—1. Document 13.

23 Kazemzadeh, *Transcaucasia*, p. 147.

24 Trumpener, *Ottoman Empire*, p. 193.

25 Ibid.

26 Ibid., p. 194.

27 Ellis, *Transcaspian Episode*, p. 52.

CHAPTER 39

1 Gwynne Dyer, "The Turkish Armistice of 1918: 2—A Lost Opportunity: The Armistice Negotiations of Moudros," *Middle Eastern Studies* (October 1972), p. 315.

2 *The Leo Amery Diaries*, Vol. 1: *1896—1929*, ed. by John Barnes and David Nicholson (London: Hutchinson, 1980), p. 194.

3 Helmut Mejcher, "Oil and British Policy towards Mesopotamia," *Middle Eastern Studies* (October 1972), p. 387.

4 C. J. Lowe and M. L. Dockrill, *The Mirage of Power*, Vol. 3: *The Documents, British Foreign Policy 1902—22* (London and Boston: Routledge & Kegan Paul, 1972), p. 553.

5 Ibid., pp. 553—4.

6 Arthur J. Marder, *From the Dreadnought to Scapa Flow: The Royal Navy in the Fisher Era, 1904—1919*, Vol. 5: *Victory and Aftermath, January 1918—June 1919* (London: Oxford University Press, 1970), p. 37.

7 Gwynne Dyer, "The Turkish Armistice of 1918: 1—The Turkish Decision for a Separate Peace, Autumn, 1918," *Middle Eastern Studies* (May 1972), p. 171, n. 30.

8 Ibid., pp. 148—9.

9 Kew. Public Record Office. Arab Bureau Papers. Foreign Office 882. Vol. 18. Document TU/18/3.

10 Dyer, "The Turkish Armistice: 1," p. 148.

11 Ibid., p. 152.

12 Charles Vere Ferres Townshend, *My Campaign* (New York: James A. McCann, 1920), Vol. 2, pp. 276 *et seq*.

13 Dyer, "The Turkish Armistice: 1," p. 161.

14 *War Memoirs of David Lloyd George*, Vol. 6: *1918* (Boston: Little, Brown, 1937), p. 278.

15 Ibid.

16 Ibid.

17 Stephen Roskill, *Hankey: Man of Secrets*, Vol. 1: *1877—1918* (London: Collins, 1970), pp. 619 *et seq*.

18 David Robin Watson, *Georges Clemenceau: A Political Biography* (London: Eyre Methuen, 1974), p. 371.

19 Dyer, "The Turkish Armistice: 2."

20 Salahi Ramsdan Sonyel, *Turkish Diplomacy, 1918—1923: Mustafa Kemal and the Turkish National Movement* (London and Beverly Hills: SAGE Publications, 1975), p. 3.

21 Erik Jan Zurcher, *The Unionist Factor: The Role of the Committee of Union and Progress in the Turkish National Movement 1905—1926* (Leiden: E. J. Brill, 1984), p. 72.

22 Watson, *Clemenceau*, p. 367.

23 Lloyd George, *War Memoirs*, Vol. 6, pp. 279–80.

24 Roskill, *Hankey*, Vol. 1, p. 609.

25 Lowe and Dockrill, *The Mirage of Power*, Vol. 2, p. 359.

26 *The Letters and Papers of Chaim Weizmann*, Vol. 8, Series A: *November 1917–October 1918*, ed. by Dvorah Barzilay and Barnet Litvinoff (Jerusalem: Israel University Press, 1977), pp. 278–9.

27 Roskill, *Hankey*, Vol. 1, p. 594.

28 Balfour's memorandum, quoted in Elizabeth Monroe, *Britain's Moment in the Middle East: 1914–1971*, rev. edn (Baltimore: The Johns Hopkins University Press, 1981), pp. 50–1.

29 Michael L. Dockrill and J. Douglas Goold, *Peace without Promise: Britain and the Peace Conferences, 1919–1923* (London: Batsford Academic and Educational, 1981), p. 146.

30 Christopher M. Andrew and A. S. Kanya-Forstner, *The Climax of French Imperial Expansion: 1914–1924* (Stanford: Stanford University Press, 1981), p. 172.

31 Briton Cooper Busch, *Britain, India, and the Arabs, 1914–1921* (Berkeley and London: University of California Press, 1971), p. 163.

32 John Darwin, *Britain, Egypt, and the Middle East: Imperial Policy in the Aftermath of War, 1918–1922* (New York: St Martin's Press, 1981), p. 160.

33 London. House of Lords Record Office. Beaverbrook Collection. Lloyd George Papers. F–205–3. Document 9.

34 Ibid. Document 7.

35 David Lloyd George, *Memoirs of the Peace Conference* (New Haven: Yale University Press, 1939), Vol. 2, pp. 665–8.

36 Frances Stevenson, *Lloyd George: A Diary*, ed. by A. J. P. Taylor (New York and London: Harper & Row, 1971), p. 174.

37 London. House of Lords Record Office. Beaverbrook Collection. Lloyd George Papers. F–39–1–10.

38 Ibid. F–205–3. Document 7.

39 Ibid. F–36–6–56.

40 *Lord Riddell's Intimate Diary of the Peace Conference and after: 1918–1923* (New York: Reynal & Hitchcock, 1934), p. 25.

41 Desmond Stewart, *T. E. Lawrence* (New York and London: Harper & Row, 1977), p. 133; T. E. Lawrence, *Seven Pillars of Wisdom* (Garden City, New York: Doubleday, Doran & Company, Inc., 1935), ch. 6.

42 William H. McNeill, *Plagues and Peoples* (Garden City, NY: Doubleday Anchor Books, 1976), p. 255.

43 *Encyclopaedia Britannica*, 14th edn, s.v. "Influenza"; *Encyclopaedia Britannica*, 12th edn, s.v. "Turkish Campaigns."

CHAPTER 40

1 Martin Gilbert, *Winston S. Churchill: Companion Volume*, Vol. 4, Part 1: *January 1917–June 1919* (Boston: Houghton Mifflin, 1978), p. 412.

2 Kenneth O. Morgan, *Lloyd George* (London: Weidenfeld & Nicolson, 1974), p. 126.

3 Charles Loch Mowat, *Britain between the Wars 1918–1940* (London: Methuen University Paperback, 1968), p. 11.

4 Gilbert, *Churchill: Companion Volume*, p. 450.

5 Martin Gilbert, *Winston S. Churchill*, Vol. 4: *1916–1922, The Stricken World* (Boston: Houghton Mifflin, 1975), pp. 179–80.

6   Howard M. Sachar, *The Emergence of the Middle East: 1914–1924* (New York: Alfred A. Knopf, 1969), p. 246.
7   Paul C. Helmreich, *From Paris to Sèvres: The Partition of the Ottoman Empire at the Peace Conference of 1919–1920* (Columbus: Ohio State University Press, 1974), p. 28.
8   Elizabeth Monroe, *Britain's Moment in the Middle East: 1914–1971*, rev. edn (Baltimore: The Johns Hopkins University Press, 1981), p. 37.
9   Ibid., p. 38.
10 Winston S. Churchill, *The Aftermath: Being a Sequel to the World Crisis* (London: Macmillan, 1941), p. 60.
11 Gilbert, *Churchill: The Stricken World*, p. 182.
12 Gilbert, *Churchill: Companion Volume*, pp. 463–4.
13 Gilbert, *Churchill: The Stricken World*, p. 194.
14 Ibid., p. 196.
15 Ibid., p. 194.
16 Kenneth O. Morgan, *Consensus and Disunity: The Lloyd George Coalition Government 1918–1922* (Oxford: Clarendon Press, 1979), p. 146.
17 John Darwin, *Britain, Egypt, and the Middle East: Imperial Policy in the Aftermath of War, 1918–1922* (New York: St Martin's Press, 1981), p. 12; *Encyclopaedia Britannica*, 15th edn, s.v. "Indian Subcontinent, History of the."
18 Gilbert, *Churchill: The Stricken World*, pp. 477–8.
19 Arno J. Mayer, *Politics and Diplomacy of Peacemaking: Containment and Counterrevolution at Versailles 1918–1919* (New York: Alfred A. Knopf, 1967), p. 139.

CHAPTER 41

1   John Maynard Keynes, *The Economic Consequences of the Peace* (New York: Harcourt, Brace & Howe, 1920), p. 38.
2   Ibid., p. 46.
3   Stephen Roskill, *Hankey: Man of Secrets*, Vol. 2: *1919–1931* (London: Collins, 1972), p. 38.
4   Paul C. Helmreich, *From Paris to Sèvres: The Partition of the Ottoman Empire at the Peace Conference of 1919–1920* (Columbus, Ohio: Ohio State University Press, 1974), p. 18.
5   Ibid., pp. 19–20.
6   Ibid., p. 94.
7   Ibid., p. 95.
8   Ibid.
9   Roskill, *Hankey*, Vol. 2, p. 72.
10 Ibid., p. 80.
11 Ibid., p. 81.
12 David Lloyd George, *Memoirs of the Peace Conference* (New Haven: Yale University Press, 1939), Vol. 2, p. 691.
13 Leonard Baker, *Brandeis and Frankfurter: A Dual Biography* (New York: Harper & Row, 1984), p. 171.
14 Christopher M. Andrew and A. S. Kanya-Forstner, *The Climax of French Imperial Expansion: 1914–1924* (Stanford: Stanford University Press, 1981), p. 197.
15 Ibid., p. 162.
16 Ibid., p. 194.
17 Ibid., p. 189.
18 Helmreich, *Paris to Sèvres*, p. 131.

19   Ibid., p. 139.
20   Lloyd George, *Memoirs*, p. 818.
21   Ibid., p. 26.
22   Lloyd George, *Memoirs*, p. 818.
23   Ibid., p. 711.
24   Ibid., p. 820.
25   Baker, *Brandeis and Frankfurter*, p. 170.
26   Roskill, *Hankey*, Vol. 2, p. 213.
27   Ibid., p. 89.
28   Daniele Varè, *Laughing Diplomat* (London: John Murray, 1938), p. 155.
29   Helmreich, *Paris to Sèvres*, p. 178.
30   *Lord Riddell's Intimate Diary of the Peace Conference and after: 1918–1923* (New York: Reynal & Hitchcock, 1934), p. 24.
31   Lloyd George, *Memoirs*, p. 491.
32   Ibid., pp. 723–4.

CHAPTER 42

1   Stephen Roskill, *Hankey: Man of Secrets*, Vol. 2: *1919–1931* (London: Collins, 1972), p. 141.
2   Jukka Nevakivi, *Britain, France and the Arab Middle East 1914–1920* (London: Athlone Press, 1969), p. 104.
3   Paul C. Helmreich, *From Paris to Sèvres: The Partition of the Ottoman Empire at the Peace Conference of 1919–1920* (Columbus: Ohio State University Press, 1974), p. 28.
4   John Darwin, *Britain, Egypt, and the Middle East: Imperial Policy in the Aftermath of War, 1918–1922* (New York: St Martin's Press, 1981), p. 172.
5   Roskill, *Hankey*, Vol. 2, p. 70.
6   Ibid., p. 115.
7   Ibid.
8   Erik Jan Zurcher, *The Unionist Factor: The Role of the Committee of Union and Progress in the Turkish National Movement 1905–1926* (Leiden: E. J. Brill, 1984), pp. 68 *et seq.*
9   Ibid., pp. 95–6.
10   David Lloyd George, *Memoirs of the Peace Conference* (New Haven: Yale University Press, 1939), Vol. 2, p. 830.
11   Nevakivi, *Britain, France and the Arab Middle East*, p. 210.
12   C. Ernest Dawn, *From Ottomanism to Arabism: Essays on the Origins of Arab Nationalism* (Urbana, Chicago and London: University of Illinois Press, 1973), p. 158.
13   Ibid., p. 178, app. 7. Cf. Elie Kedourie, *England and the Middle East: The Destruction of the Ottoman Empire, 1914–1921* (Hassocks, Sussex: Harvester Press, 1978), p. 159.
14   *Lord Riddell's Intimate Diary of the Peace Conference and after: 1918–1923* (New York: Reynal & Hitchcock, 1934), p. 112.

CHAPTER 44

1   P. J. Vatikiotis, *The History of Egypt*, 2nd edn (Baltimore: The Johns Hopkins University Press, 1980), pp. 250 *et seq.* The account provided in the text is principally based upon it and upon John Darwin, *Britain, Egypt and the Middle East: Imperial Policy in the Aftermath of the War, 1918–1922* (New York: St Martin's Press, 1981).
2   Sir James Rennell Rodd, a member of Lord Milner's mission to Egypt, 1920. *Encyclopaedia Britannica*, 12th edn, s.v. "Egypt."

3 Darwin, *Middle East*, p. 68.
4 Ibid., p. 71.
5 Durham. University of Durham. Sudan Archive. Reginald Wingate Papers. 470/7.
6 Darwin, *Middle East*, p. 77.
7 Ibid., p. 72.
8 Ibid., p. 74.
9 Ibid.
10 Vatikiotis, *Egypt*, p. 265.

CHAPTER 45

1 T. A. Heathcote, *The Afghan Wars: 1839–1919* (London: Osprey, 1980), p. 172.
2 Leon B. Poullada, *Reform and Rebellion in Afghanistan, 1919–1929: King Amanullah's Failure to Modernize a Tribal Society* (Ithaca and London: Cornell University Press, 1973), p. 239.
3 *Encyclopaedia Britannica*, 12th edn, s.v. "Afghanistan."
4 Heathcote, *Afghan Wars*, p. 179.
5 Poullada, *Reform and Rebellion*, p. 238, n. 11.
6 *Encyclopaedia Britannica*, 12th edn, s.v. "Afghanistan," according to which the treaty was concluded in 1920.
7 Poullada, *Reform and Rebellion*, p. 228.
8 Ibid., p. 247, n. 29.

CHAPTER 46

1 Briton Cooper Busch, *Britain, India, and the Arabs, 1914–1921* (Berkeley and London: University of California Press, 1971), p. 324.
2 Ibid.
3 David Holden and Richard Johns, *The House of Saud: The Rise and Fall of the Most Powerful Dynasty in the Arab World* (New York: Holt, Rinehart & Winston, 1981) p. 69; Christine Moss Helms, *The Cohesion of Saudi Arabia: Evolution of Political Identity* (Baltimore: The Johns Hopkins University Press, 1981), p. 129; J. B. Kelly, *Arabia, the Gulf and the West* (New York: Basic Books, 1980), p. 230.
4 Holden and Johns, *Saud*, p. 71; Gary Troeller, *The Birth of Saudi Arabia: Britain and the Rise of the House of Sa'ud* (London: Frank Cass, 1976), p. 142.
5 Troeller, *Saudi Arabia*, pp. 142–3; Busch, *Britain, India, and the Arabs*, pp. 328 *et seq.*; Holden and Johns, *Saud*, p. 72.
6 Helms, *Saudi Arabia*, p. 127.
7 Robert Vansittart, quoted in Busch, *Britain, India, and the Arabs*, p. 330.
8 Holden and Johns, *Saud*, p. 72.

CHAPTER 47

1 Michael L. Dockrill and J. Douglas Goold, *Peace without Promise: Britain and the Peace Conferences, 1919–1923* (London: Batsford Academic and Educational, 1981), p. 198.
2 Ibid., p. 199.
3 Ibid., p. 210.
4 Christopher M. Andrew and A. S. Kanya-Forstner, *The Climax of French Imperial Expansion: 1914–1924* (Stanford: Stanford University Press, 1981), p. 215.
5 Roderic H. Davison, "Turkish Diplomacy from Mudros to Lausanne," in Gordon A. Craig and Felix Gilbert (eds), *The Diplomats, 1919–1939* (Princeton: Princeton University Press, 1953), p. 181.

6 Stanford J. Shaw and Ezel Kural Shaw, *History of the Ottoman Empire and Modern Turkey*, Vol. 2: *Reform, Revolution, and Republic: The Rise of Modern Turkey, 1808–1975* (Cambridge: Cambridge University Press, 1977), p. 348.
7 Davison, "Turkish Diplomacy," p. 181.
8 Shaw and Shaw, *Ottoman Empire*, p. 349.
9 Davison, "Turkish Diplomacy," p. 181.
10 Shaw and Shaw, *Ottoman Empire*, pp. 352–3.
11 Davison, "Turkish Diplomacy," p. 183.
12 *Encyclopaedia Britannica*, 12th edn, s.v. "Turkey (Nationalist)."
13 Salahi Ramsdan Sonyel, *Turkish Diplomacy, 1918–1923: Mustafa Kemal and the Turkish National Movement* (London and Beverly Hills: SAGE Publications, 1975), pp. 62–5.
14 *Lord Riddell's Intimate Diary of the Peace Conference and after: 1918–1923* (New York: Reynal & Hitchcock, 1934), p. 208.
15 Michael Llewellyn Smith, *Ionian Vision: Greece in Asia Minor, 1919–1922* (New York: St Martin's Press, 1973), p. 124.
16 Dockrill and Goold, *Peace without Promise*, p. 215.
17 Smith, *Ionian Vision*, pp. 132–3.
18 Winston S. Churchill, *The Aftermath: Being a Sequel to the World Crisis* (London: Macmillan, 1941), p. 386.
19 Smith, *Ionian Vision*, p. 163.
20 Ibid., p. 164.
21 Ibid., p. 185.
22 Ibid., p. 186.
23 Ibid., p. 184.

CHAPTER 48

1 Elie Kedourie, *England and the Middle East: The Destruction of the Ottoman Empire, 1914–1921* (Hassocks, Sussex: Harvester Press, 1978), pp. 157–62.
2 Philip S. Khoury, *Urban Notables and Arab Nationalism: The Politics of Damascus 1860–1920* (Cambridge: Cambridge University Press, 1983), pp. 86–8.
3 Ibid., p. 88.
4 Christopher M. Andrew and A. S. Kanya-Forstner, *The Climax of French Imperial Expansion: 1914–1924* (Stanford: Stanford University Press, 1981), p. 204.
5 Ibid., p. 215.
6 Jukka Nevakivi, *Britain, France and the Arab Middle East, 1914–1920* (London: Athlone Press, 1969), p. 216.
7 The account in the text follows Khoury, *Urban Notables and Arab Nationalism*; and Y. Porath, *The Emergence of the Palestinian-Arab National Movement 1918–1929* (London: Frank Cass, 1974).
8 Nevakivi, *Britain, France and the Arab Middle East*, p. 216.
9 Aaron S. Klieman, *Foundations of British Policy in the Arab World: The Cairo Conference of 1921* (Baltimore: The Johns Hopkins University Press, 1970), pp. 46–7.
10 Ibid.
11 Ibid.
12 Ibid., pp. 216–17.
13 Andrew and Kanya-Forstner, *French Imperial Expansion*, p. 215.
14 Ibid., p. 216.
15 Howard M. Sachar, *The Emergence of the Middle East: 1914–1924* (New York: Alfred A. Knopf, 1969), p. 287.
16 Ibid., p. 288.

17   Klieman, *Foundations of British Policy*, p. 51.
18   Elie Kedourie, *Islam in the Modern World and Other Studies* (New York: Holt, Rinehart & Winston, 1981), pp. 85 *et seq*.
19   John Darwin, *Britain, Egypt, and the Middle East: Imperial Policy in the Aftermath of War, 1918–1922* (New York: St Martin's Press, 1981), p. 183.

CHAPTER 49

1   Christopher M. Andrew and A. S. Kanya-Forstner, *The Climax of French Imperial Expansion: 1914–1924* (Stanford: Stanford University Press, 1981), p. 220.
2   Ibid.
3   Ibid.
4   Ibid.
5   Ibid.
6   Ibid., p. 217.
7   Aaron S. Klieman, *Foundations of British Policy in the Arab World: The Cairo Conference of 1921* (Baltimore: The Johns Hopkins University Press, 1970), p. 72.
8   Oxford. St Antony's College. Middle East Centre. C. D. Brunton Papers. DS 126–DS 154.5, no. 2.
9   Ibid.
10   Ibid., no. 3.
11   Ibid.
12   Ibid.
13   Oxford. St Antony's College. Middle East Centre. F.R. Somerset Papers. DS 97.59.
14   Ibid. DS 126, DS 149, DS 154.5.
15   Ibid.

CHAPTER 50

1   Howard M. Sachar, *A History of Israel: From the Rise of Zionism to Our Time* (New York: Alfred A. Knopf, 1976), p. 123.
2   Joseph B. Schechtman, *Rebel and Statesman: The Vladimir Jabotinsky Story, the Early Years* (New York: Thomas Yoseloff, 1956), p. 328.
3   Ibid., pp. 329 *et seq.*; Sachar, *History of Israel*, p. 123.
4   Sachar, *History of Israel*, pp. 123–4.
5   Oxford. Rhodes House. Richard Meinertzhagen Diaries. Vol. 21, p. 126 (12–31–19).
6   Ibid., p. 143 (4 July 1920).
7   Martin Gilbert, *Winston S. Churchill*, Vol. 4: *1916–1922, The Stricken World* (Boston: Houghton Mifflin, 1975), pp. 484–5.

CHAPTER 51

1   H. V. F. Winstone, *Gertrude Bell* (London: Jonathan Cape, 1978), p. 207.
2   Ibid., p. 209.
3   Ibid., p. 215.
4   Ibid.
5   Elie Kedourie, *England and the Middle East: The Destruction of the Ottoman Empire, 1914–1921* (Hassocks, Sussex: Harvester Press, 1978), p. 191.
6   Winstone, *Bell*, p. 215.
7   Ibid., p. 219.
8   Jukka Nevakivi, *Britain, France and the Arab Middle East, 1914–1920* (London: Athlone Press, 1969), p. 177.

9 Winstone, *Bell*, p. 220.
10 Ibid., p. 222.
11 Howard M. Sachar, *The Emergence of the Middle East: 1914–1924* (New York: Alfred A. Knopf, 1969), p. 371.
12 Kedourie, *Middle East*, p. 192.
13 H. V. F. Winstone, *Leachman: 'OC Desert'* (London and New York: Quartet Books, 1982), p. 208.
14 Ibid., p. 215.
15 Aaron S. Klieman, *Foundations of British Policy in the Arab World: The Cairo Conferene of 1921* (Baltimore: The Johns Hopkins University Press, 1970), p. 56.
16 Kedourie, *Middle East*, p. 192.
17 Briton Cooper Busch, *Britain, India, and the Arabs, 1914–1921* (Berkeley and London: University of California Press, 1971), p. 408.
18 Oxford. St Antony's College. Middle East Centre. Leachman Papers.
19 Sachar, *Middle East*, p. 372.
20 Busch, *Britain, India, and the Arabs*, pp. 408–9.
21 Klieman, *Foundations of British Policy*, p. 57.
22 Ibid., p. 58.
23 Stephen Roskill, *Hankey: Man of Secrets*, Vol. 2: *1919–1931* (London: Collins, 1972), p. 201.
24 John Darwin, *Britain, Egypt, and the Middle East: Imperial Policy in the Aftermath of War, 1918–1922* (New York: St Martin's Press, 1981), p. 200.
25 Ibid.
26 Ibid.

CHAPTER 52

1 Kenneth O. Morgan, *Consensus and Disunity: The Lloyd George Coalition Government 1918–1922* (Oxford: Clarendon Press, 1979), p. 119.
2 Harold Nicolson, *Curzon: The Last Phase 1919–1925* (Boston: Houghton Mifflin, 1934), p. 134.
3 Ibid., p. 122.
4 Richard H. Ullman, *Anglo-Soviet Relations, 1917–1921*, Vol. 3: *The Anglo-Soviet Accord* (Princeton: Princeton University Press, 1972), p. 353.
5 Nicolson, *Curzon*, p. 138.
6 Ullman, *Anglo-Soviet Relations*, Vol. 3, p. 352, n. 11.
7 Martin Gilbert, *Winston S. Churchill: Companion Volume*, Vol. 4, Part 2: *July 1919–March 1921*, p. 1103.
8 Stephen Roskill, *Hankey: Man of Secrets*, Vol. 2: *1919–1931* (London: Collins, 1972), p. 202.
9 Ullman, *Anglo-Soviet Relations*, Vol. 3, p. 374.
10 Ibid., p. 380.
11 Ibid., p. 378.
12 Ibid., p. 377.
13 Ibid., p. 386.
14 Ibid., p. 388.
15 Professor Richard H. Ullman of Princeton University, in the work cited above.
16 John Darwin, *Britain, Egypt, and the Middle East: Imperial Policy in the Aftermath of War, 1918–1922* (New York: St Martin's Press, 1981), p. 214.

CHAPTER 53

1 Kew. Public Record Office. Arab Bureau Papers. Foreign Office 882. Vol. 23. Document M1/19/9.

2   Aaron S. Klieman, *Foundations of British Policy in the Arab World: The Cairo Conferene of 1921* (Baltimore: The Johns Hopkins University Press, 1970), p. 58.
3   Ibid.
4   *The Times*, 16 August 1985, p. 11.

CHAPTER 54

1   Richard H. Ullman, *Anglo-Soviet Relations, 1917–1921*, Vol. 3: *The Anglo-Soviet Accord* (Princeton: Princeton University Press, 1972), p. 324.
2   Ibid., p. 328.
3   Ibid.
4   Ibid., p. 329.
5   Ibid.
6   Ibid., p. 327.
7   Ibid., p. 326–7.
8   Ibid., p. 326.
9   Martin Gilbert, *Churchill: Companion Volume*, Vol. 4, Part 2: *July 1919–March 1921*, pp. 988–9.
10   Ibid., p. 989.
11   Ibid., p. 1025.
12   Martin Gilbert, *Winston S. Churchill*, Vol. 4: *1916–1922, The Stricken World* (Boston: Houghton Mifflin, 1975), p. 331.
13   Ibid., p. 371.
14   *Lord Riddell's Intimate Diary of the Peace Conference and after: 1918–1923* (New York: Reynal & Hitchcock, 1934), p. 163.
15   Ibid.
16   Ibid.
17   Ullman, *Anglo-Soviet Relations*, Vol. 3, p. 427.

CHAPTER 55

1   Richard Pipes, *The Formation of the Soviet Union, Communism and Nationalism, 1917–1923*, rev. edn. (Cambridge, Mass.: Harvard University Press, 1964), p. 1.
2   Lenin, *Collected Works*, Vol. 19, p. 254, quoted in Allen S. Whiting, *Soviet Policy in China 1912–1924* (Stanford University Press Paperback, 1968), p. 21.
3   Olaf Caroe, *Soviet Empire: The Turks of Central Asia and Stalinism*, 2nd edn (New York: St Martin's Press, 1967), p. 111.
4   Pipes, *Formation of the Soviet Union*, p. 155.

CHAPTER 56

1   Edward Hallett Carr, *The Bolshevik Revolution 1917–1923*, (Harmondsworth: Penguin, 1966), Vol. 3, p. 249, n. 1.
2   Ibid., p. 313.
3   Louise Bryant, *Mirrors of Moscow* (New York: T. Seltzer, 1923), p. 157.
4   Carr, *Bolshevik Revolution*, p. 327.
5   Ibid., p. 266, n. 2.
6   Ibid., p. 267.
7   Ibid., p. 263.
8   Ibid., p. 264.
9   Ibid., p. 268.
10   Ibid., n. 3.
11   Ibid., p. 290.

12 Leon B. Poullada, *Reform and Rebellion in Afghanistan, 1919–1929: King Amanullah's Failure to Modernize a Tribal Society* (Ithaca and London: Cornell University Press, 1973), p. 248.
13 Bryant, *Mirrors of Moscow*, p. 149.
14 Ibid., p. 160.
15 Lt.-Col. F. M. Bailey, *Mission To Tashkent* (London: Jonathan Cape, 1946).
16 Edward Allworth (ed.), *Central Asia: A Century of Russian Rule* (New York: Columbia University Press, 1967), p. 244.
17 Fitzroy Maclean, *A Person from England, and Other Travellers* (London: Jonathan Cape, 1958).
18 Richard Pipes, *The Formation of the Soviet Union, Communism and Nationalism, 1917–1923*, rev. edn (Cambridge, Mass.: Harvard University Press, 1964), p. 258.
19 Maclean, *A Person from England*, pp. 357–8; Fitzroy Maclean, *To the Back of Beyond* (London: Jonathan Cape, 1974), pp. 95–6; Olaf Caroe, *Soviet Empire: The Turks of Central Asia and Stalinism*, 2nd edn (New York: St Martin's Press, 1967), pp. 24–125.
20 Martin Gilbert, *Winston S. Churchill: Companion Volume*, Vol. 4, Part 2: *July 1919–March 1921* (Boston: Houghton Mifflin, 1978), pp. 1165–6.

CHAPTER 57

1 Martin Gilbert, *Winston S. Churchill: Companion Volume*, Vol. 4, Part 2: *July 1919–March 1921* (Boston: Houghton Mifflin, 1978), p. 938.
2 Ibid., p. 1249.
3 Ibid., p. 1261.
4 Ibid., p. 1267.
5 Ibid., p. 1269.
6 Martin Gilbert, *Winston S. Churchill*, Vol. 4: *1916–1922, The Stricken World* (Boston: Houghton Mifflin, 1975), p. 528.
7 Ibid., p. 523.
8 Ibid., p. 524.
9 Ibid., p. 527.
10 Ibid.
11 *The Letters of T. E. Lawrence*, ed. by David Garnett (London: Jonathan Cape, 1938), p. 316.
12 Lowell Thomas, *With Lawrence in Arabia* (New York and London: Century, 1924), p. 308.
13 Ibid., p. 131.
14 Ibid., p. 407.
15 John E. Mack, *A Prince of Our Disorder: The Life of T. E. Lawrence* (Boston: Little, Brown, 1976), p. 276.
16 Desmond Stewart, *T. E. Lawrence* (New York and London: Harper & Row, 1977); Mack, *A Prince of Our Disorder*; Phillip Knightley and Colin Simpson, *The Secret Lives of Lawrence of Arabia* (London: Thomas Nelson, 1969).
17 Gilbert, *Churchill: Companion Volume*, p. 841.
18 Ibid., p. 1076.
19 Gilbert, *Churchill: The Stricken World*, p. 638.
20 Ibid., p. 894.
21 Ibid., p. 545.
22 Ibid., p. 511.
23 Ibid., p. 592.
24 Ibid., p. 509.
25 Ibid., p. 217.

26 Ibid.
27 *Letters of T. E. Lawrence*, p. 291.
28 Gilbert, *Churchill: Companion Volume*, p. 1334.
29 Ibid., p. 1367.
30 Ibid., p. 1377.
31 Ibid., p. 1405.
32 H. V. F. Winstone, *Gertrude Bell* (London: Jonathan Cape, 1978), p. 235.
33 Gilbert, *Churchill: Companion Volume*, p. 1391.
34 Ibid., p. 1383.
35 Gilbert, *Churchill: The Stricken World*, p. 538.
36 Ibid., pp. 552−3.
37 Gilbert, *Churchill: Companion Volume*, pp. 1407−8.
38 Ibid., p. 1408.
39 Ibid., p. 1413.
40 Gilbert, *Churchill: The Stricken World*, p. 553.
41 Gilbert, *Churchill: Companion Volume*, p. 404.
42 Ibid., p. 1428.
43 Ibid., p. 1432.
44 Gilbert, *Churchill: The Stricken World*, p. 516.
45 Gilbert, *Churchill: Companion Volume*, p. 1414.
46 Aaron S. Klieman, *Foundations of British Policy in the Arab World: The Cairo Conference of 1921* (Baltimore: The Johns Hopkins University Press, 1970), p. 140.
47 Ibid., p. 145.
48 Ibid., p. 146.
49 Ibid., p. 156.
50 Gilbert, *Churchill: Companion Volume*, p. 1966.
51 Ibid., p. 1967.
52 Gilbert, *Churchill: The Stricken World*, p. 817.
53 Ibid.
54 Ibid., p. 818.
55 Ibid.
56 Winstone, *Gertrude Bell*, pp. 242−3.
57 Thomas Hoving, *Tutankhamun: The Untold Story* (New York: Simon & Schuster, 1978), pp. 89 *et seq.*
58 *T. E. Lawrence to His Biographer, Liddell Hart* (New York: Doubleday, Doran, 1938), p. 131.
59 Klieman, *Foundations of British Policy*, p. 215.
60 Ibid., p. 216.
61 Ibid., p. 217.
62 Ibid., p. 223.
63 Ibid., p. 217.
64 Mack, *A Prince of Our Disorder*, p. 306.
65 Klieman, *Foundations of British Policy*, p. 285−8.
66 Ibid., p. 229.
67 Ibid., p. 233.

CHAPTER 58

1 Oxford. St Antony's College. Middle East Centre. C. D. Brunton Papers.
2 Reported in *The Times*, 2 September 1921.
3 Vladimir Jabotinsky, *The Story of the Jewish Legion*, trans. by Samuel Katz (New York: Bernard Ackerman, 1945), pp. 168−9.
4 Elie Kedourie, *The Chatham House Version and Other Middle Eastern Studies*,

new edn (Hanover and London: University Press of New England, 1984), ch. 4.

5 Ibid., p. 65.
6 Ibid.
7 Ibid.
8 Martin Gilbert, *Winston S. Churchill: Companion Volume*, Vol. 4, Part 2: *July 1919–March 1921* (Boston: Houghton Mifflin, 1978), p. 1420.
9 Ibid., p. 1028, n. 1.
10 Ibid., Part 3: *April 1921–November 1922*, p. 1559.
11 Martin Gilbert, *Winston S. Churchill*, Vol. 4: *1916–1922, The Stricken World* (Boston: Houghton Mifflin, 1975), p. 597.
12 Ibid., p. 629.
13 Ibid., p. 630.
14 Ibid.
15 Kenneth W. Stein, *The Land Question in Palestine, 1917–1939* (Chapel Hill and London: University of North Carolina Press, 1984), p. 67.
16 Ibid., p. 37.
17 Ibid., p. 65.
18 Ibid., p. 37.
19 Ibid., p. 67.
20 Gilbert, *Churchill: The Stricken World*, pp. 655–6.
21 Ibid., p. 628.
22 Gilbert, *Churchill: Companion Volume*, Vol. 4, Part 3, p. 1647.
23 Ibid., p. 1659.
24 Ibid., n. 1.
25 Gilbert, *Churchill: The Stricken World*, p. 624.
26 Ibid., pp. 652–3.
27 Ibid.
28 Ibid., p. 659.
29 Ibid.
30 Shabtai Teveth, *Ben-Gurion and the Palestinian Arabs* (Oxford and New York: Oxford University Press, 1985), pp. 5, 6, 37, 47–55, 75–81.
31 Ibid., chs 5, 6, and 7.
32 Ibid.
33 Ibid., pp. 55–6; Joseph B. Schechtman, *Fighter and Prophet: The Vladimir Jabotinsky Story, the Last Years* (New York: Thomas Yoseloff, 1961), p. 324.
34 Gilbert, *Churchill: Companion Volume*, Vol. 4, Part 3, p. 2125.

CHAPTER 59

1 Walter Goerlitz, *History of the German General Staff: 1657–1945*, trans. by Brian Battershaw (New York: Praeger, 1953), pp. 231. *et seq.*
2 Salahi Ramsdan Sonyel, *Turkish Diplomacy, 1918–1923: Mustafa Kemal and the Turkish National Movement* (London and Beverly Hills: SAGE Publications, 1975), p. 83.
3 Ibid., p. 87.
4 Denis Mack Smith, *Mussolini* (New York: Vintage Books, 1983), p. 33.
5 Ibid.
6 Ibid., p. 43.
7 William Stivers, *Supremacy and Oil: Iraq, Turkey, and the Anglo-American World Order, 1918–1930* (Ithaca and London: Cornell University Press, 1982), p. 111.
8 Ibid., pp. 195–9.

9   Laurence Evans, *United States Policy and the Partition of Turkey, 1914–1924*
    (Baltimore: The Johns Hopkins University Press, 1965), p. 300.
10 Ibid., p. 303.
11 H. V. F. Winstone, *The Illicit Adventure* (London: Jonathan Cape, 1982),
    p. 348.
12 Stivers, *Supremacy and Oil*, p. 127.
13 Ibid., p. 123, n. 36.
14 Ibid., p. 126.
15 Ibid., p. 89.
16 Ibid., p. 90.
17 Sonyel, *Turkish Diplomacy*, p. 138.
18 Ibid., p. 139; Roderic H. Davison, "Turkish Diplomacy from Mudros to
    Lausanne," in Gordon A. Craig and Felix Gilbert (eds), *The Diplomats, 1919–
    1939* (Princeton: Princeton University Press, 1953), p. 193.
19 Martin Gilbert, *Winston S. Churchill: Companion Volume*, Vol. 4, Part 3:
    April 1921–November 1922 (Boston: Houghton Mifflin, 1978), p. 1656.
20 Harold Nicolson, *Diplomacy*, 3rd edn (New York: Oxford University Press,
    1964), p. 135.
21 Gilbert, *Churchill: Companion Volume*, pp. 1656–1657.

CHAPTER 60

1   Stephen Roskill, *Hankey: Man of Secrets*, Vol. 2: *1919–1931* (London: Collins,
    1972), p. 199.
2   Arnold J. Toynbee, *The Western Question in Greece and Turkey*, reprint of
    2nd edn (New York: Howard Fertig, 1970), p. 247.
3   Michael Llewellyn Smith, *Ionian Vision: Greece in Asia Minor 1919–1922*
    (New York: St Martin's Press, 1973), p. 203.
4   Ibid., p. 226.
5   Ibid.
6   Lord Kinross, *Ataturk: A Biography of Mustafa Kemal, Father of Modern
    Turkey* (New York: William Morrow, 1965), p. 307.
7   Ibid., p. 309.
8   Smith, *Ionian Vision*, pp. 228–9.
9   Ibid., p. 237.
10 Ibid., p. 271.
11 Ibid., p. 273.
12 Salahi Ramsdan Sonyel, *Turkish Diplomacy 1918–1923: Mustafa Kemal and
    the Turkish National Movement* (London and Beverly Hills: SAGE Publi-
    cations, 1975), pp. 172–3.
13 *Lord Riddell's Intimate Diary of the Peace Conference and after: 1918–1923*
    (New York: Reynal & Hitchcock, 1934), p. 385.
14 Smith, *Ionian Vision*, p. 303.
15 Toynbee, *The Western Question*, p. 152.
16 Smith, *Ionian Vision*, p. 232.
17 Toynbee, *The Western Question*, pp. 315–17.
18 Marjorie Housepian, *Smyrna 1922: The Destruction of a City* (London: Faber,
    1972), p. 166.
19 Kinross, *Ataturk*, p. 270; Stanford J. Shaw and Ezel Kural Shaw, *History of
    the Ottoman Empire and Modern Turkey*, Vol 2: *Reform, Revolution, and
    Republic: The Rise of Modern Turkey, 1808–1975* (Cambridge: Cambridge
    University Press, 1977), p. 363.
20 William White (ed.), *By-Line: Ernest Hemingway* (New York: Charles Scribner's
    Sons, 1967), p. 60.

21 Laurence Evans, *United States Policy and the Partition of Turkey, 1914–1924* (Baltimore: The Johns Hopkins University Press, 1965), pp. 374–5.
22 Ibid., p. 375.
23 Ibid., p. 344.
24 Ibid., pp. 373–4.
25 Martin Gilbert, *Winston S. Churchill: Companion Volume*, Vol. 4, Part 3: *April 1921–November 1922* (Boston: Houghton Mifflin, 1978), p. 1980.
26 Ibid.
27 Ibid., p. 1988.
28 W. K. Hancock, *Smuts: The Fields of Fire, 1919–1950* (Cambridge: Cambridge University Press, 1968), pp. 4–5.
29 Gilbert, *Churchill: Companion Volume*, pp. 1993–5.
30 Martin Gilbert, *Winston S. Churchill*, Vol. 4: *1916–1922, The Stricken World* (Boston: Houghton Mifflin, 1975), p. 829.
31 Ibid., p. 834.
32 John Campbell, *F. E. Smith: First Earl of Birkenhead* (London: Jonathan Cape, 1983), p. 606.
33 Smuts to Bonar Law. Hancock, *Smuts*, p. 130.
34 Campbell, *F. E. Smith*, p. 607.
35 Roskill, *Hankey*, Vol. 2, p. 293.
36 Robert Blake, "Baldwin and the Right," in *The Baldwin Age*, ed. by John Raymond (London: Eyre & Spottiswoode, 1960), pp. 37, 41.
37 Lord Beaverbrook, *The Decline and Fall of Lloyd George: And Great Was the Fall Thereof* (London: Collins, 1963), p. 171.
38 Riddell, *Intimate Diary*, pp. 388–9.
39 David Lloyd George, *Memoirs of the Peace Conference* (New Haven: Yale University Press, 1939), Vol. 2, p. 871.
40 Smith, *Ionian Vision*, pp. 326–8.
41 Robert Blake, *The Unknown Prime Minister: The Life and Times of Andrew Bonar Law 1858–1923* (London: Eyre & Spottiswoode, 1955), pp. 447–8.
42 Minister of Agriculture, Arthur S. D. Griffith-Boscawen, quoted in Kenneth O. Morgan, *Consensus and Disunity: The Lloyd George Coalition Government 1918–1922* (Oxford: Clarendon Press, 1979), p. 325.
43 A. J. P. Taylor, *Beaverbrook* (New York: Simon & Schuster, 1972), p. 197.
44 Gilbert, *Churchill: Companion Volume*, p. 2105.
45 Ibid., p. 2122.
46 Ibid., p. 2125.
47 Lloyd George, *Memoirs*, p. 872.

CHAPTER 61

1 Martin Gilbert, *Winston S. Churchill*, Vol. 4: *1916–1922, The Stricken World* (Boston: Houghton Mifflin, 1975), p. 892.
2 Martin Gilbert, *Winston S. Churchill: Companion Volume*, Vol. 5, Part 1: *The Exchequer Years, 1922–1929* (Boston: Houghton Mifflin, 1981), p. 236.

BIBLIOGRAPHY

This is a bibliography of my sources other than the archives and collections of private and official papers indicated in the Acknowledgments. It consists of publications only, and is limited to those that I used: the published writings that I consulted in the course, and specifically for the purpose, of writing this book. Of the titles that I list, therefore, fully half appear in the Notes; and of those that do not, many did appear in the Notes to earlier drafts of my manuscript.

It is not a comprehensive bibliography of the published literature on my subject, the creation of the modern Middle East (1914–1922) seen in the context of European world politics (1789–1922). Such a bibliography, if assembled properly, could well constitute a book in itself. It would include a multitude of germane and valuable works, some of which I have read and others not, that do not appear in the following list because I did not have occasion to examine or re-examine them in working on *A Peace to End All Peace*.

Abd Allah ibn Hussein, *Memoirs of King Abdullah of Transjordan*, ed. by Philip P. Graves (London: Jonathan Cape, 1950).

——, *My Memoirs Completed "Al Takmilah,"* trans. by Harold W. Glidden (London and New York: Longman, 1978).

Abdullah, Muhammad Morsy, *The United Arab Emirates: A Modern History* (New York: Barnes & Noble, 1978).

Adelson, Roger, *Mark Sykes: Portrait of an Amateur* (London: Jonathan Cape, 1975).

Ahmad, Feroz, *The Young Turks: The Committee of Union and Progress in Turkish Politics 1908–1914* (Oxford: Clarendon Press, 1969).

Ajami, Fouad, *The Vanished Imam: Musa al Sadr and the Shia of Lebanon* (Ithaca and London: Cornell University Press, 1986).

Allworth, Edward (ed.), *Central Asia: A Century of Russian Rule* (New York: Columbia University Press, 1967).

Amery, L. S., *The Leo Amery Diaries*, Vol. I, *1896–1919*, edited by John Barnes and David Nicholson (London, Melbourne, Sydney, Auckland, and Johannesburg: Hutchinson, 1980).

——, *My Political Life*, Vol. 2, *War and Peace: 1914–1929* (London: Hutchinson, 1953).

Anderson, M. S., *The Eastern Question, 1774–1923: A Study in International Relations* (London and Basingstoke: Macmillan Press, 1966).

Andrew, Christopher M., and Kanya-Forstner, A. S., *The Climax of French Imperial Expansion 1914–1924* (Stanford: Standford University Press, 1981).

Antonius, George, *The Arab Awakening: The Story of the Arab National Movement* (New York: Capricorn Books, 1965).

Arslanian, Artin H., "Dunsterville's Adventures: A Reappraisal," *International Journal of Middle Eastern Studies* (1980).

Asquith, H. H., *Letters to Venetia Stanley*, ed. by Michael and Eleanor Brock (Oxford and New York: Oxford University Press, 1982).

Asquith, Margot, *The Autobiography*, ed. by Mark Bonham Carter (London: Methuen, 1985).

Baedeker, Karl, *Palestine and Syria: With Routes through Mesopotamia and Babylon and the Island of Cyprus: Handbook For Travellers*, 5th edn, remodelled and augmented (Leipzig: Karl Baedeker, 1912).

Bagehot, Walter, *The Collected Works*, Vol. 8 (London: *The Economist*, 1974).

Bailey, Lt.-Col. F. M., *Mission to Tashkent* (London: Jonathan Cape, 1946).

Baker, Leonard, *Brandeis and Frankfurter: A Dual Biography* (New York: Harper & Row, 1984).

Baker, Ray Stannard, *Woodrow Wilson, Life and Letters, Princeton, 1890–1910* (Garden City: Doubleday, Page, 1927).

——, *Woodrow Wilson, Life and Letters, War Leader, April 6, 1917—February 28, 1918* (New York: Doubleday, Doran, 1939).

Beaverbrook, Lord, *The Decline And Fall Of Lloyd George: And Great Was The Fall Thereof* (London: Collins, 1963).

——, *Men and Power: 1917–1918* (London: Hutchinson, 1956).

——, *Politicians and the War 1914–1916* (London: Oldbourne Book Co., 1960).

Bein, Alex, *Theodore Herzl: A Biography*, trans. by Maurice Samuel (Philadelphia: The Jewish Publication Society of America, 1941).

Bell, Gertrude, *The Arab War: Confidential Information for General Headquarters from Gertrude Bell, Being Despatches Reprinted from the Secret "Arab Bulletin"* (Great Britain: The Golden Cockerell Press, n.d.).

Bidwell, Robin, *Travellers in Arabia* (London, New York, Sydney, and Toronto: Hamlyn, 1976).

Blake, Robert, *Disraeli* (New York: St Martin's Press, 1967).

——, *The Unknown Prime Minister: The Life and Times of Andrew Bonar Law 1858–1918* (London: Eyre & Spottiswoode, 1955).

Bodley, Ronald, and Hearst, Lorna, *Gertrude Bell* (New York: Macmillan, 1940).

Bonham Carter, Violet, *Winston Churchill as I Knew Him* (London: Eyre & Spottiswoode and Collins, 1965).

Bourne, Kenneth, *The Foreign Policy of Victorian England 1830–1902* (Oxford: Clarendon Press, 1970).

——, *Palmerston: The Early Years 1784–1841* (New York: Macmillan, 1982).

Bourne, K. C., and Watt, D. C. (eds.), *Studies in International History* (London: Longman, 1967).

Braddon, Russell, *The Siege* (New York: Viking Press, 1969).

Brandeis, Louis D., *Letters of Louis D. Brandeis*, Vol. IV, *(1916–1921): Mr. Justice Brandeis*, ed. by Melvin I. Urofsky and David W. Levy (Albany: State University of New York Press, 1975).

Brémond, General Ed., *Le Hedjaz dans la guerre mondiale* (Paris: Payot, 1931).

Brockelmann, Carl, *History of the Islamic Peoples*, trans. by Joel Carmichael and Moshe Perlmann (New York: G. P. Putnam's Sons, 1947).

Brown, L. Carl, *International Politics and the Middle East: Old Rules, Dangerous Game* (Princeton: Princeton University Press, 1984).

Buchan, John, *Memory Hold-The-Door* (London: Hodder and Stoughton, 1940).
Bullard, Sir Reader, *Britain and the Middle East, from Earliest Times to 1963*, 3rd rev. edn (London: Hutchinson University Library, 1964).
Busch, Briton Cooper, *Britain, India, and the Arabs, 1914–1921* (Berkeley, Los Angeles, and London: University of California Press, 1971).
Bryant, Louise, *Mirrors of Moscow* (New York: T. Seltzer, 1923).
Cain, P. J., *Economic Foundations of British Overseas Expansion 1815–1914* (London and Basingstoke: Macmillan, 1980).
Campbell, John, *F. E. Smith: First Earl of Birkenhead* (London: Jonathan Cape, 1983).
Caroe, Olaf, *Soviet Empire: The Turks of Central Asia and Stalinism*, 2nd edn (New York: St Martin's Press, 1967).
Carr, Edward Hallet, *The Bolshevik Revolution 1917–1923*, Vol. 3 (Harmondsworth: Penguin Books, 1966).
——, *The Russian Revolution: From Lenin To Stalin (1917–1929)* (London and Basingstoke: Macmillan, 1979).
Carrere d'Encausse, H., *Reforme et revolution chez les Musulmans de l'empire Russe, Bukhara 1867–1924* (Paris: Armand Colin, 1968).
Cassar, George H., *Kitchener: Architect of Victory* (London: William Kimber, 1977).
Cassels, Lavender, *The Struggle for the Ottoman Empire: 1717–1740* (New York: Thomas Y. Crowell, 1967).
Cecil, Algernon, *Queen Victoria and Her Prime Ministers* (London: Eyre & Spottiswoode, 1953).
Cecil, Lord Edward, *The Leisure of an Egyptian Official* (London: Hodder and Stoughton, 1921).
Cecil, Lady Gwendolen, *Life of Robert Marquis of Salisbury*, 4 Vols (London: Hodder and Stoughton, 1921–32).
Chirol, Sir Valentine, "The Downfall of the Khalifate," *Foreign Affairs* (15 June 1924).
——, "Islam and Britain," *Foreign Affairs* (15 March 1923).
Churchill, Randolph S., *Winston S. Churchill*, Vol. 2, *1901–1914, Young Statesman* (Boston: Houghton Mifflin, 1967).
——, Companion Vol. 2, Part 3, *1911–1914* (Boston: Houghton Mifflin, 1969).
Churchill, Winston S., *The Aftermath: being a sequel to The World Crisis* (London: Macmillan, 1941).
——, *Great Contemporaries* (London and Glasgow: Fontana, 1959).
——, *The World Crisis: 1911–1914* 4 Vols (London: Thornton Butterworth, 1923–1927).
Clayton, G. D., *Britain and the Eastern Question: Missolonghi to Gallipoli* (London: University of London Press, 1971).
Coles, Paul, *The Ottoman Impact on Europe* (Harcourt, Brace & World, 1968).
Cooper, Duff, *Old Men Forget* (New York: E. P. Dutton, 1954).
Cottrell, Alvin J. (ed.), *The Persian Gulf States: A General Survey* (Baltimore and London: The Johns Hopkins University Press, 1980).
Cottrell, P. L., *British Overseas Investment in the Nineteenth Century* (London and Basingstoke: Macmillan Press, 1975).
Craig, Gordon A., *Germany 1866–1945* (New York: Oxford University Press, 1978).
Craig, Gordon A., and Gilbert, Felix (eds.), *The Diplomats* (Princeton: Princeton University Press, 1953).
Cruttwell, C. R. M. F., *A History of the Great War*, 2nd edn (Oxford: Clarendon Press, 1936).
Curzon, George N., *Persia and the Persian Question*, Vol. 1 (London: Frank Cass, 1966).

Darwin, John, *Britain, Egypt, and the Middle East: Imperial Policy in the After-math of War, 1918—1922* (New York: St Martin's Press, 1981).

Davis, H. W. C., "The Great Game in Asia: 1800—1814," *Raleigh Lecture on History* (London: British Academy, 1926).

Dawn, C. Ernest, *From Ottomanism to Arabism: Essays on the Origins of Arab Nationalism* (Urbana, Chicago, and London: University of Illinois Press, 1973).

de Chair, Somerset, *The Golden Carpet* (London: Golden Cockerell Press, 1943).

de Lange, Nicholas, *Atlas of the Jewish World* (New York: Facts on File, 1984).

Djemal Pasha, Ahmed, *Memories of a Turkish Statesman: 1913—1919* (New York: George H. Doran, 1922).

——, La Verité Sur La Question Syrienne (Stamboul: IV^{ieme} Armée, 1916).

Dockrill, Michael L., and Goold, J. Douglas, *Peace without Promise: Britain and the Peace Conferences 1919—1923* (London: Batsford Academic and Educational, 1981).

Doughty, Charles M., *Travels in Arabia Deserta*, with an Introduction by T. E. Lawrence, 2 Vols (New York: Dover Publications, 1979).

Dugdale, Blanche E. C., *Arthur James Balfour*, 2 Vols (New York: G. P. Putman's Sons, 1937).

Dyer, Gwynne, "The Turkish Armistice of 1918," *Middle Eastern Studies* (May and October 1972)

Earle, Edward Meade (ed.), *Makers of Modern Strategy: Military Thought from Machiavelli to Hitler* (Princeton: Princeton University Press, 1943).

Elekdag, Sukru, "Armenians vs. Turks: The View from Istanbul," *Wall Street Journal*, 21 September 1983.

——, Letter to the Editor, *New York Times*, 11 May 1983.

Ellis, C. H., *The Transcaspian Episode: 1918—1919* (London: Hutchinson, 1963).

Emin, Ahmed, *Turkey in the World War* (New Haven: Yale University Press, 1930).

Encyclopaedia Britannica, 11th edn, s.v.
 — "Arabs"
 — "Constantinople"
 — "Hejaz"
 — "Jews"
 — "Mecca"
 — "Palestine"
 — "Russia"
 — "Syria"
 — "Turkey"

Encyclopaedia Britannica, 12th edn, s.v.
 — "Afghanistan"
 — "Egypt"
 — "Kitchener"
 — "Turkey: Nationalist"
 — "Turkish Campaigns"
 — "World War"

Encyclopaedia Britannica, 14th edn, s.v.
 — "Guerrilla"
 — "Influenza"

Ensor, R. C. K., *England: 1870—1914* (Oxford: Clarendon Press, 1936).

Evans, Laurence, *United States Policy and the Partition Of Turkey, 1914—1924* (Baltimore: The Johns Hopkins University Press, 1965).

Eversley, Lord, *The Turkish Empire, from 1288 to 1914* (New York: Howard Fertig, 1969).

Farwell, Byron, *Queen Victoria's Little Wars* (New York: Harper & Row, 1972).

Fischer, Fritz, *Germany's Aims in the First World War* (New York: W. W. Norton, 1967).

FitzHerbert, Margaret, *The Man Who Was Greenmantle: A Biography of Aubrey Herbert* (London: John Murray, 1983).

Fitzpatrick, Sheila, *The Russian Revolution* (Oxford and New York: Oxford University Press, 1982).

Fraser, T. G., *The Middle East, 1914–1979* (London: Edward Arnold, 1980).

Friedman, Isaiah, *Germany, Turkey, and Zionism: 1897–1918* (Oxford: Clarendon Press, 1977).

——, *The Question of Palestine, 1914–1918, British-Jewish-Arab Relations* (London: Routledge & Kegan Paul, 1973).

Fromkin, David, "The Great Game in Asia," *Foreign Affairs* (spring 1980).

——, *The Independence of Nations* (New York: Praeger, 1981).

Fussell, Paul, *The Great War and Modern Memory* (New York and London: Oxford University Press, 1975).

Gelfand, Lawrence E., *The Inquiry: American Preparation for Peace, 1917–1919* (New Haven and London: Yale University Press, 1963).

Gellner, Ernest, *Muslim Society* (Cambridge, London, New York, New Rochelle, Melbourne, and Sydney: Cambridge University Press, 1981).

Gilbert, Martin, *Atlas of British History* (Dorset Press, 1984).

——, *Atlas of the First World War* (Dorset Press, 1984).

——, *Atlas of Jewish History* (Dorset Press, 1984).

——, *Atlas of Russian History* (Dorset Press, 1984).

——, *Jerusalem: Rebirth of a City* (New York: Viking, 1985).

——, *Winston S. Churchill*, Vol. 3, *1914–1916, The Challenge of War* (Boston: Houghton Mifflin, 1971).

——, Companion Vol. 3, Part 1, *July 1914–April 1915* (Boston: Houghton Mifflin, 1973).

——, Companion Vol. 3, Part 2, *May 1915–December 1916* (Boston: Houghton Mifflin, 1973).

——, *Winston S. Churchill*, Vol. 4, *1916–1922, The Stricken World* (Boston: Houghton Mifflin, 1975).

——, Companion Vol. 4, Part 1, *January 1917–June 1919* (Boston: Houghton Mifflin, 1978).

——, Companion Vol. 4, Part 2, *July 1919–March 1921* (Boston: Houghton Mifflin, 1978).

——, Companion Vol. 4, Part 3, *April 1921–November 1922* (Boston: Houghton Mifflin, 1978).

——, *Winston S. Churchill*, Vol. 5, *1922–1939, The Prophet of Truth* (Boston: Houghton Mifflin, 1977).

——, Companion Vol. 5, Part 1, *The Exchequer Years, 1922–1929* (Boston: Houghton Mifflin, 1981).

Gleason, John Howes, *The Genesis of Russophobia in Great Britain: A Study of the Interaction of Policy and Opinion* (Cambridge, Mass.: Harvard University Press, 1950).

Goerlitz, Walter, *History of the German General Staff: 1657–1945*, trans. by Brian Battershaw (New York: Praeger, 1953).

Gooch, G. P., and Temperley, Harold (eds.), *British Documents on the Origins of the War 1898–1914*, 11 Vols in 13 (New York: Johnson reprint corp., 1967).

Grenville, J. A. S., *Lord Salisbury and Foreign Policy: the Close of the Nineteenth Century* (London: Athlone Press, 1964).

——, *The Major International Treaties 1914–1973: A History and Guide with Texts* (New York: Stein and Day, 1975).

Grey of Falloden, Viscount, *Twenty-Five Years, 1892–1916* (London: Hodder & Stoughton, 1925).

Grigg, John, *Lloyd George*, 3 Vols to date (London: Eyre Methuen, 1973–78, and Methuen, 1985).

Grousset, Rene, *The Empire of the Steppes: A History of Central Asia*, translated by Naomi Walford (New Brunswick, New Jersey: Rutgers University Press, 1970).

Guedalla, Philip, *Men of Affairs* (London: Hodder and Stoughton, n.d.).

Hambis, Louis (ed.), *L'Asie Centrale: histoire et civilisation* (Paris: Collège de France, Imprimerie nationale, 1977).

Hamilton, Sir Ian, *Gallipoli Diary*, 2 Vols (London: Edward Arnold, 1920).

Hancock, W. K., *Smuts*, 2 Vols (Cambridge: Cambridge University Press, 1962–68).

Headrick, Daniel R., *The Tools of Empire: Technology and European Imperialism in the Nineteenth Century* (New York and Oxford: Oxford University Press, 1981).

Heathcote, T. A., *The Afghan Wars: 1839–1919* (London, Osprey, 1980).

Heller, Joseph, *British Policy Towards the Ottoman Empire 1908–1914* (London: Frank Cass, 1983).

——, "Sir Louis Mallet and the Ottoman Empire: The Road to War," *Middle Eastern Studies* (January 1976).

Helmreich, Paul C., *From Paris to Sèvres: The Partition of the Ottoman Empire at the Peace Conference of 1919–1920* (Columbus: Ohio State University Press, 1974).

Helms, Christine Moss, *The Cohesion of Saudi Arabia: Evolution of Political Identity* (Baltimore and London: The Johns Hopkins University Press, 1981).

Hemingway, Ernest, *By-Line: Ernest Hemingway*, ed. by William White (New York: Charles Scribner's Sons, 1967).

Henty, G. A., *With Kitchener In The Soudan: A Story of Atbara and Omdurman* (New York: Charles Scribner's Sons, 1902).

Herzl, Theodor, *A Jewish State: An Attempt at a Modern Solution of the Jewish Question*, revised by J. de Haas from the translation of Sylvie D'Avigdor (New York: Maccabaean Publishing, 1904).

Hess, Moses, *Rome and Jerusalem: A Study in Jewish Nationalism*, translated by Meyer Waxman (New York: Bloch Publishing, 1945).

Hill, Stephen, "Gertrude Bell (1968–1926): A selection from the photographic archive of an archaeologist and traveller" (Department of Archaeology, The University of Newcastle Upon Tyne, 1977).

Hinsley, F. H. (ed.), *British Foreign Policy under Sir Edward Grey* (Cambridge, New York, and Melbourne: Cambridge University Press, 1977).

Hirszowicz, L., "The Sultan and the Khedive, 1892–1908," *Middle Eastern Studies* (October 1972).

Holden, David, and Johns, Richard, *The House of Saud: The Rise and Fall of the Most Powerful Dynasty in the Arab World* (New York: Holt, Rinehart & Winston, 1981).

Hough, Richard, *The Great War at Sea: 1914–1918* (Oxford and New York: Oxford University Press, 1983).

Hourani, Albert, *The Emergence of the Modern Middle East* (Berkeley, Los Angeles, and London: University of California Press, 1981).

——, *Europe and The Middle East* (Berkeley and Los Angeles: University of California Press, 1980).

——, (ed.), *Middle Eastern Affairs: Number Four*, St Antony's Papers, no. 17 (London: Oxford University Press, 1965).

House, Edward Mandell, and Seymour, Charles (eds.), *What Really Happened at Paris: The Story of the Peace Conference, 1918–1919* (New York: Charles Scribner's Sons, 1921).

Housepian, Marjorie, *Smyrna 1922: The Destruction of a City* (London: Faber and Faber, 1972).

Hoving, Thomas, *Tutankhamun: The Untold Story* (New York: Simon and Schuster, 1978).

Howard, Harry N., *The Partition of Turkey: A Diplomatic History 1913–1923* (New York: Howard Fertig, 1966).

——, *Turkey, the Straits and U.S. Policy* (Baltimore and London: The Johns Hopkins University Press, 1974).

Hunt, Barry, and Preston, Adrian, *War Aims and Strategic Policy in the Great War 1914–1918* (London: Croom Helm, and Totowa, N. J.: Rowman and Littlefield, 1977).

Hurewitz, J. C., *Diplomacy in the Near and Middle East: A Documentary Record: 1914–1956*, 2 Vols (Princeton, Toronto, London, and New York: D. Van Nostrand, 1956).

Hyde, H. Montgomery, *Carson* (Melbourne, London, and Toronto: William Heinemann, 1953).

Ingram, Edward, *The Beginnings of the Great Game in Asia 1828–1834* (Oxford: Clarendon Press, 1979).

——, *Commitment to Empire: Prophecies of the Great Game in Asia 1797–1800* (Oxford: Clarendon Press, 1981).

Ingrams, Doreen (ed.), *Palestine Papers 1917–1922, Seeds of Conflict* (London: John Murray, 1972).

Issawi, Charles, *The Economic History of Turkey: 1800–1914* (Chicago and London: University of Chicago Press, 1980).

Jabotinsky, Vladimir, *The Story of the Jewish Legion*, translated by Samuel Katz (New York: Bernard Ackerman, 1945).

Jenkins, Roy, *Asquith: Portrait of a Man and an Era* (New York: E. P. Dutton, 1966).

Jones, Thomas, *Lloyd George* (Cambridge, Mass.: Harvard University Press, 1951).

Kazemzadeh, Firuz, *The Struggle for Transcaucasia (1917–1921)* (New York: Philosophical Library, and Oxford: George Ronald, 1951).

Kedourie, Elie, *Arabic Political Memoirs and Other Studies* (London: Frank Cass, 1974).

——, *The Chatham House Version and Other Middle-Eastern Studies* (London: Weidenfield and Nicolson, 1970).

——, *The Chatham House Version and Other Middle-Eastern Studies*, New Edition (Hanover and London: University Press of New England, 1984).

——, *England and the Middle East: The Destruction of the Ottoman Empire, 1914–1921* (Hassocks, Sussex: The Harvester Press, 1978).

——, "From Clerk to Clerk: Writing Diplomatic History," *The American Scholar* (Autumn 1979).

——, *In the Anglo-Arab Labyrinth: The McMahon-Husayn Correspondence and its Interpreters 1914–1939* (Cambridge, London, New York, and Melbourne: Cambridge University Press, 1976).

——, *Islam in the Modern World and Other Studies* (New York: Holt, Rinehart & Winston, 1981).

——, "The Surrender of Medina, January 1919," *Middle Eastern Studies* (January 1977).

——, (ed.), *The Jewish World: History and Culture of the Jewish People* (New York: Harry N. Abrams, 1979).

Keep, John L. H., *The Russian Revolution: A Study in Mass Mobilization* (London: Weidenfeld & Nicolson, 1976).

Kelly, J. B., *Arabia, the Gulf and the West* (New York: Basic Books, 1980).

Kennan, George F., *Soviet-American Relations, 1917–1920*, 2 Vols (Princeton: Princeton University Press, 1956–58).

Kennedy, A. L., *Salisbury 1830–1903: Portrait of a Statesman* (London: John Murray, 1953).

Kennedy, Paul, "A Historian of Imperial Decline Looks at America," *International Herald Tribune*, 3 November 1982.

——, *The Realities Behind Diplomacy: Background Influences on British External Policy, 1865–1980* (Glasgow: Fontana, 1981).

——, *The Rise of the Anglo-German Antagonism: 1860–1914* (London: George Allen & Unwin, 1980).

——, *Strategy and Diplomacy 1870–1945: Eight Studies* (London: George Allen & Unwin, 1983).

Kent, Marian, *Oil and Empire: British Policy and Mesopotamian Oil, 1900–1920* (London and Basingstoke: Macmillan Press, 1976).

Kettle, Michael, *The Allies and the Russian Collapse March 1917–March 1918* (London: André Deutsch, 1981).

Keynes, John Maynard, *The Economic Consequences of the Peace* (New York: Harcourt Brace & Howe, 1920).

——, *Essays In Biography*, ed. by Geoffrey Keynes (New York: Horizon Press, 1951).

Khoury, Philip S., *Urban Notables and Arab Nationalism: The Politics of Damascus 1860–1920* (Cambridge, London, New York, New Rochelle, Melbourne, and Sydney: Cambridge University Press, 1983).

Kinross, Lord, *Ataturk: A Biography of Mustafa Kemal, Father of Modern Turkey* (New York: William Morrow, 1965).

——, *The Ottoman Centuries: The Rise and Fall of the Turkish Empire* (New York: Morrow Quill Paperbacks, 1977).

Klieman, Aaron S., *Foundations of British Policy in the Arab World: The Cairo Conference of 1921* (Baltimore and London: The Johns Hopkins University Press, 1970).

Knightley, Phillip, and Simpson, Colin, *The Secret Lives of Lawrence of Arabia* (London: Thomas Nelson & Sons, 1969).

Kraemer, Joel L. (ed.), *Jerusalem: Problems and Prospects* (New York: Praeger, 1980).

Langer, William L., *The Diplomacy of Imperialism 1890–1902* (New York: Alfred A. Knopf, 1951).

——, *European Alliances and Alignments 1871–1890* (New York: Alfred A. Knopf, 1956).

Laqueur, Walter, *A History of Zionism* (New York, Chicago, and San Francisco: Holt, Rinehart & Winston, 1972).

Lawrence, A. W. (ed.), *T. E. Lawrence By His Friends* (London: Jonathan Cape, 1954).

Lawrence, T. E., *Evolution of a Revolt: Early Postwar Writings of T. E. Lawrence*, ed. by Stanley and Rodelle Weintraub (University Park and London: The Pennsylvania State University Press, 1968).

——, *The Home Letters Of T. E. Lawrence and His Brothers* (Oxford: Basil Blackwell, 1954).

——, *The Letters of T. E. Lawrence*, edited by David Garnett (London and Toronto: Jonathan Cape, 1938).

——, *Oriental Assembly*, edited by A. W. Lawrence (London: Williams and Norgate, 1939).

——, *Secret Despatches from Arabia by T. E. Lawrence* (The Golden Cockerell Press, n.d.).

——, *Seven Pillars of Wisdom: A Triumph* (Garden City: Doubleday, Doran, 1935).

——, *T. E. Lawrence to His Biographers: Robert Graves and Liddell Hart*, 2 Vols (New York: Doubleday, Doran, 1938).

Leggett, George, *The Cheka: Lenin's Political Police* (Oxford: Clarendon Press, 1981).

Lenczowski, George, *The Middle East in World Affairs*, 4th edn (Ithaca and London: Cornell University Press, 1980).

Lesch, Ann Mosely, *Arab Politics in Palestine, 1917–1939: The Frustration Of A Nationalist Movement* (Ithaca and London: Cornell University Press, 1979).

Leslie, Shane, *Mark Sykes: His Life and Letters* (London, New York, Toronto, and Melbourne: Cassell, 1923).

Lewin, Moshe, *Lenin's Last Struggle*, trans. by A. M. Sheridan Smith (New York and London: Monthly Review Press, 1968).

Lewis, Bernard, *The Arabs in History*, rev. edn (New York: Harper Torchbooks, 1967).

——, *The Emergence of Modern Turkey*, 2nd edn (London, Oxford, and New York: Oxford University Press, 1968).

——, *The Middle East and the West* (New York, Hagerstown, San Francisco, and London: Harper Torchbooks, 1966).

——, (ed.), *Islam and the Arab World* (New York: Alfred A. Knopf, 1976).

Liddell Hart, B. H., *Strategy: The Indirect Approach* (New York: Frederick A. Praeger, 1954).

Liman von Sanders, Otto, *Five Years in Turkey* (Annapolis: The United States Naval Institute, 1927).

Link, Arthur S., *Wilson: Campaigns for Progressivism and Peace* (Princeton: Princeton University Press, 1965).

Lloyd George, David, *Memoirs of the Peace Conference*, 2 Vols (New Haven: Yale University Press, 1939).

——, *War Memoirs*, 6 Vols (Boston: Little, Brown, 1933–37).

Lockhart, R. H. Bruce, *The Two Revolutions: An Eye-Witness Study of Russia, 1917* (London: Phoenix House, 1957).

Lowe, C. J., and Dockrill, M. L., *The Mirage of Power*, 3 Vols (London and Boston: Routledge & Kegan Paul, 1972).

Mack, John E., *A Prince of Our Disorder: The Life of T. E. Lawrence* (Boston and Toronto: Little, Brown, 1976).

MacKenzie, Compton, *Gallipoli Memories* (Garden City: Doubleday, Doran, 1930).

——, *Greek Memories* (University Publications of America, 1987).

——, *My Life and Times, Octave Five, 1915–1923* (London: Chatto & Windus, 1966).

MacKinder, Sir Halford J., *The Scope and Methods of Geography, and the Geographical Pivot of History* (London: Royal Geographical Society, 1951).

Maclean, Fitzroy, *A Person from England, and Other Travellers* (London: Jonathan Cape, 1958).

——, *To the Back of Beyond* (London: Jonathan Cape, 1974).

Magnus, Philip, *Kitchener: Portrait of an Imperialist* (Harmondsworth: Penguin, 1968).

Manchester, William, *The Last Lion: Winston Spencer Churchill, Visions of Glory, 1874–1932* (Boston and Toronto: Little, Brown, 1983).

Marder, Arthur, J., *From the Dreadnought to Scapa Flow: The Royal Navy in the Fisher Era, 1904–1919*, Vol. 5, *Victory and Aftermath, January 1918–June 1919* (London: Oxford University Press, 1970).

Mason, Alpheus Thomas, *Brandeis: A Free Man's Life* (New York: Viking Press, 1946).

Massey, W. T., *Allenby's Final Triumph* (New York: E. P. Dutton, 1920).

May, Ernest R. (ed.), *Knowing One's Enemies: Intelligence Assessment Before the Two World Wars* (Princeton: Princeton University Press, 1984).

Mayer, Arno J., *Politics and Diplomacy of Peacemaking: Containment and Counter-revolution at Versailles 1918–1919* (New York: Alfred A. Knopf, 1967).

McNeill, William H., *Plagues and Peoples* (Garden City: Doubleday, Anchor Books, 1976).

Meinertzhagen, Colonel R., *Middle East Diary 1917–1956* (London: The Cresset Press, 1959).

Mejcher, Helmut, "Oil and British Policy Towards Mesopotamia," *Middle Eastern Studies* (October 1972).

Monroe, Elizabeth, *Britain's Moment in the Middle East: 1914–1971*, rev. edn (Baltimore: The Johns Hopkins University Press, 1981).

Moorehead, Alan, *Gallipoli* (New York: Ballantine Books, 1956).

Morgan, Gerald, *Anglo-Russian Rivalry in Central Asia: 1810–1895* (London: Frank Cass, 1981).

Morgan, Kenneth O., *Consensus and Disunity: The Lloyd George Coalition Government 1918–1922* (Oxford: Clarendon Press, 1979).

——, *Lloyd George* (London: Weidenfeld & Nicolson, 1974).

Morgan, Kenneth, and Morgan, Jane, *Portrait of a Progressive: The Political Career of Christopher, Viscount Addison* (Oxford: Clarendon Press, 1980).

Morgan, Ted, *Churchill: Young Man in a Hurry, 1874–1915* (New York: Simon & Schuster, 1982).

Morison, J.L., "From Alexander to Burns to Frederick Roberts: A Survey of Imperial Frontier Policy," *Raleigh Lecture on History* (London: British Academy, 1936).

Morris, James, *Farewell the Trumpets: An Imperial Retreat* (New York and London: Harcourt Brace Jovanovich, 1978).

Mosley, Leonard, *Power Play: Oil in the Middle East* (New York: Random House, 1973).

Mousa, Suleiman, "A Matter of Principle: King Hussein of the Hijaz and the Arabs of Palestine," *International Journal of Middle Eastern Studies* (1978).

——, *T. E. Lawrence: An Arab View* (London, New York, and Toronto: Oxford University Press, 1966).

Mowat, Charles Loch, *Britain Between the Wars 1918–1940* (London: Methuen University Paperback, 1968).

Namier, L. B., *Avenues of History* (London: Hamish Hamilton, 1952).

Nevakivi, Jukka, *Britain, France and the Arab Middle East 1914–1920* (London: The Athlone Press, 1969).

Nicholson, Harold, *Curzon: The Last Phase 1919–1925* (Boston and New York: Houghton Mifflin, 1934).

——, *Diplomacy*, 3rd edn (New York: Oxford University Press, A Galaxy Book, 1964).

Nordau, Max, *Max Nordau to His People: A Summons and Challenge* (New York: Scopus Publishing, 1941).

Norris, J. A., *The First Afghan War 1838–1842* (Cambridge: Cambridge University Press, 1967).

Nove, Alec, *An Economic History of the U.S.S.R.* (Harmondsworth: Penguin Books, 1982).

O'Brien, Terence H., *Milner* (London: Constable, 1979).

Pakenham, Thomas, *The Boer War* (New York: Random House, 1979).

Parrish, Michael E., *Felix Frankfurter and His Time — The Reform Years* (New York: Free Press, and London: Collier Macmillan, 1982).

Pinsker, Leo, *Road to Freedom: Writings and Addresses* (New York: Scopus Publishing, 1944).

Pipes, Richard, *The Formation of the Soviet Union, Communism and Nationalism, 1917–1923*, rev. edn (Cambridge, Mass.: Harvard University Press, 1964).

Porath, Y., *The Emergence of the Palestinian-Arab National Movement 1918–1929* (London: Frank Cass, 1974).

Poullada, Leon B., *Reform and Rebellion in Afghanistan, 1919–1929: King Amanullah's Failure to Modernize a Tribal Society* (Ithaca and London: Cornell University Press, 1973).

Presland, John (pseudonym for Gladys Skelton), *Deedes Bey: A Study of Sir Wyndham Deedes 1883–1923* (London: Macmillan, 1942).

Rabinowitz, Ezekiel, *Justice Louis D. Brandeis: The Zionist Chapter of His Life* (New York: Philosophical Library, 1968).

Ramsaur, Jr., Ernest Edmondson, *The Young Turks: Prelude to the Revolution of 1908* (Princeton: Princeton University Press, 1957).

Raymond, John (ed.), *The Baldwin Age* (London: Eyre & Spottiswoode, 1960).

Riddell, Lord, *Intimate Diary of the Peace Conference and after 1918–1923* (New York: Reynal & Hitchcock, 1934).

——, *The Riddell Diaries: 1908–1923*, edited by J. M. McEwen (London and Atlantic Highlands: The Athlone Press, 1986).

——, *War Diary 1914–1918* (London: Ivor Nicholson & Watson, 1933).

Ridley, Jasper, *Lord Palmerston* (London: Panther, 1972).

Robinson, Francis, *Atlas of the Islamic World since 1500* (New York: Facts on File, 1982).

Ro'i, Yaacov, "The Zionist Attitude to the Arabs 1908–1914," *Middle Eastern Studies* (April 1968).

Rose, Kenneth, *The Later Cecils* (New York, Evanston, San Francisco, and London: Harper & Row, 1975).

Rose, Norman, *Vansittart: Study of a Diplomat* (London: Heinemann, 1978).

Roskill, Stephen, *Hankey: Man of Secrets*, 2 Vols (London: Collins, 1970–72).

Round Table, *The Ottoman Domination* (London: T. Fisher Unwin, 1917).

Royle, Trevor, *The Kitchener Enigma* (London: Michael Joseph, 1985).

Sachar, Howard M., *The Emergence of the Middle East: 1914–1924* (New York: Alfred A. Knopf, 1969).

——, *A History of Israel: From the Rise of Zionism to Our Time* (New York: Alfred A. Knopf, 1976).

Said, Edward W., *Orientalism* (New York: Vintage Books, 1971).

Sanders, Ronald, *The High Walls of Jerusalem: A History of the Balfour Declaration and the Birth of the British Mandate for Palestine* (New York: Holt, Rinehart & Winston, 1983).

Schapiro, Leonard, *The Russian Revolutions of 1917: The Origins of Modern Communism* (New York: Basic Books, 1984).

Schechtman, Joseph B., *The Vladimir Jabotinsky Story*, 2 Vols (New York: Thomas Yoseloff, 1956–61).

Schuyler, Eugene, *Turkistan: Notes of a Journey in Russian Turkistan, Kokand, Bukhara and Kuldja*, edited by Geoffrey Wheeler (New York and Washington: Frederick A. Praeger, 1966).

Searight, Sarah, *The British in The Middle East* (New York: Atheneum, 1970).

Seton-Watson, Hugh, *The Russian Empire 1801–1917* (Oxford: Clarendon Press, 1967).

Seymour, Charles, *The Intimate Papers of Colonel House*, Vol. 3 (Boston and New York: Houghton Mifflin, 1928).

Shaw, Bernard, *Flyleaves*, edited by Dan H. Laurence and Daniel J. Leary (Austin: W. Thomas Taylor, 1977).

Shaw, Stanford J., "The Ottoman Census System and Population 1831–1914," *International Journal of Middle East Studies* (August 1978).

Shaw, Stanford J., and Shaw, Ezel Kural, *History of the Ottoman Empire and*

Modern Turkey, Vol. 2, *Reform, Revolution, and Republic: The Rise of Modern Turkey, 1808–1975* (Cambridge, London, New York, and Melbourne: Cambridge University Press, 1977).

Shotwell, James D., *The Great Decision* (New York: Macmillan, 1944).

Smith, Denis Mack, *Mussolini* (New York: Vintage Books, 1983).

Smith, Michael Llewellyn, *Ionian Vision: Greece in Asia Minor, 1919–1922* (New York: St Martin's Press, 1973).

Smuts, J. C., *Selections from the Smuts Papers*, Vols. 3–4, edited by W. K. Hancock and Jean Van Der Poel (Cambridge: Cambridge University Press, 1966).

——, *Selections from the Smuts Papers*, Vol. 5, edited by Jean Van Der Poel (Cambridge: Cambridge University Press, 1973).

Sonyel, Salahi Ramsdan, *Turkish Diplomacy, 1918–1923: Mustafa Kemal and the Turkish National Movement* (London and Beverly Hills: SAGE Publications, 1975).

Stanwood, Frederick, *War, Revolution & British Imperialism in Central Asia* (London: Ithaca Press, 1983).

Stavrianos, L. S., *The Balkans since 1453* (New York: Rinehart, 1958).

Steadman, John M., *The Myth of Asia* (New York: Simon and Schuster, 1969).

Steel, Ronald, *Walter Lippmann and the American Century* (Boston and Toronto: Little, Brown, 1980).

Steevens, G. W., *With Kitchener to Khartum* (New York: Dodd, Mead, 1900).

Stein, Kenneth W., *The Land Question in Palestine, 1917–1939* (Chapel Hill and London: The University of North Carolina Press, 1984).

Stein, Leonard, *The Balfour Declaration* (London: Valentine Mitchell, 1961).

Steiner, Zara S., *Britain and the Origins of the First World War* (London and Basingstoke: Macmillan, 1970).

Stevenson, Frances, *Lloyd George: A Diary*, ed. by A. J. P. Taylor (New York, Evanston, San Francisco, and London: Harper & Row, 1971).

Stewart, Desmond, *T. E. Lawrence* (New York, Hagerstown, San Francisco, and London: Harper & Row, 1977).

Stivers, William, *Supremacy and Oil: Iraq, Turkey, and the Anglo-American World Order, 1918–1930* (Ithaca and London: Cornell University Press, 1982).

Stone, Norman, *The Eastern Front 1914–1917* (London, Sydney, Auckland, and Toronto: Holder & Stoughton, 1975).

——, *Europe Transformed 1878–1919* (Fontana, 1983).

Storrs, Sir Ronald, *The Memoirs of Sir Ronald Storrs* (New York: G. P. Putnam's Sons, 1937).

Swanson, Glen W., "Enver Pasha: the Formative Years," *Middle Eastern Studies* (October 1980).

Swinson, Arthur, *North-West Frontier: People and Events, 1839–1947* (London: Hutchinson, 1967).

Sykes, Christopher, *Crossroads to Israel: 1917–1948* (Bloomington and London: Indiana University Press, 1973).

——, *Two Studies in Virtue* (London: Collins, 1953).

Sykes, Sir Mark, *The Caliphs' Last Heritage: A Short History of the Turkish Empire* (London: Macmillan, 1915).

Tabacknick, Stephen E., and Matheson, Christopher, *Images of Lawrence* (London: Jonathan Cape, 1988).

Taylor, A. J. P., *Beaverbrook* (New York: Simon & Schuster, 1972).

——, *English History 1914–1945* (Oxford: Clarendon Press, 1965).

——, *Englishmen and Others* (London: Hamish Hamilton, 1956).

——, *The First World War: An Illustrated History* (London: Hamish Hamilton, 1963).

——, *From Saravejo to Potsdam* (Harcourt, Brace & World, 1966).

——, *How Wars Begin* (London: Hamish Hamilton, 1979).

——, *How Wars End* (London: Hamish Hamilton, 1985).

——, *The Last of Old Europe: A Grand Tour* (London: Sidgwick & Jackson, 1976).

——, *Politics in Wartime and Other Essays* (London: Hamish Hamilton, 1964).

——, *Revolutions and Revolutionaries* (London: Hamish Hamilton, 1980).

——, *The Struggle for Mastery in Europe 1848–1918* (Oxford: Clarendon Press, 1954).

——, *The War Lords* (London: Hamish Hamilton, 1977).

—— (ed.), *Lloyd George: Twelve Essays* (New York: Atheneum, 1971).

—— (ed.), *My Darling Pussy: The Letters of Lloyd George and Frances Stevenson 1913–1941* (London: Weidenfeld and Nicolson, 1975).

Taylor, Robert, *Lord Salisbury* (London: Allen Lane, 1975).

Temperley, Harold, *The Foreign Policy of Canning 1822–1827: England, the Neo-Holy Alliance, and the New World*, 2nd edn (Hamden, Connecticut: Archon, 1966).

—— (ed.), *A History Of The Peace Conference Of Paris*, 6 Vols (London: Henry Froude and Hodder & Stoughton, 1920–24).

Temperley, Harold, and Penson, Lillian M. (eds.), *Foundations of British Foreign Policy From Pitt (1792) to Salisbury (1902)* (New York: Barnes & Noble, 1966).

Teveth, Shabtai, *Ben-Gurion and the Palestinian Arabs* (Oxford and New York: Oxford University Press, 1985).

Thomas, Lowell, *With Lawrence in Arabia* (New York and London: The Century Co., 1924).

Tidrick, Kathryn, *Heart-beguiling Araby* (Cambridge, London, New York, New Rochelle, Melbourne, and Sydney: Cambridge University Press, 1981).

Townshend, Charles, "Civilization and 'Frightfulness': Air Control in the Middle East Between the Wars," in Chris Wrigley, (ed.), *Warfare Diplomacy and Politics: Essays in Honour of A. J. P. Taylor* (London: Hamish Hamilton, 1986).

Townshend, Charles Vere Ferres, *My Campaign* (New York: James A. McCann, 1920).

Toynbee, Arnold J., *The Western Question in Greece and Turkey*, reprint of 2nd edn (1923) (New York: Howard Fertig, 1970).

Troeller, Gary, *The Birth of Saudi Arabia: Britain and the Rise of the House of Sa'ud* (London: Frank Cass, 1976).

Trumpener, Ulrich, *Germany and the Ottoman Empire: 1914–1918* (Princeton: Princeton University Press, 1968).

Tuchman, Barbara W., *Bible and Sword: England and Palestine from the Bronze Age to Balfour* (New York: Funk & Wagnalls, 1956).

——, *The Guns of August* (New York: Dell, 1962).

——, *The Zimmerman Telegram* (New York: Bantam Books, 1971).

Ullman, Richard H., *Anglo-Soviet Relations, 1917–1921*, 3 Vols (Princeton: Princeton University Press, 1961–72).

U.S. State Department, *Papers Relating to the Foreign Relations of the United States: The Paris Peace Conference 1919*, 13 Vols (Washington: Government Printing Office, 1942–47).

Vansittart, Lord, *The Mist Procession* (London: Hutchinson, 1958).

Varé, Daniele, *Laughing Diplomat* (London: John Murray, 1938).

Vatikiotis, P. J., *The History of Egypt*, 2nd edn (Baltimore: The Johns Hopkins University Press, 1980).

Vereté, Mayir, "The Balfour Declaration and its Makers," *Middle Eastern Studies* (January 1970).

——, "Kitchener, Grey and the Question of Palestine in 1915–1916: A Note," *Middle Eastern Studies* (May 1973).

Warner, Philip, *Kitchener: The Man Behind the Legend* (London: Hamish Hamilton, 1985).

Watson, David Robin, *Georges Clemenceau: A Political Biography* (London: Eyre Methuen, 1974).

Weber, Frank G., *Eagles on the Crescent: Germany, Austria, and the Diplomacy of the Turkish Alliance 1914–1918* (Ithaca and London: Cornell University Press, 1970).

Webster, Sir Charles, *The Foreign Policy of Palmerston, 1830–1841, Britain, The Liberal Movement and the Eastern Question*, 2 Vols (New York: Humanities Press, 1969).

Weizmann, Chaim, *The Letters and Papers of Chaim Weizmann*, Vol. 8, series A, *November 1917–October 1918*, edited by Dvorah Barzilay and Barnet Litvinoff (Jerusalem: Israel University Press, 1977).

——, *Trial and Error: The Autobiography of Chaim Weizman* (New York: Harper & Brothers, 1949).

Whiting, Allen S., *Soviet Policy in China 1912–1924* (Stanford University Press Paperback Reprint, 1968).

Wilson, Edmund, *To the Finland Station: A Study in the Writing and Acting of History* (Garden City: Doubleday, Anchor Books, 1953).

Wilson, J. M., "Sense and Nonsense in the Biography of T. E. Lawrence," *T. E. Lawrence Studies* (spring 1976).

Wilson, Trevor, *The Myriad Faces of War: Britain and the Great War, 1914–1918* (Cambridge: Polity Press, 1986).

Wilson, Woodrow, *The Papers of Woodrow Wilson*, edited by Arthur S. Link *et al.*, Vol. 41, *January 24–April 6, 1917* (Princeton: Princeton University Press, 1983).

Winstone, H. V. F., *Captain Shakespear* (London: Jonathan Cape, 1976).

——, *Gertrude Bell* (London: Jonathan Cape, 1978).

——, *The Illicit Adventure* (London: Jonathan Cape, 1982).

——, *Leachman: 'OC Desert'* (London, Melbourne, and New York: Quartet Books, 1982).

—— (ed.), *The Diaries of Parker Pasha* (London, Melbourne, and New York: Quartet Books, 1983).

Wolfe, Bertram D., *Three Who Made a Revolution: A Biographical History*, 4th rev. edn (New York: Dell Publishing, Delta Books, 1964).

Wolfers, Arnold, *Britain and France Between Two Wars* (New York: W. W. Norton, 1966).

Woodward, E. L., and Butler, Rohan, *Documents On British Foreign Policy 1919–1939*, First Series, Vols 1–24 (London: His Majesty's Stationery Office, 1947; Her Majesty's Stationery Office, 1983).

Woolley, C. Leonard, and Lawrence, T. E., *The Wilderness of Zin (Archaeological Report)* (London: Palestine Exploration Fund, 1914).

Wrench, John Evelyn, *Geoffrey Dawson and Our Times* (London: Hutchinson, 1955).

Young, Sir Hubert, *The Independent Arab* (London: John Murray, 1933).

Zeine, Zeine N., *The Emergence of Arab Nationalism with a Background Study of Arab-Turkish Relations in the Near East* (Beirut: Khayats, 1966).

Zeldin, Theodore, *France 1848–1945*, 2 Vols (Oxford: Clarendon Press, 1973–77).

Zeman, Z. A. B., and Scharlau, W. B., *The Merchant of Revolution: The Life of Alexander Israel Helphand (Parvus) 1867–1924* (London: Oxford University Press, 1965).

Zeman, Z. A. B. (ed.), *Germany and the Revolution in Russia 1915–1918* (London: Oxford University Press, 1958).

Zurcher, Erik Jan, *The Unionist Factor: The Role of the Committee of Union and Progress in the Turkish National Movement 1905–1926* (Leiden: E. J. Brill, 1984).

INDEX

Aaronsohn, Aaron: his pro-Allied position 211, 278; his achievements 278−9; his espionage activities 278, 308−9

Aaronsohn, Sarah 309

Abbas II (Abbas Hilmi Pasha), Khedive of Egypt 84, 101

Abd el Kader, Emir 336−7; 341

Abd el Kader, Said 336−7

Abdul Hamid II, Sultan 39−41, 112, 273

Abdullah, son of Hussein of Mecca: meets with Kitchener and Storrs in Cairo before the war 98−9, 101; corresponds with Kitchener on his father's behalf 102, 114; meets Storrs and Lawrence in Jeddah, and permits Lawrence to go up country 226; leads postwar expedition against Ibn Saud 425; his candidacy for the throne of Mesopotamia 437; in Transjordan 504−6, 510−14, 560, 562

Abdul Said Mir Alim Khan, Emir of Bukhara 485−7

Addison, Dr Christopher 388

Aden: administered by British India 107; included by Storrs in his plan for a new British Vice-Royalty 143

Afghanistan: British-Russian rivalry in 26−32; becomes a British protectorate 33, 99, 107; German wartime expeditions to 208; Ottoman designs on 109, 120, 170, 208, 313, 352−3, 355, 357, 363; the Third Afghan War and its settlement 415, 420−3, 453; and communist Russia 459, 461, 473, 474, 483n, 559; and Enver's revolt in Bukhara 487, 489; current conflicts in 564

Ahd, al- 99, 102, 176−8, 218, 436

Ahmed Mirza, Shah of Persia 209, 456, 460

Aitken, Sir Max, later 1st Baron Beaverbrook 234, 555−6

Albania: revolts against Ottoman rule 45; occupied by Habsburg Empire 208n

Aleppo see "Damascus, Homs, Hama and Aleppo"

Alexander, King of Greece 432

Alexandretta (Iskenderun): plans to use as British base in the postwar Middle East 140, 141, 143, 149, 192

Ali, son of Hussein of Mecca 220

Ali, Mehemet 269

Allenby, Sir Edmund, later 1st Viscount Allenby of Megiddo and Felixstowe: appointed to command Egyptian Expeditionary Force in invasion of Palestine 308; approves Lawrence's plan for use of Arab irregulars in Palestine campaign 310; leads Palestine campaign 311−13; plans attack on Syria 315; and plans for administration of territories taken from the Ottoman Empire 318, 320−2; leads Syrian campaign 332−42; and the question of French or Arab rule in Syria and Lebanon 334−43, 435; dines with Feisal in Damascus 346; and French claims to Syria 377−8; statement at Peace Conference 394−5, 396; and location of Dan ("Dan to Beersheba") 400; sent to take charge in Egypt (1919) 420; warns superiors not to disregard Feisal and Syrian Congress 437−8; and administration of Palestine 445: his policy as British High Commissioner in Egypt 502

Allenby Declaration (1922) 502, 510, 560

Amanullah Khan, King of Afghanistan 421−2, 483n

Amery, Leopold S.: at War Cabinet secretariat 224, 235; his British imperial vision and the question of a Jewish

Palestine 276–83; and the Imperial War Conference 279–83; quoted on importance of a Jewish Palestine 290–1; helps draft Balfour Declaration 293, 295; evaluates his accomplishments in 1917 300–1; discusses Sykes-Picot Agreement with Sykes 344; sees a war for Asia at hand 357–9; seeks immediate British possession of the Middle East before a cease-fire 364; fears US may accept trusteeship of Palestine 374

Amet, Vice-Admiral Jean F. C.: and armistice negotiations with the Ottoman Empire 371

Amritsar Massacre 422

Anglo-French Declaration (1918) 331, 401

Anglo-Iraqi Treaty (1922) 510

Anglo-Persian Agreement (1919) 456–9, 461

Anglo-Russian Agreement (1907) 31–3

Angora Accord (1921) 537–3

Antonius, George 279

Aqaba expedition 309–11

Arab Bulletin: described 221–2; quoted 184, 222–3; reports Hussein threatened by Ibn Saud 424; and Lowell Thomas 498n

Arab Bureau, the: creation of 170–2; opposes Sykes 194; aids in talks at Kut 200–3; views on Hussein's revolt 219, 221; and the Arab Bulletin 221–3; views 305; and Allenby's use of Feisal's forces 310–11; reports quoted 322, 328; asked by Sykes to arrange meeting with Arab leaders 329; and the Foreign Office's policy 335; and Arab independence 419; and Hussein as Caliph 426; reports (1919) on plans for a Pan-Islamic revolt against Britain 467; charged with "endangering world peace" 469–70; see also Clayton; Herbert; Hogarth; Lawrence; Walrond

Arab Club, the (Syria) 436

Arab Executive, the (Palestine) 521–2, 526

Arab Legion, the (Transjordan) 512

Arabia see specific headings

Arabian Report (Sykes) 224

Armenia: proposed US Mandate 398

Armenian Massacres (1915) 212–15

Armenian Revolutionary Federation 214

Armstrong Whitworth 55, 57, 58

Askari, Jaafar al- 220

Asquith, Herbert Henry: cruises with Churchill and others aboard Enchantress

(1912) 23–4; and the modern Middle East 26; harbors no designs on the Middle East 32, 96; and Churchill 51, 65–6; quoted on the Turkish war 73, 75; and appointment of Kitchener as War Minister 80–2; quoted 132n; favors conceding Constantinople to Russia 138–9; and Britain's Middle East goals 141–2; appoints de Bunsen committee 146; and the Dardanelles campaign 153–4; quoted on the perils of attacking Gallipoli 157; forms Coalition Cabinet 161; and the questions of what to do about Kitchener and Gallipoli 164, 165, 167, 216; orders study of "an Islamic Bureau" 170; his faltering war leadership attacked 195, 231–2; overthrown as Prime Minister 233–4; and Churchill 266n; on Herbert Samuel's plan for a Jewish Palestine and Lloyd George's support of it 269–70; defeated in the elections (1918) 384; and Russia's grievances in the Middle East 474, 539; leads his party to defeat in the elections (1922) 556; his underestimation of the Ottoman Empire 561; and Churchill 566

Asquith, Margot 54

Asquith, Violet 23–4, 53, 63, 81, 135, 566

Auda abu Tayi 309–10

Australia: role in the British imperial system 280–2, 301, 358, 530, 549n; and the Chanak crisis 550; see also specific wartime campaigns

Austria-Hungary (Habsburg Empire): and annexation of portions of the Ottoman Empire 45, 46, 49, 208n; and outbreak of First World War 45, 50, 58–9; vulnerable, says Lloyd George 134; and the Armenian Massacres 212; US delays declaration of war against 256, 259; prisoners of war in Russia 356, 360; Allied offensive against (1918) 363; and the Peace Conference 403; dissolved 434

Auto-Emancipation (Pinsker) 272n

Azerbaijan: Enver's forces fight for 209, 313, 354–6; British occupy 404; Russians recapture 482, 484, 485

Bagehot, Walter 31

Baghdad Railway project 25n

Bailey, Colonel Frederick Marshman 361

Baku: campaigns 359–60, 458; congress 482

Baldwin, Stanley 553

Balfour, Arthur James, later 1st Earl of Balfour 31, 80, 132n, 157, 234, 257, 261-2, 270, 273, 288, 293, 296, 300, 334, 345, 364, 365, 373-5, 400, 519, 520, 541, 545

Balfour Declaration (1917) 274-300, 317, 321, 322, 324, 325, 401, 445, 504, 513, 517, 520, 524-6

Balkan Confederation 74-5

Balkan League 45

Balkan Wars 43, 45, 208n, 243, 247

Barrow, Major-General Sir George 337

Beaverbrook, Lord see Aitken, Sir Max

Bedford, A. C. 534, 536

Beha-ed-Din 211

Belgium: German invasion of 80

Bell, Gertrude 35-6, 144, 323, 326, 397, 449-52, 496, 503, 507, 508n

Ben-Gurion, David 211, 526-8

Ben Zvi, Itzhak 211

Bethmann Hollweg, Chancellor Theobald von 58-9, 254

Bey, Halil 44

Bey, Rauf 371, 372

Birdwood, General William 158

Birkenhead, Lord see Smith, F. E.

Bismarck, Prince Otto von 237, 271

Boer War 38, 82, 202, 232, 235, 280, 281

Bonaparte, Napoleon, Egyptian expedition 27-8

Bonar Law, Andrew 80, 160-1, 163-5, 231, 234, 235, 266n, 295, 365, 383, 384, 387, 540, 553, 554-6

Borden, Robert 549n

Bosnia: annexation of by Austria-Hungary 45, 208n

Botha, Louis 281, 282, 549n

Brandeis, Justice Louis D. 299-300, 395, 513

Bray, Major N. N. E. 467

Brazil: and the Turkish battleships 54, 56

Breasted, James Henry 24

Brémond, Lieutenant-Colonel Edouard 225, 311

Breslau (ship) 62-8, 70-3, 119, 122

Brethren (Ikhwan) 425-6

Briand, Aristide 197, 236, 536-8

Britain/British Empire see specific headings

British East Africa 273-4, 281, 300, 308

Bronstein, Lev Davidovich see Trotsky, Leon

Brunton, Captain C. D. 12, 442-3, 516

Bryant, Louise 483

Bryce, James 213n

Buchan, John 43, 82, 93, 97, 232n, 247, 264, 280, 358

Bukhara 33, 357, 479-90

Bulgaria 34, 35, 45, 46, 49, 62, 66, 68, 74, 75, 125, 127, 134, 256, 264, 363, 364, 366-8, 373, 403

Bunsen, Sir Maurice de 142 see also de Bunsen Comittee

Cadman, Sir John 536

Caillard, Vincent 266

Cairo see Egypt/Cairo

Cairo Conference (1921) 502-7, 515, 519

Caix, Robert de 438, 439, 442

Calthorpe, Vice-Admiral Somerset Arthur Gough, 366, 369-73

Calwell, General Sir Charles 146, 147

Cambon, Jules 292-3

Cambon, Paul 192

Campbell-Bannerman, Sir Henry 31

Canada: role in the British imperial system 280-2, 530, 549n; and Chanak crisis 550

Canning, George 75

Capitulations 47, 64, 69, 267, 533

Carasso, Emmanuel see Karasu, Emmanuel

Carden, Admiral Sackville 130-2, 134-5, 150-1

Carnegie Endowment: survey of changes resulting from the war 240

Carson, Sir Edward 80, 126, 164, 232, 233-4

Carter, Howard 510n

Cartwright, Joanna and Ebenezer 268

Cavour, Count Camillo di 271

Cecil, Lord Robert 291, 293, 298, 334

Chamberlain, Austen 170, 182, 185, 552, 555

Chamberlain, Joseph 273-4, 278, 280

Chanak (Canakkale) crisis 551-5

Chauvel, General Harry 311n, 334, 335, 337-9

Cheetham, Sir Milne 85, 102, 103, 180

Chelmsford, 3rd Baron (Frederic John Napier Thesiger) 471, 472

Chicago *Daily News* 546

Chicago, University of 261

Chile: and the Turkish battleships 56

Churchill, Winston Spencer: his character and characteristics 25, 51-3, 131; his earlier political career 51-3; becomes First Lord of the Admiralty (1911) 52-3; cruises with the Prime Minister and others aboard *Enchantress* (1912); his role in creating the modern Middle

East 25, 26; and Turkish entry into the war 63−75; his role in the appointment of Kitchener as War Minister 79−83; initial views on postwar division of Middle East 96, 139, 141; plans to end stalemate in the war by flanking attack 126−131; and the Dardanelles campaign 131−7, 150−4, 168; and Sykes 147; and the Other Club 147n; and Gallipoli campaign 156−60, 165, 233; loses position at the Admiralty in the Fisher resignation crisis 160−3; serves in the army 166; quoted on Clemenceau 237; and the importance of oil 261, 354; returns to office as Minister of Munitions 265−6; aware of concerns of Jewish constituents 270; and Young Turk ideology 352; and France and Syria 378; and 1918 elections 383; becomes both War Minister and Air Minister (1919) 384; demobilization and his warning of its effects on the peace negotiations 385−9, 402, 404, 433; and the Russian civil war 404; quoted on the death of King Alexander 432; and the problem of Palestine 448; and troop withdrawals from Asia 455, 459; views on and policy towards Bolshevik Russia 404, 459, 460, 472−3, 488, 490; dissents from Lloyd George's Middle East policy 494−6; appointed Colonial Secretary (1921) 493−4; his policy as Colonial Secretary 493−530, 561; the Cairo Conference 502−6; his White Paper for Palestine (1922) 525, 560; dissents from Lloyd George's Turkish policy 530; and French support for Kemal 537−8; comes to the rescue of Lloyd George's Turkish policy 549−52, 555; defeated in the 1922 elections 556; his subsequent career 565−7
Cilicia 214−15, 396, 428, 430, 438, 536−7
Clayton, Gilbert: his military career and official positions 90−1; his abilities and his outlook 91−4, 466; his views and plans for Britain in relationship to the Arab world during and after the war 98−109, 144, 521; the al-Faruqi episode, the McMahon negotiations, and the Arab Revolt 177−85, 215, 218, 220, 224, 504n; policy differences with Sykes 193, 289; and T. E. Lawrence 226, 227, 310; policies as chief political officer to Allenby 316, 345, 377, 445; urges British

annexation of Egypt 419; his policies attacked 470; on Richmond's role in the Palestine administration 518
Clemenceau, Georges 236−8, 290, 355, 366, 371, 373, 375, 376, 378, 390, 392, 395, 399, 400, 403, 408, 436−7, 450, 493, 536
Colby, Bainbridge 535
Colonial office see Churchill
Columbia University 261
Comité de l'Afrique Française 190
Comité de l'Asie Française 190
Committee of Imperial Defence 138, 148
Committee of Union and Progress (C.U.P.) see Young Turkey Party
Congreve, General W. N. 524
Conjoint Committee 294
Conolly, Arthur 27
Constantine I, King of Greece 128, 135, 432, 433, 495, 541, 544, 545, 553, 566
Constantinople Agreement (1915) 398, 401
Cornwallis, Captain Kinahan 171, 221
Council of Four 400, 411
Cox, Sir Percy 108, 305−7, 325, 343, 488, 501, 503, 507−10
Crane, Charles 397
Crewe, 1st Marquess of (Robert Offley Ashburton Crewe-Milnes) 106, 109, 143−4
Cromer, Earl (Evelyn Baring) 84
C.U.P. see Young Turkey Party
Curtis, Lionel George 82, 232n, 235, 280
Curzon of Kedleston, 1st Earl of (George Nathaniel Curzon) 27, 182, 234, 279, 287, 295, 297, 306, 343−4, 376, 399, 423, 438, 455−9, 461, 471, 472, 496, 502, 506, 532, 534, 535, 538, 544, 545, 550−1
Cyprus 33, 35, 85, 140, 273
Czechoslovakia: French postwar relations with 538

Daily Express 554, 556
Daily Mail 82, 233, 550
Damascus: falls to the Allies (1918) 315, 334−47, 394−5
"Damascus, Homs, Hama, and Aleppo" 178−81, 183, 185, 193, 329, 336, 377, 436
Damascus Protocol, the 175−6
Daniel Deronda (Eliot) 269n
D'Annunzio, Gabriele 532
Dardanelles and the Dardanelles campaign 125, 127−38, 150−7, 159, 161, 164−6,

168, 178, 214, 231, 233, 240, 241, 267,
366, 370, 373, 398, 411, 430, 431, 500,
501, 531, 533, 547, 548, 551, 552, 554,
557, 566, 567
Dardanelles Committee 164
Dashnaktsutium (Armenian Revolutionary
Federation) 214
Dawnay, Colonel Alan 311n, 324
Dawnay, Guy 165
de Bunsen Committee (on Britain's goals in
Middle East) 146–9, 168, 191
Declaration to the Seven (1918) 331, 341,
401
Deedes, Wyndham 38–9, 66, 91–2,
132–4, 165–6, 171, 184, 186, 218, 308,
312, 406, 505, 524, 526
Delcassé, Theophile 95, 137
Denikin, General Anton Ivanovich 361,
458
Derby, 17th Earl of (Edward Stanley) 294
Dhawu-'Awn clan 112
Disraeli, Benjamin, Earl of Beaconsfield 30,
75, 82, 269–70, 280, 294n
Djavid, Mehmed 42–3, 49, 55
Djemal Pasha, Ahmed (Djemal Bey) 40,
43–4, 48, 49, 55, 58, 65, 68, 71, 72, 100,
114, 121, 175–6, 208n, 209–11,
214–15, 218–19, 278, 308, 368, 372,
461, 480, 483n
Dodge, Cleveland 260
Dulles, Allen 535–6
Dunsterville, Major-General L. C. 355–6,
359–60, 456, 458

Eastern Committee 342–5, 376, 455, 456
Egypt/Cairo 27, 28, 32–5, 74, 79–86,
88–102, 108, 109n, 110, 112, 114, 121,
122, 133, 141, 143, 155–7, 168–72, 174,
176–82, 185, 188, 191–5, 198–200,
207, 208n, 215, 218, 220–7, 237, 263,
264, 267, 268, 273, 276–8, 281, 288–9,
291, 295, 296, 308–9, 312, 316, 318,
321–3, 329–31, 341, 374, 397, 411, 415,
417–21, 428, 448, 453, 462, 467, 482,
494, 496, 501, 510, 518, 528, 533, 560,
563, 564; see also Cairo Conference
El Arish 273, 288
Eliot, George 269n
Emir of Mecca see Hussein ibn Ali
Enver Pasha: and 1908 revolt 40; British
information about his ethnic origins
incorrect 43; as a Young Turk triumvir
44; a nationalist without a nation 48;
seeks German alliance 49–50; personally

known to Churchill 55; negotiates
German alliance 58–62; offers Osman to
Germany 61; invites sending of Goeben
and Breslau to Constantinople 62–3;
pushes for Turkish entry into the war on
Germany's side 66–75; and al-Masri 99;
becomes Turkey's "vice-generalissimo"
119; leads Caucasus campaign 120–1,
128; failings as War Minister 119–23;
turns over command at the Dardanelles
to Liman 155, 160; and British
capitulation at Kut 202; wary of German
influence 207; and the Armenian
Massacres 211–14; and Djemal's offer to
the Allies 215; his political position in
1917 248–9; secret talks with Lloyd
George's emissary 266–7; his new
offensive against Russia 313–14;
al-Masri offers to overthrow 318;
campaigns in Armenia, Georgia and
Azerbaijan 351–63; his views in 1918
361; Cabinet colleagues turn against and
blame 367–9; flees Constantinople 372;
War Office still controlled by his
followers 406; rivalry with Kemal 429,
466, 482–4, 489, 542; blamed by British
for Middle East disorders 453, 466, 468;
dealings with Germany and Bolshevik
Russia 479–90, 530–1; Bukhara
campaign 485–90; death of 488
Enzeli (Persia): Soviet Russian attack on
the Caspian port of 458–9

Faruqi, Muhammed Sharif al- 173,
176–80, 183, 186, 188–9, 193, 195, 199,
219, 220, 329
Fatat, al- 102, 218, 436
Feisal, son of Hussein of Mecca, later King
of Syria, and later still, King of Iraq:
deputy from Jeddah in the Ottoman
Parliament 113; mission to
Constantinople and Damascus (1915)
174–6, 218; and al-Faruqi 178; believes
100,000 men will join Hejaz revolt (June
1916) 219; should be field commander of
the Hejaz revolt, says Lawrence 226–7;
informed of British plans to recreate a
Jewish homeland in Palestine (1917) 297;
campaigns in Arabia 309 and
Transjordanian Palestine 310–12, 328,
333; expresses sympathy for Jews and
Zionism 322, 324–5, 522; and Hussein
328–9; and the administration of
liberated Syria 333–47; and the

Damascus campaign 334—41; his dinner conversation with Allenby 346—7; importance of his contribution to Allenby's campaigns deliberately exaggerated by Lloyd George 377—8; and the peace negotiations 394—6; and the Arab leadership of independent Syria 408—9; and France 409—10; caught between the Syrian General Congress and the French 435—40; proclaimed King of Greater Syria 437, 446; defeated, deposed, and exiled by the French 439, 442; and Iraq disorders 451—4, 462; and Lowell Thomas 497; and Churchill's plan to make him ruler of Iraq 499—500, 503—10; his coronation 508; Churchill fears Turks, aided by France, will attack 537—8; Churchill and colleagues come to regard as "treacherous" 509, 562

Fisher, John Arbuthnot, 1st Baron 53, 127, 131—3, 135, 151, 153, 160—1

Fitzgerald, F. Scott: quoted 349

FitzGerald, Lieutenant-Colonel Oswald 88, 92, 94, 104, 109, 115, 126, 142, 147, 149, 170, 177, 180, 189—90, 217, 284

FitzMaurice, Gerald 41—4, 92, 198, 291, 466

Flandin, Pierre-Etienne 190—1, 288

Foch, Marshal Ferdinand 366

Fourteen Points see under Wilson, Woodrow

France see specific headings

Franchet d'Esperey, Louis-Felix-François 363—4, 366, 373, 405

Francis Ferdinand, Archduke 45

Frankfurter, Felix 395, 399

Franklin-Bouillon, Henri 537

Freemasonry 41, 468

Frunze, Mikhail 486

Fuad, Ahmed, Sultan, and later King, of Egypt, 418, 420, 560

Gallipoli 135, 156—60, 164—6, 168, 171, 175, 176, 178, 200, 207n, 214, 216, 231, 233, 248, 277, 385, 406, 549, 561

Gaster, Rabbi Dr Moses 197, 285

Gauchet, Vice-Admiral Dominique M. 371

Gaza 289, 311

George II, King of Greece 553

George V, King 23, 26, 79, 81, 182, 264, 280, 556

Georgia (Russia) 354, 355, 359, 404, 476, 484, 485

German East Africa 281, 391

Germany see specific headings

Gladstone, William Ewart 30, 138, 234, 431

Glubb, John Bagot 512

Goeben (ship) 62—8, 70—3, 119, 122, 152, 566

Goltz, Field Marshal Colman von der 201

Gorchakov, Prince Alexander Mikhailovich 29

Gordon, General Charles George 82

Gorky, Maxim 243

Gounaris, Demetrios 432, 541, 543, 553—4

Gouraud, General Henri 438—9, 511

Graham, Sir Ronald 291, 293, 295, 296

Granville Browne, Edward 198

Graves, Philip 171, 469, 525

Graves, Robert 342

Great Game in Asia, the: its history 26—32

Greek-Turkish war 431—4, 540—57

Greenberg, Leopold 273, 274, 285

Greenmantle (Buchan) 93, 97, 358

Grey, Sir Edward, later 1st Viscount Grey of Falloden 26, 31—2, 58, 70, 75, 82, 86, 95, 96, 98, 101—3, 108, 125, 127—8, 137—4, 181, 182, 185, 189, 215, 234, 274, 320, 474, 561, 562

Gulf see Persian Gulf

Habsburg Empire see Austria-Hungary

Hagana 524

Hague Convention Respecting the Laws and Customs of War on Land (1907) 406

Haig, Field Marshal Sir Douglas 386

Halil Bey 71

Halim, Prince Said, Grand Vizier 44, 58, 59, 64, 65, 67—8, 70, 72—3, 112, 134, 174—5, 248—9

Hall, Captain William Reginald 151, 196

Hama see "Damascus, Homs, Hama, and Aleppo"

Hamilton, General Sir Ian 152—3, 156, 158, 164—6, 178

Hankey, Maurice 125, 127, 131—3, 148, 151, 182, 224, 233—6, 277, 281, 283, 287, 374, 391, 393, 398—400, 403, 404, 540, 552

Harding, Warren Gamaliel 547

Hardinge of Penshurst, 1st Baron (Sir Charles Hardinge) 41, 169—70, 184—5, 326, 471

Harvard University 260, 261

Hashem, House of 112, 506, 514

Hashemites 112n, 500, 504, 505, 507, 510, 514n, 536, 562

Hashimi, Yasin al- 176, 220
Hejaz, the 101, 103, 109, 111–14, 174,
   180, 219, 220, 222–5, 227, 228, 310,
   311, 324, 326–9, 338, 340, 377, 425–6,
   451, 498n, 508, 511, 512
Helphand, Alexander Israel ("Parvus")
   242–7, 465, 467, 468, 480
Hemingway, Ernest 546
Henderson, Arthur 234
Herbert, Aubrey 121, 149, 160, 171, 181,
   193, 195, 202
Hercegovina: annexation by
   Austria-Hungary 45
Herzl, Theodore 271–4, 285
Hess, Moses 272n
Hindenburg, Paul von 254–5, 265
Hirtzel, Sir Arthur 106, 108, 141, 496–7
Hogarth, Lieutenant-Commander David
   G. 171, 185, 221, 223, 226, 320, 345–6,
   419, 470, 501
Hogarth message (1918) 401
Homs see "Damascus, Homs, Hama, and
   Aleppo"
Horne, Sir Robert 552
House, Edward Mandell 258, 260–1, 295,
   373, 390, 391; of Allied plane to partition
   the Middle East, remarks "They are
   making it a breeding ground for future
   war" 257
Hughes, Charles Evans 547–8
Hughes, William 549n
Hungary 481
   see also Austria-Hungary
Hussein ibn Ali, Sherif and Emir of Mecca,
   later King of the Hejaz: seen as a
   possible future Caliph by Kitchener and
   Kitchener's aides 98, 100–1, 143, 144,
   169, 327, 426; through Abdullah, seeks
   Britain's support (pre-1914) against the
   Young Turks 98–101; Kitchener
   corresponds with (autumn 1914) 100–5,
   173–4; India objects to Kitchener's
   dealings with 106–10; his title, his
   family, and his past history 112; the
   Turks appoint him Emir (1908) 112; his
   political position (1908–15) 112–15;
   discovers (1915) Young Turk plan to
   depose him 174; pushed by the Young
   Turk plan into conflict with the Ottoman
   Empire, seeks support from Arab secret
   societies 174–5; at urging of secret
   societies, demands British support for
   Arab independence under his kingship in
   letter to McMahon 174–5; his

correspondence with McMahon 174–80,
   182–6, 189, 218, 326, 329, 336, 401,
   504, 528; and the al-Faruqi episode
   176–81, 199; his importance in the war,
   according to Sykes 188; his
   unimportance, according to the French
   192–3; his interests in Palestine
   recognized by the Sykes-Picot Agreement
   196; revolts against the Ottoman Empire
   207, 215, 218–28, 564; in constant
   communication with the Young Turks
   with a view to changing sides in the war
   221; proclaims himself "King of the
   Arabs" 221, 222; Sykes and Picot visit
   him to roughly outline the terms of the
   secret Sykes-Picot-Sazanov Agreement
   288, 344; informed by British
   government of its plan to re-create a
   Jewish homeland in Palestine 297; and
   Sykes's draft of the proclamation to the
   people of Baghdad 306; and the design of
   his flag 315; his conflict with Ibn Saud
   326, 424–6, 453; thinks of proclaiming
   himself Caliph 327; his importance
   reevaluated by British officials 327–31,
   343, 562; complains that Feisal has
   betrayed him 328–9; and the taking of
   Damascus 334, 336, 337; and the
   administration of Syria 339; his position
   (1919) 397; the Arab Bureau's old belief
   in him as leader of an Arab confederation
   denounced in The Times 470; possible
   annexation of Transjordan by 511;
   refuses to sign treaty with Britain (1921)
   512
Husseini, Amin al-, Grand Muffi of
   Jerusalem 517–18
Husseini, Musa Kazim Pasha al- 521–2
Husseini family, al- 446

Ibn Rashid 101, 107–8
Ibn Saud, Abdul Aziz, Emir of Nejd, later
   King of Saudi Arabia 100–1, 104,
   107–8, 114, 183, 221, 326, 328, 424–6,
   462, 506, 507, 510, 514, 560, 562
Idrisi, Seyyid Mohammed al- 108
Ikhwan see Brethren
Imperial War Conference (Cabinet)
   279–82, 363
India see specific headings
India Office 91, 106, 109, 141, 144–6, 189,
   294, 467, 471, 472
Inquiry, the (US postwar plans) 260–2

Iran 354, 404, 415, 559, 564 *see also* Persia/Persian Empire

Iraq 34, 35, 42−3, 176, 184, 191, 375n, 401, 404, 408, 415, 440, 448−54, 459, 465, 495, 497, 504, 506−10, 528, 534−8, 556, 559, 560, 562−4 *see also* Mesopotamia

Ironside, Major-General Edmund 459−61, 472

Isaacs, Rufus, 1st Marquis of Reading 294

Islamic Revolutionary League 483n

Ismet Pasha, General (Inönü) 433, 541, 542

Israel 35, 214, 273, 279n, 436, 528, 563, 564

Italy 29, 43, 45, 46, 49, 74, 135, 189, 196, 256, 257, 267, 271, 290, 299, 346, 364, 365, 374, 389, 391−4, 399, 400, 404, 407, 411, 427, 428, 433, 434, 467, 531−3, 539, 546, 550−1, 565

Izzet Pasha, Field Marshal Ahmet, Grand Vizier 368−70, 372

Jabotinsky, Vladimir 277−8, 291, 446−7, 517, 524, 526−8

Jackson, Admiral Sir Henry 132−3, 153

Japan 31, 359

Jeddah 219, 222, 225, 226, 328

Jellicoe, Admiral Sir John 217

Jerusalem 305−13, 323, 332, 345, 366, 409, 445−9

Jewish Chronicle 285, 297−8

Jewish Legion 278, 291, 333, 446−7, 517, 524, 527

Jewish Peril, The (Protocols of the Learned Elders of Zion) 468−9

Jordan 35, 183, 214, 328, 436, 514, 528, 563, 564

Journal des Débats, Le 396

Joyce, Lieutenant-Colonel Pierce Charles 311n, 324

Justice, La 237−8

Kadjar dynasty (Persia) 456

Kamenev, Lev 459, 461

Karasu, Emmanuel (Emmanuel Carasso) 41−2

Kedourie, Professor Elie 179n

Kemal, Mustapha: as a Turkish commander at Gallipoli 155, 157; appointed Inspector General of the Ninth Army, embarks on a voyage to the interior (1919) 406; disobeys Sultan's order to return and rallies Turks of Anatolia around a nationalist program in revolt against the Allies 406−8; an analysis of the groups supporting his revolt 407; defeats French at Marash 408; reportedly preparing to ally with Arabs of Damascus 408; moves headquarters to Angora (Ankara) and declares National Pact 427; repeatedly defeats French (1920) 428; establishes government in Angora, and is elected president of the Grand National Assembly 428−9; sends mission to Moscow 429; his rivalry with Enver, misunderstood by British, but understood by Russians 429, 466, 482−4, 489; an enemy of Russian communism 429, 484; and Stalin 430; signs treaty with, and receives military aid from, Russia 430, 530−1; attacks British near Constantinople 430; as a threat to the Treaty of Sèvres 431−2; beginnings of war with Greece 431−4; increasingly draws France and Italy to his side 432−4; and the Arab-French conflict in Syria 438−9; blamed by British for Middle East disorders 453, 462, 466; and Armenia 484; and Afghanistan 484; and Soviet alliance structure 484; realism of his demands 521; gains support of Italy 531−2; reaches accord with France 537−8; and the Greek war 540−9; and the Chanak crisis 548−52; and the armistice of Mudanya 551 and peace talks at Lausanne 551

Kerensky, Alexander 245, 353

Kerr, Philip 235, 294, 295, 301

Keynes, John Maynard 253, 390, 391

Khedive of Egypt, the *see* Abbas II

Khiva 33

Khurma 424−5

Kim (Kipling) 27

King, Henry 397

King-Crane Commission 397

Kipling, Rudyard 27, 82, 280

Kitchener of Khartoum, 1st Earl of (Horatio Herbert Kitchener): his role in creating the modern Middle East 26; warned by Deedes of state of affairs in Turkey 66; meets with Churchill as war crisis mounts (July 1914) 79; appointed War Minister 80; his character, habits, and military career 81−3; his views on the World War and his strategy for

winning it 83; he and his aides regarded
as experts on the Middle East 83−7;
their bias 85; his aides and their views
84−95; FitzGerald writes and speaks for
him 88; his misunderstanding of Islam
and his proposal of an Arab caliphate
96−8, 564; pre-1914 dealings with
Abdullah 98−100; dealings with Hussein
(1914) 100−5, 114−15, 173−4, 426,
562; his differences with India 106−10;
and the role of the Middle East in the
war 119; and the Dardanelles expedition
124−36, 159; his plans for the postwar
Middle East 140−5, 169, 521, 539;
described by Lloyd George as a
lighthouse 126, 165; makes Sykes his
representative 146; and the de Bunsen
committee 146−9; and the Gallipoli
campaign 152−3, 156−8, 163−6, 561;
loss of Cabinet support 163−7; powers
reduced 167; and Hussein's revolt
167−8, 177−8, 180−2, 184−6, 215,
218; and creation of the Arab Bureau
170−2; and the Sykes-Picot Agreement
189−92, 194−5, 375n; mission to Russia
216−17; death of 217, 232, 234; thought
Palestine of little value 270, 278; and
Sykes 284, 289; and Wahhabi religious
revival 326n; and Arab nationalism 327
Kressenstein, Kress von 121, 289
Kun, Bela 482
Kurdistan 214, 344, 404−5, 411, 450, 451,
504, 560
Kurds 48, 212, 405, 429, 449, 450, 503−4,
528, 560, 563
Kut, siege of 201−3, 369
Kuwait 17, 107, 108, 510, 560

Labor Zionist movement 211
Lambert, George 567
Lansdowne, 5th Marquis of (Henry
Charles Keith Petty-Fitzmaurice) 317n
Lansing, Robert 254, 259−60
Last Crusade, The (Thomas) 498
Lawrence, T. E. (Lawrence of Arabia)
171, 202, 221−2, 226−7, 309−12, 322,
327, 328, 335−42, 345, 346, 379, 395,
444, 497−9, 501, 503−5, 507, 510−12,
528, 556
Leachman, Colonel Gerald 452
League of Nations 283, 291, 392, 398, 505,
526, 533, 547, 557; and Middle Eastern
Mandates 398, 411, 493, 509, 513, 526,
533, 546−7, 556, 559, 562

Lebanon 35, 36, 94, 143, 179, 183, 185,
189, 191, 192, 214, 269, 288, 290, 308,
317, 318, 325, 331, 339, 340, 344,
408−11, 436−9, 441, 442, 493, 513, 528,
563, 564
Lenin, V. I. (Vladimir Ilich Ulyanov)
241−6, 298, 351, 355, 356, 429, 459,
465, 467, 468, 474−7, 480, 482−4, 490,
495, 561
Lepsius, Pastor Johannus 213
Libya 45
Liman von Sanders, General Otto 55, 62,
68−9, 71, 119, 120, 152, 155, 158, 160,
328, 332
Limpus, Rear-Admiral Sir Arthur H. 55,
66
Lippmann, Walter 258−60, 262
Lloyd, George 165, 171
Lloyd George, David: his role in creation
of the modern Middle East 26; political
sponsor of Winston Churchill 51−2; later
blames Churchill for the war with
Turkey 74; "keen for Balkan
confederation" 74−5; Kitchener feels out
of place with 82; low opinion of Cairo
Intelligence 91; his war strategy 124−7,
134, 154n, 363; and Dardanelles
campaign 124−9, 132n, 133; describes
Kitchener 126, 165; says none of the
Great Powers covets Arabia 140; and
Gallipoli campaign 157; along with
Bonar Law, tells Asquith to form a
Coalition government 160−2; claims he
fought to get high office for Churchill
162; blamed by Churchill 162; blames
Churchill for the war and the
Dardanelles campaign 162; becomes
Minister of Munitions 163; critical of
Kitchener 163−5; meets Sykes 195;
moves away from Radicalism and
Liberals and closer to Tories 231−2;
becomes War Minister 232; overthrows
Asquith and becomes Prime Minister
233−4; his presidential style of
government 234−5; his focus on the
Middle East 234−6; influence of Milner
on 235−6; seeks postwar British
hegemony in the Middle East 235,
300−1, 266−7, 385; believes the
Ottoman Empire brought about Russia's
collapse 239; flirts with notion of
partitioning Russia 248; secret
negotiations with Turkey 249, 266−7;
and Woodrow Wilson 253−4; and

Zionism and the Balfour Declaration
263−87, 295−8; and the Palestine
campaign 289, 308, 311; and the
Mesopotamian campaign 305; opposes
Sykes-Picot Agreement 344−5, 364−5,
379; and Amery's strategy 357−9; and
negotiations for Ottoman surrender
364−6; aims to acquire Palestine and
Mosul, and to exclude France from Syria
373−9; meets with Clemenceau, who
agrees to give him Palestine and Mosul
(December 1918) 375; and the 1918
elections 383−4; claims Britain entitled
to dominant role in postwar Middle East
385; abandons his program of domestic ·
reforms in face of economic collapse
387−8; and the Peace Conference
389−411; abandons Syria to France 409,
438, 440; and the Treaty of Sèvres
427−34, 462, 472; responds to
anti-Zionism of British administration in
Palestine by appointing Samuel High
Commissioner 448; and Mosul 450; and
Persia 455; blames Curzon for Persian
involvement 459; and Bolshevik Russia
473−4; his "vendetta against the Turks"
criticized by Churchill 494−5, 529;
appoints Churchill Colonial Secretary
496; and Transjordan 505; opposes
withdrawal from Iraq 509; tells Churchill
what he and Balfour intended the Balfour
Declaration to mean 520; his
Greek-Turkish policies lose him support
of former allies 530−9; and the Greek-
Turkish war 540−8; and the Chanak
crisis 548−53; his fall from power
554−7, 566; his effect on the Middle
East 558, 565
Lloyd George, Roberts & Co.: represents
Dr Herzl and the Zionist movement 273
London Conference (1920) 403, 411
London Conference (1921) 540
London, Treaty of (1915): Italy's
agreement to join the Allies 401
Louis of Battenberg, Prince 56
Lowther, Sir Gerald 41−4
Ludendorff, Erich 255, 313, 361, 363
Luxemburg, Rosa 242, 244
Lvov, Prince G. E. 245

Macdonogh, G. M. W. 147
Macedonia: background for flourishing of
Young Turkey views 40
McKenna, Reginald 149

Mackenzie, Compton 157
Mackinder, Sir Halford 31
McMahon, Sir Henry 89, 94, 95, 115,
174, 178−80, 182−6, 189, 218, 223−5,
227, 326, 329, 336
McMahon-Hussein correspondence
(1915−16) 174−80, 182−6, 189, 218,
326, 329, 336, 401, 504, 528
Mahan, Alfred Thayer: invents the
descriptive phrase "the Middle East" 224
Mahdi, the: significance of his title 97
Malcolm, James 284−5
Malleson, Major-General Wilfred 356,
360−2, 456
Mallet, Sir Louis 44
Manchester Guardian 270−1, 286, 541
Man-eaters of Tsavo, The (Patterson) 270
Marlborough, 9th Duke of (Charles
Richard John Spencer-Churchill) 162
Marne, First Battle of 69
Maronites 35, 93, 191, 269, 340, 439
Mason, A. E. W. 82
Masri, Aziz Ali al- 99−101, 108, 177, 186,
220, 225−7, 318
Masterson Smith, Sir James 496−7
Masurian lakes, Battle of 70
Maude, Major-General Stanley 305−7
Maxwell, General Sir John 89, 91, 92, 177
Mazzini, Giuseppe 271, 531
Mecca 98, 100−1, 103−4, 106, 108−15,
140, 174, 175, 182, 190, 219, 225, 226,
228, 321, 326, 330, 334n, 435, 507, 562
Medina 101, 104, 111, 113, 114, 140, 180,
219, 225, 228, 310
Megiddo, Battle of 333
Mehmed V, Sultan 41, 109, 119, 214, 368
Mehmed VI, Sultan 368, 405−7, 411,
427−30, 449, 466, 532, 552
Meinertzhagen, Colonel Richard 12, 308,
309, 311, 316, 328, 447
Mesopotamia (Iraq) 103, 108, 140−1, 148,
149, 168, 170, 178, 183, 192, 194,
200−2, 214, 224, 231, 233, 266−7, 276,
281, 283, 300, 305−8, 323, 326, 343,
356−8, 364, 369, 387, 397, 401, 409,
411, 436−8, 449−54, 467, 469, 470, 497,
500−1, 503, 508, 528
Mesopotamia Administration Committee
307
Metaxas, Ioannis 541
Methodist Episcopal Church 547
Mexico: and Zimmerman telegram 255n
Michael, Grand Duke of Russia: refuses
the throne 245

Millerand, Alexander 95, 399, 410, 428
Milne, General George Francis 366
Milner, Alfred, Lord 13, 20, 195, 232, 234–6, 247, 248, 264, 276–81, 293–5, 301, 330, 351, 357–9, 371, 378, 420, 495–6, 502
Mirghani, Sir Sayyid Ali al- 144
Mond, Alfred 378–9
Montagu, Edwin 294–5, 297, 456, 471–2
Montenegro 45, 74
Moore, Sir Archibald 56–7
Morgan, J. P. 253
Morgenthau, Henry 211, 319
Mosul 191–2, 374, 375, 396, 450
Mubarak, Sheik of Kuwait 108
Mudros, Armistice of 371–3, 377, 390, 405, 470
Murray, General Sir Archibald 224, 289–90
Mussolini, Benito 532–3

Naqib of Baghdad, the (Sir Sayid Abdul Rachman) 507, 508
National Pact, the (Turkish) 427–8, 551–2
Navarino, Battle of (1827) 393
Newcombe, Lieutenant-Colonel Stewart F. 366–9
Newfoundland 530, 550
New Republic 258, 260, 262
New Zealand 280, 281, 301, 358, 530, 550, 560
Nicholas II, Czar 137, 139, 231, 239–49, 257, 286
Nicolson, Sir Arthur 189
Nilus, Sergei 468–9
Nixon, Sir John 200
Norris, Captain David T. 458
Northcliffe, 1st Viscount (Alfred Harmsworth) 233, 264
Nuri el-Sa'id 337–8, 451

O'Beirne, Hugh 198
"On the Quai at Smyrna" (Hemingway) 546n
Orlando, Emanuele 392, 394
Ormsby-Gore, William 235, 277–9, 293, 298, 301, 322–4, 329
Other Club 147n
Ottoman Army, 3rd 40, 120–1
Ottoman Army, 4th 121, 209
Ottoman Army, 9th 406

Ottoman Parliament 42, 44, 48, 71, 113, 368, 405, 427, 428, 437

Painlevé, Paul 236
Paléologue, Maurice 199
Palestine 42–3, 91–3, 103, 121, 142–3, 148, 149, 179, 182–3, 185, 187, 188, 190–2, 195–8, 210–11, 237, 266–74, 308–13, 316, 318, 321–5, 332, 339, 345, 358, 373–5, 377, 387, 391, 396–8, 400, 401, 408–11, 415, 435–8, 440–8, 453, 462, 466, 469, 489, 494, 500, 501, 504–7, 511–29, 534, 539, 556
Pallavicini, Johann Margrave von 213
Palmerston, 3rd Viscount (Henry John Temple) 28, 31, 75, 268–9
Pan-Islamic Propaganda Bureau 467
Pan-Turanian Movement 352, 357, 422, 466
Paris Peace Conference see Peace Conference
Parker, Colonel Alfred 171, 226
Parvus see Helphand, Alexander Israel
Patterson, Lieutenant-Colonel John Henry 277, 278
Paul I, Czar 27
Peace Conference (1919) 185, 261, 324, 338, 340, 383, 385, 390–5, 397–401, 403–4, 408, 418, 435, 450, 533, 534, 549n
Peake, Colonel F. G. 512
Persia and the Persian Question (Curzon) 455
Persia/Persian Empire 25, 29, 31, 33, 107, 138, 139, 170, 200, 208, 215, 281, 313, 325, 344, 352, 353–9, 363, 397, 454, 465, 467, 471–5, 479, 484, 559 see also Iran
Persian Gulf 34, 36, 102, 141, 148, 168, 200, 397, 411, 426, 456
Peshawar: planned Indian nationalist uprising in 421
Picot, François Georges 189–93, 195–8, 286–9, 321, 330, 340, 341, 343, 345, 379, 561 see also Sykes-Picot-Sazanov Agreement
Pinsker, Leo 272n
Pitt, William (the Younger) 28
Poincaré, Raymond 411, 538, 550, 551
Poland 210, 241, 242, 272, 295, 427, 481, 517, 538
Popolo d'Italia 532
Porte see Sublime Porte
Princeton University 261

Protocols of the Learned Elders of Zion (*The Jewish Peril*) 468–9

Radek, Karl 480, 481, 482
Rapallo, Treaty of (1922) 533
Rashid, House of 426
Raslovleff, Michael 469
Rathenau, Walter 240
Rawalpindi, Treaty of (1919) 422–3
Red Line Agreement (1928) 536n
Reshadieh (battleship) 54–6, 73
Reuters 360
Reza Khan Pahlavi, later Reza Shah Pahlavi, Shah of Iran 460
Rhodes, Cecil 280
Ribot, Alexandre 236
Richmond, Captain Herbert William 132–3
Richmond, Ernest T. 518
Riddell, 1st Baron (George Allardice Riddell) 409, 474, 545, 553
Robeck, Admiral John de 151–4, 156
Robert College 260
Robertson, Field Marshal Sir William 167, 224, 282
Robinson, Geoffrey 195, 232n
Rome and Jerusalem (Hess) 272n
Rothschild, Baron Edward 297, 379
Rothschild, James de 285
Round Table 232n, 235, 280
Rumania 34, 64, 71, 74, 125, 127, 134, 135, 538
Russell, Bertrand 125
Russia/Russian Empire (later Soviet Union): *see specific headings*
Russian Civil War 298, 360, 404, 415, 458, 473, 481
Russian Orthodox Church 36, 269
Russian Revolutions (1917) 239–49, 257, 286, 287, 344, 455, 460, 466, 469
Rutenberg, Pinhas 523, 526

St Jean de Maurienne, Agreement of (1917) 392, 401
St John Philby, H. 512
Salisbury, 3rd Marquis of (Robert Arthur Talbot Gascoyne-Cecil) 30, 273, 291
Salonika 40–1, 43, 366
Samuel, Sir Herbert 196, 197, 269–70, 294, 448, 505, 524
San Remo Conference/Agreement (1920) 403–4, 411, 534–5
Sarajevo 208n
Saud, House of 425, 506, 514

Saudi Arabia 510, 514n, 560, 564
Sazanov, Sergei 137, 139, 189–99, 214, 248
Scapa Flow (HQ of Grand Fleet) 54, 217
Scott, C. P. 270, 286
Seeckt, General Hans von 480–2, 489–90, 531
Senussi 109n
Serbia 45, 50, 58, 59, 74
Seven Pillars of Wisdom (Lawrence) 327n, 340n, 342
Seven Theses on the War (Lenin) 242
Sèvres, Treaty of (1920) 403–4, 411, 431, 432, 472, 532, 537
Sforza, Count Carlo 399, 531, 532, 551
Shaftesbury, Anthony Cooper, Earl of 268
Shah of Persia *see* Ahmed Shah and Reza Khan Pahlavi
Shakespear, Captain William Henry 107
Shaumian, Stephan 356
Sherif of Mecca *see* Hussein Ibn Ali
Shuckburgh, Evelyn 496–7, 501, 504, 511, 524
Siberia 234, 358, 359
Sidebotham, Herbert 270–1
Sikhs 422n
Sinai 91, 121, 273, 274, 277, 288, 310
Smith, F. E., later 1st Earl of Birkenhead 147n, 383, 550, 552, 555
Smuts, General Jan Christian 20, 280–3, 294, 301, 308, 358, 364, 501, 549n
Smyrna 393–4, 407, 411, 427, 430, 431, 433, 494, 532, 544–8
Socialist Second International 242
Sociéte Ottomane du Chemin de Fer Damas-Hama et Prolongements 179–80
Sokolow, Nahum 285, 286, 288, 292, 319, 516n
Somerset, F. R. 443–4
Somme, Battle of the 189, 233
Sonnino, Baron Sidney 288, 290, 392
Souchon, Rear-Admiral 62–3, 65, 71–2, 74–5
South Africa 52, 82, 232, 280, 281–3, 530, 549n, 550, 552
South Persia Rifles 209, 456
Stalin, Joseph (Joseph Vissarionovich Djugashvili) 19–20, 355, 356, 430, 475–8, 484
Standard Oil Company of New Jersey 534–6
Standard Oil Company of New York ("Socony") 453, 454, 534–6

Starosselski, Colonel 460
Steevens, George 82−3, 90, 93
Stevenson, Frances 265, 378
Stirling, W. E. 337
Storrs, Ronald 85−6, 89, 92−4, 98−105,
    107, 109, 114−15, 142−4, 168−9, 174,
    177, 180, 182, 191, 193, 194, 218, 221,
    223, 225, 226, 316, 322, 323, 325, 327,
    345, 445, 518, 521
Straus, Oscar 42, 299n
Sublime Porte: as the name given to the
    Ottoman government 37−8; see also
    specific headings
Sudan 32, 82, 84, 88−90, 97, 143, 144,
    171, 173n, 220, 222, 225, 227, 316, 322,
    477
Suez Canal 33, 79, 83, 97, 107, 114,
    121−2, 208n, 214, 276, 281, 310, 420,
    421
Sultan of Turkey see Abdul Hamid II,
    Sultan; Mehmed V, Sultan; Mehmed
    VI, Sultan
Sultan Osman I (battleship) 54−8, 60−2,
    73
Sunday Times, The 497
Sykes, Brigadier General Sir Percy 209
Sykes, Sir Mark: writes that there is no
    Turkey and there are no Turks 48; warns
    House of Commons that disappearance
    of Ottoman Empire will lead to
    disappearance of British Empire (1914)
    75; complains there is no authentic
    history of the Ottoman Empire in the
    English language 86; and French claims
    to Syria 144; his background, education,
    political career, and characteristics
    146−7; asks Churchill for a chance to
    serve "on the spot" against Turkey 147;
    appointed to serve as Kitchener's
    representative on the de Bunsen
    committee 146−9; comments on
    Kitchener 147, 190; warns Churchill that
    Turks at Gallipoli may be "formidable"
    foes 156; embarks on fact-finding tour of
    Middle East and India 167−73, 181−2;
    sees incoherence resulting from each
    government department running its own
    Middle East policies 170, 495; proposes
    creating Arab Bureau 170−3; and the al-
    Faruqi episode 180−2, 186−9; and
    Armenians 181; and Arabs 181−2;
    negotiates (with Picot) Allied partition of
    Middle East 184, 189−96;
    misunderstands what Clayton and the
    Arab Bureau asked him to accomplish in
    the negotiations 193−5; attacks Asquith,
    and meets Lloyd George, Milner, and
    the editor of The Times 195; learns of
    Zionism 196−6; joins Picot in Petrograd
    to negotiate with Russia 196−9; joins
    War Cabinet secretariat (1916) 224, 235,
    235n; publishes Arabian Report 224;
    urges support for Hussein's revolt; 224;
    urges that McMahon be replaced by
    Wingate 224; popularizes the phrase
    "Middle East" 224; and Amery 276−8,
    283; pro-Arab and pro-Zionist,
    negotiates with Zionists and seeks
    support from France, Italy, and the
    Vatican for an Allied pro-Zionist
    declaration and hopes for an Arab-
    Jewish-Armenian pro-Allied partnership
    283−98; believes imperialism "contrary
    to the spirit of the times" 290, 561; sent
    out to Egyptian Expeditionary Force
    (1917) 287−91; and the administration
    of Mesopotamia 305−6, 308; drafts
    Baghdad declaration 306; designs Arab
    flag for Hussein's followers 315;
    appointed to Foreign Office 315; officers
    on the spot disagree with him about who
    should rule the newly-occupied Middle
    East territories and about the need to
    honor pledges to France and to Zionism
    and the alliance with King Hussein
    315−45; obtains agreement of Syrian
    Arab leaders in Cairo to terms already
    negotiated with France and Hussein
    (1917) 329; writes Declaration to the
    Seven to Syrian Arab leaders in Cairo
    (1918) 331; perhaps recants his views
    379; dies 379; his wartime design for the
    postwar Middle East in large part is
    carried into effect 562; see also Sykes-
    Picot-Sazanov Agreement
Sykes-Picot-Sazanov Agreement (1916)
    189−9, 238, 257, 267, 268, 286, 288,
    291−3, 320, 329, 335, 338, 339, 342−5,
    364, 374−6, 375n, 378, 379, 401, 405,
    439, 536, 561
Symes, Captain G. S. 144, 171
Syria 27, 34, 35, 46, 84, 86, 92, 93−5, 103,
    113, 121, 137 , 140n ,143, 144, 148, 149,
    169, 175, 178−80, 183−4, 187−95, 209,
    210, 214−15, 228, 234, 237, 238, 260,
    266, 268, 287, 288, 290, 308, 310, 315,
    317, 318, 321−6, 328−32, 351, 369,
    374−9, 394−7, 401, 404, 408−11,

415—16, 418, 428, 434—43, 446, 448, 462, 469, 493, 494, 504, 505, 507, 510—13, 521, 528, 534, 537, 539, 562, 564
Syria, French League of Nations Mandate for 559
Syrian Congress, General 435—8, 451n
Syrian Istiqlal Party 436
Syrian National Party 437
Syrian Protestant College 260

Taft, William Howard 255
Talaat Bey, Mehmed 39—40, 42, 44, 48—50, 55, 58, 60—1, 68, 70—2, 151—2, 207, 210—13, 215, 248—9, 309, 318, 361, 367—9, 372, 480
Talib, Sayyid 108, 507—8
Tancred (Disraeli) 269—70
Tannenberg, Battle of 70
Tartars 356, 429
Tatler 54
Temps, Le 396
Thirty-Nine Steps (Buchan) 247
Thomas, Lowell 497—8
Tibet 31, 107
Tigris campaign (1915—16) 200—3
Times, The 80, 133, 159, 171, 195, 232n, 233, 266, 297, 298, 342, 423, 426, 452—3, 469, 470, 506, 509, 518, 524—5, 548, 552, 554, 555
Togan, Zeki Velidi 476n
Townshend, Major-General Charles Vere Ferrers 200—2, 369—71
Toynbee, Arnold 213n, 540—1, 545n
Transcaucasia 354, 355, 358, 361, 362, 471, 483, 484
Transjordan see under Palestine
Trenchard, Sir Hugh 499n, 500n, 503
Trotsky, Leon (Lev Davidovich Bronstein) 242, 244, 298, 353, 481
Trumpeldor, Captain Joseph 277, 446
Tumulty, Joseph Patrick 255
Turaba 424—5
Turkestan 48, 313, 355, 356, 358, 360, 473, 475, 477—8, 483, 485—9
Tutankhamun, tomb of 510n

Uganda: and Zionism 273—4
Ukraine 210, 242, 272, 476
United States 29, 45, 210, 211, 213, 253—63, 268, 271, 276, 278, 286, 288, 295—6, 299—300, 331, 343, 344, 367, 373—4, 377, 379, 385, 389—95,

398—400, 404, 427, 436, 457, 500, 509, 533—6, 546—8, 554, 561

Venizelos, Eleutherios 74, 127—8, 135, 393, 430—4, 540, 544, 555
Verdun, Battle of 188
Verité sur la question syrienne, La (Djemal Pasha) 209
Versailles, Treaty of 398, 480, 533, 541
Vickers 55, 57, 266
Victoria, Queen 27, 29, 291
Viviani, René 236, 248

Wafd Party (Egypt) 418
Wahhab, Muhammad Ibn Abdul 425
Wahhabis 104, 108, 326n, 328, 425, 514, 564
Walrund, Osmond 330—1
Wangenheim, Hans von 49, 59, 60—2, 64—5, 68—71, 211, 212, 243
Wassmuss, Wilhelm 209
Weizmann, Chaim 270, 285—7, 291, 293, 295—7, 319, 321, 323—5, 345, 374, 445, 513, 519, 522, 526
Wellington, 1st Duke of (Arthur Wellesley) 27, 75, 81, 216
Wellman, Guy 536
Wells, H. G. 269
Wemyss, Vice-Admiral Sir Rosslyn 225
Wilhelm II, Kaiser 58, 60, 68—9, 71, 128, 151, 255, 256
Wilson, Admiral of the Fleet Sir Arthur 153, 160, 161
Wilson, Colonel Sir Arnold T. 326, 449—53, 534
Wilson, Colonel C. E. 225
Wilson, Sir Henry 376, 383, 472, 495
Wilson, (Thomas) Woodrow: his background, character, and political career 253—4; interferes with a J.P. Morgan financing for Britain (1916) 253; opposes Allied imperial ambitions 253; attempts to negotiate a compromise peace 254—5; and the Zimmerman telegram 255n; his domestic political problems 255, 257; pushed into the war by German U-boat campaign, he plans to fight the war on political grounds of his own choosing 255—9; is worried that the public will learn of secret Allied treaties such as the Sykes-Picot Agreement 257; outlines Fourteen Points, Four Principles, Four Ends, and Five Particulars 258—9, 401; refuses to

declare war on the Ottoman Empire
259−60; seeks guidance in framing
America's plans for the postwar world
260−1; foresees "cataclysm" if the peace
"is not made on the highest principles of
justice" 262; compared and contrasted
with Lloyd George 263, 274; and the
conception of League of Nations
Mandates 283; and Brandeis, Zionism
and the Balfour Declaration 295,
299−300; and the principle of national
self-determination 331, 343−4, 346, 435,
449−50; Lloyd George's contempt for
374; meets Lloyd George in London
(December 1918) 375, 403; at the Peace
Conference 389−403, 407; falls ill 398;
defeated in his fight for Senate
ratification of the agreements reached in
Paris 398, 533, 538n; succeeded as
President by Harding 547
Wingate, Lieutenant-General Sir Francis
Reginald 89−94, 103, 104, 106, 109,
115, 144, 169, 171, 173n, 184, 218, 220,
223−5, 227, 316, 317, 318, 321, 323,
340, 344, 417−19, 466, 470
With Lawrence in Arabia (Thomas) 498n
World Zionist Congress 274, 516n

Yale University 261
Yemen, the 101
Young, Captain Sir Hubert Winthrop 225,
226, 497, 504, 511, 524
Young Turkey Party (Young Turks)
(C.U.P.) 37−8, 40−9, 58−62, 64, 67,
68, 70, 72, 99, 102, 109, 112−14, 121,
123, 174, 180, 185, 198, 207−10, 213n,
214, 218, 221, 239, 243, 245−7, 249,
266, 317n, 352, 367, 368, 372, 406, 407,
449, 461−2, 466−8, 479−81, 483, 487
Yugoslavia 34, 45, 63, 538

Zaghlul, Saad 417−20, 428
Zaharoff, Basil 266−7, 284
Zavriev, Dr 214
Zimmerman, Arthur 255
Zimmerman telegram 255
Zinoviev, Grigori 246, 482
Zionists/Zionism 42−3, 92−3, 143, 179,
196−8, 210−11, 235, 276−300, 317,
319−21, 323−5, 330, 341, 345, 374, 377,
395, 436, 437, 441−8, 466, 472, 513,
515−19, 521−8, 562
Zionist Commission (Palestine) 323−5, 518
Zionist Federation, British 285, 291, 298
Zionist-Revisionist Organization 528